Political Change in the Middle East and North Africa

Political Change in the Middle East and North Africa

After the Arab Spring

Edited by Inmaculada Szmolka

EDINBURGH
University Press

Edinburgh University Press is one of the leading university presses in the UK. We publish academic books and journals in our selected subject areas across the humanities and social sciences, combining cutting-edge scholarship with high editorial and production values to produce academic works of lasting importance. For more information visit our website: edinburghuniversitypress.com

Edinburgh University Press Ltd
The Tun – Holyrood Road
12 (2f) Jackson's Entry
Edinburgh EH8 8PJ

Typeset in 12/14 Arno and Myriad by
IDSUK (Dataconnection) Ltd,
printed and bound in Great Britain by
CPI Group (UK) Ltd, Croydon CR0 4YY

A CIP record for this book is available from the British Library

ISBN 978 1 4744 1528 6 (hardback)
ISBN 978 1 4744 1530 9 (paperback)
ISBN 978 1 4744 1529 3 (webready PDF)
ISBN 978 1 4744 1531 6 (epub)

Contents

Figures and Tables

The Contributors

Professor Ignacio Álvarez-Ossorio, University of Alicante, Spain
Colonel Víctor Bados, Ministry of Defence, Spain
Professor Rafael Bustos, Complutense University of Madrid, Spain
Professor Francesco Cavatorta, Laval University, Canada
Lecturer Marién Durán, University of Granada, Spain
Lecturer Irene Fernández-Molina, University of Exeter, UK
Lecturer Javier García-Marín, University of Granada, Spain
Lecturer Guadalupe Martínez-Fuentes, University of Granada, Spain
Dr Luis Melián, University of Salamanca, Spain
Professor Raquel Ojeda, University of Granada, Spain
Professor María Angustias Parejo, University of Granada, Spain
Professor Carmelo Pérez-Beltrán, University of Granada, Spain
Lecturer Jordi Quero, Pompeu Fabra University, Spain
Senior Research Fellow Eduard Soler, Barcelona Centre for International
    Affairs, Spain
Professor Lise Storm, University of Exeter, UK
Dr Ewa K. Strzelecka, University of Granada, Spain
Professor Inmaculada Szmolka, University of Granada, Spain
Lecturer Juan Tovar, University of Burgos, Spain
Lecturer Victoria Veguilla, Pablo de Olavide University, Spain

Acknowledgements

This book provides the results of the research project entitled 'Authoritarianism persistence and political change processes in the Middle East and North Africa region: consequences on political regimes and international scene', coordinated by the volume editor. The research is financed by the Spanish Ministry of Economy and Competitiveness (project reference CSO2012-32917) and the Regional Government of Andalucía (project of excellence SEJ-3118).

Introduction

Inmaculada Szmolka

The aftermath of the 'Arab Spring' has generated a vast amount of academic literature on the causes of the uprisings, on why some authoritarian rulers remained in power while others fell, and on the role of various actors in the processes of political change. Academic books on the Middle East and North Africa (MENA)[1] have habitually contained case studies, which occasionally lack a common conceptual and/or methodological framework. However, the change processes in the MENA region demand a systematic approach that enables comparison among countries. The key distinguishing feature of this book, therefore, is that it provides a robust academic analysis of a region that is the focus of particular international interest, using a comparative approach that analyses and explains the consequences of the political changes that have taken place since 2011, not only at national level (within political regimes), but also at regional and international level (the MENA region and western policies towards MENA countries). Thus, our book opts for a horizontal comparative analysis by theme: parties and political groups, elections, constitutional frameworks, power relations, governance, civil society, rights and freedoms, regional powers, security issues, foreign policies, and so on. In order to complement this comparative analysis, this book also employs a typology to study change processes that have taken place in specific countries in the MENA region.

Therefore, the aim of the book is to closely study regime responses and the principal transformations that have occurred in the MENA countries and in the region overall as a result of the Arab Spring, with the purpose of assessing whether the nature of power and power relations has changed since 2011.

The point of departure for this book is that political change can and often does take different directions, not all of which necessarily have to lead to regime change. Transitions may occur from authoritarianism towards democracy, but may also give rise to a reconfiguration of authoritarianism. Additionally, authoritarian rulers can undertake political reforms without democratic motivations. Thus, the broad concept of 'political change' is used in this book not only in the sense of provoking democratic developments, but also as an element in reshaping authoritarian regimes.

Firstly, the book addresses the main question of how political change affects power in authoritarian regimes: do they entail a democratic advance, or might they even lead to a reconfiguration and an increase in authoritarianism? Furthermore, it is worth asking: what have been the effects of the constitutional reforms and elections over the last five years? Have the decision-making actors and power relationships changed? Have states been strengthened or weakened by the processes of change we have seen? How are party or other representational systems now configured? What role does civil society play in democratic transitions and in the processes of change? What factors explain the poor governance of the MENA countries despite economic and political reforms? What is the current situation with regard to political rights and civil liberties, and particularly in relation to media freedom?

Secondly, the book analyses the geopolitical consequences and the reconfiguration of the political scenario of North Africa and, very notably, in the Middle East following the Arab Spring. On these points, the book attempts to provide a response to the following questions: what positions have the United States, the European Union and its member countries adopted towards the changes that have occurred in the MENA countries and in the region as a whole? Who are the hegemonic and emerging powers in the region at the present time? What position have they maintained towards the political changes occurred in each country? In what ways are relations between governments and non-state actors cooperative or confrontational? Have the identity cleavages – religious and ethnic – throughout the region become deeper, and what is their real role in the present conflicts in the MENA region? What are the challenges presented by Islamic State to the MENA countries and to the international community? Is jihadist terrorism an impediment to democratisation because it reinforces the position of authoritarian elites?

This book is organised in four parts. The first deals with the theoretical and methodological analysis of changes that have occurred since 2011 as a result of the Arab Spring: in political regimes, from a comparative politics approach (Chapter 1); and in the MENA region from an international relations perspective (Chapter 2).

In Chapter 1, Inmaculada Szmolka reflects first on the existence or not of a new wave of democratisation in the wake of the Arab Spring. It is true that simultaneity, contagion, diffusion and emulation do feature in the political dynamics of change following the Arab Spring. However, rather than a democratic tsunami, there were ebbs and flows of a 'wave of political change'

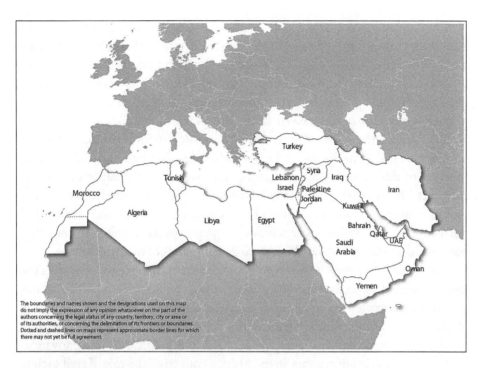

The boundaries and names shown and the designations used on this map do not imply the expression of any opinion whatsoever on the part of the authors concerning the legal status of any country, territory, city or area or of its authorities, or concerning the delimitation of its frontiers or boundaries. Dotted and dashed lines on maps represent approximate border lines for which there may not yet be full agreement.

Figure I.1 Map of Middle East and North Africa countries

that has involved differing transformative processes in each country. Secondly, the author offers a typology of political regimes as well as a classification of MENA regimes prior to the Arab Spring, in order to identify the starting point of political change. Thirdly, Szmolka defines and categorises the different types of political change processes: two general processes of political change (democratisation and autocratisation); and five specific processes of political change affecting democracies (democratic regression, democratic deepening and consolidation of democracy) or authoritarianisms (political liberalisation and authoritarian progression). And finally, the author presents the methodological framework used in this book to study political change in the MENA countries. This change is analysed with reference to three dimensions: pluralism and political competition (party/representation systems and electoral integrity); government (constitutional reforms, government and state powers, and good governance); and public rights and liberties (political rights, civil rights, rule of law and civil society).

In Chapter 2, Rafael Bustos analyses what the political transformations following the Arab Spring mean from the perspective of different international relations theories: neo-realism, institutionalism, social constructivism and critical theories. Processes of change like democratisation, political liberalisation, autocratisation, the breakdown of state authority, and covert regional and civil war are all phenomena which are associated with the Arab Spring events, but which convey very different meanings in different parts of the Middle East and North Africa. The author first points to the direct effects of foreign policy intervention in transitions to democracy worldwide, including the MENA region, notwithstanding the traditional support some non-democratic or aggressive regimes have received from consolidated democracies. Secondly, Bustos reviews the work of a number of prestigious international relations scholars on the Arab Spring and reviews how leading international relations journals of different theoretical leaning have treated the Arab Spring in the period 2011–15. He then illustrates how similar topics are treated in each theory in rather inverted ways, for example bio-security from neo-realism and critical perspectives. Thirdly, Bustos concludes on the prospects and need within international relations for further theoretical development of the Arab Spring.

Part II addresses the actors involved and the main change processes over the last five years. This includes an analysis of the transformations in party systems, the elections (from the point of view of electoral integrity), the democratising, liberalising or authoritarian effects of the constitutional reforms undertaken, changes in government and power relations within political regimes, advances or deteriorations in governance in the MENA countries, the role of civil society in processes of political change, and the current situation regarding rights and civil liberties, particularly in media and press freedom in the MENA countries.

In Chapter 3, Lise Storm examines parties and party system change across the MENA countries since December 2010. The discussion begins with a brief overview of party systems in the region on the eve of the Arab Spring, thereby providing a quick introduction to the selected cases as well as a benchmark against which to measure change. Party system change is determined via indicators such as the effective number of parties, party system fragmentation, electoral volatility and the entry of new parties into the system. The analysis of the indicators of party system change is coupled with a discussion of empirical data on the political environment during and in the immediate aftermath of the elections, including issues such as regime classification, rotation of power, coalition structures, prohibited parties and societal cleavages. The author explains how – despite the fact that some old regimes fell and elections were held – the traditionally dominant or hegemonic political parties stayed pre-eminent in a number of MENA countries. Finally, Storm shows what party system change tells us about the prospects for democracy some seven years after the outbreak of the Arab Spring.

In Chapter 4, Guadalupe Martínez-Fuentes analyses the elections held over the last five years from the point of view of electoral integrity as an analytical resource for both the classification of regimes and the detection of any change in political regime. While full democracies, defective democracies and various models of pluralist authoritarianism register varying election integrity scores, processes of political liberalisation or democratisation, as well as those of increased authoritarianism, are quite often related, respectively, to improvements or deteriorations in electoral integrity. With this premise in mind, Martínez-Fuentes focuses on the evolution of both the elections' political context and the electoral integrity level in the MENA countries since the beginning of the Arab Spring. She offers three main conclusions. The first is the heterogeneity of the MENA countries in terms of advance, regression, stability or fluctuation in electoral integrity. The second is that the behaviour of the variable 'electoral integrity' in the MENA countries has not had any relationship at all with other variables, such as the kind of regime from which the political transition emerges, the transition timing and the way the transition is conducted. The third is that the achievement of specific levels of electoral integrity in the MENA region does not always correlate with the degree of transformation achieved to date in other fields of security, rights, freedoms and good governance.

In Chapter 5, Ewa Strzelecka and María Angustias Parejo compare the constitutional reform processes that have taken place in the MENA region since the upheavals of 2011. Their analysis on the reform processes is structured around procedures (institutions and rules), consensus and dissent throughout the constitutional process, and the content of those constitutional reform processes (democratic and authoritarian mechanisms). The authors conclude that constitutional processes are relevant, but not determinant for political change. Political processes are structured by power relations, which at the same time determine the nature and scope of the constitutional changes. Many of the constitutional reforms in the last five years have been the product of strategies for survival by the respective regimes and were promoted 'top-down' through a process that, in many countries, excluded the revolutionary movements and opposition groups that were not loyal to the regime. With the exception of Tunisia (which is currently the only democratic system in the region), the scope of the constitutional amendments has been limited and has perpetuated the dominance of the authoritarian rulers.

In Chapter 6, Victoria Veguilla focuses on governments and power relationships. She studies the place governments occupy in their respective political systems, how they are perceived by their populations, and the extent to which are they capable of managing violence and imposing their authority across the whole of their national territory. Governments are responsible for the policies carried out in their countries. Thus, many of the social protests – predominantly focused on the high levels of corruption – were directed against governments. However, while governments are perceived to be the institutions responsible for meeting citizens' welfare needs, there are other non-elected institutions (formal or informal) with significant decision-making powers that are non-accountable, such as the presidents of the republic, the monarchs and other national (the armed forces in the case of Egypt; armed groups in the cases of Libya, Syria and Yemen) or international actors (such as Saudi Arabia and Iran). On the other hand, Veguilla studies changes in the power structure. The author finds evidence of greater power concentration, with the exception of the new democratic regime of Tunisia.

In Chapter 7, Raquel Ojeda and Francesco Cavatorta focus on the implementation of various policies aimed at achieving good governance in the MENA countries. Good governance is considered to be one of the most important pillars of development and democratisation processes. The logic is that when political systems become more responsive to ordinary citizens through democratic mechanisms, 'good governance' emerges and the positive effects of neo-liberal reforms begin to take hold. The authors posit that, while this might be partially true in theory – accountable governments make better policy choices than unaccountable ones – the reality has been very different on the ground. The notion of good governance has acquired rather different meanings in practice, such as, for example, the way in which state authorities actually function to meet the socio-economic expectations of citizens (ending unemployment, unfair legal systems and corruption). According to Ojeda and Cavatorta, indicators did not generally improve in the MENA region immediately following the Arab uprisings. Countries that did not experience political instability and that had improving indices before 2010 have been able to maintain them, with the exception of the indicators 'voice and accountability' and 'political stability', which have fallen due to growing security concerns. On the other hand, the authors underline that 'the lack of good governance in the MENA region is not a story of poor achievement related to criteria or adaptability, but a much broader failure of international institutional policies in the developing world.'

In Chapter 8, Carmelo Pérez-Beltrán and Ignacio Álvarez-Ossorio assess the role played by civil society and the role it should fulfil within the transition processes or wave of changes that began after the Arab Spring. Firstly, the authors demonstrate that the Arab uprisings did not occur spontaneously, but that there was, in fact, already wide experience of action, expression and mobilisation over the preceding decades, despite fierce authoritarianism, enormous social repression, fragmentation of critical movements and an absence of independent public fora. Secondly, Pérez-Beltrán and Álvarez-Ossorio produce a diagnosis of the state of civil society since 2011, with reference to the new forms of association, which are highly politicised, and analyse aspects such as: the autonomy of civil society vis-à-vis the state, civil society's mediating role between the population and the actions of the state, and its role as an alternative power base and as a pressure group in controlling political action. Finally, the authors propose a broader concept of civil society, 'much more dynamic, creative and horizontalist that involves not only hierarchical organisational structures, but also other spaces of mobilisation, real or virtual, in which the citizenry can express its social, political and economic commitment'.

In Chapter 9, Luis Melián highlights the changes in political rights and liberties across the MENA countries since 2011. He outlines the importance of taking into account the rights and liberties dimension in the definition and measurement of democracy. Melián assesses the extent to which political change has achieved the introduction of laws relating to those rights and, more importantly, the extent to which they have been applied. The author shows that, with the exception of Tunisia, the situation of civil liberties in the region is either precarious or alarming in the majority of the MENA countries, despite the reforms implemented after the Arab Spring in some countries.

In Chapter 10, Javier García-Marín explains why the MENA region has traditionally been considered a place with limited freedom of the press and details the current situation of the media five years after the Arab Spring. Thus, the author describes media systems in the region, the political and regulatory environment in which the media have to operate (censorship, media ownership, freedom to practise journalism) and the role of the Internet from a comparative perspective. For García-Marín, one of the main results of the Arab Spring has been the attempt to further control information flows. With the exception of a few countries, especially Tunisia and Algeria, almost all the governments in the region have adopted rules in the hope of controlling information in a more effective way. The most common method has been to attempt to homologise information on the Internet with information provided by traditional media and, thus, to apply the same laws to it.

Part III analyses the political consequences of the processes of change at both regional and international level. The section thus takes into account the importance of the MENA region on the international scene, the role played by international powers in the processes of political change and in the conflicts that have erupted since the Arab Spring, the configuration of new political interests, regional powers and alliances, and revised understandings of the threats facing the region and the international community.

In Chapter 11, Jordi Quero and Eduard Soler assess the impact of the internal political changes on the regional order and how regional powers have adapted to those changes. The chapter draws on the English School and constructivist theories of international relations to approach the concept of order. In order to examine changes within the existing order, the authors use alliances and amity/enmity cleavages, non-intervention, multilateralism and bilateralism, and great power management, to analyse the fundamental institutions working in the MENA region. Quero and Soler conclude that the constitutional elements of the regional order continue to operate as usual and that 'slight changes in the fundamental institutions since the Arab Spring generally respond to a more fundamental systemic change that took place in the context of the 2003 war in Iraq.'

In Chapter 12, Marién Durán and Víctor Bados examine the political, territorial and security repercussions of the self-proclaimed Islamic State (IS) for the MENA region, and particularly in Syria, Iraq and Libya. According to the authors, IS has brought a new dimension to the war in Iraq and Syria as well as to the Libyan conflict, amplifying and making the conflict more complex, establishing a new mode of governance in the conquered territories and producing a new security framework in the MENA region. Firstly, Durán and Bados focus on the type of conflict that IS has generated in the region, contributing to a new conceptualisation and characterisation of war typology, and they propose the concept of 'neo-medieval high-tech war' to describe the IS conflict. Secondly, the authors explain the government system produced by IS in the occupied territories. And, finally, they analyse the implications for security throughout the MENA region, taking into account the international community's response and the new configuration of regional and global alliances.

In Chapter 13, Irene Fernández-Molina studies the EU's and EU member states' responses to the Arab Spring. She explores the paradox of the essential continuity of the EU's policies towards the countries of the southern Mediterranean 'neighbourhood' in a context of structural and multifaceted transformation, like that of the Arab Spring. The profound regional upheavals caused by this wave of anti-authoritarian protests, revolutionary regime changes and emerging civil conflicts arguably created a 'policy window' for change in EU foreign policy. Although it has been underway since mid-2010, the 2011 revision of the European Neighbourhood Policy (ENP) was presented as the EU's paradigm shift in response to these transformations. The 'Partnership for Democracy and Shared Prosperity with the Southern Mediterranean' (March 2011) and the 'New Response to a Changing Neighbourhood' (May 2011) put a stronger and seemingly self-critical emphasis on supporting 'democratic transformation' and 'building deep democracy' in the EU's periphery by applying greater differentiation and positive ('more for more') and negative ('less for less') conditionality. However, beyond appearances, inertia and business as usual prevailed in both the underlying conceptual construction of this EU discourse, the financial practice of the ENP and other patterns of behaviour already established in the EU's bilateral relations with its neighbours.

In Chapter 14, Juan Tovar analyses the foreign policy of the US in the MENA region since the Arab Spring. US foreign policy has in large part been shaped by events in the Middle East over the last fifteen years. Following the terrorist attacks of 11 September 2001, and the initial objective of the Obama administration to adopt a more conciliatory policy toward the regimes of the region, the Arab Spring further modified the situation and a more Wilsonian perspective was adopted, leading eventually to the military intervention in Libya. The author shows how the situation changed again as the Arab Spring took a different route from that originally foreseen by US decision-makers. Doctrinal changes of particular importance, which emphasised vital and core strategic interests such as the need to fight terrorist groups, the defence of the regional status quo, and guaranteeing energy supplies were the result of the renunciation of military intervention in Syria against the regime of Bashar al-Assad. At the same time, the rise of IS in Iraq and Syria paved the way for a more important change in the administration's priorities in the region and the need for intervention in states such as Iraq, whose relative stability was previously claimed as a success by the Obama administration and a justification for the withdrawal of US troops. As Tovar points out, despite important strategic changes to the US administration's global priorities, such as the famous 'pivot to the Pacific', the reduction of its dependency on energy from the region through the adoption of technologies such as shale oil and fracking, or new challenges like the conflict in Ukraine, the Middle East will retain its vital strategic role in US foreign policy in the short and medium term.

Finally, Part IV presents the processes of political change undertaken as a consequence of the Arab Spring according to the typology established in Chapter 1. In Chapter 15, Inmaculada Szmolka studies the open democratic transition processes following the fall of the authoritarian rulers in Tunisia, Egypt, Libya and Yemen. The only successful democratisation occurred in Tunisia, thanks to agreements between political actors, concessions from a dominant party and a strong and participative civil society. On the contrary, democratic transition failed in the three other countries for different reasons: in Egypt, because of a lack of agreement between political forces, an exclusionary process led by the Islamists, and the interference of a non-accountable actor – the army – in political affairs; in Libya, due to the lack of prior institutional architecture and of experience of party participation and political groups; and in Yemen, because of the empowerment of old regime elites in the transition process and, the exclusion of revolutionary movements, the lack of consensus to address independence movement demands in the south, and antagonism between political forces and their regional backers.

In Chapter 16, Inmaculada Szmolka and Irene Fernández-Molina examine political liberalisation processes in other MENA countries such as Morocco, Jordan, Oman and Algeria. As on previous occasions, the post-2011 political liberalisation processes were planned and led by the authoritarian rulers in a top-down fashion, acting as an escape valve for authoritarian regimes to defuse social discontent. These reforms were largely cosmetic and therefore have not led to a change in the authoritarian nature of the political regimes. Although there are positive aspects, the reforms have not brought about substantial changes in power relations.

Finally, in Chapter 17, Inmaculada Szmolka and Marién Durán analyse the MENA countries that have experienced negative changes following the Arab Spring: a process of autocratisation in Turkey, authoritarian progressions in Kuwait and Bahrain, and the fragmentation of state authority in Syria and Iraq. Turkey has transited from being a defective democracy to authoritarianism (due to a concentration of power in the hands of President Erdoğan), which has been a more pronounced tendency since the attempted *coup d'état* in July 2016. Kuwait, one of the 'less authoritarian' Arab countries before 2011, has undergone an authoritarian progression as a consequence of the emir's attempts to control parliament and approve restrictive laws regarding rights and liberties. Likewise, authoritarian progression in Bahrain has been the consequence of a decline in political competition – as a result of the withdrawal of opposition movements from parliament and state repression against any type of opposition. The democratic regime established in 2005 in Iraq currently faces enormous concerns: disabling sectarism, weak governance, and the occupation of much of north-western Iraq by IS. Violence directed by al-Assad's regime against protesters provoked a civil war on several fronts and a breakdown of state authority in Syria. These conflicts in the Middle East, as well as in Yemen, have made the region unstable and represent an enormous international challenge.

Note

1. There is no single agreed-upon definition of the countries that comprise the Middle East and North Africa. In this book the region refers to the Arab countries in the north of Africa (Morocco, Algeria, Tunisia, Libya, Egypt), the *Mashriq* (Jordan, Lebanon, Syria, Iraq) and the Arabian Peninsula (Bahrain, Kuwait, Oman, Qatar, Saudi Arabia, United Arab Emirates and Yemen), together with the non-Arab countries of the Middle East (Iran, Israel and Turkey).

Part I

Chapter 1

Analytical framework for a comparative study of change in political regimes

Inmaculada Szmolka

1 Theoretical approaches to democratisation, hybrid regimes and authoritarian persistence

Over the past four decades, political change has become one of the most important fields of study in comparative politics. All of the most significant studies of so-called 'transitology', 'transition theory', or 'democratisation studies' have focused almost exclusively on Europe and Latin America, disregarding the Middle Eastern and North African (MENA) countries in their theoretical and empirical analyses (Gasiorowski 1996: 469; Montabes 1999: 62; Camau 2002: 4; Schmitter 2002: 12; Posusney 2004: 127; Bellin 2004: 142; Pace and Cavatorta 2012: 127; Valbjørn 2015: 218).

Nevertheless, some of the MENA countries felt the democratic wave unleashed by the fall of the Berlin Wall. The region experienced political liberalisation processes in the 1990s and/or in the first decade of the twenty-first century while in other parts of the world democracy suffered significant setbacks (Diamond 1996: 20). Authoritarian ruling elites planned and directed political liberalisation in each country. They were really static changes, aimed at investing the political regimes with a new legitimacy after the crisis of the Arab state in the 1980s, rather than at provoking a real transformation of the basis of authoritarian power. Regional studies analysed these liberalisation processes as a strategy for regime survival (López-García et al. 1991; Salamé 1994; Brynen, Korany and Noble 1998; Montabes 1999; Camau 2002; Schmitter 2002; Brumberg 2002 and 2005; Ottaway et al. 2002; Albrecht and Shlumberger 2004; Ottaway and Choucair-Vizoso 2008).

The democratic decline in Asian regimes that resulted from the break-up of the Soviet Union and the failed political openings in some African and Asian countries showed the weakness of the transition paradigm. The use of the term 'paradigm' was too ambitious, since what these studies really offered were not generalisations, but assumptions only applicable to certain situations and geographical areas. Many countries considered 'in transit', among them some of the MENA countries, were not in transition towards democracy, and many of the democratic transitions that were taking place did not follow the patterns laid out in the pioneering work of O'Donnell et al. (1986) (Carothers 2002).

In fact, many of the countries under consideration turned into hybrid regimes that occupy the wide and nebulous space that separates full democracy from closed authoritarianism (Carothers 2002; Schedler 2002). Hybrid regimes combine elements of democracy (such as representative institutions, elections or constitutionalism) with the practices of an authoritarian power (restricted political competition, influence of non-accountable political actors, limited political rights and public liberties) (Szmolka 2010). Academic studies of hybrid regimes were produced by writers such as Karl (1990; 1995), Diamond (2002), Wigell (2008) and, mainly, Morlino (2008) who specifically linked hybrid regimes with processes of political change.[1] Other authors conceptualised hybrid regimes in different ways, stressing either their democratic features – 'democracy with adjectives'[2] – or their authoritarian characteristics.[3]

Evidence of political change without regime change led analysts of MENA politics to focus their attention on explaining the persistence of authoritarianism in the region using cultural, economic, historical or institutionalist perspectives.[4] The concepts of 'Arab exceptionalism' (Diamond 2003: 21; Diamond 2010: 93) or 'Middle Eastern and North African exceptionalism' (Bellin 2004: 143) were coined to refer to the resistance of these countries to democratisation. Authoritarianism was characterised as robust as well as dynamic in reference to the ability of regimes to change while their authoritarian nature remained unchanged (Albrecht and Schlumberger 2004; King 2009: 5). Thus, ruling elites 'upgraded' authoritarian power to accommodate and manage changing political, economic and social conditions (Heydemann 2007).

The so-called 'Arab Spring',[5] 'Arab Springs' or 'Arab Awakening' surprised scholars, who proved unable to predict the social mobilisations or their consequences, thus casting some doubt on the validity of the theory of authoritarian resilience, mainly in relation to the weakness of civil society and the state's ability to control society (Gause 2011; Bellin 2012: 127; Lynch 2012: 1; Pace and Cavatorta 2012: 127; Brynen et al. 2012; Valbjørn 2015: 218). Specialists on the region were more concerned with explaining the persistence of authoritarianism than studying the factors that could trigger political change. Hence, scholars of the Arab world were suffering 'their own paradigm crisis' (Brumberg 2012: 29).

Therefore, the events of the Arab Spring suggest the necessity of rejecting or validating some of the assumptions of both the transition paradigm and authoritarian persistence theory (Cavatorta 2015: 136), for instance, the significance of foundational elections and constitutional reforms, the role of the coercive apparatus and authoritarian elites in political change processes, the importance of controlling territory and the monopoly on the use of the force by the state, the role of civil society to encourage political change or the influence of cultural and social context in political transitions.

This chapter offers a theoretical and methodological framework for the processes of political change that emerged as a consequence of the revolutions and protests in MENA countries. Firstly, it reflects on the existence or absence of a new wave of democratisation following the Arab Spring. Secondly, it offers a definition and a typology of political regimes as well as a classification of the regimes existing in the MENA countries before the Arab Spring, with the purpose of identifying the starting point of the political change. Thirdly, it defines and categorises different types of political change processes. And finally, it presents the methodological framework used in this book to study political change in MENA countries, both comparatively and individually in each country.

2 A fifth wave of political change, not a fifth wave of democratisation

In the wake of the revolutions, upheavals and protests that took place in North Africa and the Arab Middle East from December 2010, different processes of political change have been underway in the region, causing some academics and analysts to posit a new 'wave of democratisation' (Blaydes and Lo 2011: 2; Diamond 2011; Dobson 2011; Gershman 2011; Grand 2011).

However, can the concept of a wave of democratisation be applied to the experiences of political change in the MENA countries? Huntington (1991: 15) defined a wave of democratisation as 'a group of transitions from non-democratic to democratic regimes that occur within a specified period of time and that significantly outnumber transitions in the opposite direction during that period'. Huntington (1991: 16–26), who published his book shortly after the fall of the Berlin Wall, included the transitions in Central and Eastern Europe in the third wave of democratisation. However, we believe it more appropriate to identify these post-communist transitions as opening up a new 'fourth wave of democratisation', distinct from the one that shook southern Europe and Latin America in the 1970s and 1980s (McFaul 2002; Doorenspleet 2005; Landman 2008; Priego 2011). For his part,

Carothers (2002: 5) characterised a democratisation trend as 'a simultaneous movement in at least several countries in each region away from dictatorial rule towards more liberal and often more democratic governance'. Other authors identified a 'snowballing', 'contagion', 'emulation', 'demonstration' or 'diffusion' effect in waves of democratisation (Whitehead 2001: 3; Bunce and Wolchik 2006: 10).

Simultaneity, contagion, diffusion and emulation do feature in the political dynamics of change following the Arab Spring. Protests spread from Tunisia through the MENA countries in a matter of a few months. The success of the Tunisian and Egyptian revolutions proved that it was possible to replace authoritarian leaders who had remained in power for decades through civil protests. Protesters emulated citizens of other countries using the same slogans and strategies (occupation of cities' main squares and use of social networks as a tool to call for demonstrations). However, a democratic tsunami did not occur in the Arab world (Abdelali 2013: 198; Ahmed and Capoccia 2014: 14; Masoud 2015: 74). In fact, only Tunisia has transited from an authoritarian regime to a democratic one (Stepan 2012), while democratic transitions failed in Egypt, Libya and Yemen. At present, Egypt has returned to authoritarianism after the military coup that overthrew the democratically elected President Morsi in 2013. Transitions in Libya and Yemen drifted into an armed conflict and a state collapse. Likewise, violence directed by al-Assad's regime against protesters provoked a civil war on several fronts and a breakdown of state authority in Syria. The involvement of the self-proclaimed Islamic State (IS) and other actors in the conflict has complicated the departure of President al-Assad from power, and so, the opening of a democratic transition. IS also destabilised Iraq, a country that faces internal struggles as a consequence of sectarian policies. Other Arab regimes undertook political reforms to stave off greater demands for political participation and have not substantially altered the authoritarian nature of power (Morocco, Algeria, Jordan and Oman). In other countries, the consequences of the Arab Spring have been negative because institutional political competitiveness has diminished as a result of the withdrawal of opposition movements from parliament (Bahrain and Kuwait). And in the other Arab countries, there is no evidence of democratic progress (Lebanon) or any democratic change (Saudi Arabia, Qatar and the United Arab Emirates). In relation to non-Arab Middle East, Turkey has undergone an autocratisation process, while Iran and Israel have remained stable.

In conclusion, there has not been a wave of democratisation in the region, but rather ebbs and flows of a 'wave of political change' that has involved different processes in each country: democratisation, autocratisation, political liberalisation, authoritarian progression or even the immobility of authoritarian regimes (Szmolka 2014). Thus, different trajectories of democratisation and of authoritarianism can be identified following the Arab Spring (Volpi 2013).

In order to assess what kind of process of political change has been produced and whether there has been regime change, it is necessary to specify the start and end points, with reference to the categories of political regimes. The following section presents a typology of political regimes and a classification of the MENA countries before the Arab Spring, with a view to assessing the type and scope of political change process in each regime.

3 Political regimes

3.1 Definition and typology of political regimes

There are quite a number of definitions and classifications of the MENA regimes.[6] In most cases these conceptualisations refer to specific countries or consider one criterion for the classification of political regimes. Likewise, regional studies tend to develop their own concepts and research agendas by reasserting the exceptional nature of the cases (Bunce 2000: 721). This exceptionalism causes problems of comparability with other areas. The analytical framework applied in this book considers all countries in the MENA region and is also useful for the study of other regions, making it possible to compare processes of political change in different areas and at different times. Additionally, in comparative politics, when describing political regimes, scholars usually use democracy indices provided by such institutions as Freedom House, The Economist Intelligence Unit, Polity Project or Bertelsmann Stiftung. While we do not deny their usefulness and relevance as scientific instruments for measuring democracy or authoritarianism, it is often the case that MENA countries' scores bring about different rankings of democracy and authoritarianism (see Table 1.1 and Tables A.1, A.2, A.3 and A.4 in the Appendix).

This chapter proposes a classification of political regimes into types and subtypes. The types of political regime derive from two branches: democracy and authoritarianism. Within these, eight categories of political regime are identified. This typology will be used to define the political regimes that existed before the Arab Spring and to assess the possibility of regime change. Three analytical axes are used in order to establish the typology: pluralism and political competition, government, and public rights and civil liberties (see Table 1.2).

Table 1.1 Comparative country indices in MENA countries (before and after the Arab Spring)

Country	Freedom House scale 1 (free) to 7 (non-free)		The Economist Index scale 0 (autocracy) to 10 (democracy)		Bertelsmann Transformation Index scale 0 (failed) to 10 (highly advanced)		Polity IV scale 10 (institutional-ized democracy) to −10 (autocracy). −77 (interruption periods collapse)	
	2010	2015ᵃ	2010	2015ᵃ	2010	2016ᵃ	2010	2014ᵃ
Algeria	5.5	5.5	3.44	3.95	4.4	4.8	2	2
Bahrain	5.5	6.5	3.49	2.79	4.4	3.5	−5	−10
Egypt	5.5	5.5	3.07	3.18	4.2	3.9	−3	−4
Iran	6.0	6.0	1.94	2.16	3.5	3.0	−7	−7
Iraq	5.5	5.5	4.00	4.08	4.2	3.5	3	3
Israel	1.5	1.5	7.48	7.77	ᵇ	ᵇ	10	10
Jordan	5.5	5.5	3.74	3.86	4.0	4.0	−3	−3
Kuwait	4.0	5.0	3.88	3.85	4.7	4.4	−7	−7
Lebanon	4.0	4.5	5.82	4.86	6.3	5.7	6	6
Libya	7.0	6.0	1.94	2.25	3.2	2.4	−7	−77
Morocco	4.5	4.5	3.79	4.66	4.1	3.8	−6	−4
Oman	5.5	5.5	2.86	3.04	4.0	3.2	−8	−8
Qatar	5.5	5.5	3.09	3.18	4.2	3.8	−10	−10
Saudi Arabia	6.5	7.0	1.84	1.93	2.9	2.5	−10	−10
Syria	6.5	7.0	2.31	1.43	3.2	1.7	−7	−9
Tunisia	6.0	2.0	2.79	6.72	3.8	6.3	−4	7
Turkey	3.0	3.5	5.73	5.12	7.7	7.3	7	9
UAE	5.5	6.0	2.52	2.75	4.2	4.0	−8	−8
Yemen	5.5	6.5	2.64	2.24	4.2	2.8	−2	−77

Notes: ᵃ last data available ᵇ BTI does not include Israel
Source: prepared by the author

Table 1.2 Categories of political regimes and analytical dimensions

Category of political regime	Subcategory of political regime	Analytical dimension		
		Pluralism and political competition	Government	Public rights and civil liberties
Full Democracy		Competitive	Effective	Guaranteed
Defective Democracy		Competitive	Effective/Flawed	Guaranteed/ Diminished
Pluralist Authori-tarianism	**Quasi-Competitive and Restrictive**	Quasi-competitive	Autocratic	Restrictive
	Hegemonic and Restrictive	Hegemonic	Autocratic	Restrictive/ Very restrictive
Closed Authoritarianism		Non-pluralist	Totalitarian	Non-recognition

Source: prepared by the author

A political regime is defined here by a set of institutions and structures of power in a particular territory, the nature of access to power, and how it is exercised, the relationships and behaviours between rulers and other political actors, as well as between rulers and ruled, and the way in which the political system functions and the political processes actually take place.

The definitions for each category of political regime are:

1. Full democracy: this is a regime of government in which access to power is established by means of periodic and competitive elections, with equality of opportunity both in exercising the right to vote and in being able to stand as a candidate. The only restrictions on pluralism and participation in the social and political sphere are targeted on activities that would involve a breach of legal and constitutional principles. The government exercises its power effectively. It is politically accountable for the performance of its functions (horizontal accountability) and it is limited in the exercise of power (rule of law). Legislative, executive and judicial institutions act autonomously, without one body dominating or interfering with the core-sphere of the others (Merkel 2004: 41). This kind of regime is founded on acceptance, by the majority of the governed, of political ground rules, and on respect for minorities and human rights.

2. Defective democracy: these are political regimes which, while conducting regular and competitive electoral processes that fulfil the functions of representation and the creation of government (electoral democracies), may not have fully consolidated their progress towards full democracy (in relation to government functioning or public rights and the civil liberties situation). The reasons for democratic failure affect government and/or rights and liberties: inadequate restraints and counterbalancing of representative institutions; institutional predominance – no hegemony – of one political force that intentionally weakens the role of the opposition and reduces the possibility of rotation in government; the existence of non-accountable actors functioning as veto players (for example the army, state security agencies, or religious or ethnic groups); the presence of a foreign power supervising the country's democratic development; or the lack of full equality of rights for social, ethnic and religious groups.

3. Pluralist authoritarianism: these are regimes in which there is legal recognition of parties or political movements. Representative institutions are set up in accordance with the results of pluralist elections, but in which some political forces – that do not represent anti-democratic values – are excluded from political processes. In the same way, the correct functioning of government may be hindered by a lack of autonomy on the part of representative institutions, by an imbalance of power, or by the presence of influential actors who have no political responsibility.

Additionally, although freedoms are recognised in principle, public rights and liberties are usually curbed when the bases of political power are at risk. Depending on the extent of political competition, pluralist authoritarianism can be:

3.1 Quasi-competitive and restrictive pluralist authoritarianism: in these regimes a broad spectrum of forces takes part in politics and in elections; they are able to run for office and to be represented in institutions, resulting in social and political pluralism. Even so, specific political groups may be left out of the electoral and political race. The majority of parties or political groups accept the electoral system. Some irregularities can be observed in the electoral process, but do not influence the final election result. The autonomy of elected institutions may be reduced by the existence of unaccountable veto powers, or formal actors who centralise institutional and political process but are not democratically elected and cannot be held accountable for their actions. These quasi-competitive authoritarianisms often go hand in hand with an expansion of public freedoms, such as the right of association, freedom of expression, pluralism of the media, and so on. However, the guarantee of these rights and liberties may be constrained by limits imposed, for example, by the party in power, for reasons of national defence, for religious reasons, or by the head of state.

3.2 Hegemonic and restrictive pluralist authoritarianism: in this type of political regime the political system may be dominated by military or foreign powers, religious hierarchies, or by any other powerful group. Moreover, a formally recognised political authority, which virtually takes over all political power, may exist. Additionally, despite the fact that they may have undergone processes of political liberalisation, such as the recognition of political pluralism, only the parties or candidates who are already in power have any real opportunity of reaching positions of power and public institutions. The elections, albeit pluralist, are not competitive because significant opposition parties are excluded from them. Therefore, there is a hegemonic party or coalition in government. Furthermore, rights and liberties are restricted and are under permanent threat by the authorities. Certain ethnic, religious and regional groups may lose their civil rights, and serious conflicts involving these groups may occur.

4. Closed authoritarianism: here the rule of law does not exist, nor does the recognition of fundamental political rights or public freedoms. There is no recognition of the possible existence of political groups who might stand for interests or objectives that are different from those in power. In electoral processes, if there are any, only candidates from the political regime participate.

3.2 Classification of the MENA regimes before the Arab Spring

The preceding type of political regime in each country has to be borne in mind in order to appreciate the consequences of the processes of change after the Arab Spring. At the end of 2010 the MENA regimes were characterised as follows (see also Table 1.3):

3.2.1 Defective democracies: Israel, Turkey, Lebanon and Iraq

At the time of the Arab Spring, Israel was an electoral democracy.[7] Israeli elections were free and fair, and access was guaranteed for all political groups including Arab parties, provided that they did not deny 'the existence of the state of Israel as the state of the Jewish people'. The alternation of governments was possible and frequent, and the prime minister was usually a leader of the largest party in parliament. Israeli democracy was diminished mainly in relation to citizen rights and liberties. The Knesset has annually renewed the state of emergency since 1948. Political rights and civil liberties were extended to Jews as well as Arabs, but not equally. Arab rights were not properly protected (for example, the right to own, acquire, lease or rent property) and the rule of law was reduced by the state in order to avert the perceived threat attributed to Arabs. Arabs were recognised as a minority, but the legal framework institutionalised superior status for the Jewish ethno-national majority and it did not guarantee mechanisms to avoid decisions that could adversely affect the vital interests of the minority (Smooha 2002: 475–500).[8]

Turkey was also an electoral democracy. Elections were free and fair contests. Access to government was democratic. The Justice and Development Party (Adalet ve Kalkınma Partisi, AKP) had been the predominant party since it came to power in 2002. The elected government had the effective power to govern. The military's privileged position began to diminish under Erdoğan's government, although the military still retained a strong institutional and political influence. Turkish government pursued democratic reforms in order to meet the European Union's requirements for membership negotiations. Although all citizens had the same political rights and liberties, ethnic (Kurdish) and religious minorities were discriminated against, opposition movements were often repressed and freedom of expression and the press were restricted.

In relation to Lebanon and Iraq, both countries could be formally considered democratic before the Arab Spring. A significant degree of pluralism and political competition through competitive elections characterised their political regimes. Both Iraq and Lebanon permitted a functioning opposition to government, and had political systems designed by consensus, reflecting the multi-ethnic and multiconfessional make-up of the population. However, significant shortcomings could be found in government performance, such as governability and the lack of effective control of the territory. In Iraq, although Shiites, Sunnis and Kurds collaborated in central government, there was no real consensus on the direction of the state. The Shiite dominance of the government provoked sectarian tensions, which made government unstable in the years prior to the Arab Spring. Moreover, Iraq had a concerning human rights situation.

3.2.2 Restrictive and quasi-competitive pluralist authoritarian regimes: Morocco and Kuwait

In Morocco parties competed freely and interacted in representative institutions, elections and other political processes. The opposition could criticise the government and propose alternative agendas. However, the opposition had to observe limits imposed by the monarchy, who retained effective power; as a result, politics was not fully competitive. Some groups opted to remain outside the institutional arena as they did not believe it offered the necessary democratic conditions to enable their participation in the political game and preferred not to legitimise these power structures. Additionally, the monarchy centralised decision-making, with representative institutions only having limited powers. Finally, the exercise of civil liberties was likewise restricted whenever it threatened the foundations of political power (monarchy, Islam and territorial integrity).

In Kuwait, although political parties were officially banned, political organisations were tolerated and operated freely and had competed in elections since 1992. The universal right to vote was introduced in 2005. Observation of the elections by national and international organisations in Kuwait and public vote-counting were allowed. Seculars, Sunnis and Shiites were represented in parliament, which had legislative powers as well as the right to question and possibly dismiss ministers. The opposition usually rejected government projects and exercised tight control on the government. Nevertheless, as in Morocco, the emir had decision-making power as well as legislative and executive powers. Consequently, they were constitutional but not parliamentary monarchies like those in democratic countries.

3.2.3 Restrictive and hegemonic pluralist authoritarian regimes: Algeria, Tunisia, Egypt, Jordan, Bahrain, Yemen and Iran

In Algeria, Tunisia, Egypt and Yemen competition was limited by the hegemonic position of a party or a party coalition, by barriers to opposition activities, and by irregularities in electoral processes. Thus, the political system allowed the pluralist interaction of parties or political movements, but not access to genuine decision-making power. Elections primarily served to create parliamentary majorities to support the rulers. Furthermore, civil rights and liberties were restricted.

In Jordan the main opposition party, the Islamic Action Front, decided not to participate in the 2010 elections because of the changes in electoral legislation and the irregularities in previous elections. An official non-partisan majority dominated parliament. As in other Arab monarchies, the constitution reserved legislative and executive powers for the king. Government function was also restricted by the influence of military and security forces. In Bahrain, as in Kuwait, the regime banned political parties but allowed political associations (secular, Sunni and Shiite). The Shiite association al-Wefaq was the largest formation in the lower house of parliament. However, al-Wefaq did not participate in government, which was supported by smaller pro-government Sunni parties and independents. Parliament had a restricted capacity of control over the government. Both in Jordan and Bahrain political regimes imposed restrictions on rights and liberties.

In Iran Islamic and elected Republican institutions coexisted; however, the former clearly enjoyed supremacy. Direct elections for parliament and the president, as well as local government bodies, were undermined by the supreme leader and the Guardian Council. Religious institutions also interfered in the functioning of parliament, government and the judiciary. Regarding political competition, although there were different political societies that could run for election, there was no real pluralism. All political groups represented the values of the Islamic Republic, reform-oriented candidates were often banned and no secular opposition group could set out an alternative to the Islamic regime. Political rights and civil liberties were only nominal, and individual rights were very restricted.

3.2.4 Closed authoritarian regimes: Libya, Syria, Saudi Arabia, the United Arab Emirates (UAE), Oman and Qatar

In these countries there was no political pluralism, citizens could not express their political preferences, assemblies were of a consultative nature only, governments were formed and dissolved at the discretion of the head of state, and the exercise of civil liberties was restricted. Syria is included in this category of closed authoritarianism. Although political parties existed in Syria, only socialist parties participating in the National Progressive Front (NPF) could run for elections and be represented in parliament. The NPF was under the hegemony of the Ba'ath Party. Likewise, the constitution granted the Ba'ath Party its leadership in society and in the state. The president of the republic

Table 1.3 Classification of the MENA regimes before the Arab Spring

Categories	Countries	Pluralism and political competence	Government	Public rights and civil liberties
Defective democracy	Israel	Competitive pluralism	Effective	Restrictive
	Iraq		Flawed	
	Lebanon		Flawed	
	Turkey		Effective	
Restrictive and quasi-competitive pluralist authoritarianism	Kuwait	Quasi-competitive pluralism	Autocratic	Restrictive
	Morocco			
Restrictive and hegemonic pluralist authoritarianism	Algeria	Hegemonic pluralism	Autocratic	Restrictive
	Bahrain			Restrictive
	Egypt			Restrictive
	Jordan			Restrictive
	Iran			Very restrictive
	Tunisia			Very restrictive
	Yemen			Restrictive
Closed authoritarianism	Libya	Non-pluralist	Totalitarian	Very restrictive
	Oman			
	Qatar			
	Saudi Arabia			
	Syria			
	UAE			

Source: prepared by the author

was elected by a presidential referendum in which the sole candidate was nominated by the ruling Ba'ath Party.

4 Definition and typology of processes of political change

Political change is defined here as the transformations in a political regime that affect their rules, institutions, power relations, actor behaviours and political processes. Political change is not a linear process (Morlino 2008: 1). Even with similar starting points, whether in authoritarian or democratic regimes, political change can and often does take different directions, not all of which necessarily have to lead to regime change. From authoritarianism, the regime can move towards democracy, but the transition can also lead to a new form of authoritarianism. Therefore, it is essential to distinguish the different pathways in which political change can take place.

Two general processes of political change are identified: democratisation (from authoritarianism to democracy) and autocratisation (from democracy to authoritarianism). Five specific processes of political change are also distinguished: three affecting democracies (democratic regression, democratic deepening and consolidation of democracy); and two characterising authoritarianisms (political liberalisation and authoritarian progression). Rather than involving a change of political regime, these five processes may lead to changes in subtypes within democratic and authoritarian regimes (see Figure 1.1).

General processes:

1. Democratisation: this entails the transition from an authoritarian to a democratic regime and, therefore, the replacement of one political regime with another. In the academic literature, opinions vary as to when the democratisation of an authoritarian regime occurs. Linz and Stepan (1996: 14) pointed out four requirements for democratisation: a sufficient agreement on procedures to produce an elected government; a government that comes to power as the direct result of a free and popular vote; the government's *de facto* possession of the authority to generate new policies; and the fact that the executive, legislative and judicial power generated by the new democracy does not *de jure* share power with other bodies such as the military, or with religious leaders. Other political scientists have argued that democratisation implies the accomplishment of Dahl's (1989) requirements for polyarchy: the existence of elected officials and control over governmental decisions; frequent, free, and fair elections; universal adult suffrage; the right to stand for office; freedom of expression; access to alternative sources of information; the right to form and join independent associations; and guarantees for minorities. However, it is argued here that Dahl's conditions and Linz and Stepan's list, are insufficient. In Tunisia these conditions were met following the 2011 election; however, it was not possible to use the term 'democratisation' until 2014, as a result of the approval of a new constitution. Thus, another prerequisite for democratisation is that a large majority of parties and of citizens accept the new common framework of social and political life.

2. Autocratisation: this is the opposite concept to democratisation; specifically, the transition from a democratic to an authoritarian regime. The breakdown of democratic regimes can occur by legal means because of an abusive exercise of power, a significant restriction of political competition and/or the limitation of political rights and civil liberties. Autocratisation can also be produced as a consequence of acts of violence, such as a *coup d'état* or war. According, to Linz and Stepan (1978), the stability of democracies depends on three factors: legitimacy, efficiency and effectiveness.

Specific processes:

In democratic regimes:

1. Democratic regression: this concept is applied to full democracies that regress to become defective democracies, without the loss of the substantive democratic core (competitive elections, effective political opposition, a legitimate government that is accountable for its actions and guaranteed rights and freedoms for the majority). This situation may occur, for example, because of interference in political decision-making by non-accountable actors or through the limited impairment of citizens' rights (whether political, ethnic or religious).
2. Democratic deepening: it refers to an improvement in the quality of a democratic regime (Schedler 1998). Democratic deepening leads the transition from a defective democracy towards full democracy. This process is characteristic of countries that have recently installed a democratic regime and have improved their democratic practices, leading to full democracy first and then, if pursued, to the consolidation of democracy.
3. Democratic consolidation: this concept involves the anchoring of democratic values, institutions and practices, and therefore of the legitimacy of a democratic regime (Morlino 2003; Linz and Stepan 1996). Therefore, it is a process that is developed over time, in the context of full democracies.

In authoritarian regimes:

4. Political liberalisation: this process takes place in authoritarian contexts and is led by rulers in order to preserve the legitimacy of the regime. It implies an easing of repression and an extension of political rights and civil liberties, and thus, an increase in political competition and participation (O'Donnell et al. 1986; Mainwaring 1992). It may also involve a rotation of power. In a context of political liberalisation, the regime maintains its autocratic nature. Political liberalisation does not necessarily lead to the beginning of a transition towards democracy, and therefore does not necessarily trigger a change in political regime from authoritarian to democratic (Morlino 1985). Nevertheless, it may involve a shift from a hegemonic authoritarian regime towards a quasi-competitive one. If liberalisation is very limited or only normative, it will maintain the previous form of political authority (a quasi-competitive or hegemonic authoritarian regime).
5. Authoritarian progression: this means a deepening of the authoritarian nature of a regime. The authoritarian regime places even more limits on political competition and the exercise of political rights and civil liberties. It can occur in any category and subcategory of authoritarian regime, and may lead to a more authoritarian structure. It is also possible for a democratic transition to fail.

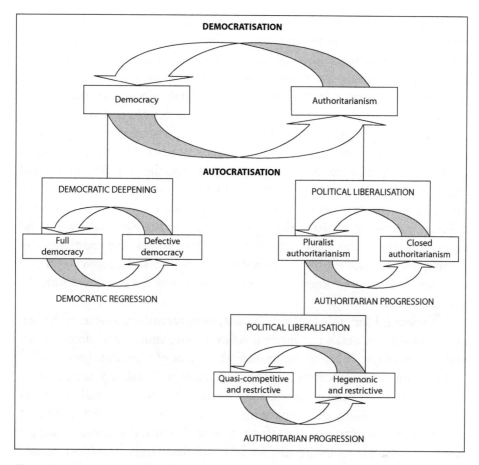

Figure 1.1 Typology of political change processes regarding political regimes

These political change processes will be analysed for MENA countries in Part III of this book.

5 Methodology for the study of political change processes

In this section a methodological framework for the study of political change in MENA regimes is offered. The aim is to provide a methodology that may be useful in evaluating the scope of political transformations and in distinguishing the types of processes of political change in each country after the Arab Spring. Political change is analysed with reference to the three dimensions that we used to classify political regimes: pluralism, government, and public rights and liberties (see Table 1.4). In each dimension, we include different variables that are used comparatively in the Part II chapters on political regimes and in relation to each country in the Part IV chapters.

In the first of these dimensions, 'pluralism and political competition', parties and party systems are analysed as well as the integrity of electoral processes. With regard to parties and party systems, political parties' legal frameworks are analysed with the aim of identifying whether there has been an increase in political pluralism and whether the main societal cleavages are represented in the creation of parties. Party system change is determined via indicators such as fragmentation, polarisation, electoral volatility and the entry of new parties into the system. We also observe interparty relations in the processes of change, bearing in mind the coalition structures and the shared or adversarial interests and strategies between parties. In relation to electoral integrity, we assess achievements in the parliamentary and presidential elections held in the MENA countries since 2011 through consensus in the electoral system and fairness, as well as the degree to which elections allow *de facto* participation, competition and the expression of political preferences, the supervision and conduct of electoral processes, and the acceptance of the electoral results by political actors.

In the second dimension of 'government', we observe three aspects of change: new constitutions and constitutional reforms, government and state powers, and good governance. Firstly, procedures, the degree of consensus (or lack of it) in the constitutional processes, and the democratic or liberalising content of the new constitutions or constitutional reforms are focused on. Secondly, elections and the accountability of government, the concentration or distribution of power between institutions, the effectiveness with which the elected rulers are able to exercise power in the absence of interference from others actors, and the state's capacity to meet the needs of its citizens (responsiveness) (Morlino 2003) are taken into account. Whether the state controls the entire territory via the legitimate use of force is also studied. Thirdly, under the heading of good governance, inclusiveness is analysed (equal treatment and equal access to public services), as well as accountability (publication of budgets and public expenditure), and transparency (fighting corruption in the public sector).

In the third dimension, 'public rights and civil liberties', the changes introduced by the new legal frameworks for rights of citizenship, the degree of success achieved in their implementation and the extent to which they represent a forward or a backward step for public rights and civil liberties are examined. Within this dimension, the main political rights surrounding participation (association, union rights and the right of assembly) and civil liberties (freedom of religious belief, speech and the press) are also analysed. Secondly, the strengthening of the rule of law through observation of the independence of the judiciary, the implementation of transactional justice, and respect for human rights are considered. Finally, the evolution of civil society resulting from the Arab Spring (the appearance of new social movements),

Table 1.4 Methodological framework to study changes in political regimes

Dimensions	Variables	Sub-variables	Democratic or Liberalising Effects
Pluralism and political competition	Political pluralism and party/representation systems	Legal framework	Increase in party supply. Possibility of parties of all tendencies to participate in politics
		Social cleavages	All social cleavages are represented in parties and political groups
	Political competitiveness	Pluralism vs hegemony	End of dominance of an hegemonic party/coalition in politics (possibility of a predominant party)
		Political alternance	Rotation in power
	Interparty relations	Coalition structures	Unified opposition platforms
		Democratic consensus	Democratic shared interests and strategies. Agreements between political forces
	Electoral integrity	Freedom for voting	Universal right to vote
		Electoral competence	Similar opportunities to run for office
		Electoral system	Acceptation of electoral system by the majority of political forces
		Fairness of election process	Mechanisms to guarantee fairness of elections (independent commissions for organising elections, international and/or national monitoring). No significant irregularities (vote-buying, intimidation, violence …)
		Social and political acceptance of electoral results	Significant turnout. Absence of political contestation of electoral results
Government	New constitutions and constitutional reforms	Procedure	Participation of majority political groups. Participation of citizenship (constitutional referendum)
		Consensus/lack of consensus	Agreed or non-agreed constitutions
		Content	Democratic or liberalising scope
	Government and state powers	Government legitimacy	Democratic election
			Accountable government
		Separation of powers	System of check and balances between institutions
		Effective power of government	Non-existence of veto players or reserved domains
			Control of the territory and legitimate use of violence
		Responsiveness	Correspondence of state to citizen needs and civil society in general
	Governance	Inclusiveness	Equal treatment and access to public services
		Accountability	Publication of budgets and public expenditure
		Transparency	Measures against corruption
Public rights and civil liberties	Rule of law	Independence of the judiciary	Increase in the autonomy of the judiciary
		Transactional justice	Implementation and consensus on transactional justice
		Human rights	Improvement in the situation of human rights
	Public rights	Right of association	New legal measures and improvements or setbacks
		Union rights	New legal measures and improvements or setbacks
		Right of assembly and demonstration	New legal measures and improvements or setbacks
	Civil liberties	Freedom of religious beliefs	New legal measures and improvements or setbacks
		Freedom of speech and opinion	New legal measures and improvements or setbacks
		Freedom of the press	New legal measures and improvements or setbacks
	Civil society	Vis-à-vis the state	Independence of the state
		Social mobilisation	Participation of social groups and citizens in processes of change

Source: prepared by the author

the autonomy of civil society vis-à-vis the state, and the role of civil society in the process of political change – the ability to mount protest action and to participate in processes of political change – are taken into account.

6 Conclusions

At the time of the Arab Spring, there was a lack of general theoretical and methodological frameworks for analysing the processes of political change that would soon take place. One problem was that the most important studies in comparative politics had ignored liberalisation processes in the MENA countries, and their assumptions were only applicable to certain situations and geographical areas (Europe and Latin America). Another was the fact that specialists on the region were more focused on explaining the persistence of authoritarianism than with studying the factors that might trigger political change in Arab countries.

So high were the expectations for political change that the Arab Spring generated, that some academics and analysts talked of a new 'wave of democratisation'. However, the initial optimism has proven unjustified. The Arab Spring does feature degrees of simultaneity, contagion and coincidence in time, but a democratic tsunami has not occurred in the Arab world. It is perhaps better to think in terms of a 'wave of political change' involving different processes and varying outcomes.

Even with similar starting points, whether in authoritarian or democratic regimes, political change can and often does take different directions, not all of which necessarily have to lead to a regime change. A regime might move from authoritarianism towards democracy, but the transition can also lead to a new form of authoritarianism. Therefore, with a typology of political regimes in mind, two general processes of political change have been identified: democratisation (from authoritarianism to democracy) and autocratisation (from democracy to authoritarianism). Furthermore, five specific processes of political change affecting democracies (democratic regression, democratic deepening and consolidation of democracy) or authoritarianisms (political liberalisation and authoritarian progression) have been identified.

This chapter has also offered an analytical framework for classifying and evaluating the processes of political change that have taken place in MENA countries. Political change has been analysed with reference to three dimensions: (1) pluralism and political competition: parties and party systems, and electoral integrity; (2) government: constitutions and constitutional reforms, government and state, and good governance; and (3) public rights and liberties: political rights, civil rights, the rule of law, and civil society.

Over the last four years, many countries in the MENA region have undertaken legal and constitutional reforms, and almost thirty elections have taken place. However, the democratising effect of these processes has been negligible in all cases except that of Tunisia. In the following chapters, the consequences of the processes of political change in various fields are examined. As will be seen, Tunisia, Egypt, Libya and Yemen all embarked on democratic transitions with varying results. The only case of democratisation is that of Tunisia, where we currently find a competitive party system, free and fair elections, a consensual constitution, a democratic government, an active civil society and an improvement in political and civil rights. In Egypt the 2013 military coup interrupted the transition and the regime regressed to a restrictive and hegemonic authoritarianism, with different actors in power. In Libya and Yemen the democratic transition has also failed and the two countries have descended into civil war. Syria also saw the outbreak of armed conflict as a consequence of the Arab Spring. The involvement of IS in the conflict complicates the departure of President al-Assad from power. IS has also destabilised Iraq. Additionally, it has to be acknowledged that the current sectarian struggle is in part the consequence of Prime Minister Nouri al-Maliki failing to respond to peaceful Sunni demands in 2012 and 2013. Lebanon has also suffered the consequences of the war in Syria: an increase in sectarian division and government instability.

Other countries, such as Morocco, Jordan, Algeria and Oman, have undergone processes of political liberalisation, although these have not altered the authoritarian nature of power. In other cases, such as Bahrain and Kuwait, there have been authoritarian progressions in political competitiveness and liberties. Finally, in the closed authoritarianisms of Saudi Arabia, Qatar and the UAE, there has been no evidence of any significant political change since the Arab Spring.

Notes

1. Morlino points to five situations: (1) stabilisation of the hybrid regime, of whatever kind ('without law', protected, limited democracy); (2) successive stabilisation of a democratic regime, which makes it possible to view the previous hybrid regime as a regime in transition towards democracy; (3) successive stabilisation of an authoritarian regime, which makes it possible to view the previous hybrid regime as a regime in transition towards authoritarianism; (4) non-stabilisation, with the regime continuing to be beset by uncertainty stemming from the period in which it was authoritarian; (5) non-stabilisation, with the regime continuing to be beset with uncertainty stemming from the period in which it was democratic (Morlino 2008: 14).
2. For example, 'delegative democracies' (O'Donnell 1994), 'electoral democracies' (Diamond 1999; Schedler 2002), 'illiberal democracies' (O'Donnell and Schmitter 1996; Zakaria 1997), 'semi-democracies' (Diamond et al. 1995; Mainwaring et al. 2000), 'defective

democracies' (Croissant and Merkel 2004), 'partial democracies' (Epstein et al. 2006), or contradictory terms such as 'authoritarian democracies' (Sakwa 1998). See the critique of this conceptualisation in Collier and Levitsky (1997).

3. For example, 'competitive authoritarianism, hegemonic, electoral, and politically-closed authoritarianism' (Diamond 2002), 'competitive authoritarianism' (Levitsky and Way 2002); 'electoral authoritarianism' (Schedler 2002, 2006), 'semi-authoritarian authoritarianism' (Ottaway 2003), 'electoral sultanism' (Thompson and Kuntz 2006), 'electoral autocratic regimes' (Wigell 2008).

4. See Bellin 2004; Posusney 2004; Ghalioun 2004; Posusney and Angrist 2005; Tessler 2002; Stepan and Robertson 2003 and 2004; Albrecht and Schlumberger 2004; Lakoff 2004; Tessler and Gao 2005: 83; Aaouzi 2006; Hinnebusch 2006; Heydemann 2007; Schlumberger 2007; King 2009; Storm 2008; Diamond 2010; Myers 2013.

5. We prefer the concept of 'Arab Spring' to 'Arab Springs' because, despite the differences and specificities of the various uprisings (structural conditions, intensity, duration and scope of the protests), as well as political demands (fall of the regimes or only changes in policies), we consider that the Arab Spring was a phenomenon with a linked origin in the countries of the region, sharing the same causes that produced the uprisings. Neither do we believe that it was a sudden 'awakening', as there was a prior awareness of the political, economic, social and cultural problems among citizens, and civil society, in the MENA countries that had developed greatly in recent decades.

6. In general: 'neo-patrimonialist regimes' (Leca and Shemeil 1983) or 'dominant-power system' (Carothers 2002). Other classifications distinguish between 'sultanist states', 'exclusionary states' and 'inclusionary states' (Kamrava 1998), 'radical republics and populist republics' and 'conservative monarchies' (Ayubi 1995), 'socialist republics' and 'liberal monarchies' (Richards and Waterbury 1990), 'one-party regimes' and 'family government' (Owen 2004; Pratt 2007), or 'traditional autocracies', 'liberalising autocracies' and 'dictatorship' (Lewis 2010). Brumberg (2002) argues that there are degrees of authoritarianism: from full autocracies to pluralist or liberalising autocracies.

7. In this book we assess the characteristics of the political regimes in relation to their territory and their nationals. Thus, we do not take into account Israel's violations of international law in its classification as a political regime, as in other countries.

8. For these reasons, Smooha (2002) characterises Israel as an 'ethnic democracy'.

References

Aaouzi, Abdelhak (2006), *Autoritarisme et aléas de la transition démocratique dans les pays du Maghreb*, Paris: L'Harmattan.

Abdelali, Abdelkader (2013), 'Wave of change in the Arab world and chances for a transition to democracy', *Contemporary Arab Affairs*, 6 (2): 198–210.

Ahmed, Amel and Giovanni Capoccia (2014), 'The study of democratization and the Arab Spring', *Middle East Law and Governance*, 6: 1–31.

Albrecht, Holger and Oliver Schlumberger (2004), '"Waiting for Godot": regime change without democratization in the Middle East', *International Political Science Review*, 25 (4): 371–92.

Ayubi, Nazih H. (1995), *Over-stating the Arab State: Politics and Society in the Middle East*, London: I. B. Tauris.

Bellin, Eva (2004), 'The robustness of authoritarianism in the Middle East: exceptionalism in comparative perspective', *Comparative Politics*, 36 (2): 139–57.

Bellin, Eva (2012), 'Reconsidering the robustness of authoritarianism in the Middle East: lessons from the Arab Spring', *Comparative Politics*, 44 (2): 127-149.

Blaydes, Lisa and James Lo (2011), 'One man, one vote, one time? A model of democratization in the Middle East', *Journal of Theoretical Politics*: 1–37.

Brumberg, Daniel (2002), 'Democratization in the Arab world? The trap of liberalized autocracy', *Journal of Democracy*, 13 (4): 56–68.

Brumberg, Daniel (2005), 'Liberalizations versus democracy', in Thomas Carothers and Marina Ottaway (eds), *Uncharted Journey: Promoting Democracy in the Middle East*, Washington, DC: Carnegie Endowment for International Peace, pp. 15–35.

Brumberg, Daniel (2012), 'Theories of transition', in Marc Lynch (ed.), *The Arab Uprisings: the Unfinished Revolutions of the New Middle East*, New York: Public Affairs.

Brynen, Rex, Bahgat Korany and Paul Noble (eds) (1998), *Political Liberalization and Democratization in the Arab World*, Boulder, CO: Lynne Rienner.

Brynen, Rex, Pete W. Moore, Bassel F. Salloukh and Marie-Joëlle Zahar (2012), Beyond the Arab Spring: *Authoritarianism and Democratization in the Arab World*, Boulder, CO: Lynne Reiner.

Bunce, Valerie (2000), 'Comparative democratization. Big and bounded generalizations', *Comparative Political Studies*, 33 (6/7, August/September): 703–34.

Bunce, Valerie and Sharon L. Wolchik (2006), 'Favorable conditions and electoral revolutions', *Journal of Democracy*, 17 (4): 5–18.

Camau, Michel (2002), 'La transitologie à l'épreuve du Moyen-Orient et de l'Afrique du Nord', *Annuaire de l'Afrique du Nord 1999*, XXXVIII: 3–9.

Carothers, Thomas (2002), 'The end of the transition paradigm', *Journal of Democracy*, 13 (1): 5–21.

Cavatorta, Francesco (2015), 'No democratic change . . . and yet no authoritarian continuity: the inter-paradigm debate and North Africa after the uprisings', *British Journal of Middle Eastern Studies*, 42 (1): 135–45.

Collier,i David and Steven Levitsky (1997), 'Democracy with adjectives: conceptual nnovation in comparative research', *World Politics*, 49: 430–51.

Croissant, Aurel and Wolfgang Merkel (2004), 'Consolidated and defective democracy? problems of regime change', *Democratization*, 11 (5): 33–58.

Dahl, Robert (1989), *Democracy and Its Critics*, New Haven: Yale University Press.

Diamond, Larry (1996), 'Is the third wave over?', *Journal of Democracy*, 7 (3): 20–37.

Diamond, Larry (1999), *Developing Democracy: Toward Consolidation*, Baltimore: Johns Hopkins University Press.

Diamond, Larry (2002), 'Elections without democracy. Thinking about hybrid regimes', *Journal of Democracy*, 13 (2): 21–35.

Diamond, Larry (2003), '¿Puede el mundo entero ser democrático? Democracia, desarrollo y factores internacionales', *Revista Española de Ciencia Política*, 9: 9–38.

Diamond, Larry (2010), 'Why are there no Arab democracies?', *Journal of Democracy*, 21 (1): 93–104.

Diamond, Larry (2011), 'A fourth wave or false start? Democracy after the Arab Spring', *Foreign Affairs*, 22 May. Available at <http://www.foreignaffairs.com/articles/67862/larry-diamond/a-fourth-wave-or-false-start> (last accessed 26 September 2011).

Diamond, Larry, Juan J. Linz and Seymour M. Lipset (1995), *Politics in Developing Countries*, Boulder, CO: Lynne Rienner.

Dobson, William (2011), 'Is this the fourth wave of democracy?', *The Washington Post*, 22 March. Available at <http://www.washingtonpost.com/blogs/post-partisan/post/is-this-the-fourth-wave-of-democracy/2011/03/22/ABKBatDB_blog.html> (last accessed 12 November 2011).

Doorenspleet, Renske (2005), *Democratic Transitions: Exploring the Structural Sources of the Fourth Wave*, Boulder, CO: Lynne Rienner.

Epstein, David, Robert Bates, Jack Goldstone, Ida Kristensen and Sharyn O'Halloran (2006), 'Democratic transitions: the key role of partial democracies', *American Journal of Political Science*, 50 (3): 551–69.

Gasiorowski, Mark J. (1996), 'An overview of the political regime change data set', *Comparative Political Studies*, 29: 469–83.

Gause, Gregory F. (2011), 'Why Middle East studies missed the Arab Spring?' Available at <https://www.foreignaffairs.com/articles/north-africa/2011-07-01/why-middle-east-studies-missed-arab-spring> (last accessed 12 November 2011).

Gershman, Carl (2011), 'The fourth wave', *New Republic*, 14 March. Available at <http://www.newrepublic.com/article/world/85143/middle-east-revolt-democratization> (last accessed 12 November 2011).

Ghalioun, Burhan (2004), 'The persistence of Arab authoritarianism', *Journal of Democracy*, 15 (4): 126–32.

Grand, Stephen R. (2011), *Starting in Egypt: the Fourth Wave of Democratization?*, Washington, DC: Brookings Institution. Available at <http://www.brookings.edu/ar/research/opinions.2011/02/10-egypt-democracy-grand/> (last accessed 12 November 2011).

Heydemann, Steven (2007), *Upgrading Authoritarianism in the Arab World*, Analysis Paper 13, Washington, DC: Brookings Institution. Available at <http://www.brookings.edu/,/media/Files/rc/papers/2007/10arabworld/10arabworld.pdf> (last accessed 20 January 2009).

Hinnebusch, Raymond (2006), 'Authoritarian persistence, democratization theory and the Middle East: an overview and critique', *Democratization*, 13 (3): 373–95.

Huntington, Samuel P. (1991), *The Third Wave: Democratization in the Late Twentieth Century*, Norman, OK: University of Oklahoma Press.

Kamrava, Mehran (1998), 'Non-democratic states and political liberalisation in the Middle East: a structural analysis', *Third World Quarterly*, 19 (1): 63–85.

Karl, Terry L. (1990), 'Dilemmas of democratization in Latin America', *Comparative Politics*, 23: 1–23.

Karl, Terry L. (1995), 'The hybrid regimes of Central America', *Journal of Democracy*, 6: 72–86.

King, Stephen J. (2009), *The New Authoritarianism in the Middle East and North Africa*, Bloomington: Indiana University Press.

Lakoff, Sandford (2004), 'The reality of Muslim exceptionalism', *Journal of Democracy*, 15 (4): 133–9.

Landman, Todd (2008), *Issues and Methods in Comparative Politics: an Introduction*, London: Routledge.

Leca, Jean and Yves Schmeil (1983), 'Cliéntelisme et patrionalisme dans le monde arabe', *International Political Science Review*, 4 (4): 455–99.

Levitsky, Steven and Lucan A. Way (2002), 'Elections without democracy. The rise of competitive authoritarianism', *Journal of Democracy*, 13: 51–65.

Lewis, Bernard (2010), *Faith and Power. Religion and Politics in the Middle East*, Oxford: Oxford University Press.

Linz, Juan J. and Alfred Stepan (1978), *The Breakdown of Democratic Regimes. Vol. 1. Crisis, Breakdown and Reequilibration*, Baltimore: Johns Hopkins University Press.

Linz, Juan J. and Alfred Stepan (1996), 'Toward consolidated democracies', *Journal of Democracy*, 7 (2): 14–33.

López-García, Bernabé, Gemma Martín-Muñoz and Miguel Hernando de Larramendi (eds) (1991), *Elecciones, participación y transiciones políticas en el Norte de África*, Madrid: Ministerio de Asuntos Exteriores.

Lynch, Marc (2012), 'Introduction', in Marc Lynch (ed.), *The Arab Uprisings: the Unfinished Revolutions of the New Middle East*, New York: Public Affairs.

Mainwaring, Scott (1992), 'Transitions to democracy and democratic consolidation: theoretical and comparative issues', in Scott Mainwaring, Guillermo O'Donnell and J. Samuel Valenzuela (eds), *Issues in Democratic Consolidation: the New South American Democracies in Comparative Perspective*, Indiana: University of Notre Dame Press.

Mainwaring, Scott, Daniel Brinks and Aníbal Pérez Liñán (2000), *Classifying Political Regimes in Latin America, 1945–1999*, Working Paper 280, Kellogg Institute. Available at <http://www.nd.edu/~kellogg/publications/workingpapers/WPS/280.pdf> (last accessed 14 June 2008).

Masoud, Tarek (2015), 'Has the door closed on Arab democracy?', *Journal of Democracy*, 26 (1): 74–87.

McFaul, Michael (2002), 'The fourth wave of democracy and dictatorship: noncooperative transitions in the postcommunist world', *World Politics*, 54 (2): 212–44.

Merkel, Wolfgang (2004), 'Embedded and defective democracies', *Democratization*, 11 (4): 33–58.

Montabes, Juan (1999), *Las otras elecciones. Los procesos y sistemas electorales en el Magreb*, Madrid: Agencia de Cooperación Internacional.

Morlino, Leonardo (1985), *Cómo cambian los regímenes políticos*, Madrid: Centro de Estudios Constitucionales.

Morlino, Leonardo (2003), *Democrazie e democratizzazioni*, Bologna: Società editrice Il Mulino.

Morlino, Leonardo (2008), *Hybrid Regimes or Regimes in Transition?*, Working Paper 70, FRIDE. Available at <http://fride.org/download/WP70-Hybrid_regimes_ENG_sep08.pdf> (last accessed 3 December 2011).

Myers, Ralph (2013), *Persistence of Authoritarianism in the Middle East and North Africa*, Munich: Grin Verlag.

O'Donnell, Guillermo (1994), 'Delegative democracy', *Journal of Democracy*, 5 (1): 55–69.

O'Donnell, Guillermo and Philippe C. Schmitter (1986): 'Defining some concepts (and exposing some assumptions)', in Guillermo O'Donnell, Philippe C. Schmitter and Laurence Whitehead, *Transitions from Authoritarian Rule: Tentative Conclusions about Uncertain Democracies*, Baltimore: Johns Hopkins University Press, pp. 6–14.

O'Donnell, Guillermo, Philippe C. Schmitter and Laurence Whitehead (1986), *Transitions from Authoritarian Rule: Tentative Conclusions about Uncertain Democracies*, Baltimore: Johns Hopkins University Press.

Ottaway, Marina (2003), *Democracy Challenged: the Rise of Semi-authoritarianism*, Washington, DC: Carnegie Endowment for International Peace.

Ottaway, Marina, Thomas Carothers, Amy Hawthorne and Daniel Brumberg (2002), *Democratic Mirage in the Middle East*, Policy Brief 20, Washington, DC: Carnegie Endowment for International Peace. Available at <http://carnegieendowment.org/files/Policybrief20.pdf> (last accessed 3 December 2011).

Ottaway, Marina and Julia Choucair-Vizoso (eds) (2008), *Beyond the Façade. Political Reform in the Arab World*, Washington, DC: Carnegie Endowment for International Peace.

Owen, Roger (2004), *State, Power, and Politics in the Making of the Modern Middle East*, London: Routledge.

Pace, Michelle and Francesco Cavatorta (2012), 'The Arab uprisings in theoretical perspective – an introduction', *Mediterranean Politics*, 17 (2): 125–38.

Posusney, Marsha P. (2004), 'Enduring authoritarianism: Middle East lessons for comparative politics', *Comparative Politics*, 36 (2): 127–38.

Posusney, Marsha P. and Michele P. Angrist (eds) (2005), *Authoritarianism in the Middle East: Regimes and Resistance*, Boulder, CO: Lynne Rienner.

Pratt, Nicola (2007), *Democracy and Authoritarianism in the Arab World*, London: Lynne Rienner.

Priego, Alberto (2011), *La primavera árabe: ¿una cuarta ola de democratización?*, Madrid: UNISCI Discussion Papers, 26. Available at <http://revistas.ucm.es/index.php/UNIS/article/view/37765/36547> (last accessed 13 December 2011).

Richards, Alan and John Waterbury (1990), *A Political Economy of the Middle East*, Boulder, CO: Westview Press.

Sakwa, Richard (1998), 'Russian political evolution: a structural approach', in Michael Cox (ed.), *Rethinking the Soviet Collapse. Sovietology, the Death of Communism and the New Russia*, New York: Pinter.

Salamé, Ghassan (ed.) (1994), *Democracy without Democrats: the Renewal of Politics in the Muslim World*, London: I. B. Tauris.

Schedler, Andreas (1998), 'What is democratic consolidation?', *Journal of Democracy*, 9 (2): 91–107.

Schedler, Andreas (ed.) (2002), 'The menu of manipulation', *Journal of Democracy*, 13: 51–65.

Schedler, Andreas (ed.) (2006), *Electoral Authoritarianism*, London: Lynne Rienner.

Schlumberger, Oliver (ed.) (2007), *Debating Arab Authoritarianism*, Stanford, CA: Stanford University Press.

Schmitter, Philippe C. (2002), 'Se déplaçant au Moyen-Orient et en Afrique du Nord, "transitologues" et "consolidologues" sont-ils toujours assurés de voyager en toute sécurité?', *Annuaire de l'Afrique du Nord 1999*, XXXVIII.

Smith, Dan (2006), *The State of the Middle East: an Atlas of Conflict and Resolution*, London: Earthscan.

Smooha, Sammy (2002), 'The model of ethnic democracy: Israel as a Jewish and democratic state', *Nations and Nationalism*, 8 (4): 475–503.

Stepan, Alfred (2012), 'Tunisia's transition and the twin tolerations', *Journal of Democracy*, 23 (2): 89–103.

Stepan, Alfred and Graeme B. Robertson (2003), 'An "Arab" more than "Muslim" electoral gap', *Journal of Democracy*, 14 (3): 30–44.

Stepan, Albert and Graeme B. Robertson (2004), 'Arab, not Muslim exceptionalism', *Journal of Democracy*, 15 (4): 140–6.

Storm, Lise (2008), 'An elemental definition of democracy and its advantages for comparing political regime types', *Democratization*, 15 (2): 215–29.

Szmolka, Inmaculada (2010), 'Los regímenes políticos híbridos: democracias y autoritarismos con adjetivos. Su conceptualización, categorización y operacionalización dentro de la tipología de regímenes políticos', *Revista de Estudios Políticos*, 147: 103–35.

Szmolka, Inmaculada (2011), 'Democracias y autoritarismos con adjetivos: la clasificación de los países árabes dentro de una tipología general de regímenes políticos', *Revista Española de Ciencia Política*, 26: 11–62.

Szmolka, Inmaculada (2014), 'Theoretical framework and models of political change processes in Arab regimes', *Anuario IEMed 2014*: 23–30. Available at <http://www.iemed.org/observatori/arees-danalisi/arxius-adjunts/anuari/anuari-2014/Szmolka_Arab_Regimes_Types_of_Process__IEMed_yearbook_2014_EN.pdf> (last accessed 2 February 2015).

Tessler, Mark (2002), 'Islam and democracy in the Middle East: the impact of religious orientations on attitudes towards democracy in four Arab countries', *Comparative Politics*, 34 (3): 337–54.

Tessler, Mark and Eleanor Gao(2005), 'Gauging Arab support for democracy', *Journal of Democracy*, 16 (3): 83–97.

Thompson, Mark and Philippe Kuntz (2006), 'After defeat: when do rulers steal elections', in Andreas Schedler (ed.), *Electoral Authoritarianism*, London: Lynne Rienner, pp. 113–38.

Valbjørn, Morten (2015), 'Reflections on self-reflections – on framing the analytical implications of the Arab uprisings for the study of Arab politics', *Democratization*, 22 (2): 218–38.

Volpi, Frédéric (2013), 'Explaining (and re-explaining) political change in the Middle East during the Arab Spring: trajectories of democratization and of authoritarianism in the Maghreb', *Democratization*, 20: (6), 969–90, DOI: 10.1080/13510347.2012.668438.

Wigell, Mikael (2008), 'Mapping "hybrid regimes": regime types and concepts in comparative politics', *Democratization*, 15 (2): 230–50.

Whitehead, Laurence (2001), 'Three international dimensions of democratization', in Laurence Whitehead (ed.), *The International Dimension of Democratization: Europe and the Americas*, New York: Oxford University Press, pp. 3–25.

Zakaria, Fareed (1997), 'The rise of illiberal democracy', *Foreign Affairs*, 76 (6): 22–43.

Chapter 2

The Arab Spring changes under the prism of international relations theory

Rafael Bustos

1 Introduction

International factors have been important in all democratising waves and especially in the most recent, although they have not been studied in great detail. This is also true for the so-called 'third democratising wave' (Huntington 1991), which includes the changes in southern Europe in the 1970s, Latin America in the 1980s, and what we shall describe here as the 'fourth wave' that affected Central and Eastern Europe in the 1990s (see Szmolka, Chapter 1). This observation is also applicable to other democratisation processes and more geographically localised political changes that took place in Asia (for example, the Philippines, South Korea, Taiwan, Mongolia and Indonesia from 1997 onwards), in sub-Saharan Africa (South Africa, Namibia, Botswana, Ghana and Senegal), and in the area of the Middle East and North Africa (MENA), such as in Algeria (1988–92), Jordan (1989–93) and Turkey (1999–2007).

Specifically, a good test of the differential treatment undertaken by international actors is provided by the Spanish (1975–82) and Algerian (1988–92) transitions – the former a great success, and the latter conflictual and anomalous, given that it gave way to another authoritarian regime (Bustos 2004). If, in the case of Spain, the generous political and financial support of the Social Democratic Party (SPD) of Willy Brandt and the German social-democratic foundation, Friedrich Ebert Stiftung, to the Spanish Socialist Workers' Party (PSOE) in the early years of the transition has been well-studied (Muñoz Sánchez 2012) and the prior knowledge that the CIA had about the failed *coup d'état* of 23 February 1982 (23-F) has been closely analysed by historians (Palacios 2010; López-Tapico 2011, among others). The details of international intervention in the process of political opening undertaken in Algeria are much less well known, despite the effort of some authors to unravel it (Thieux 2002; Moore 1994; and especially, Cavatorta 2009).

The aim of this chapter is not so much to employ an international dimension to understand transition paradigms or theories of 'resilient authoritarianism', as a large part of this book does, but rather to contribute to the analysis from the perspective of international relations' theories. It is clear that both positive and negative international influences are crucial in some cases, and essential in others, in order to move beyond the state centred framework of political science. Therefore, it makes sense to include a full chapter in this book on international processes linked to the Arab Spring. Some strong examples in different regional contexts of international processes affecting political change include the emulation and synergy generated between the Portuguese and Spanish democratic opposition (in the army, the trade unions and the press, for example) and the interactions of the Argentinian, Chilean and Uruguayan opposition starting from the women's movement. Similarly, firm pressure from external actors such as the European Economic Community and European social democratic parties to the transitions in southern Europe and Latin America as well as the Vatican and the United States in Eastern Europe has been decisive.

State support is important, but the role of international organisations (IO), which is even less researched, is also considerable. Poast and Urpelainen (2015) concluded in a recent empirical study that mere pertinence to an IO consolidated democratic regimes, particularly when they followed long military dictatorships; while it could not be said that they had an appreciable impact on the fall of authoritarian regimes. Richard Youngs (2004, 2010), on the other hand, has critically analysed the question of the European Union's promotion of democracy, along with other western actors such as governments, companies and NGOs.

Separately, the help of particular western countries to sustain and strengthen authoritarian regimes (both autocratic and totalitarian) and aggressive ethnodemocracies in the MENA region has made the implementation of processes of political opening from the top and the materialisation of popular demands from below more difficult and impractical. It is not only true to say that some of these countries are among the key beneficiaries of United States and EU aid. Israel and Egypt, for example, are among the main receivers of US military and economic aid in the world, respectively first and second in 2014 (Amoros 2015), and Morocco has been the main receiver in the southern Mediterranean of EU aid through MEDA funds between 1995 and 2006 (Natorski 2008) and the second, after Palestine, of the European Neighbourhood and Partnership Instrument between 2007 and 2013 (European Commission 2014). More importantly is that many of these countries' political economies have fallen into the perverse circle of employing hydrocarbons/remittances, foreign aid-generated income and/or rent-seeking, together with heavy arms expenditure and/or military alliances in order to protect themselves, which produces a dynamic that substantially increases the authoritarian and repressive resources of governmental regimes, thereby simultaneously generating an irresolvable 'security dilemma' (Korany et al. 1993; Anderson 1995) and making themselves less vulnerable to foreign criticism due to their apparent stability. That 'false stability' of authoritarian regimes, which are frequently in conflict among themselves, does not allow them to be consolidated as states. As Lu and Thies (2013) have demonstrated very perceptively, despite the predatory theory predictions of Charles Tilly (1990), civil and international wars have had a negative effect on the construction and consolidation of states in the Middle East and North Africa.

However, international aid can halt abruptly or in particular conditions. For example, the end of Soviet Union financial support to single-party communist regimes provoked their successive collapse in the early 1990s, something that did not occur among other single-party regimes that were not sustained by foreign support (Geddes 1999: 139–40). In other cases, only under certain conditions (an exogenous crisis of the regime and absences of alternatives to the liberal democratic model) has the US decided to withdraw its support for authoritarian governments (for example, in the Philippines and South Korea), enabling a democratic transition (Owen IV and Poznansky 2014).

In order to conclude this introduction, it can be argued that regarding the Arab Spring – in contrast with the majority of the third and fourth wave cases – neither the international (for example, the world economic crisis and tensions with Russia over the Ukraine) or regional context (armed battles in Libya, Syria and Yemen, growing Iran–Saudi Arabia rivalry) have been favourable for political change. Neither have the leading global powers or international organisations stood out for their rapid and active support of the anti-authoritarian uprisings. Furthermore, in some cases, some of these powers actually supported authoritarian regimes up until the very last moment (France in Tunisia) or impeded their fall (Russia in Syria or Saudi Arabia in Bahrain), while in other cases the responses were slow (the EU), contradictory (the US in Egypt), or showed little enthusiasm (such as that from Brussels) (see among others: Hollis 2012; Tömmel 2013). This question of direct foreign support and the regional context is analysed in Part III of this book, and so it is simply sketched out here.

2 Theories of international relations and the Arab Spring

Following the 'democratic pause' that the events of September 2001 represented, some authors predicted the start of a new democratising wave from the eruption of the Arab Spring in 2010–11 (Blaydes and Lo 2012;

Grand 2011; Howard and Hussain 2013), despite the scepticism of others (Diamond 2011). Diamond warned in 2011 that democratic processes were closing more rapidly and abruptly in a number of Arab countries than in other regions, with the unique exception of the rapid backlash of the ex-Soviet republics (Diamond 2011). In this sense, as the editor of this book points out in the first chapter, the Arab Spring involved processes of political change that could be authoritarian or democratic in nature, rather than democratisations in series, as had happened at the end of the 1980s and start of the 1990s in some countries of the region.

This chapter next turns to an analysis of these processes via the main paradigms of international relations: (neo-)liberalism; institutional liberalism; social constructivism and critical theories, by drawing on their key reference authors[1] and the main journals associated with them:[2] *International Security** (neo-realism), *Review of International Studies, International Politics** and *International Organization* (liberal institutionalism), *European Journal of International Relations** and *International Theory* (social constructivism) and *Journal of International Feminist Politics, Millennium* and the *International Political Sociology ** (critical theory).

2.1 (Neo-)realism and the Arab Spring

Neo-realism, the main paradigm of international relations, does not ignore the Arab Spring but it fundamentally conceives it in terms of power and more specifically, of state power. Power in this context is particularly measured in economic, military and technological terms. Changes in its distribution are, on the other hand, fundamental for the neo-realist theorists of international relations. They argue that an uneven distribution of resources in the international system generates different 'power structures' (Waltz 1979), which, depending on the number and capacities of the principal states of the system, will make up either a unipolar structure, a bipolar structure or a multipolar structure. The most powerful states in each possible structure determine the rules of the game of international society. The realists, attentive to historic changes, have fixed on the evolution of these structures (unipolarity, bipolarity and multipolarity), and identified both emerging states that have achieved the status of 'system powers' and those that have declined and stopped being (world) powers.

The countries of the MENA region are, clearly, peripheral in the distribution of power and although some aspire to being regional powers (Iran, Saudi Arabia, Turkey), none can be considered a power at world level. In realist thought, in which the current world structure is often defined as multipolar (although this is an object of debate within realism), no country in the MENA region would be considered a global power. However, their possession of significant energy resources (deposits and reserves), as well as their geographic location, has converted this region into a zone of world strategic importance due to its exporting capacity. These exports are directed at both developed economies and emerging countries (BRICS), which are predominantly net importers of petrol, with the notable exceptions of Russia, Canada, Brazil and Norway that are net exporters. The MENA countries attract a certain amount of global foreign investment, even though their instability impedes their continued growth. For this same reason, foreign investment is normally limited to extractive infrastructures and public utilities, thereby weakening the development of the industrial sector.

Due, among other reasons, to the MENA countries' peripheral condition, two of the main realist theorists, Kenneth Waltz and John Mearsheimer have been critical of American over-intervention and particularly scathing about US 'meddling' in Egypt and Syria, as well as in other MENA locations. This coincidence is worth noting as it emanates from two theorists who are identified with the two poles of realism: defensive (Waltz) and offensive (Mearsheimer). Waltz, who died in 2013, left us with a wake-up call over excessive American intervention in the world, at the same time as he put forward a surprising idea that was already formulated in 1980, that a world with a nuclear Iran and other nuclear powers would be more secure (Waltz 2012; Joyner 2013). Mearsheimer argues that the strategic importance of Syria and Egypt for the US has been exaggerated, as their security and freedom of action are not conditioned internationally, and can only be limited from afar by the ascent of China, for which reason, the US should not intervene in those countries (Mearsheimer 2014).[3] Along the same line, the ex-secretary of state Henry Kissinger stated he was against a possible intervention in Syria (Kissinger 2012), as Robert Gilpin had previously argued in relation to the invasion of Iraq in 2003 (Gilpin 2005).

Realism does not completely ignore other types of changes, such as internal changes, although they receive much less attention. The changes affecting the economic, demographic, military or technological power of the states, which emanate from internal transformations, also concern theoretical realists. However, political changes are less important in this sense, unless they make society more cohesive, mobilise its citizens and project that growing power abroad ('internal balancing'). Specifically, this relates to revolutionary-type processes, such as the Nasserist Revolution in Egypt or the Islamic Revolution in Iran. These political changes are an object of interest as they produce internal cohesion, civil and/or military mobilisation and a will to exercise power beyond national frontiers, by exporting, for example, the revolutionary or democratic model.

Regime changes, and more specifically democratic transitions and liberalisation policies, are not a particular focus of attention except when they are linked with other changes in state power. Hence Esther Barbé (2007) argues that analyses based exclusively on political–military structures 'are incapable of capturing change factors' (Barbé 2007: 184–5). As is well known, in line with the realist vision, all states act in accordance with the same motive: that is the search for and maximisation of power, whether it is at the minimum level, survival (defensive realism), or at the maximum (offensive realism). In other words, whatever the nature of the state, democratic or authoritarian, revolutionary or traditional, its actions on the international stage will be governed by the same key issues: namely the 'anarchy of international society' and by the capacities of global powers. Therefore, all possible changes of regime are interpreted and reduced to variations on the power of the state.

Realism holds that the appearance of revisionist states, whether revolutionary or not, have been historically responded to (in an intentional or unconscious way) by military alliances that have finished with the territorial ambitions of the rebel state, whether it be Napoleonic France, Hitler's Germany or Saddam Hussein's Iraq.

Specifically in the journal *International Security* (Massachusetts Institute of Technology (MIT), 1976–) realist authors have been most attracted to the effect of the Arab Spring on military alliances (Crawford 2011; Beckley 2015). This issue has received almost as much attention as nuclear proliferation (Braut-Hegghammer 2011; Bell 2015), alongside Waltz himself (2012) and the fight against jihadist terrorism (whether it is al-Qaeda or transnational jihadism, see Hegghammer 2010; Long and Wilner 2014). However, the journal's leading themes during the Arab Spring (2011–16) have been petrol, wars and the role of hydrocarbons in conflicts (Itzkowitz Shifrinson and Priebe 2011; Colgan 2013; Glaser 2013; Hughes and Long 2014). Also worth mentioning is an article about the majoritarian failure of regime changes by force (Downes and Monten 2013), which is a clear allusion to the policy followed by the US neoconservatives in Iraq that, as noted above, has been criticised by the leading neo-realists.

Consequently, the changes underway in the Arab world are only important to realists in the extent to which they produce variations of power in the region, modify perceptions of state security (security dilemma), or restructure alliances with foreign states that have the status of world powers (external balancing). In principle, both a country in transition and a country in conflict are considered to lose power on the world stage, in contrast to an emerging country that, because of its growth and its potential is closer to having the capacity of other powers (internal balancing). A country in conflict may also suffer intervention by other(s), end up weaker and even lose sovereignty (such as in the cases of Libya, Syria and Yemen, for example). However, if at the end of a period of democratic transition the country can become a model for the region, it may be able to increase its capacity of influence over their neighbours (soft power). Furthermore, the instauration of a democratic regime in one country can significantly alter that country's foreign policy by breaking or departing from the links its authoritarian regime had so far maintained. On the other hand, a strong legitimate political system generates cohesion and also, therefore, the capacity of mobilisation in its defence. The example of Egypt is clear. Although Egypt's failed transition has currently resulted in an authoritarian regime, as a democracy it could emerge again as a clear aspirant to regional hegemony, as has been left patent by its role as a mediator in the Gaza conflict of November 2012.

It is clear that these changes can generate distrust and fear in neighbouring states that maintain authoritarian political systems, and that fear rapid contagion. In this sense, the overthrowing of regimes and the start of regime change in the region can increase conflict not only within societies, but also between countries. This defensive response appears to have been regularly repeated in the MENA zone due to the uprisings in Bahrain, Libya, Yemen and Syria.

Finally, the ongoing transitions can have an impact on the alliances of world powers with the MENA states and lead to a potential redistribution of their areas of influence. At what point will the Tunisian transition, with Islamists playing a leading role, lead to France being displaced by the US in an area traditionally considered to be France's 'backyard'? When will French military protection for Tunisia – maintained for so long out of fear of its unpredictable Libyan neighbour – stop being necessary?

As for Syria, would not the fall of the Bashar al-Assad regime represent the loss of the last ally that Russia has in the MENA region? And is the Muslim Brotherhood not now weaving relationships with susceptible states to alter the region's political map? If not, how can the withdrawal of Hamas' support for the Syrian regime be interpreted? Is the Muslim Brotherhood not pushing, under the influence of Qatar, for a new Syria in which the Alawi minority will be replaced by Islamists from the Sunni majority? It is clear that in a potential scenario where Syria was governed by Islamist Sunnis, the country would definitively stop being within the sphere of Russian influence and move into the American zone.

2.2 Liberal institutionalism and the Arab Spring

Within liberal institutionalism there coexists a pragmatic theoretical approach – that states cooperate among themselves when they all gain something (absolute gain) – with another normative – that the opening up of trade, investments and the development of democratic values and freedom are positive historical forces that cannot be detained. The former corresponds with the utilitarian focus of the neo-liberal institutionalists (Keohane and Nye 1977; Keohane 1984) and includes international regime theorists (Krasner 1982, among others; Rittberger and Mayer 1993), while the latter relates more to idealism at the start of the twentieth century and its intellectual tradition (from Grotius, Kant, Rousseau and Wilson to the recent theorists of liberal cosmopolitanism: Beck (1944–2015), Held, Doyle and Ikenberry).[4] It is also consistent with the positivist or liberal current, dominant among internationalists or specialists in public international law.

In general, institutionalists and liberals do not enquire about the origin of international forces, such as globalisation, or whether they are guided by a specific actor; they are considered to be invisible forces, like the market in the economy or the anarchy in international society. Institutionalists and liberals are acritical of a phenomenon that, from their perspective, only seeks to eliminate barriers and obstacles to a future standardisation of the world whose consequences will be more beneficial than prejudicial. Within their optimistic conception of history and time, market forces and human freedoms can only combine to bring about a more prosperous and safe world.

The liberal institutionalist current is not only known for its emphasis on 'complex interdependence',[5] but in a more general way on globalisation, as they focus on a variety of global actors such as international organisations, NGOs, multinational companies, and so on, which operate together with states. Neo-liberal institutionalists consider the state and other actors to be rational subjects that pursue and define their objectives based on cost and benefit calculations. Institutions are created and maintained because they reduce the transactional costs of state interaction and allow information to be generated and shared. Nevertheless, there is no reason for cooperation to prevail in every circumstance; this will depend on the specific 'constellation of interest' established in a specific negotiation or international issue. These constellations of interest can take distinct forms according to the participants and the issue under negotiation; forms that the experts of game theory have sought to categorise as distinct games: competitive, cooperative and with or without coordination (Rittberger et al. 2012: 21–3).

In his empirical–rational analysis of institutions, Robert O. Keohane recently wrote that the United Nations Security Council is not the only institution with exclusive competence to maintain peace and that given its inability to abide by the 'Responsibility to Protect' (RtoP) doctrine, as well as its incapacity to reform itself, it should be complemented by a new institution, comprising of countries that are pre-committed to democracy (Buchanan and Keohane 2011).

Along similar lines, David A. Lake (2013) has evaluated the benefit to the US of maintaining alliances or hierarchies with Persian Gulf countries, taking into account not only the cost/benefit but also the type of regime. According to his analytical model, the alliances or 'hierarchies have distributive national and international consequences over coalition governments and the types of regime'. According to Lake, there is a relationship between the profits derived from that hierarchy (large/small) and the distance in citizen political preferences to the states in the alliance (short/long), on the one hand, and the type of regime that that hierarchy or alliance implies, on the other. In other words, where the profits are scarce and concentrated and the distance in the preferences are long (in the case of Central America and the Persian Gulf), the hierarchy will support autocratic friends. Conversely, where the profits are big and numerous and/or the distance between the preferences short (Western Europe), the hierarchy will support democracies. With time, the former model will generate a perverse circle, while the latter will create a virtuous circle. Under this prism and given the elevated costs of maintaining security in the Gulf region, including both the fight against terrorism and extending benefits beyond the elites, Lake recommends that the US withdraws from the zone and dismantles the structures of military and economic dependency that it has established with those countries.

In the journal *International Politics* (London School of Economics and Palgrave, 1996–), Michael Doyle (2016) and Alex Bellamy (2014) write about the RtoP in Libya and Syria. While employment of the doctrine in Libya did great harm (despite which its repeated practice will result in it becoming international common law), in Syria, opposition to the use of the RtoP is related to other factors in the neighbouring area. Doyle and Bellamy argue that neither Russia nor China have consistently raised the 'Libyan issue' in the Security Council and nor did the countries that most opposed the Libyan resolution slow down the draft proposal over Syria, and it therefore seems that IOs appear increasingly comfortable with the RtoP.

Another interesting debate raised in the journal is that of the liberal (re-)construction of states. While some articles have argued that there is a crisis in this model, liberal authors such as Hameiri (2014) contend that expansion will continue because the critics have only focused on the peace missions as an object of analysis and not the more general role that international institutions play. Regarding security, while Cerny (2015) argues that the global extension of the liberal state, where armed forces give way to police, will occur within the rule of law, Williams (2015) contends that in Afghanistan this pattern will not be successful because the Afghan army formed by NATO will finally prevail over the civil government due to the threats the country currently faces.

In contrast with the realists, liberals believe that the form of the state, its institutions and the values which govern it, are relevant for two fundamental reasons: first, to open the country internally and externally, and second, to respect the rule of law and international norms. This translates into the following liberal premise: that states with open economies tend to trade more, and more readily see cooperation as in their interest. Liberals further argue that states with open political and democratic systems prefer to resolve their differences by means of negotiation, respect norms (the rule of law) within and beyond their frontiers, and are more inclined to cooperation and peaceful interaction. These premises are summarised in the theory of 'democratic peace' or 'liberal peace', which contends that democracies do not make war among themselves, but rather prefer to trade and resolve their differences by other means (Russett 1993; Weart 1998; Doyle 2011).

While the idea of 'democratic peace' has been criticised, it continues to be a pillar of liberal institutionalism. This explains why the changes in the Arab countries are very significant, whether they are seen from the perspective of the triumph of the liberal-capitalist model and the end of history (Fukuyama), from the prism of democratising waves (Huntington), from the 'flat world' of technological globalisation (Friedman), or from the social movements of the 'network society' (Castells). In the end, have the Arab uprisings not been possible thanks to the new information technologies of the Internet, with social media at the head?

The institutionalist paradigm argues that globalisation is a blind and unstoppable force that modifies international relationships in multiple dimensions, transforming and eroding the Westphalia order that has ruled since 1648. Leading liberal author Andrew Moravcsik, who developed a 'structural theory' of liberalism, states: 'Liberals argue that the universal condition of world politics is globalisation. States are, and always have been, embedded in a domestic and transnational society, which creates incentives for economic, social and cultural interaction across borders' (Moravcsik 2010: 1).

Globalisation blurs sovereignty, de-territorialises the state and power and weakens the autonomy and independence of political communities (Baylis et al. 2011). This generates problems of complex interdependence that enables or pushes states towards international cooperation.

2.3 Social constructivism and the Arab Spring

Social constructivism is the most recent international relations theory to emerge. It was predominantly developed by Alexander Wendt (Wendt 1992; 1999), although significant predecessors include Onuf, Kratochwil, Ruggie,

Katzenstein, and contributors such as Adler, Kubalková, Reus-Smit, Barnett, Finnemore, Sikkink and the Copenhagen School[6] (in the area of security).

Constructivism shares with other critical theories a normative as well as scientific vocation. It seeks to transform social reality by revealing the interactive processes that structure the interests, objectives and finally the identity of international actors. Both vocations reject the presumed objectivity or scientific neutrality and the net separation of the object and subject. However, in contrast to critical theories, constructivism does not provide a general description of international relations nor a prognosis of how these relations will evolve. Because it is an essentially contextual and 'interactional' paradigm, the result is open, depending on the shared prior knowledge, values and experiences of the actors involved.

A central issue of social constructivism is the diffusion of norms, especially those that emanate from international organisations (Barnett and Finnemore 1999). This connects directly with the Arab Spring and relationships with actors such as the EU in this area of the world. Regarding the diffusion of values, it has been some time since European political analysts argued that the EU is a 'normative power' or even a 'normative empire' (del Sarto 2016), which diffuses values and norms throughout the world and primarily, in the Mediterranean and Arab world. The object of this liberal diffusion of ideas, apparently devoid of power and imposition, is to gradually transfer the values of democracy and the market economy.

It is clear that constructivist authors seek to distance themselves from the natural optimism of the liberals and suggest that the diffusion of norms such as democracy can have negative effects. Seva Gunitsky argues in a comparative study of the Arab Spring with the Spring of Nations (1848) and the Velvet Revolutions (1989) that this diffusion is not linear but rather a complex process of co-evolution and co-adaptation, which is characterised by dynamics that are usually contradictory. Futhermore, the diffusion is normally accompanied by a learning process of the authoritarian elite, who unleash greater repression, while specific democratic experiences are also successful (Gunitsky 2013).

Natorski (2015), for his part, has underscored that in times of crisis and uncertainty, like that which produced the Arab Spring and the institutional and economic changes in Europe (from 2010 onwards), actors such as the European Union employ social conventions such as 'epistemological coherence' as a means to give continuity to their neighbourhood policies, thereby avoiding having to make more drastic changes that would be necessary in a modified environment.

The *European Journal of International Relations* (EJIR) (European Consortium for Political Research ECPR, 1995–) frequently debates the role of the EU in the world and its power of normative diffusion, as can be seen in the article by Kunz and Maisenbacher about the promotion of women in the MENA region, and in that of Natorski about the epistemological uncertainty before the Arab Spring. This is also the case of another article about the 'twinning' policy in Egypt and Tunisia, and how this 'brotherhood' has allowed technical knowledge and efficiencies to be diffused to the administrations of the Mediterranean within a neo-liberal governance model (İşleyen 2015). Equally successful has been the normative diffusion of the Palestine Liberation Organisation since 1974, which through distinct resolutions, whether vetoed or not, has managed to develop a strong consensus within the UN Security Council that the Palestinians have a right to their own state and that this is essential for a solution, while the Israeli occupation is perceived as the main obstacle (Graubart and Jiménez-Bacardi 2016). Another key issue in the journal has been the invisibility of certain actors that has led it to overlook micro-movements, such as the Arab Spring, in which ordinary citizens and emotions are important (Sylvester 2013a; Solomon and Steele 2016). Likewise, the idea that (epistemological) silence can constitute a form of violence in the theory and practice of international relations is illustrated in the case of Yemen. The breaking of civil society's silence during the Arab Spring, argues the author, should not be interpreted as a monolithic voice in favour of individual freedom but rather as a heterogeneous group of social demands for dignity (Dingli 2015).

Arab uprisings have, although only partially, brought down the western ideological prejudice that Arabs as oriental subjects accept a good degree of autocracy and despotism. This is one of the bases of orientalism, which was so well analysed and denounced by the intellectual Edward Said (1979; 1993). The Arab Spring has demonstrated that people in the MENA region desire freedom and dignity like any other. They have sought it with strength and astonishing determination, something that has not only perplexed observers and the public of the North in general but has made these young Arabs believe still more in their possibilities.

The varying degrees of European and Western support for Arab autocracies hinged in part on that belief that these societies had resigned themselves or had adapted to live without freedoms and democracy and that therefore they could only change gradually. The spectre of a worse evil than autocracies, personified by political Islam, provided convincing arguments for diplomats to maintain pragmatic relations with anti-democratic regimes. However, once the revolutions and uprisings began, the Western 'mental veil', which could not comprehend that Arab people wanted – like other populations – to pursue liberty and freedom, started to tear.

This about-turn in perception is Copernican and clearly marks a before and after, and is what certain critics, between constructivist and critical theorists, call the 'decolonisation of thought' (Spivak 1999; Mignolo 2011; de Sousa 2014). The changes in the Arab world have forced Western thought to be deconstructed and 'decolonised' rather than continuing to see the 'other', those of the South, as different, passive, and therefore deserving of the oppressive reality that surrounds them, or as a primitive subject that must be 'civilised'. Equally the West is striving to completely reconsider North–South relations in the Euro-Mediterranean space. As the French philosopher Alain Badiou recently argued, the North cannot expect to continue giving lessons when it has so much to learn from these revolutions, and this fact shakes Western arrogance (Badiou 2012). It also implies putting an end to the paternalism of governments and societies of the North and completely re-evaluating the European model of diffusion of democratic and liberal norms.

These cognitive changes must certainly involve discussion about rights and liberties, but on both sides of the Mediterranean, because those rights and liberties are not the patrimony of particular countries and nor are they fully protected anywhere. However, the EU has been determined to continue with its 'civilising mission' on the basis of its promotion of gender equality. As Kunz and Maisenbacher accurately point out, the New European Neighbourhood Policy, launched in response to the Arab Spring, recreates a geographically and temporally distant 'other' – just at the moment in which these countries are closer to Europe than ever – whether by emphasising the incorporation of the European law 'community heritage' or democratisation processes (Kunz and Maisenbacher 2015). It is appropriate for the South to allow its civil society to be 'empowered' and become true co-participants in all Euro-Mediterranean initiatives. The changes imply that Arabs become wholly international subjects, free of illegitimate regimes but also of postcolonial relationships constructed around paternalism. To what extent is Northern paternalism receptive to the message that comes from the South and willing to reconstruct its relationships in the Mediterranean and other spaces?

2.4 Critical theories and the Arab Spring

An alternative analysis is put forward by critical theories, an umbrella term under which very distinct currents are grouped: postpositivists and post-modernists (for example, Ashley, Der Derian), feminists (Tickner, Sylvester), neo-Marxists and neo-Gramscians (Cox, Gill, Wallerstein, Van der Pijl, Ali), and cosmopolitan radicals (Linklater), who have influenced international relations as much as the theory of public international law (Kennedy, Koskenniemi, Falk, Chimni, Reus-Smit, Bachand and Lapointe).

These authors argue that globalisation is not a new phenomenon, nor distinct, but rather the deepening of a process of capitalist accumulation that started five centuries ago with the conquest of America and that has been through distinct cycles in that period of time (Wallerstein 2004). They contend that economic processes are far from being an invisible hand that produces beneficial effects: rather that globalisation and the changes in the Arab world have been induced by well-known capitalist states. Peter Gowan (2000a), for example, explains how capital deregulation was decided upon and driven by the Nixon administration following the abandonment of the gold–dollar formula and was sustained afterwards for the benefit of the economy and American banks that recycled the petro-dollars of the Middle East to lend them to southern countries; a process that served the euro-dollar markets that connected Wall Street with the City of London.

While Immanuel Wallerstein is the best known, he has not been alone in arguing that some of the Arab riots were 'remote controlled' by Washington and their European allies. On the one hand, Wallerstein argues that the disturbances are healthy and inspired in May 1968, and on the other that there are reactionaries who seek to maintain the status quo by relying on foreign allies, as has been the case in Libya (Wallerstein 2011) and in Syria (Wallerstein 2012). Other authors suggest that the US provoked the riots to gain new markets for American businesses: was it not Facebook and Twitter, American companies, which facilitated and encouraged the process? Along the same line, Kees Van der Pijl, an influential critic from the Amsterdam School of Global Political Economy, repeated the information that after the *coup d'état* in Mali, Cheikh Modibo Diarra, who was up to that time director of Microsoft for Africa, had been appointed prime minister, and that Google had contracted various human rights defenders in Arab countries (Allard, cited in Van der Pijl 2013: 13).

These authors argue that the differential approach of the US when faced on the one hand with the disturbances in Syria and Libya, and the riots in Persian Gulf countries on the other, is proof of a hypocritical US discourse that does not hide market greed. The way in which the US tolerated the crushing of the Bahrain riots at the hands of the Gulf Cooperation Council security forces, with Saudi Arabia at the head, reveals the double standards of the leading capitalist power. This is behaviour, it is argued, which openly contrasts with untiring support, in many forms, for the 'rogue states' (as US authorities describe them) of Libya and Syria.

Other theoretical neo-Marxists, such as the influential writer and journalist Tariq Ali, editor of the *New Left Review*,[7] deny that the Arab Spring represents any fundamental change and argue that the North–South relationship has not substantially varied, except among specific leaders (the Muslim Brotherhood in Egypt and Ennahda in Tunisia) who maintain links with the US (Ali 2013), but without altering their political, economic and military dependence on the North. Ali (2013) compares the Arab Spring with the advent of popular regimes in Latin America during the 2000s, which he named favourably 'the axis of hope', and argues that the current changes in the Arab world have not produced true revolutions that have replaced elites or that have been capable of slowing neo-liberalism and breaking with their foreign partners. This fact, argues Ali, is fundamentally due to the variable of foreign intervention in the MENA countries, especially of the US and its actions through their allies in the region (Israel and Saudi Arabia): 'If the Arab uprisings began as indigenous revolts against corrupt police states and social deprivation, they were rapidly internationalised as western powers and regional neighbours entered the fray' (Ali 2013: 64).

The journal *International Political Sociology* (International Studies Association, ISA, 2007–), which contains very diverse publications, has shown little direct interest in the Arab Spring (2011–16), but considerable interest in issues that cross the problematic of uprisings, interventions and conflicts in the MENA region. The reflectivist focus is dominant in the journal, which frequently deals with aspects of the intersubjective production of security, 'securitisation', vigilance and biopolitics, both in relation to emigrants (Doty and Wheatley 2013; Johnson 2013) and prisoners of war in Guantanamo (Beier and Mutimer 2014), as well as the Palestinian population under occupation. It also critically considers the legitimacy (not only legal, but also ethical and political) of the military use of drones (Gregory 2015) and the limits of private security organ-isations (for example, massive espionage, use of virtual reality by the intelligence services, immigrant detention centres, and so on). Resistance to the Palestinian occupation and in general to the processes of neo-liberal globalisation (Corry 2014), are dealt with alongside the concepts and contributions of French sociological theorists (Foucault, Bourdieu, and so on).

From feminist theories, Sylvester (2013a; 2013b) underscores the need to analyse everyday international practices from the starting point of individual experiences, both in the study of relationships in periods of peace as well as in current wars and criticises neo-realist theorists for being excessively abstract and reductionist, with Waltz at the head.

The emphasis on war as a by-product of the Arab Spring is also put forward by the school of global political economy. Authors like Van der Pijl link the stripped-down competition for capitalist supremacy with the use that the US makes of the 'industrial military complex': 'My argument in this paper is that the United States (leading the liberal West more broadly speaking) since the financial crisis of 2007–8 has been compelled to rely ever-more on its military assets to secure its global primacy' (Van der Pijl 2013: 1).

It is clear that these critical theories tend to extol and amplify the role of external actors to the point of becoming, in some cases, close to conspiracy theories. These approaches, even when not so extreme, consequently view the autonomy and decision-making will of internal actors in quite a limited way (Wallerstein), unless they produce revolutions, and underscore the importance of economic and military factors, and their interaction as determinants of international policy (Ali and Van der Pijl). Others, however, such as feminist theorists, point to political and cultural factors that underlie and feed war and conflicts: specifically the invisibility of specific actors (women) and female agency in everyday experiences, which are hidden in dominant macro-theories (neo-realism) and their narratives (Sylvester).

3 Conclusions

This chapter has shown that, unlike previous waves of democratisation, neither the regional nor the global context has been particularly favourable for the Arab Spring. This does not mean, however, that international factors related to the Arab Spring should not receive greater attention. The chapter has also demonstrated how similar topics are treated in rather inverted ways. Thus while neo-realists tend not to focus on the Arab Spring itself but rather on the possible threats that derive from it (an increase in jihadism, nuclear proliferation, and so on) and their consequences for alliances and US interests, critical theorists reverse the analysis and locate it in the economic causes and implications of armed interventions (neo-liberalism, distribution of markets, the military leverage of US hegemony) as well as the social processes of vigilance and control that are associated with the 'security obsession' (census elaboration, detention centres, massive espionage, 'biopolitics', and so on).

For their part, liberals and institutionalists move between rational calculations relating to the utility of institutions (for example, UN Security Council reform) and of US alliances in the Middle East (including its eventual withdrawal from the region) and a more or less nuanced defence of the RtoP doctrine, despite the evident lack of restraint shown in the Libyan case. Finally, the constructivist prism of 'normative diffusion' allows a less optimistic position than the liberals, by identifying contradictory processes, such as those present in the promotion of democracy. These contradictions may lead, for example, to authoritarian learning, autocratic regression and change avoidance. Likewise, constructivists question the receptivity of the 'natural transmitters of norms' (the North, the EU, and so on), as when Arab societies of the South, empowered by the Arab Spring, sent a message that shattered the dominant perception of the North (orientalism). Disruptive messages like those sent by Arab Spring actors on the self-representation of Arab societies create epistemological uncertainty and cognitive dissonance among those who take decisions. These cognitive changes imply a 'decolonisation' of Western thinking and involve a necessary discussion on rights and freedoms on both shores of the Mediterranean.

Notes

1. In order to identify the key authors of each paradigm, this chapter has basically followed the collective work *Theories of International Relations* (Arenal and Sanahuja 2015).
2. The journals on which the author has worked most closely, undertaking an exhaustive analysis of the period 2011–15 are followed by an asterisk (*).
3. Some liberal/institutionalist authors arrive at similar conclusions about the recommendable withdrawal of the US to the east of the Suez Canal. Other realists extend criticism of the role of the US in Libya and the application in that country of the doctrine of the Responsibility to Protect (RtoP).
4. See, regarding this current, the criticism of this author by Gowan (2000b).
5. A concept that is principally owed to Robert O. Keohane and Joseph Nye, who introduced it in the 1970s but then continued using it, although in a revised form (Keohane and Nye 1977; 1987; 2015).
6. Formed by Barry Buzan, Ole Waever and De Wilde, who studied the 'new security' after the Cold War and later coined the concept of 'securitisation'.
7. For a full critique of the considerations of *New Left Review* and Tariq Ali about imperialism in the MENA region, see the interview of the Irish professor of international relations and MENA specialist, Fred Halliday (2005).

References

Ali, Tariq (2013), 'Between past and future. Reply to Asef Bayat', *New Left Review*, 80: 61–74.

Amoros, Raul (2015), *The US Spends $35 Billion on Foreign Aid . . . But Where Does the Money Really Go?*, Detroit: Mondoweiss. Available at <http://mondoweiss.net/2015/11/spends-billion-foreign/#sthash.0tF3nTdZ.dpuf> (last accessed 20 April 2016).

Anderson, Lisa (1995), 'Peace and democracy in the Middle East. The constraints of soft budgets', *Journal of International Affairs*, 49 (1): 25–44.

del Arenal, Celestino and José A. Sanahuja (eds) (2015), *Teorías de las relaciones internacionales*, Madrid: Tecnos.

Badiou, Alain (2012), 'Túnez, Egipto y la chispa que incendia la llanura', in Giorgio Agamben, Jacques Rancière, Alain Badiou, Anselm Jappe, Étienne Balibar, Antonio Negri, Michael Hardt and Slavoj Žižek, *Pensar desde la izquierda. Mapa del pensamiento crítico para un tiempo en crisis*, Madrid: Errata Naturae, pp. 313–20.

Barbé, Esther (2007), *Relaciones internacionales*, Madrid: Tecnos.

Barnett, Michael N. and Martha Finnemore (1999), 'The politics, power, and pathologies of international organizations', *International Organization*, 53 (4): 699–732.

Baylis, John, Steve Smith and Patricia Owens (eds) (2011), *The Globalization of World Politics: an Introduction to International Relations*, New York: Oxford University Press.

Beckley, Michael (2015), 'The myth of entangling alliances reassessing the security risks of US defense pacts', *International Security*, 39 (4): 7–48.

Beier, John M. and David Mutimer (2014), 'Pathologizing subjecthoods: pop culture, habits of thought, and the unmaking of resistance politics at Guantanamo Bay', *International Political Sociology*, 8 (3): 311–23.

Bell, Mark S. (2015), 'Beyond emboldenment: how acquiring nuclear weapons can change foreign policy', *International Security*, 40 (1): 87–119.

Bellamy, Alex J. (2014), 'From Tripoli to Damascus? Lesson learning and the implementation of the Responsibility to Protect', *International Politics*, 51 (1): 23–44.

Blaydes, Lisa and James Lo (2012), 'One man, one vote, one time? A model of democratization in the Middle East', *Journal of Theoretical Politics*, 24 (1): 110–46.

Braut-Hegghammer, Målfrid (2011), 'Revisiting Osirak: preventive attacks and nuclear proliferation risks', *International Security*, 36 (1): 101–32.

Buchanan, Allen and Robert O. Keohane (2011), 'Precommitment regimes for intervention: supplementing the Security Council', *Ethics and International Affairs*, 25 (1): 41–63.

Bustos, Rafael (2004), *El cambio político en Argelia (1988–1992). Análisis sistémico de una transición discordante*, PhD Dissertation, Universidad Complutense de Madrid.

Cavatorta, Francesco (2009), *The International Dimension of the Failed Algerian Transition: Democracy Betrayed?*, Manchester: Manchester University Press.

Cerny, Philip G. (2015), 'From warriors to police? The civilianisation of security in a globalising world', *International Politics*, 52 (4): 389–407.

Colgan, Jeff D. (2013), 'Fueling the fire: pathways from oil to war', *International Security*, 38 (2): 147–80.

Corry, Olaf (2014), 'From defense to resilience: environmental security beyond neo-liberalism', *International Political Sociology*, 8 (3): 256–74.

Crawford, Timothy W. (2011), 'Preventing enemy coalitions: how wedge strategies shape power politics', *International Security*, 35 (4): 155–89.

Diamond, Larry (2011), 'A fourth wave or false start? Democracy after the Arab Spring', *Foreign Affairs*, 22 May. Available at <http://www.foreignaffairs.com/articles/67862/larry-diamond/a-fourth-wave-or-false-start> (last accessed 20 April 2016).

Dingli, Sophia (2015), 'We need to talk about silence: re-examining silence in international relations theory', *European Journal of International Relations*, 21 (4): 721–42.

Doty, Roxanne L. and Elizabeth S. Wheatley (2013), 'Private detention and the immigration industrial complex', *International Political Sociology*, 7 (4): 426–43.

Downes, Alexander B. and Jonathan Monten (2013), 'Forced to be free? Why foreign-imposed regime change rarely leads to democratization', *International Security*, 37 (4): 90–131.

Doyle, Michael W. (2011), *Liberal Peace: Selected Essays*, London: Routledge.

Doyle, Michael W. (2016), 'The politics of global humanitarianism: the responsibility to protect before and after Libya', *International Politics*, 53 (1): 14–31.

European Commission (2014), *European Neighbourhood and Partnership Instrument (2007–2013). Overview of Activities and Results*, Brussels: Directorate General Development and Cooperation-EuropeAid. Available at <http://ec.europa.eu/enlargement/neighbourhood/pdf/20141217-enpi-results-2017-2013.pdf> (last accessed 15 April 2016).

Geddes, Barbara (1999), 'What do we know about democratization after twenty years?', *Annual Review of Political Science*, 2: 115–44.

Gilpin, Robert (2005), 'War is too important to be left to ideological amateurs', *International Relations*, 19 (1): 5–18.

Glaser, Charles L. (2013), 'How oil influences US national security', *International Security*, 38 (2): 112–46.

Gowan, Peter (2000a), *La apuesta por la globalización: la geoeconomía y la geopolítica del imperialismo euro-estadounidense*, Madrid: Akal.

Gowan, Peter (2000b), *The New Liberal Cosmopolitanism*, IWM Working Paper 2/2000, Vienna: IWM. Available at <http://www.geocities.ws/gennarolasca/liberalcosmopolitanism.pdf> (last accessed 9 April 2016).

Grand, Stephen R. (2011), *Starting in Egypt: the Fourth Wave of Democratization?*, Washington, DC: Brookings Institution.

Graubart, Jonathan and Arturo Jiménez-Bacardi (2016), 'David in Goliath's citadel: mobilizing the Security Council's normative power for Palestine', *European Journal of International Relations*, 22 (1): 24–48.

Gregory, Thomas (2015), 'Drones, targeted killings, and the limitations of international law', *International Political Sociology*, 9 (3): 197–212.

Gunitsky, Seva (2013), 'Complexity and theories of change in international politics', *International Theory*, 5 (1): 35–63.

Halliday, Fred (2005), *Halliday Slams Tariq Ali and New Left Review over Mid-East, Imperialism*. Available at <http://www.marxsite.com/HallidayNLR.htm> (last accessed 4 April 2016).

Hameiri, Shahar (2014), 'The crisis of liberal peacebuilding and the future of statebuilding', *International Politics*, 51 (3): 316–33.

Hegghammer, Thomas (2010), 'The rise of Muslim foreign fighters: Islam and the globalization of jihad', *International Security*, 35 (3): 53–94.

Hollis, Rosemary (2012), 'No friend of democratization: Europe's role in the genesis of the "Arab Spring"', *International Affairs*, 88 (1): 81–94.

Howard, Philip N. and Muzammil M. Hussain (2013), *Democracy's Fourth Wave? Digital Media and the Arab Spring*, New York: Oxford University Press.

Hughes, Llewelyn and Austin Long (2014), 'Is there an oil weapon? Security implications of changes in the structure of the international oil market', *International Security*, 39 (3): 152–89.

Huntington, Samuel (1991), *La tercera ola. La democracia a finales del siglo XX*, Barcelona: Paidós.

İşleyen, Beste (2015), 'The European Union and neoliberal governmentality: twinning in Tunisia and Egypt', *European Journal of International Relations*, 21 (3): 672–90.

Itzkowitz Shifrinson, Joshua R. and Miranda Priebe (2011), 'A crude threat: the limits of an Iranian missile campaign against Saudi Arabian oil', *International Security*, 36 (1): 167–201.

Johnson, Heather L. (2013), 'The other side of the fence: reconceptualizing the "Camp" and migration zones at the borders of Spain', *International Political Sociology*, 7 (1): 75–91.

Joyner, James (2013), 'Kenneth Waltz' Legacy', in *New Atlanticist* (public policy blog), Washington, DC: Atlantic Council. Available at <http://www.atlanticcouncil.org/blogs/new-atlanticist/kenneth-waltz-legacy> (last accessed 6 April 2016).

Keohane, Robert O. (1984), *After Hegemony: Cooperation and Discord in the World Political Economy*, Princeton: Princeton University Press.

Keohane, Robert O. and Joseph S. Nye (1977), *Power and Interdependence: World Politics in Transition*, Boston: Little, Brown and Company.

Keohane, Robert O. and Joseph S. Nye (1987), 'Power and interdependence revisited', *International Organization*, 41 (4): 725–53.

Keohane, Robert O. and Joseph S. Nye (2015), 'Revisiting power and interdependence', *Uluslar Iliskiler*, 12 (46): 79–104.

Kissinger, Henry (2012), 'Syrian intervention risks upsetting global order', *The Washington Post*, 1 June.

Korany, Bahgat, Paul Noble and Rex Brynan (eds) (1993), *The Many Faces of National Security in the Arab World*, London: Macmillan.

Krasner, Stephen D. (1982), 'Structural causes and regime consequences – regimes as intervening variables', *International Organization*, 36 (2): 185–205.

Kunz, Rahel and Julia Maisenbacher (2015), 'Women in the neighbourhood: reinstating the European Union's civilising mission on the back of gender equality promotion?', *European Journal of International Relations*, 11: 1–23. DOI: 10.1177/1354066115621120.

Lake, David A. (2013), 'Legitimating power: the domestic politics of US international hierarchy', *International Security*, 38 (2): 74–111.

Long, Jerry M. and Alex S. Wilner (2014), 'Delegitimizing al-Qaida: defeating an "army whose men love death"', *International Security*, 39 (1): 126–64.

López-Tapico, Misael A. (2011), 'Anatomía de "un asunto interno". La actitud del gobierno estadounidense ante el 23-F', *Ayer. Revista de historia contemporánea*, 84: 183–205.

Lu, Lingyu and Cameron G. Thies (2013), 'War, rivalry, and state building in the Middle East', *Political Research Quarterly*, 66 (2): 239–53.

Mearsheimer, John J. (2014), 'America unhinged', *The National Interest*, 129: 9–30, Washington, DC: The National Interest Inc.

Mignolo, Walter D. (2011), *The Darker Side of Western Modernity: Global Futures, Decolonial Options*, Durham, NC: Duke University Press.

Moore, Pete W. (1994), 'The international context of liberalization and democratization in the Arab world', *Arab Studies Quarterly*, 16 (3): 43–66.

Moravcsik, Andrew (2010), *Liberal Theories of International Relations: a Primer*, Princeton: Princeton University Press.

Muñoz Sánchez, Antonio (2012), *El amigo alemán: el SPD y el PSOE de la dictadura a la democracia*, Barcelona: RBA.

Natorski, Michal (2008), *The MEDA Programme in Morocco 12 Years On: Results, Experiences and Trends*, Documentos CIDOB, Mediterráneo 11, Barcelona: CIDOB. Available at <http://www.cidob.org/en/publications/past_series/documents/mediterranean_and_middle_east/the_meda_programme_in_morocco_12_years_on_results_experiencesand_trends> (last accessed 7 April 2016).

Natorski, Michal (2015), 'Epistemic (un)certainty in times of crisis: the role of coherence as a social convention in the European Neighbourhood Policy after the Arab Spring', *European Journal of International Relations*, online publication before print, September, DOI: 10.1177/1354066115599043.

Owen IV, John M. and Michael Poznansky (2014), 'When does America drop dictators', *European Journal of International Relations*, 20 (4): 1072–99.

Palacios, Jesús (2010), *23-F: el rey y su secreto 30 años después se desvela la llamada "Operación De Gaulle"*, Madrid: Libroslibres.

Pastor, Manuel (2014), *Los Estados Unidos y el Rey en el 23-F*, Madrid: Kosmos-Polis.

van der Pijl, Kees (2013), *The Financial Crisis and the War for Global Governance*, Anti-capitalist Initiative. Available at <http://anticapitalists.org/2013/05/26/financial-crisis-and-war-for-global-governance/> (last accessed 4 April 2016).

Poast, Paul and Johannes Urpelainen (2015), 'How international organizations support democratization. Preventing authoritarian reversals or promoting consolidation?', *World Politics*, 67 (1): 72–113.

Rittberger, Volker and Peter Mayer (1993), *Regime Theory and International Relations*, Oxford: Clarendon.

Rittberger, Vokker, Bernhard Zangl and Andreas Kruck (2012), *International Organization: Polity, Politics and Policies*, Basingstoke: Palgrave Macmillan.

Russett, Bruce (1993), *Grasping the Democratic Peace. Principles for a Post-Cold War World*, Princeton: Princeton University Press.

Said, Edward W. (1979), *Orientalism*, New York: Vintage Books.

Said, Edward W. (1993), *Culture and Imperialism*, New York: Vintage Books.

del Sarto, Raffaella A. (2016), 'Normative empire Europe: The European Union, its borderlands, and the "Arab Spring"', *Journal of Common Market Studies*, 54 (2): 215–32.

Solomon, Ty and Brent J. Steele (2016), 'Micro-moves in international relations theory', *European Journal of International Relations*, 20 (3): 720–41.

de Sousa Santos, Boaventura (2014), *Si Dios fuese activista de los derechos humanos*, Madrid: Trotta.

Spivak, Gayatry C. (1999), *A Critique of Postcolonial Reason: Toward a History of the Vanishing Present*, Cambridge, MA: Harvard University Press.

Sylvester, Christine (2013a), 'Experiencing the end and afterlives of international relations/theory', *European Journal of International Relations*, 19 (3): 609–26.

Sylvester, Christine (2013b), *War as Experience. Contributions from International Relations and Feminist Analysis*, London: Routledge.

Sylvester, Christine (2014), 'Neorealist reductionisms', *Australian Journal of Political Science*, 49 (3): 547–51.

Thieux, Laurence (2002), *La guerra civil argelina y su impacto en las políticas exteriores de Francia y Estados Unidos respecto a Argelia (1991–1999)*, PhD Dissertation, Universidad Autónoma de Madrid.

Tilly, Charles (1990), *Coercion, Capital, and European States, AD 990–1990*, Oxford: Basil Blackwell.

Tömmel, Ingeborg (2013), 'The new Neighborhood Policy of the EU: an appropriate response to the Arab Spring?', *Democracy and Security*, 9 (1–2): 19–39.

Waltz, Kenneth N. (2012), 'Why Iran should get the bomb: nuclear balancing would mean stability', *Foreign Affairs*, 91 (4): 2–5.

Waltz, Kenneth N. (1979), *Theory of International Politics*, Reading: Addison-Wesley.

Wallerstein, Immanuel (2004), *Capitalismo histórico y movimientos anti-sistema. Un análisis de sistemas-mundo*, Madrid: Akal.

Wallerstein, Immanuel (2011), 'The contradictions of the Arab Spring', *Al Jazeera English*, 11 November. Available at <http://www.aljazeera.com/indepth/opinion/2011/11/201111 11101711539134.html> (last accessed 1 April 2016).

Wallerstein, Immanuel (2012), *The Geopolitics of Arab Turmoil*, Al Jazeera Centre for Studies, 27 September. Available at <http://www.iwallerstein.com/wp-content/uploads/docs/wallerstein-artilce-geopolitics-arab-turmoil.pdf> (last accessed 20 April 2016).

Weart, Spencer R. (1998), *Never at War: Why Democracies Will Not Fight One Another*, New Haven, CT: Yale University Press.

Wendt, Alexander (1992), 'Anarchy is what states make of it – the social construction of power-politics', *International Organization*, 46 (2): 391–425.

Wendt, Alexander (1999), *Social Theory of International Politics*, Cambridge: Cambridge University Press.

Williams, Michael J. (2015), 'State-building and the armed forces in modern Afghanistan: a structural analysis', *International Politics*, 52 (3): 305–34.

Youngs, Richard (2004), *International Democracy and the West. The Role of Governments, Civil Society, and Multinational Business*, Oxford: Oxford University Press.

Youngs, Richard (2010), *The European Union and Democracy Promotion: a Critical Global Assessment*, Baltimore: Johns Hopkins University Press.

Part II

Chapter 3

Parties and party system change

Lise Storm

1 Introduction

This chapter examines parties and party system change across the Middle East
and North Africa (MENA) since the eruption of the Arab Spring in December
2010. Hence, the discussion begins with an overview of the parties and party
systems in the region on the eve of the Arab Spring, thereby providing a quick
introduction to the cases as well as a benchmark against which to measure
change, while also anchoring the analysis in the theoretical framework outlined
previously in Chapter 1.

The units of analysis are the region's parties and party systems and, more
specifically, change to these units. That is, change within countries, the MENA
as a region as well as MENA subregions and, finally, within groups of regimes.
In short, the analysis is concerned with variance among and within countries,
and the extent to which change has occurred, whether positive or negative.

Given the focus on change, it is, of course, necessary to define how change
is understood and measured here. In line with the so-called classic studies
of parties and party systems, such as Sartori (1976) and Mair (1989; 1997),
party system change is determined via indicators such as the effective number
of parties, electoral volatility and the entry of new parties into the system. The
analysis of the indicators of party system change is coupled with a discussion
about empirical data on the political environment at election time and in the
immediate aftermath of the elections, including issues such as regime classification, rotation of power, coalition structures, prohibited parties, and societal
cleavages. Hence, the emphasis is on (in)stability and on the structure and
nature of competition in 2015 compared to that of 2010. In short, what does
party system change tell us about the prospects for democracy some seven
years after the outbreak of the Arab Spring?

With regard to the issue of party change, the analysis centres on a small handful of the region's political parties, namely (1) those that can be classified as traditionally dominant, and which have remained key operators on the scene (for example the National Liberation Front (FLN in the French acronym) in Algeria); (2) those that can be defined as new parties, whether internally or externally created,[1] which entered the party system post-2010 (Tunisia's al-Aridha (PP) is one example); and (3) the (initially) victorious Islamist parties (such as the Ennahda in Tunisia and Egypt's Freedom and Justice Party (FJP). How have these specific parties responded to the political environment established with the advent of the Arab Spring within their respective countries? And how does the success of these particular parties impact upon the prospects for democracy in the MENA?

2 The importance of parties for democracy

Democracy and political parties go hand in hand. Political parties – defined here according to Sartori's (1976: 63) minimal principles as 'any political group identified by an official label that presents at elections, and is capable of placing through elections (free or non-free), candidates for public office' – are indispensable for democracy. Research shows that without them, democracy is not only unlikely to take hold, it is also unlikely to thrive and, therefore, survive (Schattschneider 1942; van Biezen 2003; Kuenzi and Lambright 2005; Norris 2005). Hence, the state of the key political parties in the MENA, as well as the nature of the region's party systems, say a lot about the prospects for democracy in the region in the wake of the Arab Spring, which many hoped would usher in a new democratic era, and which has, in some ways, proved to be a profoundly transformative political event in a number of MENA countries.

Political parties have several functions, which can crudely be divided into two categories: firstly, representative and institutional/procedural, which are rather obvious, and secondly, a category that includes the recruitment of leaders and the organisation of parliament and government (Bartolini and Mair 2001). In other words, parties act as vehicles for citizen representation by uniting people with shared interests, structuring their voice, and therefore ultimately strengthening and empowering them. In a nutshell, it is easy for a regime to ignore the voice of a single individual, who feels s/he stands alone, but difficult to disregard the demands of a populous, organised force (Norris 2005). This rings true both outside parliament as well as within, that is, for members of the electorate as well as for the deputies serving in public office. And this is the crux of the matter. Parties are important. Parties are necessary. They cannot be replaced by 'groupings', 'alliances', 'lists' and the like. This is not simply a question of semantics, but one of representation and accountability. Without political parties, there is no democracy.

Similarly, democracy cannot be bent. Authoritarian approximations, regardless of what they are labelled, are still versions of authoritarianism; they are not subcategories of democracy. And in many cases, if not in most, authoritarian approximations do not constitute moves towards democracy, on the contrary. Usually, electoral authoritarianism, competitive authoritarianism, tutelary democracy, and illiberal democracy, along with their many siblings in the category of pluralist authoritarianism, have been introduced precisely to ensure the survival of authoritarian rule, and prevent the fostering of democracy (Schedler 2006; 2013).

Consequently, the analysis that follows focuses on countries that allow some degree of contestation, but are not necessarily democratic. Referring back to the theoretical framework in Chapter 1, the discussion spans regimes across the categories of full democracy, defective democracy and pluralist authoritarianism, while closed authoritarian regimes have been left out except for in instances where they provide useful context. The objective is accordingly to assess whether party system change, and to some extent also party change, represent significant steps towards full democracy and, in the case of Israel (the only democracy in the region, even though it is defective due to its treatment of the country's Arab population), its continued survival. Consequently, the analysis deals mainly with those MENA countries where political parties are – and were – allowed, and where competitive elections took place both prior to and following the outbreak of the Arab Spring. In short, Algeria, Egypt, Iraq, Morocco, Tunisia, Israel and Turkey are the cases – Arab and non-Arab – at the core of the discussion. That said, several other MENA countries – including Bahrain, Iran, Kuwait, Jordan, Lebanon and Yemen – will also be considered, but less closely, and from a different perspective. Rather than assessing party and party system change, the focus in these cases is the nature and extent of competition allowed prior to and in the wake of the Arab Spring, and the issue of why parties continue to be prohibited, in many cases despite the holding of competitive elections with some level of organisation, whether in the form of alliances, blocs, lists, and so on.

3 Benchmarking: the state of the MENA party systems in 2010

At the time of the outbreak of the Arab Spring in December 2010, and by the time it began to more rapidly spread across the MENA region in early 2011, none of the region's Arab regimes could be classified as democratic, although a handful did allow for both political parties and to hold competitive elections at national level – on a theoretical level, at least.

3.1 Limited pluralism

The reality is that, regardless of the holding of somewhat competitive elections and a modicum of power-sharing, on the eve of the eruption of the Arab Spring, Yemen, Tunisia and Egypt effectively had one-party systems in place following legislative elections in 2003, 2009 and 2010 respectively. A hegemonic party – the National Democratic Party (NDP) in Egypt, the Democratic Constitutional Rally (RCD in the French acronym) in Tunisia, and the General People's Congress (GPC) in Yemen – sat firmly in power, because the legislative (and presidential) elections were so heavily manipulated that there seemed no prospects of any alternation (Blaydes 2010; Martínez-Fuentes 2010; Gobe 2009; Phillips 2008). Furthermore, in the case of Yemen, legislative elections had effectively been abandoned with President Ali Abdullah Saleh postponing the scheduled 2009 elections by two years amid political tensions, which were, at times, extremely violent (Day 2012).

Somewhat more pluralist on the face of it, Turkey, Palestine and Syria all operated with two-party systems, the effective number of parties[2] (based on national election results from 2006 and 2007) amounting to 2.2 in Turkey, 2.3 in Palestine and 2.5 in Syria. That said, in Syria competition was far from genuine, and the figure of 2.5 masks the fact that Syria was effectively another case of single-party hegemony. Prior to the 2007 elections, 163 seats had been set aside for the National Progressive Front (NPF) – an alliance formed by the Arab Socialist Ba'ath Party (which won 134 of the seats, having been allocated a minimum of 130 seats) and its various satellites and crony parties. Eighty-one seats were reserved for so-called 'independents', although their distance from the regime was very limited (Ghadbian 2015). In contrast, in Palestine, competition between the two main parties, Hamas and Fatah, was extremely fierce, and there was no questioning the nature of the party system, despite allegations of fraud and manipulation (Shikaki 2006; Roy 2011). In Turkey competition was authentic too, and alternation of power a real possibility despite an electoral framework that clearly favoured the larger parties and encouraged the fielding of independent candidates due to the existence of a threshold of 10 per cent of the national vote for parties.[3] As in 2002, the 2007 elections saw the victory of the conservative Islamist Justice and Development Party (AKP), but sizeable seat shares were also awarded to the two traditionally influential parties, the Republican People's Party (CHP) and the Nationalist Movement Party (MHP). Hence, whereas Palestine was a genuine example of a two-party system, the nature of the party system in Turkey bordered on so-called 'moderate pluralism', with more than two actors standing a realistic chance of winning the elections, and competition being somewhat more centripetal.

3.2 Moderate and extreme pluralism

Moderate pluralism, defined as party systems in which the effective number of parties is in the region of three to five (Sartori 1976), was the order of the day in Algeria (5.5), while Israel (6.8), Iraq (7.1)[4], Lebanon (9.5) and Morocco (9.7) operated with party systems that could best be described as cases of 'polarised' or 'extreme' pluralism, with some being much more extreme than others. In fact, the so-called 'pluralist' party systems in place prior to the Arab Spring covered a wide variety of settings.

In Algeria, for example, the political situation was very stable. While the effective number of parties was 5.5, the party system was arguably still dominated by the two regime parties, the FLN and the National Rally for Democracy (RND), as it had been for decades. Smaller 'complacent parties', referred to as opposition parties, but effectively silent partners co-opted by the regime, were allowed the opportunity to gain a modicum of representation in parliament and some even a few seats in the cabinet, but never to an extent that these parties had any real say about how politics was conducted in the country (Volpi 2013; Willis 2014).

In neighbouring Morocco the issue of the lack of an audible voice in politics was also a major issue for the political parties. But here it was an issue for all parties. It was the king who set the political agenda, and the king who had the ultimate say about every political decision of any significance. Morocco was an executive monarchy, in which the king not only ruled, but also governed (Boukhars 2010). With the monarchy firmly entrenched, the formation – and even mushrooming – of political parties was strongly encouraged by the regime. Toothless party pluralism was seen by the regime as a means of ensuring the monarchy's position at the centre of politics, creating a democratic veneer for the electorate and the international community, and a system of spoils for the local political elite. Hence, the large number of parties contesting the legislative elections and represented in parliament and also in the cabinet did not reflect the actual division of power. Power lay firmly in the hands of the monarchy, while a slowly expanding handful of traditionally dominant parties[5] continued to support the status quo in return for privilege (Lust 2014; Storm 2013).

Although the figures for the effective number of parties in Algeria, Morocco and (as shall become evident later) Israel indicated at a first glance the existence of moderate to extreme pluralist party systems, which upon further examination turned out to be much less pluralist than initially thought, the Lebanese party system was not only highly fragmented in terms of the effective number of parties score, which was approaching ten, the system was also borderline atomised if one takes a closer look at the environment behind the figures: some twenty-one parties and groups of independents – divided between four alliances or blocs – secured seats in parliament in the country's last pre-Arab Spring elections of 2009. Two of the blocs (March 8, and Change and Reform) won around 23 per cent of the contested seats each, while the largest alliance (March 14) took 46 per cent, and the smallest (composed of pro-government independents) just short of 8 per cent. Three parties – the Future Movement (FM), the Free Patriotic Movement (FPM) and Amal – won in excess of 10 per cent of the seats, while the party spearheading the smallest alliance, the Progressive Socialist Party (PSP), secured a seat share of 5.6 per cent, which was much closer to the seat share of the vast majority of successful parties, most of which won fewer than 4 per cent.

A similar scenario to that unfolding in Lebanon, where the new Hariri government could arguably be best characterised as a compromise, which saw inclusion triumph over coherence, and breadth over strength, given its oversized nature and broad ideological span, could be found in Israel at the time of the last pre-Arab Spring elections of 2009.[6] Following strong performances at the polls by the Kadima, the Likud, Labor and Yisrael Beiteinu, which all succeeded in obtaining a seat share in excess of 10 per cent, and the ultra-orthodox Shas, which secured 9.17 per cent of the contested seats, a broad and over-sized government coalition was formed in the wake of the elections.[7] Ironically, of the five largest parties, which together controlled 78.3 per cent of the seats in the Knesset, only the Kadima did not enter the coalition, despite the party winning the elections with a seat share of 25.33 per cent to the Likud's 22.5 per cent.[8] The Kadima's origins, which began with a splinter from the Likud in 2005 and gained a number of Labor parliamentarians shortly after, partly explains why the party was not a member of the governing coalition. However, it also serves to illustrate that it would, in fact, have been theoretically possible to form a much smaller governing coalition around the Kadima: a coalition that would also have been much more ideologically coherent.

Most pluralist of them all, however, was Iraq. That is, if one can call the party system pluralist. The effective number of parties score of 7.1 at the time of the 2010 elections did not actually reflect parties but rather alliances. Within these alliances there were several parties, but the results of the individual components were never made public. Hence, while less than ten alliances were awarded seats, there were around forty parties within them. Of the alliances contesting the 2010 elections, four succeeded in winning more than 10 per cent of the contested seats, but two parties still clearly outperformed the others, namely the Iraqi National Movement, which took 28 per cent of the seats, and the State of Law Coalition, which was awarded 27.38 per cent.

4 Party system development: the Arab Spring and other factors

In the wake of the outbreak of the Arab Spring in late 2010, and the subsequent eruption of political upheaval across the MENA region in early 2011, academics, practitioners and members of the general public have questioned its impact and importance (Willis 2014; Youngs 2014; Frosini and Biagi 2015; Kausch 2015; Sadiki 2015). Initially, many hoped and thought that the unprecedented levels of political unrest experienced in the region would result in democracy finally taking hold in the MENA countries, but as time passed the expectations were dashed. But what exactly happened in terms of democratic advancement? Looking at data relating to the character of the MENA party systems, particularly the Pedersen index of electoral volatility[9], the effective number of parties, the seat share of the top two parties,[10] and the seat share of new parties entering the party system, there is no denying that the region's party systems have undergone change, although some evidently more than others as illustrated in Table 3.1.

Table 3.1 Party system change: the effective number of parties and the Arab Spring

	1-party system	2-party system	Moderate pluralism (3–5)	Extreme pluralism (6–8+)
	Egypt	Palestine	Algeria	Iraq
	Tunisia	Syria		Israel
	Yemen	Turkey		Lebanon
				Morocco
Arab Spring				
		Turkey	Algeria	Iraq
			Egypt ↑	Israel
			Libya ↑	Morocco
			Tunisia ↑	

Source: prepared by the author

At first glance, two key observations can be made from Table 3.1. Firstly, a number of countries no longer figure as there have been no competitive legislative elections held since the Arab Spring (this is the case of Lebanon, Palestine, Syria and Yemen),[11] while Libya is a new entry, as the country's first competitive legislative elections took place in 2012. Secondly, where significant party system change ocurred – measured solely on the basis of the effective number of parties and Sartori's corresponding party system categories – the trend has been in a more competitive direction. Egypt, Libya and Tunisia, the only countries witnessing such pronounced development, have all moved into the category of moderate pluralism: Egypt and Tunisia from a one-party system starting point, and Libya from a situation where free, fair competitive elections were denied and political parties prohibited.

The Pedersen index, a measure used to illustrate the level of electoral volatility in either votes or – as here – in seats, further supports the indication that the party systems in the MENA region have undergone considerable change following the Arab Spring, and while only a handful of cases have experienced significant party system change (in the sense of category leaps), most have witnessed substantial electoral volatility as voters have shifted allegiances and new parties have entered the party systems and old parties exited. While there are no precise rules stipulating what constitutes low, medium or high levels of electoral volatility, a Pedersen index above ten is generally referred to in the literature as considerable, and scores above forty as (very) high. If these cut-off points are used as a general guide, then all the MENA countries represented in Table 3.1 experienced medium to high levels of electoral volatility, that is, except for those cases that exited in the wake of the Arab Spring and the new entry of Libya (as the Pedersen index cannot be calculated for these). Nevertheless, whereas it is beyond doubt that changes to the party systems of the region have taken place, and in some cases great changes, the figures do not tell us why these changes occured, and whether they were, indeed, a product of the Arab Spring or some other factor(s). In order to determine the impact of the Arab Spring, it is therefore necessary to dig a little deeper and also take a look at the political environment, including issues such as regime classification, rotation of power, coalition structures, prohibited parties and societal cleavages.

4.1 Tunisia and Egypt: regime overthrow and party system change

Rather unsurprisingly, electoral volatility was most pronounced in Tunisia and Egypt, with scores approaching 100, as the two countries experienced great political turmoil following the fall of long-lived authoritarian regimes in late

2010 and early 2011. In both countries, the desire to see a break with the past led to the dissolution of the old regime parties (the RCD in Tunisia, the NDP in Egypt), the swift licensing of a swathe of new parties and subsequently the holding of legislative elections – all within the space of a year (Gana 2013; Korany and Rabab 2014). In Tunisia the 2011 elections, in which nineteen parties were elected (compared to seven in 2009), saw the victory of the two main opposition forces to the Ben Ali regime: Rached al-Ghannouchi's Islamist Ennahda and the liberal Congress for the Republic (CPR) under the leadership of Moncef Marzouki. While these two parties were new in the sense of contesting legislative elections, they had operated as clandestine entities during the Ben Ali regime, just as several of the other new entries into the party system had done (Perkins 2005; Storm 2013). In some cases, the so-called 'new' parties were, in fact, new constructions, but the key personalities within them were well-known figures on the Tunisian political scene. Hence, although the effective number of parties went up from 1.7 in 2009 to 4.6 in 2011, and despite a Pedersen index of ninety-nine, the political landscape was not wholly unfamiliar to the electorate.

A few years later, at the end of 2014, Tunisian voters returned to the polls to elect a new legislature following the adoption of the country's first post-Ben Ali constitution. Plagued by political unrest and strong societal division between Islamists and anti-Islamists, electoral volatility remained very high (a Pedersen index of seventy-three). Of the three newcomers (the Ennahda, the CPR and al-Aridha (PP), which had done very well in the country's first democratic elections in 2011, only the Ennahda remained a significant player. However, the Islamists were this time outperformed by the new entrant Nidaa Tounes, a party bringing together key figures and supporters of the old regime party under the leadership of Beji Caïd Essebsi (Boubekeur 2016; Brody-Barre 2013). Following presidential elections in November 2014, which were won by Essebsi, Nidaa Tounes formed a government under the leadership of prime minister Habib Essid together with a small supporting party, the Free Patriotic Union. Given Nidaa Tounes' and Essid's strong ties to Ben Ali's regime, the country appeared to have come full circle, returning to a situation where the old guard was governing, and power was effectively concentrated in the hands of one party, but with the important difference that in the post-Arab Spring era, this had happened via free, fair and competitive elections – legislative and presidential.

In Egypt things returned much to 'normal' as well, although the path taken was very different to that in Tunisia. Following Mubarak's ousting by the military, which had always played a central role in Egyptian politics, a new constitution was swiftly adopted in preparation for the holding of legislative elections and the return to civilian rule. The elections were originally scheduled for

September 2011, but were eventually postponed, officially with a view to giving new parties a better chance to establish themselves before the polls, although some observers were alleging that the decision to push the elections back a few months was instead due to the military firming up its exit guarantees (Brown and Stilt 2011; Moustafa 2012). With the former regime party dissolved, the way had undeniably been paved for party system change, and not surprisingly there was a pronounced increase in new parties readying themselves to compete in the elections. Hence, when the first free and competitive national elections in Egyptian history did eventually take place from November 2011 through to January 2012, the result was predictably a substantial growth in the party system (from eight parties to fifteen), as well as the victory of new forces, as the previously repressed Muslim Brotherhood emerged as the winner under the banner of its recently licensed electoral outfit, the FJP. In second place came another Islamist party, the brand new and more conservative al-Nour. In unison, the FJP and the al-Nour party won some 64 per cent of the contested seats, which was a considerable achievement for two newcomers, and an enormous change in fortune for the country's Islamists.[12]

The Islamist wave of success continued into the presidential elections, which saw the leader of the FJP, Mohammed Morsi, emerge victorious following a run-off against the country's former prime minister and Mubarak confidante, Ahmed Mohamed Shafik. However, Morsi's attempts to concentrate power in his own hands not long after his ascendance to the presidency, coupled with the virtually unrivalled political strength of the country's Islamist parties as a group (despite their differences) led to a second military *coup d'état* within as many years (Rougier and Lacroix 2016). Initially the military made promises of returning to civilian rule as soon as possible. Nevertheless, it quickly became apparent that it had no genuine intention of doing so, amid surprisingly few complaints. It appeared that many Egyptians – and large segments of the international community – preferred a stable Egypt under military rule to an Islamist government. The military's grip on power was eventually legitimised in spring 2014, when General Abdel Fattah al-Sisi, the architect behind Morsi's removal, won the presidential elections against the activist Hamdeen Sabahi, who was an extreme outsider.[13]

At the time the 2015 legislative elections were held, after nearly four years with no parliament *in situ*, Egypt remained under effective military rule. The elections were won by so-called independents, which had reserved 448 of the 596 seats in parliament, while party-affiliated candidates were awarded 120, and a further twenty-eight members were appointed by President al-Sisi. The Egyptian parliament had once again been reduced to the president's rubber stamp, and parties of any substance – particularly liberal or Islamist – had been dissolved or marginalised to such an extent that they were no longer major players regardless of their individual performances in the elections, which several parties argued were heavily manipulated by the military (Democracy International 2014; Rougier and Lacroix 2016). From one authoritarian regime to another, but with similar set-ups, Egypt had, indeed, come full circle.

4.2 Libya: from a party vacuum to empty moderate pluralism

Whereas Tunisia and Egypt had both come full circle – Tunisia in the sense of voting back into office key personalities from the *ancien régime*, and Egypt returning to the comfort of more overt military rule – Libya did nothing of the like. In fact, Libya went from a tightly controlled political landscape devoid of political parties and free, fair and competitive elections to an over-crowded, fragmented, disjointed and ultimately anarchic political space with more than one parliament.

Political parties in the new Libya were only of peripheral importance, however. Parties were simply a matter of box-ticking. They were a means to appease the citizenry and placate the international community, whether at the time of the country's first democratic elections in the spring of 2012, in which no less than twenty-one parties proved successful, or in the wake of the elections during the government-formation period and its aftermath. In Libya, instead, the currency was localism: specifically, tribal ties, religious extremism and brute force. The vast majority – if not all – of the parties formed in the run-up to the 2012 elections were effectively militia or tribes with local rather than national agendas. The newly established parties were lacking in political ideology and, consequently, in specific programmes. Their platforms were not based on policies aimed at building a new and united Libya or, indeed, a new and divided Libya (Tabib 2014; El Gomati 2015; Lesch 2014; Pargeter 2016). The parties were simply militia and tribal fronts – that were often also personalistic in nature – which put forward agendas based on blood and territory, as well as, of course, vehicles for the pitting of old regime forces against those it had repressed. However, these groups had suddenly become the new overlords after al-Gaddafi's demise in autumn 2011. Predictably, the 2012 elections took place in an ambience of violence and protest.

The two main parties in 2012 were the National Forces Alliance (NFA) and the Justice and Construction Party (JCP), which won 70 per cent of the contested seats between them, and they were the only two parties to obtain a seat share above 5 per cent.[14] The NFA, formed in February 2012 and headed by Mahmoud Jibril[15], who had served as rebel prime minister during the early days of the Arab Spring uprisings, brought together a wide variety of organisations, NGOs and independent personalities under a loosely defined liberal banner, calling for a democratic Libya governed by moderate Islam (St John 2015). In comparison to the NFA, the smaller JCP, which won 21.25 per cent of the seats reserved for party-affiliated candidates, can only be described as much more conservative in nature with a clear Islamist agenda, given its point of origin within the Muslim Brotherhood. In the wake of the elections, the JCP strengthened its position vis-à-vis the much larger NFA by playing a clever political game of divide and rule supporting ethnic minority candidates (for example, the Amazigh) or moderate Islamists against secular candidates fielded by the diverse, and therefore deeply divided, NFA for various high-ranking positions within the new political administration (Boduszynski and Pickard 2013; Pack and Cook 2015; St John 2015).

Regardless of the intense battle between the two top parties, there is no denying, however, that party politics remain insignificant in Libya, as do electoral politics. Most tellingly, the vast majority of the contested seats in 2012 were reserved for independent candidates, rather than those with party affiliation – a situation in sharp contrast to that in Algeria, Egypt, Israel, Morocco, Tunisia and Turkey, as well as Iraq to some extent, where independents have played a much less central role in post-2010 electoral politics. A few years later, in the summer of 2014, parties had been entirely dispensed with as the Libyan electorate headed to the polls yet again in national elections.[16] Hence, although parties were not prohibited, they had been pushed to the margins of the political system, and consequently very few now operate as anything more than empty shells (St John 2015). This situation is in sharp contrast to that in Algeria, Egypt, Israel, Morocco, Tunisia and Turkey, where independents have played a much less central role in post-Arab Spring electoral politics.

4.3 Algeria, Iraq, Israel, Morocco and Turkey: the stable party systems

In comparison to the North African cases of Egypt and Tunisia, which both experienced significant change at the party system level, whether related to the Arab Spring or as a consequence of other political events, Algeria, Iraq, Israel, Morocco and Turkey remained remarkably stable. Nonetheless, Algeria and Morocco did experience some political unrest linked to the regional unrest, and Iraq has remained in a state of turmoil since the 2003 invasion.

Morocco was perhaps the most strongly affected by the Arab Spring from this group, and was hit by large-scale political demonstrations in early 2011. The protests were chiefly organised under the banner of the Mouvement du 20 Février (20-F Movement), a collective that brought together Islamists, Berber groups and the far left in a call for political reforms (Fernández-Molina 2011; 2016). Given the disjointed nature of the 20-F Movement, the objectives of the group were somewhat unclear. Specifically, the kind of political reform that was envisaged, and how it would be arrived at, was never fully explored and, consequently, the 20-F Movement remained weak when faced with a well-organised executive monarchy used to tackling dissent, and more importantly also equipped with the means to do so effectively (Desrues 2012).

In light of the protests taking place in the larger cities across Morocco, the monarchy brought forward the date of the legislative elections originally scheduled for the following year, while also overseeing the revision and adoption of a new constitution. Both measures won the monarchy considerable goodwill among the general population, as the king came across as efficient and responsive, although in reality the king's actions did nothing good for the country's democratisation process, seeing as the monarch effectively by-passed the demo-cratically elected politicians, and ensured the passing of a new constitution, which concentrated power further in his hands (Storm 2013; Benchemsi 2012). The legislative elections which were brought forward from 2012 to 2011 saw the Moroccan electorate punish the incumbent government, which ultimately was much less to blame for the country's difficulties than the monarchy, given the distribution of power (Fernández-Molina 2016; Storm 2013).

However, that said, although the coalition government headed by Abbas el-Fassi from the Parti Istiqlal (PI) was replaced by a new government led by the Islamist Party of Justice and Development (PJD) under Prime Minister Abdelilah Benkirane, it did not alter the fact that the Moroccan party system remained much the same in the wake of the Arab Spring. Electoral volatility was reasonably low compared to much of the rest of the MENA region (Pedersen index of twenty-eight), and while the effective number of parties dropped considerably (from 9.7 to 6.6), as did the number of parties winning seats in parliament (from twenty-three to eighteen), ultimately the parties that tradi-tionally dominated Moroccan politics continued to do so, and the PJD and the PI continued to be the top two performers, increasing their combined share of seats from 30.15 per cent in 2007 to 42.3 per cent in 2011 (Storm 2007; 2013). Furthermore, the one new party to enter the country's party system in 2011, and that managed to secure more than 10 per cent of the seats, was not strictly speaking a new entity. The Party of Authenticity and Modernity (PAM), a party closely linked to the monarchy, had already contested the 2007 elections successfully as a list of so-called independents before morphing into the PAM in 2008 (Boussaid 2009).

When the unrest eventually spilled over from Tunisia and subsequently Morocco into neighbouring Algeria, it was much more muted in comparison. President Bouteflika, the long-term Algerian strongman, had anticipated its arrival, and room for manoeuvre was strictly limited. Hence, most protests were small in size and local in focus, and posed no threat whatsoever to the regime (Volpi 2013; Roberts 2015). Therefore, in Algeria, there were no reforms initiated. Elections were not brought forward and neither was the constitution amended in light of the Arab Spring, and both the government and the regime remained the same. When legislative elections were eventually held as planned in 2012, electoral volatility was moderate (Pedersen index of thirty-five) and the number of successful parties remained much the same, increasing slightly from twenty-two to twenty-six, but with the effective number of parties dropping from 5.5 to 4.1 (Storm 2013). The FLN and the RND, the two regime parties, continued to be the dominant parties, securing 59.74 per cent of the contested seats between them, which gave them the green light to continue their coalition partnership. In the wake of the elections, a few noteworthy – but ultimately unimportant – changes were made to the coalition government and the cabinet as a result of the disastrous performance of the Islamist Movement of Society for Peace (MSP), which had joined forces with other minor Islamist parties (such as the Green Algeria Alliance) and shifted its allegiance away from the regime in a highly miscalculated move just prior to the elections (Storm 2013). The prime minister, a largely impotent role, shifted from the RND's Ahmed Ouyahia to the FLN's Abdelmalek Sellal, not so much as a consequence of the election results as a reflection of the balance of power within the regime – a factor above and beyond the polls.

In Turkey the top two parties also stayed the same, and the party system remained remarkably stable despite legislative elections being held no less than three times since the onset of the Arab Spring, namely in 2011 and twice in 2015. The 2011 elections took place in an atmosphere of peace and tranquility when compared to the situation elsewhere in the region. As in 2007, the Islamist AKP emerged as the winner of the elections with the conservative CHP coming a distant second. This pattern repeated itself in the June 2015 elections, which produced a hung parliament, and again in the November 2015 elections, with the AKP and CHP together securing between 70.91 and 84 per cent of the contested seats. Electoral volatility also remained relatively low (Pedersen index of six, nineteen and eleven), and the effective number of parties varied between 2.3 and 3.1, translating into three successful parties in 2011, and four in both of the 2015 elections as the Kurdish newcomer Halklarin Demokratik Partisi (Peoples' Democratic Party, HDP) burst onto the scene.[17]

The relative stability of the Turkish party system did not imply that the country was not marred by political unrest in the post-2010 era. On the contrary, particularly from 2013 onwards, Turkey has experienced severe political difficulties as violent clashes between the police and anti-government protesters have occurred in major cities throughout the country. It is important to underscore, however, that the protests were not inspired or fuelled by the events of the Arab Spring. Rather, the root of the conflict was domestic and more recent as initial protests began as a response to urban development plans in Istanbul, but grew to reflect a nationwide concern with the Islamist government's position on secularism, allegations of political corruption and fears that the government was also increasingly curbing the freedoms of speech and assembly (Taspinar 2014; Ozkirimli 2014).

In Iraq conflict was also very much ongoing, and as in Turkey it was not inspired by the Arab Spring, but significantly predated the uprisings. The feud between the country's Shiite and Sunni communities, as well as the Kurdish power struggle, intensified in the wake of the 2003 United States invasion, and while a number of elections have taken place since then, the institutionalised party and political system which was sought remains precariously fragile. There is no denying that the atomised party system is a strong contributing factor to this state of affairs, reflecting a desire by the many previously marginalised groups to grasp some segment of power in the post-Saddam era. Rather than form larger parties representing a wider group, but necessitating leadership and a willingness to sacrifice, political parties have mushroomed around individuals and groupings, who prefer to be lord of their own formations, but join forces in loose alliances at election time with a view to maximising gains (Spencer et al. 2013; Mikail 2014; Wehler-Schök 2014). Consequently, at the time of the most recent elections in 2015, no less than forty-one parties were awarded seats in the legislature, spread out across a number of alliances, most of which did rather poorly. The effective number of parties came to 8.6, and the Pedersen index – taking into account individual parties and shifting alliances in 2015 – was a high seventy-three. The State of Law Coalition headed by Prime Minister Nouri al-Maliki and the Shiite Islamic Da'wa Party remained the country's main force with 28.05 per cent of the seats, while another Shiite alliance, the Sadrist Movement (which had contested the 2010 elections under the banner of the Independent Free Movement List) came a distant second with a seat share of 8.54 per cent. In an atomised and electorally volatile party system there was, after all, some stability to be found.

Finally, Israel – the only (defective) democratic, non-Arab state included in the sample – witnessed none of the tumult seen elsewhere in the region: not because the country was not Arab – non-Arab Turkey also experienced political violence as just discussed – but more likely as a consequence of the fact that Israel was classified as a (defective) democracy at the time the Arab Spring erupted and spread across the region. The political environment in Israel was, in other words, entirely different to elsewhere in the MENA region. This is not to say that Israel evaded politically fanned bloodshed and violent protests as the Arab–Israeli conflict was still very much ongoing, but rather that the political turmoil was not due to non-Arab Israeli citizens calling into question the legitimacy of the Israeli government. It was also not the case that there were no political differences within the Israeli political landscape; however, these played out peacefully within the context of the electoral framework. Hence, the 2013 and 2015 legislative elections saw some electoral volatility (Pedersen index of thirty-four and twenty-nine respectively), while the number of parties succeeding in winning seats in parliament came to thirteen in both elections, corresponding to 7.3 effective parties in 2013 and a slightly lower 6.9 in 2015. In 2013 one newcomer managed to secure more than 10 per cent of the contested seats as the centrist Yesh Atid won a 15.83 per cent share, making it Israel's second largest party at the time, dwarfed only by the Likud–Yisrael Beiteinu alliance, which secured 25.83 per cent. In 2015, Yesh Atid's star had nevertheless faded, and Likud, the Zionist Union (Labor and Hatnuah), the Joint List (Hadash, Balad and United Arab List) all performed better, although Yesh Atid still managed to win a respectable 9.17 per cent of the contested seats. The country's top two parties – or electoral alliances – continued to have a combined seat share just above 40 per cent, as had also been the case in the 2009 elections.

5 Party profiles: the newcomers in perspective

The various elections held across the MENA region in the wake of the Arab Spring produced a number of significant newcomers. Some new arrivals were new in the sense of newly founded, while others were simply new in terms of contesting legislative elections. In some countries these newcomers managed to win the elections and gain power, in others they merely took up a space in parliament. Rather surprisingly, however, given the call for change and the general dissatisfaction with the existing party landscape, successful and significant newcomers – defined as those winning a minimum of 10 per cent of the contested seats – were not common across the region. In several countries those in power prior to the Arab Spring, whether parties or presidents, remained in power after new elections had been held and/or as the uprisings died down. This was, for instance, the case in Algeria where the FLN and the RND maintained their long-term partnership in office, in Turkey where the legislative elections effectively continued to be a contest between the AKP and the CHP, and in Morocco where the PI remained a government force, although it was deposed as the leader of the coalition.

In contrast to the old guard, which remained significant players within the party landscape, the newcomers – at least initially – gave some hope that change was arriving in the MENA region, and that some countries were perhaps embarking upon a genuine democratisation process. However, in most instances, this was not the case, partly because democracy was never the end destination of many of the protesters, but also as a consequence of the fact that the new arrivals were few and far between, and due to the reality that several of these newcomers were made up of seasoned politicians (that is, internally created), many of whom did not have democratisation as their main priority, but rather access to power.

Of the newcomers that succeeded in obtaining a minimum of 10 per cent of the contested seats, the largest group were Sunni Islamist parties with four out of twelve newcomers falling into that category: Tunisia's Ennahda, the FJP and al-Nour in Egypt, and the JCP in Libya. Other new parties, most notably the PAM in Morocco and Nidaa Tounes in Tunisia, defined themselves largely as anti-Islamist entities (whether overtly or not) or at least as a bulwark against conservative Islamist forces (an example is Libya's NFA), while other parties could best be defined as liberal (Tunisia's CPR and Israel's Yesh Attid), outright populist (the PP in Tunisia, which is now defunct), or ethnic – even if only covertly so – as in the case of the Kurdish HDP in Turkey.

There is no arguing against the fact that Islamist forces were the big winners in the legislative elections held in the wake of the Arab Spring, both in terms of the successful creation of large new parties and with regards to seizing power. Islamist parties were clearly the new powerhouses within the party system, a trend that had begun prior to the Arab Sping, but which certainly cemented itself following the uprisings. In Turkey the AKP remained in power, capturing both the post of prime minister and the presidency. In Tunisia and Egypt the newly licensed Ennahda and the FJP, which were both made up of experienced politicians who had been prevented from contesting legislative and presidential elections on a party platform during the previous authoritarian regimes, emerged victorious from the national elections. Furthermore, in Egypt the FJP's biggest rival in the electoral contest was the newly formed conservative Islamist party, al-Nour. In Morocco the Islamist PJD, which had already established itself as a major player within the party system, won the largest share of seats and was afforded the right to form government (in the form of a coalition). This was not only the first time the PJD would be heading the government, but more importantly the first time a Moroccan government was headed by an Islamist party (Szmolka 2015).

While Islamist parties have emerged from the Arab Spring as the big winners on the party front, there is no reason to fear a so-called 'Islamist Winter', that is, Islamist parties seizing power in order to reverse the (limited) democratic gains made so far in the region, or halt the democratisation process in progress in some countries (Roy 2012; Cofman Wittes 2012; Benstead et al. 2013). Save for al-Nour, the only Salafist newcomer, all the new Islamist parties of any size are moderate in outlook. Most are strongly inspired by Hassan al-Banna's teachings, albeit to varying extents, and a number of parties have even originated from within the Muslim Brotherhood, by acting as the organisation's political arm (the FJP in Egypt and the JCP in Libya). However, what these parties really have in common is their desire to win legislative and presidential elections, to form government and to have effective power to govern. The objective of the AKP, the PJD, the FJP, the Ennahda and the JCP was and is not to seize power with a view to turn their respective states into theocracies, which would effectively see an end to their (newly acquired) powerful position within national politics. These moderate Islamist newcomers, perhaps with the exception of the JCP, are run by well-established politicians with political ambition. These are not clergymen or religious dreamers and they do not seek virtue or, indeed, democracy, but power: power within the framework of the existing political system.

6 Conclusion and perspectives: the Arab Spring, the arrival of a new democratic era?

With the eruption of the Arab Spring in late 2010, the MENA region experienced a level of political change not previously seen in the post-independence period. Presidents who had reigned for decades were suddenly deposed, constitutions which had previously been rare were now amended swiftly across the region, and wheareas popular consultations had been infrequent in the past, now the electorate was suddenly called to the polls repeatedly. Furthermore, the MENA region had long been known as hostile to democratic advances (Diamond 2010), but with uprisings spreading across the region, protesters, incumbent regimes and aspiring political leaders all called for democratisation, albeit without defining in detail how democracy was to be understood. How democracy was to be arrived at, however, was quite clear. To the aspiring political leaders and the protesters, democracy equalled the end of the incumbent regime. The incumbent regime, on the other hand, argued that democracy could best be achieved by gradually opening up the political system, but this could only be done safely by keeping the existing rulers in power as this was the only means to guarantee political stability.

6.1 Party developments

At the time, sceptics argued that this was just rhetoric and that the absence of substance was telling of the level of commitment to democracy, that is, that there was a lack of will to introduce genuine, substantial political change. Optimists, on the other hand, hoped that the fact that everyone in the region was suddenly talking about democracy, and the reality that people power had in some instances brought down long-lived regimes were an indication that the MENA region was embarking upon a process of democratisation, albeit over time. Today it is difficult not to agree with the sceptics, at least if developments on the party front are anything to go by. Despite popular uprisings and calls for democracy across the MENA region, and regardless of the fact that old regimes fell and elections were held, very few new significant actors have emerged. As discussed above, in a number of MENA countries the traditionally dominant political parties stayed pre-eminent. This was the case with the RND and the FLN in Algeria, the MP, the RNI, the UC, the PJD, the PI and the USFP in Morocco, as well as the AKP and the CHP (and to some extent also the MHP) in Turkey. This holds equally true elsewhere. In Israel the dominant parties on the scene also remain largely the same: the Likud, Labor and Yisrael Beiteinu. Furthermore, in Algeria and Egypt the military continues to be heavily involved in political life, underpinning the regime in Algeria, while outright calling the shots in Egypt. In Jordan political parties are still obscure entities, which play an insignificant role at election time, where tribal allegiances are much more relevant, and where ultimate power still lies with the king (Beck and Huser 2015), as it also does in Morocco, although political parties perform a much more prominent role in the latter.

Because the incumbent regime was overthrown in Egypt, Libya and Tunisia, most hopes were naturally pinned on these three cases. However, the new parties of any reasonable size that initially emerged in these countries largely disappeared within a few years. This was, for instance, the case with the populist PP in Tunisia,[18] which naturally fizzled out, as well as Egypt's FJP, which was shut down by the military regime following the coup of 2013. In Libya none of the parties, not even those that performed well in the 2012 legislative elections, ever came close to resembling genuine political parties. They were not vehicles for citizen representation, but rather loose political alliances based on local interests and militia or tribal allegiances, often with a charismatic leader fronting the formation.

In fact, the Arab Spring only really produced a small handful of reasonably sized parties that managed to survive for more than just a year or two; and very few of these were new entities as such, that is, hardly any were externally created. Tunisia's Ennahda and the CPR had both operated as clandestine parties during Ben Ali's regime, Morocco's PAM was already well represented in parliament, but had not contested legislative elections as a party prior to the Arab Spring, and Turkey's HDP had strong ties to previous Kurdish parties, which had ceased to exist. The genuine newcomers were Egypt's al-Nour and Israel's Yesh Attid. Of these two, al-Nour could hardly be said to be a beacon of democracy given its Salafist credentials. Hence, the only new (potential) vehicle for democracy, the only new party of any size to emerge and take hold in the MENA region, was Israel's Yesh Attid, but that party's formation was of course not related to the outbreak of the Arab Spring.

The reality that the Arab Spring did not produce a single new externally created party of any size that managed to survive for more than one legislative election does not bode well for democratic prospects in the MENA region. Parties are, after all, a cornerstone of democracy. One would have assumed that the domestic and international calls for democracy, the protest rallies and the holding of several legislative elections in a region where the electorate had not frequently had much of a voice in the past would have led to the formation of at least one or two new reasonably sized parties per country. However, it appears that political differences, tribal allegiances and a weak commitment to democracy, coupled with a domestic and international desire for political stability (Kausch 2015; Youngs 2014) contributed to a very different outcome. However, if the Arab Spring, with its unprecedented level of popular unrest across the MENA region could not produce those much-needed political parties, if the Arab Spring could not act as a catalyst for democracy, then what will it take? And where does it leave the MENA countries? At present, the prospects look bleak. The arrival of another Arab Spring in the near future is not impossible, but it does seem unlikely.

6.2 The party-barren areas of the MENA region: responses to the Arab Spring and prospects for democracy

Although the Arab Spring swept across the MENA countries, triggering – or exacerbating – political unrest from Morocco in the west to Oman in the east, and Turkey in the north to Yemen in the south, not all of these countries were equally affected, nor were all incidents of civil disobedience equally rooted in this tidal wave as illustrated above by the case of, for example, Turkey. Furthermore, where Arab Spring-related events did take place, these did not always involve political parties as in a number of the MENA countries, particularly in the Gulf region, these parties were prohibited.

In Iran the Arab Spring reignited the flame of the country's Green Movement, which had flourished in the immediate aftermath of the 2009 presidential elections as angry youths, in particular, took to the streets demanding President Mahmoud Ahmadinejad's departure (Nabavi 2012). As in 2009, the Green Movement proved that it was capable of mobilising large numbers of dissatisfied citizens. However, the protests were easily and mercilessly put down by the regime, and very few advances were made by the opposition (Furtig 2013). The same was the case in other countries across the Gulf region. In Oman, the United Arab Emirates, Qatar, Kuwait and Bahrain, vocal – and sometimes violent – disaffected members of the public were swiftly and unambiguously dealt with, and the so-called 'pro-democracy movement', which in most cases did not constitute much of a movement, but rather ad hoc gatherings of angry citizens with various grievances, made very little gains (Matthiesen 2013). The varying goals of the protesters, some dissatisfied with the level of corruption, others unhappy with the way the spoils of the political system were divided, coupled with the lack of political parties as mobilising and unifying forces, made it easy for most of the incumbent regimes to largely ignore the demonstrations.

That said, in most countries, token legislative elections were organised as a show of goodwill by the incumbent regime, but they were largely insignificant in terms of altering the balance of power. Iran held legislative elections in a parliament with very limited powers in 2012 under the watchful eye and meddling fingers of the Guardian Council. Again, no political parties took part in the contest, which was essentially a stand-off between supporters of supreme leader Ayatollah Ali Khamenei and President Mahmoud Ahmadinejad, with the former camp emerging victorious (Furtig 2013). A similar scenario unfolded in Oman in 2011 and 2015, as the electorate went to the polls to elect a toothless parliament in a contest between independent candidates from various alliances. In the UAE the emir appointed half the members of the new consultative assembly in 2015, while electoral colleges of limited representative quality elected the other half from among 330 candidates.

The state of affairs was somewhat better in Bahrain and Kuwait, where some of the so-called 'political societies' were beginning to resemble political parties, and where the level of competition was also more intense than elsewhere in the Gulf. That said, despite clear instances of electoral engineering, heated boycotts, parliaments being dissolved, elections ruled unconstitutional and further elections held, the intense political environment at election time, dividing the citizenry and candidates along religious and tribal lines in particular, did not alter the fact that real power lay elsewhere (Meijer and Danckaert 2015; Matthiesen 2013; Freer 2015).[19] In fact control lay with the emir and the ruling family, that is, with the al-Khalifas in Bahrain, and the al-Sabahs in Kuwait.

In contrast to the other Gulf states, Qatar and Saudi Arabia made little or no display of making concessions. In Saudi Arabia, where legislative elections had never taken place, no promises of any kind were made (Steinberg 2014), although municipal elections with universal suffrage and both male and female candidates were held for the first time in 2015 (Steinberg 2014). In Qatar the emir initially declared that the country's electorate would be heading to the polls in legislative elections for the first time in Qatari history sometime in 2013 (BTI 2014; Ulrichsen 2014). As the date approached, however, the elections were further postponed, allegedly to 2016, although there are presently precious few signs that such elections are likely to take place in the near future.[20]

Following the Arab Spring the Gulf region was the only area within the MENA area to prohibit political parties outright, while also making little effort to embark on a democratisation process. As discussed throughout this chapter, most other MENA states initiated some political reforms with a view to appease dissatisfied citizens, and simultaneously placate the international community. The extent of such reforms varied significantly from one country to another, with a number of states – such as for instance Algeria – hardly making any concessions at all. However, even in those countries where the scope of political reforms was minimal, competitive legislative elections were held. As had been the case for some time, many Arab states had come to use democratic processes as a means of ensuring authoritarian survival by creating a democratic veneer, thereby legitimating the regime. However, even when faced by civilian unrest inspired by the events of the Arab Spring further to the west, the Gulf states did not budge. Iran, Qatar, Saudi Arabia, the UAE, Oman, Bahrain and Kuwait remained ruled and governed in the same way as they had been prior to the Arab Spring. They did not take steps towards democracy, nor did they seek to incorporate measures that would make them qualify as defective democracies or even cases of quasi-competitive pluralist authoritarianism given the severe restrictions on organised (and formalised) contestation that remained in place even in those countries that allowed for legislative elections under full suffrage.

Notes

1. In essence, internally created parties are formed by legislators, while externally created parties originate outside the established representative institutions (Duverger 1954).
2. The effective number of parties is a measure that gives a weighted count of either electoral or parliamentary parties based on their relative strength (in vote or seat shares respectively). It is calculated as follows: $N = 1 / \Sigma_{i=1}^{n} p_i^2$, where N is the number of parties with at least one vote/seat and P_i^2 the square of each party's proportion of all votes/seats (Laakso and Taagepera 1979).
3. For more on the election framework, please refer to IFES online at <http://www.electionguide.org/elections/id/2748/> (last accessed 30 January 2016).
4. In the case of Iraq at the time of the 2010 legislative elections, the effective number of parties records the 'effective number of alliances' rather than individual parties. Within these alliances votes/seats were cast/distributed among the various members, but this data was never released.
5. The traditionally dominant parties were as follows: the Popular Movement (MP in the French acronym), the National Rally of Independents (RNI), the Constitutional Union (UC), the Istiqlal Party (PI), the Party of Justice and Development (PJD) and the Socialist Union of Popular Forces (USFP).
6. Hariri's so-called 'unity' cabinet encompassed ministers from the March 14 Alliance, the March 8 Alliance, and the bloc of pro-government independents as well as five independent ministers nominated by President Michel Suleiman (Najem 2012).
7. The cabinet (often referrred to as the 'Second Netanyahu Government') was the largest in Israeli history, originally encompassing no less than thirty ministers and nine deputy ministers. In addition to the above four parties, the coalition included The Jewish Home, a smaller Zionist party that won 2.5 per cent of the seats (Sandler et al. 2011).

8. Not surprisingly, the effective number of parties was 6.8 in 2009.
9. The Pedersen index measures net volatility, that is, the change in seat or vote share for each party from one election to another. It is calculated as the sum of the absolute changes in seat or vote shares divided by two (Pedersen 1979).
10. The performance of the top two parties is a measure frequently used in postcolonial states, particularly in sub-Saharan Africa, where elections have only been taking place for a relatively short period of time. See, among others, Kuenzi and Lambright (2001).
11. Legislative elections took place in Syria in 2012 and 2016. However, these were neither free nor fair, and competition was strictly limited.
12. The figure excludes the ten seats appointed by the Supreme Council of the Armed Forces (SCAF). The Pedersen index was 95.04 for the 2011–12 elections.
13. Sabahi finally only managed to win 4 per cent of the valid votes cast. It should be noted that several parties boycotted the presidential elections, protesting that they were not held in a truly competitive, free and fair spirit (Democracy International 2014).
14. Eighty seats were reserved for party-affiliated candidates, while the remaining 120 were set aside for so-called 'independents'.
15. Jibril belongs to the Warfalla tribe, which has often been described as having strong ties to the al-Gaddafi regime. However, several prominent Warfalla figures were in opposition to al-Gaddafi, including Jibril himself (Joffe 2013).
16. The decision to only field independent candidates was allegedly made with a view to avoiding further political tension at a time when the country was gripped by civil war and had entered into a state of anarchy, being in effect ruled by various armed militias beyond the law and with even less interest in democratic politics than the political parties (Lefevre 2014).
17. From 2014 onwards, the HDP incorporated the Kurdish Peace and Democracy Party (BDP), the successor to the Democratic Society Party (DTP), which had succeeded the Democratic People's Party (DEHAP). DEHAP was a continuation of the banned People's Democracy Party (HADEP). The HADEP, the DEHAP and the DTP had all been prohibited due to alleged ties to Abdullah Öcalan's banned Kurdistan Workers' Party (PKK).
18. It is important to highlight that Nidaa Tounes remained a key player, despite merging with a handful of other parties to create the Union for Tunisia (UPT) in 2013 and also participating in the National Salvation Front (NSF). The party contested the 2014 elections on its own slate.
19. In Kuwait all members of the legislature are elected in direct elections. In Bahrain, however, only the forty members of the lower house are popularly elected. The forty members of the upper house, which has greater powers than the lower house, are appointed by the emir.
20. Two-thirds of the members of parliament are to be directly elected, the final third to be appointed by the emir. Parties remain prohibited.

References

Bartolini, Stefano and Peter Mair (2001), 'Challenges to contemporary political parties', in Larry Diamond and Richard Gunther (eds), *Political Parties and Democracy*, Baltimore: Johns Hopkins University Press, pp. 327–43.

Beck, Martin and Simone Huser (2015), 'Jordan and the "Arab Spring": no challenge, no change?', *Middle East Critique*, 24 (1): 83–97.

Benchemsi, Ahmed (2012), 'Morocco: outfoxing the opposition', *Journal of Democracy*, 23 (1): 57–69.

Benstead, Lindsay, Ellen M. Lust, Dhafer Malouche and Gamal Solt (2013), 'Islamists aren't the obstacle', *Foreign Affairs*, 14 February.

van Biezen, Ingrid (2003), *Political Parties in New Democracies: Party Organization in Southern and East–Central Europe*, London: Palgrave Macmillan.

Blaydes, Lisa (2010), *Elections and Distributive Politics in Mubarak's Egypt*, Cambridge: Cambridge University Press.

Boduszynski, Mieczystaw and Duncan Pickard (2013), 'Libya starts from scratch', *Journal of Democracy*, 24 (2): 86–96.

Boubekeur, Amel (2016), 'Islamists, secularists and old regime elites in Tunisia: bargained competition', *Mediterranean Politics*, 21 (1): 107–27.

Boukhars, Anouar (2010), *Politics in Morocco*, London: Routledge.

Boussaid, Farid (2009), 'The rise of the PAM in Morocco: trampling the political scene or stumbling into it?', *Mediterranean Politics*, 14 (3): 413–19.

Brody-Barre, Andrea (2013), 'The impact of political parties and coalition building on Tunisia's democratic future', *Journal of North African Studies*, 18 (2): 211–30.

Brown, Nathan and Kristen Stilt (2011), *A Haphazard Constitutional Compromise*, Washington, DC: Carnegie Endowment for International Peace.

BTI (2014), *Qatar Country Report*, Gutersloh: Bertelsmann Stiftung.

Cofman Wittes, Tamara (2012), 'Learning to live with the Islamist Winter', *Foreign Policy*, 19 July.

Day, Stephen (2012), *Regionalism and Rebellion in Yemen: a Troubled National Union*, Cambridge: Cambridge University Press.

Democracy International (2014), *Egypt Presidential Election Observation Report*, Bethesda: Democracy International.

Desrues, Thierry (2012), 'Le mouvement du 20 février et le régime marocain', *L'Année du Maghreb*: 359–89.

Diamond, Larry (2010), 'Why are there no Arab democracies?', *Journal of Democracy*, 21 (1): 93–112.

Duverger, Maurice (1954), *Political Parties*, New York: Wiley.

El Gomati, Anas (2015), 'Libya's Islamists and the 17 February revolution', in Larbi Sadiki (ed.), *Routledge Handbook of the Arab Spring*, London: Routledge, pp. 118–32.

Fernández-Molina, Irene (2011), 'The monarchy vs the 20 February Movement: who holds the reins of political change in Morocco?', *Mediterranean Politics*, 16 (3): 435–41.

Fernández-Molina, Irene (2016), *Moroccan Foreign Policy under Mohammed VI, 1999–2014*, London: Routledge.

Freer, Courtney (2015), *The Rise of Pragmatic Islamism in Kuwait's Post-Arab Spring Opposition Movement*, Washington, DC: Brookings Institution.

Frosini, Justin and Francesco Biagi (eds) (2015), *Political and Constitutional Transitions in North Africa: Actors and Factors*, London: Routledge.

Furtig, Henner (2013), *Iran and the Arab Spring: between Expectations and Disillusion*, Hamburg: GIGA.

Gana, Nouri (2013), *The Making of the Tunisian Revolution*, Edinburgh: Edinburgh University Press.

Ghadbian, Najib (2015), 'Contesting authoritarianism', in Raymond Hinnebusch and Tina Zintl (eds), *Syria from Reform to Revolt. Vol. 1*, Syracuse: Syracuse University Press, pp. 91–112.

Gobe, Eric (2009), 'Deceptive liberal reforms: institutional adjustments and the dynamics of authoritarianism in Tunisia (1997–2005)', in Eberhard Kienle (ed.), *Democracy Building and Democracy Erosion. Political Change North and South of the Mediterranean*, London: Saqi Books, pp. 93–111.

Joffe, George (2013), 'Civil activism and the roots of the 2011 uprisings', in Jason Pack (ed.), *The 2011 Libyan Uprisings and the Struggle for the Post-Qadhafi Future*, Basingstoke: Palgrave Macmillan.

Kausch, Kristina (ed.) (2015), *Geopolitics and Democracy in the Middle East*, Madrid: FRIDE.

Korany, Baghat and El-Mahdi Rabab (2014), *Arab Spring in Egypt: Revolution and Beyond*, Cairo: AUC Press.

Kuenzi, Michelle and Gina Lambright (2001), 'Party system institutionalization in 30 African countries', *Party Politics*, 7 (4): 437–68.

Kuenzi, Michelle and Gina Lambright (2005), 'Party systems and democratic consolidation in Africa's electoral regimes', *Party Politics*, 11 (4): 423–46.

Laakso, Markku and Rein Taagepera (1979), '"Effective" number of parties: a measure with application to West Europe', *Comparative Political Studies*, 12 (1): 3–27.

Lefevre, Raphael (2014) 'An Egyptian scenario for Libya?', *Journal of North African Studies*, 19 (4): 602–7.

Lesch, Ann (2014), 'Troubled political transitions: Tunisia, Egypt and Libya', *Middle East Policy Journal*, 21 (1): 62–74.

Lust, Ellen (2014), 'Elections', in Marc Lynch (ed.) *The Arab Uprisings Explained*, New York: Columbia University Press, pp. 218–45.

Mair, Peter (1989), 'The problem of party system change', *Journal of Theoretical Politics*, 1 (3): 251–76.

Mair, Peter (1997), *Party System Change*, Oxford: Oxford University Press.

Martínez-Fuentes, Guadalupe (2010), 'Divisive electoral policies within authoritarian elections: the Tunisian casuistry (1989–2009)', *The Journal of North African Studies*, 15 (4): 521–34.

Matthiesen, Toby (2013), *Sectarian Gulf*, Stanford: Stanford University Press.

Meijer, Roel and Maarten Danckaert (2015), 'Bahrain: the dynamics of a conflict', in I. William Zartman (ed.), *Arab Spring: Negotiating in the Shadow of the Intifadat*, Athens, GA: University of Georgia Press, pp. 209–48.

Mikail, Barah (2014), *Avoiding Iraq's Fragmentation*, Policy Brief 178, Madrid: FRIDE.

Moustafa, Tamir (2012), *Drafting Egypt's Constitution: Can a New Legal Framework Revive a Flawed Tradition*, Paper Series 1, Doha: Brookings Institution.

Nabavi, Negin (ed.) (2012), *Iran: from Theocracy to the Green Movement*, Basingstoke: Palgrave Macmillan.

Najem, Tom (2012), *Lebanon. The Politics of a Penetrated Society*, London: Routledge.

Norris, Pippa (2005), *Political Parties and Democracy in Theoretical and Practical Perspective*, Washington, DC: National Democratic Institute for International Affairs.

Ozkirimli, Umut (2014), *The Making of a Protest Movement in Turkey*, Basingstoke: Palgrave Macmillan.

Pack, Jason and Haley Cook (2015), 'The July 2012 Libyan election and the origin of post-Qadhafi appeasement', *Middle East Journal*, 69 (2): 171–98.

Pargeter, Alison (2016), 'Libya: from "reform" to revolution', in Yahya Zoubir and Gregory White (eds), *North African Politics: Change and Continuity*, London: Routledge, pp. 178–95.

Pedersen, Mogens (1979), 'The dynamics of European party systems: changing patterns of electoral volatility', *European Journal of Political Research*, 7 (1): 1–26.

Perkins, Kenneth (2005), *A History of Modern Tunisia*, Cambridge: Cambridge University Press.

Phillips, Sarah (2008), *Yemen's Democracy Experiment in Regional Perspective*, Basingstoke: Palgrave Macmillan.

Roberts, Hugh (2015), 'Algeria: the negotiations that aren't', in I. William Zartman (ed.), *Arab Spring: Negotiating in the Shadow of the Intifadat*, Athens, GA: University of Georgia Press, pp. 145–81.

Rougier, Bernard and Stephane Lacroix (eds) (2016), *Egypt's Revolutions*, New York: Palgrave Macmillan.

Roy, Olivier (2012), 'The myth of the Islamist Winter', *The New Statesman*, 13 December.

Roy, Sara (2011), *Hamas and Civil Society in Gaza*, Princeton: Princeton University Press.

Sadiki, Larbi (2015), *Routledge Handbook of the Arab Spring: Rethinking Democratization*, London: Routledge.

Sartori, Giovanni (1976), *Parties and Party Systems*, Cambridge: Cambridge University Press.

Sandler, Shmuel, Manfred Gerstenfeld and Hillel Frisch (eds) (2011), *Israel at the Polls 2009*, London: Routledge.

Schattschneider, Elmer (1942), *Party Government*, New York: Holt, Rinehart and Winston.

Schedler, Andreas (2006), *Electoral Authoritarianism*, Boulder, CO: Lynne Rienner.

Schedler, Andreas (2013), *The Politics of Uncertainty*, Oxford: Oxford University Press.

Shikaki, Khalil (2006), 'The Palestinian elections: sweeping victory, uncertain mandate', *Journal of Democracy*, 17 (3): 116–30.

Spencer, Claire, Jane Kinnimont and Omar Sirri (eds) (2013), *Iraq Ten Years On*, London: Chatham House.

Steinberg, Guido (2014), *Leading the Counter-revolution: Saudi Arabia and the Arab Spring*, Berlin: Stiftung Wissenschaft und Politik.

St John, Ronald Bruce (2015), *Libya: Continuity and Change*, London: Routledge.

Storm, Lise (2007), *Democratization in Morocco*, London: Routledge.

Storm, Lise (2013), *Party Politics and the Prospects for Democracy in North Africa*, Boulder, CO: Lynne Rienner.

Szmolka, Inmaculada (2015), 'Inter and intra-party relations in the formation of the Benkirane coalition governments in Morocco', *Journal of North African Studies*, 20 (4): 654–74.

Tabib, Rafaa (2014), *Stealing the Revolution: Violence and Predation in Libya*, Oslo: NOREF.

Taspinar, Omer (2014), 'The end of the Turkish model', *Survival*, 56 (2): 49–64.

Ulrichsen, Kristian (2014), *Qatar and the Arab Spring*, Oxford: Oxford University Press.

Volpi, Frederic (2013), 'Algeria versus the Arab Spring', *Journal of Democracy*, 24 (3): 104–15.

Wehler-Schöck, Anja (2014), 'Frustration, fragmentation, uncertainty: Iraq on the eve of the 2014 parliamentary elections', *International Policy Analysis*, Berlin: Friedrich Ebert Stiftung.

Willis, Michael (2014), *Politics and Power in the Maghreb: Algeria, Tunisia and Morocco from Independence to the Arab Spring*, Oxford: Oxford University Press.

Youngs, Richard (2014), *Europe in the New Middle East*, Oxford: Oxford University Press.

Zartman, I. William (ed.) (2015), *Arab Spring: Negotiating in the Shadow of the Intifadat*, Athens, GA: University of Georgia Press.

Zoubir, Yahya and Gregory White (2015), *North African Politics: Change and Continuity*, London: Routledge.

Chapter 4

Elections and electoral integrity

Guadalupe Martínez-Fuentes

1 Introduction

This chapter provides a comparative study of the level of electoral integrity in elections held in the Middle East and North Africa (MENA) countries between 2011 and 2015. It seeks to meet two objectives. The first is to identify and contextualise patterns of stagnation or of negative, fluctuating or positive evolution in the period under observation. The second is to construct a panoramic ranking based on the level of electoral integrity registered in the most recent elections in those countries. With this double analysis as the point of departure, this chapter aims to clarify the current relationship between political change and electoral integrity in the MENA region.

The chapter is structured in four sections. Firstly, several key points about the conceptual, analytical and interpretative treatment of electoral integrity are reviewed. Secondly, a methodological section explains the case selection strategy and the analytical resources employed to measure, categorise and contextualise electoral integrity in the region. Thirdly, the results of the two analyses are presented in two subsections. The first throws light on the behaviour of the variable 'electoral integrity' in the last five years. The other systematises the state of the question by closely analysing the most recent elections in the region. Finally, the conclusions are highlighted.

2 Electoral integrity: conceptualisation, measurement and interpretation

Studies on stability and change in the MENA political regimes have particularly focused on the elections (Parejo 2010). This research trend has been demonstrated by the intense normative and numerous empirical works orientated towards establishing, refuting or relativising the political impact of the elections in distinct geographical areas (Edgell et al. 2015). In fact the development of studies related to stability and change in political regimes has also resulted in a boost in electoral studies dealing with 'electoral management', 'electoral governance' and 'election quality'.

Accumulated experience in both research fields has provided a new consensus about the need to refine the analysis of the electoral phenomenon in order to recalibrate its value in the framework of the behaviour of political regimes. The first point concerns the conceptual stretching of terms such as 'genuine elections', 'democratic elections' or 'free and fair elections', the significance of which has traditionally depended on the geographical and chronological coordinates in which they apply (Elklit and Svensson 1997; Davis-Roberts and Carroll 2010; Montabes and Martínez-Fuentes 2014; van Ham and Lindberg 2015). The second is a question of focus, with some arguing that the tendency to view electoral quality in terms of results and not of process is an 'erratic approach' (Elklit and Svensson 1997). The third relates to the data available, and emphasises concerns about using general indices of democracy and governance as a way to arrive at a detailed approximation of the quality of elections (Pottie 2015). The final consensus refers to the categories employed in the evaluation of the results, and argues that variations between cases and through time must not simply rely on dichotomous terms but should instead employ a continuum with a multidimensional focus (Elklit and Reynolds 2005).

As a result, recent electoral integrity studies have backed new lines of research that seek to overcome past methodological gaps. This has also opened up a new and promising debate about conceptual, analytical and interpretative terms.

The term 'electoral integrity' has some conceptual elasticity. It refers to international standards and global norms governing the appropriate conduct of elections during the pre-election period, campaign, polling day and its aftermath (Norris et al. 2013; Norris 2015), arguing that the appropriate conduct of an election is professional, impartial and transparent throughout the electoral cycle (Kofi Annan Foundation 2012). Therefore, in its negative dimension of significance, it emphasises the absence of undesirable properties in the electoral process such as electoral manipulation, electoral fraud and other types of premeditated electoral irregularities (van Ham and Lindberg 2015).

Another strength of the electoral integrity concept is its unifying double dimension, in the style of a cross-cutting concept (Nohlen 2016). Firstly, it incorporates all periods and dimensions in the electoral cycle, from the design of the legislation, the institutions and the selection of the electoral authorities, to the process of voting, recounts, diffusion of the results and audit. Secondly, it seeks correspondence between values and norms on the one hand and behaviour and results on the other.

However, this new concept also suffers from weaknesses: for example, its conceptual structure is perhaps too close to that of 'electoral legitimacy' and 'electoral credibility' (Nohlen 2016). Similarly, the 'negative dimension' of electoral integrity does not always permit a clear distinction between compliance with the law and transgression (Schedler 2002), differentiation between electoral irregularities due to human error or lack of technical capacity and planned irregularities with manipulative or fraudulent intent (Nohlen 2016), or an understanding of the extent to which some irregularities affect the electoral process in an extensive, systematic and decisive way (Elklit and Svensson 1997).

In any case, the balance between the strengths and weaknesses of the electoral integrity concept on the whole seems to be positive, as demonstrated by the wholehearted support given to it by various comparative study schools and internationally recognised institutions that specialise in electoral and opinion studies. Among the former it is worth highlighting those involved in the Electoral Integrity Project (PEI) (the University of Sydney and Harvard's Kennedy School of Government) and Varieties of Democracy project (V-Dem) (the University of Gothenburg and University of Notre Dame). Among the latter, the ACE Electoral Knowledge Network, the International Foundation for Electoral Systems (IFES), the Global Commission on Elections, Democracy and Security at the Kofi Annan Foundation, and the World Value Survey (WVS) (series 6 and 7, 2010–14 and 2016–18, respectively).

In all cases, the main concern of these institutions is in the measurement of electoral integrity as an objective phenomenon, without risk of exposure to the subjective perception of those who participate in the elections or those who observe them. In fact, it should be noted that, to date, those striving to perfect the operationalisation of the normative dimension of electoral integrity have been more effective than those seeking to standardise the measurement tools or extensively apply them in practice. ACE, IFES, the Kofi Annan Foundation, PEI and V-Dem each have their own guidelines to evaluate the phenomenon of electoral integrity, but only the latter two have managed to generate useful electoral integrity databases on a global scale.

The analytical treatment of the measurements is another dimension that is open for discussion. While it is true to say that some assume that electoral integrity operates as an explanatory variable of associated phenomenon, others see more complexity in the causality relationship by arguing that it is affected by other relevant factors. One example of the former is the belief that the legitimacy of an election and public confidence in the resulting structures of democratic governance largely depend on the actual and perceived integrity of the electoral process (IFES 2016). The latter vision, on the other hand, is represented by those who warn that the perception of the public and the relevant political actors towards electoral integrity is highly influenced by sociocultural factors, such as systemic political distrust, which allows the electoral loser and the media to reject the result of the process (Nohlen 2016).

Both positions coincide in underscoring a key question: electoral integrity must be interpreted contextually, by focusing on the characteristics and dynamics of the political regime. Firstly, from the analytical point of view, if observers view an election not as an isolated event but as part of the democratisation process, they cannot avoid considering whether the electoral competition is demonstrating qualitative improvements over previous elections and how it is contributing to that process (Elklit and Svensson 1997). Turning to the political actors involved in the electoral process, it must be borne in mind that choices over specific types of manipulation are driven by available resources and cost considerations shaped by the level of democratisation and the political context in which elections take place (van Ham and Lindberg 2015). Finally, regarding the relationship between electoral integrity and institutional engineering, it is worth emphasising that the impact of institutional reforms that aim to improve election quality is better in democratic political systems or in emerging democracies with a high or average quality of government than in authoritarian political systems with a low quality of government (van Ham and Lindberg 2015).

3 Assessing electoral integrity in the MENA countries (2011–15)

This section takes on board the conceptual and methodological considerations highlighted in the previous section in its analysis of the registered level of electoral integrity in the MENA countries between 2011 and 2015.

The selected cases fulfil two conditions. The first is that the countries have held parliamentary elections (PAE) or presidential elections (PRE) between January 2011 and December 2015. The second is the availability of electoral integrity data for these elections. Consequently, our universe of study includes: Algeria, Bahrain, Egypt, Iran, Iraq, Israel, Jordan, Kuwait, Libya, Morocco, Oman, Syria, Tunisia, Turkey and Yemen.

Table 4.1 illustrates all the observed cases, the year that each election was held and its institutional nature.

Table 4.1 Case selection strategy: elections in the MENA countries, 2011–15

	2011	2012	2013	2014	2015
Algeria		PAEᵃ		PAE	
Bahrain	PAE			PAE	
Egypt	PAE	PAE/PREb		PRE	PAE
Iran		PAE	PRE		
Iraq				PAE	
Israel			PAE		PAF
Jordan			PAE		
Kuwait		PAE	PAE		
Libya		PAE		PAE	
Morocco	PAE				
Oman	PAE				PAE
Syria		PAE		PRE	
Tunisia	PAE			PAE/PRE	
Turkey	PAE			PRE	PAE
Yemen		PRE			

Notes: ᵃ PAE = parliamentary elections ᵇ PRE = presidential elections
Source: prepared by the author from the IFES Election Guide database. Available at <http://www.electionguide.org/elections/past/> (last accessed 5 February 2016)

The databases employed to compare these cases are of a distinct type. On the one hand, we draw on two databases that offer detailed information about electoral integrity: PEI and V-Dem. In order to contextualise these values, three databases dedicated to measuring democracy and governance are employed. These are: Freedom in the World (Freedom House), the Democracy Index (The Economist Intelligence Unit) and the Democracy Ranking of the Quality of Democracy (The Democracy Ranking Association).

From the PEI the total resulting evaluation from the aggregation of its eleven subindices is adopted: electoral law, electoral procedure, boundaries, voter registration, party registration, campaign media, campaign finance, voting process, vote count, post-election and electoral authorities. This index is expressed on a scale from zero to 100 as a minimum and maximum score of electoral integrity respectively (Norris et al. 2015; Norris et al. 2016). As a database the latest version published in 2016 is employed: *The Perceptions of Electoral Integrity (PEI-4.0) Expert Survey, release 4.0.*

Regarding V-Dem, the focus has been reduced to their Clean Elections Index, expressed on a decimal scale between zero and one as the worst and best scores respectively of electoral integrity. The Clean Elections Index includes six indicators that measure the extent of registration irregularities, vote buying, ballot fraud and intentional irregularities, government-induced intimidation of opposition candidates, other types of election violence (not instigated by the government or ruling party), as well as an overall assessment as to whether the election, all things considered, should be considered 'free and fair'. Finally, two indicators are measured on an annual basis: the autonomy and capacity of the election administration body to conduct well-run elections (Coppedge at al. 2015; Teorell et al. 2016). As a database the latest version published in 2016 is employed: *Electoral Democracy Index, V-Dem [Country–Year/Country–Date] Datatset v.6.*

The indicators that most closely adhere to the electoral phenomenon and its context have been extracted from the measurement indices on democracy and governance. In the framework of Freedom in the World the focus is on the Political Rights Index, which comprises three dimensions. One corresponds directly to the electoral phenomenon (electoral process); another only partially adjusts itself to it (political participation and pluralism); and the third provides information relative to the behaviour of government resulting from the electoral process (functioning of government). The average of all of them together is expressed on a scale between one and seven, as the most positive and most negative values respectively. As a database *Freedom in the World 2012, 2013, 2014, 2015* and *2016*, referring to the years 2011, 2012, 2013, 2014 and 2015 has been employed.

In the case of the Democracy Index, the Electoral Process Index and Pluralism has been employed. This adheres closely to the electoral phenomenon, although it also incorporates aspects that transcend it: such as citizen access to the administration; their capacity to create associations; or the transfer of power mechanism once the elections are held. The total result is expressed on a scale of between one and ten, representing a less or more favourable environment for electoral governance (The Economist Intelligence Unit 2016). As a database the *Democracy Index 2011, 2012, 2013, 2014* and *2015*, referring to those same years has been employed.

Finally, when the Democracy Ranking of the Quality of Democracy is used the Political System dimension is focused on. Its Political Rights Index corresponds with that provided by Freedom House. As added information it includes indicators that relate to human rights, perceived corruption, freedom of the press, and gender equality – both present in the electoral process and resulting from it. The average of all these indices is expressed on a scale between zero and 100 as a minimum and maximum score (Campbell and Pölzlbauer 2010). As a database *Democracy Ranking 2015*, covering the periods 2010–11 and 2013–14, *Comprehensive Scoreboards and Scoreboards for the Dimensions* has been employed.

Table 4.2 illustrates the complementarity of these viewpoints, indices and registered indicators for these databases.

Table 4.2 Tools for assessing electoral integrity

Source	Freedom in the World	Contextualisation — Democracy Index	Contextualisation — Quality of Democracy	Measurement — Electoral Integrity Project	Measurement — Varieties of democracy
Index	Political Rights	Electoral process and pluralism	Political System	Perceptions of Electoral Integrity	Clean Elections Index
Focus	Electoral process Political pluralism and participation Functioning of government	Electoral process and pluralism	Political rights Civil liberties Gender equality Corruption Media freedom	Electoral integrity	Free and fair elections
Indicators	EMB[a] autonomy	Universal suffrage	Political rights (FH)	Electoral law	EMB autonomy
	Politically motivated delays in holding elections	Citizens freedom to form political/civil organisations	Civil liberties (FH)	Electoral procedures	EMB capacity
	Voter registration	Citizens freedom to form political parties	Gender Empowerment Measure/GEM (UNDP HDI)	Boundaries	Voter registration
	Party campaign freedom	Citizens access to public office	Seats in parliament held by women (UNDP HDI)	Voter registration	Government intimidation
	Voting procedure	Conditions for candidates	Press freedom (FH)	Party registration	Vote buying
	Government intimidation and other kind of intimidations	Opposition political prospect	Corruption Perceptions Index (CPI)	Campaign media	Other voting irregularities
	Vote weight	Opposition parties campaigning		Campaign finance	Other electoral violence
	Vote count	Campaign finance		Voting process	Election free and fair
	Violent coup after last elections	Voting process		Vote count	
	Legislative framework	Electorate security		Post-election react on	
	Gerrymandering	Transfer of power		Behaviour of EMB	
	Manipulation of electoral system				
	Citizens freedom to form political parties				
	Institutionalised opposition political parties				
	Opposition political prospect				
	Citizens' freedom from domination by the military, foreign powers, totalitarian parties, religious hierarchies, economic oligarchies, or any other powerful group				
	Electoral opportunities for cultural, ethnic, religious, or other minority groups				
Scale	1 max–7 min	0 min–10 max	1 min–100 max	1 min–100 max	0 min–1 max

Note: [a] EMB = Electoral Management Body

Source: prepared by the author based on Campbell and Pölzlbauer (2010), Coppedge et al. (2016a), Teorell et al. 2016, Freedom House (2016), Norris et al. (2015), Norris et al. (2016) and The Economist Intelligence Unit (2016), available at <https://www.eiu.com/home.aspx> (last accessed 21 February 2017)

Employing this broad collection of tools has as an added advantage the greatest possible coverage in temporal and spatial terms. While the Freedom in the World and the Democracy Index provide disaggregated data by year covering the complete period 2011–15, the Democracy Ranking of the Quality of Democracy undertakes its measurements in biannual periods (2010–11, 2013–14). While V-Dem offers data for the whole period, PEI only evaluates it from mid-2012. As an added difficulty, not all the indices offer information about the totality of the cases. Freedom in the World and the Democracy Index supply data for all cases, while the coverage of the other three sources is more limited. Algeria, Iran, Iraq, Jordan, Libya, Oman and Syria are not included in the Democracy Ranking of the Quality of Democracy, PEI leaves out the cases of Libya, Morocco and Yemen, and V-Dem does not include Bahrain, Kuwait and Oman.

4 Electoral integrity in the MENA countries (2011–15)

This section is divided into two parts. Section 4.1 illustrates the evolution of the electoral integrity level in each case by distinguishing the categories of regression, stagnation, progression, or fluctuation, regarding the behaviour of electoral integrity in the last five years. The sub-epigraph 4.2 highlights the electoral integrity level most recently achieved in each country in order to prepare the ranking of electoral quality in the region at the end of the observed cycle.

4.1 Electoral integrity variance and context

Table 4.3 illustrates in a systemised way the electoral integrity values registered in each case over the last five years via the indices provided by PEI and V-Dem. Data extracted from the Freedom in the World, Democracy Index and Quality of Democracy contextualise the evolution of these values. Finally, the evolution of electoral integrity under the terms progression, regression, fluctuation and stagnation are categorised. Movements of ascent or descent in decimals from the data provided by V-Dem and PEI are considered to be 'progression' or 'regression' respectively. Ascents and descents with less than such margins are valued as 'stagnation' on both indices. 'Fluctuation' is defined as the existence of contrary dynamics throughout the period under study.

Taking advantage of the existing overlap between the measurements of PEI and V-Dem (Norris et al. 2016), the behaviour of the variable electoral integrity on the continuum constructed from both sources is observed, in the cases where it is required. In the cases between 2011 and 2015 where there was

Table 4.3 Electoral integrity in the MENA countries, 2011–15: context and variance

Dimension	Source	Year 2011	2012	2013	2014	2015	EI Variance
	Algeria						
	Freedom in the World	6	6	6	6	6	
Context	Democracy Index	2.17	3	3	3	3	
	Quality of Democracy						Stagnation
EI	V-Dem	.33	.35	.36	.33	.31	
	PEI				43		
	Bahrain						
	Freedom in the World	6	6	6	6	7	
Context	Democracy Index	1.75	1.25	1.25	1.33	1.25	
	Quality of Democracy	30		24.2			a
EI	V-Dem						
	PEI				38		
	Egypt						
	Freedom in the World	6	6	5	6	6	
Context	Democracy Index	2.08	3.42	2.17	2.17	3.00	
	Quality of Democracy	27.9		31.0			Progression
EI	V-Dem	.20	.45	.49	.41	-	
	PEI				40	45	
	Iran						
	Freedom in the World	6	6	6	6	6	
Context	Democracy Index	0.00	0.00	0.00	0.00	0.00	
	Quality of Democracy						Progression
EI	V-Dem	.21	.30	.45	.53	.53	
	PEI			54			
	Iraq						
	Freedom in the World	5	5	6	5	6	
Context	Democracy Index	4.33	4.33	4.33	4.33	4.33	
	Quality of Democracy						Regression
EI	V-Dem	.54	.53	.50	.45	.39	
	PEI				44		
	Israel						
	Freedom in the World	1	1	1	1	1	
Context	Democracy Index	8.75	8.75	8.75	8.75	9.17	
	Quality of Democracy	74.2		74.2			Stagnation
EI	V-Dem	.90	.90	.90	.90	.90	
	PEI			74		72	
	Jordan						
	Freedom in the World	6	6	6	6	6	
Context	Democracy Index	3.17	3.17	3.17	3.17	3.58	
	Quality of Democracy						Stagnation
EI	V-Dem	.47	.43	.46	.49	.49	
	PEI			46			
	Kuwait						
	Freedom in the World	4	5	5	5	5	
Context	Democracy Index	3.17	3.17	3.17	3.17	3.17	
	Quality of Democracy	42.7			42.7		Stagnation
EI	V-Dem						
	PEI		51	59			

Table 4.3 Electoral integrity in the MENA countries, 2011–15: context and variance (*cont.*)

Dimension	Source	Year 2011	2012	2013	2014	2015	EI Variance
	Libya						
	Freedom in the World	7	4	4	6	6	
Context	Democracy Index	0.00	4.33	4.33	2.25	1	
	Quality of Democracy						Fluctuation
EI	V-Dem	.00	.55	.73	.60	-	
	PEI				-		
	Morocco						
	Freedom in the World	5	5	5	5	5	
Context	Democracy Index	3.50	3.50	3.50	3.50	4.75	
	Quality of Democracy	38		39.3			Progression b
EI	V-Dem	.60	.64	.65	.65	.66	
	PEI						
	Oman						
	Freedom in the World	6	6	6	6	6	
Context	Democracy Index	0.00	0.00	0.00	0.00	0.00	
	Quality of Democracy						a
EI	V-Dem						
	PEI					61	
	Syria						
	Freedom in the World	7	7	7	7	7	
Context	Democracy Index	0.00	0.00	0.00	0.00	0.00	
	Quality of Democracy						Stagnation
EI	V-Dem	.06	.06	.07	.05	.04	
	PEI				27		
	Tunisia						
	Freedom in the World	3	3	3	1	1	
Context	Democracy Index	5.33	5.75	6.17	7	7	
	Quality of Democracy	35.9			57.6		Progression b
EI	V-Dem	.59			.76		
	PEI				65/69		
	Turkey						
	Freedom in the World	3	3	3	3	3	
Context	Democracy Index	7.92	7.95	7.92	6.67	6.67	
	Quality of Democracy	53.2			50.7		Regression
EI	V-Dem	.81	.80	.77	.65	.58	
	PEI				51	45	
	Yemen						
	Freedom in the World	6	6	6	6	7	
Context	Democracy Index	2.17	3	1.33	1.33	0.5	
	Quality of Democracy	15.5			18		Progression
EI	V-Dem	.00	.32	.37	.32	.32	
	PEI						

Notes: [a] neither V-Dem nor PEI covered the elections held in Bahrain and Oman in 2011 and 2012, respectively. Hence, we cannot consider the electoral integrity variance in those countries.

[b] Electoral Integrity variance for the Moroccan Parliamentary Election 2011 is considered to be a progression in view of the data registered by V-Dem (0.51) for the previous parliamentary elections held in 2007. Similarly, electoral integrity variance for the Tunisian foundational elections 2011 is considered a progression in view of the data registered by V-Dem (0.07) for the previous parliamentary and presidential elections held in 2009.

Source: prepared by the author based on data from Freedom House (2012, 2013, 2014, 2015, 2016), The Economist Intelligence Unit (2011, 2012, 2013, 2014, 2015), Norris et al. (2016), Coppedge et al. (2016b) and the Democracy Ranking of the Quality of Democracy (2015)

only one election, the evolution of the behaviour of the variable is considered by observing the data recorded by V-Dem for the most recent elections prior to the period under study. When that prior record is unavailable the variation in electoral integrity is not categorised.

Table 4.3 reveals the heterogeneous behaviour of the variable electoral integrity. The examples of positive variation comprise: Egypt, Morocco, Iran, Yemen and Tunisia. Iraq and Turkey, for their part, have in common a negative variation in this period. Algeria, Jordan, Kuwait, Israel and Syria appear as cases of stagnation. Libya is next in this list of categories, as the only example of fluctuating electoral integrity. Bahrain and Oman are necessarily at the margin of the catalogue due to limits in the availability of data on electoral integrity for the electoral cycle 2011–15. In any case, it could be argued that the Omani case be added to the group exhibiting progression in electoral integrity, while in Bahrain everything points towards a logic of regression.

Taking on board the recommendation to interpret electoral integrity results in the light of the context of political systems, this chapter now reflects on each subgroup of countries to clarify the differences and similarities in the cases that comprise it.

4.1.1 Positive electoral integrity variance: Egypt, Morocco, Iran, Yemen and Tunisia

The existing relationship between the behaviour of the variable electoral integrity and the evolution of the political context in the countries comprising this group is heterogeneous. On the one hand, Morocco and Iran present signs of progress in terms of electoral quality as well as continuity in the political context. Egypt and Yemen, with a positive variation in terms of electoral integrity regarding the period prior to 2011, have experienced a deteriorating political context in recent times. The Tunisian case appears to be unique, with parallel advances both in terms of electoral quality and in the general process of transition to democracy.

Starting from a model of hegemonic and restrictive pluralist authoritarianism, Egypt experienced an improvement in the levels of election quality with the parliamentary elections held between 2011 and 2012 and the presidential elections in 2012. The strongly debated and finally enacted electoral reforms of the Supreme Council of the Armed Forces, the conjunction of the judiciary and the Supreme Electoral Commission as examples of supervision in the electoral processes, the authorisation – although limited – of international observers, and the legitimation and participation of previously banned or barely tolerated political forces opened up the parliamentary and presidential elections to a new framework of political competition (Szmolka 2014). Despite the multiple deficiencies detected in both polls, international observers considered them to be a progressive step towards democratic transition. However, the rapid deterioration in the political framework of coexistence between the winners and losers in the elections, due to Islamist institutional hegemony, led to an exclusionary model of transition in Egypt (Szmolka 2015). Although elections were not the cause of the country's political woes, voting threw the growing fissures in the Egyptian body politic into stark relief and sometimes aggravated them, undermining Egypt's prospects for future democratic development (Brown 2013). Consequently, the electoral cycle that began following the military coup and the ascent of General al-Sisi to the interim presidency of the country did not lead to new progress in terms of electoral integrity. The presidential elections of 2014 were boycotted by the revolutionary and Islamist sectors who considered participation to be support for a piece of theatre orchestrated by the 'powers' to simulate democratic elections, given the increase in the insecurity of the candidates and electors, the exclusion of the Muslim Brotherhood from the electoral battle and the bias of the campaign in favour of al-Sisi (Azaola 2014). Following the dissolution of the Lower House by the Egyptian Supreme Court, the parliamentary elections were postponed on numerous occasions by the interim presidency of al-Sisi. Such an imbalance in the electoral calendar was not only due to the tough technical political debates in successive proposals of the electoral law, but also the lack of interest of specific political actors in advancing the road map of the transition process (Abd Rabou 2015). Finally held in 2015, the parliamentary elections represented the last step on the road map announced by the army after ousting Morsi. The Egyptian government was relying on these elections to demonstrate to the international community its commitment to building democratic institutions (Morsy 2015). However, the result was not as positive as that desired by the authorities in terms of political legitimation. The elections merely repeated the offences of reducing political pluralism, promoting pro-regime hegemonic forces in the campaign and holding an election in an unfavourable security environment. Nevertheless, several national and international personalities have indulgently considered the results to be sufficient proof of a commitment to democratic transition (El Khawaga 2015).

In the Iranian case stability can be found in the political context and positive variation in the electoral quality between the 2009 presidential and 2012 parliamentary elections on the one hand, and the 2013 presidential elections on the other. Although there were no legal reforms between the first and the last, the Iranian political elite made it politically possible to legitimise the 2013 presidential electoral results among both the local population and the international community. With that they hoped to overcome the painful experience of the 2009 presidential elections, which was the first to be rejected by losing candidates, and was followed by massive waves of street protests against the illegitimacy of the electoral system (Zaccara and Saldaña 2015). Therefore, the 2013 presidential elections gave the impression that while the outcome would be engineered, the element of improvisation was real and hence the Iranian elections, despite their manifest limitations, should not be dismissed as mere Potemkin exercises (Maloney 2013; 2016).

Regarding the Moroccan case, again a lack of correspondence can be found between the stability of the regime and positive variation in the variable electoral integrity between the 2006 parliamentary elections and those held in 2011. The proclamation of the new 2011 constitution required legislative reform relative to the electoral process, aimed at increasing the size of the House, giving a quota of representation for young people and approving a Law of Electoral Observation (Kirhlani 2011). However, the redefinition of electoral districts was seen by Islamists as gerrymandering and intentionally oriented to reducing their possible parliamentary representation (López-García 2011). On the other hand, international observers noted classic electoral behavioural patterns in Morocco, such as the purchase of votes, the use of administrative resources for party ends, and intimidation and pressure on regime detractors (Fernández-Molina 2012). Nonetheless, the general interpretation was that the electoral process developed cleanly and with transparency in line with international standards.

Tunisia represents significant progress in electoral quality and is the only country in the MENA region that has also experienced parallel positive political changes in democratisation. Despite notable defects in organisation and transparency, the preparation and holding of the foundational Tunisian elections in 2011 symbolised a point of inflection in the electoral trajectory of the country, contributing to the key conditions that define a transition to democracy (Stepan 2012; Murphy 2013). The legalisation of political parties, the approval of new party and electoral laws, the creation of an Independent Court to audit the elections, the broad invitation to local and international election observers and the long peaceful period during the election provided a favourable framework to fully elevate its level of electoral integrity to the heights achieved in the previous elections at the start of the transition process (Montabes and Martínez-Fuentes 2014). The parliamentary and presidential elections of 2014 represented great advances in terms of democratic learning, deinstitutionalisation of the inherited authority and progress in matters of electoral integrity, thanks to a new reform of the electoral law, a more inclusive orientation and the organisational and functional improvement of the Independent Court to supervise the elections (Martínez-Fuentes 2015b). For this reason, from the point of view of international observers, the success of this second phase of the Tunisian electoral cycle represented a hopeful sign for the country's consolidation of democratic governance.

Finally, in Yemen the 2012 presidential elections took place within the terms of the agreed Transition Initiative (signed in Riyadh on 24 November 2011 by the United Nations, the United States, the European Union and the Gulf Cooperation Council). These elections represented a presidential endorsement for the only consensus candidate who stood, the previous vice-president Abd Rabbuh Mansour Hadi. The initial pact was that he assumed the presidency in a temporary way for only two years to coordinate a national dialogue and agree an electoral reform that would lead to the holding of competitive elections (Hamad 2012). However, the failure of the negotiations in the framework of the national dialogue and the conditions of instability and violence that have recently immersed the country in chaos have impeded the holding of new elections to date. In any case, and despite the uncontended nature of the 2012 elections, they represented a notable improvement on the level of electoral integrity in relation to the previous elections.

4.1.2 Negative electoral integrity variance: Iraq and Turkey

Iraq and Turkey share a negative tendency in terms of electoral integrity. However, the reasons for the behaviour of this variable differ given the varying nature of their political context.

Before the 2014 elections the political situation in Iraq acquired complex and chaotic characteristics due to deeper divisions between the Sunni, Shiites and Kurdish blocs, the growing degree of political polarisation and the self-proclaimed Islamic State (IS) advancing towards Mosul, Kirkuk, Salahaddin, al-Anbar and Baghdad (Duman 2014). In this context, the Independent High Electoral Commission, political parties and NGOs redoubled their efforts to improve election quality relative to 2010, although it is true to say that the international community already positively valued it (Ali 2014). However, the pre-election environment influenced the election process and the following developments in a negative way. This was due to a deterioration in the electoral component of this defective democracy throughout the period under observation, which arose from a growing conflict between political elites and the incapacity of authorities to guarantee the security of electors and candidates, rather than the presence of deliberately bad institutional practices. As a consequence, irregularities in the process were not sufficiently great to prevent the elections being globally interpreted in a positive way as a nation-building step.

Turkey, in contrast to Iraq, is one of the most stable countries in the region – despite its own internal difficulties with citizen protest, battles against terrorism, the Kurdish problem and their involvement in the Syrian conflict (Cagaptay and Jeffrey 2014). Also in contrast to the Iraqi case, the deterioration in Turkey's level of electoral integrity arises more because of planned electoral malpractice than a lack of competence or human resources. The 2011 parliamentary elections maintained levels of electoral integrity similar to Turkey's previous elections, despite them being held within a new normative framework. A broad package of amendments to the constitution aimed at further strengthening the guarantees of individual and human rights was adopted in a 2010 referendum. Significant changes were also introduced to election-related laws improving the overall framework for the conduct of elections. However, the new legal framework lacked clarity and uniformity, and further legal changes were considered necessary in the area of electoral as well as party law (OSCE/ODIHR 2011; FES 2011). The 2014 elections – the first presidential elections in the country – were also held under a new legal framework adopted in an expedited manner and without public consultation, and other relevant laws were not harmonised with it, resulting in a lack of clarity in the legal framework and inconsistent implementation. The electoral process registered significant defects, such as the misuse of administrative resources, the lack of a clear distinction between key institutional events and campaign activities and limited pluralistic information on political alternatives for voters, which granted the prime minister an undue advantage (OSCE/ODIHR 2014). Later, numerous alleged and documented cases of irregularity and fraud during the voting process in the 2014 local elections awoke serious national and international concerns as to whether Turkey would have a truly free and fair general election in June 2015 (Rethink Institute 2015). Finally, the quality of the June parliamentary elections, which were followed by unsuccessful attempts to form a coalition government resulting in a snap general election, and in November 2015, displayed the forecast deterioration in terms of electoral integrity. In both cases a number of Supreme Board of Elections' decisions were inconsistent with the legislation, including issues related to election administration and campaigning; media critical of the ruling party faced increasing pressure and intimidation by public figures and political actors during the election period; and media election coverage displayed a significant bias towards the ruling party. Moreover, the campaign was tainted by a large number of attacks on party offices and serious incidents, including physical attacks. Finally, various political parties and independent candidates challenged the results at different levels (OSCE/ODIHR 2015). The criticisms of international observers about the lack of transparency and integrity of the November election were especially blunt. The Parliamentary Assembly of the Council of Europe denounced the process as unfair, while the Organisation for Security and Co-operation in Europe (OSCE) said violence, especially in the country's south-east, had a significant impact on the election, and claimed that concerns over media bias and voter safety cast a 'shadow' over the results (BBC News 2015).

4.1.3 Fluctuant electoral integrity variance: Libya

In Libya the 2012 foundational elections provided Libyans with an historic opportunity to vote in meaningful national polls for the first time in almost six decades. Despite taking place in a highly insecure environment and presenting multiple deficiencies, they represented progress following a legacy of totalitarian political culture. International observers therefore interpreted the elections as a sign that the Libyans were recovering from the effects of a deadly civil war that only ended in October 2011. The 2014 parliamentary elections again suffered from evident failings, if it is true to say that they took place in a context of worsening violence that justifies the fluctuation in the level of electoral integrity. Nevertheless, international observers coincided in declaring that the 2014 parliamentary elections represented an important stage in the country's transition to democracy (Carter Center 2014). Local actors, however, were not so prone to positively interpret the election process and result. Islamist and pro-militia blocs did not accept the authority and legitimacy of the new parliament. More to the point, the Supreme Court annulled the election on unclear grounds and declared the internationally elected House of Representatives illegal and unconstitutional, complicating even more the Libyan political crisis. In sum, it is worth stating that the result of the elections – or their interpretation by certain political actors – negatively affected the transition process given that the elections failed to achieve the desired inclusiveness necessary for a truly representative body (Carter Center 2014).

4.1.4 Electoral integrity stagnation: Algeria, Jordan, Kuwait, Israel and Syria

The countries whose level of electoral integrity has experienced stagnation similarly present a common pattern of continuism regarding their respective political contexts.

In Algeria's case, there have been changes in technical–legal terms in the electoral process that do not appear to have affected the levels of electoral integrity achieved in the parliamentary elections of 2012 and the presidential elections of 2014. It is noticeable that the level of electoral quality reached in 2012 did not represent a progress in relation to previous elections, bearing in mind that these were the first elections held after the abolition of the state of emergency, the reform of the electoral law and the party law, the increase in the size of the Knesset and the electoral participation of new parties. The key to this data appears to reside in the fact that although the reforms initially gave hope of an open election, the final results darkened such illusions (Bustos 2012; Reseau Euro-Mediterranéen des Droits de l'Homme 2012). Neither did the 2014 presidential elections have a positive impact in terms of variation of levels of electoral integrity, given that they experienced party boycotts by the opposition due to suspect practices contrary to the principles of integrity, and allegations of irregularities committed throughout the process (Martínez-Fuentes 2015a).

Nor did Jordan's introduction of electoral reforms produce an improvement in terms of electoral integrity. The political opposition that backed the 2011 disturbances in Jordan shared the common demands of pushing forward an electoral reform that applied a proportional electoral formula, eliminating the effects of gerrymandering of the electoral law of 2010 and establishing an independent electoral institution that would supervise the elections (Szmolka 2014; Melián 2015). Therefore, the 2013 elections held after the revision of the party law and electoral law, was understood to be an opportunity to reduce manipulatory electoral practices given the intervention of a new independent electoral commission (Barari 2013). However, the electoral process was finally biased in favour of the regime authorities. Nevertheless, overall, international observers recognised both the important technical advances achieved in the 2013 elections as well as the key pending questions over improvement.

In Kuwait the political context is continuist not only in terms of conservation of the regime but also concerning the situation of institutional instability that has affected the country in this five-year period since the fall of the government at the end of 2011. A series of interventions by the Constitutional Court declaring the electoral process null and void led to the successive holding of parliamentary elections in February and December 2012 and in June 2013. These elections were held in a tense political environment in the face of a possible strengthening of tribal and Islamist sectors and of a significant level of violence during the electoral campaign (Okruhlik 2012; Zaccara and Saldaña 2015). The last two elections operated in line with a new electoral regulation that received similar criticisms (based on the belief that the system of constituency boundaries, proration and voting favoured candidates who were in tune with the government, and prejudiced that of their critics), which motivated both electoral boycotts by the opposition and led to similarly poor levels of electoral credibility (Boghardt 2013; Szmolka 2014).

Continuism in the electoral situation and in the way the elections developed can equally be seen in the Israeli case. The 2013 and 2015 parliamentary elections were held in the expected manner, in the context of a campaign marked by the discourse of fear and a call for strategic voting to prevent the return of the left to government, a potential strengthening of the Arab influence in the House and the possible restarting of a peace process that would end by accepting the creation of the Palestinian state (Pérez 2015). The only new element introduced in the preparations for the 2015 election was the reform of the electoral law to raise the electoral threshold from 2 to 3.25 per cent, with the aim of reducing the high level of parliamentarian fragmentation that the country traditionally produces, and which frequently makes it difficult to govern. If it is true to say that this aspect does not affect, in principle, the pattern of electoral integrity, it does nonetheless negatively condition electoral credibility, given that the Arab minority in parliament considered that this measure sought in a concealed way to favour political conditions of exclusion of the Arab sector in the House.

The struggle of the Syrian regime to resist pressure from peaceful protesters (and in fact to open war against them), jihadist terrorism, and even the efforts of international mediation, have prevented real progress in matters of electoral integrity. Syria, which began with a system of closed authoritarianism, faced 2011 with a reform of the parties law and the electoral law, which involved them legalising new parties and creating a highly decentralised judicial committee with delegations in each province to supervise the integrity of the elections. With the constitutional reform approved in the referendum of 2012, Syria also established a system of multiparty elections, the holding of presidential elections and a limitation of two seven-year presidential mandates. However, such normative innovations were purely cosmetic and were more thought of as a regime survival strategy rather than a real will to offer more pluralism and greater political responsibility (Alvarez-Ossorio 2015). Therefore, the 2012 electoral boycott and the negligible level of electoral integrity achieved in them can be interpreted as an incentive for the worsening of the violence that followed later. The 2014 presidential elections were the first that allowed the participation of more than one candidate. However, this novelty did not lead to improvements in the level of electoral quality, as they were held in the framework of an internationalised civil war and territorial occupation by terrorist forces.

4.1.5 Possible trends on electoral integrity: Oman and Bahrain

The result of the disturbances in Oman 2011 had as an immediate consequence the extension of the legislative responsibilities of the consultative assembly and the promise of a gradual implementation of elections, as the regime sought a balance between demands for political reform from young urban populations and the desire of key tribal elites and traders to maintain the status quo (Zaccara and Saldaña 2015). As a materialisation of this compromise Oman held parliamentary elections at the end of 2011 and 2015 that awoke great public interest and raised the level of competitiveness between candidates. However, international electoral observers were not authorised to participate, vote buying was tolerated by the electoral authority and there were limits on freedom of speech, assembly and association, including restrictions on citizens and civil society from associating with foreign governments (Valeri 2012; Katzman 2016). Nonetheless, taken together, the level of electoral integrity reached in these latter parliamentary elections was higher than that observed in the other Persian Gulf countries. Therefore, there is room to adventure the existence of a positive tendency in terms of electoral integrity.

Bahrain has differed from the above dynamic by being notably tougher on freedoms, rights and governance at the end of its last electoral cycle. The electoral practices observed throughout this period (partial legislative elections in 2011 and general legislative elections in 2014) have resulted in a vain attempt by the authorities to demonstrate 'democratic normality', which was in fact both empty in content and significance (Zaccara and Saldaña 2015). The behaviour of the opposition has also followed a line of continuity. Al-Wefaq, the principal Shiite opposition to the regime, withdrew its delegates from the Council of Representatives and boycotted the 2011 elections as an expression of protest, both when confronted with the political manipulation of the elections to the Council of Representatives held in 2010 and when faced with the regime's tough reprisals against the Shiite protesters who, in line with the disturbances in other countries in the region, went out on to the streets to claim equal rights with Sunni citizens. In 2013 the regime began a process of national dialogue with the opposition. However, al-Wefaq gave it up as failed and again boycotted the 2014 elections, accusing the regime of electoral fraud. For all these reasons, it could be argued that there has been a regressive tendency in terms of electoral quality.

4.2 Electoral integrity ranking

Returning to the above results, in this section the most recent score achieved by each country is considered in terms of electoral integrity and on the basis of the characteristics of their respective political contexts. Table 4.4 contrasts the countries on both scales, with the aim of facilitating the detection of correspondence or imbalance between them.

The left-hand column orders the countries in descending order of electoral integrity in virtue of the data registered in the latest elections held in each case. The following column specifies the decile in which each country is situated in terms of electoral integrity in line with the values that the PEI or V-Dem attribute it expressed on a scale of tens (PEI) or decimals (V-Dem), with the first being the highest and the sixth the lowest. The following columns allow us to contrast with the previous data the decile that each country occupies in virtue of the political context in line with the values provided by Freedom in the World, Democracy Index and Quality of Democracy, respectively expressed on a scale of units (Freedom in the World), tenths (Democracy Index) and dozens (Quality of Democracy).

Table 4.4 MENA countries ranking: correspondence between electoral integrity and political context

	Electoral Integrity Ranking	Political Context Ranking		
Country	V-Dem/PEI Decile	FW Decile	DI Decile	QD Decile
Israel	1	1	1	1
Tunisia	2	1	3	2
Morocco	2	3	2	3
Libya	2	4	5	a
Oman	2	4	6	a
Kuwait	3	3	3	3
Turkey	3	2	2	2
Iran	3	4	6	a
Jordan	4	4	4	a
Egypt	4	4	4	4
Iraq	5	3	3	a
Algeria	5	4	4	a
Yemen	6	5	6	a
Bahrain	6	5	5	5
Syria	6	5	6	a

Note: a no data available
Source: prepared by the author on the basis of Table 4.3

Table 4.4 reveals that the achievement of specific levels of electoral integrity does not necessarily correspond with the achievement of freedoms, rights and governance in the political context.

Table 4.4 allows two large groups of countries to be differentiated. On the one hand, there are those in which the level of electoral integrity corresponds with the general level of freedoms, rights and governance that contextualises the holding of elections. This is the case of Israel, Tunisia, Kuwait, Jordan, Egypt, Algeria, Bahrain and Syria. Greater levels of electoral integrity appear associated to contexts more propitiatory to quality electoral processes, as in the case of Israel, while the political contexts most hostile to the exercising of rights, freedoms and good governance are associated with lower levels of electoral integrity, as exemplified by Kuwait, Jordan, Egypt, Algeria, Bahrain and Syria.

On the other hand, countries whose level of electoral integrity does not seem to correspond with the nature of the general electoral context are also included. Among these, two casuistries can be differentiated. The first relates to the achievement of a level of electoral integrity above that expected, given the characteristics of the political regime. Morocco, Tunisia, Oman, Libya, Iran and Yemen appear in this subgroup. The second casuistry is the presentation of a lower than might be expected level of electoral integrity in relation to the defining characteristics of the regime. Iraq and Turkey are in this group.

The first dynamic has distinct reasons in each case. In Tunisia, Morocco, Oman and Iran the imbalance could be due to the support for electoral integrity fostered by the authorities to favour legitimation of the transitionary regime. On the other hand, in Libya and Yemen the imbalance seems to respond to the deterioration in the political life of the country that has entered a dynamic of escalating violence.

Separately, the second dynamic can equally be explained on the basis of a distinct logic. As has already been suggested in the previous section, the Iraqi imbalance is related to the extreme deterioration in the political system as well as worsening tensions between political elites, growing insecurity and territorial conquest by IS. On the contrary, in the Turkish case the lack of correlation could be due to a deliberate reduction in the quality of the electoral process itself in order to favour maintaining the regime in government.

5 Conclusions

Given the interest that studies about political change have in the electoral dimension this chapter has sought to facilitate comprehension of the role that elections have played in the MENA countries from 2011 to 2015. For that reason, it has focused on the variable electoral integrity, observing in a comparative and contextualised way both its evolution and the latest values it has manifested in the period. From this analysis three main conclusions can be deduced.

The first is the dynamic heterogeneity of the MENA countries in terms of advance, regression, stability or fluctuation in electoral integrity. Therefore, it cannot be said in general terms that the so-called Arab Spring has positively affected the political trajectory of the region.

The second point to underscore is that the variable electoral integrity in the MENA countries has not had any relationship at all with other variables as the kind of regime from which the political transition sets off, the transition timing and the way the transition is conducted. Therefore, this result suggests that a 'better' and predetermined political model of transformation of the quality of the electoral component in political systems does not exist.

The final significant finding is that the achievement of specific levels of electoral integrity does not always correlate with the degree of transformation achieved to date in other fields of security, rights, freedoms and good governance. Consequently, in light of this data, it is worth debating whether the expectations of democratisation that have awoken in specific countries of the region on the basis of practical progress in electoral integrity are realistic or excessively optimistic.

References

Abd Rabou, Ahmed (2015), *The Absence of the Legislative Body and the Future of Politics in Egypt*, Arab Reform Initiative. Available at <http://www.arab-reform.net/sites/default/files/20150518_AbuRabou_formatted%20final_0.pdf> (last accessed 18 February 2016).

Ali, Ahmed (2014), 'Iraq's 2014 national elections', *Middle East Security Report*, 70. Institute for the Study of War. Available at <http://www.understandingwar.org/report/iraq%E2%80%99s-2014-national-elections> (last accessed 9 March 2016).

Alvarez-Ossorio, Ignacio (2015), 'El enroque autoritario del régimen sirio: de la revuelta popular a la guerra civil', *Revista CIDOB d'Afers Internacionals*, 109: 157–76.

Azaola, Barbara (2014), *Egipto: Elecciones presidenciales, 26 y 27 de mayo de 2014*, OPEMAM. Available at <http://www.opemam.org/sites/default/files/An%C3%A1lisis%20pre-electoral%20Egipto%202014.pdf> (last accessed 18 February 2016).

Barari, Hassan (2013), *The Limits of Political Reform in Jordan. The Role of External Actors*. Berlin: Friedrich Ebert Stifung. Available at <http://library.fes.de/pdf-files/iez/10455-20140108.pdf> (last accessed 18 February 2016).

BBC News (2015) 'Turkey election: Erdoğan calls on world to respect result', (2 November). Available at <http://www.bbc.com/news/world-europe-34696489> (last accessed 12 April 2016).

Boghardt, Lori Plotkin (2013), *Kuwait's Elections: It's Not What Happens Now, but What Happens Next*, Policy analysis, Washington, DC: The Washington Institute. Available at <http://www.washingtoninstitute.org/policy-analysis/view/kuwaits-elections-its-not-what-happens-now-but-what-happens-next> (last accessed 25 February 2016).

Brown, Nathan J. (2013), 'Egypt's failed transition', *Journal of Democracy*, 24: 45–58.

Bustos, Rafael (2012), *Ficha Electoral Argelia Elecciones legislativas 10 de mayo de 2012*, OPEMAM. Available at <http://www.opemam.org/sites/default/files/FE-Argelia_Legislativas_2012.pdf> (last accessed 18 February 2016).

Campbell, David F. J. (2008), *The Basic Concept for the Democracy Ranking of the Quality of Democracy*, Vienna: Democracy Ranking. Available at <http://www.democracyranking.org/downloads/basic_concept_democracy_ranking_2008_A4.pdf> (last accessed 2 February 2016).

Campbell, David F. J. and Georg Pölzlbauer (2010), *The Democracy Ranking 2009 of the Quality of Democracy: Method and Ranking Outcome. Comprehensive Scores and Scores for the Dimensions.* Vienna: Democracy Ranking. Available at <http://www.democracyranking.org> (last accessed 7 February 2016).

Cagaptay, Soner and James F. Jeffrey (2014), *Turkey's 2014 Political Transition: From Erdoğan to Erdoğan*, Washington, DC: The Washington Institute for Near East Policy. Available at <http://www.washingtoninstitute.org/policy-analysis/view/turkeys-2014-political-transition> (last accessed 9 March 2016).

Carter Center (2014), *The 2014 Constitutional Drafting Assembly Elections in Libya. Final Report.* Available at <https://www.cartercenter.org/resources/pdfs/news/peace_publications/election_reports/libya-06112014-final-rpt.pdf> (last accessed 6 June 2016).

Coppedge, Michael, John Gerring, Staffan I. Lindberg, Svend-Erik Skaaning and Jan Teorell (2015), *V-Dem Comparisons and Contrasts with Other Measurement Projects*, Varieties of Democracy (V-Dem) Project. Available at <https://v-dem.net/media/filer_public/e7/a6/e7a638e3-358c-4b96-9197-e1496775d280/comparisons_and_contrasts_v5.pdf> (last accessed 2 February 2016).

Coppedge, Michael, John Gerring, Staffan I. Lindberg, Svend-Erik Skaaning, Jan Teorell, David Altman, Michael Bernhard, M. Steven Fish, Adam Glynn, Allen Hicken, Carl Henrik Knutsen, Kyle Marquardt, Kelly McMann, Farhad Miri, Pamela Paxton, Daniel Pemstein, Jeffrey Staton, Eitan Tzelgov, Yi-ting Wang and Brigitte Zimmerman (2016a), *V-Dem [Country-Year/Country-Date] Dataset v6*, Varieties of Democracy (V-Dem) Project. Available at <https://v-dem.net/en/data/data-version-6/> (last accessed 4 April 2016).

Coppedge, Michael, John Gerring, Staffan I. Lindberg, Svend-Erik Skaaning, Jan Teorell, Frida Andersson, Kyle Marquardt, Valeriya Mechkova, Farhad Miri, Daniel Pemstein, Josefine Pernes, Natalia Stepanova, Eitan Tzelgov and Yi-ting Wang (2016b), *V-Dem Methodology v6*, Varieties of Democracy (V-Dem) Project. Available at <https://v-dem.net/en/data/data-version-6/> (last accessed 4 April 2016).

Davis-Roberts, Avery and David J. Carroll (2010), 'Using international law to assess elections', Democratization, 17 (3): 416–41.

Democracy Ranking of the Quality of Democracy (2015), *Comprehensive Scoreboards and Scoreboards for the Dimensions*, Global Democracy Ranking. Available at <http://democracyranking.org/wordpress/2015-full-dataset-2/> (last accessed 27 February 2016).

Duman, Bilgay (2014), *The 2014 Elections, ISIS Operation and the Future of Iraq*, ORSAM Report 190. Available at <http://www.orsam.org.tr/en/enUploads/Article/Files/2014715_190raping.pdf> (last accessed 8 March 2016).

Edgell, Amanda, Valeriya Mechkova, David Altman, Michael Bernhard and Staffan I. Lindberg (2015), *When and Where do Elections Matter? A Global Test of the Democratization by Elections Hypothesis, 1900–2012*, V-Dem Working Papers 2015/8. Available at <https://v-dem.net/en/news-publications/working-papers> (last accessed 18 February 2016).

El Khawaga, Dina (2015), *The 2015 Elections: the End of Competitive Authoritarianism in Egypt?*, Arab Reform Initiative. Available at <http://www.arab-reform.net/2015-elections-end-competitive-authoritarianism-egypt> (last accessed 10 February 2016).

Elklit, Jørgen and Palle Svensson (1997), 'What makes elections free and fair?, *Journal of Democracy*', 8 (3): 32–46.

Elklit, Jørgen and Andrew Reynolds (2005), 'A framework for the systematic study of election quality', Democratization, 12 (2): 147–62.

Fernández-Molina, Irene (2012), *Ficha electoral Marruecos /Elecciones legislativas 25 de noviembre de 2011*, OPEMAM. Available at <http://www.opemam.org/sites/default/files/FE-Marruecos_Legislativas_2011.pdf> (last accessed 29 February 2016).

FES, Friedrich Ebert Stiftung (2011), *The Turkish Elections: Results and Next Steps*, FES Briefing. Available at <http://library.fes.de/pdf-files/bueros/usa/08291.pdf> (last accessed 28 March 2016).

Freedom House (2012), *Freedom in the World 2011*. Available at <https://freedomhouse.org/report/freedom-world/freedom-world-2011> (last accessed 1 February 2016).

Freedom House (2013), *Freedom in the World 2012*. Available at <https://freedomhouse.org/report/freedom-world/freedom-world-2012> (last accessed 1 February 2016).

Freedom House (2014), *Freedom in the World 2013*. Available at <https://freedomhouse.org/report/freedom-world/freedom-world-2013> (last accessed 1 February 2016).

Freedom House (2015), *Freedom in the World 2014*. Available at <https://freedomhouse.org/report/freedom-world/freedom-world-2014> (last accessed 1 February 2016).

Freedom House (2016), *Freedom in the World 2015*. Available at <https://freedomhouse.org/report/freedom-world/freedom-world-2015#.WJx3ShwnXE8> (last accessed 1 February 2016).

van Ham, Carolien and Staffan I. Lindberg (2015), 'From sticks to carrots: electoral manipulation in Africa, 1986–2012', *Government and Opposition*, 50: 521–48.

Hamad, Leyla (2012), *Ficha electoral: Yemen/Elecciones presidenciales anticipadas 21 de febrero de 2012*, OPEMAM. Available at <http://www.opemam.org/sites/default/files/FE_Yemen_Presidenciales_2012.pdf> (last accessed 21 February 2016).

International Foundation for Electoral Systems (IFES) (2016), *Electoral Integrity*. Available at <http://www.ifes.org/issues/electoral-integrity> (last accessed 6 June 2016).

Katzman, Kenneth (2016), *Oman: Reform, Security, and Elections*, US Policy Congressional Research Service. Available at <https://www.fas.org/sgp/crs/mideast/RS21534.pdf> (last accessed 10 March 2016).

Kirhlani, Said (2011), *Marruecos/Reflexiones sobre las nuevas reglas del juego electoral*, OPEMAM. Available at <http://www.opemam.org/sites/default/files/AE-Marruecos_2011_Reflexiones_sobre_las_nuevas_regla_del_juego_electoral.pdf> (last accessed 29 February 2016).

Kofi Annan Foundation (2012), Deepening Democracy: a Strategy for Improving the Integrity of Elections Worldwide. Available at <https://issuu.com/kofiannan/docs/deepening_democracy_0> (last accessed 6 June 2016)

López-García, Bernabé (2011), *Análisis pre-electoral: Marruecos/ ¿Circunscripciones a medida?*, OPEMAM. Available at <http://www.opemam.org/sites/default/files/APMarruecos_2011_Circunscripciones_a_medida.pdf> (last accessed 29 February 2016).

Maloney, Suzanne (2013), *Why Iran's Presidential Election Matters*, Brookings Topics – Middle East and North Africa. Available at <http://www.brookings.edu/blogs/markaz/posts/2013/05/20-election-matters> (last accessed 10 March 2016).

Maloney, Suzanne (2016), *Iran at the Polls: Why Today's Vote Is (and Isn't) Important*, Brookings Topics – Middle East and North Africa. Available at <http://www.brookings.edu/blogs/markaz/posts/2016/02/26-iran-election-analysis-maloney?rssid=middle+east+and+north+africa&utm_source=feedblitz&utm_medium=FeedBlitzRss&utm_campaign=FeedBlitzRss&utm_content=Iran+at+the+polls%3a+Why+today's+vote+is+%28and+isn't%29+important> (last accessed 10 March 2016).

Martínez-Fuentes, Guadalupe (2015a), 'Argelia, 2014: elecciones, partidos y sociedad civil como claves analíticas de continuidad y cambio', *Revista de Estudios Internacionales Mediterráneos*, 18: 107–36.

Martínez-Fuentes, Guadalupe (2015b), 'Política electoral transicional en Túnez 2011–2015: desinstitucionalización del autoritarismo y aprendizaje democrático', *Revista de Estudios Políticos*, 169: 235–65.

Melián, Luis (2015), 'Desarrollos políticos en el Reino Hachemí: la Primavera Árabe desde la óptica jordana', *Revista CIDOB d'Afers Internacionals*, 109: 131–56.

Montabes, Juan and Guadalupe Martínez-Fuentes (2014), 'Il cambiamento político tunesino verso la democrazia', in Guerino D'Ignazio et al. (eds), *Transizioni e Democrazia nei paesi del Mediterraneo e del Vicino Oriente*, Cosenza: Edizioni Periferia, pp. 267–286.

Morsy, Ahmed (2015), *The Egyptian Parliamentary Elections 101*, Middle East Institute. Available at <http://www.mei.edu/content/article/egyptian-parliamentary-elections-101> (last accessed 8 March 2016).

Murphy, Emma (2013), 'The Tunisian elections of October 2011: a democratic consensus', *The Journal of North African Studies*, 18 (2): 231–47.

Nohlen, Dieter (2016), 'Arquitectura institucional, contexto sociocultural e integridad electoral', *Desafíos*, 28 (I): 429–53. Available at <http://revistas.urosario.edu.co/index.php/desafios/article/viewFile/4660/3302> (last accessed 2 February 2016).

Norris, Pippa (2015), *Why Elections Fail*, New York: Cambridge University Press.

Norris, Pippa, Ferran Martínez i Coma and Max Grömping (2015), *The Expert Survey of Perceptions of Electoral Integrity, Release 3 (PEI-3)*, Sydney: University of Sydney. Available at <www.electoralintegrityproject.com> (last accessed 2 February 2016).

Norris, Pippa, Ferran Martínez i Coma, Alessandro Nai and Max Grömping (2016), *The Year in Elections, 2015*, Sydney: University of Sydney. Available at <www.electoralintegrityproject.com> (last accessed 9 March 2016).

Norris, Pippa, Richard W. Frank and Ferran Martínez i Coma (2013), 'Assessing the quality of elections', *Journal of Democracy*, 24 (4): 124–35.

Okruhlik, Gwenn (2012), 'The identity politics of Kuwait's election', *Foreign Policy*. Available at <http://foreignpolicy.com/2012/02/08/the-identity-politics-of-kuwaits-election/> (last accessed 25 February 2016).

OSCE/ODIHR (2011), *Republic of Turkey Parliamentary Elections, 12 June 2011. Final Report*. Available at <http://www.osce.org/odihr/84588?download=true> (last accessed 28 March 2016).

OSCE/ODIHR (2014), *Republic of Turkey Presidential Election, 10 August 2014. Limited Election Observation Mission*. Available at <http://www.osce.org/odihr/elections/turkey/126851?download=true> (last accessed 9 March 2016).

OSCE/ODIHR (2015), *Republic of Turkey Parliamentary Elections, 7 June 2015. Limited Election Observation Mission Final Report*. Available at <http://www.osce.org/odihr/elections/turkey/177926?download=true> (last accessed 8 March 2016).

Parejo, María Angustias (ed.) (2010), *Entre el autoritarismo y la democracia. Los procesos electorales en el Magreb*, Barcelona: Tirant lo Blanch.

Pérez, Natalia (2015), *Israel: Elecciones legislativas del 17 de marzo de 2015*, OPEMAM. Available at <http://www.opemam.org/sites/default/files/ficha%20electoral%20Israel%202015.pdf> (last accessed 23 February 2016).

Pottie, David S. (2015), Measuring Electoral Quality, The ACE Project. Available at <http://aceproject.org/ace-en/focus/measuring-electoral-quality/default> (last accessed 21 February 2016).

Reseau Euro-Mediterranéen des Droits de l'Homme (2012), *Réformes politiques ou verrouillage supplémentaire de la société civile du champ politique? Une analyse critique*. Available at <http://www.ldh-france.org/IMG/pdf/RA-RefPol-Algerie-Fr-150Dpi.pdf> (last accessed 18 February 2016).

Rethink Institute (2015), Turkey's 2015 Election Prospects, Rethink Paper 23. Available at <http://www.rethinkinstitute.org/turkeys-2015-election-prospects/ http://www.osce.org/odihr/elections/turkey/177926?download=true> (last accessed 8 March 2016).

Schedler, Andreas (2002), 'The menu of manipulation', *Journal of Democracy*, 13 (2): 36–50.

Stepan, Alfred (2012), 'Tunisia's transition and the twin tolerations', *Journal of Democracy*, 23 (2): 89–103.

Szmolka, Inmaculada (2014), 'Political change in North Africa and the Arab Middle East: constitutional reforms and electoral processes', *Arab Studies Quaterly*, 36 (2): 128–48.

Szmolka, Inmaculada (2015), 'Exclusionary and non-consensual transitions versus inclusive and consensual democratizations: the cases of Egypt and Tunisia', *Arab Studies Quaterly*, 37 (1): 73–95.

Teorell, Jan, Michael Coppedge, Svend-Erik Skaaning and Staffan I. Lindberg (2016), *Measuring Electoral Democracy with V-Dem Data: Introducing a New Polyarchy Index*, Working Paper Series 2016: 25, Varieties of Democracy Institute. Available at <https://v-dem.net/media/filer_public/f1/b7/f1b76fad-5d9b-41e3-b752-07baaba72a8c/v-dem_working_paper_2016_25.pdf> (last accessed 2 March 2016).

The Economist Intelligence Unit (2011), *Democracy Index 2011*. Available at <http://www.eiu.com/public/topical_report.aspx?campaignid=DemocracyIndex2011> (last accessed 1 February 2016).

The Economist Intelligence Unit (2012), *Democracy Index 2012*. Available at <http://www.eiu.com/public/topical_report.aspx?campaignid=DemocracyIndex12> (last accessed 1 February 2016).

The Economist Intelligence Unit (2013), *Democracy Index 2013*. Available at <http://www.eiu.com/public/topical_report.aspx?campaignid=Democracy0814> (last accessed 1 February 2016).

The Economist Intelligence Unit (2014), *Democracy Index 2014*. Available at <https://www.eiu.com/public/topical_report.aspx?campaignid=Democracy0115> (last accessed 1 February 2016).

The Economist Intelligence Unit (2015), *Democracy Index 2015. Democracy in an Age of Anxiety*. Available at <http://www.yabiladi.com/img/content/EIU-Democracy-Index-2015.pdf> (last accessed 10 February 2016).Valeri, Marc (2012), *Election Report Oman/Consultative Council 15 October 2011*, OPEMAM. Available at <http://www.opemam.org/sites/default/files/ER-Oman-Consultative-Council-2011.pdf> (last accessed 8 March 2016).

Varieties of Democracy (2016), *Electoral Democracy Index, V-Dem [Country-Year/Country-Date] Datatset v5*. Available at <https://v-dem.net/es/data/> (last accessed 2 March 2016).

Zaccara, Luciano and Marta Saldaña (2015), 'Cambio y estabilidad política en las monarquías del Golfo tras la Primavera Árabe', *Revista CIDOB d'Afers Internacionals*, 109, 177–99.

Chapter 5

Constitutional reform processes

Ewa K. Strzelecka and
María Angustias Parejo

1 Introduction

Constitutional reforms both shape and have been shaped by political changes, and as such they represent a significant area in the analysis of sociopolitical reconfigurations in the Arab world. In this chapter we analyse the different constitutional reform processes that have taken place in the Maghreb (Algeria, Morocco and Tunisia) and the Middle East (Egypt, Jordan, Syria, Yemen, Oman and Bahrain) since the uprisings in 2011. The initial hypothesis is that the constitutional reform processes have had a decisive impact on the nature and scope of the processes of political change. The existence of a democratic procedure for constitutional reform and a broad consensus – emerging from the freely expressed will of the people, and based on the covenant and model of constitutional coexistence – all represent notable indicators for the democratisation process.

The purpose of this study is to examine and compare the latest constitutional reform processes in the aforementioned nine countries in order to offer key insights into these processes and to propose a typology of the dynamics of constitutional reform, and its scope in the Arab world. The aspects for analysis include procedures (institutions and regulations), consensus and dissent during the course of the constitutional process and the content of the constitutional reforms (democratic mechanisms and authoritarian mechanisms). The emphasis is placed on the most important elements of the processes of constitutional change and of the content of the new constitutions, while paying particular attention to aspects related with the power of heads of state, the most frequently debated reforms and the advancement of gender equality and women's rights.

2 Algeria: new constitution, old status quo

In April 2011 Algeria's President Abdelaziz Bouteflika, in power since 1999, announced a constitutional reform with which he managed to mitigate popular discontent and contain the Arab Spring in his country. The first stage of this constitutional process consisted of a parallel dialogue: on one hand, with civil society, and on the other, with the political leaders. This stage was initiated in May 2011 with the aim of listening to citizens' proposals for change. The second stage began when the president created a special committee made up of five experts. All of them were university professors and worked from April 2013 to May 2014 on preparing the first constitutional reform bill, which should have taken into consideration the proposals made previously by different political and social actors. It is worth noting that the proposals from the political parties and civil society were advisory in nature rather than prescriptive and were delivered during closed-door meetings with state officials. Since they were non-binding, their implementation depended on the goodwill of the regime.

The constitutional process speeded up following the presidential elections on 17 April 2014. The six presidential candidates all viewed constitutional reform as a priority, even though they had differing views on the content of the new constitution. As Abdelaziz Bouteflika was re-elected as president, the reform process continued in accordance with his views. On 7 May 2014 the president submitted the road map for the constitutional process to the Council of Ministers, while stressing the importance of seeking consensus between political and social groups in order to broaden democracy in Algeria. Following the decisions made at this meeting, invitations were sent out on 15 May 2014 to 150 stakeholders to take part in a second round of consultations on the draft constitution. On 16 May the proposed amendments were published on the presidency's website, with the aim of promoting greater transparency and ensuring that the media and public opinion were involved in the process.

Most of the opposition parties turned down the regime's invitation to take part in the consultation, questioning the credibility and transparency of the process. Nevertheless, 134 organisations out of the 150 stakeholders invited still agreed to take part in the consolidation of the draft constitution. More specifically, the invitation was accepted by thirty out of the thirty-six prominent figures invited, fifty-two political parties out of sixty-four, and all of the thirty-seven national organisations and associations and the twelve university professors. The minister of state and the president's chief of staff, Ahmed Ouyahia, was appointed by President Bouteflika to conduct the consultation process. Thus, from 1–8 July 2014, a total of 114 meetings were held out with the representatives of different social and political groups, and some thirty written contributions were received to be taken into consideration with regard to the drafting of the reform bill. Following a review of the proposals that lasted from 14 to 28 December 2015, President Bouteflika met with a restricted council comprised of six cabinet members to finalise the draft constitution. The final draft was endorsed by the president on 28 December 2015, and subsequently approved by the Council of Ministers on 11 January 2016 (Benyettou 2015).

At the public presentation of the draft constitution, the government announced that 70 per cent of the constitution's amendments expressed the collective proposals of the political and social actors who took part in the consultation. However, this result was widely questioned by the opposition parties, who rejected the new constitution, describing it as a cosmetic change and not an in-depth reform. In spite of this criticism, the draft constitution was approved by an overwhelming majority in the two houses of parliament, thanks to the control exerted over parliament by the National Liberation Front (FLN in the French acronym), a party with close links to President Abdelaziz Bouteflika. The voting session was attended by 512 MPs from both parliamentary houses, 499 of whom voted in favour of the draft constitution, two against and with sixteen abstentions. The new constitution was enacted by President Bouteflika on 6 March 2016. On 7 February the clause implementation follow-up committee was created, a body responsible for the implementation of the constitutional amendments. However, the opposition remains sceptical about this control mechanism and the likelihood of any real change being made.

Among the most important changes introduced in the 2016 constitution are the restrictions on the president's term of office to two consecutive terms, the enlarging of the powers of parliament, the creation of an Independent Electoral Committee, an expansion of citizens' rights and freedoms, the creation of new national councils to respond to emerging issues, and the promotion of a multilingual national identity, specifically by acknowledging Amazigh as an official language together with Arabic.

With these changes, a slight alteration has taken place in the position of the president, though this reform has not substantially affected his governing powers and privileges. The president continues to enjoy wide-ranging powers, as head of state, chair of the Council of Ministers and commander-in-chief of all the armed forces of the Republic of Algeria (articles 70 and 77). He has the power to appoint the heads of the main posts in the areas of the administration, the political sphere, the judiciary, diplomats, national security and the Bank of Algeria (article 78). One significant innovation is that when appointing the prime minister, the president now requires the endorsement of a parliamentary majority (article 77). Another positive change is the return to restricting presidential mandates to two five-year terms (article 74). This restriction was modified in 2008, thereby enabling President Bouteflika to commence a third term of office in 2009 and a fourth in 2014. Thus all future presidents may govern for a maximum of ten years. It should be noted that this concession by the regime took place in a context marked by the current uncertainties from President Bouteflika's delicate state of health as well as his advanced age of seventy-nine.

The 2016 constitution also introduces significant changes to the criteria for anyone wishing to stand in the presidential elections. All presidential candidates must have solely the native Algerian citizenship and be able to prove that their parents have the native Algerian citizenship, they must not be married to anyone from a different nationality other than Algerian, they must not possess a foreign nationality, and they must have resided in Algeria for at least ten years before standing for presidential elections (article 73). These measures not only make it difficult for people of immigrant origin to advance socially and politically, they also restrict the political participation of Algerians with dual nationality and who live in diaspora, which can affect members of the opposition.

The 2016 constitutional revision introduces several improvements in issues regarding human rights, including the right to freedom of peaceful demonstration (article 41 bis), of political association (article 42 bis) and of the press (article 41 bis 2). The principle of equality and non-discrimination for reasons of gender (article 29) as well as encouraging the political participation of women (article 31) were guaranteed in previous constitutions. The new feature of the 2016 constitution is its measures for promoting gender equality in the labour market, and to encourage the promotion of women in decision-making positions in public agencies and institutions (article 31 bis 2). It also recognises the role of youth as a dynamic force in the country's development (article 31 bis 3).

3 Morocco: the monarchy's new redefinition of its control over the political scene

Over the past five decades Morocco's monarchy has shown an astonishing ability to manage and respond to social and political crises by means of constitutional revision. The constitutional reform of July 2011 took place in a context of revolts and street demonstrations by dissatisfied citizens calling for a radical change in the system. Inevitably, the hasty constitutional reform process must be viewed as a strategy of rapid reaction by the regime to the challenge represented by the emergence of an independent, unprecedented movement that challenged the existing game rules. The response by those in power to the popular demands expressed by the 20 February Movement and its support platforms extended the controversial process of liberalisation commenced in the 1990s (Parejo 2010: 92), and has been widely applauded in the international sphere as an example worthy of emulation in the Arab world. However, despite the apparent concessions, the monarchy has not ceded any of its basic prerogatives; instead it has merely redefined its control over the Moroccan political scene. This reform falls far short of achieving the 'constitutional, democratic, parliamentary and social monarchy' described in the first article of the recent 2011 constitution; it is a ruling monarchy and it has not made any change to the authoritarian nature of the regime. Morocco continues to be a quasi-competitive authoritarianism in which the autonomy of the government and the parliament has been subordinated by a monarchy of an executive and legislative nature, though a limited amount of political competition is allowed (Feliu and Parejo 2013: 88–91).

The address by King Mohammed VI on 9 March 2011 was the starting signal for the reform process. This famous royal address establishes the framework and the general guidelines for the constitutional amendments. Its two key topics were the constitutionalisation of regionalisation (Parejo and Feliu 2013) and the strengthening and balancing of powers (especially those of parliament and government), as reflected in the fourth point in the king's address to the nation.

Shortly afterwards, on 11 March, the Advisory Committee for Constitutional Reform (CCRC in the French acronym) was created, under the aegis of the lawyer Abdellatif Menouni and comprised of eighteen committee members, all appointed by the king. This committee commenced its hearings on 28 March, at which a number of political–social actors had to submit their proposals. In parallel with this committee, the Political Mechanism for Monitoring Constitutional Reform was also established, headed by the royal advisor, Mohamed Moatassime. It was officially conceived as a space for constructive debate and participation by political parties, unions and other political actors for the purpose of overseeing the draft constitution process (Desrues 2012: 370).

The final draft of the new constitution was not granted much time for debate by the parties and unions that formed part of the aforementioned Political Mechanism. An oral presentation of the draft constitution's basic principles and guidelines was given to the Political Mechanism on 7 June, though its members did not receive the full written text until 16 June. On 17 June the king announced to the Moroccan people that a referendum would be held imminently on the constitution's amendments. The consultation campaign began on Tuesday 21 June and ended at midnight on 30 June. Almost all the parties in the Moroccan political arena (including pro-government parties, the old opposition parties and new or smaller parties) participated actively in the constitutional consultation mechanism, and campaigned in favour of the new text. Only two small left-wing groups and a union (the Socialist Democratic Vanguard Party (PADS in the French acronym); the National Ittihadi Congress Party (CNI); and the Democratic Confederation of Labour (CDT)), initially decided to take part in the process of drafting the constitution, though they subsequently left the Political Mechanism. The semi-institutional opposition (the Unified Socialist Party (PSU); the Movement for the Community (MC); and the National Union of Popular Forces (UNFP)) and the non-institutional opposition (Democratic Way (VD); Justice and Spirituality; and Islamic Youth) expressed complete and open dissent with the constitutional draft process and the underlying referendum. The 20 February Movement, meanwhile, in spite of the autonomy of each of its local groups (which function by calling assembly meetings, a factor that gives rise to differences over strategy and content) decided in unison not to collaborate with either the CCRC or the Political Mechanism, and to boycott the referendum.

The referendum was held on 1 July 2011, and the official results were published after being certified by the Constitutional Council on 16 July. Voter turnout within the national territory stood at 73.46 per cent, the lowest in the history of Morocco's referendums. Final calculations, which included both the votes recorded in the national territory and abroad, showed that the 'yes' vote won, with 98.5 per cent.

One of the most notable innovations of Morocco's new political–constitutional architecture is the new status of the government. The constitutionalisation of a representative government illustrates the struggle between democratic principles and the persistence of an active monarchical power. All the constitutions have preserved (with certain nuances) an unbalanced dual executive. In 2011 a new duality emerged which featured an executive branch that was less unbalanced. The result adopted is a shared executive power which involves a necessary collaboration between the king and a head of government, while downplaying the functional and organic separation of powers and revealing the porosity that exists between the monarchy and all the other established powers.

The new constitution's harshest critics point to a series of weaknesses in the amendments. The most important of these is the fact that the centrality of the king and the concentration of his powers have not been altered. The king continues to possess great prerogatives in the executive sphere, without any political responsibility: he is the head of state (article 42), and the commander of the faithful, the highest religious authority in the country (article 41). He chairs the Council of Ministers' meetings (article 48), which determine the main strategic lines of state policy (article 49). He appoints the head of government and the members of government proposed previously by the head of government (article 47). The king is no longer sacred, but he is still inviolable (article 46), thus protecting his political–religious status.

The king maintains his legislative powers intact through the enactment of royal decrees (*dahir*) (article 42), his competence to address messages to the nation and to the parliament which 'may not be made the object of any debate' (article 52), and his authority to dissolve both houses of parliament (article 51). He controls the spheres of defence and security, and remains the supreme head of the royal armed forces and has an exclusive monopoly over military appointments (article 53) and those of ambassadors (article 55). With the aim of consolidating still further his control over state security, he heads the recently created Superior Council of Security (article 54). He has markedly increased his sphere of influence following the constitutionalisation of numerous councils (all of which he chairs), such as the Superior Council of the Judicial Power (article 56), and he appoints half of their members. In general, the king has not renounced any of his prerogatives, and continues to hold the power of veto over important decisions.

The other part of this dual executive is the government. The new government statute of 2011 enshrines a parliamentarisation of the government and the appointment of the head of government. The government emanates from the will of parliament and the investiture of the government is explicitly established once it has obtained a favourable majority vote within the House of Representatives (article 88). The constitutionalising of a representative government initiated a process of emancipation of the government from monarchical power. Some of the basic elements of majority democracy have been constitutionalised, including the appointment of the head of government within the party that emerges victorious in the legislative elections (article 47) and an asymmetrical two-chamber system. The constitution formally enshrined a two-tiered autonomy for the head of government in relation to the king: firstly, the government's responsibility to the king is removed (article 60 of the 1996 constitution), with the new constitution formally establishing the government's sole responsibility to parliament; and secondly, the head of government is granted the right to dissolve parliament (article 104). The new constitution strengthens the government's powers and degree of autonomy (the constitutionalisation of the Council of Government, article 92), but it is still weak in comparison with the king. In this respect, the government's position – less subordinate but still subordinate – can be glimpsed in the constitution's grey areas where what is known as the material constitution can come into play, and in those domains reserved for the king where the government does not exert any responsibility. The limits of governmental power can be clearly seen in the spheres of religion, security and the Council of Ministers (articles 48 and 49), which possesses 'political, strategic and symbolic competences that are more powerful than those of the Council of Government' (Parejo 2015: 40–1).

The struggle of the feminist movement and associations calling for equality between men and women has gained significant advances in terms of gender equality. One of the most important of these is the broadening of the sphere of equality recognised in article 19 which stipulates that 'the man and the woman enjoy, in equality, the rights and freedoms of civil, political, economic, social, cultural and environmental character', compared with the previous article 8 in the 1996 constitution, which only guaranteed equal political rights. Also in article 19, the state works for the realisation of parity between men and women, by including in the constitution a specific authority to promote parity and the struggle against all forms of discrimination (subsequently developed in article 164). The new constitution enshrines the state's commitment to draft and implement public policies which tackle and prevent the vulnerability of certain groups of women, mothers, children and elderly people (article 34). Gender equality is also enshrined in the state's institutional structure, with article 115 stipulating that the presence of female judges among the ten elected members must be ensured within the Superior Council of the Judicial Power, in proportion with their presence in the corps of the magistrature. Finally, the constitution includes a commitment to ensure greater participation of women in the management of local and territorial authorities (article 146).

4 Tunisia: the miracle of the constitution of compromise and consensus

The Tunisian constitution was approved on 27 January 2014. It was over two years after the election of the National Constituent Assembly (ANC in the French acronym), which was commissioned with the task of drafting a constitution within twelve months. This delay can be partly explained by the fact that the ANC exceeded its strictly constitutional mandate (Ben Achour 2014: 784) and the difficulty experienced by said body in reconciling its constitutional function with those of the legislature and governmental control. Furthermore, the constitutional paralysis was particularly caused by the intense, in-depth ideological debate on secularism that took place within a transition characterised by a scenario polarised between Islamist and secular parties (Szmolka 2015: 74). We must also consider other problematic factors such as the breakdown in security, outbreaks of terrorist violence, the political assassinations of Chokri Belaïd and Mohamed Brahmi, and the influence of regional politics (and particularly the developing events in Egypt and Libya) to understand the various political crises and incidents of institutional collapse that the political system has experienced, and which have had an impact on the constitutional process.

The current constitution of 2014 is the third in modern times and was preceded by four different texts: the Tunisian draft constitution of 8 August 2012; the draft constitution of 14 December 2012; the draft constitution of 22 April 2013; and the draft constitution of the Republic of Tunisia of 1 June 2013 (Ben Achour 2014: 784).

The various draft constitutions produced by the National Assembly in 2012 and 2013 are a symptom of the antagonistic views in Tunisian politics and society deriving from two groups that are polar opposites: the secularists and the Islamic conservatives. All the draft constitutions prompted criticism from the opposition, secularist civil society, the Tunisian Association of Constitutional Law (ATDC in the French acronym) and the Democratic Transition Study Association (ARTD). These two associations organise demonstrations and study days to denounce the serious shortcomings in the texts and the semantic and referential confusion in same, in addition to the multiple legal deficiencies and contradictions, and the backward-looking nature of its measures (Gobe and Chouikha 2014: 301–10).

The assassination of Mohamed Brahmi on 25 July 2013 unleashed a storm within the insecure, unstable and divided atmosphere of Tunisian politics. This turbulent, violent situation led to an impasse until one section of civil society committed to democratisation proposed (on 29 July 2013) a new national dialogue initiative in order to emerge from the crisis and the bipolarisation that was generating the violence (Gobe and Chouikha 2015: 261–2). This consensus legitimacy initiative was sponsored by the Tunisian General Workers' Union (UGTT), the Tunisian Union for Industry, Trade and Handicrafts (UTICA), the Tunisian League for the Defence of Human Rights (LTDH) and the Tunisia National Lawyers' Association (ONAT). This quartet proposed the idea of rearranging the main political groups represented in the ANC within the dialogue, as a kind of informal mini-parliament in which a road map was adopted to bring the transition to an end by convening legislative and presidential elections. The proposed plan featured three stages: the election, by the ANC, of a new Independent High Authority for Elections; the election of a prime minister and a new government comprised of technocrats; and speeding up the process of drafting the constitution by prioritising a rule of consensus. Finally, Ennahda, together with twenty representatives from political parties, signed the roadmap on 5 October 2013.

The path chosen for the constitutional process meant that the ANC essentially lost its control of the political agenda and the process of drafting the constitution in favour of the national dialogue and the consensus committee. This ad hoc committee was created by the ANC in early July 2013 in an effort to overcome the major differences between MPs regarding the constitutional text. Chaired by Mustapha Ben Jafar, president of the ANC and secretary general of Ettakatol, the committee were mainly comprised of the presidents of the parliamentary factions from the ANC or their representatives. This informal political arena was imposed in the final quarter of 2013 as a base for reshaping the draft constitution of 1 June 2013. After approximately twenty sessions of intensive work by the consensus committee in the last week of December focused on defusing the most controversial points, the ANC plenary debates commenced on 3 January. After many vicissitudes and negotiations, the constitution was finally approved on 26 January 2014 by an overwhelming majority: 200 votes in favour, twelve against and with four abstentions, in an atmosphere of euphoria and concord never before witnessed in the assembly (Gobe and Chouikha 2015: 262).

The constitution's painful gestation process reveals the difficulties involved for political actors with opposing views to reach consensus over their disagreements. The content of the new constitution appears to be generically in accordance with the principles of the democratic and liberal doctrine of universal human rights. Nevertheless, the constitution is the result of important concessions, sacrifice and compromise between secularists and the defenders of Islamic conservatism. It shows difficult, convoluted balances and ambiguous stipulations linked to the constitution-makers' commitment to Tunisia's Arab-Muslim particularities (Gobe and Chouikha 2015: 262–3).

One of the issues that polarised the debate, to the point of torpedoing the previous draft constitutions, is the religious question. The new constitution maintains the wording of article 1 from the 1959 constitution: 'Tunisia is a free, independent, sovereign state; its religion is Islam, its language Arabic, and its system is republican'. The constitution-makers specify the interpretive scope of the state's complex nature in article 2, which defines Tunisia as a civil state based on 'citizenship, the will of the people, and the supremacy of law'. This hybrid nature of the state is also highlighted in the constitution's Preamble, with the defence of 'Islamic-Arab identity' founded on an Islam that is open, tolerant and compatible with 'the highest principles of universal human rights', and the clear intention of 'building a republican, democratic and participatory system, in the framework of a civil state'.

The enshrinement of individual freedoms and the intervention of the state in religious matters was another of the bones of contention between secularists and Islamic conservatives. Article 6 attempted to reconcile the two – the secularists succeeded in including the principle of freedom of conscience (which represents a considerable achievement in the region, in as much as it is understood to open up the possibility for a Muslim to convert to a different religion) (Ben Achour 2014: 787) and to enshrine the state's responsibility to protect freedom of conscience at the same level as the freedom of belief and the freedom of worship. Ennahda ensured that 'the state is the guardian of religion' and is responsible for 'the protection of the sacred' (Gobe and Chouikha 2014: 321). The state safeguards a project for society based on Arab and moderate Islamic identity, and to that end it ensures the political neutrality of 'mosques, places of worship' (article 6) and 'educational institutions' (article 16). It undertakes to spread the values of moderation and tolerance, to prohibit accusations of *takfir* (apostasy) and incitement to hatred and violence (article 6), and it safeguards the right to a free public education that fosters the national and Arab-Muslim identity of the young generations (article 39).

The great obsession of the Tunisian constitution-makers in 2014 was to break with the authoritarian, personality cult provisions of the presidential system, as enshrined in the 1956 constitution and exacerbated by the many subsequent revisions. Officially, it was a mixed, half-presidential, half-parliamentary regime (Ben Achour 2014: 792), modelled on a broadly parliamentary philosophy (Gobe and Chouikha 2015: 278) that represents a kind of compromise between the two forms of government, generating a sophisticated, confused and complex relationship between a two-headed government (president of the republic and the head of government) and a single-chamber legislative body (Assembly of the Representatives of the People).

The head of state is elected by direct universal suffrage, and his term of office is restricted to two five-year terms, either successive or separate (article 75). His prerogatives include: his representative role (article 72); his ability to set general policy in specific areas, a power he shares with the head of government (article 91) and the president of the assembly (article 77); his authority to appoint the head of government, with a very limited margin of manoeuvre, and the foreign affairs and defence ministers, decided in conjunction with the head of government (article 89); his power to table new legislation, shared with a minimum of ten MPs and the head of government (article 62); his right to submit a motion of confidence to the government, and should the government fail to win this motion, the head of state may dissolve the assembly; conversely, the assembly may force his resignation (article 99).

The head of government and the government require the backing of an absolute majority in the assembly before they can be appointed by the president of the republic (article 89). Within government, the head of government is all-powerful: he can set general state policy and oversee its implementation (article 91); he heads the administration and ratifies international treaties of a technical nature (article 92); he chairs, convenes and sets the agenda for the Council of Ministers, unless it deals with issues related to defence, overseas relations or national security, in which case the session must be chaired by the president of the republic (article 93); at a legislative level he holds the right of legislative initiative, shared (as we have seen previously) with the president of the republic and a minimum of ten MPs (article 62), and he also exercises regulatory power (article 94).

The pressure exerted by progressive feminist organisations on the authorities and institutions responsible for navigating the transition and the major mobilisation campaigns it deployed (especially in 2012 and 2013) led to the issue of gender being accepted into the transition's political agenda, and consequently permeating the constitutional debate. In the constitutional sphere, the fruits of this struggle were reflected in a regulation which, to a certain degree, meets the demands of most of the feminist collective (Martínez-Fuentes 2014: 4). Thus, the women's constitutional statute of 2014: guarantees the protection, consolidation and promotion of women's accrued rights (article 46); it enshrines an equal citizenship (preamble, article 2 and article 21), in which 'male and female citizens have equal rights and duties, and are equal before the law without any discrimination' and are granted 'freedoms and individual and collective rights' (article 21); it stipulates that male and female citizens both possess the right to 'decent working conditions and to a fair wage' (article 40); in the political arena it makes a political commitment to affirmative action and states that it 'guarantees the representation of women in elected bodies' (article 34) as well as working to achieve parity between women and men in elected assemblies (article 46). Finally, the document highlights two very important achievements: the constitution includes a state commitment to 'eradicate violence against women' (article 46).

5 Constitutional development in Egypt: three changes in three years

Egypt has undergone three constitutional reform processes since 2011. The first reform was the interim constitution proclaimed on 30 March 2011 by the Supreme Council of the Armed Forces following President Hosni Mubarak's resignation from his post. The second reform involved the proclamation of the 2012 constitution, which came into force on 26 December and was devised under the hegemony of an Islamist majority within the constitutional assembly. The third reform was announced in July 2013, when the armed forces deposed President Mohammed Morsi in a coup, thus paving the way for a new constitution, adopted on 18 January 2014.

The 2012 and 2014 constitutions brought a rupture with the constitutional order of Hosni Mubarak's regime, but they did not represent a satisfactory change in democratic terms. Both documents were enacted within a context of polarisation and hostility between Islamist and secular parties (Szmolka

2015: 74), and they were used as a means to reinforce political alliances and to extend the dominant groups' advantage over their rivals (al-Ali 2016: 124). The two constitutional processes were distinguished by a lack of national consensus and the marginalisation of the opposition groups. The secular and liberal parties were marginalised following the political victory of the Islamist parties in the 2012 elections, while the Muslim Brotherhood were excluded from the transition process as a result of the military coup on 3 July 2013 and the subsequent outlawing of the Muslim Brotherhood by Cairo's Administrative Court on 23 September 2013.

The 2014 constitution, currently in force, is the result of a process established in the Constitutional Declaration proclaimed on 8 July 2013 by the interim President Adly Mansour, who replaced President Mohammed Morsi. The constitutional process was initiated by a technical committee of ten experts made up of lawyers and professors of law who, within a space of thirty days, submitted a first draft of the constitutional text, comprising 198 articles. The document was then debated and further developed by an assembly of fifty members, who proposed a constitution of 247 articles. This latter committee represented different political, social and military sectors; however, it did not include the Muslim Brotherhood, the most powerful organisation in the post-Mubarak period, and whose political arm (the Freedom and Justice Party) won three consecutive elections after 2011 (to the People's Assembly in 2011–12, the Shura Council in 2012 and the Presidency of Egypt in 2012) and two constitutional referendums (in March 2011 and in December 2012). The exclusion of the Muslim Brotherhood and the relative homogeneity of the constitutional assembly members meant 'serious disagreements would be unlikely, which was later seen when the overwhelming majority of the 247-article draft constitution was approved inside the plenary by more than 88 per cent of the total votes' (Meyer-Resende 2014: 7).

The regulations of the constitutional process had envisaged different public consultation mechanisms, but in the event these were limited to a constitutional referendum, held on 14 and 15 January 2014. The referendum was skewed in favour of a 'yes' vote, as the 'no' campaigns were repressed and intimidated by the security forces (Meyer-Resende 2014: 4–8). As a result, the constitution was endorsed by 98.1 per cent of voters, even though voter turnout was low – 38.6 per cent, only five percentage points above the turnout for the previous 2012 constitutional referendum.

While the 2014 constitution has many similarities to the one enacted in 2012, it also has significant differences. The biggest change lay in the removal of the language and the articles favoured by the Islamists in the 2012 text. The 2014 reform increased the power of the military forces, which had previously been bolstered through the prerogatives of budgetary and judicial autonomy in the 2012 constitution. One new feature was the abolition of the Shura Council. However, the 2014 reform does not go so far as to encourage separation and balance between the three powers of the state.

The 2014 constitution does not restrict the authority of the president, though his office is limited to a maximum of two four-year mandates, as stated in the 2012 constitution. The president is the head of state and has wide-ranging executive powers which he shares with the government. The problem lies in the fact that the division of responsibilities between the president and the prime minister is not explicitly stated in the constitution, which can affect the former's accountability. The president can exert significant influence over the legislature. He has the right to veto the law and to appoint up to 5 per cent of the members of the People's Assembly, a figure that becomes particularly significant when electoral results are closely fought or disputed. At the same time, parliament has the power to impugn the presidential mandate with a two-thirds majority, and if support is achieved via a popular referendum, the president may be ousted.

The 2014 constitution devotes two chapters (the second and the third) to issues related with human rights. The 2014 reform, compared with the 2012 constitution, is notable for the fact that it commits the state more explicitly to the 'agreements, covenants, and international conventions of human rights that were ratified by Egypt' (article 93) and to the principle of gender equality. What is more significative is that the 2014 constitution omitted the controversial clause of the 2012 constitution describing women in controversial terms as 'the sisters of men' (preamble). The 2014 constitution acknowledges the equality of all citizens and explicitly prohibits discrimination on the basis of sex (article 53). It stipulates that the state commits to 'achieving equality between women and men in all civil, political, economic, social, and cultural rights' (article 11). Furthermore, it must take necessary measures to ensure the 'appropriate representation of women in the houses of parliament' (article 11), though the constitution does not specify the precise mechanism through which the gender quota will be applied. The progress made in terms of women's rights is also challenged by the use of shariah law as 'the principal source of legislation' (article 2). The 2014 constitutional amendment specifies, nevertheless, that references for the interpretation of shariah are 'the relevant texts in the collected rulings of the Supreme Constitutional Court' (preamble), and do not depend on the opinions of the al-Azhar Council of Senior Scholars, as was stipulated in article 4 of the 2012 constitution. The 2014 reform also removed the controversial article 219, which broadly defined the principles of Islamic shariah, and generated concern that Salafists might make use of this mechanism to impose a restrictive view of women's rights and freedoms in society.

6 The constitutional reform promoted by the king of Jordan

The constitutional reform in Jordan was advocated by King Abdullah II in response to the mass protests of 2011, and with the aim of bringing an end to the political crisis. The Royal Committee on Constitutional Review, set up in April 2011, comprised people loyal to the regime, and did not include any representatives of the political opposition or the reformist movement (Bani Salameh and Ananzah 2015: 145; Gluck and Brandt 2015: 8). Despite the fact that King Abdullah II stated that the objectives of the constitutional reform were 'civic activism and effective public participation', the amendments were not submitted to public participatory consultation, nor were they the result of a transparent process (Gluck and Brandt 2015: 8). The forty-two amendments to the 1952 constitution, as proposed by the Committee on Constitutional Review in August 2011, were voted on by the House of Deputies and the Senate in September, and approved by royal decree on 30 September 2011 (Szmolka 2014: 130–34).

The constitutional reform of 2011 did not make any changes to the section devoted to 'The King and His Prerogatives' (articles 28–40), and thus the monarch's enormous power remained intact. The Hashemite king of Jordan is sworn in as head of state (article 30), chief executive and supreme commander of the land, naval and air forces (article 32). He is also responsible for appointing the prime minister (article 35), approving his cabinet and designating the members of the Senate (article 36). The king also has the power to dissolve both chambers of parliament, to enact and veto laws, ratify treaties, declare war, make peace, appoint judges, intervene in death penalty sentences, grant special pardons and remit sentences. The king appoints the members of the constitutional court, which was set up for the first time in Jordan as a result of the 2011 constitutional reform.

In August 2014 two new amendments to the constitution were approved, one of which granted the king an additional power – the exclusive prerogative to appoint army commanders and the heads of the intelligence services. Two years later, in April 2016, another constitutional reform was enacted which further increased the king's absolute powers. The draft amendment was drawn up by the government of Prime Minister Abdullah Ensour and was approved by the House of Deputies and the Senate with the utmost urgency, without being subjected to in-depth debate or submitted to public consultation. The reform was ratified by royal decree on 4 May 2016. As a result, changes were made to six articles of the 2011 constitution, including the approval of the controversial amendment to article 40 concerning the issuing of royal decrees, for which the requirement was abolished that such decrees be duly signed by the prime minister and the ministers concerned. The abolition of this control mechanism thus formalised the king's absolute, unilateral power to appoint the crown prince, the speaker and members of the senate, the chairman and members of the constitutional court, the chief justice, the army commander and the heads of the intelligence and gendarmerie services.

The 2016 amendments represented a backward step for the democratisation of Jordan, and went against the demands of the 2011 protest movement, which called for limitation of the monarch's absolute power. Admittedly, in 2011 the king did make some concessions in order to pacify the revolt, but in effect they were a series of superficial, nominal reforms that fell short of representing structural changes. The 2011 constitutional reform brought some selective improvements in the areas of human rights and civil liberties. For example, the use of torture was banned and safeguards for the freedom of expression were increased. However, no progress was made in the area of women's rights. The recommendation from feminist movements – that article 6 of the constitution be amended and amplified by adding the word 'gender' to the prohibition of discrimination between citizens – was ignored. This failure to explicitly prohibit discrimination for reasons of gender has hampered the reform of laws prejudicial to women.

7 Yemen: everything has changed and nothing has changed

The constitutional process in Yemen, unlike that of other countries affected by the Arab Spring, did not begin immediately after the fall of the regime. Priority was given, firstly, to establishing a national dialogue in order to lay the foundations for a future constitutional reform. The National Dialogue Conference (NDC) was convened on 18 March 2013, sixteen months after President Ali Abdullah Saleh signed a power transfer agreement brokered by the Gulf Cooperation Council, in Riyadh on 23 November 2011. The NDC lasted until 25 January 2014, producing a document over 350 pages in length, with almost 1,800 recommendations to be taken into consideration for the drafting of the new constitution. The document was the result of a consensus between 565 members of the National Dialogue. They came from different political and social sectors and represented both the traditional elites, who attempted to preserve their powers and privileges, and agents of change, who pressed for greater democratisation. The outcome of the NDC reflects the balance and the tensions between these powers, sometimes including contradictory recommendations within its final document. What is more, the NDC did not manage to reach consensus on the most important agreement as regards Yemen's future: the project for a federal state and its political-administrative division. In the final week of the National Dialogue, the Houthis withdrew from the conference in protest at the assassination, on 21 January 2014, of Ahmed Sharif al-Din, one of their representatives in the NDC. Subsequently, they denounced the NDC outcomes.

Given the difficulties involved in managing the NDC, President Abd Rabbuh Mansour Hadi attempted to drive the process forward by forming smaller and more manageable – but less representative and less accountable – working groups (Philbrick 2016: 60). The Constitutional Drafting Committee (CDC), constituted on 9 March 2014, was comprised of only seventeen members. Most of them were university lecturers, ex-diplomats and legal experts. Despite the fact that the draft constitution, issued and formally presented on 17 January 2015, was based on recommendations agreed between a broad social and political sector in the NDC, disagreement over key issues regarding the transformation of Yemen into a six-region federation served as a pretext for the non-democratic groups to block the constitutional process. Specifically, the Houthis, supported by the ousted president, Ali Abdullah Saleh, rejected the draft constitution and resorted to violence to impose their own political agenda. As a consequence, instead of convening a constitutional referendum, President Hadi was forced to sign a peace agreement with the Houthi rebels, on 21 January 2015, according to which amendments could be made to the draft constitution. Even so, the government's concessions did not succeed in preventing civil war. On 25 March 2015 an international coalition led by Saudi Arabia launched a military intervention against the Houthis in response to President Hadi's request for support. The armed conflict, which is still ongoing, unsettled the democratic transition and created concern over the future of Yemen.

The Yemeni transition to democracy was negotiated and based on national dialogue. The national authority for monitoring the implementation of NDC outcomes was established on 24 April 2014 and composed of eighty-two members. It received the draft constitution from CDC on 17 January 2015 to ensure that the new constitution was consistent with the final NDC document. This mechanism proved to be necessary, but not sufficient. It was not accompanied by the implementation of a transitional justice system that could foster reconciliation over past conflicts. Moreover, it was not backed by a genuine commitment to the democratic and peaceful methods of resolving political problems by the elites. As a consequence, the 2015 draft constitution fell victim to power struggles. The Houthis chose to carry out a coup d'état and proclaimed their own constitutional declaration, on 6 February 2015, which in fifteen articles defines a new type of transitional government in Yemen, led by a presidential committee made up of five members. This declaration was rejected by the other political actors and by the international community, though it is still being applied by the Houthis in the territories they control.

Article 1 of this document acknowledges the validity of the 1991 constitution of Yemen, as amended to 2009, providing that its measures do not come into conflict with the Houthis' constitutional declaration. Thus, the constitution of the old regime remains in force in Yemen five years after President Saleh's resignation from power.

The draft constitution of 17 January 2015 not only proclaimed a new federal system, it also significantly redefined the scope of the three state powers. At the legislative level, two houses of parliament were restructured. The Shura Council was abolished and a new Federal Council was established in its place, with 40 per cent representation assigned to the southern regions. The federal regions had their own executive authority, constituted by a regional president and a regional government. The president of Yemen was defined as a symbol of unity. He was elected for a five-year term which could only be repeated once. The president shared executive power with the vice-president. Both would be elected at the same time, though they could not be from the same region. The 2015 draft constitution considerably limited the powers of the president in comparison with the wide-ranging powers assigned to the head of state in the constitution that had been proclaimed during Ali Abdullah Saleh's regime. The president's role was reduced to a representative function and his other powers could only be exercised when previously approved by parliament. Measures were also envisaged to foster greater plurality in the selection of candidates for the presidential elections.

The 2015 draft constitution represented an important step forward in terms of women's rights and gender equality (Strzelecka 2015: 240 and 434). Following the NDC consensus-based recommendations, it included such significant improvements as guaranteeing women no less than 30 per cent of representation in various government institutions and authorities (article 76), setting a minimum age for marriage at eighteen years for both sexes (article 124), and the commitment by the state to empowering women, equal opportunities and protection from all forms of violence (article 128). The draft constitution acknowledged that all citizens should enjoy equal rights and liberties, free from discrimination for reasons of gender or other factors (article 75). Nevertheless, this article was undermined by article 135, which noted that all rights and freedoms would be guaranteed 'as long as they do not conflict with the conclusive provisions of the Islamic shariah'.

8 The farce of the 2012 Syrian constitution

The 2012 constitution was one of the main reforms adopted by the Bashar al-Assad regime in response to the popular protests which shook the country from March 2011 onwards. The constitutional reform was not the result of dialogue with the revolutionary forces, but a unilateral strategy by the regime for the purpose of retaining power (Álvarez-Ossorio 2015: 171; Heydemann 2014). On 15 October 2011 President al-Assad set up a committee comprised of twenty-nine members, including three women, which had the mission of drawing up a new constitution. The committee was comprised of legal experts, members of the regime and one single representative of the so-called 'loyal opposition' –Qadri Jamil, a communist politician who was known for his declarations in favour of reforming the system without any need to abolish the regime. The draft constitution was officially published on 15 February 2012, to be later submitted to referendum on 26 February 2012. According to official data, the draft constitution was endorsed by 89.4 per cent of voters, though a turnout of only 57.4 per cent was recorded – a rather unlikely figure if we consider that much of the country was not under the regime's control (particularly the provinces of Homs, Hama, Daraa, Idlib and Raqqa) and that the referendum was boycotted by most of the opposition and revolutionary forces (Álvarez-Ossorio 2015: 172).

The 2012 constitution introduced a package of reforms that failed to favour the democratisation of the state, but instead strengthened the authoritarian system and left intact the enormous power held by the president. In theory, the president shares executive authority with the prime minister (article 83), but in practice his power enables him to exert great control over the government. The president appoints his deputies and vice-president (article 91), the prime minister, ministers and deputy ministers (article 97), as well as supervising the implementation of all state policy (article 98). Furthermore, he may assume legislative authority when the People's Council is not in session. The president has the power to dissolve the People's Council (article 111), propose legislation (article 112) and veto laws (article 100). In addition, in his function as commander in chief of the army and armed forces (article 105), he can make decisions regarding military power, declaring war and concluding peace agreements (article 102).

The new constitution stipulates that the president may serve a maximum of two seven-year terms (article 88). However, this measure is not retroactive in its effect, which means that President Bashar al-Assad can stand again for elections and extend his mandate until 2028. What is even more worrying is the fact that the constitution allows the current president to carry on in power after his mandate has expired if no new head of state is elected (article 87). Furthermore, the criteria established for presidential candidates favour those close to the regime and represent a disadvantage for religious minorities and political dissidents who have been political prisoners or have been forced to leave the country in recent years. The constitutional text specifies that all candidates must be Muslim, enjoy civil and political rights, and must not have been convicted of a dishonourable felony (even if they were reinstated); they must have been living permanently in Syria uninterruptedly for the previous ten years, and they must not be married to a foreign woman (article 84).

The 2012 constitution made some progress in terms of greater openness to political pluralism (article 8). A positive feature was also the removal of the article 8 of the previous 1973 constitution stating that Ba'ath Party was 'the leading party in the society and the state'. The creation of a plural system, however, has not favoured democratic change; instead it has been used by the regime as a discursive tool to rebuild itself and legitimise its power.

Another of the nominal changes was the introduction of the concept 'human rights' into the 2012 constitutional text, and which did not exist in the 1973 constitution. In a positive sense, the constitutional reform endorses equality among citizens and prohibits all discrimination on the grounds of sex (article 33). The text includes the article that existed in the 1973 constitution, guaranteeing women full participation in political, social, cultural and economic life. Moreover, it acknowledges freedom as a 'sacred right' and commits the state to guaranteeing the principle of equal opportunities for all (article 33).

9 The Sultanate of Oman: the liberalisation of absolutism in the 2011 Basic Law

The Sultanate of Oman has no constitution, yet it adopted the Basic Statute of the State or Basic Law on 6 November 1996, which was amended in 2011. The 2011 reform was a political liberalisation measure issued in response to the popular protests that broke out in the sultanate in January 2011. In March 2011 Sultan Qaboos bin Said al-Said ordered that a technical committee of specialists be created to prepare the constitutional reform. The five amendments to the eighty-one articles of the Basic Law were ratified six months later, on 20 October 2011, via Royal Decree 99/2011 (Szmolka 2014: 130–4).

The constitutional process was neither transparent nor participatory, taking place as it did within the framework of an absolutist political system. What is significant about it is the fact that it was a tentative step in the transformation of an absolute monarchy into a constitutional monarchy, with several regulatory and legislative powers being ceded to the Council of Oman. Previously, both parliamentary houses – the Majlis al-Dawla (the State Council, the members of which are appointed by the sultan), and the Majlis al-Shura (the Advisory Council, made up of representatives elected via universal suffrage) – had performed a merely consultative function. At present the Council of Oman has the power to draft laws, but the sultan will always have the final word in terms of their enactment and ratification. He also has the power to dissolve the Shura Council and to call new elections, while maintaining control over parliament.

The sultan of Oman is head of state and supreme commander of the armed forces. He is also the prime minister and presides over the specialised councils, unless he delegates this function to a third party. The sultan also appoints the members of the cabinet, the state council and other senior officials of the country's general administration. He is responsible for appointing judges and Oman's foreign policy representatives as well as establishing and regulating the state administrative apparatus. He also enacts laws, signs international treaties, declares wars and makes peace.

The new feature in the 2011 constitutional amendment was the change in the process determining the succession to the throne. According to the article 6 of the Basic Law the Royal Family Council shall, within three days of the throne falling vacant, determine the successor to the throne. However, if no agreement is reached, the Defence Council, together with the chairmen of both Houses of Parliament and the chairman of the Supreme Court, along with two of his senior deputies, shall instate the person designed by the sultan in his letter to the Royal Family Council. The function of these six state officials is purely symbolic, but it implies that at least one representative of the people – the chairman of the elected Shura Council – participates in the process of confirming the legitimate successor to the throne, making the process more transparent.

The 2011 amendment did not introduce any changes in the area of human rights. It is worth noting, however, that article 17 of the Basic Law guarantees equality between all citizens, without any discrimination for reasons of 'gender, origin, colour, language, religion, sect, domicile or social status'.

10 The 2012 constitution of the Kingdom of Bahrain: a frustrated aspiration for democratic change

One of the main demands by protestors in Bahrain, where demonstrations began on 14 February 2011, was to reform the constitution to establish a constitutional monarchy where the king's powers would be of a symbolic nature. To resolve the political crisis, King Hamad bin Isa al-Khalifa convened a national dialogue, which was inaugurated on 2 July 2011 and brought together some 300 representatives from the different political groups (37 per cent), civil society organisations (36 per cent), public opinion leaders (21 per cent) and the mass media (6 per cent). The opposition was granted thirty-five seats (11.6 per cent), of which only five were assigned to the main Shiite Islamist party, al-Wefaq, which had won 45 per cent of the seats in the October 2010 parliamentary elections. Al-Wefaq's participation in the national dialogue did not last long, as on 18 July 2011 the party announced its withdrawal from the process in protest at the Sunni regime's violent repression of the Shiite protest movement. In spite of the opposition's withdrawal, the dialogue continued until late July 2011, producing as a result a package of 291 recommendations for political, social and economic reforms that were used as reference points for drafting amendments to the constitution. It is worth noting that the results of the national dialogue, on which the 2012 draft constitution was based, were approved by the government, but rejected by the opposition (Szmolka 2014: 130–4).

On 16 January 2012 King Hamad announced the constitutional amendments, which were put to the vote in both the Council of Deputies and the Shura Council in April, and subsequently ratified by royal decree on 3 May 2012. The 2012 constitutional reform was widely criticised by the opposition as insufficient, given that it did not respond to the demands formulated in the Manama Document, issued on 12 October 2011. This document was signed by five opposition parties: the Shiite Islamists of al-Wefaq, the left-wing parties (Wa'ad and the National Democratic Gathering Society), the Nationalist Democratic Assembly closely linked to the Iraqi Ba'ath Party, and al-Ikhaa, the Shiite party of Persian descendants. In spite of its importance, the document was ignored by government, thus highlighting the limits of the top-down change authorised by the king and led by the crown prince.

The amendments to the 2012 constitution did not restrict the absolute powers of the king, who is head of state, supreme commander of the defence forces, the person responsible for appointing and removing members of the Shura Council, judges, the prime minister and the ministers proposed by the latter. The hereditary succession to the throne follows the male descendants of the al-Khalifa dynasty, beginning with the firstborn son.

The constitutional reform introduced some improvements regarding the increasing of parliamentary powers, including a greater capacity to control government and the budget. However, this was not sufficient for the opposition, who aspired to having an elected government, introducing a more redistributive electoral system, abolishing the Shura Council, designated by the king, and founding an elected single-chamber parliament. The constitutional reform was also disappointing in terms of improving safeguards for human rights and for establishing specific measures to prevent discrimination against the majority Shiite population by the minority Sunni elite. Articles 1, 5 and 18 of the 2012 constitution, as stipulated in the previous 2002 version, guarantee equality between men and women and prohibit gender-based discrimination. Nevertheless, this equality is only guaranteed if it is compatible with 'the provisions of Islamic shariah' (article 5).

Table 5.1 Constitutional processes in MENA countries (2011–16)

Countries and their constitutions	Causal factor	Promoter	Representation and political interaction	Regulation that determines the process	Institutional mechanisms	Process	Reforms	Approval mechanisms	Constitutional referendum (Approved / voter turnout)
Algeria (2016)	Popular uprising	President	Controlled, conditional inclusion	– 2008 constitution – 2014 Constitutional Review Law	– Two rounds of consultations with social and political actors – 5-member experts' commission	Semi-transparent	Greater consensus, though not unanimous; mostly rejected by the opposition	– Block vote by both chambers of parliament – Enacted by the president of the Republic	No
Morocco (2011)	Popular uprising	The king	Conditional inclusion, exclusion and self-exclusion	King's address of 9 March 2011	– Advisory committee for constitutional reform – Political mechanism for monitoring constitutional reform – Royal cabinet – King	Semi-transparent	– Consensus-building between most political parties – Dissent from the semi-institutional and non-institutional opposition, and from the 20 February Movement	Referendum of 1 July 2011	Yes (98.5 per cent/ 73.46 per cent)
Tunisia (2014)	Popular uprising	– The Quartet headed by UGTT – The National Dialogue	Inclusion and consensus	– 2011 Constitutional Law 2011-6 regulating the temporary organisation of public powers – National Dialogue road map, 5 October 2013	– National Dialogue consensus committee – National constituent assembly	Almost entirely transparent	Compromise and consensus	– Voted by the National Constituent Assembly – Enacted by the president of the Republic	No
Egypt (2014)	Military coup	Interim president / military power	Non-inclusion	Constitutional declaration 8 July 2013	– 10-member technical committee – 50-member constitutional assembly	Non-transparent	Non-consensual	– Voted by the constitutional assembly – Public referendum	Yes (98.1 per cent / 38.6 per cent)

Table 5.1 Constitutional processes in MENA countries (2011–16) (*cont.*)

Countries and their constitutions	Causal factor	Promoter	Representation and political interaction	Regulation that determines the process	Institutional mechanisms	Process	Reforms	Approval mechanisms	Constitutional referendum (Approved / voter turnout)
Jordan (2011 constitution, amended in 2014 and 2016)	Popular uprising	The king	Non-inclusion	Royal decree	Royal Committee on Constitutional Review (in 2011)	Non-transparent	Non-consensual	– Voted by the Chamber of Deputies – Voted by the Senate – Royal decree	No
Yemen (2015 draft constitution)	Popular uprising	– President – The National Dialogue Conference (NDC) – NDC-related Committees	Greater inclusion	– GCC Initiative – NDC Final Document – Presidential decrees	– 565-member NDC – 17-member Constitutional drafting technical committee – 82-member national authority for monitoring the implementation of NDC outcomes	Semi-transparent	Greater consensus	– Supervised by the NDC Outcomes Monitoring Committee – Public referendum	Process interrupted by civil war
Syria (2012)	Popular uprising	President	Non-inclusion	Presidential decree	29-member constitutional committee	Non-transparent	Non-consensual	– Public referendum – Presidential Decree 94/2012	Yes (according to the governmental data: 39.4 per cent/ 57.4 per cent)
Oman (2011 Basic Law)	Popular uprising	Sultan	Non-inclusion (no political parties exist)	Royal decree	Technical committee of specialists	Non-transparent	Non-consensual	Royal Decree 99/2011	No
Bahrain (2012)	Popular uprising	The king and the crown prince	Non-inclusion	Royal decree	2011 National dialogue	Non-transparent	Greater consensus in the national dialogue between groups loyal to the regime; rejected by the opposition	– Voted by the Council of Representatives – Voted by Shura Council – Royal Decree	No

Source: prepared by the author

11 Conclusions

The initial hypothesis of this research study, that constitutional reform processes have a decisive impact on the nature and scope of processes of political change, has been partly confirmed. Constitutional processes are relevant, but not determinant for political changes of a much more complex nature. Political processes are structured by power relations, which at the same time determine the nature and scope of the constitutional changes. In Tunisia a process of transition took place in a context of deep political polarisation between secularist and Islamic conservatives. This has hampered the constitutional process, resulting in four failed attempts at drafting a new constitution. The last national dialogue initiative and the consensus committee, however, succeeded in bringing together all the different representatives of the political spectrum. They worked as the artificers of this difficult compromise and hard-to-reach consensus, both of which facilitated the miracle of the first democratically drafted constitution in Tunisia's history.

The Tunisian laboratory thus highlights the importance of negotiation, compromise and the power of informal political arenas to overcome political crises and institutional collapse. A significant, albeit certainly imperfect, democratic procedure within the constitutional reform process also took place in Yemen, where the inclusion and participation of elites and change agents produced a consensus-based draft constitution that partially, but importantly, redefined the nature and power of the regime. However, this constitutional process was interrupted and halted when one of the rebel groups violated the agreement and then civil war broke out.

The constitutional amendments in Jordan (2011), Oman (2011), Bahrain (2012) and Syria (2012), meanwhile, were the product of strategies for survival by the respective regimes, and were promoted 'top-down' through a process that excluded the revolutionary movements and all opposition groups not loyal to the regime. In the case of Egypt the hegemony of the Islamist parties, who had been elected democratically, resulted in the self-exclusion of the liberal and secular parties from the 2012 constitutional reform. Shortly after the 2013 Egyptian *coup d'état*, the use of a legal recourse to outlaw the Muslim Brotherhood enabled the old elites to get rid of a powerful rival from the 2014 constitutional process. Strategies of exclusion – or rather, the non-inclusion of specific actors in the constitutional processes – helped to ensure the survival of the authoritarian regimes in Syria and Jordan, and to shape a new form of authoritarianism in Egypt.

In Algeria the participation of different political parties and civil society in the constitutional process was restricted to consultations of a non-binding nature, and which were carried out under the guidance of the regime, as a result of which certain opposition groups turned down the government's invitation to take part in the constitutional process. The National Liberation Front, which has a large majority in both chambers of parliament and it is closely linked to President Bouteflika, wielded enough power to singularly push their position through and passed the 2016 constitutional amendments in the parliament without the opposition's support. In Morocco the process of drafting the new constitution allowed the authorities to introduce some of the political demands called for over recent years, though without losing control of the process. The reform operation refocused the debate towards a text framed within axes of reference highly influenced by the king's address of 9 March, which demarcated the outlines of the epistemic framework of what was possible. The royal palace has ably demonstrated its ability to define the agenda and the public space for discussion with an argumentative discourse based on participation and consensus. The reform process succeeded in galvanising the actors as a whole, and in placing them on one side or the other of the line of inclusion.

Tunisia, which is currently the only democratic system in the region, has constitutionalised a kind of hybrid (half-parliamentary, half-presidential) government. This includes a bicephalous executive, which shares executive and legislative powers, and enforced cohabitation spaces and a vigorous assembly which requires, on a large number of issues, the agreement of an absolute parliamentary majority and in which particular recognition is made of the scrutiny exercised by the opposition.

The wide-ranging powers held by heads of state in Syria, Jordan, Oman, Bahrain, Algeria, Morocco and Egypt have not been limited; instead, in some cases they have been expanded (Jordan), extended (the renovation of President al-Assad's mandate in Syria) or redefined (Morocco). Furthermore, significant powers have been granted to the coup perpetrators in Egypt (military elite). At the same time, a series of liberalisation reforms have been adopted, such as the introduction of political pluralism in Syria; the restriction of the presidential mandate in Algeria to two terms of office; the constitutionalisation of a representative government and a wider sphere of action for the head of government in Morocco; the granting of limited legislative power to the parliament in Oman; the enlarging of the competences of the Council of Representatives in Bahrain; the establishing of accountability mechanisms for the government and parliament in Jordan; the granting of greater legislative, regulatory and executive control powers to parliament in Morocco; the selective progress made on the issues of human rights and civil liberties in Jordan, Syria, Egypt, Algeria and Morocco; and the improved safeguards for gender equality and women's rights in Syria, Egypt, Algeria, Morocco and Tunisia.

A relatively limited impact of these liberalisation reforms until now may suggest a strategy of 'authoritarian upgrading' (Heydemann 2007) rather than democratisation. Their potential positive repercussions in terms of long-term change, however, should not be underestimated. Moreover, the important socio-economic and political developments might occur outside the bounds of the authoritarian resilience paradigm. The experience of the Arab Spring shows that even the most repressive regimes of Hosni Mubarak, Zine al-Abidine Ben Ali, Ali Abdullah Saleh and Muammar al-Gaddafi, who all made use of the mechanisms through which they were seemingly able to reconfigure authoritarian power by adopting nominally liberalising reforms, did not survive the popular uprisings (Pace and Cavatorta 2012: 127). In any event, the true scope of the political changes through constitutional reforms remains to be seen. It requires a longer-term perspective to enable us to discern how authoritarian regimes have been reconfigured; how Tunisia's young democracy is on the way to becoming gradually institutionalised and consolidated; and how the reforms have impacted on the revolutionary movements for change, particularly in those contexts that are still highly politically unstable, such as Syria and Yemen.

References

Al-Ali, Zaid (2016), 'Egypt's third constitution in three years: a critical analysis', in Bernard Rougier and Stéphane Lacroix (eds), *Egypt's Revolutions: Politics, Religion, and Social Movements*, New York: Palgrave Macmillan, pp. 123–38.

Álvarez-Ossorio, Ignacio (2015), 'El enroque autoritario del régimen sirio: de la revuelta popular a la guerra civil', *Revista CIDOB d'Afers Internacionals*, 109: 157–76.

Bani Salameh, Mohammed T. and Azzam A. Ananzah (2015), 'Constitutional reforms in Jordan: a critical analysis', *Digest of Middle East Studies*, 24: 139–60.

Ben Achour, Rafâa (2014), 'La Constitution tunisienne du 27 janvier 2014', *Revue Française de Droit Constitutionnel*, 4 (100): 783–801.

Benyettou, Wissam (2015), 'Will Algeria Start 2016 with a New Constitution? Long-awaited Constitutional Revision and the Road to Democratic Transition', ConstitutionNet, November 24. Available at <http://www.constitutionnet.org/news/will-algeria-start-2016-new-constitution-long-awaited-constitutional-revision-and-road> (last accessed 12 July 2016).

Desrues, Thierry (2012), 'Le Mouvement du 20 février et le régime marocain: contestation, révision constitutionnelle et élections', *L'Année du Maghreb*, VIII: 359–89.

Feliu, Laura and María Angustias Parejo, (2013) 'Morocco: the reinvention of an authoritarian system', in Ferran Izquierdo (ed.), *Political Regimes in the Arab World*, Abingdon and New York: Routledge, pp. 70–99.

Gluck, Jason and Michele Brandt (2015), *Participatory and Inclusive Constitution Making: Giving Voice to the Demands of Citizens in the Wake of the Arab Spring*, Washington, DC: United States Institute of Peace.

Gobe, Éric and Larbi Chouikha (2014), 'La Tunisie politique en 2013: de la bipolarisation idéologique au "consensus constitutionnel"?', *L'Année du Maghreb*, 11: 301–322.

Gobe, Éric and Larbi Chouikha (2015), 'La Tunisie de la Constitution aux élections: la fin de la transition politique?', *L'Année du Maghreb*, 13: 261–80.

Heydemann, Steven (2007), *Upgrading Authoritarianism in the Arab World*, Analysis Paper 13 (October), Washington, DC: The Brookings Institution.

Heydemann, Steven (2014), 'Syria and the future of authoritarianism', in Larry Diamond and Marc F. Plattner (eds), *Democratization and Authoritarianism in the Arab World*, Baltimore: Johns Hopkins University Press, pp. 300–14.

Martínez-Fuentes, Guadalupe (2014), 'Túnez: nueva constitución y la democracia posible', Real Instituto Elcano, *ARI* 7/2014: 1–9.

Meyer-Resende, Michael (2014), Egypt: *In-depth Analysis on the Main Elements of the New Constitution*, Brussels: Directorate-General for External Policies of the European Union.

Pace, Michelle and Francesco Cavatorta (2012), 'The Arab uprisings in theoretical Perspective: an introduction', Mediterranean Politics, 17 (2): 125–38.

Parejo, María Angustias (2010), 'Liberalización política y redefinición de la oposición: la *Kutla* y la reforma constitucional en Marruecos (1992–2006)', *Miscelánea de Estudios Árabes y Hebraicos*, 59: 91–114.

Parejo, María Angustias (2015), 'Cambio y límites del cambio en Marruecos: propuestas de reforma constitucional sobre el Gobierno', *Revista CIDOB d'Afers Internacionals*, 109: 23–44.

Parejo, María Angustias and Laura Feliu (2013), 'Identidad y regionalización: los actores políticos marroquíes ante la reforma constitucional de 2011', *Revista de Investigaciones Políticas y Sociológicas*, 12 (2): 109–26.

Philbrick, Stacey (2016), 'Yemen, five years gone', *in Reflections Five Years After the Uprisings*, POMEPS Studies, 18: 60–2.

Strzelecka, Ewa (2015), *Gender, Culture, Islam and Development: the Construction of a Political Culture of Feminist Resistance in Yemen*, PhD Dissertation, University of Granada.

Szmolka, Inmaculada (2014), 'Political change in North Africa and Arab Middle East: constitutional reforms and electoral processes', *Arab Studies Quarterly*, 36 (2): 128–48.

Szmolka, Inmaculada (2015), 'Exclusionary and non-consensual transitions versus inclusive and consensual democratizations: the cases of Egypt and Tunisia', *Arab Studies Quarterly*, 37 (1): 73–95.

Chapter 6

Government and power relations

Victoria Veguilla

1 Introduction

This chapter analyses social and political processes in Middle East and North Africa (MENA) regimes from the perspective of their stability and legitimacy. This includes both the results in terms of the possible reconfiguration of actors and the capacity of institutions to respond to social demands and manage violence. It focuses on the key institution of government, as it may have legislative and executive functions that are entirely independent of competitive democratic elections. These functions are shared with other actors, such as parliament, and – depending on the regime – with the president of the republic, monarchy, army, judicial power, or even with international organisations or foreign countries. In these latter cases, regime hybrid theory distinguishes between 'veto players' and 'reserved domains'. Both concepts involve individual or collective actors that govern without the checks and balances of other institutions, either informal 'political' actors such as the army ('veto players') (Morlino 2008; Szmolka 2010b: 115–16), or formal actors with extraordinary powers ('reserved domains') such as executive monarchies (Wigell 2008: 238; Szmolka 2010b: 116).

This chapter examines the plurality of actors that have governed in the post-Arab Spring MENA region, from a comparative perspective. It seeks to identify both formal and informal actors that have had an impact on decision-making, and therefore offers a fragmented power scenario (Signoles 2006: 240; Veguilla 2011: 240). In particular, the figure of the 'people actor' (Gobe 2012) emerges, to varying degrees depending on the country, that may participate in change process by: helping define the political agenda, accelerating or redirecting decisions, eroding or consolidating the legitimacy of specific actors – or of the process itself – and participating in ad hoc decision-making institutions. In some countries specific actors can be identified that are key to understanding how traditional authorities have lost control of their whole territory or they emerge from the decay process of the previous regime. This is the case, for example, of the militias or other armed groups in Libya, Yemen and Syria.

This chapter: (1) analyses the roles assumed by governments, but also their interaction with other actors, in the various phases of each process; (2) addresses the capacity of governments to respond (produce outputs) to social demands, linking this with their decision-making responsibilities (being accountable in government) and eventual democratic electoral legitimacy (or not); and (3) concludes by assessing their management of the legitimate use of violence.

2 Actors in the processes: decision-making and legitimacy

This section provides a chronology of political developments since the eruption of the Arab Spring and identifies the role played by governments, including their degree of stability (duration) and legitimacy (bases of support) in various processes, as well as the institutional reconfiguration of regimes (in terms of changes in their systems of checks and balances).

2.1 The differentiated role of governments in the Tunisian and Egyptian change processes

Social protests in Tunisia and Egypt led to the fall of their respective presidents: Zine al-Abidine Ben Ali on 14 January 2011 and Hosni Mubarak on 11 February 2011. In both cases, collapse occurred after the army refused to suppress demonstrations by force. However, in the case of Egypt, the army, as well as the United States government and several European countries, were in favour of the president's resignation. In fact, the trajectories of the two regimes have been very different, as well as their end results. In Tunisia the transition process began with the appointment of the president of the House of Deputies, Fouad Mebazaa, to the post of acting president, in line with that established in article 57 of the 1959 constitution. However, the transition process was led by the head of government, who formed ad hoc commissions to implement the distinct stages through which the process has passed. In Egypt, on the other hand, the transfer of powers did not follow the path prescribed in article 84 of the 1971 constitution. The actor who assumed leadership of the process was a non-constitutional military institution, the Supreme Council of the Armed Forces (SCAF), which was headed by the commander in chief of the armed forces and Mubarak's minister of defence for nearly twenty years, Marshall Mohammed Hussein Tantawi. Since the military coup that established the republic on the 23 July 1952, the army has enjoyed a privileged position in the Egyptian regime, 'a kind of "controlled" institutional autonomy based on privileges, especially economic' (Droz-Vincent 2015: 27). Additionally, the built and projected image of the army from the Nasserian era is of a guardian of the nation, which guarantees the country's stability and acts for Egypt, but also for a state that 'belongs' to them (Droz-Vincent 2015: 27). The Egyptian minister of defence chose a minister from his ranks and had an informal power of veto. The minister's role in the process can be explained by his need to guarantee his position in the political system and safeguard his corporate and economic interests. In Tunisia, however, the armed forces have played a secondary role to the security forces and have subordinated themselves to civilian authority (Droz-Vincent 2015: 27).

In both cases, the first governments following the uprisings have been on the one hand continuist and, on the other, challenged by social mobilisations. In this context the 'people-actor' (Gobe 2012) became the opposition in Tunisia that accused the government of wanting to redirect the transitionary process. The protesters groups were organised first in 'The 14th January Front', and a month later in the High Commission for the Fulfilment of the Goals of the Revolution (HCFGR), an organisation that claims revolutionary legitimacy and is recognised as an actor on the transitional road map. Strong social pressure led to Mohamed Ghannouchi, who was prime minister since 1999, dissolving his government and resigning. At this time the interim president appointed Beji Caïd Essebsi as prime minister. Essebsi was a high ranking official during the dictatorial regimes of Habib Bourguiba and his successor Ben Ali, and approved the creation of the High Commission for the Fulfilment of the Goals of the Revolution, Political Reform and Democratic Transition to drive the transition process, of which the HCFGR was planned to form a part. In Egypt the 'people-actor' also managed to achieve the resignation of the prime minister. However, in this case, it was the SCAF that accumulated executive and legislative powers during the transition process and controlled changes in the composition of the government.

The holding of competitive elections in both countries required modification of the previous electoral legislation and a change in the system of hegemonic parties – dominated by the Democratic Constitutional Rally (DCR) in Tunisia and the National Democratic Party (NDP) in Egypt – both 'illegal'– to a multiparty system. In both cases the predominant cleavage was religious and the first elections saw a clear victory for Ennahda in Tunisia and for the Freedom and Justice Party (FJP), the political wing of the Muslim Brotherhood (MB), in Egypt. The Islamist formations had strong grassroots support at the start of the protests (Burgat 2008; Allal and Geisser 2011; Steuer 2013), and their illegal status structured the debates and conditioned internal politics in both countries, which transformed them into key actors.

The Muslim Brotherhood had a complex relationship with the SCAF because it shared a similar approach as to how the transition should be carried out.

In Tunisia the victory of Ennahda with 41 per cent of the seats, in a polarised context, did not impede dialogue with other formations. This was in part because the High Commission's method favoured a scenario without absolute majorities and also because Ennahda was aware of the international suspicion that it provoked. Ennahda therefore sought to form a coalition ('the Troika') with Ettakatol and the Congress for the Republic (CPR, in its French acronym), which was in opposition during the Ben Ali regime. Ettakatol represents the Tunisian bourgeoisie and the educated middle class, while the CPR, which came second in the elections, is a formation that embraces former Islamist militants and that had demonstrated its willingness to govern with Ennahda throughout the electoral process (Gobe 2012). The opposition grew fearful that the recently formed government was going to appropriate the whole process in general, and monopolise the process of writing the constitution in particular.

In Egypt the large majority obtained in the elections by the Islamic formations panicked the opposition and army, as they would have control over the writing of the constitution. The election of the Constituent Assembly sharply divided the political actors and was the object of a number of significant judicial decisions. Eventually the Assembly was formed on 7 June 2012 with an Islamist majority and a membership reduced to thirty-nine deputies.

Since that time the two countries have gone in divergent directions. On 5 October 2013 a Tunisian road map was approved that led to the resignation of the government,[1] the formation of a technocratic transition government, approval of the constitution, adoption of an electoral law and the holding of legislative and presidential elections in 2014. In Egypt, on the other hand, the transfer of powers to a civil institution was postponed. Furthermore, a series of legal rulings reinforced the power of the judiciary in the process. The High Commission for Presidential Elections invalidated ten candidacies, for example, and the Supreme Constitutional Court declared the electoral law that governed the election of the People's Assembly unconstitutional. The SCAF therefore dissolved it and took legislative control until the following elections.

In this context, the presidential elections of June held no surprises: the leader of the FJP, Mohammed Morsi, won 51.7 per cent of the votes, which thereafter allowed him to control the political and constituent process and draft, without consensus in a divided country, the constitution that was approved in a referendum on 25 December 2012. The constitutional text of 2012 enshrined 'the instability' (de Cara 2014: 41) by including a univocal vision of society and the way to govern. The lack of consensus led to unanimous rejection by all opposition forces (liberals, nationalists, socialists and religious minorities), in a climate of growing tension and social protest.

The direction of President Morsi's mandate thereafter can be understood by his dependence on the Muslim Brotherhood, the content of the 2012 constitution and the prevailing political polarisation. From the opposition's point of view, the Islamist organisation usurped the popular will when it submitted all the elected posts to an opaque and heavily anti-democratic decision centre (Steuer 2013).

The elected president's loss of legitimacy became evident on 30 June 2013 when a massive demonstration demanded his resignation and, in part, military intervention. The coup – led by General Abdel Fattah al-Sisi, president of the SCAF[2] – took place on 3 July 2013, and immediately afterwards the 2012 constitution was suspended. Adly Mansour, president of the Supreme Constitutional Court, was appointed interim president of the republic. On 23 September 2013 the Muslim Brotherhood was declared a terrorist organisation and many of its leaders, Mohammed Morsi included, were detained.

The Tunisian constitution approved by a technocratic government in January 2014 renewed the semi-presidential form of government but introduced new balances between the executive powers (the president of the republic and head of government) and the legislative power. The new legislative authority, the People's Assembly, only requires ten members to initiate the legislative process (draft laws), which grants it a significant legislative role. Through the Constitutional Court it can also play a role, for example, in dismissing the president of the republic. Similarly, Egypt's institutional structure, following approval in January 2014 of a new constitutional text, is characterised by a semi-presidential regime in which the president exercises executive power but where the House of Representatives maintains significant influence. The Egyptian constitution gives a significant role to judicial power in the political system, specifically to the Supreme Constitutional Court, thanks to the influence of magistrates in its development (Fedtke 2014: 9). The Court recovered the legal authority to interpret article 2 of the constitution and has autonomy because it has its own system of appointments and financing. The 2014 Tunisian constitution confers no special status to the army. In Egypt, on the other hand, while the armed forces were not constitutionalised until 2012, they consolidated their authority as a political actor, thanks to the control they were able to exercise during the constitutional process.

Following approval of the respective constitutions, legislative and presidential elections took place in both countries. The legislative elections of 26 October in Tunisia were won by Nidaa Tounes, a party created in 2012 by Beji Caïd Essebsi, who then sought to form a coalition government with Ennahda, the CPR and Ettakatol. The December presidential elections also converted its leader into head of state.[3] In Tunisia, following the 2014 election, Nidaa Tounes controlled the government and the presidency, which enabled them to monopolise political power. Essebsi's executive capacity, limited to a semi-presidential system of 'counterweight government' among the institutions, was in this way reinforced. However, the constitution requires the president to renounce leadership of his or her political party – and the election of the president's son as secretary general led to some deputies leaving the parliamentary group, which modified the balance in parliament and government in favour of the Islamist party (Bobin 2016). At the time of writing a national unity government is being formed.

In May 2014 Marshall al-Sisi won the Egyptian presidential elections with 96 per cent of the vote, against a single candidate, the progressive Hamdeen Sabahi, who denounced electoral irregularities. New parliamentary elections were called for October 2015, in a 'climate of harassment of any dissident voice, whether it be Islamist or laic' (González 2015: 2). The al-Nour Party stood again but the other political formations, such as the youth movements, refused to legitimise a process that did not offer even minimum guarantees. Furthermore, the electoral law approved by al-Sisi months before the legislative elections, reinforced the mixed system of candidacies, granting only 120 seats to the list of political parties. In practice, this only consolidated personalism (local personalities) and clientelism, and ensured that parliament was structured around private rather than ideological interests (González 2015: 3).

2.2 Reformist processes controlled by the monarchic institution: Morocco and Jordan

Morocco and Jordan have carried out reform processes that have been tightly overseen by their respective sovereigns. In both countries social movements preceded these political changes. Protests against the Jordanian regime intensified in March 2011 with large demonstrations in Amman. The actors were heterogeneous and for the first time included Jordanian tribes that demanded, among other things, more responsible government (Melián 2015: 144). In Morocco, on 20 February, thousands of demonstrators took to the streets in various cities, organised by young people via various social networks and organisations (Desrues 2012). The date gave name to the opposition movement (20 February or 20-F), which subsequently united various social and political organisations as well as key personalities in Moroccan society.

Following the first protests in Morocco, King Mohammed VI created a Consultative Commission for the Reform of the Constitution, while in Jordan, King Abdullah II created the Royal Commission for Constitutional Review. In the former case, the result was a new constitutional text approved in a referendum; in the latter the result was a reform of a text whose social legitimacy was tested in the 2013 legislative elections (Melián 2015: 149). In neither case have the changes involved a substantial redistribution of power nor, therefore, a consequent loss of institutional hegemony by the monarchy. In Morocco, 'it passed from a government that was only in the hands of the king to a shared government' (Parejo 2015: 26) where the king 'conserves legislative and executive powers that are inappropriate in a democracy', such as the appointment and dismissal of the head of government, presidency of the council of ministers, the issuing of legal texts by *dahir* (royal decree), and the legal authority to dissolve parliament without the head of government's countersignature. In the case of Jordan, the changes are barely noticeable. The king is only obliged to consult the Lower House to appoint the prime minister. Besides, parliament has been strengthened in a small way through a limitation on government to approve draft laws (Szmolka 2013: 914). In neither case, however, do the changes undermine the position that the monarchies occupy at the apex of the system, nor affect in any significant way their 'reserved domains'.

The 20-F Movement and minority hard-left parties refused to participate in the Moroccan constitutional process, as they argued that the new text should emerge from a constituent assembly and sought more profound reforms. On the one hand, the remaining opposition groups participated in the process through consultative memorandums (Parejo 2015). On the other, the Jordanian opposition boycotted the institutional electoral and political reform processes. The Islamic Action Front (IAF), linked to the Muslim Brotherhood, refused to legitimise the 2013 elections, as did the minority left-wing parties.

The changes were put to the test following the legislative elections in Morocco in September 2011, and in Jordan in 2013. In the Moroccan elections the Islamist formation the Justice and Development Party (Parti de la Justice et du Développement, PJD) won the legislative elections for the first time, and Mohammed VI appointed Abdelilah Benkirane, in line with the new constitution, to form a government. However, the fragmented Moroccan party system impedes majorities and drives parties into forming coalition governments (Szmolka 2010a), which allow the monarchy to play the role of referee. The PJD sought the backing of Istiqlal, the Popular Movement and communists from the Party for Progress and Socialism to form its first government. In January 2013, however, the coalition government suffered its first internal crisis. Istiqlal demanded more protagonism within the coalition, particularly regarding ministerial posts. Fierce discussions led to a crisis that was eventually resolved without intervention by the monarchy. However, as a result the Istiqlal Party withdrew its ministers from the government and became part of the opposition. Its place was filled by ministers from the National Rally of Independents (Rassemblement National des Indépendants (RNI)) (Szmolka 2015b). The weakness of the Islamists was underscored, however, when Mohammed VI strengthened his position above the parties, and reinforced his legislative role in the system, by outlining his priorities for the new Education Law while negotiations between the PJD and the RNI to form a new government were still going on (Desrues 2014). In Jordan a government was formed on 30 March 2013, following two months of consultation between parliamentarians. The absence of the Islamic Action Front in parliament, however, undermined its legitimacy as the main opposition party was excluded.

The army has not played a leading role in either country. In Jordan the army has remained loyal to the monarchy throughout history (Melián 2015: 151). In Morocco, on the other hand, the military led two failed attacks against the monarch (Hassan II) in the 1970s, which resulted in its troops and high command being moved to Western Sahara, far from the centres of decision-making. This 'confinement strategy' was combined with an economic compensation package (Picard 2008: 322; Veguilla 2011: 265), as in the Egyptian case.

2.3 The governments questioned in the Gulf monarchies: Bahrain, Kuwait and Oman

The first Arab Spring demonstrations in the Gulf monarchies took place in Bahrain, on 14 February 2011, with daily protests for weeks against the government. The protests included both members of the Shiite majority and the Sunni minority, who were unhappy with the broken promises of political liberalisation made by King Hamad when he assumed power in 1999. The government initially gave concessions to the demonstrators: freedom for political prisoners and an amnesty for several members of opposition in exile. However, when the protests continued and spread across the country, the regime opted for strong repression, backed by 1,500 troops sent by Saudi Arabia and the United Arab Emirates (UAE). This intervention was justified by the authorities as being required to prevent Iranian influence on the protests,[4] but it was interpreted by the opposition parties (al-Wefaq, al-Wa'ad, the socialists and the Nasserists) as a foreign invasion aimed at crushing the dissidence. Al-Wefaq withdrew its eighteen members of parliament and advance partial elections in September 2011 were boycotted by opposition parties. The same occurred in November 2014 in the elections for the whole of the Council of Representatives (Zaccara and Saldaña 2015: 185–91).

In Kuwait relations between the National Assembly and the government have always been complex. The Assembly has fifty members chosen by universal suffrage, and has some control over the government, which is appointed by the prime minister and approved by the emir (Zaccara and Saldaña 2015: 187). The protests began in February by young people but the discontent quickly spread to all political opposition groups (Islamist,

Salafi, liberal and tribal). In March the opposition demanded the immediate resignation of the government and its prime minister Sheikh Nasser al-Mohammed Ahmad al-Jaber al-Sabah. The result was a governmental crisis, including the resignation of three ministers close to the royal family, who were accused of bribing parliamentarians. Demonstrations continued and, on 17 November, thousands of demonstrators entered parliament after the police employed force to break up a march that called for the resignation of the head of government – an event that led to the resignation of the prime minister. The fall of the government provoked, on 6 December, the dissolution of parliament and the appointment as prime minister of Sheikh Jaber al-Mubarak al-Hamad al-Sabah, at that time minister of defence (Szmolka 2013: 899). Disagreements between the emir and the prime minister, on the one hand, and the National Assembly, on the other, led in the following months to an institutional impasse and successive elections in which the Constitutional Court emerged as a front line political actor. The Court called for new legislative elections, declaring the parliaments that arose from the elections of February 2012 and December 2013 unconstitutional, and requiring new elections to be held that had to be regulated by the 2009 electoral law (Zaccara and Saldaña 2015: 193–4).

In Oman, where political parties are prohibited, social protests at the end of January 2011 provoked a partial change of government (six ministers) and the announcement of the reform of the Fundamental Law that would affect the Consultative Assembly (that had no legislative powers). This was a unilateral act by Sultan Qaboos bin Said al-Said, whose leadership went unquestioned during the protests, 'at least in a widespread and open way' (Zaccara and Saldaña 2015: 186). Assembly elections were held in October 2011 and October 2015, running all candidates as independents.

2.4 A 'marginal' Arab Spring?

In Saudi Arabia demonstrations were rare and concentrated in Shiite minority regions. In Qatar and in the UAE, on the other hand, there were no street demonstrations. While online protest activity on social networks has certainly been significant in all three countries[5] – and led to elections in 2011 – they produced either very limited reforms (for example, an expansion of the electoral census in the UAE) or none at all (in Saudi Arabia and Qatar).

In Algeria, on the other hand, legislative changes have either been limited and/or delayed. The ghost of the civil war, the loyalty of the army, the rentier character of its economy and the fragility of the opposition (including the Islamists) all help to understand the weak impact of the Arab Spring in this country. President Bouteflika rapidly shifted from a repressive strategy of containment to an announcement on 15 April promising political reforms in the near future. While the legal frameworks of the parties and political movements were modified in December 2011, however, there were no substantial changes (Szmolka 2013: 906). The constitutional reform, for its part, was not approved until February 2016 –with the abstention of the Workers Party and rejection by other opposition parties. Article 86 of the new text requires that the president of the republic consults parliament over the appointment of the prime minister.

In Lebanon the Arab Spring did not trigger criticisms of the political system but it underscored pre-existing conflicts (Szmolka 2013: 899). The crisis in Syria and the work of the Special Tribunal for Lebanon, established by the UN Security Council under pressure from the Bush administration to investigate the murder of Prime Minister Rafik Hariri in 2005, worsened instability in the country. The crisis centred around the withdrawal of various members of the national unity government, composed of thirty ministers pertaining to the two coalitions that polarised the political scene: on the one hand the 8 March Alliance, in which two Islamist Shiite organisations, Hezbollah and Amal, the Maronite Christians of the Free Patriotic Movement, and most recently the Druze of Walid Yumblat were grouped; and on the other the 14 March Alliance, that unites the anti-Syrian parties led by Saad Hariri.

In the non-Arab MENA countries (Turkey, Iran and Israel), the effects of the Arab Spring have been varied. In Turkey, for example, there have been protests against the authoritarian drift of the Erdoğan government,[6] while in Iran tough repression of the 'Green March' (2009 social protests that demanded political change) limited the organisation of demonstrations in 2011. In Israel, on the other hand, a youth protest movement, inspired by their Arab neighbours, railed against the lack of decent housing and the high price of basic goods. However, the Arab Spring has not led to governmental changes in any of these countries.

3 The 'social issue'

This chapter now turns to the capacity of governments to meet basic citizen demands (responsiveness), linking this analysis to their decision-making responsibilities (accountable government) and their possible democratic or non-democratic legitimation. On the one hand, this throws light on the capacity of regimes to produce outputs and respond to expectations about the role they should play in social matters, and on the other, the importance of redistributive policies in these government legitimation strategies.

3.1 Citizens' socio-economic expectations in the MENA countries

The Arab Spring in some MENA countries followed a rapid increase in sectoral social protests. In Tunisia, for example, following a long period of social demobilisation, inhabitants of the major mining towns and cities in the south-east region (Gafsa), in their majority young unemployed, in 2008 took large-scale collective action that was unique during Ben Ali's regime (Allal 2010: 107). In Egypt, from 2004, and above all from 2007 onwards, following syndicate elections in 2006, more than 1.7 million Egyptians protested in their places of work when faced with price increases and above all a deterioration in their standard of living (Duboc 2011). Between 2003 and 2004 the number of protests rose from eighty-six to 266, and tripled from 2006 to 2007, increasing from 222 to 614.[7] In Morocco since the 1990s, and more intensely during the first decade of the 2000s, sectoral protests have also increased, especially in small urban nucleus and in peripheral neighbourhoods of the large cities (Bennafla and Emperador 2010; Catusse 2011; Bogaert 2015; Bogaert and Emperador 2014).[8] Similarly, in several rentier countries there was a significant increase in sectoral protests in the period prior to the Arab Spring. In Algeria, for example, Parks (2013) identified during the first decade of the 2000s a growing tendency of Algerians to participate in local social and sectoral protests, organised by small associations seeking immediate solutions. This led to almost 9,000 riots taking place in 2009 (Parks 2013: 109).

Regional disparities and a shared perception of exclusion among the young is a constant that can be found across the MENA countries. The high rate of youth unemployment excludes a significant proportion from the system of social protection. Specifically, graduates face an eternal adolescence of dependency on their families, or a series of precarious or barely legitimate jobs. Young people have to confront a difficult situation even in the Gulf monarchies, in part due to rising housing costs in the 2000s (Flors 2012: 118–19), which impedes their economic independence until well past the age of thirty. While it is true to say that these phenomena, which provoke intergenerational tension, predominantly affect the middle class, the events that followed the death of Mohamed Bouazizi (a young Tunisian who died after immolating himself on 17 December 2010) united the 'plural' youth who shared the same feelings of marginalisation and exclusion (Flors 2012: 118–19). A further example took place in south Jordan where young unemployed people protested in 2011 and 2012 for jobs in the Jordanian phosphate business, greater access to resources distributed by the state and for admittance to specific posts (Fioroni 2015).

Joint social protests by the young over their marginalisation, exclusion and social 'declassing' (Flors 2012: 118–19) are fed by macroeconomic problems that cross many countries and highlight geographic disparities within national territories. As noted above, young people are excluded from the formal work market and therefore from social protection systems, and regimes have been incapable of facilitating access to the elite recruitment systems and therefore social mobility. In this context, various authors have identified a lack of correspondence between historically constructed expectations about the role that respective governments should play in social matters (outputs), and what they do in reality (Catusse 2006: 218; Catusse and Destremau 2010: 12; Bogaert and Emperador 2014: 177).

The developmentist and rentier paradigms (Beblawi and Luciani 1987) contribute to a better understanding of the role assumed by states in social matters following independence. From the developmentist perspective, the first stage of state construction is linked to an interventionist vision of the state in the economy (until the 1980s), a role where the state contributed to the building of social representations about 'good governance' in which governments acted as responsible actors in the provision of social welfare, thanks to the implementation in stages of 'development plans' and the incorporation into the public sector of broad sectors of the population. The rentier paradigm, on the other hand, applies to regimes with natural resources (for example, hydrocarbons), which favour redistributive policies with tax relief that along with other factors (Zaccara and Saldaña 2015) lead to greater adhesion to the regime and therefore a lower level of opposition. In both cases the policies are inflationist because they create excess administration with a growing demand for work posts, supplied through co-optation mechanisms. Public works therefore represented one of the main means of state redistribution (Catusse and Destremau 2010: 12), which has become a central axis of the social contract in each country and also a key source of postcolonial legitimacy and of aligning the population with the power structures (Bogaert and Emperador 2014: 177).

The intervention of international organisations, such as the International Monetary Fund and the World Bank, during the 1980s and 1990s (in Morocco, Jordan, Tunisia, Egypt, Yemen and Algeria) substantially reduced state redistributive capacity, which disproportionately affected the lower and lower-middle classes because of the reduction in state demand for employment and the elimination of social protection policies.[9] The generational gap is particularly acute here because the elder generation benefit from these policies while young people see their lack of access to public goods and services 'as an injustice, or as the breakdown of the contract over whom the political consent is allowed' (Bogaert and Emperador 2014: 179).

Governments have a precarious role in this scenario, as their appointment does not predominantly depend on results obtained by political formations in competitive elections. These actors emerge from contexts in which there is no electoral political pluralism and/or transparency: that is, they do not emerge from democratic processes (democratic elections) so they are not responsible to the electorate (they are non-accountable governments). Furthermore, their decision-making powers are limited by other institutional actors (heads of state or the armed forces) who in many cases have a power of veto or 'reserved domains', which makes the governmental legitimation process much more difficult. Their legitimacy is therefore eroded and they often become the target of critics and citizen dissatisfaction, who perceive them as being responsible for their situation. In Egypt, for example, the Muslim Brotherhood was made illegal following the 2013 military coup and the opposition no longer sees sufficient guarantees of transparency and impartiality to participate in the elections. Furthermore, President al-Sisi appoints the prime minister who forms the government that presents its programme to the House of Representatives (article 146). In Tunisia and Morocco, following the constitutional changes, the head of government is appointed by the president and the monarch, respectively, among the members of the political party or electoral coalition that have obtained the greatest number of seats in parliamentary elections. In Tunisia the semi-presidential regime has institutionalised a system of checks and balances that reduces the executive and legislative power of the government in favour of the president and the People's Assembly. On the other hand, in Morocco the king enjoys a hegemonic position in decision-making (he controls the political agenda), which limits the government's role despite its increased democratic legitimacy following the constitutional reform. The Lebanese constitution establishes confessional criteria for the appointment of the republic's president, the president of parliament and the prime minister. An alternative scenario exists in Jordan and the Gulf countries, where the appointment of heads of government is made by the governing monarchies. In Algeria the constitutional reform only obliges parliament to be consulted by the president for the appointment of the prime minister.

3.2 The redistributive responses of governments to protests in the context of the Arab Spring

The Arab Spring highlighted the unequal capacity of MENA governments to respond to the basic demands of citizens and, above all, their incapacity to meet the socio-economic expectations of a population that views the administration and politicians as corrupt, and questions the legitimacy of their regimes. Both in the economic contexts of structural adjustment and in rentier countries, the governing elites' redistributive policies became instruments of authoritarian consolidation, because of their capacity to co-opt elites, divide the opposition and contain dissatisfaction.

In Egypt and Morocco economic concessions to high ranking armed forces' officials (Picard 2008; Veguilla 2011) have occurred as a result of the overlapping of 'public' and 'private' sectors that explains the situation of the armed forces in the processes under analysis. Furthermore, in Morocco privatisations have reinforced the *makhzenian* modalities of government in the economic sphere (Hibou 1998: 160), thanks to uncertainty about rules and norms, which promotes discretionary decisions in favour of the most influential political and economic actors. Co-optation has become one of the key mechanisms for elite selection and control over dissidence. Similarly, in Tunisia privatisations have been employed to fragment and divide potential rivals of the regime (Hibou 1998: 160). Jordan, on the other hand, can be characterised as a model of patrimonial distribution based on wealth distribution, via subsidies, to reinforce alliances (Melián 2015: 135) and dampen dissatisfaction, above all among the population of Jordanian origin that monopolises posts in the public sector. In the Gulf countries the governing elites 'have historically silenced any demand for political change by means of a combination of distributive, co-optative and repressive mechanisms' (Zaccara and Saldaña 2015: 178).

In several MENA countries more transparent electoral processes have been accompanied by a parallel process of legitimacy erosion of the traditional institutions of representation (fundamentally the political parties and, with exceptions, the trade unions). Both processes have led to the emergence of local collectives that seek to share in the government distribution of goods and services. In Algeria and in Morocco increasing social protests have occurred together with the representative elites' loss of prestige (Catusse 2004; Parks 2013). In both cases localised protests are managed by the authorities through coercion and concession mechanisms (Bennafla and Emperador 2010; Parks 2013).

In the context of the Arab Spring, MENA governmental actors announced large-scale social and economic measures to mitigate the impact of the protests. In Algeria President Bouteflika led a containment strategy by pledging, for example, to raise public expenditure by 25 per cent, increase civil servant salaries, subsidise the price of basic products and finance measures to reduce youth unemployment (Hernando de Larramendi and Thieux 2011: 67). In Morocco and Jordan the governments announced a battery of socio-economic measures, but it was Mohammed VI and Abdullah II who announced the start of political reforms. Morocco, for example, dedicated €1,330 million to subsidise basic products, gas and petrol, contract 2,000 unemployed diplomats and broaden healthcare cover (Hernando de Larramendi and Thieux 2011: 64), while in Jordan the state invested US$125 million in basic goods and subsidies, as well as increasing civil servants' salaries. In Oman the sultan announced a 40 per cent increase in the minimum salary and the creation of 50,000 public posts; and in Saudi Arabia, where the royal family monopolises government posts, the king promised to invest €25,000 million immediately and nearly €300,000 million more in the following years in infrastructure, education and health, as well as in the creation of public employment and in better services for the unemployed (Zaccara and Saldaña 2015: 188–9).

Social expectations of welfare provision in the MENA countries continue to be strongly linked to government, to whom citizens both direct their demands for improvements and hold responsible for deterioration in their standard of living. The governments, for their part, are dependent on actors whose political responsibility and democratic legitimacy are either very limited or nil. With the exception of Tunisia, political reforms have been superficial, and so regimes have sought to contain dissatisfaction with sectoral policies aimed at specific social groups such as civil servants or unemployed diplomats. In this context, the Arab Spring clarified the continuity of states as key motors of development, a role in which they have been hegemonic since the early decades of state construction following independence. The challenge for the majority of regimes, in terms of legitimacy, is to address youth access to the labour market and reduce social inequalities, and to achieve that in the context of a crisis and with limited resources, which forces them to depend on third parties (international entities or Gulf countries).

4 The breakdown of regimes and fragmented authority

This section focuses on regime breakdown and the clear incapacity of governments to exercise control over their territory, which has forced them to compete with other actors who question their authority.

4.1 Fragmentation of actors and violence in Libya, Syria, Yemen and Iraq

In January 2011 protests in Yemen began, in February unrest erupted in Libya, and in March there were riots in Syria. The prevailing regimes in these three countries disintegrated, producing a fragmentation of actors who competed for control of territory and resources. On the other hand, in Iraq, the situation deteriorated due to the establishment of the self-proclaimed Islamic State (IS) in part of its territory (Szmolka 2015a: 15).

The profound social protests that began in Yemen in January 2011 contributed to the fall of Ali Abdullah Saleh in February 2012. Saleh had been in power since 1978, first as president of North Yemen and then from 1990 as leader of unified Yemen. The 'revolutionary youth' were also placed in a particular framework by institutional actors (fundamentally the Islamists of the Islah Party) (Bonnefoy and Poirier 2012), who were not able to get them to participate in the negotiations due to the mediating role played by the Gulf Cooperation Council. This Council influenced the transition by helping select the actors who were going to design the road map, legitimating the party in power – the General People's Congress (GPC) – and by regrouping the opposition in the Joint Meeting Parties.

Negotiations culminated with approval of the Implementation Mechanism for the Transition Process on 21 April 2011, where the Joint Meeting Parties considered the stages of the process and established the bases for the amnesty of Saleh and his family. The transfer of powers took place gradually. Abd Rabbuh Mansour Hadi, the vice-president since 1994, assumed the interim presidency and appointed Mohammed Basindawa prime minister on 27 November. Basindawa led a transitional national unity government of thirty-five members, formed in parity with members of the opposition and those loyal to President Saleh, until the elections of 21 February 2012. Basindawa continued as prime minister until the Houthi invasion of Sana'a, the Yemeni capital, on 21 September 2014.

In accordance with the road map, the only candidate for the presidency was Abd Rabbuh Mansour Hadi, who obtained 99.8 per cent of the vote. His mandate was reduced to two years, which was the period in which a new constitution had to be approved, together with a new electoral system. In March 2013 the National Dialogue Conference was created, an entity made up of 565 political and social representatives, with the objective of agreeing the bases upon which the future Yemeni constitution should be established. Their work ended in January 2014. However, the legislative and presidential elections forecast for 2014 have still not been held.

The supporters of Abdelmalik al-Houthi, leader of the political–religious movement that backed the minority Zaidi (Shiite), to which approximately a third of Yemenis formally pertain (Bonnefoy and Poirier 2012), carried out a political and military offensive in September 2014 that allowed them to take control of Sana'a, which led to President Hadi announcing his resignation on 22 January 2015. Hadi stated at the time that he was incapable of carrying out the transition process in a context dominated by armed conflict. The alliances constructed in the early period of the Yemeni Arab Spring against Saleh came together again at that time, leaving a scenario where the Houthis and Saleh's supporters (including a part of the armed forces) were pitted against the government and the al-Islah Party (Sunni). It is in this context that an international alliance led by Saudi Arabia carried out the 'Decisive Storm' military operation on the night of 26 March 2015.

In Libya, following the revolution of 17 February 2011 and the death in November of al-Gaddafi, who had been in power for over four decades, a completely different and more complex scenario emerged where a number of actors each claimed to have legitimacy to rule (either revolutionary or electoral–political following the elections of 2012 and 2014). These opposing forces sought to control the west (Tripolitania region) and the east (Cyrenaica region). In the former case militia from Zintan and Misrata fought from August 2014 for hegemony over this territory and control of the most important refinery in the country. The Zintan fighters comprise an alliance of tribes that defended the al-Gaddafi regime and won the 2014 elections on a liberal ticket, making themselves a hegemonic force in the Libyan National Congress; while the Misrata militia are a conservative alliance of tribes traditionally distant from the system who seek a different distribution of energy resources. In Cyrenaica, on the other hand, military units led by General Khafter and members of the Islamist formation Ansar al-Sharia fought for control of the main petrol ports (Mesa 2014; García-Guindo and Mesa 2015: 94–5). At this time in Libya there are no unitary or federal structures that can be described as a recognised authority beyond the alliances described.

At the start of the unrest, however, all these factions fought together against the al-Gaddafi regime, in unison with the international coalition that intervened in the country, under the mandate of the United Nations. The institution that claimed to govern the transition was the National Transitional Council (NTC), formed by leaders of the uprisings (many of whom were previously strongmen of the al-Gaddafi regime) and recognised by the UN as the only legitimate interlocutor in Libya. The NTC assumed transitional power in line with the constitutional declaration (article 1), approved on 3 August 2011, and established the rules for the first competitive elections to the General National Congress (GNC). The elections took place on 7 July 2012, after the repeal of the 1977 law that banned political parties and approval of the electoral law of 28 January. The Islamist formation the Justice and Construction Party (JCP), in contrast to the situation in Tunisia, Egypt and Morocco, did not win. Instead the election was won by the National Forces Alliance (NFA) of Mahmoud Jibril (an al-Gaddafi-regime strongman but a supporter of political reforms), who later became the first president of the NTC's Executive Committee, and interim Libyan prime minister. However, the 2012 electoral law established that the 200 seats of the GNC are chosen from among the candidates of the political formations (eighty) and among the independents (120), for which reason the minority status of the JCP, with seventeen seats, is not indicative of its real weight in votes. In practice, outcomes depend upon the stance taken by the independents.

On 9 July 2012 the GNC elected its president, Mohammed Youssef al-Magharief, and a month later the NTC renounced its transitional powers in favour of the assembly. The prime minister is also chosen by the GNC under a 'diarchical' electoral system (Haddad 2013) in which powers are poorly defined and the decision-making process is slow. Mustafa Abu Shagur, a scientist exiled in the US, was chosen to be prime minister on 12 September 2012 in a very close vote in which he benefited from the support of the JCP. However, his mandate was brief due to the lack of consensus. Twice parliamentarians from the NFA and JCP refused to approve the composition of his government, which obliged Shagur to leave his post on 7 October of the same year. The diplomat Ali Zeidan – who was close to Mahmoud Jibril – replaced him, and rapidly sought to re-establish security by appointing previous regime officials to the ministry of defence and interior (Haddad 2013).

Security was compromised by discrepancies and negotiations between, on the one hand, the authorities that claimed democratic legitimacy, and on the other, by the militias who were the self-proclaimed custodians of revolutionary legitimacy (Haddad 2013). In Libya, as in Yemen, the armed forces were divided between supporters and opponents of the regime, which placed it in a very weak situation following the fall of its leaders and when faced with the large increase in militias that, along with their respective political forces, were gradually replacing the institutional framework of the Revolutionary Committees and Popular Commissions of the al-Gaddafi era (Martínez 2014).

In May 2013 approval of the Law of Political Exclusion by a majority of Islamists and independents polarised Libyan politics, as it banned 'old regime' politicians and civil servants from exercising public functions. People in senior political posts were forced to resign (the president of the GNC, Magharief, was substituted by the Islamist Nuri Abu Sahmain), and the ministers of defence and interior, and others, such as Jibril himself, remained under suspicion. Furthermore, the road map established in the constitutional declaration was at a standstill because of an impasse between the new president of the GNC and prime minister Zeidan regarding the formation of the constituent assembly and the prolongation of the GNCs mandate. Elections to the constituent assembly took place on 20 February, and days later, a confrontation between the Tripoli and Cyrenaica authorities regarding the exportation of oil finished with the leadership of Zeidan, who was replaced by Abdullah al-Thani, the minister of defence. His mandate continued after the 25 June 2014 elections for the House of Representatives (HR). Haddad (2013) argues that the main cleavage in both elections was between the new elites who came from emblematic regions of the revolution, such as Misrata, and the previous high-ranking officials who sought to end instability. Additionally, of course, tribal cleavages persisted.

The 2012 election finished with an Islamist majority (thanks to the independents), but the results were then thrown into doubt by publication of the census, which was much reduced in comparison to previous elections. From that moment onwards, two governments co-existed in Libya that arose from separate electoral processes (in 2012 and 2014), and two distinct assemblies (the GNC and the HR): the government appointed by the GNC with Omar al-Hassi as prime minister, based in Tripoli; and the government appointed by the HR with Abdullah al-Thani as prime minister – recognised by the international community – who relocated to Tobruk for security reasons. This provoked the resignation of the Islamist GNC president, Nuri Abu Sahmain, who would not pass powers to the HR because of the location of the assembly in this city. Similarly, locating the HR in Tobruk resulted in a claim of unconstitutionality being presented by an Islamist deputy to the Libyan Supreme Court, which decided in the deputy's favour in November 2014 and invalidated the parliament that emerged from the 2014 elections. However, the chamber continued legislating and in February 2015 declared invalid the Law of Political Exclusion that had polarised Libyan politics in 2013. The dismissals and appointments that followed this repeal have not been recognised by the parties of the Tripoli government.

Libya therefore does not have any generally recognised authority, whether armed or not. Additionally, the east of Libya was declared part of IS in October 2014. In this context, while waiting for events to develop, it can be hypothesised that Libya is a failed state.

Similarly, Syria is in a catastrophic situation with both a divided territory and an armed conflict between the Syrian regime and the rebels. The insurgents comprise a mosaic of actors that lay claim to varying sources of legitimacy and who exercise, or attempt to exercise, their authority over part of the conquered territory. The Syrian regime has lost control over a substantial part of the territory, except the main cities and the coastline, where approximately 60 per cent of the population live. The groups that defend this territory include the Syrian Arab Army, which remained loyal to Bashar al-Assad, the National Defence Force, created by the government in

2012, and the Popular Committees, who are locally trained citizens who are paid by the regime to defend the areas where religious minorities and the Sunni population live. Additionally these areas are defended by Hezbollah, Palestinians and, circumstantially, Kurds. Since the start of the conflict the Syrian Free Army has been the leading armed organisation among the rebel groups, which control between 10 and 25 per cent of the territory. However, it has also become one of the weakest actors due to the loss of its troops to an Islamisation and atomisation process that has led to distinct militias, among them the al-Nusra Front, considered to be the representative of al-Qaeda in Syria. IS, on the other hand, has at times controlled around 50 per cent of the territory, specifically in a huge desert area with a very sparse population that extends from the north-east of Syria to the north-east of Iraq. IS emerged in Mosul, Iraq, in June 2014, in the same location where their losses are currently the greatest. The Iraqi army, supported by the US, Iran and the Shiite popular militias, has been able to recover almost all the major cities in which the Islamist organisation established itself.

The 'Syrian anti-authoritarian uprising' that started in March 2011 was taken as a direct challenge to Bashar al-Assad, who considered it a threat to his own survival. Consequently, the regime's immediate response was to brutally repress the demonstrators with live arms that led to opponents doing the same, in a militarisation of the uprising. In fact, one of the first measures adopted by al-Assad was the creation of a crisis cabinet formed by senior representatives of the ministries of defence and interior; therefore a security response was inevitably given to a non-security problem (Álvarez-Ossorio 2015: 163–4).

Al-Assad's regime also approved measures aimed at liberalising the political scenario by means of a constitutional reform that began with a National Committee that excluded the opposition and that did not affect the majority of presidential powers (Álvarez-Ossorio 2015: 171). This opening represented the start of political pluralism (article 8), although its consequences in practice have been very limited. In the legislative elections of 7 May 2012 the Popular Front for Change and Liberation only managed to achieve six deputies, although a number of opposition members were incorporated into the government presided over by Riyad Hijab. In the presidential elections of 3 June 2014 Hijab allowed more than one candidate to stand for the first time since the Ba'ath Party (the Syrian hegemonic formation) won power, but al-Assad won by an overwhelming majority with 88.7 per cent of the vote (Álvarez-Ossorio 2015: 172–3).

Al-Assad's response to the social protests of 2011 (both the militarisation and the closed approach of the regime) has led to heavy violence, the lack of territorial control in favour of atomised armed groups and the incapacity to address the needs of the population, which in many cases, has been forced into exile. Additionally, third countries have intervened militarily, Iran and Saudi Arabia have gained influence and the opposition in exile has lost cohesion.

5 Conclusions

The aim of this chapter has been to examine change processes in the MENA region by taking governments as a reference institution. Governments have been a special focus because of the place they occupy in their respective national institutional structures, the importance of how they are perceived by their populations and the extent to which are they capable of imposing their authority across the whole of their national territory. This perspective has led to the analysis of other actors with whom governments have interacted and who have also had protagonism.

In this sense, this chapter has demonstrated that governments have had a variable role in the distinct processes analysed, but that they share, in the majority of cases, a subordinate role in relation to other executive and legislative institutions, such as the presidents of the republic, the monarchs and other national (the armed forces in the case of Egypt, and armed groups in the cases of Libya, Syria and Yemen) or international actors (such as Saudi Arabia and Iran). In Tunisia, however, the change process has given special prominence to the government, which has been incorporated into a constitutionally designed system of checks and balances. In other countries, on the other hand, control of the change process by heads of state has been evident as they continue being hegemonic institutions thanks, among other reasons, to their capacity to appoint heads of government (in the Gulf monarchies, Jordan, Algeria and Egypt) or to exercise the power of veto (in Egypt, Morocco, Bahrain, Kuwait, Oman, Saudi Arabia, Qatar, UAE, Algeria and Jordan). In Morocco, for its part, the king is obliged under the new constitution to pass responsibility for the formation of a new government to a member of the party that has won the greatest support in the election.

It is clear that citizens continue to consider governments responsible for the policies carried out in their countries. Many of the social protests have been directed at the high levels of corruption and have called for resignations. Thus, the governments have been faced in the majority of cases with the paradox of being non-accountable actors (as their legitimacy has not come directly from competitive elections), while at the same time being perceived as the institutions responsible for meeting citizens' welfare needs.

Table 6.1 Government and powers relations in the MENA countries

	System of government	Executive-legislative relations	Veto players / reserved domains	Parliament		
				Structure	Election system of the lower house	Legislative function
Algeria	Semi-presidentialist republic (tendency to presidentialism)	Predominance of the head of state	Armed forces	Bicameralism	Direct	Yes
Bahrain	Constitutional monarchy	Predominance of the head of state	Royal family	Bicameralism	Direct	Yes
Egypt	Semi-presidentialist republic (tendency to presidentialism)	Predominance of the head of state	Head of state/armed forces	Unicameralism	Direct / designation	Yes
Iran	Islamic republic	Predominance of the head of state	Supreme leader/religious establishment	Unicameralism	Direct	Yes
Iraq	Parliamentary republic/fragmented authority	Balance	-	Unicameralism	Direct	Yes
Israel	Parliamentary republic	Balance	-	Unicameralism	Direct	Yes
Jordan	Constitutional monarchy	Predominance of the head of state	Head of state/armed forces	Bicameralism	Direct	Yes
Kuwait	Constitutional monarchy	Predominance of the head of state	Royal family	Unicameralism	Direct	Yes
Lebanon	Parliamentary republic	Balance	-	Unicameralism	Direct	Yes
Libya	Fragmented authority	-	-	-	-	-
Morocco	Constitutional monarchy	Predominance of the head of state	Head of state	Bicameralism	Direct	Yes
Oman	Absolute monarchy	Predominance of the head of state	Royal family	Bicameralism	Direct	Partially
Qatar	Absolute monarchy	Predominance of the head of state	Royal family	Unicameralism	2/3 direct 1/3 designation	No
Saudi Arabia	Absolute monarchy	Predominance of the head of state	Royal family/religious sstablishment	Unicameralism	Designation	No
Syria	Semi-presidentialist republic (tendency to presidentialism)/Fragmented authority	Predominance of the head of state	Armed and security forces	Unicameralism	Direct	Yes
Tunisia	Semi-presiden-tialist republic	Balance	-	Unicameralism	Direct	Yes
Turkey	Semi-presidentialist republic (tendency to presidentialism)	Predominance of the head of state	-	Unicameralism	Direct	Yes
UAE	Confederation of absolute monarchies	Predominance of the head of state	Dubai and Abu Dhabi emirs	Unicameralism	Indirect / designation	No
Yemen	Fragmented authority	-	-	-	-	-

Source: prepared by author from Szmolka (2011: 44–5)

Notes

1. Summer 2013 was particularly destabilising with the murders of two members of the Popular Front, which is a coalition of left-wing parties and nationalists created in September 2012. These events obliged the actors to accelerate the process by creating the National Dialogue, a kind of 'mini-parliament' that would develop the road map to holding presidential and legislative elections (Gobe and Chouikha 2015).
2. Morsi retired Tantawi a few days after his election.
3. Ennahda refused to present a candidate and maintained a neutral stance towards the competition.
4. Iranian influence in the protests was not proved in the conclusions of the report published by the Independent Research Commission appointed by the government. Available at <http://www.bici.org.bh/BICIreportEN.pdf> (last accessed 7 July 2016).
5. According to Zaccara and Saldaña (2015: 189): 'requests [via social networks] are a traditional method [of communication] in the region and the only one accepted within the strict Islamic Wahhabi tradition that ensures demands are received by the leaders'.
6. The proposal of constitutional reform to establish a presidentialist system with broad executive powers for the head of state constitutes one more step in the drift of the Turkish regime towards authoritarianism.
7. Data offered by Duboc (2011) from the NGO 'The Earth Center for Human Rights'. The author employs figures with caution and specifies that they must only be considered estimations and an indicator of protest tendencies throughout the period under analysis.
8. In Western Sahara there has also been an increase in this type of protest in the same period. See Veguilla (2009; 2016).
9. Some of these restrictions are currently being implemented. Yemen, for example, has been obliged by international organisms to eliminate fuel subsidies, which unleashed social protests against the government in 2014.

References

Allal, Amin (2010), 'Réformes néolibérales, clientélismes et protestations en situation autoritaire. Les mouvements contestataires dans le bassin minier de Gafsa en Tunisie (2008)', *Politique Africaine*, 117: 107–25.

Allal, Amin and Vincent Geisser (2011), 'La Tunisie de l'après Ben Ali. Les partis politiques à la recherche du "peuple introuvable"', *Cultures et conflits*, 2011/3 (83): 118–25.

Álvarez-Ossorio, Ignacio (2015), 'El enroque autoritario del régimen sirio: de la revuelta popular a la guerra civil', *Revista Cidob d'Afers Internacionals*, 109: 157–76.

Beblawi, Hazem and Giacomo Luciani (eds) (1987), *The rentier state*, London: Routledge.

Bennafla, Karine and Montserrat Emperador (2010), 'Le "Maroc inutil" redécouvert par l'action publique. Le cas de Sidi Ifni et Bouarfa', *Politique Africaine*, 120: 67–86.

Bobin, Frédéric (2016), 'En Tunisie, "le parti Nidaa Tounès est devenu une coquille vide"', *Le Monde Afrique*. Available at <http://www.lemonde.fr/afrique/article/2016/03/16/en-tunisie-le-parti-nidaa-tounes-est-devenu-une-coquille-vide_4883993_3212.htm> (last accessed 12 May 2016).

Bogaert, Koenraad (2015), 'The revolt of small towns: the meaning of Morocco's history and the geography of social protests', *Review of African Political Economy*, 42 (143): 124–40.

Bogaert, Koenraad and Montserrat Emperador (2014) '"The state owes us a future": the usages of "exclusion" by employment focused movements in Morocco', in Didier Chabanet and Frédéric Royall (eds), *From Silence to Protest: International Perspectives on Weakly Resourced Groups*, London: Ashgate, pp. 175–92.

Bonnefoy, Laurent and Marine Poirier (2012), 'La structuration de la révolution yéménite. Essai d'analyse d'un processus en marche', *Revue Française de Science Politique*, 5 (62): 895–913.

Burgat, François (2008), *L'islamisme au Maghreb. La voix du Sud*, Paris: Petite Bibliothèque Payot.

de Cara, Jean-Yves (2014), 'Les grandes lignes institutionnelles', in Jean-Yves de Cara and Charles Saint-Prot (eds), *L'évolution constitutionnelle de l'Égypte*, Paris: Observatoire d'Études Géopolitiques and Karthala, pp. 31–50.

Catusse, Myriam (2004), 'Les coups de forces de la représentation', in Mounia Bennani-Chraïbi, Myriam Catusse and Jean-Claude Santucci (eds), *Scènes et coulisses de l'élection. Les législatives de 2002 au Maroc*, Paris: Karthala, pp. 69–104.

Catusse, Myriam (2006), 'Ordonner, classer, penser la société: les pays arabes au prisme de l'économie politique', in Élizabeth Picard (ed.), *La politique dans le monde arabe*, Paris: Armand Colin, pp. 215–38.

Catusse, Myriam (2011), 'Le "social": une affaire d'état dans le Maroc de Mohammed VI', *Confluences Méditerranée*, 3 (78): 63–76.

Catusse, Myriam and Blandine Destremau (2010), 'L'état social à l'épreuve de ses trajectoires au Maghreb', in Myriam Catusse, Blandine Destremau and Éric Verdier (eds), *L'État face aux 'débordements' du social au Maghreb. Formation, travail et protection*, Paris: Karthala, pp. 9–32.

Desrues, Thierry (2012), 'Le Mouvement du 20 février et le régime marocain: contestation, révision constitutionnelle et élections', *L'Année du Maghreb*, VIII. Available at <http://anneemaghreb.revues.org/1537> (last accessed 15 May 2016).

Desrues, Thierry (2014), 'La fronde de l'Istiqlal et la formation du gouvernement Benkirane II: une aubaine pour la monarchie?', *L'Année du Maghreb*, 11. Available at <http://anneemaghreb.revues.org/2321> (last accessed 20 May 2016).

Droz-Vincent, Philippe (2015), 'Le rôle politique des acteurs militaires dans le monde arabe après les soulèvements', *Anuario IEMed 2015*: 26–32.

Duboc, Marie (2011), 'La contestation sociale en Égypte depuis 2004. Précarisation et mobilisation locale des ouvriers de l'industrie textile', *Revue Tiers Monde*, 5: 95–115.

Fedtke, Jörg (2014), *Analyse comparative des processus constitutionnels en Égypte et en Tunisie*, Direction Générale des Politiques Externes de l'Union, European Parliament. Available at <http://www.europarl.europa.eu/RegData/etudes/note/join/2014/433840/EXPO-AFET_NT(2014)433840_FR.pdf> (last accessed 12 May 2016).

Fioroni, Claudie (2015), 'From the everyday to contentious collective actions: the protests of Jordan Phosphate Mines Company employees between 2011 and 2014', *Workers of the World: International Journal on Strikes and Social Conflicts*, 1 (7): 30–49.

Flors, Sylvie (2012), 'Les jeunes, ces anti-héros du printemps arabe', *Anuario IEMed 2012*: 116–21.

García-Guindo, Miguel and Beatriz Mesa (2015), 'Libia: la "nueva guerra" por el poder económico', *Revista Cidob d'Afers Internacionals*, 109: 91–107.

Gobe, Éric (2012), 'Tunisie an I: les chantiers de la transition', *L'Année du Maghreb*, VIII. Available at <http://anneemaghreb.revues.org/1549> (last accessed 20 April 2016).

Gobe, Éric and Larbi Chouikha (2015), 'La Tunisie de la constitution aux élections: La fin de la transition politique?', *L'Année du Maghreb*, 13. Available at <http://anneemaghreb.revues.org/2602> (last accessed 21 April 2016).

González, Ricard (2015), 'El régimen de al-Sisi se institucionaliza', *Notes Internacionals CIDOB*, 131: 1–5.

Haddad, Saïd (2013), 'La sécurité, "priorité des priorités" de la transition libyenne', *L'Année du Maghreb*, IX. Available at <http://anneemaghreb.revues.org/1953> (last accessed 25 May 2016).

Hernando de Larramendi, Miguel and Laurence Thieux (2011), 'Los regímenes marroquí y argelino ante las protestas', *Afkar/Ideas*, 30: 64–7.

Hibou, Béatrice (1998), 'Retrait ou redéploiement de l'état?', *Critique internationale*, 1: 151–68.

Martinez, Luis (2014), 'Libya from paramilitary forces to militias: the difficulty of constructing a state security apparatus', *Policy Alternatives*. Available at <http://www.arab-reform.net/sites/default/files/Martinez%20-%20formatted%20-%20May%207.pdf> (last accessed 25 May 2016).

Melián, Luis (2015), 'Desarrollos políticos en el Reino Hachemí: la Primavera Árabe desde la óptica jordana', *Revista Cidob d'Afers Internacionals*, 109: 131–56.

Mesa; Beatriz (2014), 'Libia: la lucha por los recursos', *Documento Opinión, Instituto Español de Estudios Estratégicos*, 147. Available at <http://www.ieee.es/Galerias/fichero/docs_opinion/2014/DIEEEO147-2014_PoderEconomico_Libia_BeatrizMesa.pd> (last accessed 14 May 2016).

Morlino, Leonardo (2008), *Hybrid Regimes or Regimes in Transition?*, Working Paper, 70. FRIDE. Available at <http://fride.org/download/WP70-Hybrid_regimes_ENG_sep08.pdf> (last accessed 20 May 2016).

Parejo, María Angustias (2015), 'Cambio y límites en Marruecos: propuestas de reforma constitucional sobre el Gobierno', *Revista Cidob d'Afers Internacionals*, 109: 23–44.

Parks, Robert P. (2013), 'Algeria and the Arab uprisings', in Henry Clement and Jang Ji-Hyang (eds), *The Arab Spring: Will It Lead to Democratic Transitions?*, New York: Palgrave Macmillan, pp. 101–26.

Picard, Élizabeth (2008), 'Armée et sécurité au cœur de l'autoritarisme', in Olivier Dabène, Vincent Geisser and Gilles Massardier (eds), *Autoritarismes démocratiques et démocraties autoritaires au XXIe siècle. Convergence Nord–Sud*, Paris: La Découverte, pp. 303–29.

Signoles, Aude (2006), 'Réforme de l'état et transformation de l'action publique. Analyse par les politiques publiques', in Élizabeth Picard (ed.), *La politique dans le monde arabe*, Paris: Armand Colin, pp. 239–61.

Steuer, Clément (2013), 'Des élections révolutionnaires?', *Égypte/Monde arabe*, 10. Available at <http://ema.revues.org/3086> (last accessed 25 April 2016).

Szmolka, Inmaculada (2010a), 'Party system fragmentation in Morocco', *The Journal of North African Studies*, 15 (1): 13–7. DOI: 10.1080/13629380902727569.

Szmolka, Inmaculada (2010b), 'Los regímenes políticos híbridos: democracias y autoritarismos con adjetivos. Su conceptualización, categorización y operacionalización dentro de la tipología de regímenes políticos', *Revista de Estudios Políticos*, 147: 103–35.

Szmolka, Inmaculada (2011), 'Democracias y autoritarismos con adjetivos: la clasificación de los países árabes dentro de una tipología general de regímenes políticos', *Revista Española de Ciencia Política*, 26, julio: 11–62.

Szmolka, Inmaculada (2013), '¿La quinta ola de democratización?: cambio político sin cambio de régimen en los países árabes', *Política y Sociedad*, 50 (3): 893–935.

Szmolka, Inmaculada (2015a), 'Introducción: actores y dinámicas de cambio en el Norte de África y Oriente Próximo', *Revista Cidob d'Afers Internacionals*, 109: 7–21.

Szmolka, Inmaculada (2015b), 'Inter- and intra-party relations in the formation of the Benkirane coalition governments in Morocco', *The Journal of North African Studies*, 20 (4): 654–74.

Veguilla, Victoria (2009), 'L'articulation du politique dans un espace protestataire en recomposition. Les mobilisations des jeunes Sahraouis à Dakhla', *L'Année du Maghreb 2008*: 95–110.

Veguilla, Victoria (2011), *Politiques du poulpe à Dakhla. Action publique, ressources naturelles et dynamiques sociales*, PhD Dissertation, Institute of Political Studies in Aix-en-Provence and the University of Granada.

Veguilla, Victoria (2016), 'Social protest and nationalism in Western Sahara: struggles around fisheries and housing in El Ayun and Dakhla', *Mediterranean Politics*, DOI:10.1080/13629 395.2016.1215046.

Wigell, Mikael (2008), 'Mapping "hybrid regimes": regime types and concepts in comparative politics', *Democratization*, 15 (2): 230–50.

Zaccara, Luciano and Marta Saldaña (2015), 'Cambio y estabilidad política en las monarquías del Golfo tras la Primavera Árabe', *Revista CIDOB d'Afers Internacionals*, 109: 177–99.

Chapter 7

Good governance in MENA countries

Raquel Ojeda and Francesco Cavatorta

1 Introduction

The concept of good governance has been employed over the last two decades as a potential governing mechanism that could address the significant economic and social problems of developing countries. At the same time as improving decision-making, good governance might also chip away at authoritarian structures of power and lead eventually to democratisation. In this respect, good governance has been deemed more likely to produce positive long-term change than aggressive democracy-promotion policies that often resulted in authoritarian backlashes and domestic instability. Good governance was seen as the means by which the failure of transitology (Carothers 2002) could be 'rescued'. It is this idea of mutual reinforcement between efficient policies, accountable governments and economic development that good governance seeks to capture.

However, the notion of good governance has acquired rather different meanings in practice. Firstly, it can simply be understood as 'good government' and therefore equated with the way in which state authorities actually function to meet the socio-economic expectations of citizens almost irrespective of the nature of the political system, marginalising in this way the idea of accountability and electoral legitimacy. In short, it is similar to policy-making technocratic efficiency. Secondly, good governance can be understood as a 'complex set of institutions and processes' (Weiss 2000) that do not necessarily equate with governing, but take into account the overall functioning of a society. This implies a 'political element' whereby the nature of the political system matters. In this chapter the broader concept of good governance and World Bank indicators are employed to analyse how the Middle East and North Africa (MENA) region fares in the light of such criteria. While it should be acknowledged that international institutions have been criticised for having unrealistic or unreliable criteria in relation to good governance, this chapter argues that they do sufficiently represent what good governance should be about and in what kind of environment it should occur.

The contention here is that the lack of good governance in the MENA region is not a story of poor achievement related to criteria or adaptability, but a much broader failure of international institutional policies in the developing world. The MENA countries stand out in this respect, as there is a vast disconnect between the grievances of ordinary citizens and the policies adopted to address them. Analysis of the current socio-economic situation in the MENA countries illustrates the failure of the World Bank's good governance policy model and of the Western plan of action more broadly. It should be noted that like the European Union (Teti 2012), the World Bank itself recognises that this is the case and has begun questioning its own policies in the region. However, responsibility for the failure of good governance in the region does not rest only with international financial institutions or Western powers. These actors certainly held ingenuous beliefs about 'socio-economic recipes' that were considered to work in different political, social and cultural contexts as well as across radically different historical experiences, but local MENA political actors greatly contributed to such failure. The Arab Spring, which seemed for a brief moment to provide a degree of hope for improvement in the way MENA societies functioned, can be considered a failure in the short term and this has meant that since 2011 the socio-economic and political situation has broadly worsened. Thus, various studies on the state of governance and its indicators over the last decade, including the Arab Spring period, have demonstrated that the political, economic and social situation is no better than before the uprisings.

After this brief discussion of the logic behind the concept, application and promotion of good governance, this chapter focuses on the factors that explain its failure, both structural and contingent variables. World Bank indicators on good governance are specifically focused on, as well as the results of their application in the region over more than a decade. It should be noted, as mentioned above, that the World Bank acknowledged the need to change its approach in the light of critiques. Consequently, it launched a new strategy entitled 'Economic and Social Inclusion for Peace and Stability in the Middle East and North Africa: a New Strategy for the World Bank Group', which seeks to promote peace and social stability in the region. However, if the assumptions behind the strategy demonstrate the same lack of understanding of MENA societies as previous strategies, together with the unwillingness to confront authoritarian decision-makers, it is unlikely that it will be successful.

2 Good governance in the MENA region

The aim behind the promotion of good governance and its associated indicators by international financial institutions, but also Western governments, was to 'technocratise' difficult political relationships. This was an attempt in fact to disconnect the nature of political regimes from the implementation of efficient socio-economic developmental policies. Since the end of the Cold War, it has been problematic for Western countries to continue supporting authoritarian regimes across the globe, given that changes in the balance of power with the Soviet Union had been held as a victory for democratic ideas, freedom and the market against authoritarian rule, suppression of individual freedoms and a planned economy. The promotion of democracy – in order to spur both domestic socio-economic development in authoritarian states and international stability – became a centrepiece of Western foreign policies, at least rhetorically, in the post-Cold War period (Levistki and Way 2005). International organisations – such as the EU – as well as international financial institutions quickly followed suit and, having been in some ways liberated from the constraints of Cold War politics, began also to promote democracy as a panacea for economic underdevelopment. Despite the enthusiasm with which it was embraced and the large resources made available to democratisation programmes, democracy promotion turned out to be much more controversial and problematic than many had thought. While initial successes were achieved and pro-democracy policies in Eastern Europe and Latin America seemed to provide the empirical confirmation that spreading democracy was both possible and positive, neither democratic gains nor the outcome of foreign pro-democracy programmes seemed solidly grounded. Knack (2004) argued, for instance, that there was no real correlation between aid and democracy. Even more problematically, according to Carothers (2002), the democratisation paradigm and, consequently, the foreign policies built upon its validity did not really deliver greater liberal-democratic political systems in the long term. Following on from Carothers' intuition, a number of scholars convincingly argued that many 'newly democratic countries' were actually not that democratic – they were 'democracy with adjectives' (Collier and Levitski 1997). Some countries simply adopted democratic institutions without replacing the authoritarian core and others regressed to some form of authoritarianism after flirting with liberal democracy and finding it wanting. Levitski and Way (2002) put forward the notion of competitive authoritarianism to capture this whole phenomenon. In her work, Szmolka (2010; 2011) fine-tuned their notion and suggested differences between pluralist authoritarianisms: 'quasi-competitive authoritarianism' and 'hegemonic authoritarianism'. In any case, an academic consensus emerged that democratisation studies had to contend with many failures and shades of grey, therefore making democracy promotion much less straightforward than anticipated. In parallel with this, academics of socio-economic development began to argue that the disadvantages of neo-liberal globalisation outstripped its advantages for many ordinary citizens, with inequality increasing across the globe (Wood 1998; Galbraith 2002; Harvey 2007) and paradoxically further undermining the assumption that democracy would bring about material benefits. In short, democracy promotion did not seem to be effective, in part because local circumstances did not allow it to flourish, in part because socio-economic inequalities undermined its creation or consolidation (Manning 2005) and in part because authoritarian rulers were still perceived as useful allies in the West due to the nature of new threats arising from the end of the Cold War. One problem, for instance, was that former dominant or single-party states across Africa were able to adapt themselves to the new circumstances and hold on to power while projecting a democratic facade (Ishiyama and Quinn 2006). A similar trend was noticeable in the Arab world (Heydemann 2007). All these factors, combined with the resistance of many authoritarian rulers to the 'imposition' of global norms, ultimately rendered democracy promotion ineffective. Many Euro-Mediterranean partnership studies for instance, which were launched in 1995 by the EU to 'democratise' the Arab world, demonstrate this clearly (Pace and Seeberg 2010). It is in this context that democracy promotion by Western states and the international organisations they control was gradually replaced by a more 'technocratic approach' to address the problems of socio-economic development and stability (Schlumberger 2011). Given the politically charged atmosphere surrounding democracy promotion and its inability to compete with other foreign policy objectives such as security, the technocratic approach allowed attention to shift away from politics to instead focus on technical and depoliticised solutions in the belief that technical cooperation would eventually have positive spillover effects on the political system. The notion of good governance became useful at this moment. It became, and still is to an extent, very frequent to find references to 'good governance' in the academic literature and political speeches or documents. In many cases, the term 'good governance' is more important than democratisation or development – even though the main objective of good governance is theoretically to achieve democratisation and social and economic development – because they are believed to be mutually reinforcing. The launch of the 'Union for the Mediterranean' (Seeberg 2010), for example, clearly suggested that European countries had for once abandoned direct democracy promotion (Jourde 2008) in favour of technocratic cooperation on a range of non-political issues that would not be controversial for authoritarian Arab regimes and would strengthen, in theory, their capacity to deliver socio-economic benefits unencumbered by politics and outside political pressure. As Ishiyama and Quinn (2006: 322) argue, however, this approach is destined to fail because

> in authoritarian regimes the monopolistic state presence in the economy means the strengthening of patronage networks and the weakening of the party system. At the same time, the main objective of the party in government is sharing the benefits among its small elite or buying the opposition.

The MENA region is the location where the shift from genuine – and short lived – democracy promotion to the advancement of good governance, with its technocratic and depoliticised connotations, is clear. As most studies on the relations between Western countries and Arab regimes suggest (Yom and al-Momani 2008; Cavatorta 2009; Brownlee 2012), the key services that the latter performed for the former meant that the idea of democracy promotion was largely ignored. In fact, behind the rhetoric of engagement and progressive democratisation, authoritarian Arab regimes were simply encouraged to make cosmetic changes to give the impression that they were implementing political reforms. At the macro level, however, as Kepel (2007) convincingly argues, the struggle against 'political Islam', access to natural resources and the protection of Israel were all Western priorities that only Arab authoritarian regimes could guarantee. Therefore, it did not matter much to them what was occurring in the wider society as long as control by the authorities was exercised. Any domestic change in the Arab world would have resulted, according to Western policy-makers, in radical Islamist-led governments bent on challenging those very priorities. Arab leaders for their part played on these Western fears to ensure their survival. While this was the 'realist' game that European powers, the United States and the international organisations played, it also had to have a veneer of rhetorical liberalism. Therefore, the ideas of governance and good governance were introduced. The concepts also had the advantage of being equally applicable to Israel and semi-democratic Lebanon as a way of improving the quality of their democratic institutions and credentials.

According to the World Bank:

> governance is the process by which authority is conferred on rulers, by which they make the rules, and by which rules are enforced and modified. Thus, understanding governance requires an identification of both, the rulers and the rules, as well as various processes by which they are selected, defined and linked together and with the society generally.

This kind of aseptic and technical definition says nothing about the nature of the authority rulers have and how they acquire it, suggesting that democratic or authoritarian structures might not be very important in this respect. While the notion of good governance, according to the World Bank's definition, has a normative aspect insofar as 'in various places, good governance has been associated with democracy and good civil rights, with transparency, with the rule of law and with efficient public services', these are not a priori traits necessary for socio-economic development, but simply conditions that can be created if countries adopted the appropriate institutions. The promotion of good governance in the MENA region meant that authoritarianism could be overlooked in the short to medium term, while authoritarian leaders, under pressure from a benevolent West, slowly adopted the necessary legal, economic and political institutions that would promote socio-economic development and, in the long term, would sow the seeds for the collapse of authoritarian rule and the emergence of liberal democracy. It goes without saying that such institutional changes had to cater for the creation or consolidation of a neo-liberal market economy.

In order to monitor the progress some MENA authoritarian regimes made in the adoption of the 'correct' institutions, the World Bank, like other organisations and states, designed a number of variables and indicators. The main variables included in the definition of good governance by the World Bank are inclusiveness, accountability and transparency. For the first, it employs equal treatment and equal access to public services as indicators, without addressing the clientelistic networks behind them, which are a feature of authoritarian systems. Accountability, on the other hand, specifies the need to publish budgets and public expenditure information, for example, but not the way in which they are negotiated or the manner in which resources might be ring fenced and unaccounted for such as, for instance, in military budgets. Finally, transparency includes fighting corruption in the public sector and e-governing as indicators, but without addressing the fact that corruption within authoritarian systems is practically endemic at all levels. A breakdown of variables and indicators can be seen in Table 7.1.

As the indicators in the last five years show, the good governance approach has failed to deliver socio-economic progress in the short and medium term. Hyden (2007) argued a decade ago that good governance as a mechanism to reduce poverty in the MENA countries had not worked. It also failed to deliver progress on the political front. In many ways the Arab uprisings can be seen as a reaction against the design and implementation of good governance programmes insofar as they allowed ruling elites to implement policies that strengthened their political and economic primacy to the detriment of the majority of society, as the next section will illustrate in detail. However, the 'break with the past' that the uprisings seemed to represent did not materialise and subsequent events across the region have made the socio-economic and political situation generally worse. This is not to suggest that the uprisings were in any way illegitimate or mistimed or a priori destined to fail, but that

Table 7.1 World Bank indicators of good governance 2014 for MENA countries

	Voice and accountability[a]		Political stability and absence of violence		Government effectiveness		Regulatory quality of states		Rule of law		Control of corruption	
MENA Global Score	-0.76		-0.93		0.20		-0.31		-0.06		-0.37	
Country	Rank	Score	Rank	Score	Rank	Score	Rank	Score	Rank	Score	Rank	Score
Algeria	22.66	-0.93	10.19	-1.17	33.65	-0.51	9.62	-1.21	25.48	-0.73	31.73	-0.61
Bahrain	11.33	-1.32	14.56	-0.94	72.60	0.59	74.04	0.70	68.27	0.45	64.42	0.30
Egypt	14.78	-1.19	7.77	-1.58	20.19	-0.82	25.00	-0.75	31.25	-0.60	32.21	-0.59
Iran	4.93	-1.57	16.99	-0.91	37.98	-0.41	4.81	-1.46	13.94	-1.03	34.62	-0.57
Iraq	13.79	-1.21	2.43	-2.47	13.94	-1.13	9.13	-1.25	5.77	-1.36	5.77	-1.34
Israel	70.44	0.73	13.11	-0.99	85.58	1.16	87.50	1.21	83.17	1.11	76.44	0.82
Jordan	26.60	-0.77	26.21	-0.56	59.62	0.13	54.81	0.08	69.71	0.48	61.54	0.15
Kuwait	29.06	-0.65	52.43	0.14	47.60	-0.15	48.56	-0.13	60.10	0.05	50.00	-0.26
Lebanon	33.99	-0.42	7.28	-1.72	40.87	-0.38	46.63	-0.22	24.04	-0.76	13.46	-1.06
Libya	16.26	-1.15	4.37	-2.32	2.88	-1.64	0.48	-2.19	2.88	-1.52	1.44	-1.61
Morocco	28.08	-0.77	30.10	-0.39	48.08	-0.14	52.40	-0.01	56.25	-0.06	50.48	-0.26
Oman	19.70	-1.05	67.96	0.66	63.94	0.29	73.56	0.69	73.08	0.58	62.98	0.25
Qatar	22.17	-0.93	83.01	1.00	78.37	0.99	70.67	0.57	81.25	0.99	82.69	1.09
Saudi Arabia	3.45	-1.73	35.44	-0.24	62.02	0.23	53.37	-0.01	65.38	0.27	59.62	0.10
Syria	2.96	-1.83	0.00	-2.76	6.73	-1.44	3.85	-1.67	6.73	-1.34	2.40	-1.55
Tunisia	49.75	0.03	15.05	-0.93	48.56	-0.13	40.87	-0.35	53.37	-0.12	55.77	-0.09
Turkey	37.93	-0.32	12.14	-1.06	67.31	0.38	66.35	0.41	59.62	0.04	53.85	-0.12
UAE	19.21	-1.05	75.73	0.81	90.38	1.48	80.29	0.98	76.44	0.71	84.13	1.23
Yemen	10.34	-1.34	1.46	-2.53	7.21	-1.41	21.63	-0.84	8.17	-1.17	1.92	-1.55

Note: [a] each score of -2.5 through +2.5, with -2.5 representing the lowest and +2.5 the highest level of governance, corresponds to a range of total scores included in a rank between 0 and 100

Source: prepared by the authors based on data from The World Bank Group 2015. Available at <http://info.worldbank.org/governance/wgi/index.aspx#reports> (last accessed 7 July 2016)

domestic and international actors and circumstances – in both agency and structure – did not lead to positive change.

3 The dark side of good governance

There are a number of factors that explain the failure of good governance policies in the Middle East and North Africa and they are related to both structural weaknesses in the way in which they were thought out – erroneous theoretical assumptions – and to contingent issues related to their implementation on the ground. In terms of structural difficulties with the good governance architecture, we find a number of interlinked theoretical assumptions that are problematic.

Firstly, the institutions of good governance identified in official policy documents such as independent regulatory agencies, an autonomous judiciary, the absolute rule of law or market-oriented reforms in various economic sectors are very difficult to replicate across countries. The growth of institutions that provide good governance coincided with the historical development of leading Western countries. This is the blueprint. The policies designed to replicate the growth and success of these institutions in different contexts, which went through radically diverse historical experiences, is bound to highlight significant differences. Transplanting institutions developed and adapted over time within a specific pattern of development might not function equally well when the context changes dramatically.

Secondly, institutions of good governance focus overwhelmingly on the formal creation and adoption of institutions as if these were completely detached from the surrounding political environment. When it comes to authoritarian countries in particular, formal institutions are not necessarily the primary channels for the transmission of knowledge, information and, crucially, authority. It is not sufficient for a country to set up, for instance, an independent regulatory agency in the banking sector for it to be efficient and change patterns of clientelistic behaviour. As many authors have suggested (Hyden 2007; Andrews 2008), the importance of non-institutional factors such as patrimonialism, clientelism or tribalism must not be forgotten. Politics in authoritarian settings takes place largely through informal channels and they undermine the efficiency of whatever institution or practice of good governance might be set up. This occurs because authoritarian regimes require informality and institutions that function as 'transmission belts of decisions' made in opaque settings. The MENA countries provide countless examples of institutions created to satisfy the international community of financial donors. It is no surprise that Villoria and Izquierdo (2015: 344), when talking about good government and rules and their necessary processes and structures, underscore the need to take into account both formal and informal institutions (such as values and culture). Thirdly, the whole notion that economic development could be kick-started with the adoption of best economic practices and good governance institutions was misplaced because it did not take into account that market-oriented reforms undertaken in authoritarian contexts could be – and generally are – very easily hijacked by the ruling elites. Whether intentionally or not, market-oriented reforms have largely served the interests of the MENA ruling elites to restructure their societies and legitimate their authoritarianism through meeting the economic needs of new social groups that a rigged market economy created. In exchange for economic benefits derived from the integration of their country into the financial and global market, these new social groups coalesced around the authoritarian regime. The creation of new 'networks of privilege' (Heydemann 2004) fundamentally undermined good governance because authoritarian regimes could hide behind the requirement of international institutions and donors to carry out reforms that simply benefited one group over another while maintaining a firm grip on political power. Faith in the market is what is most striking in the policies designed within the confines of international financial institutions and while the theory might be correct, the practice has revealed significant weaknesses.

Fourthly, it has never been clearly explained from a theoretical perspective how an improvement in the quality of institutions, an end to corruption and the implementation of the rule of law could be carried out by authoritarian regimes which specifically seek to remain immutable and counter such changes. What would be the incentives for authoritarian ruling elites to dismantle a system that provides them with unrestricted access to economic and political resources? This is not a critique of the policy of engagement with authoritarian regimes, because this approach can provide useful social goods, particularly in areas of mutual interest at the international level. However, it is legitimate to ask why authoritarian regimes would willingly and without pressure introduce genuine changes that would improve the quality of institutions, which would then challenge their power. The assumption that pro-democracy and pro-market reforms would be carried out by authoritarian regimes seems erroneous or even intentionally planned to not fundamentally challenge political systems that serve the needs and interests of the Western international community.

This leads directly to the issue of the contingent weaknesses of good governance, which has to do with the specific economic policies advocated – and adopted – and their unintended consequences. In their assessment of the crisis of the MENA countries, international actors underscored the very real problems that prevented them from achieving greater socio-economic development. However, while the diagnosis might have been accurate, the solutions proposed seemed to follow a blueprint that was in no way adapted to local circumstances. For instance, the dominant role of the public sector in economic activity and the huge public employee wage bill (Saidi and Yared 2003: 3) were identified as stumbling blocks to development. Therefore, there was criticism that 'Egypt has more than six million public employees – more than the entire population of ten MENA countries – as well as per capita staffing ratios that are on par with many developed countries' (Governance News and Notes 2010: 1). Privatisation and the slashing of the state budget were offered as solutions and perhaps they might have worked well if implemented in a different setting and by a different government. However, believing that privatisation and budget reduction were 'de-politicised' issues that would be implemented efficiently was irresponsible, naïve or, at worst, cynical. As it turned out, privatisation was carried out in an opaque manner and to the benefit of members of the ruling elite with very close connections to the regime. Budget cuts deteriorated basic services, and while there was foreign investment in Egypt, its impact on (un)employment has been negligible. The regime, in an effort to strengthen its grip on power, adopted all the policies and institutions the international community suggested. However, it gutted them of any meaningful content and, in addition, increased inequality further. The paradox was of course that macroeconomic indicators seemed to suggest that the good governance model and new public management were working, while the reality of increasing inequalities went unnoticed. The Egyptian 'story' (Kienle 2001) is far from unique and has been replicated across the region from the North of Africa (Addison and Baliamoune-Lutz 2006) to Syria (Haddad 2012), and elsewhere. The slow and rigged process of public monopoly privatisations, centralised governments and absence or weakness of external accountability mechanisms – such as the media and civil society organisations – certainly represent a challenge for good governance (World Bank Group 2003), but once again the solutions offered faced contingent factors that accentuated the structural problems of the whole architecture. Two examples suffice to highlight this point.

Firstly, in most countries of the region, the international community's promotion of civil society activism failed to increase the monitoring capacity of associations. This stems in part from its refusal to engage with and support Islamist social and political activism – by far the most popular organisations in the region – as a way to pressurise governments to reform, because Islamists are considered a greater evil than authoritarian incumbents (Zakaria 2004). This decision restricted support to groups and associations with little or no public reach. Such groups would ultimately often side with authoritarian governments in its struggle against political Islam, which fundamentally undermined accountability mechanisms (Cook 2005; Jamal 2007).

Secondly, media reform and the liberalisation of the audio-visual market seemed a promising means through which accountability of state authority could occur, but once again such liberalisation did not occur fairly and, therefore, effectively. In Tunisia, for instance, liberalisation of the media benefited members of the ruling family who acquired licences to run private radio and TV channels. Although some of these media attempted to provide a soft critical voice, they were still part of a media empire in the hands of the Ben Ali ruling family (Haugbølle and Cavatorta 2012).

Furthermore, the reasons behind poor indicators in service delivery are not related to the capability of the MENA administrators. Weak government performance stems from weak governance mechanisms, especially those for public accountability (World Bank Group 2003), but reforms undertaken to improve the capacity of the public administration has faced significant problems because changes in the structure affect clientelistic networks that support the authoritarian regime. According to a recent study on Tunisia (Loschi 2016), the reform of local government sponsored by international financial institutions during the Ben Ali era to improve service delivery performance and account-ability floundered when it became clear that administrative changes put forth were simply instrumentalised by the state to retrench authoritarian practices.

Both the structural and contingent explanations mentioned above for the failure of the good governance model can be identified as causing the Arab Spring eruptions. While the political and institutional dimension of the uprisings should not be neglected – suffocating authoritarianism alienated large sectors of society – the primary causes have to be found in worsening socio-economic conditions at the micro level. It was therefore socio-economic inequalities that were central to the mobilisation of large numbers of people (Chomiak and Entelis 2012; Beinin 2012; Achcar 2013; Bogaert 2013).

The revolts are inextricably linked to the reforms that authoritarian Arab states carried out during the 2000s to conform to international norms and standards in their economic and social realms. The failure of such policies compounded an already difficult situation and, with hindsight, the uprisings were the inevitable outcome of a progressive loss of legitimacy of the state and not only of the ruling elites. It is in part because of the loss of the legitimacy of the state and its structural effectiveness in providing governance that state breakdown has occurred across the region since 2011. It is true that there are specific national dynamics at play in each case of state breakdown. The invasion of Iraq in 2003 provoked the collapse of state structures, which were then rebuilt along sectarian lines, fundamentally undermining them from the start (Benraad 2015). The war in neighbouring Syria simply accelerated the implosion of the Iraq state. International intervention altered the balance of power in the Libyan civil war in favour of the anti-al-Gaddafi faction, but the implosion of the Libyan state is due to irreconcilable differences among the winning factions on how to construct a new political system. The Syrian civil war has undermined for the foreseeable future the viability of the state, and the sectarian nature the conflict has acquired is extremely problematic. A similar scenario affects Yemen. Even in countries that have not broken down, the capacity of the state to deliver both material and produce legitimacy to the system has been severely weakened. This is also the case of Tunisia, despite the relative success of the political transition (Marzouki 2015). Therefore, the simple conclusion is that the repercussions of the Arab uprisings on good governance have been broadly negative (see again Table 7.1).

A brief overview of the post-uprising period illustrates this point. According to the World Bank, which recently published information about the current situation, 'growth in MENA is expected to be about 2.9 per cent in 2015, slightly higher than last year's 2.6 per cent, but considerably below the 4–5 per cent growth the region enjoyed from 2000–10'. In addition,

> the continuation of sluggish growth will hurt overall unemployment, now standing at 12 per cent, and household earnings in the region. The group of oil exporters is estimated to grow by around 2.7 per cent in 2015 with growth stagnation among developing oil exporters at 1.4 per cent. The Gulf countries could lose about US$215 billion in oil revenues, equivalent to 14 per cent of their combined GDP, in 2015. Growth for this sub-group is estimated at 3.2 in 2015, about half a percentage point lower than last year. Fiscal deficits continue to mount, leaving the region with a deficit of 8.8 per cent of GDP in 2015, higher than last year, and following three years of surpluses.[1]

The economic slowdown is accompanied by an increasing securitisation of politics and social life to face the numerous geostrategic challenges that have emerged since 2011, such as the refugee crisis, the internal displacement of vulnerable populations, the sharp rise in political violence and the threat of intrastate conflicts. The rise of political violence across the region and beyond has led Arab states that have survived internal collapse to focus their limited resources almost exclusively on security policy. This is true for countries in transition, such as Tunisia, and even more so for countries whose regimes face both internal threats and dissent, such as Egypt, Morocco and Algeria, or external ones, such as Jordan. In turn this increase in securitisation takes resources away from policies that promote economic growth. This chapter will now analyse individual indicators of good governance to illustrate how the uprisings have further reduced the possibilities of good governance, even in revised forms, to succeed.

4 A survey of good governance indicators

The World Bank has developed key good governance indicators by drawing on information from various sources.[2] Following criticism, the World Bank Group has decided to improve the information obtained each year in order to cover the maximum number of indicators and incorporate satisfaction interviews from citizens.[3]

4.1 Voice and accountability

Voice and accountability have certainly been reduced across the region. In states that have experienced a breakdown following uprisings, the collapse of their institutions and structures have set back the already limited liberalising reforms of the previous decade. The tentative political openings that had occurred in Libya and Syria, for instance, have floundered amidst growing violence and divisions. Immediately following the Libyan uprising, for example, the country improved its voice and accountability score, but this did not last and by 2014 the score began to fall significantly in the context of the political violence affecting the country. Syria, on the other hand, was slowly improving its score before the uprising, but this has plummeted since 2012. In states that experienced small- or large-scale demonstrations, there was significant repression in the name of security and stability, with Bahrain and Egypt's score falling significantly. These clampdowns have not only taken place through repressive means, although they have been the primary choice of rulers, but also through the tried and trusted policy of buying off dissent. This retrenchment of authoritarianism on voice and accountability has been particularly evident in Oman, Qatar, Saudi Arabia, Iran and the United Arab Emirates, but even in Iraq and Lebanon – considered quasi-democracies – which saw their scores decline. The uprisings had seemed to promise the opening up of political space across the region, permitting a multitude of political and social voices to contribute to the debate about how to solve the countries' problems. In fact, this occurred in the early days from Tunisia to Egypt, from Yemen to Bahrain and from Jordan to Morocco and Syria. However, post-uprising political violence and the inability of actors to compromise to create new political systems closed that space. The case of Egypt is particularly telling, the country having gone from holding two rounds of free and fair elections in 2012 – legislative and presidential – to a military coup that has made the country more authoritarian than at any time under Mubarak (Stacher 2016). This negative trend has been bucked in Algeria, where the ruling elites attempted to fend off greater criticism by permitting more dissent to be voiced openly, but the overall score still means that the country ranks in the bottom 22 per cent. In fact, only Tunisia has seen a marked improvement.

4.2 Political stability

Political stability has also suffered greatly following the uprisings; in fact, the indicators show that all the MENA countries are much less stable than they were in the period between 2000 and 2010. While pre-uprising stability was predicated on authoritarian practices, there was nonetheless a routinised and predictable way for ordinary citizens to interact with state authorities. Simultaneously the authorities themselves, keen on at least adopting the rhetoric of liberalisation and human rights, tended to rarely employ harsh repression. Even 'security states', such as Tunisia and Syria, began to introduce the language of rights, freedom and democracy to frame their domestic policies. While they were devoid of any meaningful content, such declarations also provided a degree of stability between state and citizens. Institutional stability also seemed to be relatively strong with routinised practices of change at the helm of the state, which was internalised by both citizens and political actors. For a time the only 'change' in the MENA region seemed to be generational renewal within the same family, with princes becoming kings in monarchies and with republics also becoming hereditary. Just as Bashar al-Assad had replaced his father in Syria, it was predicted that the same would occur in Egypt, Yemen, Libya and Tunisia (Sadiki 2010). This political stability no longer exists because states have virtually collapsed or are under such strain that their stability can only be temporary and precarious. Political stability does not even characterise Tunisia because of the fragility of the transition to democracy, although this negative score should be tempered with the knowledge that the country is building the foundations of a liberal-democratic political system that in the long run might enjoy greater legitimacy than any other regime in the region, with the possible exception of Turkey and Israel. For the moment the difficult socio-economic situation still threatens the young liberal-democratic structures in place.

4.3 Effectiveness of government

The effectiveness of governments has also been reduced generally across the MENA region, but there are notable exceptions worth examining in some detail. Effectiveness of government was never particularly strong before the uprisings and it was in part the absence of efficient government that spurred the protests, but a number of states sought to balance their increasing repression with improvements in efficiency. Algeria, Iran, Iraq, Jordan, Qatar, Saudi Arabia and even Bahrain, which experienced a significant challenge to its regime, have improved their score, albeit slightly, since the mid-2000s. It should, however, be emphasised that the quality of services the state provided was either low or non-existent even in states such as Algeria, where oil wealth would have permitted ruling elites to provide them. The small Gulf states constitute an exception to this, although it should be recognised that government effectiveness applies only to their citizens and not to the large numbers of migrant workers residing in the country. With the focus of 'surviving' states on security and with nearly collapsed (Iraq and Syria) or collapsing states (Libya and Yemen) engulfed in armed conflicts, the Arab state seems to have returned to a trait that Ayubi (1996) had highlighted in his work, namely that the Arab state is both fierce – capable of doing repression well – and weak and ineffective at the same time because it is incapable of delivering efficient services in all the other domains of state activity.

4.4 The regulatory quality of states

The regulatory quality of states and their ability and willingness to uphold the rule of law has also worsened following the uprisings because of the reduced resources available to make regulations work. Regulatory processes were weak to begin with even in pre-uprising times, as states simply instituted sham compliance with the political and economic requirements of good governance. In the post-uprising period even that facade has collapsed given the domestic and, crucially, international preoccupation with security and stability. To summarise:

> the perception of government effectiveness – the reach and quality of public service, the professionalism and independence of the civil service, the quality of policy formulation and implementation, and the credibility of the government's commitment to such policies – has declined in several ACTs (Arab Countries in Transition) between 2010 and 2012. (Economic Window 2014)

Again there are some exceptions to this general negative trend, particularly in the Gulf states. This is largely due to the need to conform to the requirements of a globalised economy insofar as these states have attempted to diversify their oil-dependent economies by attracting foreign investment. In doing so they have had to shed some of the clientelistic practices that characterised their regulatory processes and agencies. Paradoxically, Iraq and Libya have also seen their scores improve, probably in conjunction with their reinsertion into the global economy after the collapse of the respective regimes and the considerable international presence in designing new institutions.

4.5 The rule of law

The rule of law has also generally suffered in the post-uprising period. While the indicator emphasises that no arbitrary or personal decisions should be made and that citizens and rulers are subject to the law, this has demonstrably not been the case where large anti-regime demonstrations occurred (with the exception of Morocco) or where uprisings succeeded. For example, since Abdel Fattah al-Sisi took over Egypt nearly 1,000 people have disappeared at the hands of the security forces with no respect for the legal processes that are theoretically in place. While one might expect this from a country that has reverted back to authoritarian rule, similar practices have occurred in Tunisia where, since summer 2013, the government has clamped down on Salafism in all its manifestations and outside the newly established legal frameworks (Cavatorta 2015).

The end of corruption or at least a serious and sustained attempt to counter the phenomenon by the state was among the more forceful calls that emerged from Arab Spring protesters. This suggested a severe problem with corruption across the region, although it should be underscored that the term does not refer simply to traditional bribery, but also, more importantly, to the widespread belief that the socio-economic system is rigged to the benefit of the few. This sentiment has heightened in the post-uprising period as the scarcity of resources, the entrenchment of authoritarian regimes and the collapse of some states have left ordinary citizens not only devoid of confidence in state institutions, but also in the hands of militias, armed factions and security forces. These actors extract benefits from the population to sustain them, thereby making it practically impossible for the authorities to rein them in. It is no surprise that the '2010–11 Arab Barometer' found that about two-thirds of MENA respondents perceived the performance of their government in improving basic health services as 'bad' or 'very bad'. More broadly, citizens of the MENA countries say in response to surveys that their governments 'must do better in ensuring service delivery and fighting corruption' (Brixi et al. 2015: 2). Tunisia and Turkey constitute an exception here, with both countries improving slightly in recent years.

In sum, the 'good governance model', which was failing before the uprisings, should now be considered redundant in any analysis of the region.

5 Conclusion

As mentioned, this chapter has not debated the validity of the World Bank's indicators of good governance, but analysed how they came about and how they might help achieve real change. It is for this reason that we do not question the indicators per se; rather we discuss the rationale behind good governance and try to explain its failure through an analysis of its structural and contingent weakness.

The key objectives of good governance are to foster democratic regimes and promote development, but this did not occur in the region and the Arab uprisings have generally worsened the situation. Countries that did not experience political instability and that had improving indicators before 2010 have been able to maintain them with the exception of 'voice and accountability' and 'political stability', which have fallen due to growing security concerns. Israel and Turkey have maintained reasonably good indicators in all categories because they have not been affected domestically by the uprisings. The World Bank has recently proposed a new strategy to deal with the issue of good governance in the Middle East and North Africa, suggesting four potential pillars that local, national and international actors should build upon to address the concern of sliding scores. They are:

- renewing the social contract, because development must have citizens' trust, effective protection of the vulnerable, inclusive and accountable service delivery and greater participation of the private sector in order to create jobs and opportunities for young people[4]
- regional cooperation to improve collaboration between MENA countries around specific public goods and sectors such as education, water and energy
- resilience 'by promoting the welfare of refugees, internally displaced persons and host communities by focusing on building their assets'
- reconstruction and recovery related to longer-term humanitarian crises.

While these proposed solutions make sense theoretically and are certainly suggestions that could improve governance, they are as detached from the reality on the ground as the original model of good governance was. Ruling elites have neither the political incentives nor the resources to improve the quality of services. They certainly have no intention of rendering the political system more accountable, as this would undermine the very nature of the process through which they acquire enormous benefits. In this they find the tacit or open support of the international community, which is much more concerned with stability and security than with providing the resources necessary to help in the renewal of social contracts that would create employment and greater opportunities for ordinary citizens. In part this is also due to the widely held belief that market solutions actually work when the reality has demonstrated and continues to demonstrate they do not work in authoritarian Arab settings. In fact, this emphasis on the market and the reduction of the role of the state is precisely what demonstrators during the uprisings railed against. Ordinary Arab citizens seem to want more state intervention, particularly in the economic sphere.[5] All of this can be said without even considering the number of collapsed states in the region that prevent any meaningful discussion about how the socio-economic crisis affecting the Arab world could be tackled.

Notes

1. Available at <http://www.worldbank.org/en/region/mena/overview#2> (last accessed 7 July 2016).
2. For each country the sources used are: Afrobarometer, Bertelsmann Transformation Index, Freedom House Countries at the Crossroads, The Economist Intelligence Unit, Freedom House, World Economic Forum Global Competitiveness Survey, Global Integrity, Gallup World Poll, CIRI Human Rights Database, IFAD Rural Sector Performance Assessments, Institutional Profiles Database, IREEP African Electoral Index, Latinobarometro, IREX Media Sustainability Index, International Budget Project Open Budget Index, Political Risk Services and the International Country Risk Guide, Reporters Without Borders World Press Freedom Index, Vanderbilt University Americas Barometer Survey, IMD World Competitiveness Yearbook, World Justice Project, and IHS Global Insight Country Risk Rating.
3. In various World Bank tables the early years draw on fewer sources than the last.
4. Available at <http://www.worldbank.org/en/region/mena/overview#2> (last accessed 5 May 2016).
5. The survey found 66 per cent of Arab youths were increasingly concerned about falling oil prices, although 78 per cent still believed that they were entitled to subsidised energy – despite plummeting revenues. Saudi Arabia, the world's largest oil producer, is struggling to undertake large-scale economic reforms in response (ASDA'A Burson-Marsteller 2016).

References

Achcar, Gilbert (2013), *The People Want*, Berkeley and Los Angeles: University of California Press.
Addison, Tony and Mina Baliamoune-Lutz (2006), 'Economic reform when institutional quality is weak: the case of the Maghreb', *Journal of Policy Modeling*, 28 (9): 1029–43.
Andrews, Matt (2008), 'The good governance agenda: beyond indicators without theory', *Oxford Development Studies*, 36 (4): 379–407.
ASDA'A Burson-Marsteller (2016), *The Arab Youth Survey. Inside the Hearts and Minds of Arab Youth*. Available at <http://www.arabyouthsurvey.com/en/home> (last accessed 9 February 2017).

Ayubi, Nazih (1996), *Overstating the Arab State*, London: I. B. Tauris.

Beinin, Joel (2012), 'The rise of Egypt's workers', *Carnegie Papers*, Carnegie Endowment for International Peace: 1–23.

Benraad, Myriam (2015), *Iraq, la revanche de l'histoire*, Paris: Vendemiaire.

Bogaert, Koenraad (2013), 'Contextualising the Arab revolts: the politics behind three decades of neo-liberalism in the Arab world', *Middle East Critique*, 22 (3): 213–34.

Brixi, Hana, Lust, Ellen and Michael Woolcock (2015), *Trust, Voice and Incentives. Learning from Local Success Stories in Service Delivery in the Middle East and North Africa*, Overview, Washington, DC: World Bank Group.

Brownlee, Jason (2012), *Democracy Prevention. the Politics of the US–Egyptian Alliance*, Cambridge: Cambridge University Press.

Carothers, Thomas (2002), 'The end of the transition paradigm', *Journal of Democracy*, 13 (1): 5–21.

Cavatorta, Francesco (2009), *The International Dimension of the Failed Algerian Transition*, Manchester: Manchester University Press.

Cavatorta, Francesco (2015), 'Salafism, liberalism and democratic learning in Tunisia', *Journal of North African Studies*, 20 (5): 770–83.

Chomiak, Laryssa and John P. Entelis (2012), 'Contesting order in Tunisia: crafting political identity', in Francesco Cavatorta (ed.), *Civil Society Activism under Authoritarian Rule*, London: Routledge.

Collier, David and Steven Levitski (1997), 'Democracy with adjectives: conceptual innovation in comparative research', *World Politics*, 49 (3): 430–51.

Cook, Stephen (2005), 'The right way to promote Arab reform', *Foreign Affairs*, 84 (1): 91–102.

Economic Window (2014), *Strengthening Transparency and Good Governance in Arab Transition Countries*. Available at <http://www.imf.org/external/np/blog/nafida/100914.pdf> (last accessed 6 February 2016).

Galbraith, James (2002), 'A perfect crime: inequality in the age of globalization', *Daedalus*, 131 (1): 11–25.

Governance News and Notes (World Bank) (2010), 'A note from the publisher', *Middle East and North Africa Governance News and Notes* 4 (1): 1-12. Available at <http://documents.worldbank.org/curated/en/2010/01/11787521/middle-east-north-africa-mena-governance-news-notes> (last accessed 2 February 2016).

Haddad, Bassam (2012), *Business Actors in Syria: the Political Economy of Authoritarian Resilience*, Stanford: Stanford University Press.

Harvey, David (2007), *A Brief History of Neoliberalism*, Oxford: Oxford University Press.

Haugbølle Hostrup, Rikke and Francesco Cavatorta (2012), 'Vive la grande famille des medias tunisiens. Media reform, authoritarian resilience and societal responses in Tunisia', *Journal of North African Studies*, 17 (1): 97–112.

Heydemann, Steven (ed.) (2004), *Networks of Privilege in the Middle East: the Politics of Economic Reform Revisited*, London: Palgrave Macmillan.

Heydemann, Steven (2007), *Upgrading Authoritarianism in the Arab World*, Brookings Institution. Available at <http://www.brookings.edu/research/papers/2007/10/arabworld> (last accessed 26 January 2017).

Hyden, Goran (2007), 'Governance and poverty reduction in Africa', *PNAS*, 104 (43): 16751–6.

Ishiyama, John and John J. Quinn (2006), 'African phoenix? Explaining the electoral performance of the formerly dominant parties in Africa', *Party Politics*, 12 (3): 317–40.

Jamal, Amaney (2007), *Barriers to Democracy*, Princeton: Princeton University Press.

Jourde, Cédric (2008), 'The master is gone, but does the house still stand? The fate of single-party systems after the defeat of single parties in West Africa', in Edward Friedman and Joseph Wong (eds), *Political Transition in Dominant Party Systems*, London: Routledge, pp. 75–90.

Kaufmann, Daniel, Aart Kraay and Massimo Mastruzzi (2010), *The Worldwide Governance Indicators: A Summary of Methodology, Data and Analytical Issues*, World Bank Policy Research, Working Paper 5430. Available at <http://papers.ssrn.com/sol3/papers.cfm?abstract_id=1682130> (last accessed 6 February 2016).

Kepel, Gilles (2007), *Fitna: guerre au coeur de l'Islam*, Paris: Éditions Gallimard.

Kienle, Eberhard (2001), *A Grand Delusion: Democracy and Economic Reform in Egypt*, London: I. B. Tauris.

Knack, Stephen (2004), 'Does foreign aid promote democracy?', *International Studies Quarterly*, 48 (1): 251–66.

Levitski, Steven and Lucan Way (2002), 'The rise of competitive authoritarianism', *Journal of Democracy*, 13 (2): 51–65.

Levitski, Steven and Lucan Way (2005), 'International linkage and democratization', *Journal of Democracy*, 16 (3): 20–34.

Loschi, Chiara (2016), *Sweeping Too Much Dirt Under a Small Carpet? The Reform of Garbage Disposal Services in Tunisia*, PhD Dissertation, University of Turin.

Manning, Carrie (2005), 'Assessing African party systems after the third wave', *Party Politics*, 11 (6): 707–27.

Marzouki, Nadia (2015), *Tunisia's Rotten Compromise*, Middle East Research and Information Project, July 10. Available at <http://www.merip.org/mero/mero071015> (last accessed 14 January 2016).

Pace, Michelle and Peter Seeberg (eds.) (2010), *The European Union's Democratization Agenda in the Mediterranean*, London: Routledge.

Rivetti, Paola (2015), 'Continuity and change before and after the uprisings in Tunisia, Egypt and Morocco: regime reconfiguration and policymaking in North Africa', *British Journal of Middle Eastern Studies*, 42 (1): 1–11.

Sadiki, Larbi (2010), 'Wither Arab "republicanism"? The rise of family rule and the "end of democratization" in Egypt, Libya and Yemen', *Mediterranean Politics*, 15 (1): 99–107.

Saidi, Nasser and Hala Yared (2003), *eGovernment: Technology for Good Governance, Development and Democracy in the MENA Countries*, Working Papers. Economic Research Forum. Available at <http://econpapers.repec.org/paper/ergwpaper/0304.htm> (last accessed 14 January 2016).

Schlumberger, Oliver (2011), 'The ties that do not bind: the union for the Mediterranean and the future of Euro-Arab relations', *Mediterranean Politics*, 16 (1): 135–53.

Seeberg, Peter (2010), 'Union for the Mediterranean – pragmatic multilateralism and the depoliticization of European–Middle Eastern relations', *Middle East Critique*, 19 (3): 287–302.

Stacher, Joshua (2016), *Egypt Running on Empty*, Middle East Research and Information Project, 8 March. Available at <http://www.merip.org/mero/mero030816> (last accessed 16 February 2016).

Szmolka, Inmaculada (2010), 'Los regímenes políticos híbridos: democracias y autoritarismos con adjetivos. Su conceptualización, categorización y operacionalización dentro de la tipología de regímenes políticos', *Revista de Estudios Políticos*, 147: 103–35.

Szmolka, Inmaculada (2011), 'Democracias y autoritarismos con adjetivos: la clasificación de los países árabes dentro de una tipología general de regímenes políticos', *Revista Española de Ciencia Política*, 26: 11–62.

Teti, Andrea (2012), 'The EU's first response to the "Arab Spring"': a critical discourse analysis of the partnership for democracy and shared prosperity', *Mediterranean Politics*, 17 (3): 266–84.

Villoria, Manuel and Agustin Izquierdo (2015), *Ética Pública y Buen Gobierno*, Madrid: Tecnos.

Weiss, Thomas (2000), 'Governance, good governance and global governance: conceptual and actual challenges', *Third World Quarterly*, 21 (5): 795–814.

Wood, Adrian (1998), 'Globalization and the rise of labour market inequalities', *The Economic Journal*, 108 (450): 1462–82.

World Bank Group (2003), *Better Governance for Development in the Middle East and North Africa*, Washington, DC: The International Bank for Reconstruction and Development/ The World Bank.

Yom, Sean and Mohammad al-Momani (2008), 'The international dimensions of authoritarian regime stability: Jordan in the post-Cold War era', *Arab Studies Quarterly*, 30 (1): 39–60.

Zakaria, Fareed (2004), 'Islam, democracy and constitutional liberalism', *Political Science Quarterly*, 119 (1): 1–20.

Chapter 8

Civil society and social movements

Carmelo Pérez-Beltrán and
Ignacio Álvarez-Ossorio[1]

1 Introduction

Since 2011 Middle East and North Africa (MENA) region countries have been immersed in a period of turmoil as a result of the anti-authoritarian revolts that unfolded in some of them. Civil society played a crucial role in the Arab Spring, although in many cases, it did not know how or was unable to take advantage of the new turn of events to consolidate its position.

With its appeals to freedom, justice and dignity, the Arab Spring demonstrated that, unlike the assertions made by those in favour of an 'Islamic exception' (Kedourie 1992; Gellner 1994), there was nothing in Arab societies that would make them averse to democracy. Mass demonstrations initiated a period of political change that did not always lead to opening the door to democracy, but meant, in most cases, the reconstitution of authoritarianism and fragmentation of the Islamist camp (Álvarez-Ossorio 2015).

In this respect the Tunisian transition, in which the National Dialogue Quartet played an outstanding role, remains an exception. The norm, on the other hand, is marked by the preservation of the status quo (as in Algeria, Jordan and Oman), the introduction of cosmetic reforms (in Morocco, for example), a return to authoritarian dynamics (in Egypt after the return to power of the military-backed government or in Bahrain after the intervention of Gulf Cooperation Council troops), the strengthening of the rentier state (as in Saudi Arabia, United Arab Emirates and Qatar, which set policies of co-optation and redistribution in motion) and, finally, the disintegration of the state (in Libya, Syria and Yemen, countries that plunged into civil wars of a marked sectarian or tribal nature).

In general terms we can state that the main victim of this drift has been civil society, which has seen its organisations and movements systematically persecuted and its freedom of manoeuvre constrained from a legal point of view. Since 2011 some countries have restricted the channels of external funding to civil society associations (Egypt and Israel, among others) or curbed press freedom (the case of Turkey, where the daily newspaper with the largest circulation, *Zaman*, was taken over).

The objective of this chapter is to establish a general framework that will enable us to assess the situation of civil society in the MENA region, before and after the Arab Spring, and, more particularly, the role it played during the mass demonstrations recorded in 2011. We shall focus therefore on those countries that initiated processes of political liberalisation in the 1980s and 1990s in which the Arab Spring revolts took hold with greatest force, since they are spaces in which civil society has played a more prominent role. Other countries will feature less in this study because the rigid authoritarian system prevented the development of autonomous organisational structures and activism, such as Saudi Arabia and most of the Gulf monarchies.

2 Civil society, economic crisis and democratic transition

Since the creation of the modern Arab state, authoritarian regimes have sought to limit the freedom of manoeuvre of civil society, with Arab rulers systematically ignoring democratic principles such as tolerance, freedoms and pluralism. Nevertheless, civil society came back with force in the 1980s, due, above all, to the crisis of the Arab state, the breaking of the social contract between ruler and ruled, the demographic boom, the financial and economic crisis, and the awakening of minorities; in short, the erosion of the legitimacy on which the post-colonial state was established (Khader 2010: 259–67). It was then that 'religious movements, secular organizations and liberal-oriented human rights groups discovered "civil society" as a major instrument in the context of their efforts to democratically transform the political landscape' (Hamzawy 2002: 7). It was also the moment when the major international agencies and the European policies of cooperation redirected their gaze south of the Mediterranean, seeking partnership in accordance with their guiding principles to further their development projects.

Given the failure of the statist model of development and the deepening economic crisis, Arab governments were forced to apply rigid structural adjustment programmes, supervised by the International Monetary Fund (IMF) and the World Bank, in order to service runaway foreign debt. More importantly, rulers were obliged to break their social contracts with those they ruled. Morocco was the first North African country to initiate a Structural Adjustment Plan in 1983, for the purpose of dealing with an unsustainable foreign debt that had multiplied sevenfold between 1974 and 1983 (Mejjati 1996: 71–2). Algeria would follow (1986), then Tunisia (1987), Jordan (1989) and Egypt (1991). The deteriorating economic situation in Syria also led to it being obliged to introduce liberalisation measures that allowed the private sector to expand and opened up the country to foreign investment.

Bearing in mind the extreme seriousness of the economic situation, which further exacerbated the impoverished family economy, it is not surprising that popular revolts, symptomatic of a new social mobility, broke out in various countries during this period, and which were harshly put down. These were known as the 'bread riots' or 'hunger riots', which occurred in Egypt (1977), Morocco (1981), Tunisia (1984), Algeria (1988) and Jordan (1989).

This chaotic, unplanned state withdrawal from public space largely explains civil society's dynamic commitment to charity work, its direct involvement in local development and its struggle against poverty in the widest sense from the 1980s onwards (Pérez-Beltrán 2004). Given the lack of state intervention in key sectors – employment, health, food, education, the family, childhood and infrastructure – it would be civil society itself that would attempt to intervene in the domains that were hardest hit or lacked proper management. On many occasions the state institutions themselves encouraged civil society organisations to play an active role in the economic development of the country, with the further objective of preventing Islamism, which also acted in the most depressed environments, from taking greater hold.

Together with the economic crisis, another of the key factors related to the development of civil society concerned the processes of 'controlled' transition that were set in motion during this same period. Some Arab regimes, in the face of widespread questioning, were forced to introduce certain political reforms that, in the majority of cases, were merely stop-gap, cosmetic measures directed towards guaranteeing the survival of rulers who were increasingly being challenged. To prevent their collapse, the authoritarian regimes opted for a limited liberalisation policy based on the formal acceptance of a multiparty system and holding elections, even though these were neither transparent nor competitive (Álvarez-Ossorio and Zaccara 2009). This openness was authorised because, in the face of the seriousness of the crisis in which they found themselves, the regimes themselves gave the go-ahead for the reforms and allowed the mobilisation of civil society as a survival strategy (Szmolka 2011).

Accordingly, at the end of the 1980s, Algeria started the significant transition from a single to a multiparty system, which meant a brief but fruitful stage for democratic freedoms and which was interrupted by the outbreak of a traumatic civil war, which largely explains the present social ultraconservatism and authoritarianism of the Bouteflika regime. In Tunisia Ben Ali's regime took over from Bourguiba's in 1987; before adopting an iron-fist policy, he initially promoted a certain national consensus among the country's major political forces, by including such a highly representative sector as Ennahda, which was subsequently outlawed in 1992. During the first years of his mandate the strictest clauses of the Law of Association (Organic Law 88-90, 2 August 1988) were modified, which prompted the appearance of 3,500 new associations, most of them charitable, educational and sporting in nature. Not too dissimilar was the case of Egypt in 1981 with the coming to power of Mubarak, who triggered a similar process of stabilisation of the institutions and greater dynamism in the political arena, before taking an authoritarian turn. Jordan also registered reforms with the restoration of the multiparty system and the holding of the first parliamentary elections in three decades in 1989.

Within this framework that we have just outlined, the assumptions of the theory of transitology and democratisation underwent a significant development. Taking criticism of authoritarian forms of government and the rejection of the absolute pre-eminence of the state in social, political and economic life as the starting point, an attempt was made to understand the changes that Arab countries had been through, frequently taking as models the experiences of some of the Latin American countries, and, in particular, of Eastern European countries where social movements such as Solidarnosc (Solidarity) in Poland or Charter 77 in the former Czechoslovakia had managed to undermine the authoritarian nature of the regimes in power (Ayee 2004: 33). As Cavatorta stated (2012: 75): 'This meant that scholars and policymakers interpreted events in the region as steps, either forward or backward, on the straight line that inevitably takes countries from authoritarian rule towards the establishment of a liberal-democratic system.'

As for the topic that concerns us here, transitology generally awards civil society a fundamental role in delegitimising political authoritarianism, driving democratic changes, championing freedoms and as the leading actor against authoritarian regimes, to the extent that civil society and democracy are considered indissociable elements. In Camau's words, transition is considered to be 'a catalyst for a social dynamic characterised by the "resurrection" of civil society' (1999: 4). For this reason, among the manifestations of civil society, the associations and movements fighting for what we might call, generally, human rights and democratic freedoms took a leading role and, thanks to the processes of liberalisation underway, succeeded in accentuating their political dimension. For Saad E. Ibrahim, some organisations started to practise 'politics by proxy', consisting of 'articulating and debating public issues, formulating public policy alternatives and exerting pressure on decision-makers' (2002: 255).

The empowerment of organisations in defence of women's rights took place within this context, with the unfolding of a wide range of collectives, groups and associations that promoted the status of women and gender equality from diverse ideological standpoints. During this period women's organisations managed to break free from the large state structures (the national women's unions), and the political parties that brought their influence to bear on them, in order to form new, more autonomous organisational structures. Thus, the so-called 'Feminist Spring' arose, with associations such as the Arab Women's Solidarity Association, formed in 1982 by the Egyptian activist Nawal al-Saadawi, the Association for Legal Equality Between Men and Women (Algeria, 1985), the Association for the Emancipation of Women (Algeria, 1989), the Union of Feminine Action (Morocco, 1987), the Democratic Association for Moroccan Women (1985) and the Tunisian Association of Democratic Women (1989), to name just a few.

As well as activism against patriarchy and all gender inequality, these associations were characterised by their struggle in favour of the greater presence of women in political, economic and social structures and their constant demands for modernising the family codes that regulated marriage, divorce, inheritance and the custody of children. This phenomenon, however, did not extrapolate to all countries in the MENA region, since during that same period the centripetal tendencies of the mass movements were further reinforced, if that were possible, in other countries in the Middle East, as in the case of the General Federation of Jordanian Women, closely linked with the Hashemite monarchy (Abdallah 2009), or the General Federation of Iraqi Women, which was the only mass organisation permitted during Saddam Hussein's regime and became an extension of the government itself and an agent of the indoctrination of the female population (Hindi 2015: 233–5).

Another area in which significant advances were noted was in the human rights movement, which, despite the control mechanisms and other handicaps, managed to denounce human rights violations through protest campaigns, periodic visits to prisons and detention centres, drew up lists of those detained, disappeared and tortured, or investigated deaths in suspicious circumstances or places, with the details of which, many of these associations published communiqués and other documents for dissemination, as far as they were able, in various media. No less important was their activism against the lack of individual and collective freedoms, the excesses of the established regimes, the arbitrary nature of government policies and cutbacks in democracy, as well as providing legal aid to people who had been victims of abuse, torture or disappearance, or programmes to inform and make people aware of the fundamental principles of human rights. One of the first associations of this kind was the Tunisian Human Rights League, founded in 1977. In later years other organisations with similar objectives sprang up, such as the Moroccan Association of Human Rights (1979), the Arab Organization for Human Rights (1983), the Egyptian Organization of Human Rights (1985), the Moroccan Human Rights Organization (1988), the Algerian League for the

Defense of Human Rights (1987), the Palestinian Centre for Human Rights (1995), the Arab Commission for Human Rights (1998), the Amman Center for Human Rights Studies (1999) and the Bahrain Center for Human Rights (2002), among others. In order to avoid repression, many of these associations were forced to transfer their headquarters to Western or other Arab countries, as in the case of Human Rights in the Maghreb, with its headquarters in Paris, the Syrian Human Rights Committee, based in London, the Committee for the Defense of Human Rights in the Arabian Peninsula, with headquarters in Beirut and other associations related to the Sahara question or Kurdistan, such as the Association of the Families of Sahrawi Prisoners and Disappeared or the Kurdish Human Rights Project, to quote just some examples.

Within the framework of transitology and the view of civil society as an intrinsic factor in the transition from authoritarianism to democracy, Islamism is also perceived as an endogenous manifestation of this civil society; from its ethical and political view of Islam, it has not only brought together and amplified the aspirations and frustrations of the citizens in the face of authoritarian power, but also fulfilled highly important aid and charity work by means of solidarity and charity networks for the purpose of intervening both in the most poverty-stricken environments and slums and in university, trade union and professional circles. Islamist movements such as al-Ikhwan al-Muslimun (Muslim Brotherhood) in Egypt, 'Adl wa Ihsan (Justice and Spirituality) in Morocco, Da'wa (Islamic Call Party) in Iraq, Hamas in Palestine and the Gülen movement in Turkey have been highly active in domains associated with education, health and charity via the creation of a major network of private schools, health centres, legal aid bureaus, the organisation of visits to hospitals and prisons, the distribution of food and essential goods and awarding grants and aid to students. According to Ben Nefissa (2011b), 30 per cent of Egyptian associations in the 1990s had some reference to Islam in their titles and a dense network available nationwide, such as the Gamia al-Shari'ah, which had, at the time, 457 branches across Egyptian territory and controlled the activities of some 7,000 mosques. Another point to be underlined is that, within these trends, women were not only highly visible, but also demonstrated activism of prime importance, characterised by the multiple issues and spaces in which they intervened, from the theological to providing care.

3 Civil society and the persistence of authoritarianism

This process of political liberalisation was not experienced in every country, since the authoritarian regimes that were most closed off, such as the Gulf monarchies and the Middle Eastern Ba'athist republics, stubbornly resisted any type of openness to democracy. In the Syrian case, absolute control of the country by the Ba'ath Party not only prevented an autonomous civil society from emerging, but also spread an atavistic fear of any kind of anti-government political activism throughout the population. As the female activist Suhayr al-Atasi pointed out in an interview to the Arab daily *al-Sharq al-Awsat* on 16 July 2011:

> We have been subject to suppression and murder for merely calling for freedom, democracy, general freedoms, the release of all prisoners of conscience, an end to the state of emergency, and the return of all political exiles. At the time, we said that any suppression would cause the volcano to erupt.

Not too dissimilar was the case of Iraq, which, during the prolonged armed conflict with Iran (1980–8), drifted towards an increasingly authoritarian system in the hands of the immediate family of Saddam Hussein, backed by a ruthless state security apparatus.

In the 1990s the processes of openness to democracy that had started in various countries were put on ice. Regimes in Tunisia, Algeria and Egypt set various strategies in motion to regain their monopolies in the political and economic arenas. Hence, they declared political parties illegal (mainly Islamist, but also left-wing ones and any other critical sector), persecuted the opposition, manipulated elections, interfered with the judicial system and tightened control over economic resources. Hard-line policies devastated all civil society organisations focused on defending democratic freedoms and human rights, making use of highly restrictive legislation to do so. Using the Organic Law of 1992, Ben Ali succeeded in dismantling the organisational structures of the Tunisian Human Rights League, the Association of Magistrates and the National Syndicate of Tunisian Journalists by infiltrating elements close to power into these associations without their being able to do anything about it (Pérez-Beltrán 2014a). Something similar occurred in Egypt, where Law 84 of 2002 enabled the authorities to short-circuit civil society work and dissolve those organisations regarded as troublesome. According to Kausch (2009), this law amounts to

> a large set of interlocking restrictive laws and provisions, as well as the general political framework, [which] put severe restrictions on Egyptian civil society and, in particular, leave NGOs active in the field of human rights hardly any room to operate.

In the case of Bahrain, the 1989 law enabled the Bahrain Center for Human Rights to be dissolved, claiming that 'it incited hatred' by criticising the economic policy of the prime minister and accusing him of suspected corruption (Sakr 2005). In the same vein, in 2010 the Ministry of Social Development broke up the managing board of the Bahrain Human Rights Society and replaced its president with a civil servant, due to the association's criticism of violations of legal procedure suffered by detainees of the political opposition (access to lawyers, family visits, and so on) (Human Rights Watch 2013). The Saudi regime, meanwhile, tried to appropriate the discourse of human rights by establishing the National Society for Human Rights in 2004; it also encouraged an Arab Charter on Human Rights which stated, like the Cairo Declaration on Human Rights in Islam issued by the Islamic Summit Conference in 1990, that universally accepted human rights could not clash with the shariah (Islamic law) (Buendía 2013: 137–57).

In Syria the hopes generated by the coming to power of Bashar al-Assad in 2000 were soon dashed. The demands for greater freedoms and the end of authoritarianism voiced during the Damascus Spring were cut short. Apart from various forums of debate promoted by intellectuals and activists, the Committees for the Defense of Democratic Liberties and Human Rights, the Human Rights Association of Syria and the Committees for the Revival of Civil Society were also established. After some months of intense activity, most of their founders were arrested, tried and imprisoned on the charge of 'inciting sectarian strife' or 'spreading false or exaggerated news that weakens national sentiment' (Human Rights Watch 2010).

The course of history itself, which is easily verifiable, clearly demonstrated the limits and failure of the paradigm of transitology, and at the beginning of the twenty-first century the dominant theoretical trend was to highlight the persistence of authoritarianism (Carothers 2002: 17). As a result, a good proportion of the studies on the political situation in the Arab countries mainly stressed the mechanisms, strategies and dimensions of those who made use of the regimes to maintain an authoritarian system, despite keeping up a front or appearance of democracy (Hinnebusch 2006).

Transitology started from the premise that civil society could become a catalyst for democracy in the Arab world. Conversely, the paradigm of the persistence of authoritarianism interpreted civil society as not only incapable of influencing policies and eluding state control, but also as acting as an instrument at the service of the authoritarian regimes, contributing to the depoliticisation of society and the persistence of authoritarianism (Cavatorta 2012: 75–6; El Hachimi 2014: 7–8). In other words, instead of civil society promoting democratisation in Arab countries, it served to reinforce authoritarian politics, even reproducing internally the same authoritarian patterns, while the collectives and movements with greater sociopolitical mobility fighting for democratic change remain on the margins and are subject to strict control by state institutions.

Taking Egypt as a reference, Ben Nefissa (2011b) pointed out that civil society organisations operated as a sort of dismembered appendage of local government, whose role was to make up for the deficiencies of the state while participating in the official strategy of depoliticising local institutions. In short, civil society was revealed as being under the control of the state – or to peripheral structures, such as the army – and becoming a means of expression for civil servants or local elites very close to the official National Democratic Party. As Ababsa (2011) pointed out, the Jordanian case was very similar, with more than 3,145 associations in 2009, although with the distinctive feature that most of them lacked political culture and served as agencies to liaise with the state. Furthermore, these associations were generally referred to as Royal NGOs because of their close relationship with the Hashemite monarchy structures, which also favoured them when it came to obtaining funds from international agencies. In the case of Syria the NGO sector boomed in the first decade of Bashar al-Assad's government, increasing from 555 in 2002 to 1,485 in 2009, according to the Ministry of Social Affairs and Labour (Ruiz de Elvira and Zintl 2014: 335-6), although the most important ones with most resources were governmental NGOs (GONGOs) in presidential circles, such as the First Lady, Asma al-Assad's The Syria Trust for Development or Jam'iyyat al-Bustan al-Khayriyya of Rami Makhluf, the president's cousin and the leading businessman in the country.

The theoretical framework of the persistence of authoritarianism highlights two of the main characteristics shared by most civil society organisations in the MENA region: firstly, they are heavily involved in charity work associated with the sphere of human development in order to fight against poverty in its many guises, and, secondly, their local character, which favours the fragmentation of activism and hampers its capacity for mobilisation and raising political awareness (Guilmain 2014: 16–17; El Hachimi 2014: 11–14). This civil society is, in large measure, the result of certain development policies seeking to involve the network of associations in the fight against poverty by setting up local development projects, but without political leanings. It is a kind of 'solidarity economy' (Gandolfi 2013: 8) consisting of a set of activities based on the commitment of citizens yet closely coordinated with the state, which becomes an instrument of control, and without excluding collaboration with the private sector. Even in societies with long histories of mobilising people, such as Palestine, after the Oslo Accords (1993) and the establishment of the Palestinian Authority (1994), there was also a process of depoliticisation and professionalisation of civil society

> owing to its growing importance as a supplier of services and greater access to foreign financing, but also a consequence of conditions imposed by fund donors and the need to create complex financial and administrative structures to manage these new resources. (Charif 2011: 352)

This phenomenon also translates into a loss of legitimacy of the NGOs in the eyes of their traditional social bases, since they are forced to break with their past as political activists, despite the maintenance of the Israeli occupation and even the increasing number of settlements (Barreñada 2015: 221–2).

In this context Egypt set up three national councils between 2000 and 2003: the National Council for Childhood and Motherhood, the National Council for Women and the National Council for Human Rights, while Morocco instituted the National Initiative for Human Development in 2005. These cases clearly fall under the strategies highlighted earlier, since they seek to capture international aid development funds and channel economic resources, counting on civil society organisations as partners or simply taking their place. The immediate consequence of this close collaboration was dependence on the state, which became the main provider of economic resources, and also the technification and professionalisation of the social actors, with the objective of improving training and effectiveness when it came to obtaining greater funding (Bono 2010). There were other no less important consequences, such as installing a technical, depoliticised notion of 'development' and an increase in associations specialising in social benevolent activism (Ruiz de Elvira and Zintl 2014). In this respect, El Hachemi (2014:17) points out, for example, that only 2 per cent of Moroccan associations have a political agenda.

4 Civil society and the Arab Spring

The Arab Spring did not arise spontaneously, but was the result of a process that had been incubating for decades and whose principal triggers were the general discontent of the population towards their rulers and the worsening of the economic crisis. In the opinion of Abdelrahman (2011: 423), 'social and political change, whether radical or along reformist lines, does not arise from a vacuum. It is a result of a long process of accumulation, mobilization, networking and the evolution of a different, more inclusive culture'.

Revolts are built on previous experiences of mobilisation and politicisation by various vanguard movements directly involved in struggles against political and economic corruption, for wage claims, improved living conditions, gender equality, recognition of cultural diversity, promotion of human rights, and so on. The Egyptian revolution, for example, which started on 25 January 2011, was indebted to previous experiences of coalitions, such as the umbrella movement Kefaya (Enough), which came into being in 2004 as a protest against Mubarak's attempts to run for a fifth presidential mandate (Shorbagy 2007). Kefaya had unsuccessfully called for the abolition of the Emergency Law, the end to the political monopoly of the National Democratic Party, the fight against corruption and the end to violations of human rights by the security forces, demands that would be taken up again in Tahrir Square in 2011. In fact, the Egyptian activists imitated Kefaya's mobilisation tactics, including occupying the streets, the use of ICT, informal meetings, demonstrations without seeking prior authorisation and joining in as individuals (Ben Nefissa 2011b).

Although it had a religious aspect that differentiated it, the political society al-Wefaq may also be regarded as an earlier experience of mobilisation in Bahrain and as the main movement to politically oppose the monarchy under King Hamad bin Isa bin Salman al-Khalifa. From its foundation in 2001, al-Wefaq had a major track record of struggle against the regime, which was accused of breaking the promise of political liberalisation made when the king took over in 1999. From then until the mass demonstrations in Pearl Square in February 2011, this movement was characterised by significant activism against the sociopolitical discrimination to which the majority Shia population – around 70 per cent – was subjected, and the regime's aggressive policy of naturalising foreigners in order to equalise the demographic balance in favour of the Sunnis (Saldaña 2011).

During the Arab Spring, the young, who represented a third of the population, led the way in demonstrations, demanding dignity, freedom and social justice; this was only natural, given that the young and women were the social groups that suffered most from the deteriorating living conditions, unemployment and precariousness, and not only in Egypt, but also in Tunisia, Morocco, Syria, Yemen, Bahrain and other Arab countries. As the opposition activist Haytham al-Maleh had reminded the daily *al-Sharq al-Awsat* on 13 July 2011: 'We, the Syrian opposition and intellectuals, did not create the revolution. The revolution is the work of the young people. Now, they need political support and we wish to be with them in this revolution'.

In Tunisia one of the most dynamic actors in the emerging civil society was the Union of Unemployed Graduates, which was never legalised in the Ben Ali era but had more than 10,000 members by 2013 (Ketiti 2013: 152). The role of cyberactivists, most of them equally young, was crucial, as they denounced abuses of power and circumvented the strict censorship of the authoritarian regimes, obtaining an outstanding virtual activist presence, rapid access to information and greater capacity for coordination (Boughzala 2012). Youth organisations likewise played a decisive role in the success of the Egyptian revolution, especially the April 6 Youth Movement, created in 2008 to show solidarity with the strike called by the textile workers in Mahalla al-Kubra. This group became one of the most dynamic movements and with the greatest capacity for mobilisation in Egypt.

Given the success of the mobilisations, other sectors of the population joined in spontaneously, with the creative use of horizontal communication,

and what stood out most, they were independent of traditional organisational structures (NGOs, parties, trade unions, associations). Indeed, one of
the main keys to their success was that the revolts went beyond traditional
political, sectarian, tribal and class divisions, which is why they were labelled
post-ideological (Haugbølle 2012).

In Yemen men and women congregated in the so-called Change Square
to call for Saleh's downfall. The Watan Coalition – Women for Social Peace,
a network of activist women established in 2006 to 'create awareness among
other sectors of the revolutionary movement on matters of gender, as well as
form alliances with men to gain their support in promoting women's rights'
(Strzelecka 2012). Tawakkol Kerman, the activist-founder of the organisation
Women Journalists Without Chains, became one of the visible faces of the
Yemeni revolution, for which she was awarded the Nobel Peace Prize in 2011.

Similar in nature is the 20 February Movement in Morocco, an umbrella
movement of people from very disparate social sectors and ideological
tendencies calling for 'constitutional change to transform the country into a
parliamentary monarchy in which the king reigns but does not rule, as well as
the resignation of Abbas el-Fassi's government, the dissolution of parliament,
and the fight against corruption' (López-García 2011). It was a movement that
overcame traditional ideological and organisational barriers (Desrues 2012)
and where women also played a leading role and acquired visibility, becoming
symbols of the fight against regime repression and the patriarchal system that
also oppressed them.

With the exception of countries like Saudi Arabia where unions were
banned, with the argument that the state protected workers' rights (Sakr
2005), the labour movement also played a crucial role during the 2011 revolts,
although its activism in earlier years had already demonstrated its capacity
for struggle in favour of the working class (Barreñada 2013: 111–36). In
Tahrir Square the creation of the Egyptian Federation of Independent Trade
Unions (EFITU) was announced, which played a fundamental role in the
fall of Mubarak by calling a general strike that had a wide following in Cairo,
Alexandria, the Suez Canal and Mahalla al-Kubra. EFITU positioned itself in its
statutes as in favour of union freedoms, democracy, social justice, equality and
human rights. Among other issues, the 2011 uprising questioned the official
union, the Egyptian Trade Union Federation, and supported the creation of
more than 150 local independent unions (Elrazzaz 2013: 53). In Bahrain the
General Federation of Bahrain Trade Unions also played a significant role in
the popular revolt of 2011, and in Yemen the General Federation of Workers'
Trade Unions of Yemen had a leading role.

In Tunisia the Tunisian General Labour Union also has a long record of
protest in defence of the population's labour rights. Although the Ben Ali

regime managed to control its leadership, the grassroots militants maintained their 'militant, combative spirit' as the miners' protests in Gafsa in 2008 showed (Ketiti 2013: 136). On 14 January 2011 they called a general strike that was widely followed and was crucial for accelerating the Tunisian president's departure from the political scene. Although activist militancy in Algeria seemed to show greater symptoms of fatigue, even exhaustion, the major sector revolts associated with income distribution and the emergence of a new social mobilisation around autonomous unions and groups of unemployed or precarious workers should not be ignored (CCFD-Terre Solidaire and Institut de relations internationales et stratégiques 2014: 53).

5 Civil society and processes of political change after the Arab Spring

After the Arab Spring transition processes were set in motion that did not herald a fifth democratic wave, but rather the arrival of an uncertain phase of political change. Various civil society actors took advantage of the new situation to demand the adoption of a multiparty system, the holding of free elections, identifying those responsible for the repression, respect for human rights, the reform of the security apparatus and approval of new constitutions that were genuinely constitutionalist.

Nonetheless, the context for this process of political change was not a propitious one, since the social, economic and political imbalances were exacerbated, due to both internal and external factors. The deteriorating economic crisis translated into the withdrawal of investment, increasing inflation, deepening unemployment and the contraction of GDP. At the same time, the conquest of the government by Islamist parties (the Muslim Brotherhood in Egypt and Ennahda in Tunisia) polarised society and caused increasingly obvious tension between the secular and religious sectors. Finally, the irruption of jihadi groups, which attacked the security forces and the tourist sector, meant new setbacks for the newly elected governments.

The transition initiated in Tunisia after the fall of Ben Ali allowed civil society to truly blossom. In 2011–12 the number of civil society organisations increased from 10,000 to 15,000 (Ketiti 2013: 137). The blossoming was encouraged by the legal framework created by the new Decree Law on Associations, passed on 24 September 2011, which simplified the procedures for establishing or managing associations and involved no criminal sanctions (Pérez-Beltrán 2014a). The first storm clouds soon gathered on the horizon, however; prominent leaders of left-wing parties, such as Chokri Belaïd and

Mohamed Brahmi, were assassinated and Salafist groups won positions seeking to influence the transition. Growing political polarisation led Ennahda to step down and to accept the formation of a technocratic government.

Popular pressure created a new climate of understanding, thanks to which a new constitution was passed, which was undoubtedly the one that showed the most respect for the freedoms in all the Arab world. The contribution of the National Dialogue Quartet –comprising the Tunisian Human Rights League, the Tunisian General Labour Union, the Tunisian Confederation of Industry, Trade and Handicrafts, and the Tunisian Order of Lawyers – was instrumental in avoiding the collapse of the Tunisian transition, since one of the main characteristics of Arab civil society in recent years has been its direct action in the political sphere and its intention to become a mediator between the population and the state. This work was recognised with the award of the Nobel Peace Prize in 2015.

On the other hand, along with traditional development aid organisations – which continued to have a notable role as agents in the struggle against poverty – from 2011 onwards, new, more politicised associations emerged in Tunisia independent of the political parties. One such was al-Bawsala, whose objectives included: placing the citizenry at the heart of political debate, building bridges of dialogue between the political elites and voters and promoting a political ethos of good governance. For this, various observatories were launched: Marsad Madjlis to monitor parliamentary activity, Marsad Budget, to track the economic activity of the state and, from 2014, Marsad Baladiya, for users to keep abreast of municipal affairs. The young also, in conjunction with horizontalist platforms, have opted for formal types of organisation, such as the Sawti association (My Voice) and I Watch, whose objectives are to support Tunisian young people during the transition phase and to promote responsible participatory democracy. Tunisia has therefore become the main laboratory at present for investigating the nature of counterpower and the democratic strength of civil society in the MENA region.

In Egypt, on the other hand, the democratic adventure of the Muslim Brotherhood was abruptly cut short; after the overthrow of President Morsi, Abdel Fattah al-Sisi further tightened the screw of authoritarianism by restricting public freedoms. The Muslim Brotherhood, the movement that won the parliamentary elections in 2011 and the presidential elections in 2012, was outlawed and more than 20,000 leaders and sympathisers were jailed and sentenced to long prison terms. The repression did not stop there, since the April 6 Youth Movement was also outlawed and its main leaders imprisoned as they were considered a threat to national security. Leading activists, such as Alaa Abdelfatah, were also given long prison sentences. Since President al-Sisi came to power, public freedoms have regressed considerably, as is evidenced by the enactment of an anti-protest law that severely limits the right to demonstrate.

In other countries with significant protest movements, such as Morocco, Bahrain and Algeria, the situation of civil society has changed little over five years, and still lacks true structural reform to end serious problems like authoritarianism, corruption, restrictions on freedoms and discrimination against certain social sectors. To this list can be added the adoption of even more restrictive laws of association, such as the bill that the Bahraini regime sent to parliament in January 2013, allowing the authorities to refuse to authorise any association if they thought that society did not need its services or there were already other associations with similar objectives (Human Rights Watch 2013). Algeria joined the trend when it promulgated, in January 2012, a law on associations, setting up different control mechanisms by the Ministry of the Interior to prevent the development of solidly constituted social movements at a national level. Other restrictions applied to the control of economic resources, especially those from abroad, and to the introduction of vague reasons for shutting down or dissolving associations (Pérez-Beltrán 2014b). It is hardly surprising therefore that the National Coordination for Change and Democracy, which arose in 2011 as an umbrella group of different trends in Algerian civil society, should end up practically disappearing a short time later. Nonetheless, at the same time, significant social activity was mobilised around various autonomous unions and other collectives involving professionals and the unemployed, with the particular feature that they were not only concentrated on the capital or the Kabylia area, but also reached other regions in the south of the country. The major dilemma facing Algerian civil society today, however, is closely related to the direction that the country will take after Bouteflika has left the political scene.

The attempts to influence the work of NGO organisations were not restricted to the Arab countries in the MENA area, but also included Turkey and Israel. Since 2008 democracy in Turkey has suffered a notable setback due to power being concentrated in the hands of the ruling AKP, which has been translated into restrictions on freedom of the press and expression in both the print media and the social networks (Durán and García 2015: 191–211), and according to Reporters Without Borders, Turkey is, in fact, one of the countries in the world with the highest number of journalists in prison, with more than 100 in 2015. On 1 November 2015 the court ordered trustees to take control of the Koza Ipek media group with close ties to Fethullah Gülen, critical of Erdogan's government. That same month, a Turkish court sent the editor of the daily *Çumhuriyet* to prison, accused of espionage and revealing military secrets after he had denounced the involvement of Turkish intelligence services in arms trafficking with Syrian rebel groups. On 4 March

2016 the Istanbul Prosecutor's Office ordered the takeover of the management of the Feza Media Group, which included the conservative daily, *Zaman,* with the largest circulation in the country, also because of its alleged links with the illegal Gülen organisation. The newspaper had stood out for its frequent denunciations of corruption among prominent members of the Turkish government.

The major problem lies in the fact that the Turkish constitution does not fully guarantee freedom of expression, which is restricted by article 26 whenever it concerns:

> national security, public order, public safety, the protection of the basic characteristics of the republic and the indivisible integrity of the state with its territory and nation, the prevention of crime, the punishment of criminals, the retention of information duly classified as state secret, the protection of the reputation, rights and private family life of others, or the protection of professional secrets as laid down by the law, or to guarantee the proper functioning of judicial power.

As for Israel, the Knesset approved a bill in 2015 to regulate NGO activity. Its objective was none other than to muzzle human rights organisations critical of the systematic violations of human rights perpetrated by Israeli Defence Forces in the occupied Palestinian territories; these organisations included Yesh Din, B'tselem, Breaking the Silence, Adalah and Peace Now, all accused of undermining the legitimacy of Israel. According to this bill, all NGOs receiving more than 50 per cent of its financing from abroad would have to detail this information in all its reports and activities. The Association for Civil Rights of Israel considered the bill to be 'a discriminatory law that harms democracy . . . [and] supports censorship and political persecution'.

6 Conclusions

The mass mobilisation of the population during the Arab Spring undermined many of the theories that dwelt on the depoliticisation of civil society, its inability to influence the political agenda and the customary use made of it as an instrument of authoritarian regimes. Although this activism appeared to take on new forms, it was not spontaneously generated, but included an accumulation of baggage from the past, in constant relationship and tension with the state; hence, along with associations concerned with charity work and development, there also existed another more critical and politically committed type of organisation, in which the theory of the persistence of authoritarianism has not shown sufficient interest.

Likewise, the Arab Spring questions the institutionalised, structured, organisational nature of civil society that transitology usually supports. During the uprisings none of the traditional or formal civil society organisations came to the fore, either in their interventionist (NGOs) or their most contestatory dimensions (human rights organisations, Islamist groups, or more politicised platforms). It was a much more horizontal and heterogeneous movement, one that transcended ideologies and did not fit the conventional mould of civil society but demonstrated, nevertheless, that it had not lost its capacity for advocacy, was not a simple instrument in the service of authoritarian regimes and did not lack a democratic or liberalising dimension either.

The Arab Spring phenomenon demonstrates that contestatory counter-power and the ability to influence politics and promote democratic values may occur in different spaces of the hierarchical structures and organisations that characterise formal civil society. This is the reason why a good part of scientific production around these mobilisations questions or avoids the term 'civil society' to explain these new spaces of expression, and opts for other concepts such as civil activism, category of action, active citizenship, civil society in movement, and so on. This means, in short, that it is necessary to go beyond a certain reductionist view of what civil society is and to propose another concept, much more dynamic, creative and horizontalist that involves not only hierarchical organisational structures, but also other spaces of mobilisation, real or virtual, in which the citizenry can express its social, political and economic commitment. Horizontal action, decentralisation, spontaneous interaction, sociopolitical mediation and fuzzy leadership seem to be the trends in this new civil society calling for more participatory democracy.

Nor can we state that this phenomenon is one of replacement, but rather one of complementarity, because a large part of institutionalised civil society in a wide range of formal organisations and movements (associations, syndicates, unions, leagues, colleges) has, after the revolts, become that 'sounding board' for social problems that Habermas spoke of, a mouthpiece for democratic change, not without tension, with other actors on the political and institutional stage. It is also true though that the frictions between civil society, the state and official politics form part of their own idiosyncrasy.

With the exception of Tunisia, most of the Arab countries that called for a process of regime change in 2011 have ended up imposing systems just as, or more authoritarian than those in the preceding era, or worse, have degenerated into civil wars, as in Syria, Libya and Yemen. Despite this, the civil society organisations and movements exemplify a social dynamic intrinsic to Arab societies, favouring action and questioning stagnation. Although the repression of the regime and fragmentation of critical movements are elements that weigh against it, Arab civil society retains the seed of democratic freedoms and it is only a question of time and watering before it germinates, to emerge once again in search of the light.

Note

1. This research was developed as part of the project 'Las revueltas árabes: actores políticos y reconfiguración de la escena pública en el Norte de África y Oriente Medio' (CSO2012-37779), financed by the Spanish Ministerio de Economía y Competitividad.

References

Ababsa, Myriam (2011), 'Citoyenneté et question urbaine en Jordanie', in *Villes, pratiques urbaines et construction nationale en Jordanie*, Beirut: Presses de l'Ifpo, pp. 15–37.

Abdallah, Stéphanie L. (2009), 'Vers un féminisme politique hors frontières au Proche-Orient. Regard sur les mobilisations en Jordanie (années 1950–années 2000)', *Vingtième Siècle: Revue d'histoire*, 103: 177–96.

Abdelrahman, Maha (2011), 'The transnational and the local: Egyptian activists and transnational protest networks', *British Journal of Middle Eastern Studies*, 38: 407–24.

Álvarez-Ossorio, Ignacio (ed.) (2015), *La Primavera Árabe revisitada. Reconfiguración del autoritarismo y recomposición del islamismo*, Pamplona: Aranzadi Thomson Reuters.

Álvarez-Ossorio, Ignacio and Luciano Zaccara (eds) (2009), *Elecciones sin elección. Procesos electorales en el Mashreq y el Magreb*. Madrid: Ediciones del Oriente y el Mediterráneo.

Ayee, Joseph (ed.) (2004), *Les sociétés civiles du sud. Un état des lieux dans trois pays de la ZSP. Cameroun, Ghana, Maroc*, Bordeaux: Ministère des Affaires Étrangères.

Barreñada, Isaías (2013), 'Sindicatos y movimientos de trabajadores en los países árabes: entre el sistema y la sociedad civil' in Ignacio Álvarez-Ossorio (ed.), *Sociedad civil y contestación en Oriente Medio y el Norte de África*, Barcelona: Icaria, pp. 111–36.

Barreñada, Isaías (2015), 'Sociedad civil, movimientos sociales y activismo político en la Palestina post-Oslo' in Ignacio Álvarez-Ossorio (ed.), *La Primavera Árabe revisitada. Reconfiguración del autoritarismo y recomposición del islamismo*, Pamplona: Aranzadi Thomson Reuters, pp. 213–39.

Ben Nefissa, Sara (2011a), 'Les dynamiques sociales et politiques paradoxales de la promotion de la société civile en Égypte', in Anna Bozzo and Pierre-Jean Luizard (eds), *Les sociétés civiles dans le monde árabe*, Paris: La Découverte: pp. 325–40.

Ben Nefissa, Sara (2011b), 'Égypte: révolution et société civile en gestation', *Revue Humanitaire. Enjeux, Pratiques, Débats*, 29: 44–55.

Bono, Irene (2010), 'Le "phénomène participatif" au Maroc à travers ses styles d'action et ses normes', *Les Études du CERI*, 166, Paris: CERI.

Boughzala, Younès, Inès Bouzid and Jean Moscarola (2012), 'Le rôle des réseaux sociaux et des TIC dans les révolutions árabes: les résultats d'une enquête'. Available at <http://www.

lesphinx-developpement.fr/blog/wp-content/uploads/2012/04/YB_IB_JM1.pdf< (last accessed 3 January 2015).

Buendía, Pedro (2013), 'Estado, religión y derechos humanos en la sociedad civil árabe: una aproximación teórica en el marco de las revueltas árabes', in Ignacio Álvarez-Ossorio (ed.), *Sociedad civil y contestación en Oriente Medio y el Norte de África*, Barcelona: CIDOB/ Bellaterra, pp. 137–57.

Camau, Michel (2002), 'Sociétés civiles "réelles" et téléologie de la démocratisation', *Revue Internationale de Politique Comparée*, 9 (2): 213–32.

Camau, Michel (1999), 'La transitologie à l'épreuve du Moyen-Orient et de l'Afrique du Nord', *Annuaire de l'Afrique du Nord*, 38: 3–9.

Carothers, Thomas (2002), 'The end of the transition paradigm', *Journal of Democracy*, 13 (1): 5–21.

Cavatorta, Francesco (2012), 'Arab Spring: the awakening of civil society: a general overview', *Annuaire IEMed de la Méditerranée*, Barcelona: IEMed, pp. 75–81.

CCFD-Terre Solidaire and Institut de relations internationales et stratégiques (2014), *Le Baromètre 2013 des sociétés civiles. L'outre visage de la mondialisation*. Available at <http:// ccfd-terresolidaire.org/IMG/pdf/barometre-des-societes-civiles.pdf> (last accessed 23 January 2015).

Charif, Maher (2011), 'Les ONG palestiniennes et la politique', in *Les sociétés civiles dans le monde árabe*, Paris: La Découverte, pp. 341–54.

Desrues, Thierry (2012), 'Moroccan youth and the forming of a new generation: social change, collective action and political activism', *Mediterranean Politics*, 17: 23–40.

Durán, Mª Encarnación and Javier García-Marín (2015), 'Libertad de expresión y regulación mediática en la Turquía de Erdogan', in Ignacio Álvarez-Ossorio (ed.), *La Primavera Árabe revisitada. Reconfiguración del autoritarismo y recomposición del islamismo*, Pamplona: Aranzadi Thomson Reuters, pp. 191–212.

El Hachimi, Mohamed (2014), 'Société civile et démocratisation au Maroc. Le grand malentendu', *PapersIEMed*, Barcelona: IEMed.

Elrazzaz, Mohammed (2013), 'Manifestations ouvrières lors du "Printemps arabe"', in *Au tournant d'une époque. L'Europe, la Méditerranée et le monde arabe*, Stuttgart: Institut für Auslandsbeziehungen, pp. 48–53.

Gandolfi, Paola (2013), 'La société civile au Maroc: signification et issues des processus de changement sociale et politique'. Available at <http://www.cespi.it/STOCCHIERO/ Ascod-Marocco/societ%C3%A0%20civile_Gandolfi.pdf> (last accessed 20 May 2016).

Gellner, Ernest (1994), *Conditions of Liberty: Civil Society and Its Rivals*, New York: Penguin.

Guilmain, Olivier (2014), *Quelle société civile dans l'espace arabe?*, Observatoire des mutations politique dans le monde Arabe, Paris: Institut des Relations Internationales et Stratégiques.

Hamzawy, Amr (2002), 'Civil society in the Middle East. Intellectual debates and case studies' in Amr Hamzawy (ed.), *Civil Society in the Middle East*, Berlin: Hans Schiller, pp. 7–9.

Haugbølle, Sune (2012), 'Reflections on ideology after the Arab uprisings', *Jadaliyya*. Available at <http://www.jadaliyya.com/pages/index/4764/reflections-on-ideology-after-the-arab-uprisings> (last accessed 28 November 2015).

Hindi, Nadia (2015), *La relación entre el feminismo, la patria y el patriotismo/nacionalismo (wataniyya) en Iraq*, Granada: University of Granada Press.

Hinnebusch, Raymond (2006), 'Authoritarian persistence, democratization theory and the Middle East: An overview and critique', *Democratization*, 13 (3): 373–95.

Human Rights Watch (2010), '*A Wasted Decade. Human Rights in Syria during Bashar al-Assad's First Ten Years in Power*. Available at <https://www.hrw.org/report/2010/07/16/wasted-decade/

human-rights-syria-during-bashar-al-asads-first-ten-years-power> (last accessed 29 April 2016).

Human Rights Watch (2013), *Interfere, Restrict, Control. Restraints on Freedom of Association in Bahrain.* Available at <https://www.hrw.org/report/2013/06/20/interfere-restrict-control/restraints-freedom-association-bahrain> (last accessed 12 April 2016).

Ibrahim, Saad E. (1995), 'Liberalization and democratization in the Arab world: an overview' in Rex Brynen, Bahgat Korany and Paul Noble (eds), *Political Liberalization and Democratization in the Arab World. Vol. 1. Theoretical Perspectives,* London: Lynne Rienner, pp. 29–60.

Ibrahim, Saad E. (2002), *Egypt: Islam and Democracy: Critical Essays,* Cairo: The American University in Cairo Press.

Kausch, Kristina (2009), 'Defenders in retreat: freedom of association and civil society in Egypt', *FRIDE Working Paper,* 82. Available at <https://dld.omeka.net/items/show/136> (last accessed 15 December 2016)

Kedourie, Elie (1992), *Democracy and Arab Political Culture,* Washington, DC: Washington Institute for Near East Policy.

Ketiti, Awatef (2013), 'La sociedad civil en Túnez después de la caída de Ben Ali' in ECEM, *Sociedad civil y transiciones en el Norte de África,* Barcelona: Icaria, pp. 127–88.

Khader, Bichara (2010), *El mundo árabe explicado a Europa,* Barcelona: Icaria.

López-García, Bernabé (2011), *Marruecos ante el proceso de cambios en el mundo árabe,* Madrid: Real Instituto Elcano. Available at <http://www.realinstitutoelcano.org/wps/portal/rielcano/contenido?WCM_GLOBAL_CONTEXT=/elcano/elcano_es/especiales/crisismundoarabe/analisis/rie/ari46-2011> (last accessed 16 July 2011).

Mejjati, Rajaa (1996), 'Modelos de desarrollo, crisis y mutaciones socioeconómicas en Marruecos: el caso del sector informal', *Revista Internacional de Sociología,* 14: 61–81.

Pérez-Beltrán, Carmelo (2004), 'Sociedad civil y movimientos sociales en el mundo árabe', in Carmelo Pérez-Beltrán (ed.), *El mundo árabe e islámico ante los retos de futuro,* Granada: University of Granada Press, pp. 53–97.

Pérez-Beltrán, Carmelo (2014a): 'Reformas jurídicas en Túnez tras la revolución: la Ley de asociación de 2011. Estudio y traducción', *Revista Jurídica de la Universidad Autónoma de Madrid,* 30: 157–78.

Pérez-Beltrán, Carmelo (2014b): 'Reformas jurídicas en Argelia tras la primavera árabe: la nueva Ley de asociación de 2012', *Anaquel de Estudios Árabes,* 25: 177–94.

Ruiz de Elvira, Laura and Tina Zintl (2014), 'Reading socio-political transformations in Bashar al-Assad's Syria through charitable and broader social benevolent activism', *International Journal of Middle East Studies,* 46 (2): 329–49.

Sakr, Naomi (2005), 'Media and political reforms in the Gulf Cooperation Council', *Questions de communication,* 8: 67–92.

Saldaña, Marta (2011), *El Golfo ante la revolución árabe: ¿Tiempo para el cambio político?,* Madrid: Real Instituto Elcano. Available at <http://www.realinstitutoelcano.org/wps/portal/rielcano/contenido?WCM_GLOBAL_CONTEXT=/elcano/elcano_es/zonas_es/mediterraneo+y+mundo+arabe/ari55-2011> (last accessed 23 April 2016).

Shorbagy, Manar (2007), 'Understanding Kefaya: the new politics in Egypt', *Arab Studies Quarterly,* 29 (1): 39–60.

Strzelecka, Ewa K. (2012), 'Mujeres en la revolución yemení de 2011', *Revista de Estudios Internacionales Mediterráneos,* 13: 1–14.

Szmolka, Inmaculada (2011), 'Regímenes políticos híbridos. Democracias y autoritarismos con adjetivos. Su conceptualización, categorización y operacionalización dentro de la tipología de regímenes políticos', *Revista Española de Estudios Políticos,* 147: 103–35.

Chapter 9

Public rights and liberties

Luis Melián

1 Introduction

A key issue in the study of political change is the situation and evolution of rights and freedoms. Specifically, this chapter addresses the impact that the eruption of the Arab Spring has had on these liberties. In order to meet this objective it analyses primary sources, legal reforms and frameworks, and databases and research reports, such as those produced by Freedom House and Bertelsmann Stiftung.

Civil liberties and political rights form a key part of the academic literature on democracy and democratising processes; in fact any legitimate definition includes them as a fundamental and necessary condition. In this context, O'Donnell and Wolfson (2000: 549), for example, have argued that a central element of the concept of a 'political citizen' is that individuals are carriers of political and civil rights as autonomous and responsible agents. There is a close and at times diffuse relationship between civil and political liberties. In this analysis political liberties are considered to be a subgroup of civil liberties. In any case, both concepts conceive citizens to be social actors and as having agency.

The question this chapter addresses is whether political changes in the Middle East and North Africa (MENA) region reflect deepening liberalisation processes through de jure modifications of the civil liberties legislative framework, and if the response is in the affirmative, the extent to which these changes have had a *de facto* impact on regimes. In sum, it assesses whether these changes have been sufficient to represent an advance or regression in the democratic character of the region's political regimes.

This chapter has four main sections. Following this brief introduction, rights, civil liberties, their relationship to democracy, and processes of democratisation and political change are addressed from a theoretical perspective.

This section also details the sources employed and these concept's main indices and measurement models. Next, the situation and evolution of civil rights are analysed, with special emphasis on the changes that have occurred since the start of the Arab Spring. For this reason two subsections deal with the situation prior to and following the Arab Spring. Finally, the conclusions are presented.

Freedom of the press – considered to be of great importance within a political and civil rights approach – is not addressed here because it is dealt with in Chapter 10.

2 Civil liberties, political rights and democracy

Democracy is one, if not the most important, concept in the analysis of political systems and regimes. Numerous authors – Dahl (1997; 1999), Schumpeter (1962), Przeworski (1992; 2005), Przeworski et al. (2000), O'Donnell and Wolfson (2000), Linz and Stepan (1996), Diamond (1999), and many others – have sought to define democracy and the elements which comprise this concept. The definitions put forward have been classified within a range that goes from a maximalist to a minimalist (or procedural) pole. However, it is interesting to note that all definitions consider civil liberties and political rights, together with free and fair elections, to be a necessary prequisite of democracy.

On the other hand, it is important to emphasise that despite this concensus, there is no unanimous or even broad agreement over democracy's specific constitutive elements. O'Donnell and Wolfson (2000: 526) argue that there are certain freedoms of 'word, press, assembly and association' that do comprise a shared nucleus, but emphasise the arbitrary demarcation line. Even within this group of freedoms there is a debate about what has been called the 'reasonable-ness clause' (O'Donnell and Wolfson 2000: 533). This concept relates to the internal limits of where these rights and liberties are set, such as slander in the freedom of expression, the existence of organisations of a terrorist nature, or the monopoly over information itself.

In terms of civil liberties, Robert Dahl (1999: 101) argues for the need to include in any definition of democracy: freedom of expression, freedom of association, access to alternative sources of information and a concept of 'inclusive citizenship' that includes active and passive suffrage – to which might be added, from a broader perspective, other liberties that may be necessary for the effective functioning of democratic political institutions. On the other hand, Sartori (2007: 49) contributes to the debate about the nature of these freedoms and the search to transcend the dichotomy between positive and negative liberties, by arguing for the inclusion of what he calls 'protective' liberties, a liberty 'from' and therefore getting a lot closer to the category of negative liberties. Specifically, freedom of information merits a special place within this debate, as it not only depends upon a legal framework, but the social context in which it is developed. In particular, alternative news sources need to be present.

International treaties must also be taken into account. Of special relevance are the civil and political rights detailed in the International Pact on Civil and Political Rights, adopted in 1966 by the United Nations General Assembly. The UN classification includes almost all the rights and liberties mentioned above. Freedom of expression, for example, is included in article 19, and freedom of religious thought in article 18. Article 22 references the right to freedom of association while freedom of assembly is guaranteed by article 21. Article 25 relates to the right of suffrage, both active and passive. Other fundamental civil liberties are also cited, such as the inviolability of the home, the right to individual safety and physical integrity, and equable access to courts of justice.

Following this brief theoretical systemisation of civil and political liberties, this chapter now turns to the tools for their analysis and measurement. Apart from direct analysis of legal sources, it draws on established 'democracy' and 'quality of democracy' databases, which include indicators on civil liberties. These instruments generally employ a minimalist conceptualisation of democracy and have been the object of significant criticism within the academic community due to problems with their aggregation models, measurement and opacity in construction (Munck and Verkuilen 2002). Nevertheless, despite these deficiencies, these indices are of great benefit to researchers due to their comparative temporal and geographic value, and they simultaneously provide an analytical advantage for data systemisation and its quantification. However, these approximations must not substitute deep and thick qualitative research in each case, although they allow analysis of a larger number of cases and generalisations to be made.

Among the most widely used and relevant indices are those of Freedom House, the Bertelsmann Transformation Index (BTI), Polity IV (up to 2014), and the Democracy Index of The Economist Intelligence Unit. In this analysis, and to avoid duplication – particularly bearing in mind that there is a high degree of correlation among these indices (Coppedge et al. 2011) – data from Freedom House and the BTI will be predominantly employed below.

Freedom House is certainly the best known index because it includes every country in the world and dates back to 1972. It distinguishes between political rights and civil liberties on two distinct dimensions with ten and fifteen indicators, each divided into different questions. Political rights are subdivided into three dimensions: electoral processes, political pluralism, and participation and functioning of government (dealt with in detail in other chapters of this book). On the other hand, civil liberties, which are at the focus of this analysis, include four categories: freedom of expression and belief, right of association and organisation, rule of law, and personal autonomy and individual rights.

The BTI Transformation Index aggregates three components: political, economic and management transformation. The results are expressed on a range of zero to ten, with ten representing the highest degree of rights and political and civil liberties and zero their total absence. Of these, only political transformation is relevant for this study. This component comprises five parts: stateness, political participation, rule of law, stability of democratic institutions, and political and social integration. In turn, these five criteria are measured by eighteen indicators. For this analysis four indicators are taken into account which are essential to analyse civil liberties: the rule of law, the right of association and assembly, freedom of expression (on the dimension of political participation), and party systems and interest groups (on the dimension of political and social integration).

3 The post-Arab Spring civil liberties situation

This chapter next empirically analyses the evolution and current situation of civil liberties in the MENA countries. As this chapter aims to assess the role the Arab Spring played in relation to these liberties and whether they have improved, this first subsection outlines the situation in the years prior to the riots and compares it with later developments. The second analyses the situation following the political changes that took place.

Table 9.1 provides an overview and evolution of the civil liberties situation, showing the points obtained by each country on the relevant BTI indicators in 2010 and 2016. This allows for each country, and the average of these indicators for the MENA zone as a whole, to be observed.

Firstly the precarious civil liberties situation can be seen in the region as a whole, as the averages are below 4.5 (with the exception of religious freedom in 2010). The situation of these liberties has worsened in all cases except the rights associated with parties, which are slightly better, with 1.8 in 2010 and two in 2016. Overall it could be argued that the MENA area has an 'unchanging dynamic' except in Tunisia where there has been a considerable improvement in civil liberties across all indicators (except in religious freedom where it has slightly worsened; with a score of seven in 2016). Each indicator will now be analysed in detail for all cases.

Table 9.1 BTI's civil liberties scores for 2010 and 2016

Country[a]	Religious freedom		Association / assembly rights		Freedom of expression		Civil rights		Independent judiciary		Prosecution of office abuse		Party system		Interest groups	
	2010	2016	2010	2016	2010	2016	2010	2016	2010	2016	2010	2016	2010	2016	2010	2016
Algeria	6	6	5	5	6	6	5	5	2	4	2	2	4	4	5	6
Bahrain	7	6	3	2	3	2	6	4	4	3	4	4	4	2	6	6
Egypt	6	6	5	3	4	4	4	3	4	4	4	4	3	3	5	5
Iran	1	1	4	3	3	1	3	2	5	2	4	4	3	2	3	2
Iraq	5	3	7	5	5	3	4	3	3	4	3	3	2	4	3	3
Jordan	6	6	5	5	4	4	5	5	4	5	2	2	2	2	4	5
Kuwait	6	6	6	4	7	5	7	6	4	4	4	4	2	2	6	5
Lebanon	7	7	7	7	7	7	7	7	4	6	5	5	5	5	7	7
Libya	7	3	2	4	2	6	3	1	7	2	4	4	1	3	3	4
Morocco	6	6	4	4	5	4	6	5	3	2	4	4	3	3	4	4
Oman	6	5	4	2	4	2	5	3	3	2	4	4	1	1	3	3
Qatar	8	5	4	3	7	5	7	6	5	3	4	4	1	1	3	3
Saudi Arabia	2	2	2	2	3	2	4	2	4	2	4	4	1	1	3	3
Syria	7	4	2	2	2	2	2	1	4	2	3	3	1	2	3	2
Tunisia	8	7	3	7	2	6	4	5	2	6	3	3	2	5	3	7
Turkey	8	6	8	6	7	5	7	6	4	6	4	4	6	7	8	7
UAE	7	7	3	2	5	2	6	4	7	3	7	7	1	1	3	7
Yemen	6	3	6	4	4	3	4	2	4	4	6	6	4	4	5	4
MENA	4.6	3.8	3.7	3.2	3.7	2.9	4.4	2.8	3.6	3	3.6	3	1.8	2	3.8	3.6

Note: [a] BTI does not include Israel
Source: prepared by the author from BTI data

3.1 Situation prior to the Arab Spring

Non-democratic regimes have persisted since the creation of states in the MENA region. In the 1980s and 1990s diverse processes of political liberalisation began as a consequence of the so-called 'bread riots', in the context of the erosion of authoritarian pacts that sustained the political regimes (Melián 2016: 251–62). These liberal reforms, however, did not represent authentic long-term change but simply trivial cosmetic modifications.

Consequently, various authors and international agencies (Charfi 2005; PNUD 2004: 7) have pointed out the unsatisfactory situation of political rights and civil liberties in the region in which attacks on freedom of expression and opinion, strict limits on freedom of association and assembly, and the establishment of uncompetitive electoral processes have structured the political dynamic. As a result, these states have developed a public life that is in contradiction and constant tension between that established in the texts and legal frameworks and that which *de facto* structures the political game (Szmolka 2011: 47). This critical situation is in turn serverely affected by the existence of numerous 'red lines' such as those related to freedom of expression or worship, even in the academic sphere.

The overall MENA civil liberties situation in the years prior to the start of the Arab Spring was precarious and three countries – Israel, Kuwait and Turkey – obtain a score lower or equal to four on the zero–seven Freedom House scale in 2008. For 2010, as Figure 9.1 shows, Lebanon and Morocco can be added to this group but Kuwait is excluded as it has a score of five. Also in 2010, the year in which the riots erupted, Syria, Libya and Saudi Arabia score

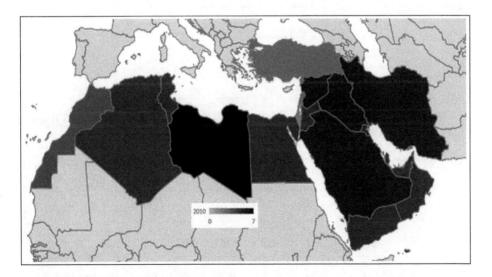

Figure 9.1 Freedom House civil liberties index before the Arab Spring (2010)

the maximum possible of six or seven, reflecting the absence of political and civil liberties in these countries. The majority of the remaining countries are in the range of 4.5 to 6.5. In fact, there were few significant changes in the whole of the region.

3.2 Post-Arab Spring: the civil liberties situation

As noted above, diverse voices during the Arab Spring called for a fifth democratising wave in the region; however, this did not occur. In fact, Figure 9.2 illustrates that between 2010 and 2016 the rights and political liberties situation barely varied in the region as a whole, and there was even a slight deterioration from 2014 onwards. However, a detailed and disaggregated analysis by country underscores significant differences in the evolution of this dimension among the MENA countries.

The Arab Spring certainly represented the start of political changes in a large number of the MENA countries. Various states reformed their constitutions and others carried out processes in line with the development of new constitutions (Szmolka 2012: 13). However, these processes rarely led to effective and authentic changes in the application of political liberties and civil rights.

Following the Arab Spring, and comparing the results to those in 2016, we can distinguish three main groups of countries: those in which there was an improvement in the situation of civil liberties and political rights, those in

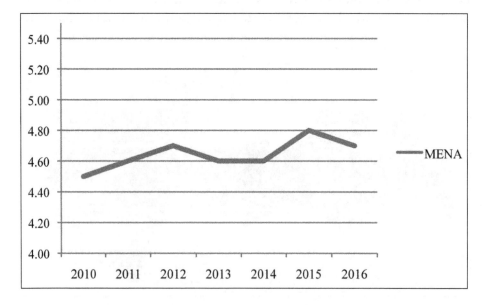

Figure 9.2 Freedom House: civil liberties post Arab Spring in the MENA region (2010–16)
Source: Prepared by the author from Freedom House data

Table 9.2 Freedom House civil liberties index, 2010–16

Country	2010	2011	2012	2013	2014	2015	2016	Evolution
Algeria	5	5	5	5	5	5	5	=
Bahrain	5	5	6	6	6	6	6	↑
Egypt	5	5	5	5	5	5	5	=
Iran	6	6	6	6	6	6	6	=
Iraq	6	6	6	6	6	6	6	=
Israel	2	2	2	2	2	2	2	–
Jordan	5	5	5	5	5	5	5	=
Kuwait	5	5	5	5	5	5	5	=
Lebanon	3	4	4	4	4	4	4	↑
Libya	7	6	5	6	5	6	6	↓
Morocco	4	4	4	4	4	4	4	=
Oman	5	5	5	5	5	5	5	=
Qatar	5	5	5	5	5	5	5	=
Saudi Arabia	6	7	7	7	7	7	7	↑
Syria	6	7	7	7	7	7	7	↑
Tunisia	5	4	4	3	3	4	3	↓
Turkey	3	3	4	3	4	4	4	↑
UAE	5	6	6	6	6	6	6	↑
Yemen	5	6	6	6	6	6	6	↑
MENA	4.5	4.6	4.7	4.6	4.6	4.8	4.7	↑

Source: prepared by the author from the Freedom House Index

which the situation worsened, and lastly the majority of countries where there were no substantial changes.

3.2.1 Countries with improvements in civil liberties: Tunisia, Egypt and Lebanon

Without doubt Tunisia has had the greatest improvement in its civil liberty scores. It is also the only country in which the Arab Spring has led to a real democratisation processs. Freedom House index shows civil liberties improving from six in 2008 to three in 2016, although religious freedom has deteriorated, as can be seen in Table 9.1. Progressive impoverishment and a worsening economic situation, together with restrictive authoritarianism in recent decades, favoured the surge in protests. It is worth underscoring that during the establishment of the modern Tunisian state following independence, Tunisia became the most advanced country in North Africa regarding political and civil liberties. As article 8 of the 1959 constitution states: 'The freedoms of opinion, expression, press, assembly and association are guaranteed and exercised under the conditions defined by law' (Pérez-Beltrán and García-Marín 2015: 72). Previously in 1956 Tunisia had established a Code of Personal Status, which is considered to be the most advanced and modern among Arab countries in relation to the development of civil liberties and, in particular, the situation of women in society (Cavatorta and Haugbølle 2012; Kaboub 2013; Pérez-Beltrán and García-Marín 2015; Perkins 2014; Pratt 2007; Willis 2012). However, the majority of these liberties and rights, especially those of a political nature, did not go beyond written statements and were subordinate to a highly repressive dictatorship that exercised its control by establishing a police state (Aleya-Sghaier 2012: 21; Daoud 2011: 2; Mabrouk 2011: 628; Martínez-Fuentes 2011: 27).

The 2014 Tunisian constitution has been defined as a 'guaranteed constitution regarding fundamental rights' (Pérez-Beltrán and García-Marín 2015: 78) and as the most coherent and credible of those that came out of the Arab Spring because of its authentic formation process (Ottaway 2014: 104). Rights related to freedom of expression and information can be found in articles 31 and 32, and article 33 establishes the right to academic freedom and scientific research (Pérez-Beltrán and García-Marín 2015: 77). Limitations on the exercise of rights and freedoms can only put in place 'for reasons necessary to a civil and democratic state and with the aim of protecting the rights of others, or based on the requirements of public order, national defence, public health or public morals' (article 49). In the religious sphere the new constitution guarantees total religious freedom, even for non-believers, although it maintains Islam as the state religion. Ennahda, the Islamist party that led the revolution, renounced the imposition of shariah as a source of law (Maddy-Weitzman 2012: 201; Zoglin 2013: 2), in favour of an Anglo-Saxon type system, in which state neutrality does not signify rejection of religion in the public sphere and against the French secularist model. The final draft of this article (article 1) on the state religion is deliberately vague and ambiguous (Carter Center 2014: 89), stating that while Tunisia's religion is Islam (Mallat 2014: 117), that should not be interpreted as making it a religious state. Separately, Decree 88-2011, relating to the regulation of associations, encourages the role of associative movements by facilitating the creation of new organisations (Pérez-Beltrán and García-Marín 2015: 82) and article 35 of the new constitution establishes the right to create trade unions. This is reflected in the improvement in Tunisia's BTI scores regarding the rights of association and assembly, which moves from three in 2010 to seven – together with Lebanon, the highest score in the region – in 2016. Separately, administration response times have been reduced and article 11.2 establishes that administrative silence will be understood as acceptance by the state. It is also worth underscoring that while there has been a notable improvement in freedom of the press, in 2014 and 2015 the government has continued to imprison journalists, mainly those with an Islamist background. One representative case was the blogger Yassine Ayari who was taken to court for criticising the army.

Egypt, on the other hand, is a very complex case to analyse. At first under Mubarak the country experienced an improvement in political liberties and took liberalising political steps towards a new supposed democratisation (Martín-Muñoz 2005: 109) by promoting political debates with the opposition in an environment of greater tolerance (Kaye et al. 2008: 30). However, these steps were not accompanied by formal changes in the existing legislation, so they remained dependent on the goodwill of the president at any particular moment. Use of the 'state of emergency' as a form of government had been employed in Egypt since the assassination of Sadat in 1981, based on article 148 of the 1971 constitution. Throughout Mubarak's government it was widely employed, especially after its institutionalisation in the constitutional reform of 2007, in which it was defended as a state tool to ensure political stability. The Mubarak regime employed this legal measure to exercise political control through censorship, constrict freedom of expression, ban demonstrations and make arbitrary political arrests (Kassem 2004: 37).

It is important to emphasise that Egypt's state of emergency under the Mubarak government was not abolished until the 2011 revolution. Although it was included in the new Egyptian constitution of 2014, it is legally circumscribed because it must be ratified within seven days by a two-thirds parliamentary majority. Furthermore, it can last for a maximum of three months and can only be extended once (Parolin 2014: 142). The new constitution was approved by referendum on 22 December 2012, although it was criticised by various sectors of society. Specifically, article 2 was the most controversial, as it established shariah as the main source of law, thereby giving a denominational character to the state. This legal religious base has been strengthened by compulsory religious teaching. These two aspects were already present in one form or another in prior constitutions and would have not been so controversial if it were not for the Islamist nature of the government. In fact, in contrast to other confessional states in the MENA region, the constitution does not require the president to be a Muslim, which is critical in a country where the Christian minority is significant. Furthermore, article 43 establishes freedom of worship, and makes special reference to the monotheist religions of Abrahamic origin. Similiarly, these religious minorities will have both legal and religious autonomy at the level of religious questions, individual and family legal status, where they will be governed by the canonical principles of Christianity and Judaism respectively (article 3).

However, General al-Sisi's *coup d'état* in 2013 represented a serious setback for public freedoms, as can be seen in the tables. Specifically, minority groups such as LGBT have been persecuted by the state, and the Muslim Brotherhood has been banned and defined as a terrorist group. Furthermore, arbitrary arrests and detentions have increased (surpassing 800 between January and February 2013), torture continues to be employed by the police (EMHRN 2014: 23), and media repression and censorship continues, such as that suffered by the famous television presenter and government critic Bassem Yousef. Additionally, there are severe restrictions on academic freedom and research has suffered, which has even affected foreign researchers working in the country, such as the case of the young Italian Giulio Regeni, murdered at the hands of the country's armed forces. Another clear example of this tougher repressive policy was the breaking up on 14 August 2013 of the Cairo camp in support of Morsi in Raba'a al-'Adawiyya Square and al-Nahda Square. This atrocity, in which the government murdered more than 1,000 demonstrators who were camping there (Human Rights Watch 2014: 6; Radinovic-Lukic and Mannheimer 2014: 20), is considered by Human Rights Watch (2014: 6) to be among the largest one-day massacres of protesters in recent history.

Additionally, the 2014 constitution prohibits the establishment of religious-based parties. In sum, in the Egyptian case it can be concluded there has been a two-stage process, with a slight improvement in the early years after the revolution being followed by a deterioration after the 2013 coup, which put the country back to the level of that prior to the riots. Table 9.1 shows how the general levels in 2016 are the same as those in 2010, or even worse as in the case of the right of assembly that has fallen from five points to three today.

In the Lebanese case changes occurred years prior to the Arab Spring during what is known as the 'Cedar Revolution' in 2005, where there were reforms that directly affected the political rights situation in the country. The rights of association and assembly, for example, which were previously restricted, experienced a considerable improvement, at the same time as the use of force was limited by the security forces with the establishment of a new Code of Conduct for the Armed Forces, adopted in 2012 (EMHRN 2014: 43). Furthermore, Lebanon has a large number of press publications, athough these are rarely independent but rather strongly connected to religious groups or sectarian leaders. On the other hand, there is great freedom of Internet access. It should be underscored, as can be seen in Table 9.1, that Lebanon has significantly better civil rights and political liberties scores than those obtained by other Arab states. Similarly this table shows that Lebanon has the best average scores regarding the selected indicators. Freedom House does not register any significant changes in the situation of these civil liberties in the country, giving it a score of 4.5.

3.2.2 Countries where there were no significant changes in civil liberties: Jordan, Morocco, Algeria, Iran and Gulf monarchies

Having analysed the small group of countries where there were some minor improvements in the extension and fulfilment of civil liberties, this chapter next turns to those countries where the Arab Spring led to no substantive improvements.

The Jordan and Moroccan kingdoms, for example, have some similarities in their evolution. Both countries pursued limited liberalisation programmes in the 1990s and they also experienced criticism of the monarchy. Furthermore, their reforms did not lead to the loss of any real crown power.

Since 2010 Freedom House has judged Jordan to have had an overall score of five, with a five in civil liberties, a six in political rights and no significant changes over time. However, from 1998 to 2010 Freedom House classified Jordan as a partially free country, which reflects a process of deliberalisation that began at the outset of the protests. Following the 2011 disturbances a constitutional reform was carried out that affected forty-two articles, but with little repercussion. Specific articles related to rights and public liberties have been revised to guarantee their fulfilment in line with the law: article 7 guarantees personal and political freedoms, article 8 punishes arbitrary detentions and prohibits torture, article 15 establishes that the state must guarantee freedom of opinion and expression, and article 16 regulates freedom of assembly and association (Szmolka 2012: 16). However, various laws in force criminalise defamation and denigration of the government. Additionally, with an anti-liberalisation dynamic, a new media law in 2011 established a censor for virtual means of communication (Susser 2013: 5). This technological area was considered to be the last bastion of liberty for independent journalists and up until that time had remained outside the control of the censor. Furthermore, specific journalists who have criticised the monarchy or uncovered corruption plots that have implicated the regime have been heavily clamped down upon. In the religious sphere, although Islam is the official religion of the state, the constitution recognises the Christian minority and guarantees them the right to worship. However, other religious minorities such as the Druze or Baha'i do not have that right formally recognised, although they are allowed to worship. In the university sphere there is freedom of expression, limited by the 'red lines' of the regime, especially if the monarchy is criticised. Additionally, there is discrimination against Jordanians of Palestinian origin, as they are prohibited to work in public service or in the country's powerful security forces.

Similarly, changes carried out by the Alawis in Morocco have not increased or guaranteed civil rights and political liberties. Table 9.1 illustrates that changes can barely be seen in this country, except for a slight deterioration in the freedoms of expression and civil rights. Changes mainly relate to reforms in response to the demands of the '20 February Movement', as the monarch promised in his speech on 9 March 2011, but which have merely been cosmetic (Parejo 2015: 24). Article 29 of the 2011 constitution guarantees freedom of assembly and association (EMHRN 2014: 56); however, red lines remain in place for political liberties related to criticism of the monarchy or any questioning of the territorial situation of Western Sahara. These same lines severely impact on press freedom in the country, as the government employs both light and heavy means of coercion and censorship on anyone who crosses them. Similar measures are used in the academic sphere where self-censorship is common for taboo subjects. Regarding religious freedom it is worth noting that the majority of the Moroccan population is Sunni Muslim and there is a small Jewish minority who are guaranteed freedom of worship. Nevertheless, the regime has employed the religious dimension to accuse critics of the monarchy of proselytising in order to expulse them from the country. On the other hand, since 2004, there has been a trade union law that guarantees the right of workers to join a union and penalises companies that prohibit them or persecute workers who become trade unionists.

Algeria has limited pluralism and a political dynamic that is strongly influenced by the memory of the bloody civil war. In fact, it is the only North African country where the Arab Spring barely had any repercussions beyond limited demonstrations, as can be seen in Table 9.1, where all the indicators are stable with the exception of interest groups, which experienced a slight improvement. Restrictions of political freedoms are significant in areas such as assembly and meetings, which are highly controlled by a state of emergency (EMHRN 2014: 12), although the government decided to lift it in 2011 during the riots in neighbouring countries. In 2014 a new media law represented a liberalising step forward by allowing private television channels to be created. However, a law against cybercrime has been used by the government to block and control what is published on the Internet. Additionally, the regime's interested use of the anti-defamation law has led to journalists who are critical of Bouteflika's policies being persecuted, such as the cartoonist Yamel Ghanem in February 2014. Also in 2014 a new Law of Association was enacted that has been heavily criticised due to the stiff requirements that it imposes on constituting new organisations. Legally, new and independent trade unions can be created, but this right has been severely restricted by the hegemonic role of the Algerian General Union of Workers, which is closely affiliated to the regime and in practice blocks new trade unions.

The Islamic Republic of Iran is another MENA state that has not experienced any significant domestic change during the Arab Spring. Civil liberties are heavily restricted and are deteriorating according to the indicators in Table 9.1, and are always below three for 2016. Regarding freedom of Internet access in recent years, despite the heavy censorship that exists in the country, band width has increased for domestic connections, which has favoured the appearance of new spaces that are relatively free of censure. The press is intimately linked to the regime, which means there is heavy censorship. Iran is a state with a Shia religious majority. However, despite the fact that Zoroastrians, Jews and Christians generally enjoy freedom to worship – religious minorities are recognised in the constitution – Sunni Muslims claim they are persecuted by the regime as it prohibits them from constructing new mosques or accessing posts in the public sector, and the minority Baha'i are systematically persecuted and imprisoned. Furthermore, freedom of association is severely restricted as only the regime can organise and authorise demonstrations. In the associative sphere, the right to join a union is limited to trade unions that are formed by the government, as other professional associations are prohibited.

The ayatollah and his government have sought, with considerable success to date, to control any riots by focusing on their foreign policy (Aras and Yorulmazlar 2014: 118), where they have sought to impose their leadership in conflicts such as that of Syria, against the interests of other Sunni states such as Saudi Arabia. Political liberties and civil rights are heavily limited by the regime. Political parties were dissolved in 1983, which means that, despite periodic elections, the country's political system is categorised as non-competitive. In Iran the right to a secret vote cannot even be assured (Zaccara 2008: 420).

The Gulf countries, and particularly the six monarchies that comprise the Gulf Cooperation Council, do not have any significant electoral tradition. Only Bahrain and Kuwait, which have held municipal and legislative elections since the creation of their states in 1961, have a greater tradition in this sense, followed distantly by the Sultanate of Oman. Furthermore, all these monarchic countries heavily restrict political freedoms such as the right to both active and passive suffrage. The situation for women is particularly alarming in this regard. There is also a generalised prohibition of political parties, as well as the right to association. Among these countries the Arab Spring especially affected Bahrain as there was strong public demand to improve rights and political liberties in the country as well as direct political participation (Zaccara and Saldaña 2013: 181–5). However, the riots in Bahrain have not led to any significant changes. As noted above, Kuwait has enjoyed the greatest level of political liberties in the Gulf since its foundation, and more specifically since 1991 as a consequence of the first Gulf War, despite the restrictions of basic civil liberties such as the press, as all media are either state controlled or owned by individuals who have close links to the monarchy. Recent limits to freedom of expression are also worth noting, such as the law introduced in February 2014 that criminalised any monarchic insult. Additionally, the heavy persecution faced by Bahrain's Shia religion has increased further since 2014.

Similarly, Kuwait punishes insults of the king, Islam or the government, which clearly limits freedom of expression. However, in the religious sphere minorities, including the Shia, enjoy a high degree of freedom to worship. Regarding unions, despite the law guaranteeing trade union liberties, in practice freedoms are limited because there is only one state union, and professional trade unions are restricted to one for each branch of work. In sum, it can be said that the riots increased state investment and led to minor economic reforms, but led to little change in the area of civil liberties (Zaccara and Saldaña 2013: 194).

3.2.3 Countries where the situation of civil liberties worsened: Turkey, Yemen, Syria, Libya, Iraq and Israel

On the other hand, the Arab Spring has led to deteriorating political and civil rights in a number of countries. Turkey, for example, has undergone a process of autocratisation regression in recent years (see Szmolka and Durán, Chapter 17), which has placed severe limits on freedom of expression, particularly in relation to the Kurdish conflict (EMHRN 2014: 96). For example, following the Justice and Development Party's (AKP) win at the 2002 general elections, a liberalising process began that prompted various academics to categorise it as a tutelary democracy (Esen and Gumuscu 2016); and it was even suggested that the 'Turkish model' was one to follow by other MENA countries. This model was based on the balance of the triad formed by democracy, Islam and the market economy (Rodríguez 2011). However, following the 2013 demonstrations in Gezi Park, Istanbul, a change of direction was detected in Turkish policy with tendencies towards hard-line Islamist conservativism (Özbudun 2014: 156). This occurred to such a degree that currently there are various research projects that specifically focus on the regime's authoritarian drift in recent years (Esen and Gumuscu 2016: 2). This change has meant a profound deterioration in rights and political freedoms, with an increase in arbitrary detentions, a lack of fair trials and excessive use of force and state censorship (Özbudun 2014: 161). Censorship, in particular, has become highly visible in recent months, academic critics of the regime have been persecuted, dissent 'securitised' and freedoms of expression and association heavily restricted. New laws have been enacted that have led to a dramatic rise in people being investigated for defamation, for example, from thirty-eight in 2011 to over 450 in 2015 (Esen and Gumuscu 2016: 10–13). Journalists and academics are especially closely monitored. Specifically, they are harrassed by the security forces, judged for any opinions broadcast against the Erdoğan regime and persecuted for discussing sensitive subjects, such as the Kurdish minority. In August 2013 Turkey's journalist association published a report denouncing these political persecutions and the precarious situation of journalists in the country due to governmental manipulation and attacks.

Regarding religion, since 2014 an increase in hate speech has been noticed in the media towards the Jewish, Orthodox Christian and Armenian minorities, despite the fact that the constitution guarantees them freedom of worship. Furthermore, the Alevi minority, who are non-Sunni Muslims, lack official protection and have been victims of hate crimes.

One common result of the Arab Spring for a number of the MENA countries was a civil war and the practical destruction of the state. In Yemen, for example, following the initial success of the protests with President Saleh's resignation, the country collapsed into a civil war with strong ethnic and religious elements, making it impossible to speak of a single state in the Weberian sense. Furthermore, the government systematically violates freedoms of expression and press, and as a result the indicator has fallen from four to three in Table 9.1. The country has, for example, expelled foreign journalists and shut media considered to be close to former President Saleh, who is an ally of the Houthis in the war against the Hadi government. Similarly, academic freedom has been seriously threatened by political polarisation in the country's universities. In the religious sphere Islam is the official religion of the state and shariah is established as the main source of law. Nonetheless, freedom of worship for small religious minorities has been respected in the country. On the other hand, Syria and Libya represent a further two examples where the Arab Spring protests have resulted in armed conflict, disappearance of the state framework and loss of control of the territory.

The Libyan dictatorship of Colonel al-Gaddafi experienced a similar lack of liberties and basic political rights, as well as the persistent violation of human rights. One example is the impunity that the dictator enjoyed and another is the total prohibition of any type of protest (EMHRN 2014: 49). Following the 'victory' of the riots and the fall of the president, Libya has become a 'large black hole' in North Africa where civil liberties have been severely affected, not only by government regulations but also by self-censorship and the fear that various violent groups have been strengthened in the country. However, this rentier state with a strong dependency on oil has fallen into total chaos since the fall of al-Gaddafi. Since that time there have been at least two separate governments and parliaments in the country – one Islamist established in the city of Tripoli and the other that is internationally recognised and based in the coastal city of Tobruk. The situation has changed following the formation of a national unity government at the start of 2016, whose future is uncertain.

Nevertheless, there is no effective control of the territory as a consequence of strong tribal fragmentation in the country. In this situation dozens of rebel groups have flourished, making any discussion about political rights and civil liberties meaningless.

For its part, the Syrian regime has restricted basic political rights such as assembly and association (EMHRN 2014: 77). Syria lives under constant martial law that has permitted systematic abuse of the few legal rights established. The state exercises total control over public and private life through coercive and repressive mechanisms such as the omnipresent *mukhabarat*, which functions as a kind of repressive and omniscient panopticon (Álvarez-Ossorio and Gutiérrez de Terán 2009: 266). In July 2000 the arrival of President Bashar al-Assad awoke hope of political change, which became known as the Damascus Spring, but it had no real democratising effect (Álvarez-Ossorio 2012: 23). In fact, the regime continued to exercise strict control over public life and limited political liberties. Following the eruption of the riots in 2011 and the start of the now long civil war, the situation of political rights and civil liberties has greatly deteriorated from what was already a problematic situation. In the areas controlled by the regime the war has worsened and repression increased, and in the areas under Islamic State (IS) control the situation is alarming.

Due in part to the complete collapse of Syrian state control, the Iraqi state has lost territory to IS. IS has plunged Iraq into a religious conflict, and so despite the fact that freedom of belief is theoretically guaranteed in the constitution, the reality is that both Shia and non-Muslim minorities are being persecuted and massacred in the country. This deteriorating situation is reflected in its BTI indicator for religious freedom (Table 9.1), which has fallen from five in 2010 to three in 2016. Following the United States' occupation the country has continued to use summary imprisonment, and torture is widespread (PNUD 2004: 4). The al-Maliki government persecutes the press, and journalists who are critical of the president are imprisoned. In this sense, the threat of IS and the discourse of terror has been employed to cut civil liberties and freedom of communication.

Israel is a very complex case due to its occupation of Palestine. While the traditional measuring tools take into account the functioning of the system in relation to Israeli citizens, the introduction of the Arab variable inevitably modifies the results of any research. Certainly, Israel has a high degree of freedom of expression and press, even when the media directly criticise Israeli government policy. However, in 2011 a law that criminalised favouring an Israel boycott was approved, and organisations that commemorate the *Nakba* can be fined or have their financing removed. This law has been denounced in Israeli courts by human rights groups in the country. Nonetheless, there persist serious restrictions on the right to assembly and association, and particularly in contexts linked to the Arab–Israeli conflict, which is established as a red line of national policy. These limitations of political rights increased following the riots in the MENA region, even though the Arab Spring did not directly affect Israeli society. Together with restrictions on freedom of association, the number of arbitrary arrests increased and there has been excessive use of force against peaceful demonstrations, as occurred during the Negev Bedouin protests when they were faced with settlement plans in their territory (EMHRN 2014: 29). Similarly, the UN development programme has denounced Israel's systematic and repeated violation of Palestinians' human rights by, for example, seriously restricting ther civil and political liberties (PNUD 2004: 3).

4 Conclusions

Firstly, the central role that civil liberties play in the analysis of political regimes must be underscored and so should their eventual transformation processes. This is especially important when seeking to describe and classify the political regimes under study. It is beyond doubt that political science has paid special interest to the concept of democracy and the elements that define it. Among those elements, minimalist and procedural definitions have played a leading role thanks to their analytical and comparative capacity. However, in many cases the analysis of political regimes has exclusively focused on electoral procedures and their development, leaving aside equally important dimensions, such as civil liberties, which include fundamental civil and political rights like freedom of expression, assembly and association, religious freedom, freedom of information and the rights of trade unions, among others.

This chapter has focused on the importance of these civil liberties in the context of the Arab Spring, and in particular on the evolution of these liberties from 2011 as key to explaining what really occurred in the region and the political repercussions of the uprisings. Various conclusions can be drawn regarding the civil liberty situation in the MENA region following the Arab Spring. As Tables 9.1 and 9.2 illustrate, the situation of these countries barely changed after 2010 and then only to reflect a deteriorating situation from 2014. A disaggregated analysis shows some variation although the majority of countries have remained reasonably stable, within their precarious situation, regarding these rights and liberties for decades.

Only Tunisia has considerably improved rights and liberties with an improvement of -2 on the Freedom House index between 2010 and 2016. Lebanon for its part continues to lead the field in civil liberties in the region, although not as a result of the Arab Spring. On the other hand, a number of countries have clearly deteriorated, with falls of over a point in the case of Bahrain and Yemen.

In sum, it can be concluded that the situation of civil liberties in the region is either precarious or alarming in the majority of the MENA countries. Furthermore, with the exception of Tunisia, the Arab Spring has not led to a substantive improvement despite the reformist ambition of some countries, and has even led to a significant deterioration in various cases, as has been demonstrated above.

References

Aleya-Sghaier, Amira (2012), 'The Tunisian revolution: the revolution of dignity', *The Journal of the Middle East and Africa*, 3 (1): 18–45.

Álvarez-Ossorio, Ignacio (2012), 'The Syrian uprising. Syria's struggling civil society', *Middle East Quaterly*, 19 (2): 23–32.

Álvarez-Ossorio, Ignacio (2015), 'El enroque autoritario del régimen sirio: de la revuelta popular a la guerra civil', *Revista CIDOB d'Afers Internacionals*, 109: 157–76.

Álvarez-Ossorio, Ignacio and Ignacio Gutiérrez de Terán (2009), 'La república hereditaria Siria: el fracaso de una transición', in Ferrán Izquierdo (ed.) *Poder y regímenes en el mundo árabe contemporáneo*, Barcelona: CIDOB, pp. 265–300.

Aras, Bulent and Emirhan Yorulmazlar (2014), 'Turkey and Iran after the Arab Spring: finding a middle ground', *Middle East Policy*, 21 (4): 112–20.

Carter Center (2014), *Le processus constitutionnel en Tunisie 2011–2014*, Atlanta. Available at <http://www.cartercenter.org/resources/pdfs/news/peace_publications/democracy/tunisia-constitution-making-process-french.pdf> (last accessed 18 May 2016).

Cavatorta, Francesco and Rikke H. Haugbølle (2012), 'The end of authoritarian rule and the mythology of Tunisia under Ben Ali', *Mediterranean Politics*, 17 (2): 179–95.

Charfi, Mohamed (2005), 'Las libertades en el mundo árabe', *Afkar/Ideas*, 6: 80–2.

Coppedge, Michael, John Gerring, David Altman, Michael Bernhard, Steven Fish, Allen Hicken, Matthew Kroenig, Staffan I. Lindberg, Kelly McMann, Pamela Paxton, Holli A. Semetko, Svend-Erik Skaaning, Jeffrey Staton and Jan Teorell (2011), 'Conceptualizing and measuring democracy: a new approach', *Perspectives on Politics*, 9 (2): 247–67.

Dahl, Robert (1997), *La Poliarquía. Participación y Oposición*, Madrid: Tecnos.

Dahl, Robert (1999), *La Democracia. Una guía crítica para los ciudadanos*, Madrid: Taurus.

Daoud, Abdelkarim (2011), 'La révolution tunisienne de Janvier 2011: une lecture par les déséquilibres du territoire', *EchoGéo, Sur le Vif*. Available at <https://echogeo.revues.org/12612> (last accessed 14 February 2016).

Diamond, Larry (1999), *Developing Democracy: Toward Consolidation*, Baltimore: Johns Hopkins University Press.

El-Issawi, Fatima (2011), 'The Arab Spring and the challenge of minority rights: will the Arab Revolutions overcome the legacy of the past?', *European View*, 10 (2): 249–58.

EMHRN (2014), *Freedom of Assembly under Threat Muzzling Dissent in the Euro-Mediterranean Region*, Copenhagen.

Esen, Berk and Sebnem Gumuscu (2016), 'Rising competitive authoritarianism in Turkey', *Third World Quarterly*, 6597 (March): 1–26.

Human Rights Watch (2014), *All According to Plan. The Rab'a Massacre and Mass Killings of Protesters in Egypt*. Available at <https://www.hrw.org/report/2014/08/12/all-according-plan/raba-massacre-and-mass-killings-protesters-egypt> (last accessed 18 May 2016).

Kaboub, Fadhel (2013), 'The making of the Tunisian revolution', *Middle East Development Journal*, 5 (1): 1–21.

Kassem, Maye (2004), *Egyptian Politics. The Dynamics of Authoritarian Rule*, London: Lynne Rienner.

Kaye, Dalia D., Frederic Wehrey, Audra K. Grant and Dale Stahl (2008), *More Freedom, Less Terror? Liberalization and Political Violence in the Arab World*, Santa Monica, CA: Rand Corporation.

Linz, Juan J. and Alfred Stepan (1996), *Problems of Democratic Transition and Consolidation: Southern Europe, South America, and Post-Communist Europe*, Baltimore: Johns Hopkins University Press.

Mabrouk, Mehdi (2011), 'A revolution for dignity and freedom: preliminary observations on the social and cultural background to the Tunisian revolution', *The Journal of North African Studies*, 16 (4): 625–35.

Maddy-Weitzman, Bruce (2012), 'Historic departure or temporary marriage? The left-Islamist alliance in Tunisia', *Dynamics of Asymmetric Conflict: Pathways toward terrorism and genocide*, 5 (3): 196–207.

Mallat, Chibli (2014), 'Constitutionalism in 2014: basic rights in Egypt and Tunisia', *Anuario IEMed 2014*. Available at <http://www.iemed.org/observatori/arees-danalisi/arxius-adjunts/anuari/anuari-2014/Mallat_Costitution_Tunisia_Egypt_baisc_Rights_IEMed_yearbook_2014_EN.pdf> (last accessed 18 May 2016).

Martín-Muñoz, Gema (2005), *El Estado Árabe. Crisis de legitimidad y contestación islamista*, Barcelona: Edicions Bellaterra.

Martínez-Fuentes, Guadalupe (2011), 'El proceso revolucionario tunecino: tiempos, contextos y actores', in Ignacio Gutiérrez de Terán and Ignacio Álvarez-Ossorio (eds), *Informe sobre las revueltas árabes: Túnez, Egipto, Yemen, Bahréin, Libia y Siria*, Madrid: Ediciones del Oriente y del Mediterráneo: pp. 28–57.

Melián, Luis (2016), *Procesos de cambio político tras la Primavera Árabe. Un estudio comparado de los casos de Túnez, Egipto y Jordania*, PhD Dissertation, University of Salamanca.

Munck, Gerardo and Jay Verkuilen (2002), 'Conceptualizing and measuring democracy: evaluating alternative indices', *Comparative Political Studies*, 35 (1): 5–34.

O'Donnell, Guillermo and Leandro Wolfson (2000), 'Teoría democrática y política comparada', *Desarrollo Económico*, 39 (156): 519–70.

Ottaway, Marina (2014) 'Constitutional models vs political reality: the making of Arab constitutions after the uprisings', *Anuario IEmed 2014*. Available at <http://www.iemed.org/observatori/arees-danalisi/arxius-adjunts/anuari/anuari-2014/Ottaway_Constitutions_Arab_Uprising_Models_international_standards_IEMed_yearbook_2014_EN.pdf> (last accessed 13 February 2016).

Özbudun, Ergun (2014), 'AKP at the crossroads: Erdoğan's majoritarian drift', *South European Society and Politics*, 19 (2): 155–67.

Parejo, María Angustias (2015), 'Cambio y límites en Marruecos: propuestas de reforma constitucional sobre el Gobierno', *Revista CIDOB d'Afers Internacionals*, 109: 23–44.

Parolin, Gianluca P. (2014), 'The 2014 Constitution of Egypt: nn overview', *Anuario IEMed 2014*. Available at <http://www.iemed.org/publicacions/historic-de-publicacions/anuari-de-la-mediterrania/sumaris/avancaments-anuari-2013/The%202014%20Constitution%20of%20Egypt%20_Med2014.pdf> (last accessed 18 May 2016).

Pérez-Beltrán, Carmelo and Javier García-Marín (2015), 'Las libertades públicas en Túnez tras las Revueltas de 2011'. *Revista CIDOB d'Afers Internacionals*, 109: 69–90.

Perkins, Kenneth (2014), *A History of Modern Tunisia*, Cambridge: Cambridge University Press.

PNUD (2004), *Informe sobre Desarrollo Humano 2004. La libertad cultural en el mundo diverso hoy*. Available at <http://hdr.undp.org/es/content/informe-sobre-desarrollo-humano-2004> (last accessed 18 May 2016).

Pratt, Nicola (2007), *Democracy & Authoritarianism in the Arab World*, London: Lynne Rienner.

Przeworski, Adam (1992), *Democracy and the Market. Political and Economic Reforms in Eastern Europe and Latin America*, Cambridge: Cambridge University Press.

Przeworski, Adam (2005), 'Democracy as an equilibrium', *Public Choice*, 123: 253–73.

Przeworski, Adam, Michael E. Álvarez, Jose Antonio Cheibub and Fernando Limongi (2000), *Democracy and Development. Political Institutions and Well-Being in the World, 1950–1990*, Cambridge: Cambridge University Press.

Radinovic-Lukic, Marta and Edgar Mannheimer (2014) *Egypt : Military vs. Revolutionary. Why Structures Are Stronger than Individuals*, Lunds Universitet. Available at <lup.lub.lu.se/student-papers/record/4227604/file/4227607.pdf> (last accessed 18 May 2016).

Rodríguez, Carmen (2011), *¿Turquía Como Modelo Para Las Transiciones Árabes?*, ARI 118/2011, Madrid: Real Instituto Elcano. Available at <http://www.realinstitutoelcano.org/wps/portal/rielcano/contenido?WCM_GLOBAL_CONTEXT=/elcano/elcano_es/zonas_es/mediterraneo+y+mundo+arabe/ari118-2011> (last accessed 18 May 2016).

Sartori, Giovanni (2007), *Elementos de Teoría Política*, Madrid: Alianza Editorial.

Schumpeter, Joseph (1962), *Capitalism, Socialism and Democracy*, New York: Harper & Row.

Susser, Asher (2013), 'Is the Jordanian monarchy in danger?', *Middle East Brief*, (72): 1–8.

Szmolka, Inmaculada (2011), 'Democracias y autoritarismos con adjetivos: la clasificación de los países árabes dentro de una tipología general', *Revista Española de Ciencia Política*, 26: 11–62.

Szmolka, Inmaculada (2012), 'Factores desencadenantes y procesos de cambio político en el Mundo Árabe', *Documentos CIDOB, Mediterráneo y Oriente Medio*, 19. Available at <http://www.cidob.org/content/.../1/.../DOCUMENTOS_WEB_MEDITERRANEO_19.pdf> (last accessed 18 May 2016).

Willis, Michael (2012), *Politics and Power in the Maghreb. Algeria, Tunisia and Morocco from Independence to the Arab Spring*, New York: Columbia University Press.

Zaccara, Luciano (2008), 'La situación de los derechos humanos y libertades políticas en Irán', *Anuario Asia Pacífico*. Available at <http://www.anuarioasiapacifico.es/pdf/2008/cultura1.pdf> (last accessed 16 May 2016).

Zaccara, Luciano and Marta Saldaña (2013) 'Cambio y estabilidad política en las monarquías del Golfo tras la Primavera Árabe', *Revista CIDOB d'afers internacionals*, 109: 177–99.

Zoglin, Katie (2013), 'Tunisia at a crossroads: drafting a new constitution', *Insights*, 17 (18). Available at <https://www.asil.org/insights/volume/17/issue/18/tunisia-crossroads-drafting-new-constitution> (last accessed 15 January 2016).

Chapter 10

Media and media freedom

Javier García-Marín

1 Introduction

Any approach, academic or not, to the Middle East and North Africa (MENA) region stumbles upon a feature common to all but one of the countries that compose it: the lack of freedom. Indeed, a glance at any comparative politics handbook immediately shows us that the prevailing political regimes in the area are referred to in various ways, but almost never as 'fully democratic'. And one of the fundamental components of any liberal democracy is freedom of expression, which is usually represented through a system of plural media. Liberal theories, for example, have always emphasised the importance of independent journalism when it comes to limiting the abuse of power. Thus, it is not unreasonable to say that there can be no real democracy without freedom of expression, or freedom of expression without free media. It is only in these circumstances that citizens have the opportunity to receive accurate information and diverse viewpoints in relation to the political sphere. However, an initial examination of the media in the region indicates that the lack of freedom and the presence – omnipresence, even – of censorship or self-censorship prevail over any kind of recognition of rights. Of course, as discussed throughout this analysis, this situation results in citizens looking for alternatives. Specifically, we are thinking here about satellite television, a phenomenon from the mid 1990s. Satellite television has led to a creative explosion of media companies in the region, which have established a shared system and to some extent have become a haven for diversity of opinion. The triumph of these channels is analogous to using the Internet as a source of news – another great success for the plurality of information in the region. In addition, these new media move to the rhythm of the news and combine two factors: immediacy and technology. The result has been a media environment that changes almost every year, making any analysis obsolete in the medium term.

The objective of this analysis therefore is to explore the region's media systems in order to assess the sources of information available to civil society. The chapter is divided into four parts, which provide: firstly, an account of the political and regulatory environment in which the media have to operate; secondly, a description of traditional media; thirdly, an overview of satellite television, which is paramount in the region; and fourthly, an analysis of Internet access in the region. A cross-cutting focus to describe those systems has been necessary in order to deal with such an extensive region; hence no system in particular is going to be described, but rather the common characteristics of all of them.

2 Freedom of expression in the MENA countries

The most important factor in determining the nature and extent of freedom of expression in the media is the degree of pluralism and political freedom in a given society. Media systems have been overlooked on many occasions in studies of comparative politics, as it was felt that they were directly dependent on the general political situation. Hence, media system studies have been considered to be a secondary tool to approach political socialisation, regardless of their role in the formation of civil society or the differing media systems among similar political structures.

As can be seen in Table 10.1, in the MENA countries the media face very significant challenges and the treatment of public information is characterised by a lack of freedom. Of course, there are differences between countries: from those which might be considered 'partly free' by Freedom House, such as Lebanon, Kuwait and – less convincingly – United Arab Emirates (UAE), to those that are clearly not free, and which impose a high level of censorship, or self-censorship, such as Yemen or Saudi Arabia. On the other hand, Israel can be argued to be a separate case, as defective democracy in the area; nonetheless, there are concerns about media freedom in the country.

As indicated above, Table 10.1 shows how media and political systems are correlated, indicating that the situation of the media might be extrapolated to the whole society. However, this is by no means always the case. The example of Tunisia may be illustrative: on the one hand, in 2015 Freedom House considered it to be a democratic country (Table 10.1); on the other, Reporters Without Borders (Reporters sans frontières, RSF) currently argue that media freedom is a concern in the country, and compare it with Algeria, Oman or Morocco. The same can be applied to Israel. Lebanon, in contrast, is considered to be the home of the most liberal media in the region, but it is only partly-free.

Table 10.1 Press freedom in MENA countries

Country	RSF – 2010	RSF – 2015	FH – 2010	FH – 2015
Algeria	47.33 (133)	36.63 (119)	5.5	5.5
Bahrain	51.38 (144)	58.69 (163)	5.5	6.5
Egypt	43.33 (127)	50.17 (158)	5.5	5.5
Iran	94.66 (175)	72.32 (173)	6	6
Iraq	45.58 (130)	47.76 (156)	5.5	6
Israel	23.25 (86)	32.09 (101)	1.5	1.5
Jordan	37.00 (120)	42.07 (143)	5.5	5.5
Kuwait	23.75 (87)	30.84 (90)	4	5
Lebanon	20.50 (78)	31.81 (98)	4	4.5
Libya	63.50 (160)	45.99 (154)	7	6
Morocco	47.40 (135)	39.19 (130)	4.5	4.5
Oman	40.25 (124)	38.83 (127)	5.5	5.5
Qatar	38 (121)	35.35 (115)	5.5	5.5
Saudi Arabia	61.50 (157)	59.41 (164)	6.5	7
Syria	91.50 (173)	77.29 (177)	6.5	7
Tunisia	72,50 (164)	38.68 (126)	6	2
Turkey	49.25 (138)	44.16 (149)	4	3.5
UAE	23.75 (87)	36.73 (120)	5.5	6
Yemen	82.13 (170)	66.36 (168)	5.5	6

Sources: reports from and Reporters sans frontières 2010 and 2015 (Press Freedom: the bigger the number, less press freedom) and Freedom House 2011 and 2016 (Freedom of the World: 1 more freedom – 7 less freedom)

Furthermore, the most striking result of Table 10.1 is the comparison between 2010 and 2015 – that is to say before and after the so-called Arab Spring. Indeed, out of the eighteen countries, twelve show a regression in the press freedom index and eight in political freedom. The situation only improves in six countries for the media (Morocco, Algeria, Tunisia, Libya, Yemen and Qatar) and three for freedom in general (Tunisia, Libya and Turkey) – hardly a positive outcome of the processes of political change.[1]

3 Traditional media

Table 10.2 shows that the media have high penetration in almost all countries surveyed, especially in television, perhaps with the exception of Yemen. The penetration of satellite television in the region is also worth highlighting, as it is one of the highest proportions in the world and will have significant effects in terms of plurality of information.

Table 10.2 Media penetration, 2012–15

Country	Newspaper titles	Newspaper circulation (x 1000)	TV penetration (household (HH))	Satellite TV penetration (HH)	Mobile penetration	Broadband penetration (HH)
Bahrain	8	189	97%	96%	202%	105%
Egypt	21	5,360	96%	42%	86%	7.9%
Iraq	12	250	80%	a	87%	0.1%
Jordan	8	313	95%	76%	110%	33%
Kuwait	18	1,053	99%	90%	149%	81%
Lebanon	17	389	93%	88%	76%	36%
Libya	1	75	76%	a	232%	10%
Morocco	22	673	90%	64%	109%	10%
Oman	9	274	90%	95%	182%	14%
Qatar	3	211	92%	75%	204%	101%
Saudi Arabia	15	1,685	98%	86%	168%	36%
Syria	5	413	93%	74%	53%	1%
Tunisia	8	370	94%	89%	114%	29%
UAE	14	1,019	95%	46%	267%	93%
Yemen	3	170	64%	a	48%	3.2%

Note: a no data available
Source: Dubai Press Club (2013)

The written press in the MENA countries is constrained by factors applicable to all the media listed in the Table 10.2 (which are explained below), as well as poor literacy levels in the region (as low as 67.1 per cent in Morocco and 65 per cent in Yemen).[2] However, as occurs in the rest of the world, the press has a dual role: it is not only a means of communication to citizens, but also often gives a lead to other media through its editorials. Thus, the press is considered to be one of the most influential mass media, and it is therefore tightly controlled.

In the case of newspapers, we can divide them into three categories: those owned by governments, those owned by political parties and the independent press. However, very few of the media outlets belonging to the latter group can be considered truly independent; they are often owned by the elites who have or seek political power (or its benefits). Qatar, for example, has six newspapers, all of them technically independent, but in the hands of members of the ruling family or people with close ties to that family. In Saudi Arabia newspapers can be privately owned, but are restricted because they can only be established by royal decree. Rugh (2004; 2007) prefers to speak of different press typologies rather than the plurality and role of the media in the countries analysed.[3] Each of the typologies proposed involve varying relations between the media and politicians, but are based on common conditions for the entire region: a weak economic base, high politicisation and a pan-Arab cultural influence. Likewise, the author indicates some equally common consequences: political patronage, fragmentation, geographic concentration in the capitals of each state, the low credibility of journalists and the importance of oral communication.

Overall, governments in the area seek to maintain control of political discourse, especially when it is perceived as a threat to the established order, although the degree of control varies from country to country. In addition to direct censorship, usually directed at controlling information entering each country from abroad, Whitaker (2009) points out that control is established through different bureaucratic and legal tools, such as the control of licences, press laws or defamation laws. This whole network is aimed at controlling the press, and is applicable to other national media companies. The cases of Israel and Turkey are very different. In the former case, the real problems arise when journalists deal with the situation of the Palestinian people in the occupied territories. In the latter, most control measures over the media relate to the crime law and the recent anti-terrorist law (Durán and García-Marín 2015).

3.1 Licences and regulatory bodies

The MENA countries have historically been characterised by tight government control over both the print and broadcast media sectors. Although the notion of independent regulation is slowly starting to emerge in a few countries, no country has to date put in place a fully independent system. Iraq was the first country in the region to move in this direction, and steps to do so in Tunisia are relatively advanced. In many countries in the region –including Jordan and even the relatively liberal Lebanon – regulation of the print media, which usually involves something akin to a licensing requirement, is undertaken directly by the government, usually by the Ministry of Information or its equivalent. In other countries, such as Egypt, the print media are regulated by a separate body, the Supreme Press Council (SPC), but for the most part these bodies are firmly under government control.

A more common model in the region is to establish a separate broadcast regulator, such as the High Authority for Audio-visual Communication (HACA) (or the Haute Autorité de la Communication Audiovisuelle) in Morocco, the Audio-Visual Commission (AVC) in Jordan, the National Council for Audio Visual Media (NCAVM) in Lebanon or the High Audio Visual Office in Turkey (RTÜK). In most countries, including the four noted above, these bodies are under firm government or official control. In Morocco, for example, the king partially appoints (five out of nine, including the chairman) the members of HACA while in Jordan the Commission simply makes recommendations to the cabinet, which takes the final decision as to the licensing or otherwise of broadcasters. Since 2005 in Turkey, however, members of RTÜK are selected by parliament.

Two exceptions to this scenario of otherwise strict government control are Tunisia and Iraq. In Tunisia historically, authorisation to establish a new broadcaster was subject to ministerial approval and the licences were signed by the prime minister. A new law, adopted in November 2011, created the Independent High Authority for Audiovisial Communica-tion (Haute Autorité Indépendante de la Communication Audiovisuelle, HAICA). The independence of HAICA is expressly guaranteed in the law, and its funding is also protected against political interference. Members are nominated by a range of different social actors (the president, the courts, the parliament, journalists and media owners), thereby ensuring that they are not subject to the control of any one political actor. Members hold tenure for six years, which is non-renewable, and may be removed only by a unanimous decision by the other members (Pérez-Beltrán and García-Marín 2015).

Basically, the licence creates an appearance of freedom to allow the existence of independent media without direct government censorship, but the regulatory system provides several avenues of government interference under threat of licence withdrawal. That is, the media can be disciplined by employing technical tools, such as violating the terms of the licence, even though the real reason is offending the government (hence the importance of an independent regulatory body).

The conditions for obtaining a licence vary in each country, from purely bureaucratic to very arduous. In Mubarak's Egypt it was necessary for ten people to deposit US$100,000 each in a government account to begin the process of applying for a newspaper licence. Such a process could take years and no interest rate for the deposited money was paid. At that time newspapers were created in Cyprus to circumvent these measures, although they were considered to be foreign publications and therefore subject to censors before their release in the country. Capital deposit requirements are common in most of the MENA countries.

3.2 Media laws

In virtually all countries of the region there are press or media laws that impose limits on what can and cannot be published. The rules tend to be very vaguely defined, allowing for broad interpretation. For example, article 9 of the Saudi Arabian Media Law 2003 establishes that '[Publications] shall observe objective and constructive criticism that aims at public interest and which is based on facts and evidence.' Or the Yemeni Press and Publications Law of 1990, which includes the following prohibitions:

- anything that harms the Islamic faith and its principles or the diminishing of religion
- anything that causes tribal, sectarian, racial, regional or ancestral discrimination; or that can spread a spirit of dissent and division among the people or the call to apostasy
- anything that leads to the spread of ideas contrary to the principles of the Yemeni Revolution, are detrimental to the nation or distorts the image of the Yemeni Islamic heritage or Arab unity
- criticising the head of state, or attributing statements or images unless such statements or images were taken during a public speech. This is not necessarily applied to objective and constructive criticism.

These points reflect the sensitivities of most Arab countries. Similarly, the reform of the Kuwaiti 2006 press law criminalises the publication of material critical of the constitution, the emir, Islam, or anything that incite acts that offend public morals or religious sensitivities. One of the few positive trends that can be identified is that defendants are facing (hefty) fines instead of prison sentences. Restrictions may be quite specific to each country: in Qatar news of bankruptcies are prohibited, while in Bahrain the media law establishes that the press must not find 'fault against the right of a king or president of an Arab or Islamic state or any other state which the Kingdom of Bahrain has mutual diplomatic representation' (Duffy 2014: 27). The Press Law 93/95 of Egypt is usually considered the best example of these extreme limitations, to the point of making journalists responsible for the accuracy of the information, even when that information has come from foreign agencies (Eickelman and Anderson 2003: 24). Opposition to this law was so great that Hosni Mubarak abolished it a few years later.

3.3 Laws against defamation

Defamation laws are frequently employed as a tool to protect senior officials from media criticism. Defamation is usually categorised as a civil matter in many countries in the region, although people are also often punished under the criminal law, which can lead to imprisonment. For example, in 2009 the report of the International Press Institute stated:

> Defaming or insulting state officials continues to carry prison time in many MENA countries. In Algeria, defamation of high officials and state organs has been criminalised since 2001, and as of February 2006, it is illegal to criticise actions by security forces in that country. In Jordan, defamation is punishable only with a fine; however, insulting the king or the royal family carries a sentence of up to three years. Criticising the head of state, undermining public morality, defaming individuals or misrepresenting Yemeni or Arab heritage are all illegal in Yemen. Similar legislation also exists in Egypt, Saudi Arabia, Libya, Tunisia, Morocco, Chad, the United Arab Emirates, Qatar and Oman.[4]

Unfortunately, little has changed since then. In some cases the concept of defamation has both been extended and blurred, and can extend beyond individuals to other countries or to concepts such as religion itself. For example, since the start of 2015, the RSF has registered many cases of journalists being harassed in Morocco or accused of defamation for criticising government policy or for covering sensitive matters involving government officials.[5]

3.4 Advertising revenue

One key element when assessing the independence of the media in any society is the degree of financial autonomy. Logically, independent media revenues can come from three sources: circulation revenue, advertising or subsidies.

With regard to circulation revenue in the region, the Arab Media Outlook 2009–2013 estimated that no single media outlet in the region made any profit because of its limited reach (Dubai Press Club 2010). On the other hand, it is worth noting that investment in advertising in the Arab world averages only US$22 per person (compared to 462 in North America and 273 in Western Europe), representing 1.5 per cent of the world total. Therefore, subsidies are the real protagonists, whether from the state or from families who own the media (both concepts can be confusing sometimes, as in the case of Al Jazeera and the Qatari elite). For example, some authors estimate that in 2003 total income of the (combined) Arab newspapers was lower than that of *The New York Times* alone, and the sum of the salaries of all journalists in Saudi Arabia was less than that of the annual salary of the famous American journalist Peter Jennings (Rugh 2004: 5). According to the most recent Arab Media Outlook (2012–15) (Dubai Press Club 2013), thirteen years later the situation had improved, but it is still among the least-developed advertising markets in the world, lagging well behind North America, Western Europe, Asia Pacific, Latin America and Central and Eastern Europe (for example, advertising spend per capita is thirty times less than in North America or almost twenty times less than in Western Europe, regions where traditional media outlets struggle for survival).

All of the above limitations go well beyond article 19 of the International Covenant on Civil and Political Rights. Article 19 says that any restriction on freedom of expression must be the subject of a law and must be necessary for the purposes specified in paragraph 3 of the article, which include 'protection of national security or of public order, or of public health or morals'. In other words, the authorities must demonstrate that the information threatens national security or satisfies one of the other criteria specified in the covenant.

4 Media regulation changes

In spite of the lack of positive changes shown in Table 10.1, some countries in the MENA region have initiated modifications in media laws. Table 10.2 summarises changes in these laws across the region during the last five years, and the difference in media freedom (according to Freedom House). Most countries have a prejudicial environment for media freedom, however, that does not necessarily respond to changes in media laws. Therefore, those changes are not a clear indicator of a worsening situation for freedom of expression. However, in those countries where the situation has improved, the regulatory framework has changed (with the exception of Iran where improvement is minimal). As there are no democracies in the region any change in media freedom has to be achieved through legal changes. However, these changes are not necessary for a situation to worsen since the tools used to constrain the media (as seen above) are varied and sometimes governments prefer to use subtler means to achieve their goal, usually through varying legislation such as anti-terrorism laws. Nonetheless, three groups can be identified from Table 10.3, namely countries where: media freedom improved, the legal framework changed and media freedom worsened, and without any legal change media freedom deteriorated.

The first group comprises countries such as Morocco, Algeria, Tunisia, Libya and Qatar (and, to a much lesser extent, Yemen and Iran). The Tunisian case is the most promising in the region, especially following the creation of the independent regulatory body (HAICA), as mentioned above. However, Algeria is perhaps the country where the situation is improving to the greatest extent. Algeria's 2012 Media Law abolished prison sentences for press-related offences and also opened up the media to private ownership. In 2013 three new private

Table 10.3 Media law changes, 2010–15

Country	Regulatory changes 2010–15	Media freedom difference 2010–15[a]
Algeria	Yes	-14
Bahrain	Yes	+19
Egypt	Yes	+31
Iran	No	-2
Iraq	No	+26
Israel	-	-
Jordan	Yes	+23
Kuwait	Yes	+3
Lebanon	No	+20
Libya	Yes	-6
Morocco	Yes	-5
Oman	No	+3
Qatar	Yes	-6
Saudi Arabia	No	+7
Syria	No	+4
Tunisia	Yes	-38
Turkey	No	+11
UAE	No	+33
Yemen	Yes	-2

Note: [a] positive (+) sign represents less media freedom
Source: Media Freedom by Freedom House

television stations opened without prior permission, ending the government's monopoly on broadcast media. However, these stations were given posterior government approval by a law passed by the Algerian parliament on 20 January 2014. Nonetheless, substantial legal restrictions on press freedom remain. Significant fines are still a constraint on journalists, limiting their coverage of particular subjects such as state security.

Besides the Tunisian and Algerian cases (where the situation is still very difficult), the real extent of those changes for journalists or media outlets has, at best, yet to be seen. Morocco might be a good example, where not one but three media laws were reformed in November 2014. While this step represented a big improvement on the former legislation, the reforms failed to dismantle the 'red lines' forbidding criticism of Islam, the king and other members of the royal family. Yemen also finalised a freedom of information law in 2012, becoming only the second Arab country, after Jordan, to enact such legislation. Freedom of information advocacy groups welcomed the law, although the actual degree of implementation remains unclear. In Qatar – the first country in the region to abolish the Ministry of Information that was responsible for controlling, directing and censoring media, in 1995 – a controversial 'cyber law' introduced new restrictions on Internet freedom in May 2013. Similarly, in Libya recent changes are curtailing the freedom of expression that was partly won after the 2011 revolution. In 2012 a media law was passed that bans insults against the people of Libya or its institutions. This law also prohibits criticism of the country's 2011 revolution and glorification of the deposed former leader Muammar al-Gaddafi. Nonetheless, even with the civil war, media freedom is greater in 2015 than under the closed dictatorship of al-Gaddafi.

The second group is formed by countries where legal changes are accompanied by a worsening situation for freedom of expression: Egypt, Jordan, Bahrain and Kuwait.

Egypt is, perhaps, the country where changes were most profound and, at the same time, least encouraging. The 2014 constitution contains several provisions regarding freedom of expression (article 65), access to information (article 68), and the media (articles 70, 71 and 72). The constitution also calls for the establishment of independent regulatory bodies tasked with supporting and developing both private and state-owned media and administering all relevant regulations. However, these positive elements are seriously undermined by a variety of exceptions and ambiguities (as is common in the region). Article 71 authorises media censorship 'in times of war or general mobilisation'. The same article, which ostensibly eliminates jail terms for media offences, leaves room for imprisonment for crimes related to incitement of violence, discrimination and defamation. The constitution notably fails to specify the composition and appointment procedures for regulatory bodies, meaning future legislation could create structures that enable political influence. Moreover, the existing press laws and penal code remain in place, including an array of articles that can be used to imprison journalists. For example, defamation is a criminal offence, and sentences of up to five years in prison can be imposed for blasphemy, or 'exploiting religion by spreading, either in words, in writing, or by any other means, extreme ideas for the purposes of inciting strife, ridiculing or insulting [the Abrahamic faiths] or a sect following it, or damaging national unity'.[6]

In Jordan a law passed in September 2011 allows journalists who report on corruption without 'solid facts' to be fined. An amendment to the Press and Publications Law of September 2012 introduced restrictions on Internet content and led to the blocking of 200–300 websites and blogs in June 2013.

In Bahrain the law prohibits the distribution of any publication without written approval from the authorities. The Information Affairs Authority monitors national media, which it can (and does) censor. Nonetheless, changes were considered necessary following the political unrest in early 2011. In August 2013 the government declared an 'emergency media strategy' to counter what it deemed to be false reporting on the country's political crisis.[7] The new legislation follows a zero tolerance approach, which means on the one hand increased monitoring and the presence of the Information Affairs Authority in social media, while on the other hand the state-run Bahrain News Agency has been promoted as 'the main source of information for local and international media outlets'. Internet access is subject to restrictions and a number of websites remain inaccessible within Bahrain. Bahrain's blogging scene is very active and diverse; however, it is under permanent scrutiny by the authorities.

Finally, Kuwait, though still heading the list of Arab states by a significant margin, saw its position downgraded due to legal changes: in May 2014 a new telecommunications law, according to Human Rights Watch, 'gives the government sweeping powers to block content, deny access to the Internet, and revoke licenses without giving reasons'.[8]

The final group comprises countries that have not undertaken legal changes and that also have a more negative environment for media freedom. It is also the most numerous group, including: Saudi Arabia, Oman, Iraq, UAE, Syria, Lebanon and Turkey. Each of these countries has a deteriorating media freedom situation, with the worst being Lebanon, where the increasing polarisation of the political sphere has resulted in less independence and pluralism of opinion within the media. Nevertheless, Lebanon remains a more or less safe place for journalists. In contrast are the cases of Iraq and Syria due, of course, to their conflictive situation. These conflicts may be employed, however, to tighten control over the media: for example, the Iraqi authorities ordered the closure of forty-four news media outlets operating in Iraq in June 2012, including the BBC, Voice of America and the United States-funded Radio Sawa. In June

2014, following the offensive of Islamic State (IS), the Iraqi Media and Communication Commission sent a list of guidelines for the media. This included a ban on meeting and interviewing individuals wanted by judicial authorities as well as on broadcasting messages issued by armed groups.

Gulf countries have also increasingly being trying to control media outlets. While Bahrain and Kuwait have changed media laws to that end, others have not felt it to be necessary. In Saudi Arabia, for instance, the government moved to increase its control over independent blogs and web sites, demanding that these too obtain official licences. On the other hand, the case of Oman is even more concerning. The period between February 2013 and January 2015 confirmed the dramatic crackdown on freedom of expression that took place in the country, perpetuating what the United Nations Special Rapporteur Maina Kiai called a 'pervasive culture of silence and fear affecting anyone who wants to speak and work for reforms in Oman'.[9] And, while the UAE constitution guarantees all citizens 'freedom to hold opinions and expression of the same' as well as 'freedom of communication', the government continued to severely restrict freedom of expression. Existing laws prohibit both criticism of the ruler and any speech that may encourage or create unrest, and they authorise censorship of domestic and foreign publications to remove criticism of the government or statements that are deemed threatening to social stability. A new anti-terrorism law passed in August 2014 contains clauses that can be used to further restrict rights. Article 14 punishes with death or life sentence acts 'intended to undermine the stability, safety, unity, sovereignty or security of the state'. Article 15 provides for temporary imprisonment for 'whoever declares by any public means his enmity to the state or regime, or his non-allegiance to the leadership'.

Turkey is a special case. Considered to be a defective democracy at the start of the period under study, it is still one of the countries with the most restrictive media freedom environment. Not only does the constitution limit freedom of speech (especially through articles 26 and 28), but also further restrictions can be added through the ordinary legislative procedure. Turkey has been particularly severe with regard to these limits, resulting in a maze of rules, many of broad interpretation, which pose a very real impediment to the exercise of freedom of expression and publication. Among the laws and codes that stand out due to their widespread use, are the following: the penal code, the Press Law and the Anti-terror Law. The specificity of the Turkish case is that the media is limited by those laws, rather than by ordinary media regulations. In fact, the red lines that have existed in previous years, such as the debate on the Armenian genocide or Kurdish nationalism, have practically disappeared, but control of the media has intensified, leaving a paradoxical situation (Durán and García- Marín 2015).

5 Pluralism in the media: satellite television

The Arab satellite television industry is unique in the world, mainly due to the fragmentation of its audiences, with 250 million people and about twenty dialects.

However, it was from the unquestionable success of CNN to report directly on the ground in the 1991 Gulf War, that governments and Arab business elites understood the potential that satellite television could have. Since that time several clusters have arisen, with the biggest being the Middle East Broadcasting Centre (MBC), founded in 1991 in London. Following the example of MBC, several other groups were created such as Orbit Communications, Arab Radio and Television, the Lebanese Broadcasting Corporation, Star Asia, Al Mayadeen and Al Jazeera. The model has been very successful in the region and in 2014 there were an estimated 450 Pan-Arab satellite channels, with thirty-two of them devoted exclusively to news (Dubai Press Club 2013: 46–7). However the beginnings of satellite television services were not without problems. Orbit (owned by the Saudi group Al-Mawarid), for example, linked with the BBC to create a news service in Arabic, where the BBC maintained editorial control. Nonetheless, because of the existing controls over the media in the Middle East mentioned above, the association was short lived: a difference of opinion about an incident in Saudi Arabia caused Orbit to break the agreement with the BBC in 1996. Dozens of journalists dismissed following the suspension of the channel would almost immediately be hired by the newly formed Al Jazeera in Qatar.

However, satellite television, while free from many of the above controls, is also limited by state interference in the region (even Al Jazeera, the media outlet that tends to break most taboos and to criticise Arab governments, is sensitive to the national political environment of its home country, Qatar). Firstly, because satellite television companies are owned by the ruling elites' families (see Table 10.4). Secondly, and as occurs with other media in the region, no channel makes a profit without subsidies. In fact, five channels (MBC 1, MBC4, MBC 2, Saudi TV1 and Al Arabiya) account for a 47 per cent share and the remaining 53 per cent is distributed among hundreds of different channels. And even among those channels, advertising revenues are very low – 60 per cent lower than European revenues (Dubai Press Club 2010: 50–1).

However, following several political incidents between various Arab governments and media companies, especially Al Jazeera, the Arab information ministers adopted a regulatory charter (The Arab League Satellite Broadcasting

Table 10.4 Ownership of selected media companies in Gulf countries

Media group	Ownership	Headquarters
Arab Media Group	Part of TECOM, which is part of Dubai Holdings. UAE government	Dubai, UAE
Orbit Communications Company	Mawarid Holding (private company chaired by Prince Khaled al-Saud)	Manama, Bahrain
Middle East Broadcasting Centre (MBC)	Investment funds. Major shareholder Prince Abdul Aziz bin Fahd (Saudi Arabia)	Dubai, EAU
Al Jazeera	Partly funded by the House of Thani (Qatar royal family)	Doha, Qatar

Source: prepared by the author from companies' data

Charter) on 12 February 2008.[10] These rules allow them to penalise companies that attack political leaders or emit socially unacceptable content. It also covers a broad spectrum, from news and political programmes to sport and entertainment. The strategy followed has been twofold: on the one hand, it seems to want to placate moderate Islamist groups, to prohibit or limit sexual content and to prevent advertising related to alcohol consumption. On the other hand, it addresses the nationalist need to protect 'the Arab identity from the harmful effects of globalisation'. And finally, it seeks popular support by offering citizens the right to information, including the right to watch some competitive sports free via government channels, even though private channels have exclusive rights (this is a direct attack on intellectual property and the bottom line of any media outlet: its profits). However, the key aim of the document is to ban content that undermines 'social harmony, national unity, public order or traditional values' – very similar to those words referred to above when media laws were discussed. However, the implementation of these regulations has been uneven across the Arab League countries. Qatar, for example, refused to sign the charter because of potential problems with their domestic law. The Lebanese government on the other hand only interpreted the charter as a set of guidelines and principles that was not mandatory.

Nilesat and Arabsat are among the satellite operators in the region that can be involved in conflictual situations. The former is located in Egypt and the latter in Saudi Arabia. The charter theoretically allows the governments of those countries to 'ban' the 'awkward' channels, although such actions could lead to political consequences. Mubarak's Egypt demonstrated its ability to do so by disconnecting three satellite television channels in February 2008.[11]

Even eight years later the true scope of the charter has yet to be seen, but it would not be surprising to find an increase in self-censorship across the region. In any case, satellite television is now one of the widely available means of getting unbiased information to the Arab public.

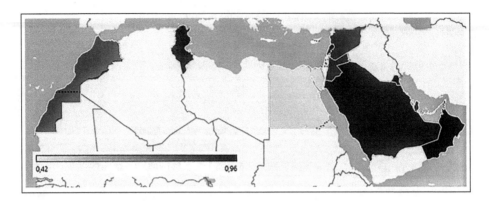

Figure 10.1 Satellite television penetration rate per household

6 The emergence of the Internet: a change in the media structure?

The Internet is perhaps the most significant recent change in communication processes across the planet. Internet access in the Middle East and North Africa is uneven, although, as Table 10.5 shows, almost all rich Gulf countries have very high penetration rates. However, in countries with limited financial resources, or in conflict, such as Yemen and Syria, this penetration is much less, but still significant.

The Internet changes communication processes as it is not a media in itself, but rather a new platform for information exchange, be it political, social, entertainment, and so on. In the MENA countries some of the tools that have emerged from the Internet have become very popular, such as blogs or social networks (Table 10.5), which have a very high penetration rate, probably because they are not bound by the constraints that traditional media face, and are therefore a bastion of freedom. The 2012 Arab Media Outlook report specifically highlighted the fact that the Internet is one of the most popular sources of information among those who buy newspapers in the region. In particular, the concept of bloggers' news is particularly important in the MENA countries. This means that competition in news media comes not only in the form of official news and news websites, but also from individual bloggers. This concept is increasingly popular in the region as it provides a platform for freedom of expression, although several countries have imposed filters or have arrested bloggers under various charges. In fact, it could be argued that with complete control of the traditional media assured, reining in the Internet is seen as the next big task for some countries. Initially unprepared for dealing with the Internet, an excellent tool for circumventing censorship, the most despotic regimes are now quickly making up for lost time and, with the help of surveillance technology sold by leading Western companies, are realising the Internet's potential for state control.

As Table 10.5 shows, Freedom House has an index on Freedom on the Internet that 'measures the subtle and not-so-subtle ways that governments and non-state actors around the world restrict our intrinsic rights online'.[12] The index is based on three categories: obstacles to access, limits to content, and violations of user rights. While not as extensive as their other indexes, it covers a substantial number of the MENA countries. Furthermore, according to Freedom House's 'Freedom in the World' reports, there is not a single country in the region where citizens enjoy a free environment on the Internet, with criticism of the authorities (present in all countries) being the most censored topic, surpassing even blasphemy.

Table 10.5 Internet and social media penetration

Country	Facebook penetration	Twitter penetration	Internet penetration	Freedom on the Net
Algeria	8.02%	0.12%	27.8%	a
Bahrain	16.35%	4.67%	96.4%	72 not free
Egypt	10.33%	0.61%	54.6%	61 not free
Iran	a	a	57.2%	87 not free
Iraq	7.04%	0.14%	33.0%	a
Israel	55.4%	-	74.7%	a
Jordan	22.83%	1.31%	86.1%	50 partly free
Kuwait	17.74%	7.60%	78.7%	a
Lebanon	19.03%	2.57%	80.4%	45 partly free
Libya	8.72%	0.22%	37.4%	54 partly free
Morocco	10.17%	0.25%	60.6%	43 partly free
Oman	11.58%	1.31%	78.6%	a
Qatar	24.68%	3.76%	91.9%	a
Saudi Arabia	13.14%	6.48%	65.9%	73 not free
Syria	a	a	28.1%	87 not free
Tunisia	19.51%	0.31%	49.0%	38 partly free
Turkey	52.8%	a	59.6%	58 partly free
UAE	28.15%	4.89%	93.2%	68 not free
Yemen	1.86%	a	22.6%	a

Note: a no data available
Sources: Facebook and Twitter users above thirteen years old. Arab Social Media Report 2014; Internet penetration from internetworldstats.com data for 2015; and, 'Freedom on the Net' by Freedom House 2015

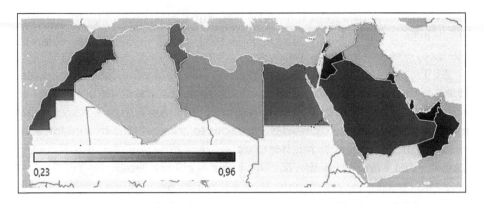

Figure 10.2 Internet penetration in MENA countries

In fact, authorities that feel threatened by domestic reform efforts or criticism following the overthrow of authoritarian regimes in Tunisia, Egypt, Libya and Yemen in 2011 have fiercely cracked down on freedom of expression and online journalism in particular. The Internet is no longer as welcoming to independent journalism as non-democratic governments erase the legal distinctions between expression online and offline. The digital space for independent journalism and free speech is likely to be constricted further by the impact of restrictive laws, surveillance and ensuing self-censorship.

In this environment, laws against disrupting public order and 'spreading false news' have been passed or updated to apply to online expression in the name of preserving stability, preventing terrorism and avoiding anarchy. Journalists who breach these regulations face criminal penalties, sometimes including lengthy prison sentences and fines.

In some cases, the filtrate is openly recognised and legislated for accordingly. For example, in Saudi Arabia, the cabinet passed a set of rules for the Internet (Resolution 229 in 13/8/1425, in 2004), which among other things forbade users to publish or access:

- any material that contravenes legislation or fundamental principles, or violates the sanctity of Islam and its benevolent law or public decency
- any material contrary to the state or its system
- reports or news that harm the Saudi armed forces without the approval of the competent authorities
- any material harmful to the dignity of the state or heads of diplomatic missions accredited in the kingdom, or that harms relations with those countries
- any false information concerning officials and private or public institutions that can hurt them personally or to those institutions or their integrity
- any libellous or defamatory material against individuals.

More importantly, the Internet service providers (ISPs) have to direct their traffic through the Internet national service unit at King Abdul-Aziz City for Science and Technology.

Kuwait, meanwhile, passed a law in 2014 that would empower authorities to block websites and restrict access to the Internet without providing a reason under the guise of protecting public morals, health or national security. Kuwait has one of the highest per capita Twitter usage rates in the world, and critics saw this as an effort to curb discussion on sensitive topics and election coverage with the threat of harsh penalties, including prison sentences.

In Qatar an ambiguous cybercrime law passed in September 2014 imposes heavy fines and prison sentences on anyone found guilty of violating social values by publishing 'news, pictures, audio or video recordings related to the personal or family life of individuals, even if true'. Like many such laws in the region, it includes prohibitions on spreading false news but also includes penalties for creating or managing a website to do so. By criminalising the creation and dissemination of a range of vaguely defined content, it opens journalists and others up for prosecution for engaging in routine reporting and commentary.

7 Conclusions

As seen throughout this chapter, the MENA countries have configured a dual system of communication media. The first group comprises the traditional structure, which is made up of national television, newspapers and radio stations. The promotion of diversity has not been a priority in the Arab world, and in most countries national laws seek to control information in that system. In fact, the main objective of the licensing of broadcasters or print media outlets has been to ensure loyalty to the governing regime and an understanding that the owner would not engage in criticism of government or officials. Due, perhaps, to that control, a second group of media outlets parallel to the national structure has been created, which may be described as pan-Arab (outside the Arab world that is Iran, Turkey or Israel, no such system exists) and that is composed mainly of satellite television.[13]

The data analysed in this chapter clearly illustrates that one of the results of the Arab Spring has been the attempt to further control information flows. With the exception of a few countries, especially Tunisia and Algeria, almost all the governments in the region have adopted rules in the hope of controlling information in a more effective way. The most common method has been to attempt to homologise information on the Internet with information provided by traditional media and, thus, to apply the same laws to it. In fact, regional governments consider that one of the causes of political change was the free flow of information on the Internet, so a significant part of the new media laws has been to control it. For example, countries such as Turkey and Saudi Arabia have been especially active in their attempt to control social media.

Hence, media outlets in the region face a series of challenges that have led to limitations on totally free enterprises and the delivery of unrestricted communication services to citizens. All of the countries in the area are in serious breach of these standards, even Israel, the only country with a legitimate claim to democracy in the region. While there has been some progress recently, particularly in terms of respect for freedom of expression, the need for comprehensive media law reform in the region remains pressing and very substantial. Unless structural protection for media freedom is provided through legal reform, it is extremely unlikely that any gains for freedom of expression will be long lasting.

Of course, this does not mean that citizens are unable to obtain political information through other channels than those accepted by governments. As shown above, satellite television is a first fracture in the closed ecosystem, but events in recent years suggest that it is not entirely free from attempts at regularisation and control. Nonetheless, there are other tools to serve the public that can be treated as sources of information and, therefore, as media: namely the Internet and all its facets. Today networking via social media is considered to be one of the main sources of political information for citizens, particularly among the youth, who have instinctively and quickly adapted to these changes and technological advances; in fact, the average age of users is rarely over thirty. The question, however, is to what extent are these new tools important? A clear response is very difficult because analysis of the information received and emitted is extremely complex. We would argue that it is desirable that the new media can somehow be an antidote to authoritarianism. Discourse and debates in that media are often fascinating, but its political importance, even after the Arab Spring, has still to be demonstrated. It is unclear how civic pluralism translates into political power, and whether it does.

However, we not are talking about a few channels (or even hundreds) reaching citizens in a unidirectional way, but millions of pages and dozens of different tools that compete for the attention of users. It is in some ways an á la carte service, with constantly changing protagonists, and is therefore extremely difficult to control. That has led to speculation about the effects of the Internet on social movements, and especially the great convulsions of 2010--11. From the field of journalism and media studies the reaction has been to exaggerate, perhaps, the effects of social networks. That could lead, in turn, to some academics rejecting any effect. Data from the Arab Social Media Report suggest that, perhaps, we should find some midpoint: that social networks have not had an absolute role in these riots – which, after all, were carried out by people, not tools – but neither can it be said that they did not play a role. As noted above, in an environment where the media are heavily censored and without access to conflict zones, social networks functioned as disseminators of information, facilitating the protests, at least initially, by broadcasting information beyond local and national areas. This last idea connects us with the concept of censorship. Censorship, as shown throughout this chapter, is omnipresent in the region, either officially or through other conduits seeking self-censorship by journalists. However, in the light of new media and social networking, is this model of censorship sustainable? Is it effective? We argue that it is clearly not, and its effectiveness will be increasingly undermined as Internet access grows. Therefore, current regimes have to get used to surviving without imposing controls on information, or it will flow regardless of the filters employed. The first step taken by authoritarian governments is often not very promising: the closure of websites, more censorship, attempts to redirect web traffic, and so on. However, the digital world has sufficiently demonstrated that any form of control (digital rights management, copy protection, and so on) can be overcome by skilled computer users and ingenuity. To date many of these regimes have used repression as a means of control, especially towards bloggers, but this seems impossible to continue in societies that are rapidly moving towards universal access to information.

Notes

1. The situation in Libya and Turkey has significantly worsened during 2016 though.
2. Statistics from UNICEF, available at <http://www.unicef.org> (last accessed 27 January 2017).
3. Rugh speaks of three different types of relationship between media and governments in the area: mobilisation, loyalist and diverse. In countries classified as having a mobilisation type the regime not only prevents the media from expressing any opposition or deviation from the official line on politically sensitive matters, but it actively uses the media as a tool to mobilise popular support for its political programmes. The countries in the 'loyalist' media group also have political systems in which there are no political parties or competitive elections, and furthermore, the political environment does not encourage dissent to be expressed against the government. But the regime adopts a more passive attitude toward the media than is the case in mobilisation systems, and does not seek to aggressively exploit the media to activate the public for specific political purposes, as the mobilisation system does. In the third group of countries, a very different political environment leads to a 'diverse' media system. Contrasting and competing political parties or groups can express their views relatively freely. Some restrictions on freedom of expression exist in the laws, but they are relatively minimal or not strictly enforced (Rugh 2007: 6–7).

4. Available at <http://www.freemedia.at/newssview/article/middle-east-and-north-africa-overview.html> (last accessed 30 June 2016).
5. Available at <https://rsf.org/en/news/monarchys-red-lines-gag-moroccos-independent-media> (last accessed 30 June 2016).
6. Freedom House 2015. Available at <https://freedomhouse.org/report/freedom-press/2015/egypt> (last accessed 30 June 2016).
7. Available at <http://www.bna.bh/portal/en/news/575628> (last accessed 30 June 2016).
8. Available at <https://www.hrw.org/world-report/2015/country-chapters/kuwait> (last accessed 3 July 2016).
9. Availableat<http://www.ohchr.org/en/NewsEvents/Pages/DisplayNews.aspx?NewsID=15036&LangID=E> (last accessed 3 July 2016).
10. Available at <http://www.arabmediasociety.com/UserFiles/AMS%20Charter%20Arabic.pdf> (last accessed 3 July 2016).
11. Available at <http://www.aljazeera.com/focus/2008/08/20088791952617974.html> (last accessed 13 July 2016).
12. Available at <https://freedomhouse.org/report-types/freedom-net> (last accessed 13 July 2016).
13. In both cases Arab media is primarily Arab, so it can only be understood in their cultural and social context. For example a study by Shahira Fahmy (2010), which compared photographs published by *Al Hayat* and the *Herald Tribune* on the 2001 attacks on the US and the subsequent war in Afghanistan, showed how each medium tended to emphasise the human drama in their culturally closest scenario. Thus, *Al Hayat* published more images in that framework (emphasising human suffering) while reporting on Afghanistan and less when informed of the US attacks. And the opposite occurred when the US case was analysed.

References

Dubai Press Club (2010), *Arab Media Outlook 2009–2013*, Dubai: DPC.
Dubai Press Club (2013), *Arab Media Outlook 2012–2015*, Dubai: DPC.
Dubai School of Government (2011), *Arab Social Media Report*, Dubai: DSG.
Duffy, Matt J. (2014), 'Arab media regulations: identifying restraints on freedom of the press in the laws of six Arabian Peninsula countries', *Berkeley Journal of Middle Eastern and Islamic Law*, 6 (1): 1–31.
Durán, Marién and Javier García-Marín (2015), 'Libertad de expresión y regulación mediática en la Turquía de Erdogan', in Ignacio Álvarez-Ossorio (ed.), *La Primavera Árabe Revisitada*, Madrid: Aranzadi, pp. 191–212.
Eickelman, Dale and Jon Anderson (eds) (2003), *New Media in the Muslim World: the Emerging Public Sphere*, Bloomington: Indiana University Press.
Fahmy, Shahira (2010), 'Contrasting visual frames of our times: a framing-analysis of English and Arabic language press coverage of war and terrorism', *International Communication Gazette*, 72 (8): 695–717.
International Press Institute (2009). *Middle East and North Africa Institute*. Available at <http://www.freemedia.at/index.php?id=227&tx_ttnews[tt_news]=4137&tx_ttnews[backPid]=190&cHash=1813c5cb1a> (last accessed 2 February 2015).

Pérez-Beltrán, Carmelo and Javier García-Marín (2015), 'Las libertades públicas en Túnez tras las revueltas de 2011', *Revista CIDOB d'Afers internacionals*, 109: 69–90.

Rugh, William A. (2004), *Arab Mass Media: Newspapers, Radio and Television in Arab Politics*, Westport: Praeger.

Rugh, William A. (2007), 'Do national political systems still influence Arab media?', *Arab Media and Society*, 2. Available at <http://www.arabmediasociety.com/?article=225> (accessed 15 June 2006).

Whitaker, Brian (2009), *What's Really Wrong with the Middle East*, London: Saqi Books.

Part III

Chapter 11

Regional order and regional powers in the Middle East and North Africa

Jordi Quero and Eduard Soler

1 Introduction

Since the initiation of the various revolutions, upheavals and protests in late 2010 in the Middle East and North Africa (MENA), many have discussed the international dimension of these events. However, it seems most of that analysis has engaged in 'second image reversed' questions or how the international system impacts on the domestic politics of the states (Bush 2015). As suggested by Valbjørn (2015: 74), there have been very few attempts at developing theoretical perspectives on the impact of the so-called Arab Spring on international relations in the region.

Among those who have accepted that challenge there is no clear-cut opinion on the repercussions of the events. For some authors, the Arab Spring represented a change in the regional order as they 'finally and definitively reshap[ed] the post-colonial regional order' prompting the inception of an 'emerging regional order' (Rózsa 2013: 16); triggered a 'rapid change of the regional system' (Legrenzi 2015: 29); or embodied 'the contours of a change in the Arab regional order not seen since the 1967 war' (Malmvig 2012: 1). Some even argued that 'there was no meaningful Arab or Middle East regional order' before the uprisings; 'there is still not one today (. . .) [as the region] has no cooperative, political, security or economic framework' (Salem 2012: 10) and there is 'no movement toward building any architecture of regional order' (Salem 2014: 6). Contrarily, some other scholars saw continuity as 'some key aspects of regional politics continue to operate along familiar lines' as 'regional regimes [were] still playing with the old playbook, even as societies have changed dramatically' (Ryan 2015: 42).

This chapter aims at analysing the political consequences of the processes of political change in the MENA for the regional system. Particularly, it assesses whether and to what extent those internal political changes have triggered a shift in the regional order of the MENA subsystem and its institutions and how regional powers have adapted to those changes. The chapter draws on the English School and constructivist theories of international relations to approach the concept of order. It firstly discusses the impact of the Arab Spring on the 'constitutional structure' of the regional order, following Reus-Smit's well-known contribution on the hierarchical structure of international society. Next, it examines whether we have witnessed a change within the existing order. In order to do so, it analyses what has changed in relation to some of the fundamental institutions working in the MENA region (alliances and amity/enmity cleavages, non-intervention, multilateralism and bilateralism, and great power management). It argues that slight changes in the fundamental institutions since the Arab Spring generally respond to a more fundamental systemic change that took place in the context of the 2003 war in Iraq. However, despite attempts to challenge it, the constitutional structure of the regional order is intact.

2 The Arab Spring and the constitutional structures of the MENA's regional order

The study of the notion of international order has been one of the driving forces of international relations, most probably only comparable to that of anarchy. Bull (1995: 8) initially defined order as 'a pattern of activity that sustains the elementary or primary goals of the society of states, or international society'. Since then, the English School of International Relations – but not only that – has advanced alternative definitions nuancing and widening Bull's theoretical framework.[1] At the same time, the concept of order and its constitutive elements have provided a profitable and prolific theoretical framework not only for the analysis of the global system but also for examining regional subsystems. Among many others, contributions by Fawcett and Hurrel (1995), Lake and Morgan (1997), Ayoob (1999) and Alagappa (2002) have provided regionalised applications of these notions in their efforts to offer a comprehensive picture of regional subsystems. In the case of the MENA regional subsystem, analogous theoretical frameworks have been most notably adopted by Binder (1958), Barnett (1995), Hinnebusch (2003) and Buzan and González-Peláez (2009) in describing and analysing the reality of the whole subsystem.

In order to fully understand the impact of the Arab Spring over the regional order,[2] this chapter firstly applies Christian Reus-Smit's (1997) constructivist notions of the constitutional structure of international society applied at regional scale. For Reus-Smit, international society comprises a set of international institutions[3] divided hierarchically in three different layers. The first, called the 'constitutional structure', is made up of

> coherent ensembles of intersubjective beliefs, principles, and norms that perform two functions in ordering international societies: they define what constitutes a legitimate actor, entitled to all the rights and privileges of statehood; and they define the basic parameters of rightful state action. (Reus-Smit 1997: 566)

The 'constitutional structure' groups three different constitutive metavalues: a collective acceptance about the moral purpose of the centralised political organisations forming the system, an arranging principle of sovereignty and norms of procedural justice among the units (Reus-Smit 1997: 556).

The Arab Spring, despite representing a historical breakthrough, did not provoke a substantive change in the regional 'constitutional structure'. The first constitutive value is the 'moral purpose of the state' defined as 'the reasons that historical agents hold for constructing and maintaining autonomous political units' based on 'a conception of the individual or social "good" served by autonomous political organisations' (Reus-Smit 1997: 566). A large amount of scholarship has been produced discussing the modern state-formation period in the MENA and the reasons behind its formation, the historical evolution of this form of political organisation, different forms that exist in the region and the challenges posed by normative alternatives such as pan-Arabism or pan-Islamism (Rogan 2013; Khoury and Kostiner 1991). Societies in the region conceive the state not only as a security provider and the institutionalised cornerstone of a national differentiated identity but also as a key economic actor that aims to provide, or actively foster the conditions for, economic welfare for its population.

None of the political demands expressed by critical actors in the uprisings articulated their demands around the idea of modifying the state as the main form of political organisation or its social purpose. No alternative to it was even part of the discussion; almost all the demands were framed in terms of taking the state as an established fact and only putting forward prescriptions on how its internal political structure should be modified or who should run the institutions. Likewise, none of the changes that have occurred at domestic level since 2011 seems to indicate the *raison d'être* of the state nor its condition as the only legitimate form of organising autonomous political communities were put into question by emerging political actors. The state as it was known, therefore, continues to be the only option available to effectively join contemporary international society.

The second constitutive element is the 'organising principle of sovereignty', a corollary of the 'moral purpose of the state'. Broadly speaking, this second element encompasses established principles through which each constituent unit differentiates itself from another (Ruggie 1983: 274). It is contingent on historical and spatial factors. In contemporary international society, sovereignty is the organising principle that establishes the foundation of how to differentiate 'political units on the basis of particularity and exclusivity, creating a system of territorially demarcated, autonomous centres of political authority' (Reus-Smit 1997: 567). Similarly to that said about the former, sovereignty continues to be unchallenged as an organising principle of political units. Following the terminology introduced by Krasner (1999), the result of the historical process where regional actors accepted – or were forced to accept – the concept of Westphalian sovereignty appears unchallenged to date. Not only is the state the hegemonic form of political organisation and its 'moral purposes' remain but also political units are differentiated from each other through territoriality: claiming exclusive decision (sovereign) rights over non-overlapping pieces of land ultimately enforced by their exclusive monopoly of legitimate use of force within that estate.

No change to this constitutional element has taken place due to the events since late 2010. It is true that some emerging actors are proposing *de facto* territorial modifications or the creation of sovereign-like entities within previously existing states. This is the case of quasi-autonomous city-states such as Misrata in Libya, the strengthening of Kurdish political projects in Syria and Iraq, and the revival of secessionism in southern Yemen. However, these endeavours do not challenge the primacy of the principle of sovereignty and the form of statehood. Some of these movements ultimately seek to constitute new states. Others aim to be part of a more decentralised political structure within already existing sovereign states. And actors that do propose alternatives to the principle of sovereignty lack the capacity to jeopardise the principle itself and its application, while the remaining actors in the system adhere to it and take it as legitimate.

The last constitutive element is the set of 'norms of pure procedural justice'. Reus-Smit (1997: 567) defines them as the collection of 'correct procedures that "legitimate" or "good" states employ collectively to formulate basic rules of interstate conduct'. Independently of the fairness of the outcomes, this notion appeals to ideas of procedural justice and how the units of the system decide to order their social relations. It is difficult to assess the continuity of this constitutional element as, unless a profound systemic change occurs (for instance, after total systemic war), changes generally take place over long periods of time. Two possible events might trigger substantial changes on the 'norms of procedural justice': the incorporation of a new actor to the system with the capacity to challenge these procedural relational norms or, related to situations described by Krasner (1983) and regime theory, the evolution of those procedural norms after a period of active or passive erosion of them by actors within the system (mismanaging their application, distorting its purpose and finding alternative channels to carry out their purposes).

In the case of the MENA region, as discussed below, the Arab Spring has not produced the emergence of any hegemonic actor with the capability of challenging former norms of procedural justice, nor has it represented a turning point in a long-lasting erosion process dating back to before 2011. Even actors who formerly question this and other fundamental institutions of the regional order, revolutionary Iran being the best example, do so within the order itself (these are actors who challenge how the system works but do so within the system; they do not renounce their part in it, nor fully abandon the advantages and responsibilities associated with the prevailing order).

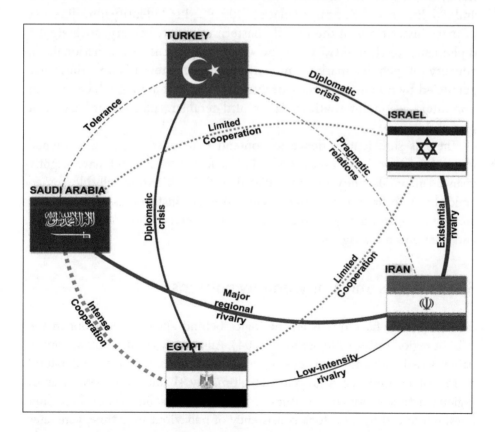

Figure 11.1 Relations of the Middle East regional powers (2015)

3 The Arab Spring and the fundamental institutions of the MENA's regional order

Besides the 'constitutional structure', Reus-Smit states that the constitutive hierarchy of modern international institutions is made up of two other layers that lie on top of the 'constitutional structure'. The mezzo level incorporates the 'fundamental institutions', meaning 'those elementary rules of practice that states formulate to solve the coordination and collaboration problems associated with coexistence under anarchy' (Reus-Smit 1997: 557). This concept could be equated to that of 'primary institutions' provided by the English School. These are 'deep and relatively durable social practices (...) shared among the members of international society but also seen among them as legitimate behaviour' (Buzan 2014: 16–17). Elaborating on this concept, Bull (1995) argued that five primary institutions function at the level of contemporary international society: balance of power, international law, diplomatic mechanisms, managerial system of the great power and war. Buzan and González-Peláez (2009: 92–116) identify nine different primary institutions of the Middle Eastern interstate society: sovereignty, diplomacy, territoriality, great power management, war, nationalism, equality of people, market and environmental stewardship. These are paralleled by nineteen primary derivate institutions among which we find non-intervention, international law, multilateralism, alliances or balance of power.

There is sufficient evidence to contend that most of the fundamental institutions have been untouched while a few others might have slightly changed in long-lasting processes initiated in 2003, which only fully blossomed amid the Arab Spring. The fundamental/primary institutions analysed here are: alliances and amity/enmity patterns, non-intervention, multilateralism and great power management.

3.1 Alliances and amity/enmity patterns

Several authors have discussed the logics behind alliance behaviour in the MENA region (Walt 1990; Lebovic 2004). Alliances, as well as amity/enmity patterns that on many occasions represent their basis, might be understood as formal or informal arrangements ultimately shaping the behaviour of regional actors at primary institutions level. The consolidation of these fault lines, reinforced by an actor's consistency of behaviour over time, generates expectations on how international actors are going to respond to specific events. Such expectations ultimately order relations among actors as they reduce uncertainty and contribute towards manufacturing a communicative framework that establishes the limits of commonly accepted behaviour where unexpected outcomes are less common.

Traditionally, one of the great driving forces behind alliance logics in the Middle East – besides strict regime survival – has been the fracture between status quo and revisionist powers. As shown by Hinnebusch (2003: 18), revisionism has been endemic in the MENA subsystem as it has traditionally been 'rooted in irredentist conflicts over identity and borders or in reactions against Western penetration and expressed by suprastate ideologies – Arabism, Zionism, Islam, and so on'. Such a label could be applied to various regional powers throughout contemporary history, most notably Egypt from the July Revolution (1952) to the Camp David Agreements (1978), Syria and Iraq under Ba'athist regimes (from 1963, the former, and between 1968 and 2003, the latter) and the Islamic Republic of Iran (since its inception in 1979). On the other side of the spectrum, status quo powers, better represented by Turkey, Iraq before the 1958 Abdel-Karim Qassim's July revolution, Iran before 1979, Saudi Arabia and the Trucial States, were formed or 'typically ruled by landed, tribal, or commercial elites who consolidated their power with Western aid or have a stake in Western markets and who therefore look westward for protection from revisionist neighbours' (Hinnebusch 2003: 19).

Since 2003 increasing assertive foreign policies on the two shores of the Persian Gulf have nurtured the status quo versus revisionist powers fracture to manifest itself more intensely in the regional subsystem – Iran representing the spearhead of the so-called 'Axis of Resistance' and Saudi Arabia the status quo power par excellence. The United States-led invasion of Iraq in 2003 and the subsequent collapse of the Iraqi state amid a civil war-like environment in 2006–7 represented a significant shift in the regional subsystem in two different ways. Firstly, it represented an inflection point for the American commitment with the Middle East regional security system. At least since the Kuwait War, the regional system lived under a hegemonic peace by relying on the US. Under that rationale, Washington carried the burden of being the external security provider granting survival to the units of the system and ultimately enforcing the status quo. After the 2003 war in Iraq, and partly as a response to the so-called 'Iraq Syndrome' (Mueller 2005) and the 'pivot to Asia' strategy, the US repeatedly expressed its intentions to reduce its commitment to maintaining the security system while requesting that regional powers assume that responsibility. Secondly, the disappearance of Iraq as a regional power allowed for Iran's 'return' to regional politics. Since the 1979 Iranian revolution the Iraqi Ba'athist government acted as a counterbalancing power, and became a cornerstone of those Arab regimes – especially in the Persian Gulf – that saw Tehran and its revolutionary appeal as a threat to their own regime survival. The 2003 war thwarted the former regional power to continue assuming this role in the regional subsystem. This prompted a niche of opportunity for a more assertive and decided Iranian foreign policy in the MENA region, echoed by analogous Saudi foreign policy. This renovation of the status quo/revisionist divide led to scholars referring to this situation as the 'New Arab Cold War' between Riyadh and Tehran (Ryan 2012; Gause III 2014).

The Arab Spring triggered, in a first stage, a new logic of alliances based on varying degrees of animosity towards the rising regional influence of the Muslim Brotherhood. This overlapped rather than substituted previous amity/ enmity patterns related to the confrontation of status quo and revisionist powers. In a second stage, the region witnessed the revival of long-standing regional rivalries, often described in sectarian terms (Sunni versus Shia) but which would be better framed as the new expression of the old status quo versus revisionist cleavage.

A new cleavage of regional confrontation erupted in 2011. Some actors came together around their shared sympathies with the Muslim Brotherhood and/or their willingness to raise their regional influence by profiting from domestic regime changes. Between 2011 and roughly 2013, Turkey, Qatar, Egypt and Hamas formed a new informal alliance whose *raison d'être* was common support for Muslim Brotherhood branches and similar political movements (Ryan 2015: 44). Saudi Arabia and the United Arab Emirates stood facing them, with the occasional support of Jordan. This traditionalist axis perceived the Muslim Brotherhood and its political-religious ideology as a direct threat to the survival of their own autocratic regimes had the Egyptian revolution become an 'inspirational model' (Malmvig 2012: 2), as the newly formed pro-Muslim Brotherhood alliance combined 'financial, military and demographic power with the Islamist ideology, transnational permeability and organisational skills' (Salloukh 2013: 44). Specifically, the former posed a normative challenge to the religious basis of their legitimacy as unquestionable rulers in their countries.

The pro-Muslim Brotherhood bloc clearly suffered a setback in light of Egypt's July 2013 *coup d'état* that brought Mohammed Morsi's government to an end, illegalised the Muslim Brotherhood, criminally prosecuted its members and inaugurated the al-Sisi presidency. These changes were highly welcomed by the anti-Ikhwan bloc. Their strong commitment with the new government was demonstrated through, for instance, King Abdullah II of Jordan visiting Cairo within twenty-four hours of the regime change, or Saudi Arabia and the UAE pumping up to US$25 billion in foreign aid into al-Sisi's regime –to substitute Qatar after it suspended its former equivalent financial commitments (Ryan 2015: 44).

For different reasons, the domestic political shift was received in Ankara and Tehran as a hammer blow and both countries condemned the *coup d'état* (Stein 2015: 70). From Turkey's perspective, it was a major blow to the informal pro-Muslim Brotherhood alliance. Not only had it lost a key pillar but following that event Egypt turned into a radical stronghold against the Muslim Brotherhood not only domestically but region wide. From Iran's perspective, it brought Egypt back into the pro-Saudi camp.

Besides this new temporary cleavage, the Arab Spring offered a perfect space for further manifestations of the old status quo versus revisionist division, represented now by Saudi Arabia and Iran. Saudi Arabia's reactions towards the Arab Spring were motivated by the consecution of three critical goals: 'to insulate the kingdom from the winds of the Arab Spring, protect the survival of monarchical regimes and undermine Iran's power in the region' (Salloukh 2013: 40). This agenda led to highly ambivalent reactions. Dependent on the country affected by the uprising the al-Saud family concomitantly supported revolutionary movements – for instance in Libya against al-Gaddafi or in Syria against the al-Assad regime, as discussed below, aimed at jeopardising revisionist regimes – and reactionary efforts – in Bahrain or Yemen, isolating the Gulf from regime change waves (Ryan 2014: 28; Malmvig 2012: 1). As pointed out by Khoury (2013: 77), these ambivalent reactions were manifestations of Riyadh's dilemma: 'having to fend off the turmoil from their own shores while jumping into the fray where their interests clearly lie in favour of one side or the other and with the overall goal of containing the situation'.

The Arab Spring offered Saudi Arabia the opportunity to put into practice a more assertive foreign policy, broadening its scope beyond the Gulf. This is one of the many examples of what has been named as a competitive multipolarity in the Middle East (Kausch 2014). In Libya, despite not undertaking a leading role like the UAE, Saudi Arabia backed the United Nations Security Council-sanctioned NATO-led 2011 military intervention that called a halt to Muammar al-Gaddafi's long-lasting autocratic regime. In Bahrain, amid social protests that threatened the continuity of the Sunni al-Khalifa monarchy, Saudi Arabia, together with the UAE, sent the Gulf Cooperation Council's (GCC) Peninsula Shield Force on 15 May 2011. This was justified by depicting the uprisings as the result of undercover actions by Iran-backed Shia elements (Salloukh 2013: 41) and, consequently, was a clear Saudi warning to any foreign intervention in its direct vicinity (Rózsa 2013: 26). In Syria the al-Saud monarchy has systematically supported the opposition to the regime, mainly through financing and equipping different groups within the Free Syrian Army (Gause III 2015: 16). For Riyadh, the collapse of the al-Assad regime in Damascus was understood to be a crucial step in thwarting Iranian power projection in the Levant and a necessary step to cut 'the umbilical land cord' between Tehran and Hezbollah and Hamas (Salloukh 2013: 38). In the case of Yemen, one of the central theatres of the popular uprisings since almost the beginning, Saudi actions initially aimed at smothering and controlling a pacific transition of power from Ali Abdullah Saleh to Abd Rabbuh Mansour Hadi. Once the Houthi tribal group's –conceptualised by Riyadh as a mere pawn of Iran – rebellion broke out and with the accession to the throne of King Salman bin Abdulaziz in January 2015, the Saudis decided to lead a military operation in the summer of that year (Decisive Storm) aimed at eradicating the possibility of the establishment and consolidation of any Houthi-led government in Yemen (Khoury 2013: 77; Salloukh 2013: 40–1).

The Islamic Republic of Iran's reaction to the uprisings was no less ambivalent than that of Saudi Arabia. Its assertive foreign policy could be understood in Syria, Yemen and Egypt. In Syria its support to the al-Assad regime reached the point of deploying elements of the Revolutionary Guard (Pasdaran) on the southern border of the country to, at least, offer its military expertise to regime forces and Hezbollah. Similarly, in Yemen, Tehran provided support to the Houthis who confronted Hadi's government. In Egypt, as suggested by Fürtig (2014: 30), Tehran 'launched a charm offensive and tried to create the perception of an "equal footing" between the two Islamic centres'. It aimed at persuading the newly formed Morsi government to join its efforts in confronting what they understood to be common threats from status quo and extra-regional powers (mainly Saudi Arabia and the US, respectively).

However, as can be seen, the present cleavage is far more related to status quo/revisionist logic than sectarian confrontations for identity survival. The examples above demonstrate that the issue again is opposing conceptions about how the regional order should be and the role of external extra-regional powers in it. Additionally, part of the story might be better explained by power confrontations between two different poles – amid a multipolar situation. The two poles had no problem in engaging with actors on the other side of the sectarian spectrum if this might gain some kind of advantage in front of the other competing pole. Good examples of this might be Saudi collaboration with Shiite political groups opposing raising Iranian influence in Iraq, Iranian support of the Sunni group Hamas or Tehran's quick rapprochement to Egypt after the 2011 revolution (understanding that the largest Sunni political organisation in the world, the Muslim Brotherhood, might be a good revisionist ally in facing status-quo powers). As suggested by Malmvig (2015), we might be witnessing a se-curitisation process of sectarian affiliations; yet the instances when this securitisation process takes places might be arbitrary – not encompassing all the potential cases in the region – depending on the logic of the status quo versus revisionist cleavage.

3.2 Non-intervention

The primary institution of non-intervention refers to the international law con-suetudinary principle forbidding states to intervene, directly or indirectly, in the domestic affairs of other states. This is recognised as a primary institution of the global order and, as such, operates in the MENA subsystem (Buzan and González-Peláez 2009: 93–6). However, respect of the norm by regional actors has repeatedly been put to the test because, as pointed out by Halliday (2009: 15), it seems the MENA countries have a greater predisposition to intervene – to a greater degree than in any other region of the globe – in each other's internal affairs. Notwithstanding this, the non-intervention principle is fundamental in ordering state relations in the MENA region as it still constrains actors' behaviour by imposing limits on their foreign actions, and forcing them to justify any deviation in its observance or pay a 'legitimacy price' in front of other actors in the system.

Since 2003, in the context of the end of the American hegemonic peace and the inauguration of more assertive foreign policies by regional actors, the continuity of this institution has been further brought into question. The Arab Spring – with wars in Libya, Syria, Yemen, Bahrain and the participation of regional and extra-regional powers in all of them – seemed to paint an even more conflictive picture. This chapter argues that the fundamental institution has not changed since the Arab Spring, as some of the above-mentioned events might not be considered a violation of the principle and, even in situations which might have deviated from the norm, interventions have been considered unacceptable behaviour against the system.

The foreign military intervention in the 2011 Libyan civil war, involving NATO countries as well as Jordan, Qatar and the UAE, can hardly be considered a violation of the non-intervention principle according to international law: the UN Security Council Resolution S/RES/1973 authorised the use of force in Libya and consequently there is no room for such consideration. In the case of Bahrain a formal invitation by the al-Khalifa ruling family was the trigger of the Peninsula Shield Force intervention in May 2011. Therefore, again from an international law perspective, this case cannot be considered a violation of the non-intervention principle as there is a request from the legitimate government of the country to other nations, which, accordingly, are permitted to intervene militarily in Bahrain. Foreign intervention in the 2015 war in Yemen also followed some vague petitions in that respect by President Abd Rabbuh Mansour Hadi to prevent the Houthis from taking over the country. However, most importantly, Saudi Arabia, Qatar, the UAE, Morocco and the remaining Arab countries involved, justified their intervention by appealing to informal collective security mechanisms. That is, while it might be considered a violation of international law – there is no UN Security Council resolution authorising the use of force under Chapter VII – the actors have been forced to justify their intervention by putting forward an argument about collective security. The fact that countries deviating from the non-intervention norm understand they have to provide justification for this misconduct is clear evidence that the principle is still in place and accepted as a part of correct international behaviour. The opposite case might be Syria where both regional and international powers have repeatedly intervened in the country and supported different factions in the conflict with little respect for this principle.

Therefore, the non-intervention principle acts as a solid red line for regional actors' foreign policy even if some practices might indicate otherwise. There is room to argue that the Arab Spring might have created perfect incentive structures for regional actors to be more adventurous in their foreign relations with other countries as their conceptualisation of upheavals and uprisings triggers a common concern related with potential spillover effect, thus interpreting external events as an internal threat (Khoury 2013: 74). However, the cases analysed might in fact confirm that the institution of non-intervention is still in place as all actors remain in agreement about its purpose – linked with sovereignty – and its violation is understood to be an illegitimate course of action, condemned by all, and forcing wrongdoers to provide justification or pay a legitimacy price.

3.3 Multilateralism

Multilateralism is also recognised as a fundamental institution of the regional order (Buzan and González-Peláez 2009). The Arab Spring was temporally seen as a catalyst for regional multilateral and bilateral institutionalised cooperation, including in the critical field of security. Helle Malmvig (2013: 30) indicated that

> in 2011 and early 2012 there was still widespread belief in the potential for more regional integration and cooperative security mechanisms, especially with regard to the role that the Arab League and sub-regional forums such as the Union of the Maghreb or GCC could play.

Somehow, these expectations faded away with the same rapidity as hopes for a region-wide push for democratisation evaporated.[4]

There were two drivers for regional cooperation during this 'regionalist parenthesis' or 'regionalist illusion' that started in 2011 and ended two years later: political change, and regional conflicts and transnational security threats (Fawcett 2013: 201). The impact of the former was tangible in North Africa and less so in the Middle East. In fact, political openings coincided with (failed) attempts to resuscitate the Arab Maghreb Union (AMU) and also with calls to improve bilateral relations (Hernando de Larramendi and Fernández-Molina: 2015). For instance, in July 2011 the king of Morocco, on the anniversary of his coronation, called for an improvement in relations with Algeria and advocated reopening a border between the two countries. The decision by the newly appointed minister of foreign affairs of Morocco, Saad-Eddine El Othmani, to visit Algiers in January 2012 on his first official visit abroad was along the same lines. Despite some positive diplomatic responses from Algiers, such reconciliation did not take place. On the contrary, Algerian–Moroccan relations deteriorated, including several incidents on the border in 2014. Similarly, it is also worth noting that in 2012 the recently appointed president of Tunisia, Moncef Marzouki, tried to resuscitate the AMU, increasingly referred to as the Maghreb Union as a gesture towards the Amazigh population. Marzouki toured the region and announced his willingness to host a Maghreb summit in Tunisia in 2012. As time went by, however, it became clear that Marzouki's plans were not met with the same enthusiasm in other capitals of the region.

Regional conflicts and transnational security threats have also fostered further cooperation in the Maghreb region, not through multilateral but rather bilateral mechanisms. A good example of this dynamic might be, for instance, Algeria and Tunisia cooperation on border control and counter-terrorism in light of threats emanating from a close-to-collapsed Libya.

This second element, cross-border insecurity, also played an important role in understanding other multilateral institutions' responses to the events unfolding since 2011, namely the role of the League of Arab States (LAS), for instance, in the Libyan and Syrian conflict. The leaders of the LAS decided to play a more active role in regional affairs. In Libya, for example, they called the UN Security Council to establish a no-fly zone which, somehow, provided regional legitimation to the approval of the 1973 Resolution which not only authorised the international community to establish a no-fly zone but also to use all means necessary (except foreign occupation) to protect civilians. With regards to Syria, early attempts to mediate with the Bashar al-Assad regime were unsuccessful and the LAS decided, first, to suspend Syria's membership and then impose economic sanctions on an Arab country for the first time in its history. Later on, in December 2011, an Observer Mission was deployed in Syria and, in light of its reports, the LAS urged the International Criminal Court to hold those responsible for crimes in Syria accountable.

As Korany (2013: 93) pointed out, this involvement proved that 'even the LAS – that fossilised regional organisation – cannot escape the winds of change' and that the new interventionism of the LAS 'reflects a change in both its initial conception and its general behaviour'. He also acknowledged that 'the LAS has mirrored, rather than triggered, the regional power structure' (Korany, 2013: 94). Similarly, the changing regional dynamics since 2013 (the ousting of Mohammed Morsi, the irruption of the organisation Islamic State, the escalation of tension between Iran and Saudi Arabia), have also resulted in formalised regional initiatives to address security threats. While the fight against this terrorist organisation pushed some Arab countries into joining forces, intra-regional rivalries have undermined, as has happened many times before, the capacity of the LAS to play a greater role, both as a force for regional integration and also as a mediating or conflict-resolution actor.

Concurrently, non-institutionalised multilateral mechanisms of cooperation prevailed in Yemen. Before 2015 states in the region, most notably some Gulf countries and the GCC, channelled cooperation mechanisms to address the increasingly challenging situation in Yemen through multilateral institutions. Up to that point, in November 2011, the Council had successfully brokered a power transfer deal with former President Saleh that inaugurated Hadi's transitional presidency and smothered social unrest in the country. Additionally, and following some of the requisites stated in the November 2011 deal, the GCC was responsible for launching the 2013–14 National Dialogue Conference aimed at social and political reconciliation. It is only since 2015, after the failure of reconciliation attempts and the Houthi offensive reaching Sana'a in September 2014, that countries willing to get involved in responding to the situation on the ground opted for non-institutionalised channels of multilateral cooperation. Saudi-led missions Decisive Storm and Restoring Peace, with the involvement of Morocco, Egypt, Jordan, Kuwait, Qatar, Bahrain, Sudan and the UAE, were designed as ad hoc military missions that did not fall under the umbrella of either the GCC or the LAS. It is true that the Yemeni intervention triggered some intensive conversations in May 2015 in Sharm el-Sheikh about the creation of a Joint Arab Force in the framework of the LAS; however, these ended unsuccessfully for various reasons (Gaub 2015).

3.4 Great power management

Great power management appeals to 'the special responsibilities that the great powers have, given their resources and interests, to manage the system' (Buzan and

González-Peláez 2009: 100). This fundamental/primary institution recognises the privileged position that some actors have in the system and the prevailing order – its configuration and evolution, its survival and its potential change. It proposes that, despite the principle of sovereign equality, great powers generally assume further responsibilities (also entangled with their greater privileges) and their voices have a greater impact on how international life is conducted in the system.

In the case of the MENA region, great power management has two dimensions: one internal, that looks at the special responsibilities regional powers have vis-à-vis the regional system and its order; and one external, that investigates the privileged positions of global superpowers in managing the regional system.

3.4.1 Intraregional great power management: the cases of Egypt and Qatar

Exploring the impact of the Arab Spring over the intraregional dimension of great power management compels us to look at the structure of power in the region, and specifically at how the power is distributed among the actors in the Middle East and North Africa. The structure of this system has traditionally been defined as a multipolar situation with five medium or regional powers taking the reins of its management: Egypt, Saudi Arabia, Iran, Turkey and Israel.

If we accept the idea that great powers have special status in managing the reality of the subsystem, in order to discover any potential change in this fundamental/primary institution, we must look at the appearance or disappearance of regional powers and the attitude of all poles towards this privileged position. In this context, this section examines two main questions: whether the domestic political changes in Egypt represented a shift in its more introspective approach; and to what extent Qatar was able to seize the Arab Spring to upgrade its status to regional power.

The 2001 and 2013 domestic regime changes in Egypt sparked two different levels of interrogations. The first, linked with foreign policy analysis, demanded whether and to what extent new domestic post-revolutionary elites would reconceptualise the country's national interest (Legrenzi 2015: 27). The second, related with systemic approaches, questioned the possibilities of Egypt becoming a pole of regional power (Malmvig 2012: 2) after its relatively voluntary retreat from great power management responsibilities since 1979.

The victory of the Muslim Brotherhood in the electoral process following the 2011 revolution 'provided [Egypt] a regional, if not international, cross-border dimension and leadership' (Rózsa 2013: 24). Mohammed Morsi's new government pursued a renewed independent regional voice, which sought a fine balance between promoting its own representative-based model of political Islam in the face of Arab autocratic regimes and maintaining some distance with revisionist powers like Iran. The quest for stability might be better observed in specific foreign actions undertaken by Cairo during that period. In his first trips abroad President Morsi visited Saudi Arabia, the People's Republic of China and the Islamic Republic of Iran. In Riyadh he reassured the kingdom's authorities that his government did not seek regime change region-wide. In Tehran the president took the opportunity to distance Egypt from revisionist powers by not paying the supreme leader Khamenei a visit – even if he was invited to – and by making anti-al-Assad regime remarks in front of the Iranian leadership (Rózsa 2013: 25).[5] The new government also manifested its willingness to approach Turkey as Morsi participated in the national congress of the ruling Erdoğan's Justice and Development Party (AKP) and labelled Turkey 'a source of inspiration for the whole Middle East' (Khoury 2013: 79).[6] Finally, it also comforted Tel Aviv, fearful of the emergence of a revisionist power in its southern border, by managing and overseeing the November 2012 truce between Hamas and Israel.

Nevertheless, as suggested before, Egypt's new foreign policy generated mistrust and suspicion among some states in the region, mainly Saudi Arabia and the UAE. But this situation did not last long. The counter-revolutionary upheaval in 2013 brought to power a new political-military elite which recuperated pre-2011 foreign policy priorities: the government of al-Sisi integrated into the status quo axis, by approaching Saudi Arabia and turning its back on Iran and Qatar. Ultimately, Cairo's quest for an independent voice was substituted by a traditional 'Egypt first approach', renouncing major involvement in regional power management structures besides those issues that were strictly connected with its neighbours (that is, in effect, caring only about Libya's future and the Sinai Peninsula situation). The only exception to that quasi-introspective policy was its regional campaign against the Muslim Brotherhood, conceptualised as an internal threat to al-Sisi's regime survival.

The case of Qatar is completely different as it has never been part of the regional great power management structures. Since the late 1990s Sheikh Hamad bin Khalifa al-Thani, the then king of Qatar, started implementing policies that showed his willingness to twist some of his father's fundamental ideas about his country's role in the world. Sheikh Hamad considered that Qatar 'needed to fundamentally change its position to become a leading, moderate, internationally focused, socially developing, knowledge-led country' (Roberts 2012: 235). This general idea was translated into a quest-for-status oriented foreign policy, which, in the absence of hard power capabilities, was articulated around public diplomacy and soft power projection. On the one hand, Qatar designed and implemented self-branding worldwide campaigns around non-sensitive highly popular issues like sports (1995 FIFA Under-20 World Cup,

2015 Men's Handball World Championship, 2022 Football World Cup) and culture (the Islamic Museum of Art, the Tribeka Film Festival) (Roberts 2012: 236). On the other, and not a minor issue, the sheikhdom launched the television channel Al Jazeera in 1996, which has given Doha a tool to transmit its messages – crucially on regional political issues – to the households of all the countries throughout the MENA region.

Another critical pillar of its status-seeking foreign policy was related to projecting the image of Qatar as an impartial mediator and peace broker. Following article 7 of the 2003 constitution's mandate encouraging international mediation initiatives (Ulrichsen 2013: 1), the sheikhdom has carried out significant mediation enterprises based on an increasingly regional perception of neutrality. Among the many examples, those worth mentioning might include: Yemen in 2008 and 2010 – where Qatar was able to broker various ceasefires between the Houthi rebels in the north and the central Yemeni government, Lebanon in 2008 – with the 21 May Doha Accord reducing tensions between Fouad Siniora's government and Hezbollah, and Darfur reaching the 2010 ceasefire between the government and the Justice and Equality Movement (Ulrichsen 2013: 2; Akpinar 2015).

The Arab Spring offered Qatar an opportunity to further advance this particular agenda while introducing some adjustments to it. Indirectly, Qatar had a role in the spread of the revolutionary message through the active coverage of Al Jazeera channel network of the events in the region. In parallel, Doha actively participated in regime changes by stabilising with financial aid Mohammed Morsi's government (Salloukh 2013: 42). In the case of the Syrian conflict, it provided funds and logistic support to the opposition forces fighting the al-Assad regime, most notably to the different branches and armed forces linked with the Muslim Brotherhood, after orchestrating Syria's suspension of membership in the LAS (Salloukh 2013: 42). In Libya, Qatar contributed with fighters and logistic support to the implementation of the NATO-sponsored no-fly zone (Khoury 2013: 76) and funded the anti-Gaddafi rebel faction that today constitutes the Islamist government in Tripoli (Roberts 2012: 237). All this contributed to the emergence of a general perception of Qatar as a new centre of regional influence in the region 'playing a regional role far beyond its means' (Ryan 2014: 28).

However, Qatar's regional outreach triggered tensions with Riyadh that ultimately undermined Doha's advantageous position in the regional subsystem. Inserted into the logic of the 'for versus against' Muslim Brotherhood described above, Saudis and Emiratis viewed with concern any Qatari support to Muslim Brotherhood-type actors mainly in Syria, but also in Egypt, Libya or Palestine (Salloukh 2013: 44). As pro-Muslim Brotherhood support dissipated – especially following the al-Sisi coup – and the new Saudi leadership under

King Salman and Deputy Crown Prince Mohammad prompted more assertive interventionist policies in the regional system, the differentiated voice of Doha faded progressively under Riyadh's traditional hegemonic rhapsody. The abdication of King Hamad in favour of his son, Tamim, also led to a downscaling of Qatar's foreign policy ambitions. Therefore, it might be argued that Qatar attempted to be part of the great power managerial framework but was forced to recalibrate its ambitions by a more assertive Saudi Arabia.

From a theoretical standpoint, the cases of Egypt and Qatar remain interesting as they pose a stimulating question still to be solved: the impact on the system of a great power who voluntarily moves away from great power management frameworks to self-imposed silence (the difference between having the means to exercise power and using them); the contingent nature of national interest shifts in domestic regimes might automatically trigger a change in national priorities and whether a country with almost no hard power capabilities can become part of the great power management institutions using only its soft power and, consequently the impact of soft power-hubs over the structure of a system.

3.4.2 Extra-regional great power management: the case of Russia

The MENA regional order has been traditionally characterised by a high level of penetration by external powers (Brown 1984). Besides wide-ranging discussions on the diminishing impact of key extra-regional powers in the region, namely the US and the European Union, or the future involvement of emerging powers like China and India, the effects of the Arab Spring, and particularly the war in Syria, prompted questions on the irreversibility of Russia's return to the MENA region and its effects over the regional order.

Russia is not a newcomer. The Russian Empire fought several wars against the Ottomans and the Persians, and Moscow motivations were threefold: territorial gains and the establishment of some sort of control over transcontinental trade and strategic routes; to project itself as the main protector of Christian Orthodox communities in the Middle East; and to balance the rise of other European powers (the Austrians in the Balkans, the French in the Levant and the British in Asia). In its new form as the leading force of the Soviet Union, Russia developed intensely close relations with Egypt, Algeria, Libya and Syria in various areas including training, military cooperation, infrastructure and industrialisation, among many others. However, the only Arab country to be formally part of a Soviet alliance was southern Yemen. In fact, when looking at the impact of Cold War dynamics in this region, analysts pointed out that its effects ended earlier in the Middle East than in any other region of the world (Halliday 1995: 100) and that the Middle Eastern regional order proved to be quite autonomous as Arab and Middle Eastern states were able to play with global rivalries or, to put it differently, the two superpowers found themselves at the mercy of domestic and regional dynamics (Hinnebusch 2003). The 1990s and to some extent part of the 2000s were depicted as the years of the 'contraction of Russia' (Halliday 1995: 136). However, this period might be over.

The Russian return to the Middle East can be framed in terms of changes in the global order, with the (re)emergence of non-Western global powers that are challenging the post-Cold War unipolar order. In the Middle East the literature has focused on the role of the BRICS (Brazil, Russia, India, China and South Africa) as investors and traders but also incipiently on security issues (Huber et al. 2013). The renewed Russian presence in the region can also be seen as a response to a potential or effective alternation of the regional order in the Middle East. Although all the attention has been put on the war in Syria, it was NATO's intervention in Libya, based on the UN Security Council Resolution 1973, that marked a turning point in Russia's re-evaluation of their role in the MENA region (Zvyagelskaya 2014: 233). Russia decided not to veto that resolution but denounced the fact that it evolved into a regime-change operation and that the penetration of Western interests in Libya was undertaken at the expense of Russia's pre-existing stake. This gave Russia additional rhetorical ammunition to stand with Bashar al-Assad.

Russia's involvement in Syria confirmed it as a key external player. Its support to al-Assad in the form of economic and military supplies and, since September 2015, with an intense airstrike campaign that modified the power balance among the contenders, was fundamental to sustain the regime. This also allowed Russia to reinforce military cooperation with other regional actors such as the Iraqi government and several Kurdish groups. Simultaneously, Russia played the diplomatic game. While Moscow vetoed all the initiatives of the UN Security Council that could have paved the way to enforcing no-fly zones or even a wider military intervention, it also brokered a deal to dismantle the chemical weapons arsenal in September 2013 and a ceasefire in February 2016. Thus, despite renewed Russian–Western rivalry, Moscow and Washington were able to find compromises on Middle Eastern issues. This is true for Syria but also for the multilateral negotiations on the Iranian nuclear deal.

How did the renewed involvement of Russia in the Middle East modify its relations with the regional powers? It translated into open confrontation with Turkey and an indirect rivalry with Saudi Arabia on Syria, but also over oil prices. The effect on Iran is ambivalent. While both are on the same side in the Syrian war, the disagreement over Syria's future could even lead to competition for the leadership of what has often been called 'the axis of resistance', which is non other than the 'anti-Western block'. In contrast, it has brought Russia closer to Egypt, particularly when tensions between Cairo and Washington were at their height. And Israel has also made an effort to revitalise bilateral relations with Russia as a response to a confidence crisis with the West in relation to the end of sanctions on Iran.

Finally, it must be stressed that Russian policies in this region have a lot to do with the country's domestic concerns and its global ambitions. On the first dimension, it is worth remembering that Russia was very reticent to back the early demonstrations on the Arab streets as they created a precedent that could be emulated by Russian activists. A parallel with the colour revolutions in Eastern Europe was often mentioned and, consequently, the uprisings in Arab countries were often interpreted as Western manipulations. Still on the domestic front, Russia was also concerned by prospects of continued instability close to its borders, aggravated by the presence of Russian and Central Asian fighters in the ranks of different jihadist organisations. On the global front Russia seized the various crises in the Middle East to project its own vision of the world order, denouncing interference in the domestic affairs of third countries and demanding that regional players – but even more the West – treat Russia as a global power again.

4 Conclusions

This chapter argued that the Arab Spring did not trigger a change in the type of order itself but a change within the regional order, categorised as a situation where 'the basic principles continue to apply but their manifestation alters' (Alagappa 2002: 64). The constitutional elements of the regional order continue to operate as usual. The upheavals have not modified the state as the uniquely legitimate form of political organisation and its moral purpose, nor sovereignty, as the unquestionable organising principle of the regional system that helps in differentiating each of its units. Norms of procedural justice are not brought into question any more than they have traditionally been; contestants articulate their challenges within the system itself and in no case represent a critical mass to foster changes.

Alternatively, various minor changes have been observed in some fundamental or primary institutions of the regional order. Traditional alliances and amity/enmity cleavages were temporary challenged by the emergence of a new fracture line: supporters and opponents of the Muslim Brotherhood's regional role. However, this new cleavage progressively blurred and made way for the consolidation of traditional status quo versus revisionist power logics, wrongly presented on many occasions as a mere sectarian clash led by Saudi Arabia and Iran. The non-intervention principle continues to be a fundamental institution of the regional order although wars in Libya, Syria, Yemen and the GCC intervention in Bahrain might suggest the opposite. The intervening actors have presented their actions on the ground as legitimate and complying with international law. The use of multilateral cooperation mechanisms might have increased since 2011 (particularly in the framework of the LAS and the GCC) but recent events may signal a return to the prevalence of non-institutionalised multilateral forms of cooperation (Yemen being the best example). Finally, the Arab Spring raised expectations of potential changes in the multipolar system by bringing new actors into the great power management. The emergence of Qatar and the return of Egypt (if it ever left its regional power's status and responsibilities) might have temporarily challenged the pre-2011 great power management institution but, to date, it is only the reappearance of Russia that might represent a long-lasting change in how this fundamental institution works, particularly if the US commitment to regional security further diminishes.

Notes

1. See, for instance, Hall (1996), Cox and Sinclair (1996), Ikenberry (2000), Keene (2002).
2. This chapter opts for the concept of order provided by Alagappa (2002: 39): 'a formal or informal arrangement that sustains rule-governed interaction among sovereign states in their pursuit of individual and collective goals', emphasising 'rule-governed interactions' rather than Bull's goals of the society.
3. Reus-Smit (1997: 557), quoting Keohane (1989: 3), defines institutions as having a 'persistent set of rules (formal and informal) that prescribe behavioural roles, constrain activity, and shape expectations'.
4. The link between democratisation and regional cooperation are also apparent when comparing the parallel debates on the region's exceptionality. For many years the failure to materialise regional cooperation was framed within a broader trend in which this region would be immune to the tendencies affecting other parts of the world (Aarts 1999: 911). Thus, an analysis of cooperation dynamics in the Middle East connects with a broader debate on the lack (or failure) of democratisation processes and the resilience of authoritarianism in Arab and Middle Eastern countries.
5. This was an important setback for Tehran as it saw the Arab Spring in general, and specifically the triumph of the Muslim Brotherhood in Egypt, as 'an opportunity for the Iranian regime to gain external legitimisation for its Islamic republican model' (Stein 2015: 70).
6. The Muslim Brotherhood–AKP solidarity relations are fundamentally underpinned by the pro-active Turkish position amid the 2011 Egyptian revolution – requesting Hosni Mubarak to step down – as well as a common sense of shared history as Islamist movements violently suppressed by domestic regimes categorised as 'Western pawns'.

References

Aarts, Paul (1999), 'The Middle East: a region without regionalism or the end of exceptionalism?', *Third World Quarterly*, 20 (5): 911–25.

Akpinar, Pinar (2015), 'Mediation as a foreign policy tool in the Arab Spring: Turkey, Qatar and Iran', *Journal of Balkan and Near Eastern Studies*, 17 (3): 252–68.

Alagappa, Muthiah (2002), 'The study of international order', in Muthiah Alagappa (ed.), *Asian Security Order: Instrumental and Normative Features*, Stanford: STU, pp. 33–69.

Ayoob, Mohammed (1999), 'From regional system to regional society: exploring key variables in the construction of regional order', *Australian Journal of International Affairs*, 53 (3): 247–60.

Barnett, Michael N. (1995), 'Sovereignty, nationalism, and regional order in the Arab states system', *International Organization*, 49 (3): 479–510.

Binder, Leonard (1958), 'The Middle East as a subordinate international system', *World Politics*, 10 (3): 408–29.

Brown, Carl L. (1984), *International Politics and the Middle East: Old Rules, Dangerous Game*, London: I. B. Tauris.

Bull, Hedley (1995), *The Anarchical Society: a Study of Order in World Politics*, New York: Columbia University Press.

Bush, Sarah (2015), 'Forms of international pressure and the Middle East', *International Relations Theory and a Changing Middle East, POMEPS Studies* 16: 13–15.

Buzan, Barry (2014), *An Introduction to the English School of International Relations*, Cambridge: Polity Press.

Buzan, Barry and Ana González-Peláez (2009), *International Society and the Middle East: English School Theory at the Regional Level*, Basingstoke/New York: Palgrave Macmillan.

Cox, Robert W. and Timothy J. Sinclair (1996), *Approaches to World Order*, Cambridge: Cambridge University Press.

Fawcett, Louise (2013), 'Alliances and regionalism in the Middle East', in Louise Fawcett (ed.), *International relations of the Middle East*, Oxford: Oxford University Press, pp. 185–204.

Fawcett, Louise and Andrew Hurrel (eds) (1995), *Regionalism in World Politics*, Oxford: Oxford University Press.

Fürtig, Henner (2014), 'Iran: winner or loser of the Arab Spring?', in Henner Fürtig (ed.), *Regional Powers in the Middle East: New Constellations after the Arab Revolts*, New York: Palgrave Macmillan.

Gaub, Florence (2015), *Stuck in the barracks: the Joint Arab Force*, Brief Issue, 31, Brussels: EUISS.

Gause III, F. Gregory (2014), *Beyond Sectarianism: The new Middle East Cold War*, Brookings Doha Center Analysis Papers, 11, Doha: Brookings Institution.

Gause III, F. Gregory (2015), 'Ideologies, alliances and underbalancing in the new Middle East Cold War', *International Relations Theory and a Changing Middle East, POMEPS Studies* 16: 16–20.

Hall, John A. (1996), *International Orders*, Cambridge: Polity Press.

Halliday, Fred (1995), *The Middle East in International Relations*, Cambridge: Cambridge University Press.

Halliday, Fred (2009), 'The Middle East and conceptions of "international society"', in Barry Buzan and Ana González-Peláez (eds), *International Society and the Middle East: English School Theory at the Regional Level*, Basingstoke: Palgrave Macmillan, pp. 1–23.

Hernando de Larramendi, Miguel and Irene Fernández-Molina (2015), 'The evolving foreign policies of North African states (2011–2014): new trends in constraints, political processes and behavior', in Yahia H. Zoubir and Gregory White (eds), *North African Politics: Change and Continuity*, London: Routledge, pp. 245–76.

Hinnebusch, Raymond (2003), *The International Politics of the Middle East*, Manchester/New York: Manchester University Press.

Huber, Daniela, Vladimir Bakhtin, Li Guofu, P. R. Kumaraswamy and Arlene Clemesha (2013), *The Mediterranean Region in a Multipolar World. Evolving Relations with Russia, China, India, and Brazil*, Mediterranean Paper Series, Washington, DC: GMF and IAI.

Ikenberry, G. John (2000), *After Victory. Institutions, Strategic Restraint and the Rebuilding of Order after Major Wars*, Princeton: Princeton University Press.

Kausch, Kristina (2014), *Competitive Multipolarity in the Middle East*, IAI Working Papers, 10, Rome: IAI.

Keene, Edward (2002), *Beyond the Anarchical Society: Grotius, Colonialism and Order in World Politics*, Cambridge: Cambridge University Press.

Keohane, Robert O. (1989), *International Institutions and State Power*, Boulder, CO: Westview Press.

Khoury, Nabeel A. (2013), 'The Arab Cold War revisited: the regional impact of the Arab uprising', *Middle East Policy*, 20 (2): 73–87.

Khoury, Philip S. and Joseph Kostiner (eds) (1991), *Tribes and State Formation in the Middle East*, Oakland: University of California Press.

Korany, Bahgat (2013), 'The Middle East since the Cold War' in Louise Fawcett (ed.), *International Relations of the Middle East*, Oxford: Oxford University Press, pp. 77–100.

Krasner, Stephen (ed) (1983), *International Regimes*, Ithaca: Cornell University Press.

Krasner, Stephen (1999), *Sovereignty: Organized Hypocrisy*, Princeton: Princeton University Press.

Lake, David A. and Patrick M. Morgan (eds) (1997), *Regional orders: Building Security in a New World*, University Park: Pennsylvannia State University Press.

Lebovic, James H. (2004), 'Unity in action: explaining alignment behavior in the Middle East', *Journal of Peace Research*, 41 (2): 167–89.

Legrenzi, Matteo (2015), 'New dimensions of security and regionalism in the Middle East', *International Relations Theory and a Changing Middle East*, POMEPS Studies 16: 27–31.

Malmvig, Helle (2012), *The Arab Uprisings and the New Geopolitics of the Middle East*, IEMed Focus Article, 77, Barcelona: IEMed.

Malmvig, Helle (2013), *Ambiguous Endings. Middle East Regional Security in the Wake of the Arab Uprisings and the Syrian Civil War*, DIIS Report, 23, Copenhagen: DIIS.

Malmvig, Helle (2015), 'Coming in from the cold', *International Relations Theory and a Changing Middle East*, POMEPS Studies 16: 32–5.

Mueller, John (2005), 'The Iraq syndrome', *Foreign Affairs*, November/December.

Reus-Smit, Chris (1997), 'The constitutional structure of international society and the nature of fundamental institutions', *International Organization*, 51 (4): 555–89.

Roberts, David B. (2012), 'Understanding Qatar's foreign policy objectives', *Mediterranean Politics*, 17 (2): 233–9.

Rogan, E. (2013), 'The emergence of the Middle East into the modern state system', in Lousie Fawcett (ed.), *International Relations of the Middle East*, Oxford: Oxford University Press, pp. 21–43.

Rózsa, Erzsébet (2013), *Geo-Strategic Consequences of the Arab Spring*, IEMED Papers, Barcelona: IEMed.

Ruggie, John G. (1983), 'Continuity and transformation in the world polity: toward a neorealist synthesis', *World Politics*, 35 (2): 261–85.

Ryan, Curtis R. (2012), 'The new Arab Cold War and the struggle for Syria', *Middle East Report*, 42 (262). Available at <http://merip.org/mer/mer262/new-arab-cold-war-struggle-syria> (last accessed 12 November 2015).

Ryan, Curtis R. (2014), 'Inter-Arab politics and international relations in the Middle East', in *Reflections on the Arab Uprisings, POMEPS Studies* 10: 27–30.

Ryan, Curtis R. (2015), 'Regime security and shifting alliances in the Middle East', in *International Realtions Theory and a Changing Middle East, POMEPS Studies* 16: 42–6.

Salem, Paul (2012), 'The regional order', in Sinan Ülgen, Nathan J. Brown, Marina Ottaway and Paul Salem (eds), *Emerging Order in the Middle East*, Washington, DC: Carnegie Endowment for International Peace, pp. 10–15.

Salem, Paul (2014), *The Middle East in 2015 and Beyond: Trends and Drivers*, Policy Foc. Washington, DC: Middle East Institute.

Salloukh, Bassel F. (2013), 'The Arab uprisings and the geopolitical of the Middle East', *The International Spectator*, 48 (2): 32–46.

Stein, Ewan (2015), 'Beyond "geosectarianism"', *International Relations Theory and a Changing Middle East, POMEPS Studies* 16: 68–70.

Ulrichsen, Kristian C. (2013), *Qatar's Mediation Initiatives*, NOREF Policy Brief, Oslo: NOREF.

Valbjørn, Morten (2015), 'International relations theory and the new Middle East: three levels of a debate', *International Relations Theory and a Changing Middle East, POMEPS Studies* 16: 74–9.

Walt, Stephen M. (1990), *The Origins of Alliances*, Ithaca: Cornell University Press.

Zvyagelskaya, Irina (2014), *Russia and the Arab Spring*, IEMed Mediterranean Yearbook 2014, Barcelona: IEMed.

Chapter 12

The political and security repercussions of Islamic State in the MENA region

Marién Durán and Víctor Bados

1 Introduction

Processes of political transformation can come about either through peaceful or violent change. Several factors can affect the way these processes take place in a particular scenario. In this regard, favourable external factors such as international or regional context can promote non-violent changes in transitions to democracy (Whitehead 2001; Calatrava 2012: 140). Conversely, situations with vacuums of power can mean violence becomes a key component that favours the presence of terrorists or insurgents. These elements are capable of destabilising a region and controlling specific areas in order to overthrow governments to establish new states or other forms of political organisation. They can take advantage of the absence of sustainable states and they usually have a political aim: to end state organisation as a form of government and create a new structure or another nation. In this way violence can generate processes of change which have serious political and security implications.

Since the so-called Arab Spring, the Middle East and North Africa (MENA) region has experienced extremely complicated political changes. A common factor among these countries is that the conditions to promote democracy have been insufficient in the region. Only in one case, that of Tunisia, is it possible to argue that the revolts have led towards a democratic transition. In the other countries, either the changes have been insubstantial, or they have ended in civil wars, such as in Syria and Libya, with serious implications for the growth of the self-proclaimed Islamic State (IS). The Syrian conflict, for example, has turned into the cruellest and bloodiest since World War II for the number of civilian victims, displaced people and refugees. There is also a sense of continuity with previous conflicts due to the significant level of cruelty. Iraq is destabilised and divided and Libya has serious problems in establishing a legitimate government, with some areas declaring loyalty to IS, as we will analyse in more depth below.

The establishment of IS[1] on 29 June 2014 has had a major impact on political progress and security alike. The expansion of IS has transformed the regional dynamics of the MENA region as well as triggering processes of political and territorial change.[2] It has also generated very serious security threats, both in the latter region and beyond, due to a wave of followers and spillover worldwide (Marsili 2016: 86). In this way IS has brought a new dimension to the war in Iraq and Syria as well as to the Libyan conflict in: amplifying and making the conflict more complex, with related implications for security; establishing a new mode of governance in the conquered territories; and producing a new security framework in the MENA region.

These three issues are analysed in this paper. We aim to study in detail the political and security implications of IS. Following a brief contextualisation of the origins and goals of IS, we analyse: (1) the repercussions for security: the IS type of conflict; (2) the government imposed in the occupied territories; and (3) the implications for security throughout the MENA region by focusing on two main domains: the response to the threat by the international community, and the new configuration of regional and global alliances. In the context of a lack of studies, our key contribution is an analysis of IS's conflict typology.

2 Islamic State conflict: origins and objectives

The so-called Islamic State, or Islamic Caliphate of Iraq and the Levant, was proclaimed ninety years after Mustafa Kemal Ataturk abolished it in March 1924. The current caliphate is meant to symbolise the past greatness of other Islamic caliphates.[3] It aims to revive or claim through war, conflict and the destabilisation of fragile states, a glory or a lost 'Golden Age' in order to establish itself as a global actor (Nuruzzaman 2015). Over a year and a half following its inception in Iraq, immediately after the 2003 United States invasion, IS expanded into Syria in 2013. Since then it has rapidly advanced to conquer vast territories of both countries, which include a population of roughly eight million people in total, thanks to a growing army of 30,000 troops. In the occupied territories IS has been perceived by many as a legitimate actor. It applies shariah law and exercises totalitarian governance. It acts, *de facto*, as a state without international recognition and endangers the existence of other states in the MENA region (Jordán 2015: 111).

How did IS achieve this rapid advance in such a short period of time? The answer is not simple, but if we look back in history we find some revealing information. For example, Halil Inalcik's study on the origins of the traditional Islamic State details the substantial Ottoman advance from the thirteenth century. The Ottomans aspired to the rich and fertile land of the Byzantines. A war for resources broke out and it drove the Ottomans to make dazzling advances through the Anatolian peninsula. The rapid victory of the Islamic Ottoman State was due to them offering more resources to the Byzantine population than that provided by their own lords pursuing a conciliatory policy towards Christians and, also, taking advantage of the lack of unity between the Latin and Orthodox Churches. In search for more territory the Gaza, 'Holy War', was launched in order to legitimise the war against Byzantium (Inalcik 1973: 6–15).

IS also had and still has a very clear territorial objective in which it rejects the colonial political map of the Middle East following World War I. In this context it seeks to unite the territories divided by the Treaty of Sykes–Picot (1916) so as to build a new state by taking advantage of the fragile states of the MENA region and impose a rigid interpretation of the shariah.

However, that goal cannot be achieved without effective tools. IS possesses a powerful instrument: the execution of a war that spares no material or human resources. It is a method of warfare with both classic and new elements. It has historical and chronological continuity with the past (that is the restoration of the caliphate), which includes mythical speeches to attract followers, and a mix of obsolete military means that coexist with the latest technologies. We will now analyse this effective and powerful tool to dissect and scrutinise IS's signs of identity.

3 Repercussions for security: IS war as a typology of conflict

The participation of IS in the MENA region conflict has reversed the decreasing trend of international conflicts in both frequency and intensity, a tendency which had developed since the fall of the Iron Curtain. IS's internal actions across the countries in which it operates, as well as the extreme external and global impact of their actions, has drawn the attention of governments and media in a similar way. Study groups such as the Uppsala Conflict Data Programme (UCDP) at the University of Uppsala, currently identifies the Middle East as the most violent region in the world due to the fighting in Syria and Iraq (Melander 2015: 7). War, armed conflict, crisis, terrorism, barbarism, extreme violence, genocide, extortion, slavery and sexual violence, black market, refugees and displaced persons crisis, mercenaries and international intervention, are some of the repeatedly heard and read words associated with the IS phenomenon. Most are familiar terms in the media due to the ruthless wars of the 1990s in the Balkans, African Great Lakes and Caucasus.

It is worth raising the question about whether we can categorise these variables and features in the same way Mary Kaldor did with her concept of the 'new wars' from the case studies of Bosnia and Caucasus, and especially based on the paradigmatic model of Bosnia (Mello 2010: 6). Or should we categorise the IS conflict as a 'proxy war',[4] 'hybrid war',[5] 'spectator-sport war'[6] or 'fourth-generation conflict',[7] as suggested by other authors?

The typologies that proliferated in the 1990s to describe conflicts of various kinds, although in essence very similar, can provide some clarification on this matter. What, then, are the similarities and differences between the current conflict and those of the early 1990s or even with respect to the preceding wars? And more significantly, against what typology should we compare the IS conflict among the wide variety of denominations we have noted? We have opted to primarily focus on the concept of 'new wars' to carry out our analysis. The reasons are overwhelming: because it is considered to be the most unifying,[8] prominent and detailed concept with the greatest impact, as well as being the most commonly cited term by scholars when analysing contemporary conflicts (Malantowicz 2013: 52). Despite the detractors,[9] and even though some authors who write on this issue, such as Herfried Münkler, have clearly stated that the concept of 'new wars' is not so new but 'the return to something very old', it is quite clear that the conflicts that arose in the 1990s had some unique features (Münkler 2005: 2).

After reviewing the works of Kaldor, and those of the 'new wars-positioned' authors such as Münkler, Snow, Van Creveld, Bellamy, Hoslti, Duffield, Eppler, Mandel, Singer and Luttwak, we have established and brought together a series of categories on the new wars: actors, causes, methods and strategies, forms of financing, complex emergencies, geographical framework, and legal legitimate framework, in order to come up with a comprehensive definition of 'new wars':

> Those conflicts taking place in a geographical territory which is restricted to the conflict within the state, but with transnational implications; the causes of these conflicts are often identity (religious, ethnic) and contention for resources. The objectives are consistent with the causes since they are related to a particularistic identity. The multiplicity and fragmentation of the internal actors involved in the conflict (regular armed forces, criminal groups, self-defence units …) result in complex emergencies requiring humanitarian and military response. This in turn leads to an internationalisation of the conflict due to globalisation, and generates as a result of the latter, some forms of financing that may be described as 'the new economy of war' (looting, extortion, foreign aid, black market). The assets, methods, tactics and strategies of fighting are characterised by violence against civilians, by asymmetry in the conflict, as being hybrid in the way warfare develops, as having a different level of tolerance to casualties and finally, what we describe as the legitimate-legal framework of these conflicts. There is also an erosion of the monopoly of violence and a complete rejection of international law leading to practices and methods of senseless violence that may be categorised as barbarism. (Bados and Durán 2015: 33)

We will empirically analyse this conceptual framework to decide whether we are witnessing another 'new war' conflict or if there are substantial differences as far as this analytical framework is concerned. Table 12.1 shows the variables

Table 12.1 Categories, variables and indicators of 'new wars-type conflicts'

Categories	Variables	Indicators	Result
Actors	Multiplicity and fragmentation of the internal actors	Regular armed forces	Yes
		Paramilitary groups	Yes
		Self-defence units	Yes
		Insurgent groups, rebels	Yes
		Terrorist groups	Yes
		Warlords	Yes
Causes	Religious, tribal or linguistic identities	Clan/tribe	Yes
		Language	Yes
		Religion	Yes
		Otherness	Yes
	Fighting for resources/greed	Chance of economic benefit	Yes
Methods and strategies	Violence against civilians	Civilian casualties	Yes
		Military casualties	Yes
		Forced displaced people	Yes
	Asymmetry	Difference in weapons and means	Yes
		Difference in training standards	Yes
		Difference in economic resources and logistics	Yes
		Difference in recruiting capability	Yes
	Hybridity	Coexistence of high-tech weapons with obsolete conventional arms	Yes
		Concurrence of conventional combat with insurgent tactics	Yes
		Blurred line between combatants and non-combatants	Yes
	Different tolerance to casualties	Degree of tolerance to casualties	Yes
	Terrorism		Yes
Ways of finance	New economy of war	Looting, pillage, robbery	Yes
		Extortion	Yes
		Corruption	Yes
		External support	Yes
		Black market	Yes
Complex emergencies	Humanitarian response	NGOs, volunteer expatriates	No
		Agencies of United Nations in warfighting zone	No
	International military response	Foreign regular forces and International actors	Yes
		Foreign mercenaries	Yes
		Foreign irregular forces' intervention outside of international law	Yes
Geographic framework	Conflicts based and not based on the state	Conflict not based on the state	Yes
		Within a state / civil and internationalised conflict	Yes
Legal–legitimate framework	Erosion of the monopoly of violence	Rebel groups controls the territory	Yes
		Warlords	Yes
		Other private actors	Yes
	Barbarity	Torture and execution of prisoners of war	Yes
		Sexual violence	Yes
		Genocide/ethnical cleansing	Yes
		Mass murders	Yes

Source: Bados and Durán (2015)

associated with indicators related to the signs of identity of these types of conflicts. This sort of operationalisation allows us to reach the granularity of the conflict to be able to identify substantial differences that might reveal some kind of 'newness'.

After having illustrated synthesised 'new war' features in Table 12.1, we will now analyse if the IS conflict across the MENA region fits the definition of 'new wars', has elements of other typologies, or might even display new signs of identity.

Firstly, regarding the category of actors, we have highlighted the variable 'multiplicity and fragmentation of the internal actors'. The IS conflict is distinguished not only for its complexity, due to the large number of combatants, but also for its internal divisions. Key indicators witnessed on the IS battlefield include: the involvement of regular armed forces from different countries (Russia, US-led coalition of sixty countries, the Bashar al-Assad army, the ineffective Iraqi army (Jordan 2015: 127), self-defence units (Kurdish and Christian-Assyrian forces trained by coalition and other external actors), insurgent groups (the so-called Syrian opposition and IS army) and the creation of militias and non-state actors by proxy states such as Iran. We will now focus on IS, which although considered to be an insurgent group, aspires to political power as a priority (Pollard et al. 2015: 4), in order to hold on to its regular and professionalised forces. Despite being an amalgam of various factions from the Iraq war, the current leader Abu Bakr al-Baghdadi has succeeded in consolidating an army by acquiring new capabilities, expanding and professionalising it over the last seven years, beginning from when the conflict broke out in Syria. Today IS is the largest and richest jihadist organisation with clear objectives, a cohesive leadership structure, discipline, and experienced cadres from the former Iraqi army (Jordan 2015: 123). They also have an established and continuous recruitment system, good logistics, competitive wages, social assistance for soldiers' families, strong military and ideological training, and high morale (Pollard et al. 2015: 9).

Secondly, regarding the causes of conflict, we have identified two variables that also meet the 'new wars' typology: religious identities and the fight for resources. The political and religious context is a strong motivation for this form of political violence (Kaplan and Costa 2015: 932). The proclamation of the caliphate provides a frame of reference and membership for Sunni Muslims. However, that proclamation, in terms of statehood and religion, conflicts with alternative interpretations of Islam and previously existing entities, other Muslim states and (Marsili 2016: 86), particularly with nations such as Saudi Arabia, who are considered to be the guardians of Islamic holy places (Philips 2014: 497). The struggle for resources is another major cause of the IS conflict. The control of oil wells has been one of the main objectives of IS in order to finance the war and achieve their political goals.

The third category relates to methods and strategies. It is essential to understand the key issues of the IS conflict in Syria and Iraq and, in particular, that variables such as violence against civilians, asymmetry, hybridity, different tolerance to casualties and terrorism have been identified. Firstly, this conflict has produced more casualties (460,000), internally displaced people (IDP, 6.5 million) and refugees (REF, 4.7 million) than any other since World War II (eleven million).[10] The first IS advance in Iraqi Kurdistan alone provoked one million IDP (Phillips 2014: 496), millions of refugees in Turkey, Jordan, Lebanon, and innumerable uncontrolled flows of people escaping to Europe. As for the existence of asymmetry in the conflict, a dissimilarity can be observed in weaponry and means (especially air assets), a dissimilar level of training between IS and Iraqi units, unequal economic resources, and disparate recruitment capacity, as IS has been able to recruit both local and foreign fighters from ninety different countries (Lister 2014: 23), in addition to its capacity to recruit women from all over the world.

The appeal of IS for young people is greater than al-Qaeda had at its inception (Kaplan and Costa 2015: 927, 929). There are also hybrid indicators (such as the mixture of conventional fighting with insurgent tactics (Jordán 2015: 126). IS possess sophisticated and high-tech weapons (from those originally provided by the US to the Iraqi armed forces) (Phillips 2014: 496), and not only 'leftovers' as Münkler pointed out as being characteristic of the 'new wars' (Münkler 2005: 98). 'Hybrid' in this context represents the coexistence of means, materials and weapons of different generations and technology, not only within IS forces, but also in contrast with the Western countries' armies and air forces in particular. Likewise, the variable of different levels of tolerance to casualties between IS and Western armies is also significant because it represents a gap in the conception of death, and therefore accentuates the asymmetrical nature of the struggle. The IS's disregard for its own lives, coupled with the rapid adaptation of military tactics and modern weapons render them difficult to defeat (Paasche and Gunter 2016: 12). Finally, their resort to terrorist actions, not only in the MENA region, but also in Europe and Africa, is amplifying and expanding the conflict and producing changes in other security contexts. Consequently, this category once analysed falls clearly into the definition of 'new wars'.

Moving onto the fourth category, its forms of funding are also representative of a new war economy – not a legitimate economy, as noted in the 'new wars' concept. Key identified indicators in this domain include looting, robbery, extortion, corruption, foreign aid and use of the black market. The IS conflict clearly meets all these criteria. IS exploit various sources of income such as selling oil on the black market (their main source of financing), kidnapping Westerners, selling antiquities, extortion, raising taxes in the controlled territories and taking advantage of agricultural resources (Lister 2014: 2).

Similarly, in the fifth category, complex emergencies, IS has provoked an international military and humanitarian response, but the latter in neighbouring countries. In fact, the humanitarian response in the conflict zone itself is nonexistent. The United Nations Refugee Agency (UNHCR) and NGOs operate in bordering countries and, specifically, there have been some humanitarian initiatives undertaken by the UN and the Red Cross in the form of food distribution. However, there is no NGO presence in those countries because they are unsafe. It is worth noting, regarding this point, that there is a substantial difference with the Bosnia case, as a paradigm of 'new war', as in Bosnia there was a broad array of international actors both during the war and in the stability operations afterwards, both at state, non-state and international level (Kaldor 1999). With regard to the international military response to IS, there are foreign regular forces (from Russia and the US-led coalition but without 'boots on the ground') as well as a high number of foreign mercenaries who participate in the conflict attracted by IS salaries, housing and sex slaves (mainly from Morocco, Tunisia and Libya).

Concerning the geographical framework where the conflict takes place, there is a useful typology provided by UCDP. In accordance with its classification, we could categorise the IS conflict as an internationalised intrastate conflict, which makes it similar to 1990s warfare. The military action occurs across two states (Iraq and Syria) with various external branches, as well as an impressive internationalisation in terms of the number and variety of actors involved. As for the external ramifications of the conflict, it is also interesting to note that the current battle between IS and the Democratic Union of Kurdistan is a conflict that is not based on the state (Melander 2015: 2). All things considered we can describe it as an internationalised intrastate conflict.

Finally, with regards to the legitimate legal framework, the IS conflict clearly meets the two key indicators displayed in Table 12.1. Firstly, there is a strong erosion of the legitimate monopoly of violence caused by rebel groups controlling a third of Iraq and Syria. Secondly, there is a widespread practice of barbarity, which is used as a tool to strengthen loyalty to the group (Bellamy 2002). This method includes torture, the cruel execution of prisoners (decapitation and crucifixion), violence and the sexual slavery of women and children, systematic rape, forced marriages and compulsory religious conversions (especially for female Yazidis), ethnic cleansing and the murder of almost entire populations who do not surrender to their demands (Paasche and Gunter 2016: 11). Furthermore, they also spread terror by posting and broadcasting videos of their barbarities on the Internet (Karadoç 2014: 600). Regarding sexual violence, we find the capitalising of women as spoils of war. Nonetheless, this issue is far from new; in fact it is as old as war itself. However we can talk about a 're-sexualisation of this type of violence', by emphasising that even though it is a very important feature of the new wars, it is to be acknowledged that it is a regression to the war tactics of the Early Middle Ages. What is this difference between this sexual violence and that of the new wars? In the IS case, it can be categorised as ethnic cleansing as a strategy of organised warfare, as the affected populations will 'voluntarily' move elsewhere (Münkler 2005: 107–9).

Following this analysis it seems clear that the IS conflict meets the new wars criteria, even though some indicators, such as the barbarism, are stronger than others. Is it possible to identify different elements in contrast to the Balkan wars as a paradigm of Kaldor's new wars that is not present in our analysis of the table? The answer is 'yes'. In addition to the issues already noted, such as differences in the analysis of the variables and indicators (for example, changes in the international military response, participation without international auspices, the strategy of forced marriages, compulsory religious conversions and the issue of women as spoils of war), we identify the following that do not fit neatly into Table 12.2.

Firstly, we would like to add an indicator that we call 'expansionism', which is an expression that has been materialised by the caliphate. Perhaps it is the most relevant as it is used as an influential tool by some sectors of the Muslim world. The announcement of the caliphate in June 2014 – a political and religious system that provided IS with morale and materials – allowed them to gain followers across the MENA region and even beyond. By bringing to life something past, by linking it to the Ottoman Caliphate – which was abolished ninety-two years ago – and other areas with an Islamic steward proclaimed in the Middle Ages, they were able to claim continuity with a glorious history.

However, the IS sphere of influence, support and adherence across MENA countries is to be regarded as fable in terms of its internal sociopolitical impact, except for Libya and Yemen where IS-oriented organisations are playing a key role in those countries' internal dynamics and clashes for power.

In Libya the danger is more acute. The country's chaotic situation constitutes a perfect breeding ground for dozens of militias that freely operate with the help of thousands of uncontrolled weapons present on its soil. Among these armed groups that are active along the Mediterranean coast in places such as Sirte or Derna, we find some that have pledged loyalty to IS, who now control significant financial resources. Consequently, IS is not only gaining ground in the country that is under the rule of the caliphate, but also clearly affecting the political stability of Libya, by challenging the establishment of the government. In the early months of 2016, IS doubled its combat forces in Libya thanks to the arrival of fighters from countries like Sudan, Tunisia and Turkey. This situation has led to the US carrying out airstrikes against IS training camps, killing dozens of terrorists.

Yemen is another country with comparable conditions to those in Iraq and Syria in the sense that the Shiite government is unable to control the territory owing to the loyalty of some jihadi groups operating across the country. Yemen has become a battlefield between Houthi (Shiites) rebels and an Arab coalition, led by Saudi Arabia, in which IS has become more important as a key actor in the conflict. The organisation has carried out terrorist bomb attacks on two mosques in Sana'a city centre, with close to 150 deaths. The mosques were controlled by militia Houthis supported by Iran; the Houthis control much of the country. IS has also conquered four territories: Sana'a, Sabua, Jadramat and, most recently, a territory in the Gulf of Aden, which they have named 'Ulaia'.

For the other MENA countries the situation is not uniform in the sense that some governments have been able to cope with the threat posed by IS-loyal groups while in others IS is affecting internal political stability. In the former group, arrests of alleged IS members and the dismantling of terrorist cells have taken place in Tunisia, Algeria and Morocco. Notably these operations are particularly concentrated in Tunisia, where the conservative mainstream is not in total control and where opportunities for democratisation are greater (Jordán 2015:125). Additionally, Tunisia is the country that has suffered most from terrorist acts.

In Egypt the situation is different regarding IS, which is represented by the group Ansar Bait al-Maqdis, Wilayat Sina (Sinai Peninsula), having changed its name after pledging allegiance to IS in 2014. It mainly operates in the north of Egypt's troubled Sinai Peninsula, by attacking Israel, Egyptian security forces, oil and gas infrastructure and personnel and, on one occasion, tourists. The group, whose strength is estimated to be between 1,000 and 2,000 fighters, blew up a Russian airplane travelling from Sharm el-Sheikh to Saint Petersburg on 31 October 2015, killing all of its 224 passengers.

Secondly, IS has developed a successful information operations campaign based on a powerful communication strategy with significant use of social networks. The use of the Internet to recruit, and also to attract international media, has turned the protagonists of this conflict into active users of social networks such as Twitter and other Internet resources such as YouTube or other websites, with some of their material becoming viral. They also publish their own magazine, *Dabip*, where their ideas, campaigns and victories are proclaimed, and the terror spread through the webcasting of executions and murderers. They know how to disseminate ideology and produce extraordinary propaganda to attract affiliates and develop branches in the MENA region, Europe (France, Belgium, Spain and the United Kingdom) and other remote areas (Nigeria, Indonesia).

Table 12.2 New categories, variables and indicators of the IS conflict

Categories	Variables	Indicators
Methods and strategies	Expansionism	Caliphate
	New technologies	Media propaganda Social networks
Complex emergencies	International military response	Foreign regular forces without international auspices
Legal–legitimate framework	Barbarity	Forced marriages Forced conversions

Source: prepared by the authors

The information strategy comprises four areas, which are determined and supported by core messages and subsequent strategic narratives. The first is based upon getting support, both personal and financial; the second is focused on uniting all Sunnis on the battlefield; the third seeks to spread fear among its adversaries, both internal and external; and the fourth seeks to publicise the effectiveness of the organisation by broadcasting its achievements and direct actions.[11]

The proposal for the new variables and indicators that IS fulfils are shown in Table 12.2.

How can we consider these differentiating elements in relation to the new wars typology? Can they fit into existing new conflicts' denominations or do we need to create a new typology? What should we call the war where IS is present? In view of the newly identified indicators coupled with those from the 'new wars' analysis set out in Table 12.1, we propose a new conceptualisation for this conflict: 'neo-medieval high-tech war'. This 'neo-medieval high-tech war' includes the features of 'new wars', but adds new indicators. Therefore, the IS conflict is a type of warfare that encapsulates multiple traditional signs of identity from the conflicts of past decades, plus new indicators that have clear characteristics of the past, the Middle Ages and the twenty-first century.

4 Type of governance exerted by IS in the controlled areas: strengths and weaknesses

We have analysed the features of the IS conflict in the field of security that allowed us to approach the issue from the viewpoint of the type of conflict, in order to propose a new definition. This new conceptualisation is a powerful tool because: (1) it refines the conflict's signs of identity in comparison to other definitions, which permits a more precise and pragmatic analysis for the decision-making process; and (2) all indicators identified as key to help build this conceptualisation allow IS to reach its political end-state: it means that designated violent actions, through war, have the maximum political impact in order to ultimately achieve the creation of an Islamic state. And they succeeded in doing it. This state controls large territories as noted. Once a territory is conquered, IS takes into consideration several substantial elements to exert its dominance: the continuity of funding sources, the capacity of law enforcement, legitimacy and a sense of belonging (Pollard et al. 2015: 14; Nuruzzaman 2015). Therefore, its aim is clearly political.

In fact, IS has always stressed the political dimension over the military. The self-proclaimed Islamic State runs a significant political and economic organisation, even though its features are only known by indirect sources. Be that as it may, it seems that they have created a context to provide what the Arab Spring was unable to (Kaplan and Costa 2015: 929) and accomplish a key objective: legitimacy. But, how or what tools they have used to attain legitimacy? There is nothing new; firstly, we analyse how they have exercised government to gain authority (which is their strength) and secondly, we explore the weaknesses of its political organisation.

First of all, although the exercise of power is totalitarian (mass executions of dissenters and a rigid interpretation of shariah law), they have managed to gain the local population's hearts and minds by providing them with material and non-material goods. As a matter of fact, although some populations were afraid in the beginning, their perception has changed over time. It can be observed that they mix mythical speech (past glories of the caliphates and a strict shariah), with a fairly rational discourse (Durán and Ávalos 2013). Let's look more closely at this mix of religion and supply of material goods. On the one hand, the caliphate provides a religious and political sense of belonging. This can easily be confirmed by the number of franchises that have pledged allegiance to IS and the territories keen to join them. In this system the shariah courts control: the prohibition of drugs, alcohol, snuff, gambling and non-Islamic music; clothing; gender separation; and the destruction of impious shrines. Police forces receive training (both men and women) to maintain law and order and monitor full compliance with the shariah. This rapid mobilisation and organisational structure has come about due to the wages on offer.

One key goal of IS is to supply the same services that many states provide to their citizens: infrastructure, postal services, free health care, soup kitchens, loans, Islamic schools for boys and girls (food and free gifts), and even subsidies for commodities such as bread or transportation. They also have filled the power vacuum of the municipal administration, creating new institutions or taking advantage of the old ones to remodel them. In the occupied territories they have created their own police, set up their own education system, established courts with a strict interpretation of shariah, provided a health system, social services and a public administration within the context of a fair redistributive system (Pollard et al. 2015: 13). All of these actions have changed the perception of the population. Where does IS get the funding to provide all of these services? They have a well-organised taxation system and varied and interesting funding sources. Their system of funding began operating before the Islamic state was proclaimed. Mosul was and is the financial source of IS. Its primary sources are oil and gas, but it has other resources such as agriculture, water, cotton, electricity, kidnappings, external donations, extortion, and so on. It also controls industries, ranging from water, electricity and gas to local factories, bakeries and municipal services. This fact has placed IS in position 161 out of the 214 world economies. They are richer than Burundi, Liberia and Belize (Pollard et al. 2015: 12). Therefore, with all these resources at their disposal, it is not difficult to win the hearts and minds of populations and to simultaneously build a mythical discourse on the basis of fully rational actions. However, in the exercise of power not all their features are strengths. We can point to a number of indicators that can lead to significant weaknesses; specifically, we highlight four of these.

The first two indicators are related to weaknesses in the realm of ideology. Firstly, even though their exercise of power may be described as totalitarian, we should make a number of clarifications about it. Concerning the political situation in the 1930s, Francis Fukuyama stated that 'there were two very powerful ideologies that were openly anti-democratic: fascism and communism'. Nowadays the author says that 'the Islamic State and other Muslim fundamentalist groups are much weaker than Nazi Germany or the Soviet Union'.[12] Secondly, IS maintains a coalition with Sunni Arab tribes and former Ba'ath Party cadres who, although ideologically distinct, have a common objective – to oust the Shiite government. These ties were established within Iraqi prisons in the years that the balance of power began to change in favour of the Shiites (Jordán 2015: 119). Those links are essential for IS, since former Ba'ath cadres are trained and educated professionals of the former Saddam Hussein army and administration. Thirdly, they lack international recognition and a legitimate economy (Pollard 2015: 2). As noted, the proclamation of the caliphate challenges the international nation-state order and clearly shows a war economy or a new war typology. All of this has led to both a regional and international military response against IS which, to some extent, undermines its capabilities and chances of success. Moreover, a war economy cannot be sustained indefinitely. Finally, its elites enjoy maximum autonomy in the state. This means that there is no control of the state by the citizens, and therefore the imposed political regime is to be considered a dictatorship or, more specifically, totalitarian. The survival of these regimes can only be sustained by the provision of significant material resources to the population.

5 New security framework in the MENA region

The emergence of IS on the international scene has transformed the security framework and international relationships in the MENA region, with particular signs of identity that differ from the previous status. The features of the conflict analysed above, together with the IS's political objectives and exercise of government in the occupied areas, have resulted both in a different international response to the conflict, and in a new configuration of alliances in the region.

On the one hand, the changes have been motivated by the absence of a consensus or of coordinated international response, which has had an enormous impact on the relationships and geopolitics in the region. This circumstance has created a vacuum of power which has been seen by some countries as an opportunity to pursue their own national agendas. On the other hand, the fighting has highlighted divergences not only between the Shiite and Sunni countries, but also among various countries with regards to particularly sensitive issues, such as the question of the Kurds. This situation has added complexity to the conflict, making any resolution more difficult to achieve.

These changes can be assessed in two main domains as mentioned above: the international response to the threat by the international community, and the new scenario of regional and global alliances.

5.1 International response

The international response to counter the IS threat can be viewed as weak in terms of large organisations such as the UN, NATO or the European Union, as well as a lack of coordinated action from the big powers to achieve a specific goal.

In this context, the UN Security Council has limited its response to passing a resolution strengthening legal measures against those doing business with terrorist groups. It targets mainly IS militants and it has called on states to fight 'a global and unprecedented threat to international peace and security'. The text does not provide any legal basis for military action, although a coalition of nations – and Russia – are already bombing IS in Syria and Iraq. A similar approach was adopted after the terrorist attacks in Paris when the UN adopted a resolution condemning this terrorist act of violence. The resolution determines that IS constitutes 'a global and unprecedented threat to international peace and security'. After the attack in Brussels in March 2016 members of the Security Council stressed the need to take measures to prevent and suppress the financing of terrorism, terrorist organisations and individual terrorists, in accordance with Resolutions 2199 (2015) and 2253 (2015).

However, NATO – unlike in the previous major crises that occurred after 1989 where its participation was active (as in the Balkans, Iraq and Afghanistan) – did not take any measures against IS this time. The Alliance's inaction triggered the formation of an ad-hoc US-led coalition following the NATO Summit in Wales in June 2014. It is significant to note that all twenty-eight NATO allies are involved in that coalition.

As for the EU, the global financial crisis made European policy-makers look inward, led to a renationalisation of foreign policy, and stalled the evolution of a common foreign and security policy for the following years (Kausch 2014: 4). Thus, the EU has once again proved how ineffectual the policies of common security have been, not to mention those on counterterrorism and immigration. The inability to cope with the flood of hundreds of thousands of war refugees who are arriving in Europe via the Mediterranean Sea[13] has meant that each country has adopted measures on a unilateral basis in the aforementioned three areas based on their own national interests and political agendas.

In this context, following the Paris attacks of November 2015, countries are coordinating their military responses either within the coalition, or individually, such as Russia, Turkey or China, within a framework where combat troops have explicitly been ruled out by the countries involved, as they exclusively rely on air power. However, the prolonged nature of this campaign has led many to reignite the debate about whether the coalition is doing enough and whether 'boots on the ground' is the next logical step.

5.2 The new alliance framework

Since 2000 the US has followed in the MENA region the so-called Orientalist (Karakoç 2014: 597) strategy based on Sunni-based, Israel-biased and anti-Iranian policies whose prominent actors and allies were Saudi Arabia, Turkey and Israel. By encouraging the ambitions of states that intend to become dominant powers in the Middle East, the US determined to become more active in the MENA region.

However, the emergence of IS has constituted a severe challenge to that policy and it has modified the regional dynamics, alliances and politics in the region, representing a threat to Saudi Arabia, Turkey and Israel, as well as to the US. Nevertheless, the approach and proxies used to fight the menace of IS are very different. While Saudi Arabia is an existential issue in terms of Shiite–Sunni confrontation, Turkey, reticent in the beginning, started to consider IS a threat after the terrorist bombing in Ankara. Conversely, Israel considers it to be a containable rather than a strategic threat because IS cannot challenge Israel's own organised military forces, with Iran remaining as the primary threat.

Table 12.3 The new game of alliances in the Middle East

Actor Country interest	IS	Bashar al-Assad	Kurds
US	Defeat	Defeat	Support
Russia	Defeat	Support	Support
China	Defeat	Support	Slight support
Iran	Defeat	Support	Support
Israel	Defeat	Defeat	Not relevant
Saudi Arabia	Defeat	Defeat	Not relevant
Turkey	Defeat	Defeat	Defeat

Source: prepared by the authors

As for the US, fighting against IS has given it new partners in the region, such as Iran and the Kurds, which is a change of approach that has led to direct confrontation with its former allies. Taking sides with Iran, predominantly as a consequence of the nuclear deal,[14] represents a challenge to Israeli and Saudi Arabian policies, while support to the Kurds collides with Turkey's interests. Therefore, former partners in the region such as Israel, Saudi Arabia and Turkey are now considered ineffective in the fight against IS. Their place has been taken by the Kurds, which are considered to be more suitable,[15] and by Iran as a necessary 'travelling companion' to counter the IS threat in Syria.

Furthermore, the objective of the US and its allies in the coalition is based upon not only seeking the defeat of IS, but also in overthrowing Bashar al-Assad – a stance in clear opposition to Iran and other external powers, such as Russia and China. These powers, together with Iran, have shown that the fight against IS is a way to gain a good geopolitical position in the MENA region, and as a clear 'pro-Shiite' policy that includes keeping Bashar al-Assad, in opposition to the coalition's stated objective. An outline of the new alliance framework is shown in Table 12.3, where conflicting positions can be identified.

6 Conclusions

Throughout this chapter we have aimed to study the political and security implications that the actions of IS are generating. Over the past two years IS has become a global actor that has changed dynamics across the MENA region and has caused external shocks and spillover that have impacted on world politics and the international security framework. The study has focused on: (1) the type of conflict in which IS is involved; (2) the type of governance practices in the occupied territories; and (3) the new security framework.

Firstly, the most important and novel contribution provided by the chapter on security has been the analysis of the IS conflict typology in the MENA region that shows specific signs of identity. We have further scrutinised the broad security problems that the war is causing. Once various indicators were analysed and some differentiations identified with respect to the features of the 'new wars' concept – in use since the late 1990s – we have come to the conclusion that a new name for this war can be put forward. Our proposal is 'neo-medieval high-tech war'. This is a war that combines old and traditional warfare characteristics with the latest technological advances, sometimes highly effectively employed, such as the communication campaigns and propaganda broadcast through social networks.

Secondly, the most important political priority set by IS, is to establish a caliphate and act like a state. In this regard it has been our goal to analyse the strengths and weaknesses of IS. We consider that its major strength is the way it has gained legitimacy among the populations in the occupied territories. However, its greatest weakness is on the ideological side – both the survival of its own ideology on the one hand, and the ideological differences with the groups with whom they have signed alliances, on the other.

Finally, we have analysed the impact of the new security framework. The main results are markedly different from those of the 1990s in which the major international organisations in the field of security and defence played a more active role in conflicts (the UN, NATO and the EU). Moreover, the emergence of IS has also led to a new configuration of alliances in the Middle East, where the Kurds and Iran have come to play a different role in US foreign policy and thus have altered the relationship and set of alliances in the region.

Therefore, we can propose a new typology of conflict with many similarities and some differences with regard to those of recent decades, namely an insurgent and terrorist group which occupies vast territories and rules as a government for the first time in history. It has also triggered new global configurations with a changed pattern of international response and the modification of regional and global alliances. All of this allows us to conclude that we are witnessing a highly concerning growing political issue with severe repercussions for global security.

Notes

1. The current Islamic State was named 'Islamic State of Iraq and Syria' (ISIS) and has had different names. It is also now known as DAESH. In 2006 it was called Islamic State of Iraq (ISI) and self-named in 2013 as 'Islamic State of Iraq and the Levant' (ISIL) because of its involvement in the war in Syria. In June 2014 they proclaimed the caliphate as Islamic State.

2. IS controls territories in Iraq, Syria, Sinai and eastern Libya. It also has members in Morocco, Lebanon, Jordan, Turkey, Israel and Palestine and wants to extend its power in Libya, Egypt (Sinai), Saudi Arabia, Yemen, Algeria, Afghanistan and Pakistan (Marsili 2016: 87)

3. For instance, IS condemns the last caliphates and the Ottoman Empire for their deviance from a pure form of Islam (Marsili 2016: 87).

4. War performed among various regional and/or global powers without a direct confrontation among each other but through mercenaries, guerrillas and regular troops which take sides.

5. The hybrid form of warfare clearly shows the following four differentiators: the use by opponents either simultaneously or in a combined way of conventional troops, irregular forces, terrorist acts and organised crime. It also focuses on the effective control of the field of information and introduces elements of uncertainty and brutality (Hoffman 2007: 3).

6. We point out that the 'spectator-sport warfare' definition is described as such on the basis of Western intervention and the importance of air power as a transcendental resource. There could be other contentious issues that characterise these wars and perhaps they might not be applied to the IS conflict, such as the fact that they are based on the location of conflicts that meet the requirement of desirability for Western powers (McInnes 2006).

7. The term 'fourth-generation wars', predominantly describes the decentralised nature of war. It is characterised as a conflict in which the lines between war and politics, military and civilians are not so clear. These types of wars can be summarised by four general traits: (1) fighting in a complex context in a low intensity conflict; (2) tactics and techniques of previous generations are employed; (3) it is fought through a range of social, economic and military policy networks; (4) it involves a mix of national, international, transnational and subnational actors (Lind et al. 1989: 2–11).

8. The 'new wars' concept also includes features and indicators visible in the types of conflicts previously identified (such as the hybrid war, sport-spectator, proxy and fourth-generation war among people).

9. Kalyvas (2001), Newman (2004), Lacina and Gledistch (2005) are, among others, the main detractors of the 'new wars' followers as they basically defend the idea that there are no substantial differences between the 'new' and 'old' wars.

10. For casualties, information has been employed from the Syrian Centre for Policy Research (SCPR). It claims that the true figure is 470,000 – almost double the UN estimate. Available at <http://www.economist.com/news/middle-east-and-africa/21693279-how-many-people-has-syrias-civil-war-killed-quantifying-carnage> (last accessed 23 February 2016). For refugees and IDP, information has been employed from UNHCR. Available at <http://data.unhcr.org/syrianrefugees/regional.php> (last accessed 23 February 2016).

11. 'DAESH information campaign and its influence. Results of the study', IntelCenter. Available at <http://www.stratcomcoe.org/daesh-information-campaign-and-its-influence-1> (last accessed 30 July 2016).

12. Fukuyama interview. Available at <http://www.elmundo.es/cronica/2016/02/02/56ab 9adcca4741fd408b4606.html> (last accessed 18 February 2016).

13. One million refugees arrived in Europe in 2015 and 110,000 refugees in 2016 (UNHCR). Available at <http://data.unhcr.org/mediterranean/regional.php> (last accessed 24 February 2016).

14. Nuclear agreement between Iran and the P5+1 group of world powers – the US, UK, France, China and Russia, plus Germany.

15. 'Our non-ally in Ankara', *The Wall Street Journal*, 15 September 2014.

References

Bados, Victor and Marién Durán (2015), 'Las nuevas guerras: una propuesta metodológica para su análisis', *Unisci Journal*, Universidad Complutense de Madrid, 38: 9–35.

Bellamy, Alex (2002), 'The great beyond: rethinking military responses to new wars and complex emergencies', *Defence Studies*, 2 (1): 25–50.

Calatrava, Adolfo (2012), *¿La estabilidad del autoritarismo? Análisis de los procesos de cambio político en Asia Central: estudio de los casos de Kazajistán, Kirguistán y Uzbekistán. La importancia de los factores externos*, PhD Dissertation, University of Granada.

Durán, Marién and Antonio Ávalos (2013), *Culturas Cruzadas en Conflicto. Militares poblaciones locales en misiones internacionales: los casos de Afganistán y Líbano*, Granada: University of Granada Press.

Hoffman, Frank (2007), *Conflict in the 21st Century: the Rise of the Hybrid Wars*, Arlington: Potomac Institute for Policy Studies.

Inalcik, Halil (1973), *The Ottoman Empire: the Classical Age 1300–1600*, London: Phoenix.

Jordán, J. (2015), *El Daesh*, Instituto Español de Estudios Estratégicos, La internacional yihadista, Madrid: Ministerio de Defensa: 109–47.

Kaldor, Mary (1999), *New and Old Wars: Organized Violence in a Global Era*, Stanford: Stanford University Press.

Kalyvas, Stathis N. (2001), 'New and old civil wars: a valid distinction?', *World Politics*, 54: 99–118, DOI: 0.1353/wp.2001.0022.

Kaplan, Jeffrey and Christopher P. Costa (2015), 'The Islamic State and the new tribalism', *Terrorism and Political Violence*, 27 (5): 926–69.

Karakoç, Jülide (2014), 'The failure of indirect Orientalism: Islamic State', *Critique*, 42 (4): 597–606, DOI: 10.1080/03017605.2014.984500.

Kausch, Kristina (2014), *Competitive Multipolarity in the Middle East*, Istituto Affari Internazionali, IAI working paper 14/10.

Lacina, Bethany and Nils P. Gledistch (2005), 'Monitoring trends in global combat: a new dataset of battle deaths', *European Journal of Population*, 21 (2–3): 145–66.

Lind, William S., Keith Nightengale, John F. Schmitt, Joseph W. Sutton and Gary I. Wilson (1989), 'The changing face of war: into the fourth generation', *Military Review*, 69 (10): 2–11.

Lister, Charles (2014), *Profiling the Islamic State*, Brookings Doha Center Analysis Paper, 13, Doha: Brookings Institution.

Malantowicz, Artur (2013), 'Civil war in Syria and the "new wars" debate', *Amsterdam Law Forum*, 5 (3): 52–60.

Marsili, Marco (2016), 'The Islamic State: a clash within the Muslim civilization for the new caliphate', *Studies in Conflict & Terrorism*, 39 (2): 85–105.

McInnes, Colin (2006), *SpectatorSport War: the West and Contemporary Conflict*, Boulder, CO: Lynne Rienner.

Melander, Erik (2015), *Organized Violence in the World 2015. An Assessment by the Uppsala Conflict Data Program*, UCDP, Paper 9.

Mello, Patrick (2010), 'In search of new wars', *European Journal of International Relations*, 12: 1–13.

Münkler, Herfried (2005), *Viejas y 'nuevas guerras'. Asimetría y privatización de la violencia*, Madrid: Siglo XXI.

Newman, Edward (2004), 'The new wars debate: a historical perspective is needed', *Security Dialogue*, 35: 137–89.

Nuruzzaman, Mohammed (2015), 'The challenge of the Islamic State', *Global Affairs*, 1 (3): 297–304.

Paasche, Till F. and Michael M. Gunter, (2016), 'Revisiting Western strategies against the Islamic State in Iraq and Syria', *The Middle East Journal*, 70 (1): 9–29.

Pollard, Stacy E., David A. Poplack and Kevin C. Casey (2015), 'Understanding the Islamic State's competitive advantages: remaking state and nationhood in the Middle East and North Africa', *Terrorism and Political Violence*, DOI: 10.1080/09546553.2015.1094306.

Phillips, Andrew (2014), 'The Islamic State's challenge to international order', *Australian Journal of International Affairs*, 68 (5): 495–8.

Shaw, Martin (1999), 'War and globality: the role and character of war in the global transition', in Ho-Won Jeong (ed.), *Peace and Conflict: a New Agenda*, Hampshire: Ashgate Publishing, pp. 61–80.

Whitehead, Laurence (2001), 'Three international dimensions of democratization', in Laurence Whitehead (ed.), *The International Dimension of Democratization: Europe and the Americas*, New York: Oxford University Press, pp. 3–25.

Chapter 13

EU and EU member states' responses to the Arab Spring[1]

Irene Fernández-Molina

1 Introduction

International relations (IR) and geopolitics have taken a discreet back seat in the academic discussion of political change in the Middle East and North Africa (MENA) in the aftermath of the so-called Arab Spring. On the one hand, a good deal of comparative politics scholarship has endeavoured first to establish the empirical record and later to theorise the causal origins, mobilisation and diffusion dynamics, and diverging outcomes of the 2011 popular uprisings in various countries of the region. In keeping with a largely domestic focus, this literature has somewhat overlooked the role of foreign and transnational actors and forces in shaping the political evolution of MENA states, even though the latter have been described for decades as being distinctively 'penetrated' – 'the most penetrated international relations subsystem in today's world' (Brown 1984: 4). Only some comparative analyses of post-2011 trajectories have acknowledged the 'international variable' – from dependence on 'Western' support and international financial institutions to foreign military intervention and competitive interference by rival regional powers – to be one of the key set of factors accounting for variation in the domestic power balances between regimes and opposition forces, and the ensuing outcomes of the uprisings (Hinnebusch 2015b). On the other hand, the emerging IR literature on the consequences of, and responses to, the Arab Spring at regional and international levels (Fürtig 2014; Ryan 2014; Mason 2014) has still not thoroughly addressed the puzzle of causal links between external factors and domestic effects (Yom 2015: 699).

The aim of this chapter is to examine the involvement of one – or one set – of the external actors that have historically shown greatest capacity to 'penetrate' the MENA region, namely the European Union and its member states, during a critical juncture or 'moment of truth' such as the Arab Spring and its aftermath. The role of the EU has gone relatively unnoticed in the literature on international relations of the Middle East in comparison with the prominence traditionally granted to the United States and the recent surge of attention to the 'return' of Russia to the region. By contrast, a wealth of publications has been devoted to the EU's reaction to the Arab Spring within EU foreign policy studies (for example Peters 2012; Biscop et al. 2012; Teti 2012; Behr 2012a; Behr 2012b; Horst et al. 2013; Pace 2014; Van Hüllen 2015). This chapter will provide a critical review of mainly the latter strand of literature, yet seeks to alleviate its usual self-absorption and inevitable Eurocentrism by bridging the gap with scholarship on international relations of the Middle East (Fawcett 2013; Hinnebusch 2015a).

In trying to make sense of this abundant and disparate body of scholarship, the chapter will engage with two debates. The first relates to the debate on change and continuity within EU–MENA relations after what many have described as a moment of multifaceted 'flux' (Whitman and Juncos 2012) and 'crisis' (Natorski 2015) as well as a 'critical juncture' in historical institutionalist terms (Boogaerts et al. 2016). At the time, the perception of breach of normality and uncertainty came from almost all fronts: 2010–11 brought together the apex of the Eurozone crisis, a far-reaching internal legitimacy crisis and questioning of the European integration process in its entirety, the institutional novelties entailed by the entry into force of the Lisbon Treaty in the area of EU foreign policy –including the establishment of the new European External Action Service (EEAS) and the reinforced and double-hatted responsibilities of the Union's High Representative for Foreign Affairs and Security Policy (HR) – and the sudden destabilisation of the EU's southern Mediterranean 'neighbourhood'. The positive reading was that, by creating a widely acknowledged level of 'cognitive uncertainty', the wave of domestic and regional transformations of the Arab Spring could expectably open a 'policy window' for innovation in EU foreign policy (Bicchi 2007). This situation could even favour the EU's regional actorness in terms of opportunity, or 'factors in the external environment of ideas and events which constrain or enable actorness' (Bretherton and Vogler 2006: 24). However, research published in subsequent years has almost been unanimous in ruling out any far-reaching change occurring thereafter in the EU's foreign policy towards the MENA region. Paradoxically, and counterintuitively, such unprecedented and manifold crises did not precipitate policy change but fundamental continuity (Natorski 2015).

The second related debate, which will be outlined in the next section, concerns the identities and roles that most shape – or best describe – the EU's behaviour as a regional power in the southern Mediterranean. The long theoretical fencing battle between advocates of more liberal/idealist and more realist understandings of the EU's international action has been decried as being ultimately irrelevant and 'sterile' (Cavatorta and Rivetti 2014: 623) Eurocentric navelgazing. Still, the premise in this chapter is that this generalising hook and point of reference remains useful as long as it is brought down to earth and specified by the empirical analysis of concrete policy areas and case studies. In line with this view, the contention informing the pages that follow is that the answers to the two aforementioned overarching questions – on EU foreign policy change and continuity in the aftermath of the Arab Spring, and on the most discernible EU international identity – need to be similarly qualified and complexified.

The first step to providing a more accurate and nuanced picture of the EU's response(s) to the Arab Spring is to consider the latter in plural and distinguish between crisis management and strategic components. The jigsaw of political and institutional frameworks within which the EU deals with the MENA region and individual third states – from the Common Foreign and Security Policy (CFSP) and the Common Security and Defence Policy (CSDP) to the European Neighbourhood Policy (ENP) and the Union for the Mediterranean (UfM) – also needs to be taken into account in this disentanglement exercise. Roughly speaking, crisis management responses were those produced by the EU in the short term in reaction to specific events or developments in the MENA countries: 'Crisis management . . . has a shorter time frame and implies a degree of urgency and immediacy, aiming to stop escalation and/or deal with the consequences of a rapidly worsening situation' (Whitman and Wolff 2012: 6). These responses involved resort to diplomatic and military instruments whose use had to be decided on an intergovernmental basis in the framework of the CFSP, with the Council serving as the main institutional focus and the HR as the most visible common face. On the other hand, strategic or structural responses were envisaged for the medium and long term, and involved the full range of instruments of the EU's foreign policy and external action (Smith 2014: 44–66), chiefly aid, trade and mobility, thus granting a greater role to the Commission. The encompassing political framework that comprised strategic responses was the ENP – one of the EU's most prominent 'structural foreign policies' (Keukeleire and Delreux 2014: 28) – and decision-making was mixed and policy-specific – depending on whether each measure fell within community (supranational) or CSFP (intergovernmental) competences.

The argument of this chapter is that the EU's response(s) to the Arab Spring can be best described as hybrid and is (are) closely reflective of the very hybridity of the EU's international identity (Bretherton and Vogler 2006: 58). On the one hand, despite genuine normative impetuses, a largely realist approach and exclusive identities and roles prevailed in crisis management and short-term reactions driven by intergovernmental decision-making. On the other hand, a more 'liberal' outlook and inclusive identities and roles were embodied in strategic or long-term responses in the framework of the ENP, although the latter's inherent contradictions and lack of innovation in relation to past policies eventually deprived them of the value-based and progressive effect envisaged on paper.

The remainder of the chapter is structured as follows. Firstly, after reviewing the debate on the identities and roles of the EU as a regional power in the southern Mediterranean, the EU's crisis management responses to the Arab Spring will be evaluated by disentangling their normative and realist components in the cases of three different groups of MENA countries – those having witnessed regime change, civil conflict and regime resilience. Secondly, this range of initiatives will be contrasted with strategic responses in which the EU seemed to give precedence to liberal, inclusive and normative approaches. Thirdly, a brief section will examine the EU's return to crisis mode in managing the massive Syrian refugee inflows that were framed as a 'crisis' and took the 'fortress Europe' identity to its utmost degree from 2015 onwards.

2 The debate about the EU's identities and roles as a regional power in the Mediterranean

In order to frame the argument that the EU's crisis management and strategic responses to the Arab Spring were shaped by predominantly realist/exclusive and liberal/inclusive approaches, respectively, an overview needs to be provided of the debate on the identities and roles of the EU as a regional power in the MENA. In a particularly insightful streamlining of the discussion on the complex and hybrid 'nature of the beast', Charlotte Bretherton and John Vogler (2006) distinguish between inclusive and exclusive identities – and external roles resulting from them. The former are built upon conviction on the uniqueness of the EU as a polity (compared to conventional nation states) and its value-based foundations, which are claimed to inform the EU's external action in a positive or at least well-intentioned way. By contrast, exclusive identities and roles are based on the need to prioritise the self-interest and draw the boundaries of what remains a finite and select club, thus erecting barriers between insiders and outsiders, at times through practices of active othering (Bretherton and Vogler 2006: 46). This selfish and restrictive behaviour towards the outside world ties in better with realist and structuralist understandings of the EU's external action.

As regards the liberal/inclusive dimension of the EU's relations with the southern Mediterranean or MENA, the conception of the EU as a 'civilian power' (Duchêne 1972) captures quite appropriately the profoundly liberal nature of the Euro-Mediterranean Partnership (EMP) as it was conceived of in the mid-1990s, as well as the thrust of its partial successors, the ENP and the UfM. The EMP project was very much in line with François Duchêne's (1972: 47) contention that 'lacking military power [was] not the handicap it once was' in a time of growing economic interdependence and international significance of low politics, non-state actors and ideational influences. In a sense, the three mutually reinforcing liberal logics of transformation underpinning the EMP – economic (neo-)liberal reform (macroeconomic stabilisation, trade liberalisation), political democratisation (good governance, democracy, human rights) and multilateral/ regional cooperation (Adler et al. 2006: 58-66) – were civilian (as opposed to military) means to ultimately achieve a security objective, which is to strengthen the EU's safekeeping by expanding its home-grown security community beyond its borders to the southern shore of the Mediterranean.

Along the same lines but more up to date, the influential notion of the EU as a 'normative power' with a distinctive 'ability to shape conceptions of "normal" in in-ternational relations' (Manners 2002) had a direct bearing on the work of authors who have analysed the EMP as an inherently constructivist policy. According to them, the radical originality of the EMP lay in its ideational dimension and boldness to think the previously unthinkable, that is, in its ambition to forge a new shared identity and invent a somewhat counter-intuitive or 'antinatural' region encompassing the two shores of the Mediterranean (Adler et al. 2006). Besides the region-building experiment, the 'normative power' concept in its liberal or soft constructivist derivations has explicitly underlain a plethora of studies on the EU's promotion of human rights and democracy in the MENA. This is a logical consequence of Ian Manners' (2002) emphasis on the value-based internal sources of the EU's international normative influence and his identifica-tion of peace, liberty, democracy, rule of law and human rights as being the five core values. In practice, however, empirical testing has often led to discouraging conclusions, highlighting the EU's failure to live up to its own normative promises and ubiquitous contradictions: between words and deeds, between different policies and objectives, between self- and external perceptions, and so forth.

Altogether, even when adopting critical perspectives, a large part of the literature on EU–MENA relations has revolved around the roles of the EU as a liberal/ inclusive actor, chief among which are those of 'model' (of regional integration, peace and prosperity), 'promoter of norms' (human rights, democracy and development cooperation) and 'counterweight' to US influence (Bretherton and Vogler 2006: 56–7). Nevertheless, there are also a number of authors who have directly rejected the central premise by questioning the assumption that the EU acts as a 'force for good' in international politics in general and Euro-Mediterranean relations in particular. As opposed to the liberal 'socialisation/inclusion view', the so-called 'realist' 'hegemony/domination view' (Attinà 2003) reminds us of the structural asymmetry of the relationship between the two shores of the Mediterra-nean and the predominance of EU agency in all forms and frameworks of bilateral and multilateral cooperation within this area, even when the delusional ideas of 'partnership' and 'co-ownership' have been invoked. According to this approach, the origins of contemporary EU foreign policy towards the MENA can be traced back to the neo-liberal turn of capitalism in the 1970s and pervasive insecurity within this region in the 1990s. European and Eurocentric responses to both of these challenges have been consented by southern elites and governments even at the expense of their countries' general interests – as in the case of asymmetric trade liberalisation and EU agricultural protectionism – as part of typical 'client' behaviour in a situation of international hegemony (Attinà 2003). Considering all of its norm diffusion and socialisation components, EU action can be construed as that of a 'benevolent' or 'half-way hegemon' that is 'trying to enforce a halfway hegemonic strategy' (Costalli 2009: 336).

These arguments are reminiscent of Johan Galtung's classic structuralist account of the European Community as an emerging 'capitalist superpower' with potential neocolonial leanings (Galtung 1973). Arguably, in few places like in the MENA does EU hegemony go so much hand in hand with the bloc's historical heritage as a 'postcolonial power' (Fisher Onar and Nicolaïdis 2013: 284). In addition, the most unmistakably exclusive identity of the EU in its relations with this region is that of 'fortress Europe', which encompasses restrictive behaviour ranging from the trade sphere to EU enlargement and, most infamously today, immigration and asylum policies. While regular practices in the latter area are 'evidently inconsistent with the inclusive, value-based understandings of EU identity' (Bretherton and Vogler 2006: 49), their exclusionary and unprincipled nature is significantly aggravated in what are framed as moments of 'crisis'. On a different note, a final neither/nor conceptualisation falling between inclusive and exclusive EU identities and roles is that of 'market power' (Damro 2012). This intendedly non-normative alternative places the focus on the market basis of the EU's identity – the fact that, deep down, it remains 'fundamentally a large single market' – and the power it exercises by means of the externalising of its economic and social market-related policies and regulatory measures.

3 Crisis management responses to the Arab Spring

Overall, when confronted with this range of identities and roles, the EU's crisis management and short-term responses to the Arab Spring appear to have been dominated by a prevailingly realist and exclusive approach, even though they included a significant number of normatively inspired initiatives. To be fair, both the boldest and the most cynical European reactions to the wave of Arab uprisings in early 2011 were led by the governments of individual EU member states, thus calling into question the extent to which they can be attributed to the EU proper. At the same time, the intergovernmental nature of decision-making in the framework of the CFSP made collective decisions subject to the foreign policy preferences of member states and especially of the 'big three' (Germany, France and the United Kingdom). The recurring problem of EU foreign policy actorness returned to the fore, as in every moment of international crisis. Fragmented responses often revealed the prevalence of bilateral ties and approaches over multilateral intra-EU coordination of positions vis-à-vis third countries. 'Geoclientelism', or 'patron-client like relationships between EU member states and certain non-EU countries or groups of countries' (Behr and Tiilikainen 2015: 27), built at times on postcolonial underpinnings, also played a role in determining which were the most involved and influential actors in each specific crisis. The following sections address the EU's immediate responses to the Arab Spring events in each of its Arab southern Mediterranean partners – encompassed by the southern dimension of the ENP – which can be divided for this purpose into three groups, namely countries where the 2011 revolutions led to regime change (Tunisia and Egypt), where the uprisings degenerated into civil conflicts (Libya and Syria) and where regime continuity prevailed (Morocco, Jordan and Algeria). Arab states that were less affected by the Arab Spring domestically (Lebanon and Palestine) or fall outside the scope of the ENP (Gulf Cooperation Council members, Iraq and Yemen) will not be considered.

3.1 Coming to terms with regime change: Tunisia and Egypt

The immediate EU response to the first revolutionary outbursts in Tunisia and Egypt in January 2011 essentially consisted of joint statements by the HR Catherine Ashton and the Commissioner for Enlargement and ENP Štefan Füle. This traditional diplomatic instrument was handled in a centralised way from Brussels, since neither the EU delegations to the aforementioned countries nor channels for bilateral political dialogue existing in the framework of the respective EMP association agreements (association councils and association committees) were visibly put into use. The EU representatives' declaratory activism started from quite cautious and softly worded statements – like the one whereby Ashton and Füle simply conveyed 'concern about the events' and called for 'restraint in the use of force' in Tunisia almost one month after the self-immolation of a street vendor had sparked escalating popular protests and violent state repression (EU 2011a) – and took on a more overtly normative and pro-democracy tenor only a posteriori – expressing 'support and recognition to the Tunisian people and their democratic aspirations' (EU 2011b) after the revolution had overthrown President Ben Ali. Subsequently, both the Foreign Affairs Council (31 January) and the European Council (4 February) expressed sympathy and support for the budding Tunisian democratic transition. The former agreed a CFSP decision to impose individual sanctions ('restrictive measures') and an economic asset freeze on the members of the Ben Ali family (Council of the EU 2011a; Lannon 2012: 12). Ashton then travelled to Tunis and assured the interim government that the

EU wanted to be 'Tunisia's strongest ally in their move towards democracy' (EU High Representative 2011a).

Seven months later these promises were to lead to the establishment of an EU–Tunisia Task Force, co-chaired by the HR and the interim Tunisian prime minister Mohamed Beji Caïd Essebsi, in order to coordinate European and international financial support for the Tunisian transition. EU Election Observation Missions were dispatched to monitor the Tunisian Constituent Assembly elections in October 2011. Throughout 2012 and 2013, as Tunisia became distinguished as the only success story left of post-Arab Spring democratisation in the region, bilateral relations would be stepped up through the signing of a new action plan (replacing the one from 2005) and a largely symbolic Privileged Partnership.

At the revolutionary outset, however, while EU institutions struggled to come to terms with a never imagined and rapidly evolving chain of events, the European reaction with distinct postcolonial – or neocolonial (Kallander 2013: 118) – connotations, which provoked the most outrage and somehow set the tone for critical external perceptions, was that of French foreign minister Michèle Alliot-Marie, who offered the 'expertise' (*savoir-faire*) of French security forces in policing techniques to support Ben Ali. While Alliot-Marie had to resign out of embarrassment, other members of her cabinet and counterparts from the Italian government similarly talked about the Tunisian autocrat in understanding and conciliatory terms (Pace 2014: 977). In parallel, Italy was starting to witness a substantial increase in the number of migrants crossing the Mediterranean from Tunisia to the island of Lampedusa, which would certainly contribute to securitising its national approach to the North African uprisings and bringing the EU's 'fortress Europe' identity back in by extension. The 'uneasy' migration situation in the Mediterranean region was raised in late February 2011 by the Justice and Home Affairs Council and the interior ministers of six southern EU member states, pushing the European Commission to take action and ensure the 'full mobilisation' of EU instruments such as Frontex with the joint operation Hermes 2011 (European Commission 2011a). Overall, the more normative stance on the Tunisian revolution on which the EU ended up collectively settling sharply contrasted with the realist and exclusive approach of member states, especially the southern – and most involved – ones. The problem is that, when weighed against each other, the latter tended to take precedence in terms of visibility and ultimately undermined the former's credibility.

The international reactions to the Egyptian uprising against President Hosni Mubarak, which erupted over one month after the one in Tunisia, arguably benefited from the accelerated learning process that had just taken place. Although statements by the HR started again from the standard and mild 'call on all parties to exercise restraint' (EU 2011c), this time the EU institutions were swifter in siding with the protesters. The Foreign Affairs Council recognised 'the legitimate democratic aspirations and grievances of the Egyptian population', and called for 'the Egyptian authorities to embark on an orderly transition through a broad-based government leading to a genuine process of substantial democratic reform' less than one week after the beginning of protests (Council of the EU 2011a). HR Ashton also endeavoured to play a more visible and active role of coordination (Behr 2012b: 79). During her visit to Cairo in late February, she said that the EU stood 'ready to accompany the peaceful and orderly transition to a civilian and democratic government' (EU High Representative 2011c). Individual sanctions in the form of asset freezing and restrictive measures against key members of the Mubarak regime were adopted in March by the Council in the framework of the CFSP.

The EU's toolkit and measures announced in order to support a democratic transition in Egypt were similar in principle to those offered to Tunisia, except that the intergovernmental consensus between EU member states notably suffered from the subsequent parliamentary electoral victories of the Muslim Brotherhood's Freedom and Justice Party as well as the election of Mohammed Morsi as president in June 2012. The unprecedented empowerment of Islamist forces that occurred in the post-Arab Spring context was difficult to digest and prone to securitisation especially by southern EU member states. Conversely, the Muslim Brotherhood's leadership were keen on searching for 'Western' recognition and establishing themselves as interlocutors of both the US and the EU (Hernando de Larramendi and Fernández-Molina 2015: 263–4), as demonstrated by Morsi's prompt visit to Brussels in September 2012. EU institutions were receptive to pursuing this inclusive normalisation route and demonstrated their commitment to promote bilateral cooperation by setting up an EU–Egypt Task Force two months later. However, Morsi's constitutional declaration placing the presidency above judicial review rang alarms and led some member states and the European Parliament to call for the freezing of EU aid to Egypt. The major crisis that was to maximise dilemmas and polarise positions was the military coup with wide civilian backing that overthrew Morsi in July 2013, since supporters of both sides similarly invoked normative arguments relating to democracy and the rule of law. Even then, the EU institutions, along with member states such as the UK, Germany and Sweden, avoided purely realist stances and decried the 'military intervention' (not called a coup) in relatively strong terms. The EU representatives even tried to play a mediating role, with HR Ashton becoming the first foreign diplomat to meet the deposed Morsi in his secret detention place and the EU Special Representative for the Southern Mediterranean region, Bernardino León, attempting to broker a deal between the Muslim Brotherhood and the new incumbent military authorities (Pinfari 2013).

3.2 Civil conflicts and the intervention dilemma: Libya and Syria

Overall, in spite of an unsurprising measure of fragmentation and inconsistency, the EU's collective reactions to the Tunisian and Egyptian revolutions and regime changes included some genuine normative inputs. By contrast, the uprisings in Libya and Syria, which soon degenerated into armed civil conflicts and thus fully fell within the framework of EU crisis management, were more difficult to accommodate with democracy promotion objectives even at the rhetorical level. They particularly brought to the fore the problematic link between the ENP and EU crisis management (Koenig 2016) and the persistence of the famous 'capability–expectations gap' (Hill 1993) surrounding the EU's role as a security provider in its near abroad. Still, a crucial difference between these two cases is that the 2011 military action in Libya promoted by France and the UK – outside the EU framework – was in principle led by the liberal norms of humanitarian intervention and responsibility to protect, while responses to the war in Syria never crossed the line of realist caution.

The European response to massive violent crackdown on Libyan protesters by the regime of Colonel Muammar al-Gaddafi epitomised a singular combination of normative rationale and intergovernmental paralysis over the use of force. Two EU member states, namely France and the UK, immediately took the lead in condemning the killing of civilians and advocating a military intervention to impose a no-fly zone in order to protect them, which was eventually authorised by the United Nation Security Council Resolution 1973 in mid-March 2011. President Nicolas Sarkozy's normative u-turn was all the more striking after having defended Ben Ali and Mubarak against the tide (Echagüe, Michou and Mikail 2011: 332–3). However, this dynamic policy entrepreneurship fell short of forging – if not seeking – a substantial intra-EU consensus. Firstly, France got in before the other EU countries in unilaterally recognising Libya's National Transitional Council, the opposition force that was leading the revolt against al-Gaddafi, as the legitimate representative of the Libyan people. Secondly, when the military option started to take shape, 'no one apparently seriously considered intervention under the framework of the CSDP', which was replaced by that of NATO once again in the EU's immediate neighbourhood (Menon 2011: 75). Thirdly, the UN Security Council vote on Resolution 1973 included a much talked-about abstention by Germany, which at the time occupied a seat as a non-permanent member but decided to break ranks with the two other 'big' EU states.

In a sense, expectations that the EU would address this crisis as a primarily normative power, most notably involving humanitarian intervention, clashed with its inability to go beyond its traditional role as a civilian power (Koenig 2014). The lowest common denominator, that is, the only two areas in which there was consensus and unified EU action from the outset, were humanitarian aid and sanctions against the al-Gaddafi regime. Later on, once NATO's air strikes campaign was already underway, the Council of the EU agreed on a face-saving operation in the framework of the CSDP, EUFOR Libya, which would aim at supporting humanitarian assistance 'if requested by the UN Office for the Coordination of Humanitarian Affairs (OCHA)' (Council of the EU 2011b). The irony is that this unusual condition was never met and thus EUFOR Libya was never deployed. From the autumn of 2011 onwards, after the fall of al-Gaddafi and the termination of the NATO operation – and in an already supposedly post-conflict setting – the EU stepped up its engagement with Libya by inaugurating a full-fledged EU delegation in Tripoli and launching the EU Border Assistance Mission (EUBAM) Libya, a CSDP civilian mission aimed at supporting border control by the country's security forces with a typical liberal state-building approach. However, all of these initiatives were to be thwarted by the relapse of the civil conflict in 2014–15, when the EU's role returned to the back seat, becoming limited to supporting the UN-led peace talks (P5+5) between the Libyan factions (Koenig 2016).

In the case of Syria, despite a comparable starting point and level of regime violence, the international response to the Arab Spring uprising sharply diverged from the Libyan script and was in fact largely meant to prevent its repetition – since veto powers Russia and China, in particular, rejected the overstretching of the doctrine of the Responsibility to Protect and the exceeding of the terms of the UN Security Council resolution which had made the NATO intervention result in regime change in Tripoli. As a result, even though HR Ashton acknowledged in August 2011 'the complete loss of Bashar al-Assad's legitimacy in the eyes of the Syrian people and the necessity for him to step aside' (EU 2011i), the EU's actual response focused more than ever on the lowest common denominator consisting of humanitarian aid and targeted sanctions. These two elements constituted the civilian dimension of the EU's normative power in a situation of conflict in which the use of military instruments seemed to be excluded.

The distinctive feature of this situation was that the tightening EU sanctions agreed by the Council in the framework of the CFSP over several rounds from May 2011 onwards reached an unprecedented level: 'The EU deployed the virtual entirety of measures in the sanctions toolbox within less than a year' (Portela 2012: 2). Firstly, these included diplomatic sanctions such as the suspension of the 2008 EU–Syria draft Association Agreement (never signed) and all bilateral cooperation under the ENP. Other areas affected by EU sanctions were finances, trade, travel and transport, and arms (Boogaerts et al. 2016). However, while this comprehensive package somewhat contributed to weakening the Syrian regime during the first years of the conflict (2011–14), its overall effectiveness was qualified by the fact that al-Assad and his clique managed to adapt to such pressure without their survival being ultimately jeopardised (Seeberg 2015).

In parallel, various forms of military intervention were put on the table at different points in time by EU member states such as France and the UK, yet never under an EU (CSDP) framework. France recognised the Syrian National Council and proposed to establish a humanitarian corridor in late 2011, while both France and the UK called for a partial lifting of the arms embargo in order to deliver weapons to 'moderate' rebels in March 2013 and expressed their willingness to support the air strikes campaign against the al-Assad regime announced by the US after chemical weapons attack in Ghouta in August of the same year – which eventually never took place (Koenig 2016). Only a game-changer such as the daunting rise of the Islamic State group and its proclamation of a worldwide 'caliphate' in mid-2014 would be able to hasten US-led military airstrikes in Syrian territory with the support of an international coalition that ended up including the majority of EU member states (UK, France, Germany, Italy, Poland and Denmark initially, plus seventeen more later).

3.3 Endorsing regime continuity: Morocco, Jordan and Algeria

A final grouping of countries within the EU's southern Mediterranean neighbourhood is made up of those that witnessed domestic unrest and anti-authoritarian protests in the context of the Arab Spring but managed to preserve regime continuity thanks to constitutional reforms and other top-down political adjustments. The EU's policies towards what appeared to be its most stable southern neighbours did not enter crisis mode nor fall under EU crisis management proper; they largely stuck to 'business as usual' in the framework of the ENP and under the institutional leadership of the Commission. In terms of domestic power struggles, the EU considered that its best bet was on the side of incumbent authorities irrespective of the credibility of their commitment to democratic reforms, which reflected a predominantly realist and non-normative approach.

The EU's political endorsement of the reformist path followed by its two monarchical southern Mediterranean partners was apparent in statements by HR Ashton and Commissioner Füle. Significantly enough, in the case of Morocco, the first EU declarations in 2011 did not respond to the unprecedented pro-democracy protests organised by the so-called 20 February Movement but to King Mohammed VI's ensuing announcement of a constitutional reform, which was described as a 'qualitative leap' and a 'commitment to further democratisation' 'in line with the ambitions of the Advanced Status' (EU 2011d). The accelerated constitution drafting process launched in Rabat was accompanied by an extensive diplomatic and public relations campaign that targeted mainly the EU and key EU member states such as France, the UK and Spain. As a result, the new constitutional text that was approved by referendum in early July was commended from Brussels as a 'significant response to the legitimate aspirations of the Moroccan people' (EU 2011g). The EU Special Representative León repeatedly stated that Morocco was 'a good example that fundamental reforms can be made maintaining stability', 'as an evolution, not revolution', and described this country as a 'reference' or a 'leader' for the entire region (Fernández-Molina 2015: 146–7).

Along the same lines, one month after the first demonstrations in Jordan, the HR limited herself to praising King Abdullah II's 'political and economic reform agenda' (EU High Representative 2011b). She subsequently reiterated the EU's willingness 'to continue to support Jordan politically and economically, and in every way possible' (EU 2011f). The king's announcement of a constitutional amendment and the replacement of his prime minister under corruption allegations were similarly applauded by EU representatives as part of a 'reform path to meet the aspirations of the Jordanian people' (EU 2011h). In practical terms, the EU's overall satisfaction with stability-oriented reforms in Morocco and Jordan translated into the selection of these two countries – along with post-revolutionary Tunisia and Egypt – as front-runners for the new mid- and long-term cooperation opportunities offered as incentives by the 2011 revision of the ENP, namely the Support to Partnership, Reforms and Inclusive Growth (SPRING) financial programme ('money'), the negotiation of Deep and Comprehensive Free Trade Areas (DCFTAs) ('market') and the signing of Mobility Partnerships ('mobility'). The flagrant asymmetry between the domestic political changes witnessed in these four countries over the previous year did not prevent them from being put on an equal footing (Fernández-Molina 2016). The 'new monarchical exceptionalism' (Yom and Gause III 2012) was certainly reinforced by the EU's realist prioritisation and rewarding of stability.

On the other hand, in spite of regime continuity and stability being upheld, Algeria did not receive these first-class EU offers. Bilateral relations were relatively strengthened, yet starting from a more backward point of departure and according to the equal partnership approach that this wary and conditionality-averse neighbour had always requested from Brussels. As a novelty, the Arab Spring context, by coupling considerable domestic unrest with a new perception of regional encirclement by the Algerian regime, pushed the latter into improving its hesitant relations with the EU. After having refused to participate in the ENP for years, the authorities in Algiers suddenly agreed to start negotiating a bilateral action plan and invited an EU Election Observation Mission to monitor the parliamentary elections in May 2012. The EU, which had welcomed the lifting of the state of emergency and the political and socio-economic reforms announced by President Abdelaziz Bouteflika in mid-April 2011 (Council of the EU 2011c), responded very positively to a novel cooperative turn that seemed to increase its limited leverage on this country (Darbouche and Dennison 2011). More importantly, this rapprochement suited the European security interest in having a capable regional partner to rely on in order to face 'the new challenges of instability, poverty and arms proliferation in the Sahel region' (European Commission 2011d; Dennison 2012). Fulfilling a long-held Algerian desire, a memorandum of understanding on a Strategic Energy Partnership was concluded in mid-2013. In sum, in spite of some exceptional normatively inspired decisions – such as the EU's refusal to send another observation mission to the presidential elections of April 2014 – the EU's approach to this awkward relationship continued to be essentially shaped by a realist approach and security interests.

4 Strategic responses to the Arab Spring

Against this diverse and volatile backdrop, moving beyond crisis management to long-term planning did not seem to be an easy task for any international actor. However, the EU was impelled by its self-identity and external expectations to attempt to respond to the 'historic challenge' of the Arab Spring as both a normative and a strategic actor. In a much-quoted speech at the European Parliament in late February 2011, Commissioner Füle engaged with a previously unheard-of soul-searching exercise: 'Too many of us fell prey to the assumption that authoritarian regimes were a guarantee of stability in the region. This was not even realpolitik. It was, at best, short-termism' (European Commission 2011a). Following this admission, the EU was quick to announce what was intended to be its strategic response to the Arab Spring in March 2011. The ENP was the political framework that encompassed it, since the UfM remained largely inactive and there was no proper multilateral response (Behr 2012b: 80). The key document that embodied such expectedly thorough and long-term rethinking of EU–MENA relations was a joint communication by the European Commission and the HR entitled 'A Partnership for Democracy and Shared Prosperity with the Southern Mediterranean' (European Commission/HR 2011a). This would be complemented almost three months later by another joint communication on 'A New Response to a Changing Neighbourhood' (European Commission/HR 2011b), which reflected the results of the 2011 comprehensive revision of the ENP in all of its dimensions. In fact, the ENP review process was already underway in 2010 well before the outbreak of the Arab Spring, which calls into question the extent to which it really represented a response to the latter.

Both of these major strategic region-wide documents in the framework of the ENP explicitly embraced the EU's identity as a normative power and as having a liberal and inclusive outlook with regard to relations with the southern Mediterranean countries. The reference to 'democracy' in the title and the wording of the former communication's first overarching objective – 'democratic transformation and institution-building, with a particular focus on fundamental freedoms, constitutional reforms, reform of the judiciary and the fight against corruption' – were very telling (European Commission/HR 2011a: 3). The 'New Response' communication similarly stated that the main aim of the revised ENP was to 'provide greater support to partners engaged in building deep democracy – the kind that lasts' (European Commission/HR 2011b: 2). Both documents purported to pursue this normative horizon by means of the ENP's usual incentive-based and differentiated approach as well as greater positive conditionality ('more for more') depending on each neighbour's progress in terms of democracy and the rule of law.

The three main incentives of rewards offered to southern Mediterranean neighbours by the 'Partnership for Democracy and Shared Prosperity' were famously summarised by HR Ashton as the 'three Ms': 'money', 'market' (or 'market access') and 'mobility' (EU 2011e). 'Money' basically referred to the provision of funding according to value-based criteria through new programmes such as SPRING, the Civil Society Facility and the European Endowment for Democracy. The SPRING programme was launched in September 2011 as part of the European Neighbourhood and Partnership Instrument (ENPI) with the aim of addressing the most pressing socio-economic needs and supporting the 'transition to democracy' in southern Mediterranean countries (European Commission 2011c: 1). The allocation of funds should be based 'on an assessment of progress in building and consolidating deep and sustainable democracy and on needs' (European Commission 2011b: 7). This rationale was in line with the EU's longstanding aspiration to exercise its normative power through practices of project-funding as well as with Manner's (2002) consideration of 'transference' (exchanges of goods, trade, aid and technical assistance) as one of the procedures for the diffusion of EU values. In practice, however, the choice of the first recipients of SPRING funding – Tunisia, Egypt, Morocco and Jordan – virtually blurred the lines between countries where a genuine democratic transformation seemed to have started and the traditional 'good students' of the EU that had merely experienced continuity-oriented authoritarian reforms.

The major new 'market' incentive, which would supposedly enable the southern neighbours' gradual integration into the EU Single Market, was the offer to launch negotiations on DCFTAs made to Tunisia, Egypt, Morocco and Jordan in December 2011, when the Council approved the negotiating directives for the Commission. DCFTAs were meant to broaden and upgrade the trade provisions of the respective bilateral association agreements in two ways, namely by extending trade liberalisation to formerly uncovered areas such as services, public procurement, investment protection, competition and intellectual property rights, and reducing non-tariff barriers posed by industrial standards, technical regulations or sanitary and phytosanitary measures. In reality, the novelty of this economic instrument was qualified by two facts: (1) DCFTA negotiations with Ukraine had already been underway since 2007–8, which was supposed to be a test case for all Eastern Partnership countries; and (2) some of the core elements of DCFTAs, such as trade in services, had already been long under discussion with advanced southern partners such as Morocco (Fernández-Molina 2015: 149). The post-Arab Spring EU offer thus largely amounted to a relabelling exercise. In terms of EU international identity, DCFTA negotiations primarily embodied that of market power, yet incorporating some normative connotations as a result of the EU's deeply embedded liberal assumption of a mutually reinforcing relationship between economic (neo-)liberal reform (including trade liberalisation) and political democratisation.

As far as 'mobility' is concerned, the new offer to negotiate Mobility Partnerships in keeping with the 2011 Global Approach to Migration and Mobility reflected the EU's concern to avoid being seen as 'fortress Europe'. Mobility Partnerships are non-binding political agreements between a third country, the European Commission and some interested EU member states, which typically outline a roadmap with mid- and long-term cooperation objectives in four areas: mobility and legal migration; preventing and combating illegal migration (including border management); the migration-development nexus; and international protection of refugees and asylum-seekers. In short, the migration cooperation packages proposed to southern (and eastern) neighbours involved a well-calculated combination of inclusive and exclusive elements. While the former prevailed on paper, there was a widespread perception that the first and foremost EU concern – and the only bargaining chip for southern Mediterranean countries – was the signing of readmission agreements by the latter (including citizens of third countries or stateless persons who entered the EU from their territory). The deal could be summed up as readmission agreements in exchange for visa facilitation plus financial and technical support. Commonalities with the DCFTA offer included the limited originality of this instrument, which had already been created by the 2005 Global Approach to Migration and negotiated with most of the EU's eastern neighbours, and the choice of front-runners (Tunisia, Egypt, Morocco and Jordan). Only Egypt declined the EU offer (Carrera et al. 2012: 14). Despite some unsurprising resistance, Mobility Partnerships were eventually concluded with Morocco, Tunisia and Jordan in 2013–14, respectively. These negotiations are illustrative of the way in which 'interests and identity interlock in EU foreign policy' and 'the EU can be both normative and realist at the same time' (Limam and Del Sarto 2015: 14).

'Money', 'market' and 'mobility' were supplemented by other EU foreign policy instruments such as electoral observation. This was in line with the provision included in the 'Partnership for Democracy and Shared Prosperity' communication that 'a commitment to adequately monitored, free and fair elections should be the entry qualification for the Partnership' (European Commission/HR 2011a: 5). EU Election Observation Missions (EOMs) were deployed to monitor the Tunisian Constituent Assembly elections of October 2011, the Algerian parliamentary elections of May 2012, the Libyan General National Congress elections of July 2012, the Jordanian parliamentary elections of January 2013, the Egyptian presidential elections of May 2014 and the Tunisian parliamentary and presidential elections of October–December 2014.

5 Managing refugee inflows: back to the 'crisis' square one

Migration and border control policies would add a definitively counter-normative coda to the EU's response to the Arab Spring, especially from 2015 onwards. Regional instability, borderline chaos and the collapse of the EU's externalised controls in countries such as Tunisia and Libya had already altered long-settled irregular migration patterns and routes from North Africa to Europe, leading the EU to reframe growing crossing attempts of the Mediterranean as a 'migration crisis' as of 2011 (Jeandesboz and Pallister-Wilkins 2016). 'Tragic' shipwrecks such as that in Lampedusa in October 2013 provoked an ever-contradictory combination of humanitarian moral outrage and securitising reflexes. The external dimension of EU home affairs such as migration and asylum policies became reinforced and formalised as part of the agenda of the Foreign Affairs Council. After the drowning of hundreds of migrants in the Mediterranean in April 2015, the statements of EU institutions took a markedly normative tone and became full of references to 'EU values', 'moral duty' and common European 'responsibility': 'The EU no longer has any alibi, all the member states no longer have any alibi', said HR Federica Mogherini (EU High Representative 2015a).

Tensions between the EU's barely reconcilable discourse and practices became even more apparent when refugees fleeing the war in Syria – and unable to reach EU territory through safe routes – came to the forefront. This unprecedented refugee inflow made the EU and EU member states face the unintended consequences of an underdeveloped and ineffective Common European Asylum System (CEAS) based on the Dublin Regulation, which provides that third-country nationals can only apply for asylum in the first EU state they step on: Syrian refugees became stuck and forcibly warehoused in south-eastern European countries which were incapable of coping with the challenge. The first attempted common 'exceptional response' of the EU that was guided by normative concerns and aiming at intra-European burden-sharing was the Commission's proposal for the resettlement of 40,000 refugees from Italy and Greece, which never achieved the required intergovernmental consensus as several member states fiercely resisted the quota system. The other side of the coin was the launch of the military CSDP operation EUNAVFOR Med, which included a controversial plan to search and destroy (empty) migrant smuggling boats departing from Libya, provided that the UN Security Council and the coastal states concerned gave their consent. Still, in spite of this security component, the EU institutions' red line at that time was that 'no refugees or migrants intercepted at sea [would] be sent back against their will', as 'their rights under Geneva conventions [would] be fully honoured' (EU High Representative 2015b).

In September 2015 the global wave of emotion provoked by the viral picture of a dead Syrian child on the Turkish coast pushed the EU and EU member states to raise their normative stakes. Strong calls for EU 'solidarity' came from the Council, the HR and the Commission alike: 'If leaders do not demonstrate good will, solidarity will become an empty slogan and will be replaced by political blackmail, divisions and a new blame game' (European Council 2015). 'Only in this way we will have the possibility to face this issue, this urgency, this dramatic event, being faithful to our European values – the values of respect of human rights and solidarity' (EU High Representative 2015c). The European Commission put forward a second emergency mechanism to relocate a further 120,000 asylum seekers from Italy, Greece and Hungary, which this time for a while seemed to get closer to receiving the member states' backing. However, the Commission's efforts to play a brokering role and promote a more comprehensive package of responses to the refugee inflow – including also a permanent relocation mechanism, a common European list of safe countries of origin, measures to make return policy more effective and the external dimension of the ongoing crisis (European Commission 2015) – ended up running into the wall of EU member states' self-interest and realist tendencies.

After the failure of the Commission's relocation plan, the EU's short-lived normative turn came to an end and an undisguisedly exclusive and securitising approach prevailed. The president of the European Council, Donald Tusk, made clear that the EU's priority should be the protection of the its external borders and blurred the lines between refugees and economic migrants (Maurice 2015). This stance of the intergovernmental voice of the EU paved the way for the infamous EU–Turkey deal, reached in March 2016, which enabled the massive forced resettlement of refugees from Greece to Turkey, a country with a questionable human rights record and a non-signatory to the 1951 Refugee Convention. The combination of a crisis management framing and ultimately intergovernmental decision-making resulted in the most cynical embodiment of 'fortress Europe' ever imaginable.

6 Conclusions

In sum, this chapter has shown the duality and hybridity of the EU's reaction to the Arab Spring by comparing and contrasting crisis management and strategic responses. The bottom line is that the former have been more dominated by intergovernmental decision-making and realist and exclusive approaches, while the latter have been presented on paper as those of a would-be normative, liberal and inclusive supranational actor. However, an even more problematic conclusion is that the strategic responses contained significant inner contradictions and a noteworthy lack of innovation that ultimately led to the opposite effects of that intended. Observers have related this counter-intuitive absence of policy change with the widespread diagnosis of failure of the ENP as a 'structural foreign policy' (Keukeleire and Delreux 2014: 28), which is in turn explained by: firstly, the decline of region-building and growing bilateralisation and differentiation of the EU's relations with southern Mediterranean countries (Bicchi 2014); secondly, the non-consideration of alternatives to utilitarian and rational-choice instruments of EU external influence (incentives, conditionality and differentiation) in spite of acknowledgment of their limitations; thirdly, the waning of the EU's own relevance in this region in the competition with other increasingly influential external actors such as the Gulf states, Russia and China; fourthly, the EU's self-absorption in its own economic and identity crisis; and fifthly, a return among EU member states to an emphasis on national perspectives. More constructivist and critical arguments about the EU's inner resistance to change highlight the role of prejudices embedded in the EU actors' understandings of the MENA region (Pace 2014), their unquestioned and reductionist (neo-)liberal conception of 'democracy' (Teti 2012; Teti et al. 2013) and the paralysing effects of the EU's obsession with coherence (Natorski 2015).

This chapter's assessment of the EU's strategic responses to the Arab Spring is also mixed in terms of the contrast between realist/exclusive and liberal/inclusive elements. The selection of front-running southern Mediterranean countries for the allegedly new EU offers of 'money' (SPRING), 'market' (DCFTAs) and 'mobility' (Mobility Partnerships) revealed a non-normative stability bias and a tendency to confuse the closeness of a country's ties with the EU with its willingness for domestic reform (Behr 2012a: 21). In addition, long-term migration policies also demonstrated a barely disguised predominance of exclusive tendencies, and an obsession with readmission over any proper global approach. More generally, and critically, the dichotomy between crisis management and strategic foreign policy needs to be qualified so as not to obscure structural factors, the entanglement between crisis and routine practices – the former often building on the latter – and the role of 'crises' in consolidating new routine practices (Jeandesboz and Pallister-Wilkins 2016).

Table 13.1 EU responses to the Arab Spring events in seven countries

				Tunisia	Egypt
Pre-existing bilateral framework				Association Agreement (1995/1998), ENP Action Plan (2005)	Association Agreement (2001/2004), ENP Action Plan (2007)
Crisis/conflict management		Diplomatic instruments (CFSP)	Traditional diplomacy	Statements (2011)	Restraint in use of force → support for democratic transition	Restraint in use of force → support for democratic transition
			Mediation		Mediation Muslim Brotherhood/ al-Sisi
			Support to international organisations		
			Sanctions	Asset freeze	Asset freeze, embargo on equipment used for internal repression
		Military instruments	CSDP missions		
		Humanitarian aid			
Political dialogue & recognition				Task Force (2011)	Task Force (2012)
Strategic responses/ European Neighbourhood Policy (ENP)	Contractual relations/ ENP Action Plans			New ENP Action Plan, Privileged Partnership (2012)	
	Economic instruments		Financial assistance ('money')	SPRING	SPRING
			Trade relations ('market')	Negotiations DCFTA	Offer for negotiation of DCFTA
	Others		Mobility	Mobility Partnership (2014)	Offer of Mobility Partnership (declined)
			Electoral observation (EU EOMs)	Constituent Assembly, Oct 2011; parliamentary, Oct 2014; presidential, Nov–Dec 2014	Presidential, May 2014

Source: prepared by the author

Morocco	Jordan	Algeria	Libya	Syria
Association Agreement (1996/2000), ENP Action Plan (2005), Advanced Status (2008)	Association Agreement (1997/2002), ENP Action Plan (2005)	Association Agreement (2002/2005)	No contractual framework, negotiations Framework Agreement (2008–11)	Cooperation Agreement (1978), draft Association Agreement (2008–)
Support for constitutional reform and referendum	Support for constitutional amendment and new PM	Support for lifting of state of emergency and political and socio-economic reforms	Strong condemnation of use of force against civilians, support for UNSC resolutions	Call for al-Assad to step aside
			EU Special Envoy for Libya (2014)	
			Support for UN-led peace talks (P5+5)	Support Joint Special Representative UNSG & Arab League
			Asset freeze, service ban, travel ban, arms ban, suspension of negotiations of Framework Agreement	Asset freeze, investment ban in energy sector, ban on financial assistance to government, trade restrictions, travel ban, arms ban, suspension of bilateral cooperation, freezing of draft Association Agreement
			EUFOR Libya (2011, not deployed), EUBAM Libya (2013), EUNAVFOR Med (2015)	
	Humanitarian aid for Syrian refugees		Humanitarian aid for displaced persons	Humanitarian aid for refugees
	Task Force (2012)		Opening EU Delegation (2011), joining UfM as observer (2013)	Recognition of opposition forces (2012)
New ENP Action Plan (2013)	Protocol to EU–Jordan Association Agreement	Negotiations ENP Action Plan (2012–), MoU Strategic Energy Partnership (2012)		
SPRING	SPRING			
Negotiations DCFTA (2013–), agricultural trade agreement (2012)	Preparatory process for negotiations DCFTA			
Mobility Partnership (2013)	Mobility Partnership (2014)			
	Parliamentary, Jan 2013	Parliamentary, May 2012	General National Congress, July 2012	

Note

1. This chapter draws also on part of the results of the research project 'The International Dimension of Political Transformations in the Arab World' (CSO2014-52998-C3-3-P).

References

Adler, Emanuel, Federica Bicchi, Beverly Crawford and Raffaella A. del Sarto (eds) (2006), *The Convergence of Civilizations: Constructing a Mediterranean Region*, Toronto: University of Toronto Press.

Attinà, Fulvio (2003), 'The Euro-Mediterranean partnership assessed: the realist and liberal views', *European Foreign Affairs Review*, 8 (2): 181–99.

Behr, Timo (2012a), *After the Revolution: the EU and the Arab Transition*, Paris: Notre Europe.

Behr, Timo (2012b), 'European Union's Mediterranean policies after the Arab Spring: can the leopard change its spots?', *Amsterdam Law Forum*, 4 (2): 76–88.

Behr, Timo and Teija Tiilikainen (eds) (2015), *Northern Europe and the Making of the EU's Mediterranean and Middle East Policies*, Farnham/Burlington, VT: Ashgate.

Bicchi, Federica (2007), *European Foreign Policy Making toward the Mediterranean*, New York: Palgrave.

Bicchi, Federica (2014), '"Lost in Transition": EU foreign policy and the European Neighbourhood Policy post-Arab Spring', *L'Europe en Formation*, 371: 26–40.

Biscop, Sven, Rosa Balfour and Michael Emerson (2012), *An Arab Springboard for EU Foreign Policy?*, Brussels/Ghent: Egmont/Academia Press.

Boogaerts, Andreas, Clara Portela and Edith Drieskens (2016), 'One swallow does not make spring: a critical juncture perspective on the EU sanctions in response to the Arab Spring', *Mediterranean Politics*, 21 (2): 205–25.

Bretherton, Charlotte and John Vogler (2006), *The European Union as a Global Actor*, Abingdon/New York: Routledge.

Brown, L. Carl (1984), *International Politics in the Middle East: Old Rules, Dangerous Game*, Princeton: Princeton University Press.

Carrera, Sergio, Leonhard Den Hertog and Joanna Parkin (2012) *EU Migration Policy in the Wake of the Arab Spring: What Prospects for EU-Southern Mediterranean Relations?*, Centre for European Policy Studies/MEDPRO.

Cavatorta, Francesco and Paola Rivetti (2014), 'EU–MENA relations from the Barcelona process to the Arab uprisings: a new research agenda', *Journal of European Integration*, 36 (6): 619–25.

Costalli, Stefano (2009), 'Power over the sea: the relevance of neoclassical realism to Euro-Mediterranean relations', *Mediterranean Politics*, 14 (3): 323–42.

Council of the EU (2011a), *Press Release. 3065th Council Meeting. Foreign Affairs*, 31 January.

Council of the EU (2011b), *Council Decides on EU Military Operation in Support of Humanitarian Assistance Operations in Libya*, 1 April.

Council of the EU (2011c), *Sixième Session du Conseil d'Association UE-Algérie. Déclaration de l'Union Européenne*, 20 June.

Damro, Chad (2012), 'Market power Europe', *Journal of European Public Policy*, 19 (5): 682–99.

Darbouche, Hakim and Susi Dennison (2011), *A 'Reset' with Algeria: the Russia to the EU's South*, European Council on Foreign Relations.

Dennison, Susi (2012), *The EU, Algeria and the Northern Mali Question*, European Council on Foreign Relations.

Duchêne, François (1972), 'Europe's role in world peace', in Richard Mayne (ed.), *Europe Tomorrow: Sixteen Europeans Look Ahead*, London: Fontana/Collins, pp. 32–47.

Echagüe, Ana, Hélène Michou and Barah Mikail (2011), 'Europe and the Arab uprisings: EU vision versus member state action', *Mediterranean Politics*, 16 (2): 329–35.

EU (2011a), *Statement by EU High Representative Catherine Ashton and European Commissioner for Enlargement Štefan Füle on the Situation in Tunisia*, 10 January.

EU (2011b), *Joint Statement by EU High Representative Catherine Ashton and Commissioner Štefan Füle on the Events on Tunisia*, 14 January.

EU (2011c), *Statement by the EU High Representative Catherine Ashton on the Events in Egypt*, 27 January.

EU (2011d), *Joint Statement by EU High Representative Catherine Ashton and Commissioner Štefan Füle on Morocco's Future Constitutional Reform*, 10 March.

EU (2011e), *Remarks by EU High Representative Catherine Ashton on Arrival to the Extraordinary European Council*, 11 March.

EU (2011f), *Remarks by HR Catherine Ashton after her Meeting with Minister of Foreign Affairs of Jordan, H. E. Mr Nasser Judeh*, 16 June.

EU (2011g), *Joint Statement by High Representative Catherine Ashton and Commissioner Štefan Füle on the Referendum on the New Constitution in Morocco*, 2 July.

EU (2011h), *Statement by High Representative Catherine Ashton on the Constitutional Amendment in Jordan*, 17 August.

EU (2011i), *Declaration by the High Representative, Catherine Ashton, on Behalf of the European Union on EU Action Following the Escalation of Violent Repression in Syria*, 18 August.

EU High Representative (2011a), *Remarks by the High Representative/Vice-president Catherine Ashton at the End of her Visit to Tunisia*, 14 February.

EU High Representative (2011b), *Remarks by the EU High Representative Catherine Ashton during her Visit to Jordan*, 16 February.

EU High Representative (2011c), *Remarks by Catherine Ashton, EU High Representative for Foreign Affairs and Security Policy and Vice-president of the European Commission, at the End of her Visit to Egypt*, 22 February.

EU High Representative (2015a), *Remarks by High Representative/Vice-president Federica Mogherini upon Arrival at the Foreign Affairs Council*, 20 April.

EU High Representative (2015b), *Statement by High Representative of the European Union for Foreign Affairs and Security Policy, Ms Federica Mogherini, at the Security Council Briefing on Cooperation between the UN and Regional and Sub-regional Organizations in Maintaining International Peace and Security*, 11 May.

EU High Representative (2015c), *Remarks by High Representative/Vice-president Federica Mogherini following the Informal Meeting of the EU Foreign Ministers, Gymnich*, 5 September.

European Commission (2011a), *Speech on the Recent Events in North Africa by Štefan Füle, European Commissioner for Enlargement and Neighbourhood Policy*, 28 February.

European Commission (2011b), *Action Fiche for the Southern Neighbourhood Region Programme Support for Partnership, Reforms and Inclusive Growth (SPRING)*, 26 September.

European Commission (2011c), *EU Response to the Arab Spring: the SPRING Programme*, 27 September.

European Commission (2011d), *Statement by Commissioner Štefan Füle following his Meeting with Abdelkader Messahel, Deputy Foreign Minister of Algeria*, 8 December.

European Commission (2015) *Refugee Crisis: European Commission Takes Decisive Action*, 9 September.

European Commission/HR (2011a), *Joint Communication: a Partnership for Democracy and Shared Prosperity with the Southern Mediterranean*, COM(2011) 200 final, 8 March.

European Commission/HR (2011b), *Joint Communication: a New Response to a Changing Neighbourhood*, COM(2011) 303 final, 25 May.

European Council (2015), *Remarks by President Donald Tusk before his Meeting with Prime Minister of Hungary Viktor Orbán*, 3 September.

Fawcett, Louise (ed.) (2013), *International Relations of the Middle East*, Oxford: Oxford University Press.

Fernández-Molina, Irene (2015), *Moroccan Foreign Policy under Mohammed VI, 1999–2014*, Abingdon/New York: Routledge.

Fernández-Molina, Irene (2016), 'EU–Maghreb relations', in Tobias Schumacher, Andreas Marchetti and Thomas Demmelhuber (eds), *The Routledge Handbook on the European Neighbourhood Policy*, Abingdon/New York: Routledge.

Fisher Onar, Nora and Kalypso Nicolaïdis (2013), 'The decentring agenda: Europe as a post-colonial power', Cooperation and Conflict, 48 (2): 283–303.

Fürtig, Henner (ed.) (2014), *Regional Powers in the Middle East: New Constellations after the Arab Revolts*, New York: Palgrave Macmillan.

Galtung, Johan (1973), *The European Community: a Superpower in the Making*, London: Allen and Unwin.

Hernando de Larramendi, Miguel and Irene Fernández-Molina (2015), 'The evolving foreign policies of North African states (2011–2014): new trends in constraints, political processes and behavior', in Yahia H. Zoubir and Gregory White (eds), *North African Politics: Change and Continuity*, Abingdon/New York: Routledge, pp. 245–76.

Hill, Christopher (1993), 'The capability–expectations gap, or conceptualizing Europe's international role', Journal of Common Market Studies, 31 (3): 305–28.

Hinnebusch, Raymond (2015a), *The International Relations of the Middle East*, Manchester: Manchester University Press.

Hinnebusch, Raymond (2015b), 'Conclusion: agency, context and emergent post-uprising regimes', Democratization, 22 (2): 358–74.

Horst, Jakob, Annette Jünemann and Delf Rothe (eds) (2013), *Euro-Mediterranean Relations after the Arab Spring: Persistence in Times of Change*, Farnham/Burlington, VT: Ashgate.

Jeandesboz, Julien and Polly Pallister-Wilkins (2016), 'Crisis, routine, consolidation: the politics of the Mediterranean migration crisis', Mediterranean Politics, 21 (2): 316–20.

Kallander, Amy A. (2013), '"Friends of Tunisia": French economic and diplomatic support of Tunisian authoritarianism', in Nouri Gana (ed.), *The Making of the Tunisian Revolution: Contexts, Architects, Prospects*, Edinburgh: Edinburgh University Press, pp. 103–24.

Keukeleire, Stephan and Tom Delreux (2014), *The Foreign Policy of the European Union*, New York: Palgrave Macmillan.

Koenig, Nicole (2014), 'Between conflict management and role conflict: the EU in the Libyan Crisis', European Security, 23 (3): 250–69.

Koenig, Nicole (2016), 'The EU in Libya and Syria: at the Crossroads of ENP and crisis management', in Tobias Schumacher, Andreas Marchetti and Thomas Demmelhuber (eds), *The Routledge Handbook on the European Neighbourhood Policy*, Abingdon/New York: Routledge.

Lannon, E. (2012), *The Responses of the European Union to the Changes in its Neighbourhood*, Euromed Survey 2011, Euro-Mediterranean Policies and the Arab Spring. Available at

<http://www.iemed.org/publicacions/historic-depublicacions/enquesta-euromed/euromed-survey-2011/qua_rep8_lannon.pdf> (last accessed 6 June 2016).

Limam, Mohamed and Raffaella A. Del Sarto (2015), *Periphery under Pressure: Morocco, Tunisia and the European Union's Mobility Partnership on Migration*, European University Institute/Robert Schuman Centre for Advanced Studies.

Manners, Ian (2002), 'Normative power Europe: a contradiction in terms?', *Journal of Common Market Studies*, 40 (2): 235–58.

Mason, Robert (ed.) (2014), *The International Politics of the Arab Spring: Popular Unrest and Foreign Policy*, New York: Palgrave Macmillan.

Maurice, Eric (2015), 'Tusk: "Wave of migrants too big not to be stopped"', *EU Observer*, 3 December.

Menon, Anand (2011), 'European defence policy from Lisbon to Libya', *Survival*, 53 (3): 75–90.

Natorski, Michal (2015), 'Epistemic (un)certainty in times of crisis: the role of coherence as a social convention in the European Neighbourhood Policy after the Arab Spring', *European Journal of International Relations*, 14 (2): 195–230.

Pace, Michelle (2014), 'The EU's interpretation of the "Arab uprisings": understanding the different visions about democratic change in EU–MENA relations', *Journal of Common Market Studies*, 52 (5): 969–84.

Peters, Joel (ed.) (2012), *The European Union and the Arab Spring: Promoting Democracy and Human Rights in the Middle East*, Maryland and Plymouth: Lexington Books.

Pinfari, Marco (2013), 'The EU, Egypt and Morsi's rise and fall: "strategic patience" and its discontents', *Mediterranean Politics*, 18 (3): 460–6.

Portela, Clara (2012), *The EU's Sanctions against Syria: Conflict Management by Other Means*, Egmont Royal Institute for International Relations, Egmont Security Policy Brief 38.

Ryan, Curtis R. (2014), 'Inter-Arab relations and the regional system', in Marc Lynch (ed.), *The Arab Uprisings Explained: New Contentious Politics in the Middle East*, New York: Columbia University Press, pp. 110–23.

Seeberg, Peter (2015), 'The EU and the Syrian crisis: the use of sanctions and the regime's strategy for survival', *Mediterranean Politics*, 20 (1): 18–35.

Smith, Karen E. (2014), *European Union Foreign Policy in a Changing World*, Cambridge: Polity.

Teti, Andrea (2012), 'The EU's first response to the "Arab Spring": a critical discourse analysis of the Partnership for Democracy and Shared Prosperity', *Mediterranean Politics*, 17 (3): 266–84.

Teti, Andrea, Darcy Thompson and Christopher Noble (2013), 'EU democracy assistance discourse in its "new response to a changing Neighbourhood"', *Democracy and Security*, 9 (1–2): 61–79.

Van Hüllen, Vera (2015), *EU Democracy Promotion and the Arab Spring: International Cooperation and Authoritarianism*, New York: Palgrave Macmillan.

Whitman, Richard G. and Ana E. Juncos (2012), 'The Arab Spring, the Eurozone crisis and the Neighbourhood: a region in flux', *Journal of Common Market Studies*, 50: 147–61.

Whitman, Richard G. and Stefan Wolff (eds) (2012), *The European Union as a Global Conflict Manager*, Abingdon and New York: Routledge.

Yom, Sean (2015) 'The Arab Spring: one region, several puzzles, and many explanations', *Government and Opposition*, 50 (4): 682–704.

Yom, Sean L. and F. Gregory Gause III (2012), 'Resilient royals: how Arab monarchies hang on', *Journal of Democracy*, 23 (4): 74–88.

Chapter 14

The foreign policy of the United States following the Arab Spring

Juan Tovar

1 Introduction

This chapter aims to analyse President Barack Obama's foreign policy in the Middle East and North Africa (MENA) region. Specifically, it responds to the following questions: (1) Does the Obama administration have a coherent doctrine or strategy towards the region? (2) What place does the MENA region occupy in the list of foreign policy priorities of President Obama? (3) How should the regional policy of President Obama, who now faces his final period as president of the United States, be assessed?

The structure of this chapter addresses these questions. The next section focuses on the discourse and key strategic documents of the Obama administration. The purpose is to identify the place that the MENA region has in the order of priorities of his foreign policy. The following section analyses the foreign policy of the North American power towards some of the states affected by the Arab Spring. It then goes on to analyse the participation of the US in various conflicts that have marked this change process before exploring the question of the nuclear agreement with Iran and its effects on Israel, which is one of the main allies of the US in the region. The final section pulls together the conclusions.

2 The MENA region in US foreign policy

The 'Arab Spring' produced enormous transformations that have affected not only the regimes that make up the region, but also the regional status quo that had prevailed for decades, as well as the international relations of an area that has been strategically relevant for the US since the time of Presidents Eisenhower and Carter. This process has forced the Obama administration to define its position. It has mostly adapted to events by varying its policy in function of the strategic interests at play, without completely ignoring the values and ideals considered key to the administration. These values and ideals are defended by ideological groups such as the liberal interventionists and neoconservatives and respond to foreign policy traditions such as Wilsonian idealism (Mead 2002: 1–29; Smith 2008: 66–74; Tovar 2014: 325–48; Vaisse 2010: 1–20; Walt 2011) that had so much influence over the regional policy of Obama's immediate predecessor with the Freedom Agenda and the Iraq War (Rice 2005; Traub 2008; Packer 2005; Haass 2010; Mann 2004).[1]

Previous to the 'Arab Spring' Obama's key objectives had focused on: the need to withdraw from Iraq; the anti-terrorist fight against al-Qaeda (marked by the actions of special forces and drone attacks); successive attempts to disuade Iran from its nuclear programme and; attempts by the US president to distance himself from the foreign policy of his predecessor. In fact, President Obama initiated a reconciliation process with the Arab and even Islamic world, as can be seen in strategic documents such as the 2010 National Security Strategy and – particularly – in the famous Cairo speech of 4 June 2009. In this speech the US president returned again to some of the key aspects of his inaugural address in relation to regional adversaries such as Iran, revealing to be receptive to an agreement. He also expressed his wish to conclude a fair peace deal between the Israelis and Palestinians and distance himself from President George W. Bush's policies of democratic expansion, while arguing for the compatibility of Islam with democracy and human rights. On the other hand, he showed himself to be against the imposition of any form of government. Additionally, he talked about the need to combat terrorism.[2]

The 2010 National Security Strategy specifically cited Israel as an ally of the US, reaffirming American commitment to its security. It also mentions Saudi Arabia, Egypt and even Jordan as key allies, as well as the Gulf Cooperation Council as a relevant regional organisation with which it can cooperate. In the sphere of values and ideals, the strategy includes the will of the US to pressure states in the region to carry out political reforms and defend rights, such as that of freedom of speech, association and demonstration. It also emphasises support to individuals and to that part of the civil society that seeks to defend those rights. The strategy's most specific challenges stress the need to oblige states, such as Iran, to: fulfil their international obligations and to strengthen the Non-Proliferation Nuclear Treaty; fight against al-Qaeda; transition Iraq towards a 'sovereign and responsible' state – including the withdrawal of troops; strengthen Iraq's civil capacities and create long-term associations between the authorities and the people; and obtain a solution based on the two-state system to resolve the conflict between the Israelis and Palestinians. These objectives would also be brought together and firmed up in the Quadrennial Defense

Review 2010, with the important addition of rebalancing US presence in the region in line with the above, without damaging regional feelings. Few of these objectives would finally be met.[3]

Furthermore, in this context it is worth emphasising the growing importance granted to the well known 'pivot' to the Pacific, which some administration decision-makers, such as Secretary of State Hillary Clinton and the national security adviser Tom Donilon, argued was necessary for world order as a consequence of China's ascent.[4] However, the series of uprisings that occured in key MENA states modified these plans, obliging the US to focus again its attention on an increasingly convulsed region.

The speech of President Obama on 19 May 2011 offered a more intimate vision to that of his immediate predecessors, by arguing for the compatibility of values such as democracy and human rights, and for the population of countries undergoing a process of change to show that the US is on their side and not defending a status quo that he defines as 'unsustainable'. Furthermore, Obama distinguished countries such as Tunisia or Egypt from those in which regimes recurred to the use of force, such as Libya – arguing that 'had we not acted along with our NATO allies and regional coalition partners, thousands would have been killed' – or Syria. On the other hand, he proved to be more understanding towards Bahrain's government in its legitimate defence of the rule of law and in preventing Iran taking advantage of an unstable situation.[5]

Taken together, small advances in the democratisation of states such as Egypt, Yemen, Libya and Syria – altogether with growing regional instability – obliged the US to modify its views. In his speech to the United Nations on 25 September 2013, the vision that the US president offered was now much more pessimistic than in the past. After renouncing military intervention in Syria because of the alleged use of chemical weapons, he moved to a policy founded on a more limited presence and in defence of key strategic interests, acknowledging failures in the Libyan intervention of 2011. If it is true to say that Obama continued to defend values such as democracy and human rights, he was also much more sceptical about what the US could achieve in these processes of change when acting unilaterally. Consequently, he stressed four key objectives: to prevent aggression of external powers in the region; to assure the free flow of energy; to dismantle terrorist cells in the region; and to prevent the use or proliferation of weapons of mass destruction.[6]

US strategic documents increasingly reflected the challenge of the deteriorating regional situation and the rise of the self-proclaimed Islamic State (IS). If both in the Strategic Defense Guidance 2012 and in the Quadrennial Defense Review 2014, the Asia–Pacific region and the 'pivot' still appeared to have a pre-eminent place, this latter document furthermore warned about the possible risks of the influence of the Iranian nuclear plan, expressing the evident danger associated with terrorism that the state situation in Libya and, especially, Syria represented as a 'pole of attraction for global jihad'.[7] This stance would be expressed in a much more direct way in the National Security Strategy 2015, which drew together some of the key problems emanating from the Arab Spring such as: competition between the Sunnis and Shiites; US strategy in the fight against IS; the conflict in Yemen; and the risks for the success of the Tunisian transition.[8]

The evolution in the administration's discourse and strategic documents offer a first snapshot in response to the questions posed above, which, however, should be contrasted with the actual foreign policy actions that we shall analyse in the following sections.

3 The position of the Obama administration towards the Arab Spring: the cases of Tunisia, Egypt and Yemen

In order to understand the US stance, as well as its diverse reaction to events in various states, it is first necessary to analyse the interests at play when examining its statements. In the Tunisian case, for example, because of the low level of US interest in the country and influence on the government, support for the changes came quite promptly and already, by January 2011, there was condemnation expressed at the repression exercised by the regime. Following Zine al-Abidine Ben Ali's exit, and due to the relative instability that Tunisia had recently experienced, the US conceded aid. The US$610 million dedicated to various ongoing programmes is merely of symbolic and political nature (Arieff and Humud 2015: 15–17). Nonetheless, given the later deterioration of the transition process in other countries, Tunisia has been praised as a model of emerging democracy in the region by President Obama. In fact, in a speech together with former president Mohamed Beji Caïd Essebsi – after recognising some common interests such as the fight against terrorism and the need to stabilise Libya – Obama highlighted his intention to designate the country as one of the leading US non-NATO allies.[9]

The case of Egypt is very different. The pressure from the youths who gathered in Tahrir Square and who put the Mubarak regime up against the ropes led to a wider debate about the position the US should take. It should not be forgotten that since the Camp David Agreement in 1978, Egypt has been an outstanding ally of the US in the region and a guarantor of stability in relations with Israel. Furthermore, it is worth emphasising that the military and economic aid offered to the Egyptian army by the US had greater influence and gave more capacity of maneouvre in Egypt than in Tunisia. In fact, Mubarak's role is specifically mentioned by President George W. H. Bush and his national security adviser, Brent Scowcroft, in their memoirs, in establishing a coalition that would eventually expel the Iraqi troops from Kuwait in the context of the Gulf War (Bush and Scowcroft 1998: 61).

With these antecedents it is not surprising that an internal debate was generated that led to the division of the administration into two groups, one composed of the most veteran members of the administration, such as Clinton, Gates and Biden, who favoured a more cautious approach, while younger advisers argued for supporting the movement for democratic change. In this context, some leading US allies such as Israel and especially Saudi Arabia were totally against allowing Mubarak to fall. Finally, the position of the latter group prevailed and the US president appealed for a peaceful and orderly transition that should start 'now', smoothing the road for the Egyptian army to withdraw support from its old *ra'is* (president)[10] (Mann 2012: 264–69).

From that moment on, events would make the US relationship with Egypt much more complex. The first Egyptian presidential elections would shortly afterwards lead to a period of transition headed by Marshall Tantawi's military junta, and then to the victory of Mohammed Morsi – who was a candidate of the Freedom and Justice Party, linked to the Muslim Brotherhood – in the 2012 presidential elections. Egypt's relationship with the US became increasingly difficult throughout this period, as the US reaction to the assault on the Israeli embassy in Cairo demonstrated. This attack was carried out by protesters who had previously demonstrated against the slowness of the military junta's democratic changes. Moreover, in a September 2012 interview, Obama said about President Morsi's government: 'I don't think we would consider them an ally, but we don't consider them an enemy' – something that was unthinkable in the case of Mubarak.[11]

America's position after the *coup d'état* of July 2013 that brought down Morsi, and the assumption of power by Abdel Fattah al-Sisi, was not at all simple, as it was obliged to choose between the ideals that it extolled and US key strategic interests in Egypt. Following these events greater pragmatism can be observed by the US in the release, with certain qualifications, of US$3 billion that is traditionally granted to the Egyptian army, which was not wholly delivered in 2013 as a result of the coup (Wittes 2015). This pragmatism would also lead Secretary of State John Kerry to visit the Egyptian capital on three occasions – November 2013, June 2014 and August 2015 – and offer recognition to the government. However, the secretary of state continued to express his reservations on matters of human rights and state security, particularly in the Sinai region.[12]

In the short term the US relationship with Egypt clearly seems destined to take different turns marked by a preference for a democratic government that respects human rights on the one hand, but also by the magnitude of the strategic interests at play, such as: the fight against terrorism; the support that regional allies like Saudi Arabia and the United Arab Emirates (UAE) give to the Egyptian government; the rapprochement of powers such as Russia or China to Egypt; and the limited US capacity to influence the development of events in Egyptian policy after the al-Sisi coup.[13]

The cases of Bahrain or Yemen reflected a different US position to that of Egypt or Libya, because Obama accepted Saudi Arabia's justificatory argument for intervention in Bahrain, and the legitimate interest of the al-Khalifa family in protecting the state of law against the theoretical Iranian threat, as expressed in his speech of May 2011. It is also worth highlighting the support, although reluctant, of the US for Saudi actions in Yemen against the Houthi minority, after having pushed hard and participated in long negotiations in 2011 for the removal of President Ali Abdullah Saleh. In both cases the security interest, the base of the fifth fleet in Bahrain, the anti-terrorist fight, the fragility of the state in Yemen, and the deteriorating relationship with their Saudi allies, explain the US posture.[14]

4 The armed conflicts of the Arab Spring: Libya, Iraq and Syria

Some of the most significant protests that took place during the Arab Spring were the armed conflicts that emerged from the resistance to political change of some autocratic regimes, such as those of Libya or Syria. To these it is worth adding the case of Iraq, which is undergoing a fragile process of state building. In each of these cases the US has seen itself obliged to intervene to a greater or lesser degree without solving the problems generated.

The first of these conflicts was in Libya that constitutes, to date, the first and only uninherited military intervention undertaken in a direct way by the US administration. Following the start of the protests in Libya, their leader Muammar al Gaddafi began a campaign of repression against his opponents, accompanied by verbal statements that made the Libyan rebels fear a possible genocide, as the opposition appeared to be at the point of being defeated by the advance of the Libyan army towards Benghazi, a key stronghold in the uprising. At that moment various European leaders such as David Cameron and Nicolas Sarkozy – the latter influenced by the writer Bernard-Henri Lévy, who would become a nexus with the Libyan opposition – requested in various private messages and public statements to President Obama his participation in the establishment of a no-fly zone. These leaders reminded Obama of the effort made by the British and French armies in Afghanistan. The goal aimed by Cameron and Sarkozy was to put an end to the human rights abuses of the Libyan regime (Mann 2012: XI; Clinton 2014: 368–9).

The internal process of US decision-making presented, in the case of Libya, various specificities that distinguish it from other crises that the US administration has faced. The secretaries of state and defence, Hillary Clinton and Robert Gates, had chosen to collaborate since they joined the administration – uniting forces in the administration's decision-making processes – in order to strengthen their position (Gates 2014: 283; Clinton 2014: 24–5). In the case of Libya, Hillary Clinton aligned herself with the US ambassador at the UN, Susan Rice, and with the special assistant to the president and senior director running the Office of Multilateral Affairs and Human Rights at the National Security Council, Samantha Power, in support of intervention. Robert Gates, on the other hand, aligned himself with Vice-president Joseph Biden, the national security adviser Donilon and the adviser to the president on terrorism questions, John Brennan. Biden, Donilon and Brennan argued for prudence, as they saw the US being immersed in another military intervention in an Arab state and warned that the Libyan rebels may have links with al-Qaeda. The support given to the idea of military intervention in Libya by the Arab League and the increasing likelihood of obtaining a resolution from the UN Security Council to authorise a no-fly zone, meant that the US president opted for intervention. President Obama approved a US intervention of short duration – 'days, not weeks' – leaving greater visibility to the US' European allies (Mann 2012: 281–301). The intervention in Libya gave rise to an unfortunate expression of debated origin: 'leading from behind', that crystallised the Obama opposition's criticism to his foreign policy lack of leadership on international issues (Rogin 2011).[15]

When Robert Gates, the secretary of defence, learned about the president's final decision to intervene in Libya he disagreed, as he confirmed in his memoirs, and confided to his staff that he had considered resigning over the Libya issue. He told them he had decided not to leave because he was so close to the end of his tenure anyway; 'it would just look petulant', he said (Gates 2014: 522). Gates would take advantage in his departing speech to criticise Europe's low level of commitment in defence expenditure and its poor performance throughout the intervention.[16]

When justifying the decision to intervene in Libya, the US president employed two arguments: the first was the need to prevent a massacre of the opposition if al-Gaddafi's army arrived in Benghazi – arguing that the fact that one cannot intervene in all cases does not mean that one cannot intervene in Libya; and the second to prevent other dictators, who had the same problems as the Libyan leader, opting for the use of force to maintain power. In any case, on 17 March 2011, the vote on the UN Security Council Resolution to establish a no-fly zone in Libya was approved with five abstentions – Brazil, Russia, India, China and Germany – and a campaign of bombardment quickly began that in the end would not restrict itself to the area of the no-fly zone, sheltering under the concept of 'all necessary means'. This intervention ended by provoking regime change, which included the violent death of al-Gaddafi in October 2011. According to Mann (2012: XII–XIII), the decision to go beyond the no-fly zone was taken in a direct way by the US president, when faced with the insufficiency of the strategy to finish with the regime's human rights abuses. The use of force in Libya was criticised by some emerging powers, especially Russia and China, which questioned the concept of 'Responsibility to Protect' – a doctrine that has not been employed since that time. The action in Libya needs to be explained, in fact, because a similar intervention did not take place in Syria.[17]

Following the Libyan intervention, and in contrast to what occured in other cases, such as Afghanistan and Iraq, there was no externally imposed state-building process. The country remained in the hands of various militias and governments that were too fragile to restore order, with the well-known consequences for security, migration and energy, the growing presence of IS, and the destabilisation of other states in the region, such as Mali. Additionally, the US ambassador to Libya, Christopher Stevens, was murdered in the course of a visit to Benghazi by a group of Libyan extremists on 11 September 2012. This act was condemned by President Obama, who then withdrew diplomatic personnel from Libya, reinforced the security of US diplomatic legations abroad, announced the opening of an investigation into the attack, and sent in troops. Furthermore, Secretary of State Hillary Clinton's management of the crisis was questioned during the 2015 electoral campaign. It also meant that Susan Rice was not appointed as secretary of state, due to the controversy generated by her remark characterising the origins of the Benghazi events as the result of 'spontaneous protests' in response to the video of the American pastor Terry Jones burning the Qur'an (Clinton 2014: 382–415). Libya, currently divided in two governments, supported by different militias and by other regional powers such as Egypt and the UAE in the latter case, faces some uncertain negotiations in order to form a united government. As a consequence, some analysts have described the intervention in Libya as 'Obama's Libya debacle' (Kuperman 2015: 66–77). The US president himself has recognised its failures in his speeches to the UN in September 2013, 2015 and in an interview in *The Atlantic* in April 2016, which have notoriously contributed to his pessimistic vision about the situation in the Middle East. In his own words: 'Libya is a mess' (Goldberg 2016).[18]

It is important to highlight in this respect that the growing presence of IS in Libya and particularly around Sirte represents a potential risk that could justify a new international intervention. In fact, the US bombarded an IS camp in Libya and eliminated one of its leaders in November 2015. This could be an indicator of similar actions to come, which introduces enormous uncertainties over the future of Libya.

Syria has been one of the supposed keys to understanding the Obama administration's foreign policy in the region. Despite attempts that began in 2009 to improve relations with the al-Assad regime (Sharp 2010: 1), the administration has gradually modified its posture since the start of the Arab Spring. At first Obama asked President al-Assad to lead a transition to democracy; afterwards he said al-Assad had to go; and then he discussed the possibility within his administration of arming the rebels who fought against al-Assad's regime – a step that Obama had always previously been reticent about. Faced with internal pressure to intervene in Syria, Obama drew a 'red line' by saying that the use of chemical weapons would change his decision. When in August 2013 the Syrian regime was accused of using them in a Damascus suburb controlled by the rebels, President Obama announced an intervention of various days against the regime. This action was finally aborted because of strong opposition from the public; its rejection by key allies, such as the British government after losing the vote in parliament; and strong internal divisions within the US Congress and administration –with the US ambassador to the UN, Samantha Power, and the White House chief of staff, Dennis McDonough, holding contrary positions both for and against. The final decision against intervention was taken by the president himself, following a conversation with McDonough, despite the opposition of the majority of Obama's cabinet who argued that the intervention was necessary in order to maintain 'American credibility'. Finally, a Russian proposal was adopted as a result of statements by the secretary of state about how the intervention could be avoided and a conversation between Obama and Putin at the G20 Summit in Saint Petersburg held on 5–6 September 2013. The deal was negotiated bilaterally between Russia and the US with the acquiescence of the Syrian regime. This proposal included the destruction of the regime's chemical weapons and new peace talks in Geneva that would end with the US president constructing a more realist international policy towards the region. Furthermore, the increasingly bitter conversion of the Syrian conflict into a fight between the regime and diverse jihadist groups, such as al-Nusra or the rising IS, would lead the US into a new intervention in Syria – not against al-Assad's regime, but instead against IS. The decision not to stand by the red line that the administration itself had drawn would be criticised, not only by its political and ideological opponents, but also by various analysts who previously had been in greater harmony with US foreign policy. Despite everything, the US president refused to apologise for a decision that could have led to entry into a new unwinnable conflict in the Middle East. 'I am very proud of this moment,' said Obama (Goldberg 2016).[19]

US policy in Syria and Iraq specifically converge over IS. The evolution of events, which have accelerated since the fall of Mosul in May 2014, belied the president's statements about a 'sovereign, stable and self-reliant Iraq' as a consequence of the US troop withdrawal in December 2011. Faced with the Yazidi siege in Iraq and, in order to protect citizens and US property, President Obama announced an air bombardment campaign on 7 August 2014, which quickly broadened following the NATO Summit in Cardiff of 4–5 September, with the announcement of a four-point strategy against IS. The strategy included measures of a political, military, diplomatic and humanitarian nature, with the explicit aim of finishing with IS. Very quickly IS moved to the centre of US concerns, as President Obama confirmed in his speech to the UN in September 2014, where he identified IS as one of the biggest global threats, together with Ebola and Russian aggression in the Ukraine, stating that IS only understand the use of force and that the final objective was its disappearance. Later, in Obama's State of the Union speech addressed in January 2015, he urged Congress to approve the use of force against this organisation that would be presented in February 2015.[20]

Despite this new approach, which always rejected the possibility of putting 'boots on the ground' in order to prevent subsequent disasters, the strategy against IS has not been free from debate and controversy in the framework of what could be called the crisis over President Obama's foreign policy, especially when faced with the apparent lack of results after the conquest by IS of Ramadi in Iraq and Palmyra in Syria. In this context, leading figures and ex-members of Obama's administration, such as the US chairman of the Joint Chiefs of Staff, Martin Dempsey, and the ex-secretary of defence, Robert Gates, contended that an air campaign per se would not be effective and that there would be a need to put 'boots on the ground', while the the ex-secretary of state, Hillary Clinton, argued publicly for a harder policy toward Syria, according to her position in the internal debates of the administration in favour of training and equipping a non-extremist rebel force to fight against the Syrian regime (Clinton 2014: 460–4). At the same time some Republican leaders, like John McCain, who is closer to a neoconservative position, criticised the premature withdrawal of US troops from Iraq in 2011 and the decision not to stand by the red line statement in relation to the use of chemical weapons in Syria. He also criticised the new direction regarding regime change and al-Assad, reactivating the ideological debate on foreign policy despite the consensus existing about the need to fight IS, which did not exist in the case of Libya. These differences have sharpened as a consequence of the presidential electoral campaign and the participation of Russia in the Syria war in support of the al-Assad regime, followed by the Paris attacks that caused the deaths of 130 people, the consequent negotiations to establish an international coalition against IS that includes Russia – a priori rejected by Obama given the support to al-Assad – and the tensions between Russia and Turkey as a consequence of the bringing down of a Russian fighter plane.

Up to this moment, the intervention of Turkey in northern Syria after the coup attempt, has led to coordinated operations with the US against IS, despite their differences over the Kurdish militias. On the other side, the US and Russia have been negotiating and reaching an agreement to bring about a ceasefire in Syria and joint attacks on IS and al-Nusra with limited consequences, due in part to the 'deep mistrust' between both powers and the continuous violations of the ceasefire, denounced by both parties.[21]

5 The nuclear pact with Iran and relations with Israel

Debate about Obama's foreign policy has also been conditioned by the negotiations and agreement that the US has arrived at with the Iranian regime over their nuclear programme, which has produced great controversy and also affected the relationship of the US with its regional allies, such as Israel and Saudi Arabia, and the arguments over the conflicts in Iraq and Syria. It is important to emphasise here that Israel has traditionally been one of the most important allies of the US in the Middle East and is, furthermore, an influential actor when the US takes any decisions in the region. Similarly, it has enjoyed the support of powerful private interest groups that are particularly influential in Washington's political circles such as the American Israeli Public Affairs Committee (AIPAC), which has significant support in the US Congress in the same way as it had with past administrations, such as those of George W. Bush and Clinton (Mearsheimer and Walt 2006: 40–53).

Following years of diplomatic confrontations, threats, sanctions – developed with the clear protagonism of Brennan, at that time deputy national security adviser for Homeland Security and Counterterrorism, and assistant to the president – and even the sabotaging of Iranian nuclear installations via a computer virus (Sanger 2013: xi–xxii and 188–225) the nuclear negotiations held in Geneva by the 5+1 group (the five permanent members of the UN Security Council plus Germany), led to the announcement of a preliminary agreement and then a definitive deal on 13 July 2015, presented by the US president himself as the 'lesser evil'. When asked about the reasons behind the deal, Obama responded that it is more about it being needed to prevent a new conflict rather than a possible improvement in relations between the US and Iran. Furthermore, he suggested that Iran and the Saudis should 'share' the Middle East in a kind of 'cold peace' (Goldberg 2016).[22]

There was an immediate reaction against the agreement with Iran and both regional allies, Israel and Saudi Arabia, and Democrat and Republican legislators opposing it. The Israeli prime minister Benjamin Netanyahu gave a highly critical speech before the US Congress that led to unease in the administration, in the context of an already difficult relationship due to the lack of progress in the peace process with the Palestinians, in spite of attempts by the secretary of state John Kerry to achieve advances. Despite the afore-mentioned disagreements the administration had maintained its support traditionally granted to its ally, expressed in the generous US$3 billion of aid granted annually in defence material, without taking into account the partici-pation in defence programmes such as the missile inteceptor 'the Iron Dome'. The secretary of defence, Ashton Carter, sought to offer guarantees that would dissipate the fears of the Israeli prime minister, such as offering to increase the previously mentioned aid by the secretary of defence and arguing that the 'US will continue strengthening the security of its allies and friends in the region, especially Israel, to help them defend themselves against any aggression, and will monitor Iran's influence in the region' – without too much impact, however, on Israeli's stance towards the agreement. On the other hand, the Saudis started to develop a more independent foreign policy and demonstrated their displeasure with the US policy towards Iran by the absence of King Salman at the summit with the US president and with various Gulf state leaders at Camp David on 12 May 2015. To this it is worth adding the criticisms of Republican leaders in Congress, such as Senator John McCain, who described the agreement as risky and dangerous, arguing that the guarantees in it were insufficient, and that there was a potential danger of Iran increasing its regional influence with the ending of sanctions.[23]

It is worth highlighting, in this regard, European and Russian manouevres to improve economic relations with Iran, as has been clearly seen during President Rohani's January 2016 tour through various European states, as well as the effects that the ending of sanctions will have on the future development of the Iranian economy. Equally, the consequences of an increase in Iranian oil production in a relatively saturated market, distinguished by reduced oil prices, has been speculated upon (Zakaria 2016). In sum, not all the sanctions that hang over Iran have been removed, and the US itself has announced the establishment of new measures related to the Iranian programme for the development of inter-ballistic missiles, whose continuation Iran has defended. Neither is it likely that differences in matters of regional policy between the US and its allies will disappear anytime soon. However, despite the political and personal differences of the US president and Israeli prime minister, the recent agreement reached by the US and Israel that increases the military aid conceded until 2028 with annual payments of US$3.8 billion – less than the amount demanded by Benjamin Netanyahu and without the special arrangement of spending the 26 per cent of the amount in the development of Israel's defence industry – demonstrates the solid relations between both powers.[24]

One direct consequence of the Iranian nuclear deal is its participation in the long sought-after resolution of the Syrian conflict, as for the first time it was invited to peace talks held in Vienna at the end of October and middle of November 2015 – rather late given the importance of its role as a regional power and as a leading defender, together with Russia, of al-Assad. It is to be seen whether the Iranian agreement (together with the re-establishment of relations with Cuba, one of the factors that, according to some analysts, will help to mark the future legacy of President Obama) contributes towards the resolution of some of the more important regional problems or whether it will become, as in the Libyan case, one of Obama's greatest fiascos.[25]

6 Conclusions

The analysis leads us, firstly, to question whether the Obama administration has a coherent doctrine or strategy towards the MENA region. The president's speeches, such as that at West Point in May 2014, and his responses in interviews, such as that given to Thomas Friedman in *The New York Times* on 15 July 2015 or those to Jeffrey Goldberg, published in the April 2016 issue of *The Atlantic*, do not offer a clear response.[26]

Furthermore, the administration's stance – during and after the Arab Spring – highlights enormous contrasts, but also double standards. In fact when what occured in Bahrain (marked by US support for the royal family of the Gulf Emirates first, and the intervention of Saudi Arabia and other Gulf states to maintain the status quo afterwards) or the US' reluctant support of the Saudi intervention in Yemen is contrasted with the support for the change processes that took place in Tunisia and Egypt or the rejection of the coup attempt in Turkey – despite the apparent lack of confidence in President Erdoğan – there is little room for any doubt. This reflects a careful balance between the defence of US interests that the theory of political realism prescribes – namely the defence of national interest – (Mearsheimer 2001: 1–54) and the values and ideals of the American people, symbolised by Wilsonian idealism, and its 'mission' of 'making the world safe for democracy' as part of the American identity, following a constructivist perspective (Wendt 1992: 391–425). This balance in the US president's foreign policy obliges him to find distinct solutions for different contexts.

In sum, and despite the fact that it is difficult to identify any type of coherent US foreign policy doctrine or strategy, there are some concepts that help illuminate the development of Obama's stance. The most important of these is not that represented in any way by the unfortunate expression of 'leading from behind', frequently expressed by critics of the administration to characterise

Obama's international policy, but rather that of 'nation-building at home'. This focuses on the need to internally strengthen the US, before intervening in foreign conflicts or constructing – democratic – states abroad.

Furthermore, US foreign policy towards the MENA region has been influenced by the president's increasingly pessimistic and Hobbesian view about the development of the change process following the Arab Spring and the limitations of the US to influence it. Nor has the negative approach of regional leaders, both allies and adversaries – starting with the Saudis – contributed towards changes in Obama's foreign policy or the belief that the US should increase its involvement in other regions, while nonetheless being obliged to continue in them (Goldberg 2016).

A second interesting aspect is the position that the MENA countries occupy in the Obama administration's order of priorities. This question is pertinent in relation to the approach developed by the US administration during the years of the 'pivot to the Pacific'. The MENA region, on the other hand, with the failure of its democratising processes and America's increasing difficulty to influence events, seems to have become an 'abandoned territory' in which the US is destined to solely focus on the defence of its most relevant strategic interests, such as guaranteeing the free flow of energy and the fight against terrorism.

However, the ascent of IS and the 'aggressions' of great powers such as Russia in Ukraine, have obliged the Obama administration to review its immediate strategic priorities, as stated in Obama's 2014 speech to the UN. As a consequence the MENA region is at the centre of a debate between ideological groups in the US, and IS has become one of its main threats, as reflected in its foreign policy and in recent influential strategic documents, maximised by recent events in Paris and San Bernardino. This is despite the US president, himself, not considering IS to be 'an existential threat for the US' and stopping the Russian intervention in Syria, 'not a US business' (Goldberg 2016).

Finally, it is worth assessing US foreign policy in the context of a president and administration in its final stage. This is not a simple task and it must address various aspects. One of the most positive has been the president's self-restraint, which has prevented the repetition of serious past mistakes in the belief that the US was capable of shaping events in the region. In this context it is important to emphasise the very necessary abandonment of Wilsonian policies in the expansion of democracy, which has produced such poor results in the past, such as in the Iraqi case, despite the dismay that this stance will represent for neoconservative and liberal interventionists alike.

Another achievement that is worth mentioning is the agreement over Iran's nuclear programme, which opens the doors to further possible collaborations with the Iranian regime on matters of mutual interest, as has already been shown in the peace talks over Syria in Vienna. This agreement has had collateral effects, such as the worsening of US relations with some of its traditional allies in the region, such as Saudi Arabia and Israel, who argue that the agreement strengthens Iran, who they consider a serious threat in regional politics.

However, not all of President Obama's policy decisions have been positive. The intervention in Libya has clearly been a disaster that was provoked by the administration itself, with all its consequences for matters of regional and international security, migration and energy. Al-Gaddafi's old regime was substituted, in the end, by a series of militias and governments incapable of controlling the territory, which furthermore led to the intervention of regional actors such as Egypt and the UAE, contributed to the expansion of IS and toughened the position of emerging powers in the face of humanitarian interventions, now questioned for their bad results.

The Syria conflict is another example of errors made. In this case, Western policy was trapped between 'the rock' of a regime considered to be an adversary in the past for the US and some regional allies such as Israel, and 'the hard place' of a divided opposition, on occasion extremist and untrustworthy, supported by US allies like Qatar, Saudi Arabia and Turkey, which have resulted in the generation of a breeding ground for the expansion of IS.

Iraq has been the focus of heavy criticism towards the administration, in this case focused on the supposedly precipitated withdrawal of US troops in 2011. This criticism is only partially fair because nothing makes one think that continuing US involvement would have done anything more than 'freeze' the existing situation, and because prior to an eventual and inevitable later withdrawal, the Nouri al-Maliki government in any case would have carried out the sectarian policy for which it has been so criticised.

Neither has the strategy against IS in either territory led to a clear solution. The strategy employed against al-Qaeda, founded on special troops and drone attacks, will not be sufficient to beat an entity that controls territory, population and a government that exercises control over both. Once the threat was identified a strategy had to emerge to confront it. Now there are authors such as Walt (2016: 50–64) who have raised the possibility of a strategy of containment if IS consolidates itself as a state.

The US, in November 2016, is going into a period of presidential elections where the challenges of the MENA region and especially of IS have been some of the few issues of international policy debated between the Democratic and Republican Party candidates to the presidency. These candidates, and especially some of the protagonists of US foreign policy, such as Hillary Clinton, must keep in mind the reasons for the success and failure of the decisions taken in the past when acting in a region that has shown itself to be particularly difficult for the protection of US interests and the spread of its ideals and values abroad.

Among the objectives for Obama's successor will be: the need to continue combatting extremist groups like IS; addressing the growing presence of great powers like Russia and China; improving relations with some key regional allies such as Saudi Arabia, Egypt and Turkey; and integrating Iran into regional and global policy – as well as knowing how to take advantage of both powers' common interests, such as the need to halt IS.

Addressing these challenges will be fundamental for the development of a successful foreign policy towards a region that, despite the original intentions of the US president, will continue to have primary strategic importance for the US in the short and medium term.

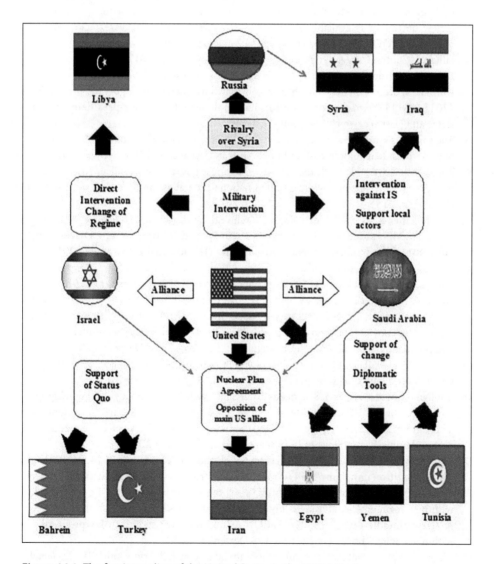

Figure 14.1 The foreign policy of the United States in the MENA Region

Notes

1. Eisenhower and Carter speeches, available at <http://www.presidency.ucsb.edu/ws/index. php?piard=11007&st=&st1> (last accessed 10 December 2015) and <http://www.jim-mycarterlibrary.gov/documents/speeches/su80jec.phtml> (last accessed 10 December 2015). About George W. Bush see his second inaugural speech, available at <http://www.inaugural.senate.gov/swearing-in/address/address-by-george-w-bush-2005> (last accessed 10 December 2015).

2. The speech is available at <https://www.whitehouse.gov/the-press-office/remarks-president-cairo-university-6-04-09> (last accessed 23 November 2015).

3. The strategy document is available at <https://www.whitehouse.gov/sites/default/files/ rss_viewer/national_security_strategy.pdf > (last accessed 25 November, 2015). The review document is available at <http://history.defense.gov/Portals/70/Documents/ quadrennial/QDR2010.pdf> (last accessed 25 November 2015).

4. Hillary Clinton speech is available at <https://2009-2017.state.gov/secretary/ 20092013clinton/rm/2011/11/176999.htm> (last accessed 27 November 2015). Tom Donilon Speech is available at <https://obamawhitehouse.archives.gov/the-press-office /2013/03/11/remarks-tom-donilon-national-security-advisor-president-united-states-an> (last accessed 27 November 2015).

5. The speech is available at <https://www.whitehouse.gov/the-press-office/2011/05/19/ remarks-president-middle-east-and-north-africa> (last accessed 20 November 2015).

6. The speech is available at <https://www.whitehouse.gov/the-press-office/2013/09/24/ remarks-president-obama-address-united-nations-general-assembly> (last accessed 20 November 2015).

7. The documents are available at <http://archive.defense.gov/news/Defence_Strategic_ Guidance.pdf> (accessed 28 November 2015) and <http://archive.Defence.gov/ pubs/2014_Quadrennial_Defence_Review.pdf> (last accessed 28 November 2015).

8. The strategy document is available at <https://www.whitehouse.gov/sites/default/files/ docs/2015_national_security_strategy.pdf> (last accessed 30 November 2015).

9. Available at <https://www.whitehouse.gov/the-press-office/2011/01/14/statement-president-events-tunisia> (last accessed 5 December 2015). Essebsi speech is available at <https://www.whitehouse.gov/the-press-office/2015/05/21/remarks-president-obama-and-president-essebsi-tunisia-after-bilateral-me> (last accessed 5 December 2015).

10. The speech is available at <https://www.whitehouse.gov/the-press-office/2011/02/01/ remarks-president-situation-egypt> (last accessed 10 February 2016).

11. 'Mohamed Morsi warns US it needs to change Middle East policy', *Daily Telegraph*, 23 September 2012. Available at <http://www.telegraph.co.uk/news/worldnews/ africaandindianocean/egypt/9561363/Mohammed-Morsi-warns-US-it-needs-to-change-Middle-East-policy.html> (last accessed 29 December 2015).

12. 'Egypt declares el-Sisi winner of presidential election', *CNN*, 4 June 2014. Available at <http://edition.cnn.com/2014/06/03/world/africa/egypt-presidential-election/> (last accessed 29 December 2015). 'EU's Ashton on surprise visit to Egypt for talks with new regime', *Al-Arabiya*, 17 July 2013. Available at <http://english.alarabiya.net/ en/News/middle-east/2013/07/17/EU-s-Ashton-on-surprise-visit-to-Egypt-for-talks-with-new-regime-.html> (last accessed 29 December 2015).

13. 'China, Egypt, consolidate ties After Sisi's attendance at military parade', *The Diplomat*, 9 September 2015. Available at <http://thediplomat.com/2015/09/china-egypt-

consolidate-ties-after-sisis-attendance-at-military-parade/> (last accessed 29 December 2015). 'Russia, Egypt sign deal on construction of Egypt's first nuclear plant', *CNN*, 19 December 2015. Available at <http://edition.cnn.com/2015/11/19/middleeast/russia-egypt-nuclear-deal/> (last accessed 29 December 2015). 'Hagel: US has "limited influence" over Egypt', *The Hill*, 19 August 2013. Available at <http://thehill.com/video/administration/317675-hagel-us-influence-in-egypt-limited> (last accessed 29 December 2015).

14. As regards Bahrain, see Obama speech at note 5. 'Amid uprising, Yemen president quits after 33 years', *NBC News*, 23 November 2011. Available at <http://www.nbcnews.com/id/45413404/ns/world_news-mideast_n_africa/t/amid-uprising-yemen-president-quits-after-years/> (last accessed 29 December 2015). 'Arabia Saudí lidera una operación militar árabe en Yemen', *El País*, 26 March 2015. Available at <http://internacional.elpais.com/internacional/2015/03/26/actualidad/1427327690_787380.html> (last accessed 29 December 2015). 'Saudi Arabia says king won't attend meetings in US', *The New York Times*, 10 May 2015. Available at <http://www.nytimes.com/2015/05/11/world/middleeast/saudi-arabia-king-wont-attend-camp-david-meeting.html?_r=0> (last accessed 29 December 2015).

15. 'Obama takes hard line with Libya after shift by Clinton', *The New York Times*, 18 March 2011. Available at <http://www.nytimes.com/2011/03/19/world/africa/19policy.html?pagewanted=all&_r=0> (last accessed 29 December 2015).

16. The speech is available at <http://archive.defense.gov/Speeches/Speech.aspx?SpeechID=1581> (last accessed 10 December 2015).

17. The speech is available at <http://www.whitehouse.gov/the-press-office/2011/03/28/remarks-president-address-nation-libya> (last accessed 10 December 2015). The UN Resolution is available at <http://www.un.org/es/comun/docs/?symbol=s/res/1973%20(2011)> (last accessed 10 December 2015). 'Putin's Russia set against regime change in Syria', *Reuters*, 28 January 2012. Available at <http://www.reuters.com/article/us-syria-russia-un-idUSTRE80R08B20120128> (last accessed 29 December 2015). Regarding al-Gaddafi's death see <http://www.whitehouse.gov/the-press-office/2011/10/20/remarks-president-death-muammar-qaddafi> (last accessed 10 December 2015).

18. President Obama's condemnation speech is available at <https://www.whitehouse.gov/the-press-office/2012/09/12/remarks-president-deaths-us-embassy-staff-libya> (last accessed 3 February 2016). 'Susan Rice withdraws from consideration as secretary of state', *CNN*, 14 December, 2012. Available at <http://edition.cnn.com/2012/12/13/politics/rice-withdraws-secretary-of-state/> (last accessed 29 December 2015). 'Looted Libyan arms in Mali may have shifted conflict's path', *The New York Times*, 7 February 2013. Available at <http://www.nytimes.com/2013/02/08/world/africa/looted-libyan-arms-in-mali-may-have-shifted-conflicts-path.html> (last accessed 29 December 2015). 'Why Clinton's Benghazi testimony is critical for campaign', *NBC News*, 20 October 2015. Available at <http://www.nbcnews.com/politics/2016-election/lid-why-clintons-benghazi-testimony-critical-campaign-n448076> (last accessed 29 December 2015). President Obama speeches are available at note 6 and <https://www.whitehouse.gov/the-press-office/2015/09/28/remarks-president-obama-united-nations-general-assembly> (last accessed 7 February 2016).

19. The speeches are available at <https://obamawhitehouse.archives.gov/blog/2011/08/18/president-obama-future-syria-must-be-determined-its-people-president-bashar-al-assad> (last accessed 13 December 2015) and <http://www.whitehouse.gov/

the-press-office/2012/02/04/statement-president-syria> (last accessed 13 December 2015). 'Off-the-cuff Obama line put the US in bind on Syria', *The New York Times*, 4 May 2013. Available at <http://www.nytimes.com/2013/05/05/world/middleeast/obamas-vow-on-chemical-weapons-puts-him-in-tough-spot.html> (last accessed 29 December 2015). 'Syria crisis: Cameron loses Commons vote on Syria action', *BBC News*, 30 August 2013. Available at <http://www.bbc.com/news/uk-politics-23892783> (last accessed 29 December 2015). A poll about the intervention is available at <http://www.gallup.com/poll/164282/supportsyria-action-lower-past-conflicts.aspx> (last accessed 15 December 2015). 'Obama's uncertain path amid Syria bloodshed', *The New York Times*, 22 October 2013. Available at <http://www.nytimes.com/2013/10/23/world/middleeast/obamas-uncertain-path-amid-syria-bloodshed.html> (last accessed 29 December 2015). In relation to the critics see <https://twitter.com/RichardHaass/Status/373999717602312192> (last accessed 30 December 2015).

20. President Obama's speech is available at <https://www.whitehouse.gov/the-press-office/2011/10/21/remarks-president-ending-war-iraq> (last accessed 15 December 2015). President Obama's speeches are available at <https://www.whitehouse.gov/the-press-office/2014/08/07/statement-president> (last accessed 20 December 2015), <https://www.whitehouse.gov/the-press-office/2014/09/05/remarks-president-obama-nato-summit-press-conference> (last accessed 20 December 2015), <https://www.whitehouse.gov/the-press-office/2014/09/24/remarks-president-obama-address-united-nations-general-assembly> (last accessed 20 December 2015) and <https://www.whitehouse.gov/the-press-office/2015/01/20/remarks-president-state-union-address-january-20-2015> (last accessed 20 December 2015). President Obama's strategy against IS is available at <https://www.whitehouse.gov/the-press-office/2014/09/10/fact-sheet-strategy-counter-islamic-state-iraq-and-levant-isil> (last accessed 20 December 2015).

21. 'US special operations forces arrive in Syria to advise Turks in ISIS fight', *The New York Times*, 16 September 2016. Available at <http://www.nytimes.com/2016/09/17/world/middleeast/us-troops-syria-isis.html?_r=0> (last accessed 18 September 2016).

22. The agreement is available at <https://medium.com/@ObamaWhiteHouse/introduction-fcb13560dfb9#.pra8jtl9j> (last accessed 23 December 2015). President Obama's speech is available at <https://www.whitehouse.gov/the-press-office/2015/08/05/remarks-president-iran-nuclear-deal> (last accessed 23 December 2015).

23. Prime Minister Netanyahu's speech is available at <https://www.washingtonpost.com/news/post-politics/wp/2015/03/03/full-text-netanyahus-address-to-congress/> (last accessed 23 December 2015). 'How John Kerry built a peace process for Israel–Palestine, then watched it burn', *New Statesman*, 21 July 2014. Available at <http://www.newstatesman.com/politics/2014/07/how-john-kerry-built-peace-process-israel-palestine-then-watched-it-burn> (accessed 29 December 2015). 'Critics of Iran deal ramp up campaign', *The Financial Times*, 9 September 2015. Available at <http://www.ft.com/intl/cms/s/0/bf18622c-570b-11e5-9846-de406ccb37f2.html#axzz3vkeD1ATZ> (last accessed 29 December 2015).

24. 'US sanctions Iran's ballistic missile program', *USA Today*, 17 January 2016. Available at <http://www.usatoday.com/story/news/politics/2016/01/17/us-sanctions-irans-ballistic-missile-program/78930672/> (last accessed 5 February 2016). The memorandum is available at <https://www.whitehouse.gov/the-press-office/2016/09/14/fact-sheet-memorandum-understanding-reached-israel> (last accessed 21 September 2016). 'US and Israel reach agreement on unprecedent amount of military aid', *The Washington Post*, 13 September 2016. Available at <https://www.washingtonpost.com/world/

national-security/agreement-on-military-aid-for-israel-expected-within-days/20
16/09/13/50847ad8-79c1-11e6-bd86-b7bbd53d2b5d_story.html?utm_term=.
56fdd801bf06> (last accessed 21 September 2016).
25. 'After a US Shift, Iran has a seat at talks on war in Syria', *The New York Times*, 28 October
2015. Available at <http://www.nytimes.com/2015/10/29/world/middleeast/syria-
talks-vienna-iran.html> (last accessed 29 December 2015). 'Why the Iran deal is so
huge for Obama's legacy', *The Washington Post*, 31 July 2015. Available at <https://www.
washingtonpost.com/news/the-fix/wp/2015/07/31/why-the-iran-deal-is-huge-for-
obamas-legacy/> (last accessed 29 December 2015).
26. The speech is available at <https://www.whitehouse.gov/the-press-office/2014/05/28/
remarks-president-united-states-military-academy-commencement-ceremony>
(last accessed 31 December 2015). The interview is available at <http://www.nytimes.
com/2015/07/15/opinion/thomas-friedman-obama-makes-his-case-on-iran-nuclear-
deal.html?_r=0> (last accessed 31 December 2015).

References

Arieff, Alexis and Carla E. Humud (2015), *Political Transition in Tunisia*, Congressional
Research Service, 10 February, 1–22. Available at <https://www.fas.org/sgp/crs/row/
RS21666.pdf> (last accessed 23 December 2015).
Bush, George H. W. and Brent Scowcroft (1998), *A World Transformed*, New York: Vintage
Books.
Clinton, Hillary (2014), *Hard Choices*, New York: Simon and Schuster.
Gates, Robert (2014), *Duty: Memoirs of a Secretary at War*, New York: Alfred A. Knopf.
Goldberg, Jeffrey (2016), 'The Obama doctrine', *The Atlantic*, April. Available at <http://
www.theatlantic.com/magazine/archive/2016/04/the-obama-doctrine/471525/#1>
(last accessed 29 March 2016).
Haass, Richard N. (2010), *War of Necessity, War of Choice: a Memoir of two Iraq Wars*, New
York: Simon and Schuster.
Kuperman, Alan J. (2015), 'Obama's Libya Debacle', *Foreign Affairs*, 94 (2), March/April:
66–77.
Mann, James (2004), *The Rise of the Vulcans: the History of Bush War's Cabinet*, New York:
Penguin Books.
Mann, James (2012), *The Obamians: the Struggle Inside the White House to Redefine American
Power*, New York: Viking.
Mead, Walter R. (2002), *Special Providence: American Foreign Policy and How it Changed the
World*, New York: Routledge.
Mearsheimer, John J. (2001), *The Tragedy of Great Power Politics*, New York: Norton & Co.
Mearsheimer, John J. and Stephen M. Walt (2006), 'The Israel lobby and US foreign policy',
Middle East Policy, XIII (3): 29–87.
Packer, George (2005), *The Assassin's Gate: America in Iraq*, New York: Farrar Strauss and Giroux.
Rice, Condoleezza (2005), 'The promise of democratic peace', *The Washington Post*, 11 December.
Available at <http://www.washingtonpost.com/wp-dyn/content/article/2005/12/09/
AR2005120901711.html> (last accessed 23 December 2015).
Rogin, Josh (2011), 'Who really said Obama was "leading from behind"?', *Foreign Policy*, 27
October. Available at <http://foreignpolicy.com/2011/10/27/who-really-said-obama-
was-leading-from-behind/> (last accessed 9 March 2016)

Sanger, David E. (2013), *Confront and Conceal. Obama's Secret Wars and Surprising Use of American Power*, New York: Broadway Paperbacks.

Sharp, Jeremy M. (2010), *Syria: Background and US Relations*, Congressional Research Service, 26 April. Available at <http://fpc.state.gov/documents/organization/142735.pdf> (last accessed 8 March 2016).

Smith, Tony (2008), 'Wilsonianism after Iraq', in John G. Ikenberry (ed.), *The Crisis of American Foreign Policy: Wilsonianism in the Twenty-first Century*, Princeton: Princeton University Press, pp. 66–74.

Tovar, Juan (2014), *La política exterior de Estados Unidos y la expansión de la democracia*, Valencia: Tirant lo Blanch.

Traub, James (2008), *The Freedom Agenda: Why America Must Spread Democracy (Just Not the Way George Bush Did)*, New York: Farrar, Straus and Giroux.

Vaisse, Justin (2010), *Neoconservatism: the Biography of a Movement*, Cambridge, MA: Harvard University Press.

Walt, Stephen M. (2011), 'What intervention in Libya tells us about the neocon–liberal alliance', *Foreign Policy*, 21 March. Available at <http://foreignpolicy.com/2011/03/21/what-intervention-in-libya-tells-us-about-the-neocon-liberal-alliance/> (last accessed 29 December 2015).

Walt, Stephen M. (2016), 'EI/Daesh, nuevo Estado revolucionario', *Política Exterior*, XXX (169), January/February: 50–64.

Wendt, Alexander (1992), 'Anarchy is what states make of it: the social construction of power politics', *International Organization*, 46 (2): 391–425.

Wittes, Tamara C. (2015), 'The politics of restoring Egypt's military aid', *The Washington Post*, 2 April. Available at <https://www.washingtonpost.com/blogs/monkey-cage/wp/2015/04/02/the-politics-of-restoring-egypts-military-aid/> (last accessed 29 December 2015)

Zakaria, Fareed (2016), "From Iran to Nigeria, cheap oil means perilous politics", *The Washington Post*, 4 February. Available at <https://www.washingtonpost.com/opinions/from-iran-to-nigeria-cheap-oil-means-perilous-politics/2016/02/04/aefcdbb8-cb76-11e5-a7b2-5a2f824b02c9_story.html> (last accessed 5 February 2016).

Part IV

Part IV

Chapter 15

Successful and failed transitions to democracy

Inmaculada Szmolka

1 Introduction

Democratic expectations awoken by the Arab Spring have not been met after five years. The democratising wave that many political analysts forecast in 2011 has not taken place as a consequence of the popular protests and revolutions. Today the only established democracy in the Middle East and North Africa (MENA) region after the Arab Spring is Tunisia, and that is still on the path of consolidation. On the other hand, democratic transitions in Egypt, Libya and Yemen have failed. In other countries the authoritarian power structure has remained intact, and even Turkey's defective democracy has recently suffered a process of autocratisation.

The persistence of authoritarian political regimes, however, does not mean that changes have not taken place in the respective political systems (Rivetti 2015: 5). Political reforms, mainly of an institutional nature, have occurred in many MENA countries. As on previous occasions, authoritarianism has 'upgraded' itself to ensure the survival of political regimes (Heydemann 2007).

In this book, the broad concept of 'political change' is employed. In Chapter 1 political change was defined as the transformation of a political regime that affects rules, institutions, power relations, actor behaviours and political processes. That chapter presented a typology of processes of political change, not all of which have necessarily led to regime change. On the one hand, two broad processes were identified: democratisation (from authoritarianism to democracy) and autocratisation (from democracy to authoritarianism). And, on the other, five specific processes of political change were highlighted, which are either related to democracies (democratic regression, democratic

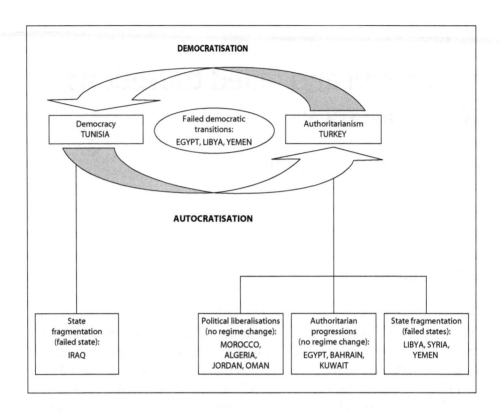

Figure 15.1 Typology of political change processes in MENA countries following the Arab Spring

deepening and consolidation of democracy) or authoritarianism (political liberalisation and authoritarian progression).

The aim of the chapters in Part IV is to identify the type of political change processes that have taken place in each country (see Figure 15.1). The reach of those transformations are evaluated through three dimensions of political regime analysis that were highlighted in Chapter 1: pluralism and political competition, government function and public rights and liberties.

This chapter focuses on four countries that as a consequence of the Arab Spring undertook transition processes from authoritarianism to democracy: with success (Tunisia) or with failure (Egypt, Libya and Yemen). Chapter 16 examines political liberalisation processes in other MENA countries such as Morocco, Jordan, Oman and Algeria. And, finally, Chapter 17 analyses MENA countries that have experienced negative changes following the Arab Spring: authoritarian progressions (Kuwait and Bahrain) or the fragmentation of state authority.

Table 15.1 Classification of the MENA regimes (2016)

Categories	Countries	Pluralism and political competence	Government	Public rights and civil liberties
Defective democracy	Israel	Competitive	Effective	Diminished
	Lebanon		Flawed	
	Tunisia		Effective	
Restrictive and quasi-competitive pluralist authoritarianism	Morocco	Quasi-competitive pluralism	Autocratic	Restrictive
	Turkey			
Restrictive and hegemonic pluralist authoritarianism	Algeria	Hegemonic pluralism	Autocratic	Restrictive
	Bahrain			Very restrictive
	Egypt			Very restrictive
	Jordan			Restrictive
	Kuwait			Restrictive
	Iran			Very restrictive
Closed authoritarianism	Oman	Non-pluralist	Totalitarian	Very restrictive
	Qatar			
	Saudi Arabia			
	UAE			
Failed states	Iraq	Competitive	Fragmented	Very restrictive
	Libya	–		
	Syria	–		
	Yemen	–		

Source: prepared by the author

2 A successful democratisation: consensual and participative transition in Tunisia

The departure of Zine al-Abidine Ben Ali, on 14 January 2011, opened a window of opportunity for regime change. The Tunisian transition followed the sequence of stages detailed by the transitology paradigm: reform of party and electoral laws, the holding of founding elections, approval of a new constitution, formation of a democratic government and acceptance and legitimation of the electoral results and the rules of the political game (O'Donnell et al. 1986).

However, engaging with these institutional political processes is insufficient for democratisation, as the case of Egypt shows. The Tunisian transition was possible thanks to agreements between political actors in a polarised political scenario, concessions made by a dominant party and a strong and participative civil society (Szmolka 2015). Despite the Islamist Ennahda (Renaissance) Party winning a majority in the October 2011 elections, this did not result in other political forces being excluded from the transition process. Not without difficulty, Tunisian political actors negotiated and came to agreements throughout the democratic transition process. Once the transitional steps were decided, the parties agreed the election rules, terms and functions of the constituent assembly. Secondly, the constituent assembly passed a provisional constitution containing 26 articles on 10 December 2011, setting out the powers of the prime minister, head of state and parliament (Law on the Interim Organisation of Public Powers). Later, on 28 September 2013, as a consequence of a blockage in the constitutional process and after weeks of negotiations, Ennahda and the opposition parties signed an agreement establishing a road map that called for the resignation of the government and the formation of a non-partisan transitional government, the adoption of the constitution, the passage of an electoral law and the holding of legislative and presidential elections (Martínez-Fuentes 2015a). As a result of this partisan consensus, the national assembly was able to approve the democratic constitution at its plenary session on 26 January 2014. Also, on 29 January 2014, Tunisia's parliament approved a technocratic caretaker government tasked with holding legislative and presidential elections, which took place at the end of 2014.

The Tunisian transition was not only inclusive in terms of political forces but also regarding the involvement of civil society in the change process. On the one hand, citizen mobilisation was not only limited to the time of the revolution in January 2011, but also continued throughout the transition process as a consequence of the social and political unrest. The Tunisian demonstrations gathered strength in 2013 because of the murders of two prominent opponents, Chokri Belaïd and Mohamed Brahmi, who died on 6 February and 25 July 2013, respectively. Many of the protests were organised by the Tunisian equivalent of the Egyptian Tamarrod (Rebellion) and the National Salvation Front, an umbrella group of opposition parties and movements campaigning for the resignation of the government, the dissolution of parliament and a democratic transition. On the other hand, the role of civil society was key in breaking the stalemate in the Tunisian transition in summer 2013. The National Dialogue Quartet, driven by four civil society organisations,[1] achieved an agreement between the parties that permitted approval of the constitution and the formation of a caretaker government to organise new legislative and presidential elections.

Table 15.2 Models of the transitions in Tunisia and Egypt

	Dimensions			
	Veto actors	Competition and political interaction	Consensus on political processes	Popular mobilisation and civil society participation
Tunisia	None	Inclusive	Consensual	Participatory
Egypt	Army	Exclusionary	Non-consensual	Participatory

Source: prepared by the author

2.1 Increase in pluralism and fair elections

One of the first consequences of the Tunisian revolution was the licensing of new parties in the early months of the transition through Decree 87-2011 on 24 September 2011 (Gana 2013). By the time the October 2011 elections took place, Tunisian authorities had approved the registration of 116 political parties, of which only eight had existed before the Arab Spring. Approximately eighty parties, in addition to independents, submitted candidate lists in districts across the country (National Democratic Institute 2011). On the other hand, the Tunisian revolution represented the end of Ben Ali's hegemonic party, the Democratic Constitutional Rally (Rassemblement Constitutionnel Démocratique, RCD). In March 2011 the Tunisian Court of the First Instance, on request of the Interior Ministry, abolished the RCD, which had been suspended by the army on 6 February, by applying article 18 of the Organic Law 88-32 of 3 May 1988. This led to the current multiparty system where all ideological tendencies are recognised, can compete in elections and be represented in parliament.

Foundational elections symbolise one of the key conditions for transition to democracy (Stepan 2012). The first polls for the election of the constituent assembly were held on 23 October 2011. The High Commission for the Fulfilment of the Goals of the Revolution, Political Reform and Democratic Transition, representing all major parties as well as professional and civil society associations, was given the task of drawing up the new electoral code. The High Commission agreed to adopt a proportional representation system (employing the largest remainder formula), to use administrative divisions as constituencies, and to have candidates chosen from closed and blocked 'zipper' lists (Decree 35, 10 May 2011, relates to the election of the national constituent assembly). The aims were to encourage plurality and a broad consensus. Of eligible voters, 52 per cent participated (86 per cent of registered voters and 16 per cent unregistered), and as a result Ennahda, which was banned under the Ben Ali regime, won 37 per cent of the votes and 41.5 per cent of the seats in the constituent assembly. Notably, the other competing political parties accepted the electoral results. A great effort was made to guarantee pluralism and to avoid the electoral fraud of past elections. The Independent High Authority for the Elections carried out the review of the electoral census, coordination and supervision of the elections (Decree 27, 18 April 2011). Additionally, delegates of the parties and candidates, and international organisations were authorised to attend and observe. The elections were viewed as fair, transparent, properly conducted and competitive (Carter Centre 2012: 2; Murphy 2013).

Once the constitution was approved, the constituent assembly was dissolved and elections were held, on 26 October 2014, to the Assembly of the Representatives of the People. The turnout was 67 per cent of registered voters. Nidaa Tounes (Tunisia's Call), a coalition of secularists, leftists, liberals and officials of the Ben Ali regime,[2] came first with eighty-six seats (37.56 per cent), while Ennahda only won sixty-nine seats (27.79 per cent), twenty fewer than in 2011. Fourteen other parties are also present in the Assembly of the Representatives.

Presidential elections were held in two rounds on 23 November and 21 December 2014. Mohamed Beji Caïd Essebsi, the Nidda Tounes candidate, won the presidential race against the incumbent Moncef Marzouki in the second round with 55.68 per cent of the vote. Ennahda decided not to endorse a presidential candidate, in order not to monopolise the whole political scene. Electoral turnout was high: 70 per cent in the first round and 60 per cent in the second. International organisations reported improvements in the legislative and presidential elections following problems of transparency and regulation in the 2011 elections (Martínez-Fuentes 2015a and 2015b).

In sum, greater pluralism, the competitive character of the elections, acceptance of the electoral results by competing political forces and the possibility of government alternation through the ballot box confirm Tunisia to be on the democratic path.

2.2 Democratic governments and a consensual constitution

2.2.1 Tunisian governments following the Arab Spring

In the five years since the 2011 revolution seven governments have led Tunisia, of which the first two governed in the early months of the transition, two were appointed as a result of agreements between parties to unlock a political crisis, two emerged as the result of elections and the last government as a consequence of a vote of no confidence in the head of government, Habib Essid.

After the departure of Ben Ali, on 18 January 2011, Prime Minister Mohamed Ghannouchi assumed the presidency of the republic, according to article 56 of the constitution that stipulated an interim presidency in case of the temporary or provisional absence of the president. However, to prevent Ben Ali's return, article 57 on the president's total incapacity was applied. Thus, on 14 January 2011, the Constitutional Council appointed the speaker of the Lower House, Fouad Mebazaa, as acting president. Ghannouchi retained his post as prime minister and formed two governments until his resignation on 27 February 2011 as a result of ongoing street protests. On 7 March 2011 Essebsi chaired a new government. He issued a decree suspending the 1959 constitution and regulating the interim functions of state institutions (Martínez-Fuentes 2011).

Following the October 2011 elections Hamadi Jebali, a former political prisoner and general secretary of the Islamic party Ennahda, was appointed head of government on 14 December 2011. He formed his cabinet with two secular political forces, the Democratic Forum of Labour and Liberties, known as Ettakatol (pan-Arabist) and the Congress for the Republic (Congrès pour la République, CPR) (centre/left wing). The Assembly had previously chosen Moncef Marzouki, leader of the CPR, as president of the republic, with the support of three governmental coalition parties. Jebali resigned on 19 February 2013, as all parties – including his own Ennahda Party – rejected his proposal to form a technocratic government after the crisis that followed the murder of a prominent member of the opposition and the consequent impasse in the constitutional process. Following the resignation of prime minister Jebali, Ali Larayedh, previously minister of the interior and a member of Ennahda, was appointed head of government on 14 March 2013, with the same parties remaining in the governmental coalition. On 9 January 2014 Larayedh resigned to give way to a caretaker government, which was to implement the political agreement between government and opposition parties in order to unblock the democratic transition. Larayedh was replaced by an independent, Mehdi Jomaa, on 29 January 2014.

Following the holding of presidential elections in 2014 the elected President Essebsi appointed the independent Habib Essid as head of goverment and gave him the responsibility to form a government on 6 February 2015. Essid formed a coalition government made up of independents (twelve members), Nidaa Tounes (eight members), the Free Patriotic Union (UPL) (three members), Afek Tounes (Tunisian Horizons) (three members) and Ennahda (one member).

Lastly, on 30 July 2016, the Assembly of the Representatives passed a motion of no confidence in Essid. As a consequence, Youssef Chahed was appointed head of government and was tasked to form a unity government.

President Essebsi and political parties had agreed a new unity government to overcome political divisions in the ruling coalition and address the challenges of the economy and security.

Therefore, throughout the Tunisian transition, governments have been formed as a result of political consensus or electoral results, which have guaranteed their democratic legitimacy. Similarly, a peaceful alternation in government has been possible from the Troika government headed by Ennahda to that of Nidaa Tounes.

2.2.2 The 2014 Tunisian constitution

The shift from an authoritarian regime to a democratic government in Tunisia has been made possible by the approval of a constitution written by a constituent assembly and agreed by all political forces, though not without passing through a long and difficult process. As noted above, the constituent assembly was democratically elected on 23 October 2011. While a commission was given the task of drafting a constitution for the constituent assembly, it proved very difficult to reach a consensus on the content. The commission finished its final draft at the end of June 2013, and the constitutional project passed to the national constituent assembly. Following the agreement between Ennahda and the opposition parties, the constitution was voted in by an overwhelming majority of the constituent assembly's members on 26 January 2014. The next day the president of the republic and the head of the national assembly signed the country's new constitution.

The most controversial aspects of the constitution's content were the rights of women and the place of Islam in the state and society (Ben Achour 2014: 787). The constitution recognises equality of rights and responsibilities (article 20) and guarantees parity between men and women in all elected assemblies (article 46). Islamic and secular political forces comprise a confessional state, recognising Islam as the state religion (article 1), but there is no reference to Islamic shariah as a source of legislation. Freedoms of belief, worship and conscience are guaranteed by article 6 and the state has responsibility to protect them. Arriving at an agreement on the type of executive power was also a complex process. Ennahda insisted on a parliamentary system while other parties proposed a presidential structure. In the end, a semi-presidential government system was established in the constitution. Executive power is shared between the president of the republic and the head of government. The president of the republic is elected by universal suffrage for a term of five years (article 74). His or her power is limited, although s/he retains important prerogatives, notably in defence and foreign affairs (article 76). The government is responsible to parliament at the time of its formation (article 88), and can also be dismissed following a motion of no confidence, which requires the subsequent approval of another head of government (article 96).

In short, the Tunisian constitution has followed a procedure of democratic approval, in which only a referendum has been missed. The polarised debate about the confessional nature of the state and its compatibility with democracy is currently closed. In its content, the Tunisian constitution is in line with democratic standards regarding the separation of powers and the recognition of rights and liberties.

2.3 Government effectiveness and governance

Besides the transitional challenges, government functioning has been marked by economic and security problems resulting from terrorist attacks. Nevertheless, the state exercises control over the entire territory and possesses a total monopoly on the use of force. The advent of democracy has not met citizen expectations of economic and social development. This may provoke political instability and government ineffectiveness that could put democracy at risk in Tunisia.

In relation to governance, great efforts have been made in order to improve transparency and to fight against corruption. The Good Governance and Anti-Corruption Commission was created in late 2012 and included in the 2014 constitution. The constitution also guarantees the right of citizens to information and a 2011 information law requires public institutions' internal documents to be made available on request to the public. However, transparency is improvable: Tunisia received a score of thirty-eight and was ranked seventy-six out of the 168 countries assessed on the 2015 Corruption Perceptions Index (Transparency International 2016).[3]

2.3 Limited improvements in public rights and civil liberties

Political rights and civil liberties have improved in the last five years, although the situation could be significantly better. A new law on associations was passed on 24 September 2011, which simplified the procedures for establishing or managing associations. The new legal framework led to an increase in associations (from 10,000 to 15,000 in 2011–12) (see Pérez-Beltrán and Álvarez-Ossorio, Chapter 8). Nonetheless, several civil society organisations have been closed down over concerns related to terrorism and security. On the other hand, in March 2014, President Moncef Marzouki lifted the state of emergency imposed during the 2011 revolution. However, following the attack on presidential guards in the capital, a state of emergency was declared again in November 2015, conferring exceptional powers on Tunisian authorities to prohibit public gatherings, strikes, demonstrations and to control the press. Also, on 25 July 2015 Tunisia's assembly of representatives adopted a new counter-terrorism law, which gives the security forces broad and vague monitoring and surveillance powers, extends incommunicado detention from six to fifteen days for terrorism suspects, and permits courts to close hearings to the public and allow the identities of witnesses to be withheld from defendants (Human Rights Watch 2016b).

Regarding freedom of opinion, expression and publication, international organisations have reported journalists being arrested or convicted for defamation, Internet users and bloggers tried or anti-government activists jailed, usually over 'security'. The establishment of the Independent High Authority of Audiovisual Communication (HAICA) was hailed as a major step towards free and pluralistic media in Tunisia. However, HAICA's independence has been subject to debate due to its alleged politicisation, especially during the elections (Freedom House 2016a).

Lastly, the national constituent assembly passed the Organic Law on Establishing and Organising Transitional Justice in December 2013. According to the law, a Truth and Dignity Commission was established in June 2014, to look into human rights violations committed since 1956. Major advances have been made in some of the investigations and compensation has been paid to the victims of past crimes. However, transitional justice is not currently a priority in Tunisia due to the economic and security situation. In particular, the presence of members of the old regime in Nidaa Tounes does not seem propitious for the investigation of human rights abuses. On 14 July 2015 the government approved a draft Law on Economic and Financial Reconciliation, strongly supported by President Essebsi. If enacted, the law will offer amnesty to officials of the former Ben Ali regime and protect the economic and financial elite from prosecution (Human Rights Watch 2016b).

In brief, political rights and civil liberties have considerably improved following the Tunisian revolution. Freedom House offers a positive assessment on all variables of 'civil liberties'. However, further improvements are necessary, above all in relation to the rule of law (see Table A.1 in the appendix). Diminished rights and freedoms, like economic and security problems, are a threat to democracy in Tunisia.

3 The exclusionary and non-consensual transition in Egypt

The case of Egypt shows that the holding of competitive elections and approval of a constitution does not inevitably lead to the establishment of a democratic regime (Brown 2013: 46). In Egypt it is necessary to distinguish between two different processes of political change during the last five years. The first is a democratic transition that failed due to three main factors: a lack of understanding between polarised political forces (secular and Islamist); the exclusionary politics implemented by the Islamists; and the interference of a non-accountable actor – the army – in political affairs (Szmolka 2015). Secondly, there is a process of autocratisation following the 2013 military coup, which implies the return to a restrictive and hegemonic authoritarianism, such as that of the Mubarak era.

Following the fall of President Mubarak, on 11 February 2011, the Supreme Council of the Armed Forces (SCAF) assumed power and led the democratic transition until the Islamist Mohammed Morsi was named president of the republic. Morsi proved unable to make concessions and reach agreements with other political forces, choosing instead to impose his own political constitution of 25 December 2012, which was rejected by liberal, nationalist and progressive groups. Widespread social and political mobilisation against Morsi's hegemonic politics served as a pretext for the military coup of 3 July 2013, in which he was ousted. The military then aborted the process of democratisation and established a new authoritarian regime, with characteristics similar to Mubarak's system: a hegemonic pluralist and restrictive authoritarianism.

3.1 From competitive multipartyism to the return of hegemonic pluralism

The first steps of the political transition were positive in the sphere of political pluralism. On 28 March 2011 the SCAF approved Decree 12, which reformed specific articles of the 1977 Law 40 on political parties. Furthermore, on 16 April 2011, the Supreme Administrative Court dissolved the National Democratic Party (NDP), which had been the Egyptian hegemonic party since its creation in 1978. Numerous political parties were created at the start of the transition. Specifically, forty-two parties and four electoral coalitions (the liberal/left-wing Egyptian Bloc, the Islamic Alliance, the Continuous Revolution and the Democratic Alliance) ran in the elections for the first democratically elected People's Assembly.

Elections for the two parliamentary houses passed through a number of stages, which involved the People's Assembly (on 28–9 November, 14–15 December, and 3–4 January); and the Shura (Consultative) Council (29 January to March). The Islamist Freedom and Justice Party (FJP), the political wing of the Muslim Brotherhood (MB), came first at the People's Assembly elections, with 38 per cent of the votes and 43.4 per cent of the directly elected seats. However, the elected People's Assembly was suspended, following the Supreme Constitutional Court's ruling, on 14 June 2012, which found the electoral system to be partially unconstitutional.[4]

Presidential elections took place in 2012: the first round on 23–4 May, and the second on 16–17 June. Mohammed Morsi, Chairman of the FJP, took office on 30 June 2012, with 51.5 per cent of the votes in the second round of these elections. The turnout of 46.4 per cent in the first round, and 51.8 per cent in the second, cannot be considered high, taking into account that they were the first free presidential elections, and that legislative elections had averaged 65 per cent. The low participation rate appears to suggest an electorate unwilling to choose between an Islamist candidate and Ahmed Mohamed Shafik, the prime minister appointed by Mubarak at the start of the January 2011 revolution. Nevertheless, both the 2012 presidential and the 2010–11 legislative elections were considered free and fair by the Supreme Electoral Commission, local judges and national and international non-governmental organisations (Carter Center 2012: 2).

Thus, in the post-revolutionary phase there was a broadening of pluralism and political competence, although this produced a highly polarised situation between Islamist and secular parties. However, a further problem in the competition for power was that the army did not remain neutral during the transition, but instead acted as a 'veto player' in the political process. First, it established itself as a driver of the transition, concerned with its own interests, and later it intervened directly in the coup of 3 July 2013, when President Morsi ignored the ultimatum of the army to reconsider its exclusionary political policy. As O'Donnell et al. (1986) have pointed out, in authoritarian systems with military bases, the army will seek to lead the transition, and if it is unable to do that, it will establish itself in strong opposition to it (Melián 2016).

Following the military coup the new regime sought institutional legitimacy firstly through the approval of a new constitution, and later through the holding of presidential and legislative elections (Rougier and Lacroix 2016). It therefore reversed the sequence of stages of the previous transition period. The presidential elections took place on 26 May 2014, although the original military road map had called for parliamentary elections to be held first. Only two candidates managed to fulfil the formal requirements to present themselves for election: Abdel Fattah al-Sisi, former military commander-in-chief and minister of defence, and Hamdeem Sabahi, leader of the Egyptian Popular Current, a leftist secular party. Al-Sisi won an overwhelming victory with 96.9 per cent of the vote, although the official participation rate only reached 46 per cent. The presidential elections, however, cannot be considered to have been free and fair. International organisations denounced the harassment suffered by Sabahi supporters, the lack of impartiality of the High Elections Commission and the absence of control by electoral observers (Democracy International 2014).

The last elections for the People's Assembly took place on 18 October and 22 November 2015, depending on each governorate. However, the elections were invalid due to the exclusion of the FJP, which represent a significant electoral sector of Egyptian society.[5] A new majority electoral system was established by the interim president, Adly Mansour, on 5 June 2014.[6] Several party leaders criticised the new system, arguing that it gives individuals (whether independent or affiliated to a party) greater chances over political parties and empowers old networks, based on family and business ties, at the expense of political parties (Morsy 2015). The election led to 351 independents winning representation and two parties closest to the regime obtaining most seats: the Free Egyptians Party (sixty-five) and the Nation's Future Party (fifty-three). On the other hand, the Salafist al-Nour (Party of the Light), which backed the military coup of 2013 and sought to fill the electoral gap left by the JFP, only won eleven seats. Egyptians showed their political disaffection and their rejection of the elections with an official turnout of only 28 per cent. The elections were supervised by judicial authorities that, according to constitutional mandate, are in charge of these processes during the ten years that follow the establishment of the constitution. However, the electoral integrity of these elections was questioned and key relevant international organisations did not participate in the monitoring.

3.2 Autocratic government functioning

3.2.1 Concentration of power in the Morsi and al-Sisi regimes

On 11 February 2011 President Hosni Mubarak was forced from his post following persistent protests. As the transition literature highlights, the rupturing of the pact between the authoritarian leaders and the principle regime support group – the army in the case of Egypt – was indispensable to open the democratic transition process. Mubarak's regime fell when the army – probably unhappy with Mubarak's plan to allow his son Gamal to succeed him – decided not to suppress the social protests. This also fulfils the thesis of the paradigm of authoritarian persistence, which highlights the need to control the mechanisms of coercion for regime survival (Bellin 2004 and 2012). After the deposing of Mubarak the SCAF decreed the suspension of the 1971 constitution and the dissolution of the two parliamentary chambers, and assumed presidential and legislative powers.

Following presidential elections held in May and June 2012, the SCAF transferred executive power to President Morsi. Morsi also exercised legislative power by presidential decree, with no legislative branch check on his power due to the dissolution of the People's Assembly in June 2012 following a Supreme Constitutional Court ruling. On 24 July 2012 President Morsi appointed Hesham Qandil, an independent, as prime minister. In the new government there were three members of the Muslim Brotherhood, although most ministers came from the former government.

The military coup of 3 July 2013 ousted President Morsi. The SCAF appointed the president of the Supreme Constitutional Court, Adly Mansour, as interim president and directed him to approve a new constitution and organise elections. Following the May 2014 presidential elections Abdel Fattah al-Sisi assumed power. The 2014 constitution structured a semi-presidential regime in Egypt. Nevertheless, it was in fact a presidential type regime, in detriment to parliament and the prime minister.

Despite the fact that parliament can theoretically control government – the People's Assembly may impeach the president and can pass a no-confidence vote against any member of government or its head – its docility converted it into an institution at the service of government that makes it in practice un-accountable, given that there is no real possibility of it being removed either through elections or by parliament. Therefore, it is effectively an autocratic government in which there is no possibility of a peaceful rotation of government and separation of powers.

On the other hand, the judiciary has traditionally been more independent from the executive. Morsi sought to reduce the power of the judiciary by for example issuing the declaration on 22 November 2012 that aimed to prevent judicial review of presidential decisions. Additionally, the 2012 constitution reduced the size of the Supreme Constitutional Court by almost half and the Islamist-dominated Shura Council – at that time parliament's only chamber – reduced the mandatory judicial retirement age from seventy to sixty, which, if enacted, would have removed all but one of the remaining Supreme Constitutional Court judges, the whole of the Supreme Judicial Council, and the entire senior leadership of the judiciary (Risley 2016). Under al-Sisi, however, the judiciary recovered its authority. Judges played an important role in the first draft of the 2014 constitution, which was prepared by a committee of ten jurists. According to the 2014 constitution, the judiciary self-selects its members and senior officers, including the prosecutor general (articles 189 and 193). Similarly, the Supreme Constitutional Court selects its own members and chief justice (article 193). Some recent rulings may indicate that Egyptian courts are seeking to rein in the judiciary's influence – for example, the July 2016 ruling on the maritime border demarcation agreement under which the Egyptian government ceded the Red Sea islands of Tiran and Sanafir to Saudi Arabia.

Lastly, the government has fallen short due to its incapacity to meet citizens' basic needs and because of the corruption that directly implicates members of the army. The 2015 Corruption Perceptions Index ranks Egypt eighty-eight out of 168 countries and gave it a score of thirty-six points (Transparency International 2016). Corruption is a severe problem across the MENA region. As Ojeda and Cavatorta pointed out in Chapter 7, corruption does not refer simply to traditional bribery, but also 'to the widespread belief that the socio-economic system is rigged to the benefit of the few'.

3.2.2 The non-consensual constitutions of 2012 and 2014

In any transition process towards democracy the establishment of a durable political and social framework accepted by a broad majority is essential. However, Egypt's two constitutions approved in 2012 and 2014 marginalised political rivals and lacked the necessary national consensus (al-Ali 2016: 124).[7]

The procedure for approval of the 2012 constitution forecast that a constituent assembly would write a constitutional draft that would be ratified later in a referendum (Moustafa 2012). The Constituent Assembly was elected between November 2011 and January 2012, and comprised an equal number of parliamentarians and civil representatives. However, on 10 April 2012, the Assembly was invalidated by the High Administrative Tribunal, as it was not considered to be representative of Egyptian society, due to Islamist control of the body. At the beginning of June the People's Assembly agreed new principles for electing new members of the Constituent Assembly and, so, the constitutional process was in theory unblocked. However, secular and progressive members left the Assembly and denounced the imposition of the Islamist majority, especially because of their insistence on shariah as a source of law. On 30 November the constitutional project was approved by the remaining members of the Constituent Assembly and alternate members. Ignoring strong social opposition, President Morsi called a constitutional referendum for 15 and 22 December 2012, and saw the constitution confirmed with 63.8 per cent of votes, although only 32.9 per cent of the electorate participated. On 25 December 2012 the president of the republic signed the constitution and it came into force.

The 2012 constitution included positive aspects such as guaranteeing fundamental rights and freedoms, the distribution of power between institutions (through a semi-presidential governmental system), the limitation of presidential terms (two terms of four years each, article 133) and freedom of religion (although only Islamism, Judaism and Christianity were specifically mentioned, article 43). On the other hand, the constitution consolidated the Islamic nature of the state and confirmed the use of shariah as the main source of legislation (article 2). In addition, the new constitution 'sustained and even enhanced the institutional and social foundations of the military's power' (Brumberg 2012: 49). Thus, in order to gain military loyalty, the constitution conferred significant powers on the army. For example, seven of the fifteen members of the Higher Defence Council are from the military (article 197), and they have the legal authority to control the armed forces' budget and review laws that affect it. The constitution also established that the minister for defence must come from the army (article 195) and that military courts can judge civilians accused of crimes against the army (article 198).

After the ousting of Morsi on 3 July 2013, the 2012 constitution was suspended. On 8 July the interim president, Adly Mansur, issued a constitutional declaration authorising a temporary constitution to structure the interim period until a new constitution could be approved. A committee of ten appointed jurists proposed a constitutional draft, which was discussed and approved by a committee of fifty members appointed by the interim president, representing all sectors of Egyptian society. The constitutional referendum took place on 14–15 January 2014, with 98.1 per cent of voters showing their approval. It is necessary to emphasise the plebiscite character of the constitutional referendum as al-Sisi qualified his candidacy in the presidential elections on a clear victory for the 'yes' vote in the referendum. Nevertheless, the referendum turnout was low, at 38.1 per cent of eligible voters. The fast approval process for the new constitution seems to suggest that the new regime was pursuing constitutional legitimacy.

The current constitution has not fundamentally changed Morsi's version. Islam continues to be the state religion and shariah the main source of legislation (article 2). The constitution also prohibits political parties being formed on the basis of religion or discrimination based on sex, origin or on sectarian or geographic grounds (article 74). The 2014 constitution maintains the prerogatives of the army included in the 2012 constitution. The major change to the 2012 constitution aimed to restore the powers of the presidency. The president is the head of the state, the head of the executive branch and the supreme commander of the armed forces (articles 139 and 152). He or she appoints 5 per cent of the members of the House of Representatives and has the right to issue or object to laws (article 123), the prime minister, and the ministers of justice, interior and defence in the event that the government is chosen from the party or the coalition that holds a plurality of seats in the House of Representatives (article 146). In exchange, the House of Representatives may propose to withdraw confidence from the prime minister and ministers by majority, and from the president of the republic by approval of two-thirds of its members (article 161).

In brief, both the 2012 and 2014 constitutions lack democratic approval, as they were developed without the input of contrary political groups and were not supported by a broad social majority in the constitutional referendum. Regarding content, there is an imbalance of power in favour of the president although the current constitution contains basic democratic principles, such the guaranteeing in principle of citizens' rights and liberties. However, there is a lack of adjustment between what is formally written in the constitution and the autocratic exercise of power in the country.

3.2.3 Regression in the exercise of rights and freedoms

Since President al-Sisi came to power, rights and public freedoms have regressed further than under Mubarak. Political opposition is practically impossible, because any critical expression or activity against the government or the armed forces is suffocated. Human rights organisations report the use of torture, enforced disappearances, illegal arrest, mistreatment of detainees and death penalties for regime opponents. Judges have made harsh decisions against the current government's political adversaries, which reveal the judiciary's politicisation. Therefore, the rule of law is in question.

The freedoms of assembly and peaceful demonstration have been restricted since the 2013 military coup. Demonstrations in support of the deposed President Morsi, for example, were severely put down, resulting in more than a thousand deaths. Law 107 issued in November 2013 grants security officials discretion to ban any protest or meeting of more than ten people on very vague grounds, including meetings related to electoral campaigning. It also allows police officers to forcibly disperse any protest, with the threat of heavy prison sentences (Human Rights Watch 2013). Furthermore, the new counterter-rorism law gives the president the power to 'take any necessary measures to ensure public order and security'.

Freedom of association and syndication is also currently restricted. The Muslim Brotherhood has been banned and more than 20,000 leaders and sympathisers jailed and sentenced to long prison terms. Similarly, the April 6 Youth Movement was outlawed and its leaders imprisoned. On the other hand, independent trade unions proliferated following the 2011 uprising, but the government has not officially recognised them and the activities of those that do exist have been controlled, even though the 2014 constitution guarantees the right to form independent syndicates and unions (article 76). Likewise, the trade union strikes of 2014 were severely put down by the security forces. Successive governments have prepared draft laws on syndication since 2011 but none have been adopted, so the 1976 law continues to be in force (Human Rights Watch 2016a).

The Egyptian authorities have cracked down on free speech by arresting and imprisoning journalists and online critics. One specific problem is that the constitution itself authorises censorship of the media during times of war or social mobilisation (article 71). Additionally, the counterterrorism law imposes heavy fines on journalists whose reporting on terrorism differs from official statements (Freedom House 2016b).

4 Failed democratic transition: failed state in Libya

The uprising against al-Gaddafi's regime fuelled a seven-month civil war that culminated in the leader's death on 20 October 2011. Western governments intervened in the armed conflict to help ensure the rebels' victory over pro-al-Gaddafi forces and the United Nations Security Council (UNSC) approved a 'no-fly zone', which was overseen by NATO (UNSC Resolution 1973 of 17 March 2011).[8]

The Libyan road map for transition towards democracy included, like in the Tunisian and Egyptian cases, holding founding elections and the approval of a constitution, which has not occurred to date. The absence of prior institutional architecture and of experience of party and political participation represented an insuperable obstacle for the country's democratisation. The rejection of the electoral results in the second legislative elections by the Islamists led to the failure of the transition process and the establishment of two governments and two parliaments. Libya became immersed in a destabilising political and military confrontation that led to an anarchic state, characterised by the fragmentation of power and weak and contested government legitimacy (Buzan 2012). In order to progress from this situation, in March 2016 rival political forces agreed a transitional unity government, known as the Government of National Accord (GNA). According to the political agreement, the House of Representatives (HR) had to conduct a formal vote on the composition of the proposed GNA and amend the constitutional declaration. However, many members of the HR and militias have still not accepted this new government structure.

4.1 From the absence of pluralism under al-Gaddafi's regime to a belligerent pluralism

Given that political parties did not exist under al-Gaddafi, their creation was one of the first challenges of the democratic transition. In January 2012 the

National Transitional Council (NTC) abolished a 1972 ruling prohibiting political parties and, on 25 April 2012, issued a party law. This law banned political parties founded on religion, region or ethnicity, although it only lasted a week as the decision was then reversed. However, the newly established parties never came close to resembling genuine political parties as they were lacking in political ideology and, consequently, in specific programmes for the future of Libya. They were not vehicles for citizen representation, but rather loose political alliances based on local interests and militia or tribal allegiances, often with a charismatic leader fronting the outfit (see Storm, Chapter 3; Lesch 2014; Pargeter 2016).

Despite this, following the death of al-Gaddafi, the emerging political forces reached agreements on several key points: approval of the electoral system, holding of the first competitive elections, formation of a transitional coalition government representing the main political trends (independent, liberal and Islamist), approval of the procedure for drafting the constitution and recognition of Libya's multicultural identity (Arab, Amazigh, Tuareg and Toubou).

The first competitive polls took place on 7 July 2012, to elect the General National Congress (GNC). Previously, on 28 January 2012, the NTC had issued Law 4/2012 to regulate the electoral system. However, the electoral law was difficult to develop due to: the geographical and demographic peculiarities (a sparse population in a huge territory, concentrated near the coast), tribal and regional cleavages, the lack of previous regulations regarding administrative divisions and parties in electoral processes, and the weakness of the state and society in the wake of the armed conflict. The text of the law went through substantial and protracted revisions as a result of the debate that ensued when the drafts were presented. Finally, a parliament of 200 members was established, elected by a parallel system. In accordance with this system, 120 seats were assigned by simple majority, in uninominal districts reserved for independent candidates (in a 'first-past-the-post' system) and by a system of non-transferable vote in multi-member districts, while eighty seats were distributed via a proportional 'largest remainder system' for candidatures in closed 'zipper' lists, which respected equality between the sexes. Additionally, electoral districts were demarcated by taking into account population density and geography (Szmolka 2014). The result was that thirty-nine of the eighty seats were won by the National Forces Alliance (the NFA was formed in February 2012 by Islamic groups, civil society organisations and representatives of the Amazigh, Tuareg and Toubou communities and was led by Mahmoud Jibril, who was a rebel prime minister during the civil war). The Muslim Brotherhood's Justice and Construction Party (JCP) came in second with seventeen seats. The remaining twenty-four seats under the proportional representation system went to nineteen small parties, which took fewer than three seats each.

An additional 120 seats were filled under the majority system, in which only independent candidates stood. The independents tipped the scales in favour of an Islamist majority in the GNC. A total of thirty-three women were elected. Despite the difficulties in the electoral process, the elections were assessed as fair by the Electoral High Commission, which comprises judges, lawyers, young people, women and human rights activists. Additionally, judicial control of the electoral process was established and international observers were permitted. In line with the transitional road map, on 8 August 2012, the NTC transferred legislative power to the elected parliament (Pack and Cook 2015).

A second election was held on 20 February 2014, in this case to elect a Constituent Assembly. According to the constitutional declaration of 2011, the GNC was responsible for the appointment of a sixty-member commission to draft the constitution (article 30). However, two days before the 2012 elections, the NTC established that the constituent assembly would be elected by the people and not appointed (third amendment of the constitutional declaration). Nevertheless, on February 2013, the Supreme Court invalidated this amendment as it had not been passed by a majority of two thirds of votes, as required by the constitutional declaration. Finally, on 10 April 2013, a political agreement confirmed the election system for the Constituent Assembly. The sixty members of the Constituent Assembly were deliberately non-partisan and were charged with drafting a constitution within eighteen months of their election.

On 25 June 2014 the third elections took place for the HR, which was intended to replace the GNC. The HR was elected by a majority system, rather than by the mixed electoral system employed in 2012. All candidates stood as independents in the 2014 elections to avoid further political violence, unlike in 2012 where candidates could also be put forward by political parties (Lefevre 2014). Amid violence, turnout fell from 62 per cent in 2012 to 42 per cent in 2014. The Islamists lost the elections and refused to recognise the new parliament. On November 2014 the Tripoli-based Supreme Court declared the HR to be illegal and voided the election result. However, the international community recognised the legitimacy of the elections, which were supervised by the UN. Fierce political and military opposition forced the newly elected parliament into exile in Tobruk as well as the newly formed government. The HR was forecast to appoint an interim president, enact a new constitution and publish an electoral law to elect a new parliament.

4.2 A divided and ineffective government

Libya has had a number of governments in the last five years. The first was the rebel interim government formed, on 27 February 2011, by anti-al-Gaddafi forces in

Benghazi: the NTC. The NTC brought together members of the military, tribal leaders, Islamists of various tendencies, communists, Nasserists, monarchists and liberals, and was led by the chairman Mustafa Abdul Jalil and Prime Minister Mahmoud Jibril (from 5 March to 23 October 2011). After the death of al-Gaddafi, Ali Tarhouni was named acting prime minister for a month. On 24 November 2011 Abderrahim al-Kib was appointed to form a new government, which lasted until 14 November 2012 when the GNC approved prime minister Ali Zeidan's cabinet. On 11 March 2014, following two *coup d'état* attempts, the GNC voted to remove Zeidan, naming the minister of defence Abdullah al-Thani as interim prime minister. On 13 April 2014 al-Thani resigned after an attack on his family. In May 2014 the GNC elected Ahmed Maiteeq prime minister in a disputed vote in the assembly. However, on 9 June 2014 the Libyan Supreme Court ruled that the procedure had been invalid, and al-Thani returned to power.

Following the 2014 legislative elections and the Islamists rejection of the election results, the Libyan government divided into two parliaments and cabinets. Both parliaments adopted new laws but it was unclear to what extent they were enforced. On September 2014, while the HR reappointed al-Thani as prime minister, dissidents in Tripoli appointed Omar al-Hassi, who was then replaced by Khalifa al-Ghawi on 31 March 2015. The political dispute then led to a civil war in May 2015 between various militias aligned with the two governments. Amid the armed conflict the Constituent Assembly, which appears to enjoy the recognition of both the GNC and the HR, published a preliminary draft constitution in October 2015.

Additionally, regional actors became involved in the Libyan conflict. While Qatar and Turkey sided with the Islamists, Egypt, Saudi Arabia and the United Arab Emirates supplied arms to the Libyan army, commanded by General Haftar, and supported the Tobruk government. Further complications include the fact that Islamic State (IS) took control of several Libyan cities, and many fighters loyal to al-Qaeda in the Islamic Maghreb continue to operate in Libya.

On 17 December 2015 the United Nations Support Mission in Libya (UNSMIL) brokered a ceasefire and a peace agreement between members of the HR and the new GNC. Under the terms of the agreement, a nine-member presidential council and a seventeen-member interim government of national accord was formed in order to hold new elections within two years. The HR remained as a legislative and advisory body, and was renamed the State Council. On 31 March 2016 Fayez al-Sarraj formed a unity government in Tripoli. However, to date, the agreement has failed to end hostilities or build faith in government institutions.

In sum, since al-Gaddafi every government has been contested, and the state has therefore been incapable of exerting effective control over the country as a whole.

4.3 An impossible exercise in rights and liberties

There was an improvement in public rights and liberties after the fall and death of al-Gaddafi. However, the situation stalled and deteriorated due to problems in the transition process.

The interim government passed a law on freedom of assembly in December 2012 (Law 65/2012 on guidelines for peaceful demonstrations). However, the law failed to include guarantees and imposed severe restrictions on the right to assembly (Human Rights Watch 2014). Demonstrations have been frequent since 2011, though marches have often ended in violence. The ongoing disturbances have seriously discouraged peaceful assemblies (Freedom House 2016c). Moreover, violence has impeded civilian access to food, health care, water, sanitation and education. There are approximately 435,000 internally displaced people in Libya: many of those have been uprooted more than once and over 100,000 reside in makeshift camps, schools and warehouses (Amnesty International 2015).

The law on freedom of association has yet to be adopted and so there is no law that specifically regulates civil society organisations. Libya's 1953 penal code is still in force and contains articles that undermine freedom of association, due to broad and ambiguous definitions and the criminalisation of acts by local and international NGOs. Additionally, the code offers the possibility of the death penalty for anyone who establishes or participates in unlawful organisations (Human Rights Watch 2014).

Media freedom significantly increased after the fall of the al-Gaddafi regime. However, the ongoing armed conflict has considerably worsened its legal, political and security situation. Specific laws restrict freedom of expression: for example, on 22 January 2014 the GNC passed Decree 5/2014, 'concerning the cessation and ban on the broadcasting of particular satellite channels', which allowed authorities to ban stations that criticise the government. And, on 5 February 2014 the GNC announced Law 5/2014 under which 'harming' the February 17 revolution of 2011 became a criminal offence (Human Rights Watch 2014). Therefore, the ability of journalists to undertake critical investigative work has been undermined. Journalists and media offices have been attacked on several occasions, not only by non-state actors, but also occasionally by the national security forces (Freedom House 2015).

Lastly, the rule of law is in doubt in Libya because of widespread violence and because the legal system is barely functioning. Courts in several cities are closed and judges and lawyers have been attacked and abducted. People seen as being loyal to al-Gaddafi have been detained for years without charge or trial (Amnesty International 2015). The Special Procedures Law (38/2012) enacted in May 2012 gave anti-al-Gaddafi revolutionaries immunity against prosecution for serious crimes, including war crimes and crimes against humanity, if they were believed necessary to the success of the 2011 uprising (Human Rights Watch 2014).

5 The aborted transition in Yemen

Anti-government protests grew strongly in Yemen in 2011. Beside socio-economic improvements, demonstrators demanded the resignation of President Ali Abdullah Saleh and of his family members from their respective public offices, the revocation of the constitution, the dissolution of parliament, the establishment of an interim government, the arrest of those responsible for corruption and repression, and a new security system (Hamad 2011: 105). Social unrest led to fighting breaking out on several fronts among, on the one hand, factions loyal to the regime and, on the other, dissident sectors of the army, particular tribes (supporters of Sheikh Sadiq al-Ahmar) and al-Qaeda militants in the Arabian Peninsula. In April 2011, backed by the United States, the European Union and the UN, the Gulf Cooperation Council (GCC) agreed that President Saleh should resign on 23 November 2011, after several failed proposals. According to the deal, Saleh had to transfer his presidential powers to Vice-president Abd Rabbuh Mansour Hadi, in exchange for immunity for himself, his family and his close collaborators.

Yemen chose a different model of transition to Tunisia, Egypt and Libya. Firstly, the authorities followed a reformist route that included power-sharing between the old regime elites and the traditional opposition parties. The interim president Hadi represented an element of continuity with the previous regime, in which he had served as vice-president since October 1994. The counterweight to Hadi was provided by the appointment of the independent Mohammed Basindawa, on 27 November 2011, as prime minister. Similarly, the provisional government that emerged in the aftermath of Saleh's resignation was formed in such a way as to ensure parity between representatives of the General People's Congress (GPC) – the hegemonic party since Yemen's unification in 1990 – and the opposition parties. Secondly, the Yemeni transition inverted the traditional sequence of stages to install democracy. Yemen chose to reach an initial consensus among the different social and political forces before embarking on the process of approving the constitution and holding legislative and presidential elections. And, thirdly, the Yemeni democratic transition had strong international backing. The UN oversaw the transitional process and sent a special envoy for Yemen, Jamal Benomar.[9]

5.1 The failed pluralist consensus

The party system under Saleh's regime can be characterised as hegemonic pluralism exercised by the GPC. Unlike Tunisian and Egyptian hegemonic parties, the Yemeni GPC remained in power after President Saleh's resignation, and participated in the transition towards democracy. On the other hand, opposition party unity facilitated dialogue with the government. The opposition parties had worked together since 2001, mainly with the aim of reforming the electoral system. In 2005 five parties had come together to form the Joint Meeting Parties: the Islamist Islah (Reform), the Yemen Socialist Party (the former single party of South Yemen), Al Haqq (Zaidi), the Nasserist Unionist Party and the Union of Popular Forces. The Joint Meeting Parties participated in the GCC plan and supported it, while the majority of the revolutionary protest movement and the Houthis – a social movement from northern Yemen – rejected it. Similarly, opposition parties participated in the unity government with parity of representation, and supported the candidacy of the acting president Abd Rabbuh Mansour Hadi as the sole consensus candidate in the 2012 presidential elections (Hamad 2011: 87 and 106).

In order to achieve consensus for the new political regime, and in line with the GCC plan, the National Dialogue Conference (NDC) was created, which operated from March 2013 to January 2014. It comprised 565 representatives, which included both sexes as well as people from the conservative elite and the new social and political movements. The NDC also incorporated Houthi rebel representatives from the north and from the southern separatist movement. Such diversity led to internal tensions and conflict, with the old elite seeking to preserve its power and privilege, while new political actors from progressive movements pushed for more democratic change in order to establish a modern, civil and egalitarian state (Strzelecka 2015). The NDC produced a report with approximately 1,400 recommendations for a new constitution and suggested the extension of Hadi's term of office for a further year to oversee the democratic transition. Following the end of the NDC's work, on 9 March 2014, President Hadi announced the creation of the Constitutional Drafting Commission (CDC) to draft the new constitution.

However, the initial consensus among the political forces ruptured in 2014, which led to armed conflict among, on the one hand, the Houthis and those close to ex-President Saleh and, on the other, President Hadi's internationally recognised government and his ally party, Islah. Although planned in the transitional road map, the conflict made the holding of the legislative and presidential elections impossible. Therefore the only elections that have taken place in five years were those in 2012 to legitimise Hadi's interim presidency.

5.2 Yemeni governments following the Arab Spring

One consequence of the persistent protests was that Saleh announced on 2 February 2011 that he would not run for re-election in the elections planned for 2013 and that he would not pass power to his son. On 20 March Saleh dismissed his whole cabinet but remained in a caretaker role with the intention of forming a new government. However, on 4 June, Vice-president Abd Rabbuh Mansour Hadi took over as acting president after a bomb attack on Saleh and other members of government and parliament. Saleh flew to Saudi Arabia to be treated for his injuries, declared the transfer of power as temporary and returned to the country on 23 September. Finally, however, on 23 November, after several failed attempts, Saleh signed the agreement proposed by the GCC, under which he would resign and transfer the presidency to Hadi in exchange for immunity. On 21 January 2012 the House of Representatives approved the immunity law.

In line with the agreement, presidential elections took place on 21 February 2012, with Abd Rabbuh Mansour Hadi as the only candidate. Hadi received 99.8 per cent of the vote with a 64.8 per cent turnout. The agreement foresaw a two-year presidency to draft a new constitution, reform the electoral system and hold parliamentary and presidential elections in 2014.

However, the Houthis took Sana'a in September 2014 and forced President Hadi and his government to resign. The Houthis' success was possible because of their alliance with former President Saleh's network, which included core factions from the Yemeni military and an extensive tribal network (Zimmerman 2016). The Houthis and Saleh also benefited from social discontent due to government corruption and the poor standard of living. In November 2014 Hadi and the Houthis signed an agreement sponsored by the UN, which stipulated a new cabinet headed by an independent, Khaled Bahah. On 17 January 2015 the CDC presented the final constitutional draft. The Houthis rejected the constitutional text, mainly because of the division of the territory into six federal states, and took up arms. In February 2015 the Houthis proposed their own constitution, dissolved Yemen's parliament and announced the formation of their own interim government. In March of the same year President Hadi withdrew his resignation and relocated his government to Riyadh (Saudi Arabia).

The Yemeni war led to a wider regional conflict. Since March 2015 an international coalition – led by Saudi Arabia and backed by the US, United Kingdom and France – has intervened in Yemen by supporting Hadi's government. On the other hand, Iran and the Lebanese Hezbollah back the Houthis with funding, training and weapons. Therefore, the Yemeni conflict has become a 'proxy war' of the regional struggle between Saudi Arabia and Iran (Zimmerman 2016).

In short, Hadi's governmental authority is challenged by various sectors, such as the young, the Houthis, Saleh's supporters, secessionists from South Yemen, al-Qaeda in the Arabian Peninsula and the so-called IS in Aden and Abyan. On the other hand, due to security threats and the weakness of the Yemeni economy, the state has been incapable of meeting the basic needs of its citizens. The country is therefore in a humanitarian crisis.

5.3 Worsening situation of rights and liberties

It is impossible to seriously discuss rights and liberties given the current situation of armed conflict in Yemen. In theory, freedoms of assembly and association are constitutionally guaranteed. However, a new law on association drafted in 2014 could not be approved because of the war. Several NGOs have closed and others have had serious difficulties operating in the country.

The only legal change to rights and liberties has come about by the Freedom of Information Law in 2012. However, media censorship and self-censorship remain. The authorities frequently harass journalists who are reporting on the violence (Freedom House 2015d). Also, the government blocks websites they deem offensive and in general Internet penetration is low, which is related to poor literacy levels and economic failings (see García-Marín, Chapter 10).

Regarding the rule of law, the executive routinely interferes in the judicial sphere. Furthermore, judges do not see their rulings enforced, particularly those issued against prominent tribal or political leaders. Lacking an effective court system, citizens often resort to tribal justice or direct appeals to executive authorities. National and international agencies also report arbitrary detention, torture and abuse of detainees by the security forces. All parties to the conflict have committed war crimes and other serious violations of international law (Amnesty International 2016).

In conclusion, Yemen has not transited towards democracy from a hegemonic and restrictive authoritarianism. At present Yemen can be characterised as an anarchic and failed state.

6 Conclusions

Four countries began to transition towards democracy following the Arab Spring: Tunisia, Egypt, Libya and Yemen. However, of those only Tunisia has shifted from hegemonic authoritarianism to a democratic regime. Democratic progress in Tunisia was possible thanks to agreements between political actors, concessions from a dominant party and a strong and participative civil society. On the other hand, despite the Egyptian transition taking place in a similar scenario of polarisation between Islamist and secular parties, Egypt failed in its democratic passage due to a lack of agreement between political forces, an exclusionary process led by the Islamists, and the interference of a non-accountable actor – the army – in political affairs. Therefore, Egypt continues to be a hegemonic and restrictive pluralist authoritarian state, as it was in the Mubarak era. The Egyptian case shows that electoral pluralism and participatory rights are insufficient conditions to guarantee a democratic transition.

On the one hand, a movement towards democracy has been aborted in Libya and Yemen, and in fact has led to fragmented state institutions and ongoing armed conflicts. In Libya the lack of prior institutional architecture and of experience of party participation and political groups represented an insurmountable obstacle for democratisation. On the other hand, the model of democratic transition that was carried out in Yemen was favourable to the achievement of democracy. It sought a broad social and political consensus for the new state before holding elections and approving a constitution, and had the involvement of the international community in the design and implementation of the transitional road map. However, empowerment of old regime elites in the transition process and, on the other hand, the exclusion of revolutionary movements, the lack of consensus to satisfy the demands of the independence movement in the south, and antagonism between political forces and their regional backers have doomed the democratic transition to failure.

Notes

1. The Tunisian General Labour Union (Union Générale Tunisienne du Travail, UGTT), the Tunisian Human Rights League (Ligue Tunisienne des Droits de l'Homme, LTDH), the Tunisian Union for Industry, Trade and Handicrafts (Union Tunisienne de l'Industrie, du Commerce et de l'Artisanat, UTICA) and the Tunisian Bar Association.
2. In May 2014 the NCA narrowly defeated the proposed article 167 of the election law, which would have continued to disqualify members of the old ruling party who served in the government under Ben Ali from participating in politics.
3. The scale ranges from zero (a highly corrupt country) to 100 (very clean). Rank one is occupied by the most transparent country.
4. The electoral law was passed by the council of ministers on 25 September 2011, and enacted by the SCAF two days later, after a partial revision. This law established a complex parallel system for the election of the people's assembly, whereby two thirds of the candidates were elected under the largest remainder formula in closed and blocked lists, and a third by a simple majority of nominal candidates. At first, independent candidates could only be elected by a simple majority and parties could not stand for seats reserved for independents. This approach was rejected by all the political parties, which led to it being reformed on 1 October to allow parties to compete for seats distributed by a simple majority, while not giving independents the same chance. However, this was considered unconstitutional by the Supreme Constitutional Court.

5. The FJP was dissolved and the Muslim Brotherhood was declared to be a terrorist organisation on 23 September 2013.

6. Of 567 representatives, 420 members are elected through competition over individual constituencies; 120 are elected from larger multi-seat constituencies based on a winner-takes-all closed list system; and twenty-seven members (5 per cent) are appointed by the president. Both political parties and independents can run for both the single member and list seats (Morsy 2015).

7. At the start of the transition, on 19 March 2011, a partial constitutional reform was carried out by referendum. The objective was to provide the framework for holding legislative and presidential elections. As a result of the referendum, the SCAF published the constitutional declaration, containing sixty-three articles that were to remain in force until the approval of the constitution.

8. Other international measures were taken, such as the arms embargo, an order by the International Penal Court to detain al-Gaddafi for crimes against humanity, and the recognition of the National Transitional Council (NTC) by various countries, and so on.

9. See the secretary-general's statement of 21 May 2012 and the United Nations Security Council Resolution 2014 of 21 October 2011, Resolution 2051 of 12 June 2012 and Resolution 2140 of 26 February 2014.

References

Al-Ali, Zaid (2016), 'Egypt's third constitution in three years: a critical analysis', in Bernard Rougier and Stéphane Lacroix (eds), *Egypt's Revolutions: Politics, Religion, and Social Movements*, New York: Palgrave Macmillan, pp. 123–38.

Amnesty International (2015), *Libya 2014/2015*. Available at <https://www.amnesty.org/en/countries/middle-east-and-north-africa/libya/report-libya/> (last accessed 30 June 2016).

Amnesty International (2016), *Yemen 2014/2015*. Available at <https://www.amnesty.org/en/countries/middle-east-and-north-africa/yemen/report-yemen/> (last accessed 30 June 2016).

Bellin, Eva (2004), 'The robustness of authoritarianism in the Middle East: exceptionalism in comparative perspective', *Comparative Politics*, 36 (2): 139–57.

Bellin, Eva (2012), 'Reconsidering the robustness of authoritarianism in the Middle East: lessons from the Arab Spring', *Comparative Politics*, 44 (2): 127–49.

Ben Achour, Rafâa (2014), 'La constitution tunisienne du 27 janvier 2014', *Revue Française de Droit Constitutionnel*, 4 (100): 783–801.

Brown, Nathan J. (2013), 'Egypt's failed transition', *Journal of Democracy*, 24: 45–58.

Buzan, Barry (2012), *People, States, and Fear: the National Security Problem in International Relations*, Brighton: Wheatsheaf Books.

Carter Center (2012), *Final Report of the Carter Center Mission to Witness the 2011–2012 Parliamentary Elections in Egypt*. Available at <http://www.cartercenter.org/resources/pdfs/news/peace_publications/election_reports/egypt-2011-2012-final-rpt.pdf> (last accessed 26 September 2012).

Democracy International (2014), *Preliminary Statement: Egypt's 2014 Presidential Elections*. Available at <http://democracyinternational.com/resources/preliminary-statement-egypt-s-2014-presidential-election/> (last accessed 24 May 2016).

Freedom House (2016a), *Tunisia Report 2016*. Available at <https://freedomhouse.org/report/freedom-world/2016/tunisia> (last accessed 2 September 2016).

Freedom House (2016b), *Egypt Report 2016*. Available at <https://freedomhouse.org/report/freedom-world/2016/egypt> (last accessed 2 September 2016).

Freedom House (2016c), *Libya Report 2015*. Available at <https://freedomhouse.org/report/freedom-world/2016/libya> (last accessed 30 June 2016).

Freedom House (2016d), *Yemen Report 2015*. Available at <https://freedomhouse.org/report/freedom-world/2015/yemen> (last accessed 1 July 2016).

Gana, Nouri (2013), *The Making of the Tunisian Revolution*, Edinburgh: Edinburgh University Press.

Hamad, Leila (2011), 'Yemen: de la revolución pacífica a las luchas por el poder', in Ignacio Gutiérrez De Terán and Ignacio Álvarez-Ossorio (eds), *Informe sobre las revueltas árabes*, Madrid: Ediciones del Oriente y del Mediterráneo.

Heydemann, Steven (2007), *Upgrading Authoritarianism in the Arab World*, The Brookings Institution, Analysis Paper 13: 1–37. Available at <http://www.brookings.edu/,/media/Files/rc/papers/2007/10arabworld/10arabworld.pdf> (last accessed 20 January 2016).

Human Rights Watch (2013), *Egypt: Deeply Restrictive New Assembly Law*. Available at <https://www.hrw.org/news/2013/11/26/egypt-deeply-restrictive-new-assembly-law> (last accessed 27 June 2016).

Human Rights Watch (2014), *Libya: UPR Submission September 2014*. Available at <https://www.amnesty.org/en/countries/middle-east-and-north-africa/libya/report-libya/> (last accessed 30 June 2016).

Human Rights Watch (2016a), *Egypt: Unshackle Workers' Right to Organize*. Available at <https://www.hrw.org/news/2016/04/30/egypt-unshackle-workers-right-organize> (last accessed 20 September 2016).

Human Rights Watch (2016b), *Tunisia: events of 2015*. Available at <https://www.hrw.org/world-report/2016/country-chapters/tunisia> (last accessed 27 June 2016).

Lefevre, Raphael (2014), 'An Egyptian scenario for Libya?', *Journal of North African Studies*, 19 (4): 602–7.

Lesch, Ann (2014), 'Troubled political transitions: Tunisia, Egypt and Libya', *Middle East Policy Journal*, 21 (1): 62–74.

Martínez-Fuentes, Guadalupe (2011), 'La transición democrática post-benalista: procedimiento y alcance del cambio político en Túnez', *Revista Jurídica de la Universidad Autónoma de Madrid*, 23: 119–34.

Martínez-Fuentes, Guadalupe (2015a), 'Legitimidad gubernamental y movilización ciudadana en contextos de cambio: estudio comparado de Egipto, Túnez y Marruecos', *Revista CIDOB d'Afers Internacionals*, 108–9: 45–67.

Martínez-Fuentes, Guadalupe (2015b), 'Política electoral transicional en Túnez (2011–2014): desinstitucionalización del autoritarismo y aprendizaje democrático', *Revista de Estudios Políticos*, 169: 235–65.

Melián, Luis (2016), *Procesos de cambio político tras la Primavera Árabe. Un estudio comparado de los casos de Túnez, Egipto y Jordania*, PhD Dissertation, University of Salamanca.

Morsy, Ahmed (2015), *The Egyptian Parliamentary Elections*, Middle East Institute, 26 January. Available at <http://www.mei.edu/content/article/egyptian-parliamentary-elections-101> (last accessed 15 June 2016).

Moustafa, Tamir (2012), *Drafting Egypt's Constitution*, Doha: Brookings Institution.

Murphy, Emma C. (2013), 'The Tunisian elections of October 2011: a democratic consensus', *The Journal of North African Studies*, 18 (2): 231–47.

National Democratic Institute (2011), *Final Report on the Tunisian National Constituent Assembly Elections*. Available at <https://www.ndi.org/files/tunisia-final-election-report-021712_v2.pdf> (last accessed 11 March 2012).

O'Donnell, Guillermo, Philippe C. Schmitter and Laurence Whitehead (1986), *Transitions from Authoritarian Rule: Tentative Conclusions about Uncertain Democracies*, Baltimore: Johns Hopkins University Press.

Pack, Jason and Haley Cook (2015), 'The July 2012 Libyan election and the origin of post-Qadhafi appeasement', *Middle East Journal*, 69 (2): 171–98.

Pargeter, Alison (2016), 'Libya: from "reform" to revolution', in Yahya Zoubir and Gregory White (eds), *North African Politics: Change and Continuity*, London: Routledge, pp. 178–95.

Risley, David (2016), *Egypt's Judiciary: Obstructing or Assisting Reform?*, Middle East Institute Policy Focus 2016–4. Available at <http://www.mei.edu/content/at/egypt%E2%80%99s-judiciary-obstructing-or-assisting-reform> (last accessed 29 June 2016).

Rivetti, Paola (2015), 'Continuity and change before and after the uprisings in Tunisia, Egypt and Morocco: regime reconfiguration and policymaking in North Africa', *British Journal of Middle Eastern Studies*, 42 (1): 1–11.

Rougier, Bernard and Stephane Lacroix (eds) (2016), *Egypt's Revolutions*, New York: Palgrave Macmillan.

Stepan, Alfred (2012), 'Tunisia's transition and the twin tolerations', *Journal of Democracy*, 23 (2): 89–103.

Strzelecka, Ewa (2015), *Género, Cultura, Islam y Desarrollo. Construcción de una Cultura Política de Resistencia Feminista en Yemen*, Granada: University of Granada Press.

Szmolka, Inmaculada (2014), 'Political change in North Africa and Arab Middle East: constitutional reforms and electoral processes', Arab Studies Quarterly, 36 (2): 128–48.

Szmolka, Inmaculada (2015), 'Exclusionary and non consensual transitions versus inclusive and consensual democratizations: the cases of Egypt and Tunisia', *Arab Studies Quarterly*, 37 (1): 73–95, DOI: 10.13169/arabstudquar.37.1.0073.

Transparency International (2016), *Corruption Perceptions Index 2015*. Available at <http://www.transparency.org/cpi2015> (last accessed 7 July 2016).

Volpi, Frédéric (2013), 'Explaining (and re-explaining) political change in the Middle East during the Arab Spring: trajectories of democratization and of authoritarianism in the Maghreb', *Democratization*, 20: 6, 969–90, DOI: 10.1080/13510347.2012.668438.

Zimmerman, Katherine (2016), *Signaling Saudi Arabia: Iranian Support to Yemen's al Houthis*, Critical Threats, 15 April. Available at <http://www.criticalthreats.org/yemen/zimmerman-signaling-saudi-arabia-iranian-support-to-yemen-al-houthis-april-15-2016> (last accessed 23 June 2016).

Chapter 16

Political liberalisation processes

*Inmaculada Szmolka and
Irene Fernández-Molina*

1 Introduction

This chapter focuses on political liberalisation processes undertaken in parallel in other Middle East and North Africa (MENA) countries such as Morocco, Jordan, Oman and Algeria. As the analyses of transitional and dynamic authoritarianism underscored, political liberalisation acts as an escape valve for authoritarian regimes to defuse social discontent. As on previous occasions, the political reforms that took place from 2011 onwards were planned and led by the authoritarian rulers in a top-down fashion, with varying degrees of political and social support. These post-Arab Spring processes focused mainly on two aspects: reforms of the constitution and party and electoral laws (none of which had any significant impact on the distribution of power though), and changes in each regime's degree of representation and/or political participation. Only in the case of Morocco did these changes produce alternation in government although, as shall be seen, even there the repercussions were limited by the need for the election-winning party to form a coalition government and because of royal interference in the executive. Overall, the post-2011 political liberalisation processes have been largely cosmetic and therefore have not led to a change in the authoritarian nature of the political regimes. Such a pattern suggests overall continuity with previous reforms launched in these and other Arab states in the 1990s and the 2000s, and poses the question as to the continuing relevance of the literature on authoritarian resilience (Brumberg 2002; Albrecht and Schlumberger 2004; Heydemann 2007) which seemed to be relatively (temporarily) overruled by the events in 2011 (Bellin 2012). This chapter aims to lay the foundations for a more nuanced understanding of political change in the absence of regime change by presenting an empirical stocktaking of the post-2011 reforms in Morocco, Jordan, Oman and Algeria. The evidence gathered largely supports the argument that the lack of democratic change should not be confused with plain and simple authoritarian continuity (Cavatorta 2015).

2 Significant political reforms without regime change in Morocco

Of the countries that began political liberalisation processes after the Arab Spring, the changes in Morocco have been the most significant, although even there they have not led to a democratisation of the regime. As a result of the popular protests in Morocco, driven by the 20 February Movement (20-F Movement) (Hoffmann and König 2013; Desrues 2013), King Mohammed VI drove forward a package of political reforms in 2011: changes to the law on political parties, approval of a new constitution, reform of the law for the election to the House of Representatives, early elections – the most competitive seen so far – and the appointment of a new head of government from the winning party in the elections (Dalmasso 2012). However, despite these positive changes, the king retains the majority of his legislative and executive powers. Given this situation, a number of political forces still refuse to participate in the political game. Therefore, the Moroccan regime continues to be defined as quasi-competitive and restrictive pluralist authoritarianism.

2.1 The quasi-competitive multiparty system and the 2011 elections

Morocco has had a multiparty system since its independence in 1956, although its structure is conditioned by 'red lines' set by the regime (the monarchy, Islam and the territorial integrity of the state). Although the opposition can criticise the government and propose alternative programmes, Morocco's monarchy has designed a fragmented multiparty system in order to prevent any single hegemonic group challenging royal power. However, while there is broad political pluralism in Morocco, there are parties and movements that do not participate in the political game either because they are banned by the regime or they exclude themselves, as they do not have trust in the democratic guarantees. The leading non-parliamentary opposition group is the Islamist al-Adl wa al-Ihsan (Justice and Charity) movement, which is illegal, although tolerated by the authorities. Other Islamist groups face state harassment and are banned from the political process, such as the al-Badil al-Hadari Party (Party of the Civilisational Alternative).

Party regulation was modified by the Organic Law 29-11 of 22 October 2011. The new law established democratic standards in relation to the constitution of parties, the principles of organisation and administration, financing (public and private) and control, the union and merger of parties, and the sanctioning system. The 2011 party law, like its predecessors in 2002 and 2006, prevented the formation of parties on religious, linguistic, ethnic or regional grounds, or, more generally, on any discriminatory basis contrary to human rights. Likewise, political parties must not impinge on the Muslim religion, the monarchical regime, constitutional principles, democratic foundations or the national unity and territorial integrity of the kingdom. Each of these limits on political parties is confirmed in the new constitution approved in July 2011. Despite these restrictions, the Moroccan regime tolerates formations that represent Islamist or Berber interests.

The social protests triggered early elections – almost one year earlier than forecast – to the House of Representatives, on 25 November 2011. For that reason a new law relating to the assembly was issued (Organic Law 27-11, 14 October 2011), which partially reformed the electoral system. Similarly, a new distribution of constituency seats was approved (Decree 2-11-603 of 19 October 2011), which had in the past been detrimental to the Islamists of the Justice and Development Party (Parti de la Justice et du Développement, PJD) (Szmolka 2010). The new electoral law increased the number of members of the House of Representatives from 325 to 395, of which 305 seats are chosen in nine-two local constituencies; sixty seats are elected in one national constituency, which the parties have reserved for a closed women's list since 2002; and thirty seats for a new national district of young people up to the age of forty years, in a concession to the 20-F Movement. On the other hand, the proportional largest remainder method (Hare method) was maintained, as well as the closed and blocked lists, and although the electoral barrier of 6 per cent remained in local constituencies, it dropped to 3 per cent in the national constituency of women, and the under forties constituency (Szmolka 2014).

The elections had a quasi-competitive character as various forces refused to participate in the process due to their opposition to the political regime. In fact, the 20-F Movement, various parties and illegal Islamist organisations (al-Adl wa al-Ihsan, al-Umma), banned entities (al-Badil al-Hadari), various left-wing parties (the Unified Socialist Party, the Socialist Democratic Party and Annahj Democrati) and the Amazigh Democratic Party (Fernández-Molina 2011b: 7) called for an election boycott. Nevertheless, the elections were contended by a large number of political formations: thirty-one parties presented candidatures in local constituencies and nineteen on national lists

(Ministère de l'Intérieur 2011).[1] Significant progress in electoral competitiveness was confirmed by observers – the new *dahir* (royal decree) 1-11-62 of 29 September (promulgation of Law 30-11) established the types of independent and neutral electoral observers. In order to comply with this new regulation, powers were given to the newly established National Council on Human Rights– the successor of the Consultative Council on Human Rights, which had played a role in previous elections – for the accreditation of national and international observers. Furthermore, inspectors and party representatives were allowed to be present. However, in spite of greater supervision of the electoral process, harassment of defenders of the boycott was denounced and there were isolated instances of vote-buying. Regarding participation, 70 per cent of Moroccans of voting age registered on the electoral census and 45.5 per cent of those went to vote; a low turnout but higher than in the 2007 elections (37 per cent) (Fernández-Molina 2011b: 8). However, it is also important to highlight the invalid votes at 22.3 per cent. Such a high level of invalidity and low electoral mobilisation during a period of change cannot exclusively be attributed to socio-demographic factors, but must have a political explanation, such as rejection of the monarchy's reform process.

The House of Representatives was again renewed on 7 October 2016. To this purpose, on 19 July 2016, parliament approved a partial reform of the parties law (Law 21-16) and of the organic law relating to the House of Representatives' election (Law 20-16), with the aim of allowing joint electoral party lists and reducing the electoral barrier to 3 per cent in local constituencies.

2.2 The preservation of royal powers: the 2011 constitution and Benkirane's coalition governments

The procedure for approval of the 2011 constitution provides an idea of the restrictions placed on political change in Morocco. As in previous constitutional processes, reform was driven by King Mohammed, who announced it in a speech to the nation on 9 March 2011. Two days after the royal speech a Constitutional Reform Advisory Commission – a technical commission of jurists and political scientists – was formed and tasked with writing a report on constitutional reform. Political parties were given the opportunity to have their proposals studied by the constitutional commission, which delivered its report to the king on 10 June. Finally, a constitutional referendum was held on 1 July 2011 (Maghraoui 2011; Fernández-Molina 2011a).

The new constitution garnered strong political support from the parties represented in parliament and similarly, citizens largely endorsed it in the referendum (98.5 per cent voted in favour, with 72.65 per cent voter participation). However, the 20-F Movement rejected the reforms, calling for a constituent assembly to be established and for further-reaching constitutional reform. One advance, nonetheless, is that the king would now have to appoint a head of government from the party that obtained most seats in the legislative elections. Although this was an important constitutional modification, it should be underscored that since the 1992 constitutional reform the new government already needed to have parliamentary confidence. Additionally, the 2011 constitution increased the powers of the head of government beyond that enjoyed previously.

Regarding the head of state, the king was no longer deemed 'sacred'. Nevertheless, the constitution continued to recognise him as the 'commander of the faithful' (article 41) and therefore, the most powerful religious authority in the country. His status was now 'inviolable' (article 46) and thus, he would not be accountable to any other institution. On the other hand, the king maintained significant legislative and executive powers, including: the appointment of the head of government and ministers (following a proposal from the head of government); the capacity to dismiss one or more members of the government (article 47); chairing the Council of Ministers (article 48); the power to dissolve parliament (article 51) after simply informing the head of government (article 96); proclamation of the state of emergency (article 59); the prerogative to initiate revision of the constitution and submit it directly to referendum (article 172); the role of commander-in-chief of the armed forces (article 53); the appointment of ambassadors (article 55); presidency of the new Superior Council of Security, Superior Council of the Judicial Power, and the Higher Council of Ulemas (article 54, 56 and 41); the right to appoint six of the twelve members of the Constitutional Court (article 130); and so on (see Madani et al. 2012). In brief, the constitution consolidates the king's 'reserved domains' and his centrality in the political system.

In the field of rights and liberties, the 2011 constitution gave citizens the right to present motions on legislative matters and to petition public entities (articles 14 and 15), reinforced the independence of the judiciary (articles 107–28), introduced Title XII on good governance and officially recognised the *Tamazight* (Berber) language (article 5).

On the other hand, article 1 refers to decentralisation and 'advanced regionalisation' as a new model of territorial organisation, the latter being a concept that does not exist in comparative law. However, the so-called advanced regionalisation process in Morocco was not a direct consequence of the 2011 social protests, as it began a year previously and formally concluded with approval of the 2015 regionalisation law (Organic Law 111-14) (Szmolka 2016).

In line with the 2011 constitution, on 29 November 2011, following the November legislative elections, Mohammed VI appointed Abdelilah Benkirane, the general secretary of the PJD, as head of government. This represented the first time that the Islamists had been allowed to accede to government. This was possible thanks to the fact that the PJD had followed a reformist strategy and collaborated with the monarchy (Tomé 2013). The Islamist party had come first in the elections held four days earlier, with 22.8 per cent of the vote, and 27.1 per cent of the seats in the House of Representatives. However, in order to obtain the necessary parliamentary support, the PJD had to form a government with three other political forces: the Istiqlal Party (PI), the Party of Progress and Socialism (PPS) and the Popular Movement (MP). The government also included 'independent' ministers who actually reported to the king rather than the head of government. Therefore, the governmental power of the Islamists was counterbalanced by the presence of other parties and individuals from the king's inner circle.

This coalition government was to last 279 days. On 9 July 2013, after three months of disagreements between the PI and the PJD, five of the six PI ministers presented their resignations to the head of government, and withdrew from the coalition. This governmental crisis was caused by a change of leadership in the PI. A new executive could not be appointed until three months later, on 10 October 2013. The PJD remained as the lead party in the new government, along with the MP and the PPS, and these were joined by the National Rally of Independents (Rassemblement National des Indépendants, RNI), the third largest political force in the House of Representatives (Szmolka 2015).

However, the two Benkirane governments have not triggered democratic change in Morocco, mainly due to the necessary 'cohabitation' between government and the king (Hernando de Larramendi 2013), which gives a small margin of decision-making autonomy to the former. Many state policies are determined through royal commissions and the king has exclusive powers in matters of religion, security and strategic policy choices. At the same time, the leading Moroccan parties have not strongly pressurised the monarchy to give up these legislative and executive powers, as was made patent in the constitutional reform process.

Regarding governance, the Islamist-led government raised hopes that they would combat widespread corruption. However, this remained a problem, both in public life and in the business world. Morocco has a score of thirty-six and is ranked eighty-eight out of 168 countries surveyed in the 2015 Corruption Perceptions Index (Transparency International 2016).[2] One of the deepest structural impediments to reducing corruption is the king's own role in the economy as the major stakeholder in the country (Freedom House 2016a).

In sum, advances have been made in Morocco as there is now a rotation of power as a consequence of quasi-competitive elections. Nevertheless, the constitution consecrates the powers and centrality of the monarchy. The lack of government autonomy means that the regime remains authoritarian, although with a larger degree of pluralism and party competition than others in the MENA region.

2.3 The lack of improvement in public rights and civil liberties

Civil liberties and rights improved significantly during the last years of the reign of Hassan II (1961–99) and the early period of Mohammed VI. Nevertheless, rights and freedoms in Morocco have deteriorated within the last decade.

Freedoms of assembly, association and syndication are guaranteed under the constitution. Demonstrations are frequent and generally tolerated, especially when they relate to socio-economic concerns, such as those led by unemployed graduates and unions. However, the government sometimes uses administrative delays and other methods to suppress or discourage unwanted peaceful assembly, and is capable of using excessive force to disperse demonstrations (Bertelsmann Stiftung 2016a). Civil society and independent non-governmental organisations (NGOs) are active, but the authorities monitor Islamist groups, arrest suspected extremists, and harass other activists. Islamist groups and organisations supporting self-determination for Western Sahara generally have difficulties registering –which is necessary to access government funds or accept contributions – or carrying out their activities (Human Rights Watch 2016).

Freedom of expression is generally respected, although control is exercised over the press and social networks. Parties and the independent press enjoy a significant degree of freedom, as long as journalists do not cross the three red lines of the state (the monarchy, Islam and Moroccan sovereignty over Western Sahara). Instead of censure, the regime tends to assert control through the threat of heavy fines for the defamation of public figures and institutions, and for publishing articles that question Morocco's territorial integrity. Additionally, the regime can curtail sources of press funding and persuade companies not to purchase advertising space in critical publications. Following the Arab Spring the government committed itself to reforming the press law in order to expand press freedom. On 23 December 2015, the Government Council approved a draft press code (88-13), although to date the law has not been submitted to parliament for final approval and adoption.

The rule of law is defective in Morocco. The judiciary is not independent of the monarchy, and the courts are regularly used to punish government opponents. Arbitrary arrest and police brutality, including torture, still occur, and are rarely investigated (Freedom House 2016a).

3 Jordan: political reforms without consensus and democratic improvements

During the spring of 2011 Jordanian protesters called for: a constitutional monarchy to limit the king's powers; elected governments; reform of the security forces; and the formation of a Constitutional Court. In order to ease the social pressure on the regime, King Abdullah II promised political reforms (Barari and Satkowski 2012; Ryan 2012; Tobin 2012). On 14 March 2011 he appointed a National Dialogue Committee and tasked it with finding a consensus over revision of the party and election laws. Additionally, on 27 April 2011, the king created the Royal Committee on Constitutional Review. However, the opposition, grouped under the National Front for Reform, rejected all these initiatives.[3]

3.1 A very limited multipartyism

The manipulation of the electoral law, the absence of a genuine parliamentary opposition (Ryan 2011) and a pro-regime parliament have all contributed to maintaining the hegemonic pluralist system in the last five years.

The aim of the reform of Jordan's party law in June 2012 was to foster a multiparty system, but without significant effects. Although political parties have been allowed in Jordan since 1992, the political system has predominantly relied upon nonpartisan tribal formations. Changes to the party law reduced many bureaucratic obstacles while increasing the demographic and geographic requirements meant to ensure that new political parties enjoy nationwide support (the minimum number of members required to form a party rose from 250 to 500). On the other hand, the authority to licence political parties is no longer vested in the Interior Ministry, although it heads the ad hoc committee that takes the decision.

The electoral law has been reformed twice since 2011: in June 2012 and in March 2016. Electoral manipulation has traditionally been employed in Jordan to limit the role of political parties in favour of tribal representation. The opposition had demanded a party list system and proportional representation instead of the single non-transferable vote (SNTV, 'one person, one vote' system) which had governed the 2010 elections. However, the 2012 electoral reform had very limited impact on the multiparty system, although the highly criticised 'virtual (non-geographical) districts' were eliminated and a new national constituency of closed lists restricted for political parties was established (Burtoff 2015: 46). The national constituency accounted for only twenty-seven out of 150 members of parliament (18 per cent). The remaining seats were left open to independent candidates in forty-five local electoral districts (nine were allocated to Christians, three to Circassians, nine to Bedouins, eighty-seven to Muslims and fifteen seats to women). Each voter had two ballot papers. One vote would be cast for a party list in which candidates were to be selected through proportional representation in a single nationwide constituency, while the other vote would be for a candidate selected through the old SNTV system. In sum, the electoral system continued to reinforce the patron–client relationship by over-representing rural districts, whose residents are generally from the East Bank (supporters of tribal elites). On the other hand, urban areas continued to be under-represented, where the vote of the Palestinians is located (mainly supporters of opposition parties).

Under the 2012 electoral reform, elections for the House of Deputies took place on 23 January 2013, with a voter turnout of 56.7 per cent. The main opposition parties did not contest the elections and rejected the constitution and electoral reforms. Nevertheless, sixty-one parties or movements contested the election for the twenty-seven seats filled under the proportional system. Twenty-two won seats: three were won by the Islamic Centrist Party; two each by the Stronger Jordan, the Homeland and the National Union Party; and, one each by the eighteen remaining parties (Inter-parliamentary Union 2016). The remaining 108 seats were occupied by independents. Thus, the House of Deputies once again had an absolute majority of loyalists, tribal members and conservatives. In relation to electoral integrity, an independent commission for the supervision of elections was established to oversee the process. However, international observers assessed both the political campaign and the elections as non-competitive due to: the unfair electoral system, an opposition boycott, vote buying, and the electoral influence of tribal elites and independent businessmen loyal to the regime (Bank and Sunik 2014).

In March 2016 the two houses of parliament passed a new electoral law. The number of seats of the House of Deputies was reduced from 150 to 130, of which fifteen are allocated to women. The 2016 election law is based on the open proportional list of twenty-three electoral districts, in which candidates can run for election on one large multi-member ticket. Eligible voters have a number of votes equal to the number of seats allocated for their district. During the elections, each eligible voter votes for a multi-member list as a whole and for individual candidate of their choice from the same ticket (*The Jordan Times*, 13 March and 23 May 2016). With the endorsement of the law, on 29 May 2016, the king dissolved the House of Deputies and called for early elections, on 20 September 2016. On 11 June 2016 the Islamic Action Front (IAF) announced that it would compete in the elections, in contrast to the 2010 and 2013 boycott, citing an ample majority of party members who supported involvement in the upcoming election. In addition, the IAF's participation in politics should reduce regime pressure on the party and reinforce the weakened organisation.

3.2 Government changes and constitutional reforms increasing royal powers

After 2011 elections continued to play a very limited role in Jordan's government formation, although the House of Deputies now had to show confidence in any new government before it could formally take office. The prime minister and his cabinet were formed by independents, many of whom had already been in charge of ministerial portfolios in previous governments. The social unrest during the Arab Spring led to several government reshuffles. On 1 February 2011 the prime minister Samir al-Rifai resigned and the king appointed Marouf al-Bakhit, who formed a new government of independents. A few months later, in October 2011, al-Bakhit was replaced after being accused of corruption during an earlier tenure as prime minister. Next, three different prime ministers were subsequently nominated in the period leading up to the 2013 elections: Awn Shawkat al-Khasawneh (17 October 2011), Fayed al-Tarawneh (26 April 2012) and Abdullah Ensour (11 October 2012). After the general elections in January 2013, King Abdullah reappointed Ensour, on 9 March 2013, who formed his second cabinet and who was sworn in before the king later that month. A period of relative stability followed until 29 May 2016, when, on the same day of the dissolution of parliament, the king named Hani al-Mulki as caretaker prime minister to organise the elections scheduled for September 2016.

On the other hand, the three constitutional changes that occurred in Jordan following the Arab Spring, in 2011, 2014 and 2016, not only consolidated the previous distribution of power in favour of the king, but also increased the latter's discretionary powers. Following the report of the Royal Committee on Constitutional Review, a partial reform of the constitution was approved by the two parliamentary chambers in September 2011. The constitutional reform was rejected by the opposition, yet this was no obstacle to the parliamentarian endorsement as the main opposition party, the IAF, did not have parliamentary representation in the House of Deputies (as a consequence of its election boycott of 9 November 2010). Forty-two articles of the constitution were amended, providing for: the establishment of a Constitutional Court (articles 58–61); control of the elections by an independent commission (article 67); the resolution of electoral disputes in civil courts (article 71); curtailing of government powers to pass provisional laws (article 94); more guarantees for public rights and liberties articles (articles 7, 8, 11, 15, 16 and 18); a lowering of the age limit to become a member of parliament (article 75); the establishment of a procedure for putting ministers on trial (article 55); and amendments to various jurisdictions (religious, civil, special, and the State Security Tribunal for crimes of treason, espionage and terrorism (articles 98, 100, 101, 109 and 110). Nevertheless, the constitutional changes did not respond to the key democratic demand: to curtail royal powers. The monarch retains the right to: choose and dismiss the prime minister; to appoint the Senate; to dissolve the bicameral National Assembly at his discretion; to delay parliamentary elections for up to two years; to rule by royal decree during periods in which parliament is not in session; and to appoint the judges and provincial governors. On the other hand, the powers of the House of Deputies remain limited. The lower chamber may approve, reject, or amend legislation proposed by the cabinet, but has little power to initiate or enact laws without the assent of the Senate, which is wholly appointed by the king. The government is accountable not only to parliament, but also to the king (Yom 2013; Köprülü 2014).

The August 2014 reform vested the king with the absolute power to appoint the chairman of the Joint Chiefs of Staff and director of the General Intelligence Department. Additionally, a second amendment expanded the authority of the Independent Elections Commission to supervise and manage all elections. In May 2016 a new constitutional reform removed the need for any countersignature by the prime minister or ministers to appoint the crown prince, the regent, Senate speaker and members, chairman and members of the Constitutional Court, the chief justice, the commander of the army, and the heads of Intelligence and the Gendarmerie (article 40). Both amendments were adopted without meaningful debate in parliament or society. Therefore, the separation of powers is only normative, as both parliament and the government are subordinate to royal power. Similarly, there is also an informal and non-accountable institution, Diwan al-Maliki (the Royal Hashemite Court), which functions as a parallel administrative structure directly under the king's authority (and in parallel to the state bureaucracy) (Bertelsmann Stiftung 2016b).

In the field of governance, one of the main social demands was to fight corruption in the context of the economic privatisation process. The Jordanian government responded by creating the National Integrity Commission in December 2012 to investigate allegations, while the Privatisation Review

Committee, formed in January 2013, was tasked with reviewing the privatisation of state-run enterprises, which has been a source of scandals in the past. Additionally, Prime Minister Ensour launched a five-year anti-corruption strategy in June 2013. Jordan is considered to be the fourth most transparent country in the MENA region – after Qatar, the United Arab Emirates and Israel – ranked forty-five out of 168 countries surveyed in the 2015 Corruption Perceptions Index (Transparency International 2016).

3.3 Restricted rights and liberties

Rights and liberties are theoretically guaranteed for all Jordanian citizens; however, they are severely restricted in practice, and East Bank Jordanians in particular enjoy better political and socio-economic conditions. In relation to the freedom of assembly, on 23 March 2011 parliament modified the 2008 Public Gatherings Law, abolishing the need for the governor's authorisation to be sent to the Interior Ministry and only requiring forty-eight hours' notice by organisers. There have been frequent demonstrations against the government and its policies, and the police have dispersed protesters on many occasions. The constitution safeguards freedom of union (article 23f), although workers still require government permission to strike. Jordanians also have the right to association, but they have to seek prior authorisation from the Ministry of Social Development. NGOs are banned from supporting associations with political objectives, and all board members must be vetted by state security (Freedom House 2016b).

The freedoms of expression and of the press are restricted by numerous laws that criminalise defamation, offence to the state's 'reputation and dignity', insulting religious belief, and inciting ethnic and sectarian strife. Any reports on the king and the royal family require prior authorisation before publication. The Press and Publications Law mandates 'media objectivity'. However, the government pressurises editors to control the media and harasses journalists by threatening them with detention or other legal measures. Self-censorship is widespread, particularly when reporting on the royal family, foreign leaders and specific societal taboos. Most broadcast news outlets remain under state control, although satellite dishes and the Internet provide residents with access to foreign media. An amendment to the Press and Publications Law of September 2012 introduced restrictions on Internet content, which led to the blocking of approximately 300 news websites in June 2013. Nevertheless, these have since been unblocked after registering with the Ministry of Commerce and obtaining licenses from the Department of Press and Publications (Freedom House 2016b; Bertelsmann Stiftung 2016b).

The courts are subject to executive influence through the Justice Ministry and the Higher Judiciary Council, most of whose members are appointed by the king. The judges' interpretation of the law is mostly in line with that approved by the monarchy. There are three types of courts: civil, special (such as military/state security) and religious. In early 2014 the government limited the jurisdiction of the State Security Council to the serious crimes of espionage, drugs, terrorism, treason and counterfeiting. However, the 2014 amendments to the 2006 antiterrorism law broadened its scope to include non-violent offences, such as using information networks to support, promote, or fund terrorism, as well as any acts that may harm Jordan's relations with a foreign country (Bertelsmann Stiftung 2016b).

4 Oman: insignificant political reforms

In Oman the Arab Spring demonstrations began on 17 January 2011, in Muscat. Shortly afterwards they spread to other cities, mainly to the industrial port city of Sohar and to Salalah. The political regime initially tolerated the peaceful protests, but later police and security forces used excessive force. The social contract in Oman is based on the rentier model: there are no income taxes and extensive social-welfare benefits for citizens because the state has traditionally relied upon the export of oil and gas (Worral 2012). As a result of the unrest, several measures were taken in the social sphere: there was an increase in the minimum wage and student grants; a second public university was established; a Public Authority for Consumer Protection to monitor prices was set up; new jobs were created in the public sector, and so on. Political measures were also implemented: the Royal Oman Police had their prosecuting powers removed; the Ministry of National Economy, seen by protesters as a hotbed of corruption, was abolished; a National Audit Committee was established to tackle corruption; the cabinet was reshuffled;[4] and the Basic Law was reformed to increase parliament's legislative and regulatory powers (Worral 2012). Even so, the protests continued during 2012 and the authorities responded repressively to peaceful demands made by social movements, unions and professional organisations.

Neither the protests nor reforms have led to any real political liberalisation. The sultan continues to wield absolute power, parliament is not autonomous, there is no political pluralism or real competition in elections and there is not even a minimum guarantee of political rights and civil liberties. Therefore, Oman remains a closed authoritarian regime.

4.1 Elections without pluralism and political competition

Political parties remain banned in Oman and neither are there organised political movements that participate in the institutional arena. Political representation is provided by the regime seeking to create a balance between the country's diverse tribal, regional and ethnic interests in the parliament and in the Council of Ministers. Organised opposition barely exists.

Since political parties are banned in Oman, all candidates run as independents. Elections to the Majlis al-Shura (Consultative Council) have taken place twice since the Arab Spring: on 15 October 2011 and on 25 October 2015. No electoral reforms preceded the holding of elections. Omanis would elect members of the Majlis al-Shura (eighty-four in 2011 and eighty-five in 2015) in sixty-one constituencies by plurality vote to serve four-year terms. In the 2011 elections the context of the Arab Spring led to a broad electoral choice (1,100 independent candidates) and a high turnout (76.6 per cent). However, in the 2015 elections both the number of candidates who ran for office (596) and the turnout (56.6 per cent) decreased. Tribal alliances and political patronage invariably explain which candidates are elected (Zaccara and Saldaña 2015: 192). The Omani elections cannot be considered as competitive for several reasons: the absence of parties in the electoral processes, the interdiction of public meetings during the electoral campaign and the lack of electoral monitoring.

4.2 The monopolisation of power by the sultan

On 20 October 2011, without previous debate, Sultan Qaboos bin Said al-Said issued a *dahir* amending several provisions of the Basic Law of the State. One of the amendments concerned the succession process, a sensitive issue due to the fact that no successor had been chosen, despite the sultan's health problems and age (he was born in 1940). Articles 5 and 6 of the Basic Law detail the process required to confirm the appointment to the throne of the person designated by the former ruler in the absence of agreement between members of the Royal Family Council.

Furthermore, the reform of the Basic Law expanded the powers of the Council of Oman, which is composed of elected Majlis al-Dawla and the appointed Majlis al-Shura. However, parliament acts in practice as an advisory body, due to its limited legislative and executive powers and its government-friendly composition. According to the 2011 reform both chambers can propose, review and amend draft laws passed by the Council of Ministers before submitting them to the sultan. However, if there are amendments by any chamber on the draft law, the sultan may refer it back to parliament for reconsideration of the amendments (article 58 bis 35). Additionally, members of both chambers may later question 'service ministers' (article 58 bis 43), but not ministers involved in national sovereignty (foreign affairs, defence, finance, interior and oil). Members of the Council of Ministers are only accountable to the sultan (article 52). Likewise, the sultan retains the power to dissolve parliament (article 58 bis 19) and issue royal decrees that have the force of the law when parliament is in recess or dissolved (article 59 bis 39).

The sultan has enormous executive powers, because besides being the head of state, he is also prime minister, and is in charge of the ministries of interior, defence, foreign affairs and finance. He is also supreme commander of the armed forces and the governor of Oman's central bank. The sultan appoints the Council of Ministers, which functions as his cabinet. The judiciary is not independent and remains subordinate to the sultan and the Ministry of Justice. The sultan makes all judicial appointments and presides over the Supreme Judicial Council, which, in turn, oversees the courts and formulates all related policy.

On the other hand, the sultan of Oman has a total monopoly on the use of force and control over the whole territory. Political particularism remains in the southern region of Dhofar, although there is currently no questioning of Omani national unity following the area's insurgency in the 1970s (Valery 2009: 248).

In the governance sphere, protesters have expressed their anger against the corrupt political elite. In response, Sultan Qaboos removed long-serving ministers perceived to be corrupt and issued a decree ordering the State Financial and Administrative Audit Institution to increase transparency and efficiency within government ministries. Government officials are required by law to declare their assets and sources of wealth. However, the majority of cabinet members, senior office holders and some prominent members of the ruling family are still directly involved in businesses that benefit from public contracts. Oman was ranked sixty out of 168 countries surveyed in the 2015 Corruption Perceptions Index (score forty-five) (Transparency International 2016).

4.3 No progression on rights and liberties

The situation of civil rights and liberties remains unsatisfactory in Oman. The right to peaceful assembly within limits is provided for by the 1996 Basic Law. All public gatherings require official permission, and the government has the authority to prevent organised public meetings without any appeals process. The Penal Law (article 137) was amended by royal decree in October 2011 to provide for the possibility of jail sentences for gatherings that 'seek to affect' the public system. Additionally, the penal reform allows the arrest and detention of individuals by public prosecutors without an arrest warrant and for up to thirty days without charge for 'crimes related to national security or mentioned in the anti-terrorism law'. This reform led to a considerable number of protesters being detained or convicted in connection with the social protests, although the sultan pardoned them in March and July 2013. However, the Omani government has continued to arrest critics and activists and has significantly invested in the security sector, with the aim of strengthening political control and pre-empting further unrest (Bertelsmann Stiftung 2016c).

The right of association is recognised, but all organisations must receive the approval of the Ministry of Social Development, which puts barriers in the way of independent NGOs. All kinds of political associations are banned. Private sector workers, but not government employees, have the right to form trade unions, undertake collective bargaining and strike.

The freedoms of expression and of the press are very limited. The government censors any content on the media and Internet that it deems offensive, particularly relating to politics, culture or sex. Editorial policies generally reflect the views of the government. The government also influences the privately owned press through subsidies. In a further example of state repression in Oman, a number of social websites, blogs and Facebook accounts have been shut down and bloggers sentenced to jail since the eruption of the Arab Spring (Bertelsmann Stiftung 2016c).

5 Long-term political reforms in Algeria

The Arab Spring has also had social repercussions in Algeria where demonstrations and a wave of self-immolations have taken place in various parts of the country since the end of 2010. However, memories of the civil war of the 1990s limited the force of the protests. The government quickly contained the unrest, reduced food prices and introduced measures to mitigate unemployment. On 24 February 2011 the government lifted the state of emergency declared in 1991 following the victory of the Islamic Salvation Front in the first round of the legislative elections. In 2012 parliament approved various laws relating to political parties, associations, media and elections (Zoubir and Aghrout 2012; Volpi 2013; Boserup et al. 2014), and in February 2016 a promised new constitution came into force.

5.1 The persistence of bicephalous hegemonic pluralism

In December 2011 two Algerian parliamentary chambers passed a new law on political parties (Law 12-04). The most significant development was that now political groups could go to court to appeal if the Interior Ministry did not permit their application to create a new party. As in the past, the new party law continued to ban the formation of political groups on religious or ethnic grounds and does not allow those found guilty of terrorist acts to exercise party leadership. Although the law prohibits the formation of parties on the basis of religion or ethnic identity, in reality some parties can easily be grouped within these criteria.

Following the approval of new party legislation, about twenty political groups were legalised and forty-four participated in the May 2012 elections (Zoubir and Aghrout 2012). As in the case of Morocco, in Algeria there are a broad range of parties with various ideological tendencies, although some significant political forces do not participate in the political game, or do it in an intermittent way, as they do not believe it is democratic, such as the Amazigh Socialist Forces Front (Front des Forces Socialistes, FFS) and the Rally for Culture and Democracy (Rassemblement pour la Culture et la Démocratie, RCD). In June 2014 other secular and Islamist parties, civil society organisations and public figures created the National Coordination for Liberties and Democratic Transition, an opposition platform that seeks to obtain real democracy in Algeria.

The renewal of the National People's Assembly (NPA) took place on 10 May 2012, in line with the duration of the parliamentary mandate. Previously, a new electoral law had been passed (Organic Law 12-01, 12 January 2012) together with a presidential decree that fixes the number of seats per electoral district (Decree 12-01, 15 January 2012). Further electoral changes resulted in an increased number of seats (from 389 to 462), greater control of the electoral process (judicial supervision of voting, transparent ballot boxes, access to vote-counting by parties and candidates, and so on) and the removal of restrictions from standing for election placed on members of the government and elected representatives who had abandoned their political affiliation. The proportional system, in the forty-eight electoral districts corresponding to the *wilayas* (provinces), as well as in the four districts for voters residing abroad and the 5 per cent threshold, remained unchanged. In addition, a law regulated women's representation in elected bodies which, in the case of the NPA, was organised in accordance with the size of the electoral district (Law 12-03, 14 January 2012).

The most prominent aspects of these elections were voter apathy, greater transparency in the electoral process and the continuing hegemony of the regime parties. The Constitutional Council announced a turnout of 43.14 per cent. Although this represented a rise in turnout (35.65 per cent in 2007), the percentage of blank and invalid votes also increased (from 13.78 per cent in 2007 to 18.24 per cent in 2012) (The Carter Center 2012). The National Commission for Election (NCES) was formed to oversee the process, with the participation of representatives of political parties and judges. There were also international observers from the European Union, the African Union, the Arab League, the United Nations and the Islamic Cooperation Organisation. While foreign observers declared the elections free and fair, opposition candidates and some human rights groups argued that the Ministry of the Interior manipulated the results. Similarly, the NCES denounced the lack of control in the *wilayas* where votes had been cast at polling stations and then transported by the town councils. As a consequence of the official results, fifteen parties – which won a combined twenty-nine seats – boycotted parliament. The electoral arena therefore remained dominated by the two regime parties, which won the overwhelming majority of seats: the National Liberation Front (Front de Libération Nationale, FLN) (220 seats, 47.6 per cent of total seats) and the National Democratic Rally (Rassemblement National Démocratique, RND) (sixty-nine seats, 14.7 per cent of total seats). The Islamist Green Algeria Alliance – bringing together Movement of Society for Peace (Mouvement de la Société pour la Paix, MSP), , Ennahda and al-Islah) – came only third, a result that distinguished Algeria from the Islamist victories in Tunisia, Egypt and Morocco. The FFS, who had boycotted the legislative elections since 2002 but decided to contest elections in 2012, came fourth.

The results of the presidential election held on 17 April 2014 were even more questionable. Several parties boycotted the elections, among them the RCD – as in the 2012 elections – and the Islamist MSP. President Abdelaziz Bouteflika, who only appeared once in the electoral campaign, was re-elected for a fourth term with 82 per cent of the vote, from a 42 per cent official turnout. International organisations were not allowed to monitor the elections and Ali Benflis, Bouteflika's main rival, made accusations of voter fraud (Djabi 2014; Werenfels 2014).

In July 2016 parliament approved a revision of the law on the electoral regime in order to guarantee electoral transparency and a further law to establish an Independent High Instance of Election Monitoring. Nevertheless, hegemonic pluralism persists in Algerian politics, which is dominated by two political forces that alternate at the head of government (the FLN and RND), while the opposition remains fragmented and continually debates whether or not to participate or remain at the margins of the political game.

5.2 Continuity in the regime's powers

The government coalition remained after the 2011 social protests, but in the wake of the 2012 elections the MSP withdrew from the cabinet to form the Green Algeria Alliance with other Islamist parties. Following the NPA elections the prime minister changed from Ahmed Ouyahia (RND) to Abdelmalek Sellal (FLN), not so much as a consequence of the election results, but as a reflection of variations in the balance of power within the regime (see Storm, Chapter 3). After the presidential elections Bouteflika reappointed Sellal as prime minister for a second term.[5] Currently, the cabinet is comprised, as usual, by the FLN and the RND, together with the refounded social democratic Algerian Popular Movement (previously known as the Union for Democracy and Republic) and the Tadjamou Amel al-Djazair (Rally of Algerian Hope, a split from the MSP), the only two parties which accepted Sellal's offer to participate in the cabinet.

The constitution adopted by parliament on 6 February 2016 does not change the foundations of state power, but included several progressive aspects, such as: the recognition of the *Amazigh* language as official alongside Arabic; a two-term limit for the presidency –lifted in 2008 to allow Bouteflika to run for a third time; the presidential obligation to nominate a prime minister from the largest party in parliament; an enlargement of parliamentary powers; the creation of an independent electoral commission; recognition of the roles of women and youth; and an explicit guarantee of the freedoms of assembly and the press. Nevertheless, other controversial aspects were also either included (such as the prohibition on anyone with dual nationality running for key offices), or remained in place (such as the appointment of one-third of the members of the Council of the Nation – the upper legislative house – by the president).

In Algeria power is less concentrated, in contrast with other regimes in the region. Therefore, bargaining and factionalism are the hallmarks of the political decision-making process. On the one hand, the president has lost his centrality in the political system – as a consequence of his age and two strokes in recent years – in favour of his inner circle. On the other, there are two hegemonic parties instead of only one, that alternate as heads of government. The military and intelligence services continue to play a significant role in politics. Nevertheless, the president and his supporters have reduced their influence in the last years, dissolving the Department of Intelligence and Security (Département du Renseignement et de la Sécurité, DRS) and jailing or dismissing top army officials, such as General Mohamed Mediène in September 2015, who led the DRS over the last twenty-five years (PGI Intelligence 2015).

High-level corruption, often linked to officials and the military, is a major problem. In 2014, Algeria dropped to eighty-eight out of the 168 countries listed in Transparency International's 2015 Corruption Perceptions Index (in the same position together with Egypt and Morocco).

5.3 Limited reforms of freedoms and liberties

The law on associations (Law 12-06), issued in 2012, has been widely criticised for continuing to restrict the registration, funding and functioning of civil society organisations. Permits and application submissions are required to establish and operate NGOs. New partnership agreements are required to cooperate with foreign NGOs, but these relationships remain largely unauthorised. Additionally, restrictions on donors and foreign NGOs were reinforced in the Law on Associations of 2012. Freedom of assembly is also restricted and the government has continued to forcibly disrupt and discourage public gatherings and protests by citing security concerns, although the state of emergency was lifted in 2011 (Freedom House 2016c).

There is a considerable freedom of expression in Algeria, as in Morocco. Individuals and the press can criticise government and its policies. Changes in the press and media laws in recent years include the 2012 Media Law, which abolished prison sentences for press offences and also opened up the media to private ownership, although authorities had tolerated several private broadcasters for years. New private television stations opened in 2013 and a new law was passed by parliament on 20 January 2014 relating to this issue. However, significant fines still act as a constraint on journalists, limiting their coverage of certain subjects, such as state security. Bloggers are also subject to defamation suits, and several have been fined. The state maintains control over much of the press through control of the printing and advertising industry (Bertelsmann Stiftung 2016c).

6 Conclusions

The authoritarian structure of the ruling elite persists in MENA countries that carried out processes of political liberalisation in the aftermath of the Arab Spring. As in the past, and in line with the claims of the literature on authoritarian resilience, these regimes have basically 'upgraded' themselves (Heydemann 2007) to address domestic social discontent and, to some extent, to meet international expectations. A real will to cede legislative and executive power from authoritarian rulers to citizen representatives cannot be perceived, so the possibility of gradual regime reform towards democracy is, at best, uncertain.

In the cases of Morocco and Algeria the political liberalisation processes have brought with them a greater offer in terms of the number of political parties, and in the case of Morocco greater electoral integrity and a change in the relationship between the main opposition party and the monarchy. Nevertheless, several groups have opted to remain outside the institutional arena, preferring not to legitimise these power structures. In Jordan, despite the modification of the parties and electoral law, a deepening of the party system has not taken place, and the links of tribal representation continue being more important than that of the parties. Similarly, the opposition has rejected all the reforms undertaken by the monarchy and has boycotted the elections that have taken place. Meanwhile, in Oman, parties continue to be prohibited and organised opposition is insignificant.

As part of these political liberalisation processes, there have been constitutional reforms in all four countries, with varying degrees of political participation and consensus. Although there are positive aspects, the constitutional reforms have not brought substantial changes in power relations. Decision-making falls on the head of state, most notably in Oman where the sultan completely monopolises power. In Morocco and Algeria parliaments are more representative and have a greater capacity of control over the government than in Jordan and Oman, where the elected and unelected chambers are broadly pro-governmental.

On the other hand, unlike in other MENA countries, these four states possess a total monopoly on the use of force and the security apparatus have complete control over national territory, which represents a quite exceptional degree of stability in the current regional context. Governments have strengthened their focus on security issues at the expense of the rule of law. The opposition has had to observe the limits imposed. Nevertheless, civil society activism has significantly increased in the years following the uprisings and mobilisation around a number of issues is much higher than it used to be (Cavatorta 2015: 143). In sum, the reforms undertaken have not led to a change in the typology of the political regimes. Therefore, there is quasi-competitive and restrictive pluralist authoritarianism in Morocco, hegemonic and restrictive pluralist authoritarianism in Algeria and Jordan, and closed authoritarianism in Oman.

Notes

1. Available at <http://www.elections2011.gov.ma/fr/index.html> (last accessed 15 December 2015).
2. The scale ranges from zero (a highly corrupt country) to 100 (very clean). Rank one is occupied by the most transparent country.

3. The National Front for Reform brought together the Islamic Action Front (IAF) and left-wing parties, as well as union representatives and independent figures.
4. On 26 February 2011 the sultan reshuffled the cabinet by dismissing ministers widely perceived as corrupt. A larger cabinet reshuffle took place on 7 March, in which sixteen of the twenty-nine members were replaced, including, significantly, a number of elected members of the Majlis.
5. Sellal stepped down in March 2014 in order to lead the re-election campaign of the ailing President Bouteflika. Yosef Yousfi was nominated as acting prime minister.

References

Albrecht, Holger and Oliver Schlumberger (2004), '"Waiting for Godot": regime change without democratization in the Middle East', *International Political Science Review*, 25 (4): 371–92.

Bank, André and Anna Sunik (2014), 'Parliamentary elections in Jordan, January 2013', *Electoral Studies*, 34: 291–379.

Barari, Hassan and Christina Satkowski (2012), 'The Arab Spring: the case of Jordan', *Ortadogu Etütleri*, 3 (2): 41–57.

Bellin, Eva (2012), 'Reconsidering the robustness of authoritarianism in the Middle East: lessons from the Arab Spring', *Comparative Politics*, 44 (2): 127–49.

Bertelsmann Stiftung (2016a), *Morocco Country Report*, Gütersloh: Bertelsmann Stiftung.

Bertelsmann Stiftung (2016b), *Jordan Country Report*, Gütersloh: Bertelsmann Stiftung.

Bertelsmann Stiftung (2016c), *Oman Country Report*, Gütersloh: Bertelsmann Stiftung.

Bertelsmann Stiftung (2016d), *Algeria Country Report*, Gütersloh: Bertelsmann Stiftung.

Boserup, Rasmus A., Luis Martinez and Ulla Holm (2014), *Algeria after the Revolts: Regime Endurance in a Time of Contention and Regional Insecurity*, Danish Institute for International Studies, DIIS Report.

Brumberg, Daniel (2002), 'Democratization in the Arab world? The trap of liberalized autocracy', *Journal of Democracy*, 13 (4): 56–68.

Burtoff, Gail (2015), 'Coordination failure and the politics of tribes: Jordanian elections under SNTV', *Electoral Studies*, 40: 45–55.

The Carter Center (2012), *People's National Assembly Elections in Algeria*. Available at <https://www.cartercenter.org/resources/pdfs/news/peace_publications/election_reports/algeria-may2012-final-rpt.pdf> (last accessed 19 September 2016).

Cavatorta, Francesco (2015), 'No democratic change . . . and yet no authoritarian continuity: the inter-paradigm debate and North Africa after the uprisings', *British Journal of Middle Eastern Studies*, 42 (1): 135–45.

Dalmasso, Emanuela (2012), 'Surfing the democratic tsunami in Morocco: apolitical society and the reconfiguration of a sustainable authoritarian regime', *Mediterranean Politics*, 17 (2): 217–32.

Desrues, Thierry (2013), 'Mobilizations in a hybrid regime: the 20th February Movement and the Moroccan regime', *Current Sociology*, 61 (4): 409–23.

Djabi, Nacer (2014), *Algeria: the Man and the Regime*, Arab Reform Initiative, Policy Alternatives.

Fernández-Molina, Irene (2011a), 'Between the 20 February Movement and monarchic reformism. Who holds the reins of political change in Morocco?', *Mediterranean Politics*, 16 (3): 435–41.

Fernández-Molina, Irene (2011b), *Ficha electoral:Marruecos. Elecciones legislativas 25 de noviembre de 2011*, OPEMAM. Available at <http://www.opemam.org/sites/default/files/FE-Marruecos_Legislativas_2011.pdf> (last accessed 8 May 2013).

Freedom House (2016a), *Morocco Report 2015*. Available at <https://freedomhouse.org/report/freedom-world/2016/morocco> (last accessed 7 July 2016).

Freedom House (2016b), *Jordan Report 2015*. Available at <https://freedomhouse.org/report/freedom-world/2016/jordan> (last accessed 12 July 2016).

Freedom House (2016c), *Algeria Report 2015*. Available at <https://freedomhouse.org/report/freedom-world/2016/algeria> (last accessed 11 July 2016).

Hernando de Larramendi (2013), 'El islamismo político y el ejercicio del poder tras el despertar árabe: los casos de Egipto, Túnez y Marruecos', in *El islamismo en (R)evolución: movilización social y cambio político, Cuadernos de Estrategia*, 163: 71–116.

Heydemann, Steven (2007), *Upgrading Authoritarianism in the Arab World*, The Brookings Institution, Analysis Paper, 13. Available at <http://www.brookings.edu/,/media/Files/rc/papers/2007/10arabworld/10arabworld.pdf> (last accessed 20 January 2009).

Hoffmann, Anja and Christoph König (2013), 'Scratching the democratic façade: framing strategies of the 20 February Movement', *Mediterranean Politics*, 18 (1): 1–22.

Human Rights Watch (2016), *Morocco and Western Sahara*. Available at <https://www.hrw.org/sites/default/files/morocco.pdf> (last accessed 19 September 2016).

Inter-parliamentary Union (2016), *Jordan*. Available at <http://ipu.org/parline-e/reports/2163_E.htm> (last accessed 12 July 2016).

Köprülü, Nur (2014), 'Jordan since the uprisings: between change and stability', *Middle East Policy*, 21 (2): 111–26.

Madani, Mohamed, Driss Maghraoui and Saloua Zerhouni (2012), *The 2011 Moroccan Constitution: a Critical Analysis*, Stockholm: International IDEA.

Maghraoui, Driss (2011), 'Constitutional reforms in Morocco: between consensus and subaltern politics', *The Journal of North African Studies*, 16 (4): 679–99.

Martínez-Fuentes, Guadalupe (2011), 'La transición democrática post-benalista: procedimiento y alcance del cambio político en Túnez', *Revista Jurídica de la Universidad Autónoma de Madrid*, 23: 119–34.

Melián, Luis (2016), *Procesos de cambio político tras la Primavera Árabe. Un estudio comparado de los casos de Túnez, Egipto y Jordania*, PhD Dissertation, University of Salamanca.

PGI Intelligence (2015), *Algeria: Political Manoeuvring Reduces Influence of Powerful Intelligence Agency*. Available at <https://pgi-intelligence.com/news/getNewsItem/Algeria-Political-manoeuvring-reduces-influence-of-powerful-intelligence-agency/569> (last accessed 19 September 2016).

Ryan, Curtis R. (2011), 'Political opposition and reform coalitions in Jordan', *British Journal of Middle Eastern Studies*, 38 (3): 367–90.

Ryan, Curtis R. (2012), 'The armed forces and the Arab uprisings: the case of Jordan', *Middle East Law and Governance*, 4 (1): 153–67.

Szmolka, Inmaculada (2010), 'Party system fragmentation in Morocco', *The Journal of North African Studies*, 15 (1): 13–37, DOI: 10.1080/13629380902727569.

Szmolka, Inmaculada (2014), 'Reformas políticas sin cambio de régimen en Marruecos', in Paloma González-Gómez del Miño (ed.), *Tres años de revoluciones árabes. Procesos de cambio: repercusiones internas y regionales*, Madrid: La Catarata: pp. 61–84.

Szmolka, Inmaculada (2015), 'Inter- and intra-party relations in the formation of the Benkirane coalition governments in Morocco', *The Journal of North Africa Studies*, 20 (4): 654–74, DOI: 10.1080/13629387.2015.1057816.

Szmolka, Inmaculada (2016), 'Western Sahara and the Arab Spring', in Raquel Ojeda-García, Irene Fernández-Molina and Victoria Veguilla (eds), *Global, Regional and Local Dimensions of Western Sahara's Protracted Decolonization*, New York: Palgrave Macmillan.

Tobin, Sarah (2012), 'Jordan's Arab Spring: the middle class and anti-revolution', *Middle East Policy*, 19 (1): 96–109.

Tomé, Beatriz (2013), 'Terrenos de convergencia versus terrenos de diferenciación: la dialéctica entre el sistema marroquí y el Partido de la Justicia y el Desarrollo'. *Paper presented at the XI International Conference of Spanish Political Science Association*, Seville, 18–20 September.

Transparency International (2016), *Corruption Perceptions Index 2015*. Available at <http://www.transparency.org/cpi2015> (last accessed 7 July 2016).

Valery, Marc (2009), *Oman: Politics and Society in the Qaboos-State*, London and New York: Hurst and Oxford University Press.

Volpi, Frédéric (2013), 'Algeria versus the Arab Spring', *Journal of Democracy*, 24 (3): 104–15.

Werenfels, Isabelle (2014), *The Risks of Playing for Time in Algeria: Internal Strife over Key Choices after the Presidential Election*, Stiftung Wissenschaft und Politik, SWP Comments.

Worrall, James (2012), 'Oman the "forgotten" corner of the Arab Spring', *Middle East Policy Council, Journal Essay*, XIX (3). Available at <http://www.mepc.org/journal/middle-east-policy-archives/oman-forgotten-corner-arab-spring> (last accessed 31 March 2016).

Yom, Sean L. (2013), 'Jordan: the ruse of reform', *Journal of Democracy*, 24 (3): 127–39.

Zaccara, Luciano and Marta Saldaña (2015), 'Cambio y estabilidad política en las Monarquías del Golfo tras la Primavera Árabe', *Revista d'Afers Internacionals*, 108: 177–99.

Zoubir, Yahia H. and Ahmed Aghrout (2012), 'Algeria's path to reform: authentic change?', *Middle East Policy*, 19 (2): 66–83.

Chapter 17

Autocratisation, authoritarian progressions and fragmented states

Inmaculada Szmolka and Marién Durán

1 Introduction

This final chapter focuses on Middle East and North African (MENA) countries that have experienced negative changes following the Arab Spring. This trend can be placed within the overall context of a process of 'democratic involution' that has taken place since the start of the twenty-first century, as identified and described by Francis Fukuyama (Fukuyama 2016: 26). The five countries studied here show that the Arab Spring has simply deepened this tendency.

Firstly, Turkey's evolution from a defective democracy in 2011 into a quasi-competitive and restrictive pluralist authoritarianism is examined (a situation that has been further aggravated since the attempted *coup d'état* in July 2016). Secondly, countries with an authoritarian progression are analysed. These countries include Bahrain, which has sought to carry out political reforms, and Kuwait, which has undergone an authoritarian progression as a consequence of the emir's attempts to control parliament and approve restrictive laws regarding rights and liberties. Finally, this chapter provides an assessment of the fragmentation of the Iraqi and Syrian states, which occurred as a consequence of the presence of the self-proclaimed Islamic State (IS) in north-western Iraq and the civil war in Syria.

2 The process of autocratisation in Turkey

Turkey has become a significant case study for comparative politics. First hailed as a democratic example for the Arab world when the riots began in 2011, it soon became a country of international concern because of its growing authoritarianism. Turkey experienced a democratic evolution when

Recep Tayyip Erdoğan and his Justice and Development Party (Adalet ve Kalkınma Partisi, AKP) came to power in 2002 (Özbudun 2007; Rodríguez et al. 2013; Durán 2013; Önis 2015). Specifically, Prime Minister Erdoğan began by carrying out a process of economic and political reforms in order to foster Turkey's rapprochement with Europe, reduced the army's power in the political arena, expanded rights and freedoms, and contributed to Kurdish integration in Turkish society and politics. Nevertheless, his aim to transform the parliamentary system of governance into a hyper-presidential one, the repression of the Gezi Park protests in June 2013, corruption scandals involving government ministers, severe restrictions on freedoms of expression and the press, and repression in all spheres following the failed *coup d'état* on 15 July 2016, bear all the characteristics of emergent authoritarian rule. Therefore, the political change experienced by Turkey in recent years has been dramatic: from being a defective democracy in 2011 with positive steps towards democratic consolidation, it has now been downgraded to a quasi-competitive and restrictive pluralist authoritarianism. Has Turkey suffered a contagion or emulation of its neighbours' political dynamics? Or is its current situation the result of a combination of regional dynamics and internal processes?

2.1 Quasi-competitive pluralism and competence

Unlike in neighbouring countries, party legislation and/or electoral rules did not substantially change in Turkey after the Arab Spring. In fact, Turkey has long had a strong electoral tradition since its first elections in 1950. However, there are several continuity elements that today partially limit pluralism and political accountability, including: the election requirement that a party must obtain at least 10 per cent of valid votes nationally to have parliamentary representation, maintenance of the rules on the closure of political parties and restrictions on funding for political parties and election campaigns, which limit electoral transparency and accountability (Hakyemez and Akgun 2002; European Commission 2015: 8).

Since the Arab Spring, four elections have taken place in Turkey: the presidential election of 10 August 2014 and three parliamentary elections on 12 June 2011, 7 June 2015 and 1 November 2015. In accordance with a constitutional reform in 2007, the Grand National Assembly's (GNA) term was reduced from five to four years. The constitutional reform also introduced the direct national election of the president for a five-year term with the possibility of one renewal – rather than appointment by members of parliament – which has strengthened the role of the president in the

Turkish political system. In fact this has turned out to be a key reform that has allowed Erdoğan to control state institutions.

After the Arab Spring elections to the GNA were held on 12 June 2011. The election was preceded by a limited electoral reform in order to reduce the age for parliamentary eligibility from thirty to twenty-five, to make it easier for citizens to vote, and to guarantee the transparency of the electoral process. Turnout was high at 83.16 per cent of registered voters. For a third time, the AKP won the election with an absolute majority of seats (326 seats, 59.27 per cent) and only two other parties obtained parliamentary representation: the Republican People's Party, with 135 seats, and the Nationalist Movement Party, with fifty-three seats. Thirty-six independents were also elected, many of them members of pro-Kurdish parties who hoped to win 10 per cent of the votes in the province where they stood for election.[1] As a result of the election, Erdoğan formed a new government on 6 July 2011 led by the AKP (Aydın-Düzgit 2012).

The first pluralist and direct presidential elections took place on 10 August 2014. Despite the Gezi Park protests in June 2013 and the December 2013 corruption allegations against members of the government, Erdoğan, the incumbent prime minister, was elected president, against two other candidates, with an absolute majority in the first round (57.79 per cent) (Kalaycioğlu 2015: 157). The turnout was 74.13 per cent. Opposition parties and international organisations criticised media bias in favour of Erdoğan and the unequal distribution of campaign resources, due to the (mis)use of public funds (OSCE 2014).

On 7 June 2015 the GNA was renewed with a record 84 per cent turnout. The AKP again won the elections, but lost its absolute majority in parliament for the first time since 2002. The pro-Kurdish Peoples' Democratic Party (HDP) succeeded in reaching the 10 per cent national threshold necessary to obtain seats in parliament (with 13 per cent of the vote and 14.4 per cent of seats). According to international observers, basic election freedoms were respected but some negative incidents were reported, including: attacks on candidates and party offices, the president's lack of impartiality during the electoral campaign, use of public resources to support the AKP, pressure on the media and the apparent bias of the Radio and Television Supreme Council (RTÜK). However, talks to form a government coalition failed and so the elections had to be repeated on 1 November 2015. This time the AKP won an overall parliamentary majority to form a government with 317 seats (57.6 per cent), with a new record turnout of 85.2 per cent. HDP's parliamentary representation fell to 10.7 per cent of the seats. The electoral campaign was affected by the terrorist attack in Ankara on 10 October 2014, and again by violence against candidates, party offices and staff, and pressure on the media.

In sum, pluralism was reduced at the expense of the Kurdish parties because of the high threshold required to achieve representation. The integrity of the elections was also undermined due to the advantages enjoyed by Erdoğan and the AKP.

2.2 A hyper-presidential form of government, despite the absence of a constitutional reform

Following Erdoğan's election as president, he sought to adopt a new constitution to establish a presidential system of governance – although he has needed thirteen parliamentarians to add to the AKP's 317 votes to make any constitutional change. However, as all the opposition parties are currently against moving towards a presidential system, he still requires the vote of defecting members of parliament.

Nonetheless, the Turkish political system functions in some aspects as a *de facto* presidential system with a hyper-presidential trend (Durán 2016: 10). The checks and balance system is biased in favour of the president, which now even brings into question the independence of the judicial power. The role of prime minister has lost its leading institutional and political role in the executive since Erdoğan assumed the presidency. In fact, Ahmet Davutoğlu resigned as prime minister in May 2016 due to the imbalance in power between the president and prime minister.

As a consequence of the AKP's absolute majority, parliament lacks effective oversight of the executive. The president has the power to veto legislation, and key laws are frequently prepared by government and adopted with little consultation or debate in parliament. There has been no improvement in parliament's supervision of public spending, and the military and intelligence services lack parliamentary accountability (European Commission 2015). Regarding the judicial power, in 2013 legislative changes to the Upper Council of Judges and Prosecutors were introduced. The Council plays a crucial role in the promotion and transfer to other locations of, and disciplinary proceedings against, judges and prosecutors. Thus, judges and prosecutors who were investigating cases of corruption were replaced by pro-government legal figures (Özbudun 2015: 46; Durán 2016: 12 and 16–17).

However, systemic change has gone beyond institutional control; dominance over other actors, such as the Kurds and the military, has also been evident. Specifically, Erdoğan has used terrorist attacks on Turkish territory and the Syrian crisis to reinforce his presidential power and strengthen his stance towards the Kurdistan Workers' Party (PKK), both in Turkey and northern Iraq.[2]

On the other hand, the army has traditionally been a homogeneous institution and a veto-player in Turkish politics and so has acted as a constraint on government authority. Since the proclamation of the republic in 1923, the military has seen itself as the guardian of Turkey's secularism and democracy. Nevertheless, it has had its influence considerably reduced in the political system, not only because of the arrival of the AKP to government (through constitutional and other legal reforms in 2003 and 2004), but also because the Turkish military has an interest in resembling Western armies to help gain European Union membership for Turkey. However, the *coup d'état* attempt on 15 July 2016 has made evident the complexity and significant plurality of factions and divergent interests within the army (pro-AKP Islamists, pro-Gülen Islamist and pro-Kemalists) in the last decade.

Regarding transparency and governance, a number of serious corruption cases implicating the government came to light in December 2013. As there is no committee with the necessary technical expertise to follow up reports from the Turkish Court of Accounts, the auditing of public expenditure has remained superficial. Undue influence by the executive in the investigation and prosecution of high-profile corruption cases continues to be a major concern (European Commission 2015). Turkey received a score of forty-two (out of 100) and was ranked sixty-two out of the 168 countries assessed in the 2015 Corruption Perceptions Index (Transparency International 2016).

2.3 Restrictions on rights and liberties

The deterioration of rights and freedoms underscores the growing trend towards authoritarian rule in Turkey. The Gezi Park protest in July 2013 became a turning point in this sense, because since then many proposed demonstrations have not been given authorisation, and when they have taken place the police have frequently used excessive force. On 27 March 2015 the GNA passed two laws (that is, the Amending Police Powers and Duties Law, and the Law on the Gendarmerie's Organisation, Duties and Authorities) that restricted freedom of assembly with the aim of preserving national security and maintaining public order in the country. The laws augmented police authority during protests, including allowing them to use lethal force or extend detention periods (Esen and Gumuscu 2016: 14). The first mass authorised rally took place on 24 July 2016, which was organised to condemn the coup attempt and support democracy. Freedom of association is also restricted, mainly to restrict pro-human rights associations and pro-Kurd protests. The state response to terrorism and the government campaign against the PKK has also given rise to serious concerns over human rights violations and regression on the rule of law. Despite this, civil society has remained active and involved in many spheres of public life.

New laws have restricted freedom of expression, such as the March 2015 Internet Law, which has been used to block Twitter and Facebook without a court order on a broad range of grounds: protection of life, safety of property, national security, public order, prevention of crime and safeguarding of general health (European Commission 2015). Blocking mainly occurred during the corruption scandals of 2013 and the local elections in March 2014. Freedom of expression is also undermined through: arbitrary and restrictive interpretations of the legislation; attacks on opposition figures; the closure of critical media; and frequent court cases against journalists, writers or social media users (Duran and García-Marín 2015). All these pressures have led to growing self-censorship (European Commission 2015; Freedom House 2016a).

In sum, the situation of rights and liberties has deteriorated considerably since 2013, and particularly since the 2016 coup attempt. On 20 July 2016 Erdoğan declared a state of emergency for ninety days. Mass arrests followed the failed coup with more than 11,000 detained, including soldiers, police, judges, civil servants and journalists. School teachers and university heads were suspended and education and health institutions were closed. Many of those arrested were accused of being supporters of Fethullah Gülen, an exiled Muslim cleric accused by the Turkish government of being behind the attempt to overthrow the regime. The authorities also ordered the closure of 131 media outlets in the aftermath of the failed coup (Anadolu, 27 July 2016; BBC, 25 July 2016; Reuters, 23 July 2016).

3 Authoritarian progressions: Bahrain and Kuwait

3.1 Bahrain: political reforms, but less pluralism and liberties

Shiite social protests – which can partially be explained by issues related to identity – have been significant since their eruption on 14 February 2011 (Alshehabi 2014; Gengler 2013). Rather than demand the end of the monarchy, Bahrain's protesters sought constitutional changes and improvements in rights and liberties. However, demonstrations were harshly repressed by the regime with the help of a military intervention by a 'loyal' Gulf Cooperation Council (GCC), led by Saudi Arabia in March 2011 to support King Hamad bin Isa bin Salman al-Khalifa (Louër 2013; Nuruzzaman 2013; Albrecht and Ohl 2016). Thus, Bahrain was one of the Arab countries in which the consequences of the Arab Spring ended with negative impacts, specifically with the decline of institutional political competitiveness and the further repression of political movements.

After smothering the protests, on 29 June 2011, King Hamad formed the Bahrain Independent Commission of Inquiry (BICI), and tasked it with investigating the crackdown. Its report was released on 23 November 2011 and confirmed the Bahraini government's use of torture and other forms of abuse on detainees. Also, on 1 July 2011, the king established the National Dialogue Commission as a forum for the discussion and promotion of reform. Taking into account some of the proposals suggested by the National Dialogue Commission, the king reformed the constitution on 3 May 2012.

3.1.1 Decreasing pluralism

There has been a notable fall in pluralism and political competition in Bahraini public life since the advent of the Arab Spring. In 2011 opposition movements were represented in parliament despite political parties being banned. However, the Arab Spring changed relations between the opposition and the regime. For example, the main opposition group, the Shiite al-Wefaq coalition, left parliament to signal its objection to the repression. Consequently, al-Wefaq did not participate in the partial elections of 24 September 2011 (first round) or 8 October 2011 (second round), held to fill the eighteen seats of the Council of Deputies that had been vacated by them. Other political forces such as al-Menbar (a Sunni Islamist movement, linked to the Muslim Brotherhood) and Wa'ad (a secular leftist movement) also boycotted the partial elections. The success of the boycott was highlighted by the opposition, which provided data on the low voter turnout (16.3 per cent) (Zaccara and Saldaña 2015: 183).

The National Dialogue started on 2 July 2011 and involved over 300 organisations. However, the main opposition movements comprised only twenty-five of the 300 seats. Al-Wefaq walked out of the National Dialogue two weeks after it started. The dialogue was relaunched in 2012, but al-Wefaq again abandoned it in February 2013, following the arrest of several of its leading members in late 2012.

Al-Wefaq also maintained its electoral boycott in the 22 and 29 November 2014 general elections. The party did not agree with the electoral system, particularly the make-up of the constituencies, which put a limit on the Shiite voting weight to avoid a majority for al-Wefaq in the Council of Deputies (Zaccara and Saldaña 2015: 183). The Bahraini government's reaction was to suspend the groups' activities for three months and to arrest its president, Ali Salman, on December 2014, on charges of inciting violence and supporting the overthrow of the government. Thus, pro-government independents won thirty-seven of the forty lower house seats, and the leading Sunni societies took the remaining seats (Freedom House 2016b).

Three more opposition groups boycotted the elections, claiming that major flaws in the voting process would affect the electoral outcome (Bertelsmann Stiftung 2016a). Another nine political societies contested the elections, but they only represented thirty-six of the 266 candidates. Of these, only two societies obtained seats: two from the Salafi al-Asalah and one from the Sunni al-Menbar (IFES 2016).[3] Therefore, pro-government candidates again dominated the Council of Deputies. The official average turnout was 59.78 per cent, mainly from the Sunni electorate.

In sum, there is very little political competition in Bahrain due to the harassment of opposition groups, a biased electoral system, unfree and unfair elections and, as a consequence, the opposition's self-exclusion from institutions.

3.1.2 Family government in Bahrain

Constitutional reform was the main result of the promised political reforms in Bahrain. The main objective of the constitutional amendments was to strengthen the National Council, which is formed by the Council of Deputies (lower house) and the Advisory Council (upper house), by speeding up the passage of laws and increasing legislative control over the government. Further changes include a parliamentary vote of confidence on new governments, motions to censure the government, the possibility of setting up commissions of inquiry and of questioning ministers in plenary sessions, and the king's obligation to consult the heads of the two parliamentary houses before dissolving parliament. However, government accountability to parliament is restricted because the king can remove the government or dissolve the assembly if there is a no-confidence vote. The legislative power of the Council of Deputies also remains limited. The upper house is appointed by the king, and parliament can only pass legislation that has been approved in both chambers. Additionally, royal decrees can only be approved or rejected, but not amended, by parliament.

Regarding the government, the king has discretion in the choice of the prime minister and appoints all ministers of government. The prime minister, Khalifa bin Salman al-Khalifa, the king's uncle, has been in office since 1971 and the most important posts are occupied by al-Khalifa family members. Furthermore, the judicial system is headed by members of the ruling family. Although the power of the king is absolute, it is constrained by factionalism within the royal family, who function as a 'veto player' (Gengler 2013). As in the case of Oman, negotiation and agreements are necessary in the government decision-making process on key issues.

In sum, there is no separation of powers or system of checks and balances. Additionally, the government is not democratically elected and there is no possibility for alternation.

3.1.3 Deteriorating rights and liberties

The situation of rights and liberties has deteriorated considerably in Bahrain in recent years. The 2002 constitution guarantees freedom of assembly. However, citizens must obtain a licence to hold demonstrations – which is regularly denied – and the police often use violence to break up political protests, most of which occur in Shiite areas. In 2013, at the recommendation of BICI, the government created a police ombudsman to investigate allegations of excessive use of force. As a result, several police officers were sentenced to prison. Nevertheless, in August 2014 the king issued an emergency law banning all protests and public gatherings in the capital Manama. The exercise of freedoms of association and syndication is also highly restricted. NGOs have to obtain a permit from the Social Development Ministry, and political associations are not allowed. Bahrainis have the right to establish labour unions, but not foreign workers. Strikes are often banned and the harassment of unionised workers is common (Freedom House 2016b).

Freedom of expression is nonexistent. The regime clamps down heavily on political dissidence (Beaugrand 2016). Amendments passed in 2013 and 2014 to the country's anti-terrorism legislation have been used to keep political opponents in detention either without charge, or accused of inciting violence and jeopardising the stability of the country. The media are controlled by the government through prior censorship. The press law (issued in 1965, with several amendments since) and a law issued in February 2014 allow journalists to be imprisoned for criticising the king or Islam or for threatening national security. Additionally, the Internet is subject to restrictions and permanent scrutiny by the authorities. Many journalists and bloggers are currently imprisoned (Bertelsmann Stiftung 2016a).

3.2 Kuwait: absence of political reforms and a decrease in pluralism and liberties

Protests against government corruption and growing authoritarianism have been constant in Kuwait since 2011. In contrast to other countries in the region, the regime never initiated any process of political reform. Nevertheless, the 'Kuwaiti Spring' has had other consequences for the political system and its distinctively participative and competitive political culture (Segal 2012): governmental and parliamentary instability (various governmental crises and the holding of three elections in two and a half years); attempts by the emir to control parliament; a reduction in pluralism and political competition due to the opposition's refusal to participate in elections; and a reduction in public liberties due to new restrictive laws in this sphere. For these reasons, Kuwait has had an authoritarian progression from a quasi-competitive and restrictive pluralist authoritarianism towards a hegemonic and restrictive pluralist authoritarianism.

3.2.1 Fewer political powers in parliament

Organised political parties are not allowed in Kuwait, although political movements can participate in politics. These quasi-parties include secular and leftist nationalists, Shiites, Salafi Islamists and the Islamic Constitutional Movement, affiliated to the Muslim Brotherhood. During the protests there were demands for the legalisation of parties, but the government did not respond to these calls.

Three electoral processes have taken place following the Arab Spring. First, elections were held on 2 February 2012 after the early dissolution of the National Assembly brought about the downfall of the government in December 2011. For the first time the opposition dominated the National Assembly (thirty-five of the fifty seats of the legislature), elected with a turnout of 62 per cent. However, the Constitutional Court annulled the electoral results because it argued that the decree that dissolved the previous parliament in December 2011 was unconstitutional (Albloshi 2016).

Elections were repeated on 1 December 2012. Before the elections, on 19 October 2012, the emir decreed an amendment to the electoral law, which was rejected by the opposition and caused intense protests again (Ulrichsen 2014). According to the reform, parliamentary representatives would be elected in plurinominal constituencies of ten seats each through a single vote from the voter, rather than through the block vote system that had been previously agreed in which each voter casts four votes. The electoral change facilitates the co-optation of candidates by members of the ruling family (Dazi-Heni 2015) and makes the building of electoral coalitions difficult.[4] Consequently, the opposition boycotted the elections and challenged the electoral amendment in the Constitutional Court. The election returned a pro-government parliament, although, on 16 June 2013, the Court invalidated its results on procedural grounds and called for a new election.

Therefore, a third election was held on 27 July 2013. This time several opposition figures decided to participate, while others again boycotted the electoral process. Turnout rose to 52 per cent from the record low of 39 per cent in the December 2012 elections. The Sunni pro-government candidates maintained a parliamentary majority, but the liberals, Shiites and Salafists also obtained seats. More government-friendly figures joined the National Assembly after a special election in June 2014 to replace five members who had stepped down in protest after being refused the opportunity – by a majority in the National Assembly – to question the prime minister about political corruption (Bertelsmann Stiftung 2016c).

3.2.2 Government instability and weakening of the checks and balances system

In Kuwait protesters directed their criticisms against the government, predominantly because of corruption among its members, which provoked various governmental crises. The prime minister and the main government departments (defence, interior and foreign affairs) are in the hands of senior al-Sabah princes. The first crisis occurred on 31 March 2011, when three ministers belonging to the royal family resigned, after being accused of paying bribes to parliamentarians. However, the accusation of corruption was predominantly directed at the prime minister, Sheikh Nasser. The crisis came to a head on 17 November 2011 when thousands of protesters entered the parliament building after police had used force to break up a march demanding that the prime minister step down. Finally, Sheikh Nasser resigned on 28 November 2011. The defeat of the government led to the dissolution of parliament and to the appointment of Sheikh Jaber al-Mubarak al-Hamad al-Sabah as prime minister, who had been defence minister up until that time. After the third elections, on 28 July 2013, the emir re-appointed al-Sabah as prime minister, who formed a new cabinet. However, citizens' demands for the government ministers' resignation only played a marginal role in governmental changes that are, in the final instance, the product of royal intra-family conflict (Dazi-Heni 2015).

Checks and balances in Kuwait have traditionally been more robust than in other Gulf monarchies, both formally and in practice. According to the 1992 constitution, parliament can veto the appointment of the prime minister,[5] conduct inquiries into government actions and pass motions of no confidence against any member of the cabinet. Parliament can also overturn decrees issued by the emir when the National Assembly has not been in session. Although legislative power rests with parliament, the emir can demand that a bill be reconsidered, in which case the assembly must confirm it by a two-thirds majority. Furthermore, as cabinet members are ex officio members of parliament (consisting of fifty directly elected members), the government can block parliamentary initiatives together with pro-government members of parliament. On the other hand, the emir can dissolve parliament –as has been done on several occasions before the end of the parliamentary term – but has to organise new elections within sixty days.

3.2.3 Restrictions on rights and liberties

Kuwaitis used to enjoy a high level of rights and liberties compared to other monarchies in the Gulf, especially in press freedom. However, this situation changed after the Arab Spring. Gatherings and demonstrations are frequent, but they have often been violently dispersed by the police. The Kuwaiti government regularly restricts the registration and licensing of NGOs, and thus freedom of association is limited (Bertelsmann Stiftung 2016c). Authorities have detained opposition figures for denouncing the high level of corruption. The regime has also persecuted critics, journalists and Internet users in recent years. A new telecommunications law, approved in 2014, gives the government sweeping powers to block content and deny access to the Internet, and revoke licences without giving reasons (Human Rights Watch 2016a).

4 Fragmented and failed states: Syria and Iraq

4.1 Syria

After five years of war in Syria, a solution to the conflict still seems distant. Mass protests started on 15 March 2011 in Syria to demand President Bashar al-Assad's resignation, lift the emergency law, release political prisoners, end corruption, legalise political parties, equal rights for Kurds and broaden political freedoms, such as freedom of the press, speech and assembly. As a consequence of the government's violent crackdown, the social protests escalated into an ongoing armed conflict among various competing opposition and regime forces. On 29 July 2011 several defecting Syrian officers formed the Free Syrian Army and many civilians took up arms to join the opposition. Nevertheless, the majority of the military and the powerful security agencies remained loyal to the regime. The emergence of IS added a further dimension to the conflict. Additionally, other regional and international actors have been involved in a proxy war. The Syrian government receives technical, financial, military and political support from Russia, Iran and Iraq as well as from Lebanese Shiite Hezbollah militias fighting in support of the Syrian regime.

Despite the armed conflict and disintegration of the state, al-Assad maintains a minimum governing structure and has carried out several formal changes, such as reform of the party law and constitution, adaption of the country's modes of economic governance and restructuring of its military and security apparatus (Heydemann 2014; Szmolka 2014). Thus, Syria remains categorised as a closed authoritarian state – even though the country has recently held elections – because of the absence of an authentic opposition, the concentration of powers in the president's hands and the persistent violation of human rights (Sotimano 2016).

4.1.1 Cosmetic pluralism and political competitiveness

Before the Arab Spring, only socialist parties participating in the National Progressive Front (NPF), under the hegemony of the Ba'ath Party, could run for elections and be represented in parliament. On 5 August 2011 Decree 100-2011 on political parties was passed, which aimed to recognise new political forces. Nevertheless, the Parties Affairs Committee still maintains control over party legislation and authorises new political parties. Additionally, the party law forbids parties based on religion, tribal affiliation or regional interests, as in other Arab countries. On the other hand, in November 2011, al-Assad appointed a committee to draft a new constitution, which was approved by a referendum on 27 February 2012.[6] New provisions allow for pluralism and the democratic exercise of power through elections. Similarly, the constitutional reform formally ended the monopoly of the Ba'ath Party as leader of the state and of Syrian society. Despite the formal adoption of pluralism, the exercise of genuine opposition inside the country is impossible. In exile, the Syrian National Coalition was recognised in 2012 as the representative of the Syrian people by the Arab League, many European countries and the United States. However, the opposition has been incapable of establishing a front that is cohesive and respected by the military factions that fight against the regime (Álvarez-Ossorio 2015: 170).

There have been two People's Council elections held in the last five years: on 7 May 2012 and on 13 April 2016. Eight parties contested the 2012 elections besides the National Progressive Front, which was already in existence (and led by the Ba'ath Party). The result of the election was a 'government-friendly' parliament. Only five seats were won by the main opposition coalition, the Popular Front for Change and Liberation (PFCL), formed by two parties. The NPF occupied 168 seats (134 for the Ba'ath Party) and seventy-seven were won by non-partisan candidates.

The elections on 13 April 2016 took place while a new round of discussions were held in Geneva between the al-Assad regime and the Syrian opposition to seek a political agreement that would lead to a transition government, approval of a constitution and the holding of legislative and presidential elections. The elections called by al-Assad were seen as an attempt by the president to strengthen his position in the negotiations. The pro-presidential National Unity Alliance won 200 of the possible 250 seats.[7] This time, the PFCL boycotted the election, along with most of the opposition parties.

On the other hand, on 3 June 2014, Syria held the first presidential multicandidate elections in government-held areas. According to the Supreme Constitutional Court of Syria, the turnout was 73.42 per cent and al-Assad was re-elected for a third presidential term with 88.7 per cent of the vote.

These three elections, however, were not considered free and fair because of the ongoing war, the nominal opposition and the absence of independent election monitoring.

4.1.2 Illegitimate and non-effective government

The 2012 constitution did not impact on the power relationships in Syria, because the changes were normative and very limited. Besides adopting the principle of political pluralism, the constitutional reform limited presidential terms to two seven-year periods of office, meaning that al-Assad could remain in power until 2028, following the presidential elections of 2014. The head of state still retains significant prerogatives, such as the designation and removal of the prime minister and the cabinet, the authority to initiate and veto laws, and legislative power when the People's Council is not in session. The powers of parliament have not increased with the constitutional reforms. There is no political debate on laws and policies in the parliamentary arena and parliament is basically an instrument of support for the government.

On the other hand, Syria is fragmented into several authorities that rule their respective territories. After five years of war al-Assad has control of 40 per cent of Syrian territory. Obviously, the state cannot provide citizens with basic services and goods even in the state-held areas. The remaining territory is ruled by a multitude of armed factions, including the moderate opposition, the Syrian Islamic Front, Jabhat al-Nusra (al-Qaeda's affiliate in Syria until July 2016), IS and Kurdish units. In January 2014 the Kurdish

Democratic Union Party and allied parties established a transitional administration in the three northern regions where they have declared the Kurdish autonomous region of Rojava. They have formed councils similar to ministries and introduced a new constitutional law (Human Rights Watch 2016b).

Regarding governance, corruption within the al-Assad regime is very high and has increased due to the ongoing war. Syria was ranked 154 out of 168 countries and territories surveyed in the 2015 Corruption Perceptions Index (with a score of eighteen points) (Transparency International 2016).

4.1.3 Impracticable exercise of rights and liberties

In times of war, when the rule of law is non-existent, it is impossible to talk of rights and liberties. Since March 2011 over a quarter of a million Syrians have been killed, 4.8 million have been forced to leave the country, 7.6 million are internally displaced, and 12.2 million have required humanitarian assistance (UN Refugee Agency and UN Office for the Coordination of Humanitarian Affairs 2016).[8] There has not been a decisive international intervention to protect civilian and human rights because geopolitical interests have taken priority (Lombardo 2015).

The intelligence and security apparatus continue to punish any political opposition. Human rights organisations report torture, arbitrary arrests, enforced disappearances, deaths in custody and other serious violations by government forces. IS and Jabhat al-Nusra have been responsible for systematic and widespread offences, including targeting civilians, kidnappings and executions. Kurdish armed forces and other non-state groups have also committed abuses (Human Rights Watch 2016b).

The government enacted anti-terrorism laws (Laws 19, 20 and 21) on 2 July 2012, which restrict rights and liberties. Freedom of expression remains under strict control. All media are required to obtain permission to operate from the interior ministry. The state controls major newspapers, while private media in government areas are generally owned by figures closely associated with the regime. A number of national and international journalists have been kidnapped or murdered. Additionally, the regime exercises strong control over the Internet. In relation to the right of association, NGOs have serious difficulties in their work and authorities generally deny registration to organisations with reformist or human rights missions. Control of the unions by the Ba'ath Party, compulsory membership of the General Federation of Trade Unions and the violent context make labour relations impossible (Freedom House 2016d).

4.2 A weakened state: Iraq

Citizens have mobilised against the government for five years in Iraq. Protests began in 2011 as a result of high unemployment, poor living conditions, insecurity, corruption and the inefficacy of government, and the occupation by the US army, which withdrew before 31 December 2011 as planned. In response to the demonstrators, Prime Minister Nouri al-Maliki announced electricity subsidies, investigations of corruption cases, improvements in national security and a constitutional limit for the term of the prime minister. However, new protests erupted in 2013. Unlike in 2011, this time the protesters were Sunni Arabs who felt marginalised and harassed by the al-Maliki government. They denounced anti-terrorism laws being used to indiscriminately arrest Sunnis and abusive De-Ba'athification laws, and demanded the resignation of Prime Minister al-Maliki. At the end of 2013 the security forces violently cracked down on a sit-in at Ramadi, alleging the protest camp was a potential shelter for al-Qaeda. Demonstrations erupted again in August 2015 in several cities across Iraq due to poor living conditions, sectarian politics and endemic corruption.

Thus, the uprisings have aggravated a process of regime erosion by mobilising sectarian and ethnic identities and exposing the country's geopolitical rivalries and interventions, giving rise to transborder movements, such as IS, which has occupied a part of Iraqi territory. The resulting state fragmentation, continuing violence and terrorist acts have constrained democratic consolidation in Iraq (Saouli 2015: 315) and increased the already significant state fragility. Today Iraq is ranked eleventh (of 178 countries) in the Failed State Index 2016 (Fund for Peace 2016).

Despite this, democratic practices such as the holding of elections and the formation of government have not been interrupted, as a result of consensus agreements among parties to ensure institutional stability. On the other hand, there has not been any significant political reform since the Arab Spring and, for example, the Federal Council (the upper house planned in the 2015 constitution to represent regional interests) has never been formed.

4.2.1 A fragmented and polarised pluralism

The Iraqi party system is characterised by ethnic–sectarian cleavage, high fragmentation and polarisation. Therefore, electoral alliances and governmental coalitions are essential in Iraq.

In the midst of political instability and violence, legislative elections were held on 30 April 2014 as scheduled. Even political parties have become more professional despite the deep conflicts afflicting the country (Harmes 2016). Previously, the electoral system had been partially reformed following fierce parliamentary debate. The largest remainder system was replaced by the Sainte-Laguë method due to a ruling by the Supreme Court of Iraq that the former method discriminated against smaller parties. The Independent High Electoral Commission (IHEC) supervised the electoral process, and further monitoring was provided by political parties, Iraqi non-governmental organisations (NGOs) and international observers. The elections were reported as competitive, free and fair.

The resulting Council of Representatives (CR) was reasonably plural, although dominated by Shiite parties. The State of Law party, which was the incumbent prime minister al-Maliki's coalition, emerged as the largest bloc (with 95 of the 328 seats). A further two Shiite coalitions were placed second and third: the al-Ahrar Kutla (Liberal Bloc) linked to the cleric Muqtada al-Sadr (thirty-four seats) and al-Muwatin Etelaf (Citizen Alliance) (thirty-one seats). The other seats were occupied by the Sunni coalition Muttahidun (United for Reform) (twenty-eight seats), the Kurdistan Democratic Party (KDP) (twenty-five seats), the secular nationalist coalition al-Wataniya (twenty-one seats), the Patriotic Union of Kurdistan (PUK) (twenty-one seats), the Arabiyya Alliance (ten seats) and the Kurdish Movement for Change (Gorran) (nine seats).[9] The turnout was 52 per cent.

4.2.2 Flawed government functioning and weakened state capacity

One of the main brakes on the development of democracy in Iraq has been the lack of an inclusive government and the concentration of power in the prime minister's hands, mainly by Nouri al-Maliki. Al-Maliki occupied the premiership on 20 May 2006, after the first democratically elected prime minister, Ibrahim al-Jaafari, was forced to resign. Following the elections, on 21 December 2010, al-Maliki again formed a government thanks to the support of the 'largest bloc' in the CR even though his party did not win the elections. His government included ministers from all main blocs. However, al-Maliki tried to centralise power, at the expense of parliament and both Kurdish and Sunni political forces, and achieved a Supreme Court ruling that deprived the CR of its legislative power in 2011. As a result, all new laws had to be proposed by the Council of Ministers first. His monopolisation of power contributed to sectarian tensions: a growing Kurdish nationalism and the Sunni insurgency. Disaffection with al-Maliki grew even within the Shiite parties because of the corruption, insecurity, and growth of IS, which took Mosul in June 2014.

After the victory of the State of Law coalition in the 2014 elections, a number of al-Maliki's members of parliament withdrew their support and forced him to accept the nomination of Haider al-Abadi, a member of his own party, as prime minister. The US also pushed for the replacement of al-Maliki, conditioning greater military assistance on the nomination of another prime minister. On 11 August 2014 al-Abadi received the approval of the CR. He formed a unity government with a power-sharing agenda among the three main communities and reformed plans to fight corruption and improve public services. Additionally, al-Abadi reached an agreement with the Kurdistan Regional Government (KRG) over the distribution of oil revenues, introduced a plan for rebuilding the Iraqi security apparatus and a national reconciliation project (through the establishment of the National Guard Force and the amendment of the De-Ba'athification Law), and launched a military campaign to recapture territories under IS control (Bertelsmann Stiftung 2016b). As a consequence of new protests in 2016, al-Abadi submitted a further reform package to the CR to fight against corruption and put an end to the sectarian quota system. On 27 February 2016 Shiite leader Muqtada al-Sadr led a massive protest to demonstrate against strong corruption and the PM's reform plans. In order to reduce the social and political pressure, al-Abadi partially reshuffled his cabinet, including the non-party members. However, the protests calling on al-Abadi to form a government of technocrats have continued to date in a bid to push forward reforms stalled by government inefficiency, corruption and power struggles among independents. Nonetheless, the prime minister faces opposition from various political parties.

As stated in the 2005 constitution, Iraq has a parliamentary system of government and a separation of powers between the legislative, executive and judicial branches. However, the ability of the Council of Representatives to supervise the cabinet was eroded by the former prime minister, al-Maliki. Additionally, during his second term in office, he regularly relied on the support of the Federal Supreme Court, which has exclusive jurisdiction to interpret the constitution, and routinely appeared to rule in favour of the government. This situation has changed significantly under the premiership of Haider al-Abadi, as the role of parliament is now much stronger than it was (Bertelsmann Stiftung 2016b).

The functioning of Iraqi democracy has been undermined by the state's inability to exert its authority across national territory (Ahram 2016). The federal government has lost control of a large part of Iraq, which is ruled by IS and other groups. Nor does the Iraqi state have a monopoly on the use of the force. The Kurdish Peshmerga forces hold *de facto* control over the three Kurdish-Iraqi provinces and act as the army of the KRG.[10]

On the other hand, the government has limited administrative capacity to respond to citizens' basic demands and to assure security in the country. In territories under IS control, services are even more poorly delivered (Bertelsmann Stiftung 2016b). The Fund for Peace ranked Iraq in eleventh place among fragile states in positions of 'high alert'. Regarding governance, corruption is one of the major problems in the Iraqi public sector. Iraq is ranked 161 out of 168 countries surveyed in Transparency International's 2015 Corruption Perceptions Index; the worst score in the MENA region (together with Libya).

4.2.3 The regression of rights and liberties

Iraq has deteriorated considerably in terms of public rights and liberties since 2011. While freedom of assembly has regularly been exercised, many demonstrators have been arrested, above all in Sunni protests. In October 2014 a draft law on the Freedom of Expression, Assembly and Peaceful Demonstration, written in 2012 under the former prime minister al-Maliki, was returned to parliament. The law allowed officials to restrict freedom of assembly to protect 'public interest' and 'the general order or public morals', without defining what these terms actually cover (Bertelsmann Stiftung 2016b).

As a consequence of the IS occupation in 2014, the government issued 'mandatory guidelines' to assure favourable coverage of the Iraqi security forces and control information about IS advances. Additionally, Iraqi authorities have closed news media outlets, banned satellite channels and arrested journalists.

The rule of law in particular is very weak. The Iraqi judiciary is subject to political manipulation, especially by the executive branch. Human rights organisations have denounced detention without cause, mistreatment and even the torture of detainees. Under the IS occupation, detainees in contested areas have been summarily executed. The death penalty is frequent, often with inadequate due process. Freedom of belief is guaranteed in the constitution, but the reality is that both Shiite and non-Muslim minorities are being persecuted and massacred in the country.

5 Conclusions

A fifth wave of democratisation has not taken place as a consequence of the Arab Spring. As pointed out at the beginning of this chapter, the trend across the world since the beginning of the twenty-first century has been towards democratic involution. Many of the MENA governments have considered or interpreted protest as a question of security and not as a political question and/or an opportunity to become more democratic, and this has often resulted in violent state responses. Thus, social conflict has been transformed into violent conflict and war in some countries.

Aside from Tunisia, which has undergone a successful process of transition towards democracy, no MENA country has experienced significant democratic improvements that have involved regime change. Rather, in general terms, regressive political change has taken place. An authoritarian structure and institutional weakness persists in the majority of the political systems in the MENA countries. In fact, the most liberal and secular Muslim country in the region, Turkey, has even transited from being a defective democracy to pluralist authoritarianism since 2012. Similarly, in Bahrain and Kuwait, there have been authoritarian progressions, leaving behind the democratic hopes that were present at the beginning of the century. Finally, Syrian protests led to an ongoing war, which has involved not only national, but also regional and international actors. Thus, Syria is currently a failed state, while Iraq is also at severe risk of becoming a failed state and a more authoritarian country.

In consequence, a generalised autocratic tendency in the MENA countries has joined the global trend of democratic backsliding. Specifically, a typology for the five case study countries in this chapter might be that: Turkey can be considered near to a quasi-competitive authoritarian state, with the main regressions being in rights and freedoms and power concentration, which have predominantly affected the independence of the judicial power. Bahrain might be described as a restrictive and hegemonic pluralist authoritarian regime, considering the repression and notable deterioration in freedoms and rights and the loss of political competitiveness. Kuwait could be labelled a hegemonic authoritarian state due also to significant degeneration in specific areas such as pluralism. Finally, a typology of political regime cannot be provided for Syria and Iraq, as these countries have severe problems with the nature of their states, and are unable to control large swathes of their territory.

This negative trend shows that the patterns were similar across all the countries considered in this chapter. If the revolutions began by demanding the end of authoritarianism, free elections, respect for human rights, freedom of expression, and ultimately more democratic societies, the results have been very different from that expected. The current situation across all countries is less pluralism, less freedom and more power concentration.

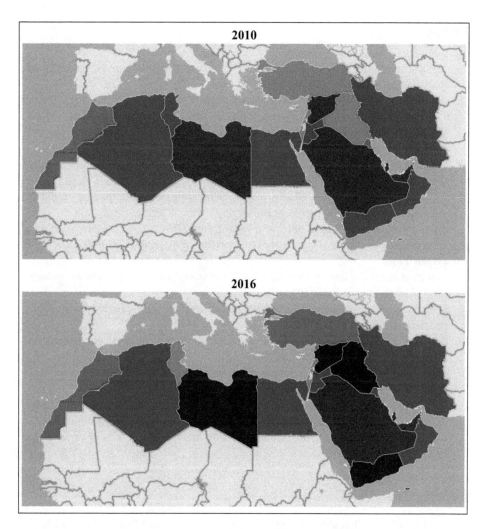

Figure 17.1 MENA political regimes before (2010) and after (2016) the Arab Spring

The colour scale goes from light to dark grey in this order: Full democracy, defective democracy, restrictive and quasi-competitive pluralist authoritarianism, restrictive and hegemonic pluralist authoritarianism, closed authoritarianism and failed states

The boundaries used here do not imply the expression of any opinion whatsoever on the part of the authors concerning the legal status of any country, territory, city or area or of its authorities, or concerning the delimitation of its frontiers or boundaries. Dotted and dashed lines on maps represent approximate border lines for which there may not yet be full agreement

Source: prepared by Inmaculada Szmolka and Javier García-Marín for this book

Notes

1. Available at Inter-parliamentary Union, <http://ipu.org/parline-e/reports/arc/2323_11.htm> (last accessed 5 July 2016).
2. The PKK and the government had been in an official ceasefire since March 2013. During this time the government conducted negotiations with the imprisoned head of the PKK, Abdullah Öcalan. However, violence has erupted again in south-eastern Turkey between the PKK and state security forces.
3. Available at <http://www.electionguide.org/elections/id/2483/> (last accessed 25 July 2016).
4. The right to vote for four candidates makes the building of alliances among candidates and political groups easier (Albloshi 2016).
5. In this event, parliament must select from among three alternatives of the emir's choosing.
6. According to official data, 57 per cent of the electorate took part, and 87 per cent of voters were in favour.
7. Data available at the Inter-parliamentarian Union at <http://ipu.org/parline-e/reports/2307_E.htm> (last accessed 18 July 2016).
8. Available at <http://www.unocha.org/syrian-arab-republic/syria-country-profile/about-crisis> (last accessed 18 July 2016).
9. Data available at the Inter-parliamentarian Union at <http://ipu.org/parline-e/reports/2151_E.htm> (last accessed 19 July 2016).
10. Disagreements between the federal government and the KRG have been common for over a decade due to the fact that the KRG act as a quasi-state (Soguk 2015). Discord arose again in June 2014 because of Kurdish President Barzani's decision not to share Kurdish oil production (as required by the Iraqi constitution) in exchange for reimbursement of 17 per cent of the total nationwide budget and his announcement to hold a referendum on Iraqi Kurdistan independence.

References

Ahram, Ariel (2016), 'Republic of Iraq', in Mark Gasiorowski and Sean L. Yom (eds), *The Government and Politics of the Middle East and North Africa*, Boulder, CO: Westview Press, pp. 235–70.

Albloshi, Hamad H. (2016), 'Sectarism and the Arab Spring: the case of the Kuwaiti Shi'a, *The Muslim World*, 106 (1): 109–26.

Albrecht, Holger and Dorothy Ohl (2016), 'Exit, resistance, loyalty: military behavior during unrest in authoritarian regimes', *Perspectives on Politics*, 14 (1): 38–52.

Álvarez-Ossorio, Ignacio (2015), 'El gran juego sirio. Irán versus Arabia Saudí', in Ignacio Álvarez-Ossorio (ed.), *La Primavera Árabe revisitada. Reconfiguración del autoritarismo y recomposición del islamismo*, Pamplona: Thomson Reuters Aranzadi, pp. 169–88.

Alshehabi, Omar H. (2014), 'Radical transformations and radical contestations: Bahrain's spatial-demographic revolution', *Middle East Critique*, 23 (1): 29–51, DOI: 10.1080/19436149.2014.896596.

Aydın-Düzgit, Senem (2012), 'No crisis, no change: the third AKP victory in the June 2011 parliamentary elections in Turkey', *South European Society and Politics*, 17 (2): 329–46.

Beaugrand, Claire (2016), 'Deconstructing minorities/majorities in parliamentary Gulf states (Kuwait and Bahrain)', *British Journal of Middle Eastern Studies*, 43 (2): 234–49.

Bertelsmann Stiftung (2016a), *Bahrain Country Report*, Gütersloh: Bertelsmann Stiftung.

Bertelsmann Stiftung (2016b), *Iraq Country Report*, Gütersloh: Bertelsmann Stiftung.

Bertelsmann Stiftung (2016c), *Kuwait Country Report*, Gütersloh: Bertelsmann Stiftung.

Buzan, Barry (2012), *People, States, and Fear. The National Security Problem in International Relations*, Brighton: Wheatsheaf Books.

Dazi-Heni, Fatiha (2015), 'The Arab Spring impact on Kuwaiti "exceptionalism"', Arabian Humanities, 4. Available at <http://cy.revues.org/2868> (last accessed 14 April 2016).

Durán, Marién (2013), 'Turquía: El camino hacia la democracia', *Revista Española de Ciencia Política*, 32: 11–42.

Durán, Marien (2016), 'Institutional changes in Turkey: the presidentialization of Turkish politics and its influence in democratic regression', *Paper presented at the 24th World Congress of Political Sciences*, Poznan, Poland.

Durán, Marien and Javier García-Marín (2015), 'Libertad de expresión y regulación mediática en la Turquía de Erdogan', in Ignacio Álvarez-Ossorio (ed.), *La Primavera Árabe revisitada. Reconfiguración del autoritarismo y recomposición del islamismo*, Pamplona: Thomson Reuters Aranzadi, pp. 191–212.

Esen, Berk and Sebnem Gumuscu (2016): 'Rising competitive authoritarianism in Turkey', *Third World Quarterly*, 37 (9): 1581–606, DOI: 10.1080/01436597.2015.1135732.

European Commission (2015), *Commission Staff Working Document Turkey Report 2015*. Available at <http://ec.europa.eu/enlargement/pdf/key_documents/2015/20151110_report_turkey.pdf> (last accessed 5 July 2016).

Freedom House (2016a), *Turkey Report 2015*. Available at <https://freedomhouse.org/report/freedom-world/2016/turkey> (last accessed 11 July 2016).

Freedom House (2016b), *Bahrain Report 2016*. Available at <https://freedomhouse.org/report/freedom-world/2016/bahrain> (last accessed 25 July 2016).

Freedom House (2016c), *Kuwait Report 2016*. Available at <https://freedomhouse.org/report/freedom-world/2016/kuwait> (last accessed 26 July 2016).

Freedom House (2016d), *Syria Report 2016*. Available at <https://freedomhouse.org/report/freedom-world/2016/syria> (last accessed 27 July 2016).

Fukuyama, Francis (2016), *Los orígenes del orden político. Desde la Prehistoria hasta la Revolución Francesa*, Barcelona: Planeta.

Fund for Peace (2016), *Fragile States Index*. Available at <http://fsi.fundforpeace.org/rankings-2016> (last accessed 30 June 2016).

Gengler, Justin J. (2013), 'Royal factionalism, the Khawalid, and the securitization of "the Shia problem" in Bahrain, *Journal of Arabian Studies*, 3 (1): 53–79, DOI: 10.1080/21534764.2013.802944.

Hakyemez, Yususf S. and Birol Akgun (2002), 'Limitations on the freedom of political parties in Turkey and the jurisdiction of the European Court of Human Rights', *Mediterranean Politics*, 7: 54–78, DOI: 10.1080/713869654.

Harmes, Adam (2016), 'Political marketing in post-conflict elections: the case of Iraq', *Journal of Political Marketing*, 1–32, DOI: 10.1080/15377857.2016.1193834.

Heydemann, Steven (2014), 'Syria and the future of authoritarianism', in Larry Diamond and Marc F. Plattner (eds), *Democratization and Authoritarianism in the Arab World*, Baltimore: Johns Hopkins University Press, pp. 300–14.

Human Rights Watch (2016a), *Kuwait. Events of 2015*. Available at <https://www.hrw.org/world-report/2016/country-chapters/kuwait> (last accessed 27 July 2016).

Human Rights Watch (2016b), *Syria. Events of 2015*. Available at <https://www.hrw.org/world-report/2016/country-chapters/syria> (last accessed 18 July 2016).

Kalaycıoğlu, Ersin (2015), 'Turkish popular presidential elections: deepening legitimacy issues and looming regime change', *South European Society and Politics*, 20 (2): 157–79, DOI: 10.1080/13608746.2015.1046264.

Lombardo, Gabriele (2015), 'The responsibility to protect and the lack of intervention in Syria between the protection of human rights and geopolitical strategies', *The International Journal of Human Rights*, 19 (8): 1190–8, DOI: 10.1080/13642987.2015.1082833.

Louër, Laurence, (2013), 'Sectarianism and coup-proofing strategies in Bahrain', *Journal of Strategic Studies*, 36 (2): 245–60, DOI: 10.1080/01402390.2013.790314.

Nuruzzaman, Mohammed (2013), 'Politics, economics and Saudi military intervention in Bahrain', *Journal of Contemporary Asia*, 43 (2): 363–78, DOI: 10.1080/00472336.2012.759406.

Önis, Ziya (2015), 'Monopolising the centre: the AKP and the uncertain path of Turkish democracy', *The International Spectator*, 50 (2): 22–41, DOI: 10.1080/03932729.2012.1015335.

Özbudun, Ergun (2007), 'Democratization reforms in Turkey, 1993–2004', *Turkish Studies*, 8: 179–96.

Özbudun, Ergun (2015), Social Change and Political Participation in Turkey, Princeton, Princeton University Press.

OSCE, Office for Democratic Institutions and Human Rights (2014), *Republic of Turkey Presidential Election, 10 August 2014.* Available at <http://www.osce.org/odihr/elections/turkey/126851?download=true> (last accessed 5 July 2016).

Rodríguez, Carmen, Antonio Ávalos, Hakan Yilmaz and Ana Planet (eds) (2013), *Turkey Democratization Process*, London and New York: Routledge.

Saouli, Adham (2015), 'Back to the future: the Arab uprisings and state (re)formation in the Arab world', *Democratization*, 22 (2): 315–34, DOI: 10.1080/13510347.2015.1010813.

Segal, Eran (2012), 'Political participation in Kuwait: dīwāniyya, majlis and parliament', 2 (2): 127–41, DOI: 10.1080/21534764.2012.735457.

Soguk, Nevzat (2015), 'With/out a state, Kurds rising: the un/stated foreign policy and the rise of the Kurdish Regional Government in Iraq', *Globalizations*, 12 (6): 957–68, DOI: 10.1080/14747731.2015.1100857.

Sotimano, Aurora (2016), 'Building authoritarian "legitimacy": domestic compliance and international standing of Bashar al-Asad's Syria', *Global Discourse*, 6 (3): 450–66.

Szmolka, Inmaculada (2014), 'Political change in North Africa and the Middle East: constitutional reforms and electoral processes', *Arab Studies Quarterly*, 36 (2): 128–48.

Transparency International (2016), *Corruption Perceptions Index 2015.* Available at <http://www.transparency.org/cpi2015> (last accessed 7 July 2016).

Ulrichsen, Kristian C. (2014), 'Politics and opposition in Kuwait: continuity and change', *Journal of Arabian Studies*, 4 (2): 214–30, DOI: 10.1080/21534764.2014.974323.

Zaccara, Luciano and Marta Saldaña (2015), 'Cambio y estabilidad política en las Monarquías del Golfo tras la Primavera Árabe', *Revista d'Afers Internacionals*, 108: 177–99.

Appendix

Table A.1 Freedom House classification of MENA countries (2010 and 2015)

Country		Dimensions		Political rights			Civil liberties			
		Political rights (1–7)	Civil liberties (1–7)	Electoral process (max. 12)	Political pluralism and participation (max. 16)	Functioning of government (max. 12)	Freedom of expression and belief (max. 16)	Associational and organisational rights (max. 12)	Rule of law (max. 16)	Personal autonomy and individual rights (max. 16)
Algeria	2015	6	5	4	4	3	7	4	5	7
	2010	6	5	4	4	3	7	6	5	7
Bahrain	2015	6	7	2	2	3	2	1	1	6
	2010	6	5	3	6	4	8	3	3	7
Egypt	2015	5	6	2	4	2	5	4	2	7
	2010	6	5	1	4	2	7	2	4	7
Iran	2015	6	6	3	2	2	2	1	3	4
	2010	6	6	a	a	a	a	a	a	a
Iraq	2015	6	6	8	5	1	5	4	0	4
	2010	5	6	7	5	2	5	4	1	4
Israel	2015	2	1	12	14	10	12	10	11	11
	2010	2	1	a	a	a	a	a	a	a
Jordan	2015	5	6	2	6	3	7	4	6	8
	2010	6	5	2	5	3	7	3	6	8
Kuwait	2015	5	5	2	7	5	6	4	7	6
	2010	4	4	4	9	6	8	6	7	6

Country	Year									
Lebanon	2015	4	5	2	9	3	11	7	5	7
	2010	5	3	5	9	3	12	8	6	9
Libya	2015	6	6	5	3	0	6	3	1	5
	2010	7	7	0	1	0	1	0	0	6
Morocco	2015	5	4	5	7	3	8	6	6	7
	2010	5	4	4	6	4	8	6	6	8
Oman	2015	6	5	2	2	2	5	3	4	5
	2010	6	5	2	2	2	6	3	4	5
Qatar	2015	6	5	2	2	3	8	2	4	4
	2010	6	5	2	2	3	8	2	4	4
Saudi Arabia	2015	7	7	0	0	1	3	0	2	2
	2010	7	6	0	0	1	4	0	3	2
Syria	2015	7	7	0	0	0	2	0	0	0
	2010	7	6	0	0	1	2	0	1	5
Tunisia	2015	1	3	12	16	8	13	10	9	11
	2010	7	5	1	3	1	4	2	4	8
Turkey	2015	3	4	10	10	6	8	5	7	9
	2010	3	3	a	a	a	a	a*	a	a
UAE	2015	6	6	1	2	2	4	2	3	4
	2010	6	5	1	2	2	8	3	4	4
Yemen	2015	6	6	3	4	2	6	3	2	5
	2010	6	5	4	4	3	7	3	3	5

Note: * no data for 2010

Source: prepared by Inmaculada Szmolka and Lucía García-del Moral for this book

Table A.2 The Economist classification of MENA countries (2010 and 2015)

Country	Year	Classification	Rank	Overall score	Dimensions				
					Electoral process and pluralism	Functioning of government	Political participation	Political culture	Civil liberties
Algeria	2015	Authoritarian	117	3.96	3	4.29	5	3.13	4.41
	2010	Authoritarian	125	3.44	2.17	2.21	2.78	5.63	4.41
Bahrain	2015	Authoritarian	146	2.79	1.25	3.21	2.78	4.38	2.35
	2010	Authoritarian	122	3.49	2.58	3.57	2.78	5.00	3.53
Egypt	2015	Authoritarian	134	3.18	3	2.86	3.33	3.75	2.94
	2010	Authoritarian	138	3.07	0.83	3.21	2.78	5.00	3.53
Iran	2015	Authoritarian	156	2.16	0.00	2.86	3.33	3.13	1.47
	2010	Authoritarian	158	1.94	0.00	3.21	2.22	2.50	1.76
Iraq	2015	Hybrid regime	115	4.08	4.33	0.07	7.22	4.38	4.41
	2010	Hybrid regime	111	4.00	4.33	0.79	6.11	3.75	5.00
Israel	2015	Flawed democracy	34	7.77	9.17	7.14	8.89	7.5	6.18
	2010	Flawed democracy	37	7.48	8.75	7.50	8.33	7.50	5.29
Jordan	2015	Authoritarian	120	3.86	3.58	3.93	3.89	4.38	3.53
	2010	Authoritarian	117	3.74	3.17	4.64	3.33	3.75	3.82
Kuwait	2015	Authoritarian	121	3.85	3.17	4.29	3.89	4.38	3.53
	2010	Authoritarian	114	3.88	3.58	4.29	3.33	4.38	3.82
Lebanon	2015	Hybrid regime	102	4.86	4.42	2.14	7.78	4.38	5.59
	2010	Hybrid regime	86	5.82	7.92	3.93	6.67	5.00	5.59

Country	Year	Regime type							
Libya	2015	Authoritarian	153	2.25	1.00	0.00	1.67	5.63	2.94
	2010	Authoritarian	158	1.94	0.00	2.14	1.11	5.00	1.47
Morocco	2015	Hybrid regime	107	4.66	4.75	4.64	3.89	5.63	4.41
	2010	Authoritarian	116	3.79	3.50	4.64	1.67	5.00	4.12
Oman	2015	Authoritarian	142	3.04	0.00	3.93	2.78	4.38	4.12
	2010	Authoritarian	143	2.89	0.00	3.57	2.22	4.38	4.12
Qatar	2015	Authoritarian	134	3.18	0.00	3.93	2.22	5.63	4.12
	2010	Authoritarian	137	3.09	0.00	3.21	2.22	5.63	4.41
Saudi Arabia	2015	Authoritarian	160	1.93	0.00	2.86	3.33	3.13	1.47
	2010	Authoritarian	160	1.84	0.00	2.86	1.11	3.75	1.47
Syria	2015	Authoritarian	166	1.43	0.00	0.00	2.78	4.38	0.00
	2010	Authoritarian	152	2.31	0.00	2.50	1.67	5.63	1.76
Tunisia	2015	Flawed democracy	57	6.72	7	6.07	7.78	6.88	5.88
	2010	Authoritarian	144	2.79	0.00	2.86	2.22	5.63	3.29
Turkey	2015	Hybrid regime	97	5.12	6.67	5.36	5	5.63	2.94
	2010	Hybrid regime	89	5.73	7.92	7.14	3.89	5.00	4.71
UAE	2015	Authoritarian	148	2.75	0.00	3.57	2.22	5.00	2.94
	2010	Authoritarian	148	2.52	0.00	3.57	1.11	5.00	2.94
Yemen	2015	Authoritarian	154	2.24	0.50	0.36	4.44	5.00	0.88
	2010	Authoritarian	146	2.64	1.33	1.79	3.89	5.00	1.18

Source: prepared by Inmaculada Szmolka and Lucía García-del Moral for this book

Table A.3 Bertelsmann Transformation Index for MENA countries (2010–15)

Country	Year	Political Transformation Index	Stateness	Political participation	Rule of law	Stability of democratic institution	Political and social integration
Algeria	2015	4.8	7.2	4.5	4.2	3.0	50
	2010	4.37	7.0	4.3	4.3	2.0	4.3
Bahrain	2015	3.48	6.5	1.8	3.5	2.0	3.7
	2010	4.42	7.8	2.5	4.5	2.0	5.3
Egypt	2015	3.93	6.2	3.2	3.5	2.0	4.7
	2010	4.22	7.0	3.5	4.3	2.0	4.3
Iran	2015	2.97	5.5	2.5	2.5	2.0	2.3
	2010	3.50	5.8	3.3	3.3	2.0	3.0
Iraq	2015	3.45	3.2	4.5	3.5	3.0	3.0
	2010	4.22	4.0	5.8	4.0	5.0	2.3
Jordan	2015	4.03	6.2	3.8	4.5	2.0	3.7
	2010	4.02	7.0	3.8	4.0	2.0	3.3
Kuwait	2015	4.38	7.5	3.5	4.8	2.5	3.7
	2010	4.68	8.0	4.8	5.0	2.0	3.7
Lebanon	2015	5.70	6.2	6.0	5.2	5.0	6.0
	2010	6.25	6.5	6.3	6.3	6.0	6.3
Libya	2015	2.38	1.8	3.8	1.8	2.0	2.7
	2010	3.20	7.5	1.5	3.0	2.0	2.0
Morocco	2015	3.83	6.8	3.5	3.2	2.0	3.7
	2010	4.05	6.8	3.5	4.0	2.0	4.0
Oman	2015	3.22	7.8	1.8	2.2	2.0	2.3
	2010	3.98	8.3	3.0	4.0	2.0	2.7
Qatar	2015	3.83	8.0	2.8	3.8	2.0	2.7
	2010	4.20	8.8	3.8	4.5	2.0	2.0
Saudi Arabia	2015	2.52	5.5	1.5	2.2	1.0	2.3
	2010	2.87	6.0	1.8	3.3	1.0	2.3
Syria	2015	1.70	2.2	1.8	1.5	1.0	2.0
	2010	3.23	7.0	2.3	2.3	2.0	2.7
Tunisia	2015	6.30	7.5	7.5	5.5	5.5	5.5
	2010	3.78	8.0	2.5	3.8	2.0	2.7
Turkey	2015	7.25	7.8	7.2	6.2	8.0	7.0
	2010	7.70	8.0	7.8	7.3	8.0	7.3
UAE	2015	3.95	8.5	1.8	4.0	2.5	3.0
	2010	4.15	8.3	3.0	4.5	2.0	3.0
Yemen	2015	2.82	2.8	3.0	3.0	2.0	3.3
	2010	4.23	6.3	4.3	4.0	2.0	4.7

Source: prepared by Inmaculada Szmolka and Lucía García-del Moral for this book

Table A.4 Policy IV Project classification of MENA countries (2010 and 2014)

Country	Year	Classification	Polity	Democracy	Autocracy
Algeria	2014	Anocracy	2	3	1
	2010	Anocracy	2	3	1
Bahrain	2014	Autocracy	-10	1	6
	2010	Autocracy	-5	0	10
Egypt	2014	Anocracy	-4	1	4
	2010	Anocracy	3	0	4
Iran	2014	Autocracy	-7	0	7
	2010	Autocracy	-7	0	7
Iraq	2014	Anocracy	3	4	1
	2010	Anocracy	3	4	1
Israel	2014	Democracy	10	10	0
	2010	Democracy	10	10	0
Jordan	2014	Anocracy	-3	2	5
	2010	Anocracy	-3	2	5
Kuwait	2014	Autocracy	-7	0	7
	2010	Autocracy	-7	0	7
Lebanon	2014	Democracy	6	6	0
	2010	Democracy	6	6	0
Libya	2014	Autocracy	-77	0	7
	2010	Autocracy	-7	-77	-77
Morocco	2014	Anocracy	-4	0	6
	2010	Autocracy	-6	1	5
Oman	2014	Autocracy	-8	0	8
	2010	Autocracy	-8	0	8
Qatar	2014	Autocracy	-10	0	10
	2010	Autocracy	-10	0	10
Saudi Arabia	2014	Autocracy	-10	0	10
	2010	Autocracy	-10	0	10
Syria	2014	Autocracy	-9	0	7
	2010	Autocracy	-7	0	9
Tunisia	2014	Democracy	7	1	5
	2010	Anocracy	-4	7	0
Turkey	2014	Democracy	9	8	1
	2010	Democracy	7	9	0
UAE	2014	Autocracy	-8	0	8
	2010	Autocracy	-8	0	8
Yemen	2014	Anocracy	-77	1	3
	2010	Anocracy	-2	-77	-77

Source: prepared by Inmaculada Szmolka and Lucía García-del Moral for this book

Index

Note: references to notes are indicated by n